# Fireworks® 2 Bible

# Fireworks® 2 Bible

Joseph Lowery

IDG Books Worldwide, Inc.
An International Data Group Company

Foster City, CA ✦ Chicago, IL ✦ Indianapolis, IN ✦ New York, NY

**Fireworks® 2 Bible**

Published by
**IDG Books Worldwide, Inc.**
An International Data Group Company
919 E. Hillsdale Blvd., Suite 400
Foster City, CA 94404
www.idgbooks.com (IDG Books Worldwide Web site)

ISBN: 0-7645-3334-7

Printed in the United States of America

10 9 8 7 6 5 4 3 2 1

1B/SX/QY/ZZ/FC

Distributed in the United States by IDG Books Worldwide, Inc.

Distributed by CDG Books Canada Inc. for Canada; by Transworld Publishers Limited in the United Kingdom; by IDG Norge Books for Norway; by IDG Sweden Books for Sweden; by IDG Books Australia Publishing Corporation Pty. Ltd. for Australia and New Zealand; by TransQuest Publishers Pte Ltd. for Singapore, Malaysia, Thailand, Indonesia, and Hong Kong; by Gotop Information Inc. for Taiwan; by ICG Muse, Inc. for Japan; by Norma Comunicaciones S.A. for Colombia; by Intersoft for South Africa; by Eyrolles for France; by International Thomson Publishing for Germany, Austria and Switzerland; by Distribuidora Cuspide for Argentina; by LR International for Brazil; by Galileo Libros for Chile; by Ediciones ZETA S.C.R. Ltda. for Peru; by WS Computer Publishing Corporation, Inc., for the Philippines; by Contemporanea de Ediciones for Venezuela; by Express Computer Distributors for the Caribbean and West Indies; by Micronesia Media Distributor, Inc. for Micronesia; by Grupo Editorial Norma S.A. for Guatemala; by Chips Computadoras S.A. de C.V. for Mexico; by Editorial Norma de Panama S.A. for Panama; by American Bookshops for Finland. Authorized Sales Agent: Anthony Rudkin Associates for the Middle East and North Africa.

For general information on IDG Books Worldwide's books in the U.S., please call our Consumer Customer Service department at 800-762-2974. For reseller information, including discounts and premium sales, please call our Reseller Customer Service department at 800-434-3422.

For information on where to purchase IDG Books Worldwide's books outside the U.S., please contact our International Sales department at 317-596-5530 or fax 317-596-5692.

For consumer information on foreign language translations, please contact our Customer Service department at 800-434-3422, fax 317-596-5692, or e-mail rights@idgbooks.com.

For information on licensing foreign or domestic rights, please phone +1-650-655-3109.

For sales inquiries and special prices for bulk quantities, please contact our Sales department at 650-655-3200 or write to the address above.

For information on using IDG Books Worldwide's books in the classroom or for ordering examination copies, please contact our Educational Sales department at 800-434-2086 or fax 317-596-5499.

For press review copies, author interviews, or other publicity information, please contact our Public Relations department at 650-655-3000 or fax 650-655-3299.

For authorization to photocopy items for corporate, personal, or educational use, please contact Copyright Clearance Center, 222 Rosewood Drive, Danvers, MA 01923, or fax 978-750-4470.

**Library of Congress Cataloging-in-Publication Data**

Lowery, Joseph (Joseph W.).
  Fireworks 2 bible / Joseph Lowery.
    p.   cm.
  Includes index.
  ISBN 0-7645-3334-7 (alk. paper)
  1. Computer graphics.   2. Fireworks (Computer file)
  I. Title.
T385.L695   1999
006.6–dc21                                      99-36224
                                                    CIP

is a registered trademark under exclusive license to IDG Books Worldwide, Inc., from International Data Group, Inc.

# ABOUT IDG BOOKS WORLDWIDE

Welcome to the world of IDG Books Worldwide.

IDG Books Worldwide, Inc., is a subsidiary of International Data Group, the world's largest publisher of computer-related information and the leading global provider of information services on information technology. IDG was founded more than 30 years ago by Patrick J. McGovern and now employs more than 9,000 people worldwide. IDG publishes more than 290 computer publications in over 75 countries. More than 90 million people read one or more IDG publications each month.

Launched in 1990, IDG Books Worldwide is today the #1 publisher of best-selling computer books in the United States. We are proud to have received eight awards from the Computer Press Association in recognition of editorial excellence and three from Computer Currents' First Annual Readers' Choice Awards. Our best-selling ...For Dummies® series has more than 50 million copies in print with translations in 31 languages. IDG Books Worldwide, through a joint venture with IDG's Hi-Tech Beijing, became the first U.S. publisher to publish a computer book in the People's Republic of China. In record time, IDG Books Worldwide has become the first choice for millions of readers around the world who want to learn how to better manage their businesses.

Our mission is simple: Every one of our books is designed to bring extra value and skill-building instructions to the reader. Our books are written by experts who understand and care about our readers. The knowledge base of our editorial staff comes from years of experience in publishing, education, and journalism — experience we use to produce books to carry us into the new millennium. In short, we care about books, so we attract the best people. We devote special attention to details such as audience, interior design, use of icons, and illustrations. And because we use an efficient process of authoring, editing, and desktop publishing our books electronically, we can spend more time ensuring superior content and less time on the technicalities of making books.

You can count on our commitment to deliver high-quality books at competitive prices on topics you want to read about. At IDG Books Worldwide, we continue in the IDG tradition of delivering quality for more than 30 years. You'll find no better book on a subject than one from IDG Books Worldwide.

John Kilcullen
Chairman and CEO
IDG Books Worldwide, Inc.

Steven Berkowitz
President and Publisher
IDG Books Worldwide, Inc.

IDG is the world's leading IT media, research and exposition company. Founded in 1964, IDG had 1997 revenues of $2.05 billion and has more than 9,000 employees worldwide. IDG offers the widest range of media options that reach IT buyers in 75 countries representing 95% of worldwide IT spending. IDG's diverse product and services portfolio spans six key areas including print publishing, online publishing, expositions and conferences, market research, education and training, and global marketing services. More than 90 million people read one or more of IDG's 290 magazines and newspapers, including IDG's leading global brands — Computerworld, PC World, Network World, Macworld and the Channel World family of publications. IDG Books Worldwide is one of the fastest-growing computer book publishers in the world, with more than 700 titles in 36 languages. The "...For Dummies®" series alone has more than 50 million copies in print. IDG offers online users the largest network of technology-specific Web sites around the world through IDG.net (http://www.idg.net), which comprises more than 225 targeted Web sites in 55 countries worldwide. International Data Corporation (IDC) is the world's largest provider of information technology data, analysis and consulting, with research centers in over 41 countries and more than 400 research analysts worldwide. IDG World Expo is a leading producer of more than 168 globally branded conferences and expositions in 35 countries including E3 (Electronic Entertainment Expo), Macworld Expo, ComNet, Windows World Expo, ICE (Internet Commerce Expo), Agenda, DEMO, and Spotlight. IDG's training subsidiary, ExecuTrain, is the world's largest computer training company, with more than 230 locations worldwide and 785 training courses. IDG Marketing Services helps industry-leading IT companies build international brand recognition by developing global integrated marketing programs via IDG's print, online and exposition products worldwide. Further information about the company can be found at www.idg.com. 1/24/99

# Credits

**Acquisitions Editors**
Kathy Yankton
Debra Williams Cauley

**Development Editor**
Laura E. Brown

**Technical Editor**
Ram Ganesh

**Copy Editors**
Bill McManus
Jennifer H. Mario
Timothy J. Borek

**Production**
IDG Books Worldwide Production

**Proofreading and Indexing**
York Production Services

**Cover Design**
Murder By Design

# About the Author

**Joseph W. Lowery** has been writing about computers and new technology since 1981. He is the author of *Dreamweaver 2 Bible* and *Buying Online For Dummies* (IDG Books Worldwide). He has also written books on using the Internet for business and HTML, and has contributed to several books on Microsoft Office. Joseph is currently Contributing Editor for GadgetBoy, an online consumer review service, as well as Webmaster for a variety of sites. Joseph and his wife, dancer/choreographer Debra Wanner, have a daughter, Margot.

*For the ever-growing artist in my brother, Allen Mark Lowery.*

# Foreword

When we first set out to make Fireworks, we didn't know what the software was going to look like or features we were going to have. We didn't even know what we were going to call it! All we knew was that we were going to identify and solve the problems that professional Web developers were having in producing and integrating graphics into their Web site production workflow.

The very first thing we noticed was that the people we spoke to and visited were spending a large amount of time flipping between many applications to create, edit, composite, optimize, and animate their Web graphics. Invariably, once the ideas were presented to the clients, there were changes that required repeating the whole process again, turning what should be simple edits into major undertakings. So we set out to bring all of the utilities and tools that people were using together in a single environment that would not only complete the individual tasks involved but also give the user the benefit of keeping everything completely editable all the time.

But we still hadn't gotten to some of the workflow issues with what the designers do with their graphics once they've designed them. They needed to have hotspots, they needed to have different parts of their images in different formats, and they needed to have JavaScript rollovers and buttons. So the designers would create images, give them to the coders, and then through the skill and hard work of the coders, the graphics could be reconstructed into something similar to what the designer intended. But chopping up these graphics, reassembling them, and giving them interactivity was also something that took far too much energy to maintain. So Fireworks comes to the rescue! We added hotspot tools, slicing tools, and JavaScript rollovers. And of course, in keeping with Fireworks' philosophy, all of these things are editable all the time.

And it seems that all that listening was worth it! Fireworks has received rave reviews and numerous awards from different shows and publications. But the most gratifying thing to me is seeing Web sites that were produced by people using Fireworks, and hearing from the people who produced them.

And that brings us to Fireworks 2!

Very quickly after Fireworks 1 came out, we learned that the biggest features that people used in Fireworks 1 were the optimization, slicing, image map, and rollover tools, but that they wanted to do even more once they saw the possibilities we had opened up to them. Others wanted us to add features important to their workflow that we had missed in Fireworks 1. So we did the wise thing, and listened.

The result of all those customer requests were

- ✦ Disjoint rollovers
- ✦ User customizable HTML output templates
- ✦ A Behaviors panel for controlling the interactive properties of Web objects
- ✦ Scanning
- ✦ Color locking
- ✦ Scripted batching
- ✦ Styles

We also found that people wanted more interaction between their Web site creation software and their graphics software, so we decided to make Fireworks into Dreamweaver's best friend. Some of the things we added between Fireworks and Dreamweaver were

- ✦ HTML that works flawlessly with Dreamweaver
- ✦ Quickly Optimizing graphics using Fireworks from within Dreamweaver
- ✦ Direct Dreamweaver Library output, so Dreamweaver will update your entire site automatically (this one is really cool!)
- ✦ An easy way for Dreamweaver to launch Fireworks to edit an image, and have Fireworks edit the original source

So what will the future bring? One thing is certain: it will bring change. Many technologies are on the verge of being feasible and mainstream, and we are constantly listening to hear what people want to do with them. It will also bring workflow problems that people either didn't have, or didn't notice, previously. Our job will be to help you solve them.

But the thing I want you to remember is that the most important feature of our software is our users. We dedicate ourselves to making the time to visit Web developers, participate in our newsgroup, and read our wishlist so we know what you think the future is all about. If you still have questions and comments after reading Joseph's book, please drop us a note at wish-fireworks@macromedia.com. I guarantee it'll be read.

*— Dennis Griffin*
VP, Fireworks Development
Macromedia, Inc.

# Preface

Remember that burst of pleasure when you first realized how exciting the Web could be? I'll let you in on a little secret. Macromedia's Fireworks makes creating graphics for the Web fun again. Images produced with Fireworks are as sophisticated and rich as those created with any other combination of programs, plus they're Web-ready — as optimized as possible and bundled with HTML and JavaScript code for amazing interactive effects.

I'll be the first to admit my bias. I'm a power Dreamweaver user, and it seems only natural to combine Macromedia's premier Web authoring tool with its graphic solution. But while I'm confessing, let me also note that I have no patience for tools that don't do the job. The wonderful revelation about Fireworks is that this program eliminates production bottlenecks I didn't even know existed — all while producing stunning imagery.

When I set out to write this book, I decided to really push Fireworks. Rather than using it merely to optimize a series of images (which is does superbly) or create a compact animation (ditto) from work created in other programs, I used Fireworks exclusively for all image manipulation and creation. Consequently, both my productivity and my creativity went through the roof. *Fireworks 2 Bible* was designed to give you all the information and techniques you need to achieve the same results.

## Who Should Read This Book?

The Web is, without a doubt, one of the key phenomena of our time, and it's attracted an enormous amount of talent, both artistic and technical. After all, how often does a new mass medium appear? The range of Web designers extends from first-generation artists drawn to the exciting Internet possibilities to print professionals who need to expand their creative horizons. *Fireworks 2 Bible* talks to all those groups, offering solutions to everyday graphics problems as well as providing a complete reference for the program.

# What Hardware and Software Do You Need?

*Fireworks 2 Bible* includes full coverage of Fireworks 2. If you don't own a copy of the program, the CD-ROM contains a demo version for your trial use. Written to be platform-independent, this book covers both Macintosh and Windows 95/98/NT versions of Fireworks 2.

Macromedia recommends the following minimum requirements for running Fireworks on a Macintosh:

- ✦ Power Macintosh
- ✦ MacOS 7.5.5 or later
- ✦ 24MB of available RAM with Virtual Memory turned on
- ✦ 60MB of available disk space
- ✦ Color monitor capable of 640 × 480 resolution and 256 colors
- ✦ Adobe Type Manager 4 or later, if you work with Type 1 fonts
- ✦ CD-ROM drive

Macromedia recommends the following minimum requirements for running Fireworks on a Windows system:

- ✦ Intel Pentium processor, 120 MHz or equivalent
- ✦ Windows 95/98, NT 4.0 (with Service Pack 3) or later
- ✦ 32MB of available RAM for Windows 95 or 98; 40MB of Ram for Windows NT
- ✦ 60MB of available disk space
- ✦ 256-color monitor capable of 640 × 480 resolution
- ✦ Adobe Type Manager 4 or later, if you work with Type 1 fonts
- ✦ CD-ROM drive

Please note that these are the minimum requirements. As with all graphics-based design tools, more capability is definitely better for using Fireworks, especially in terms of memory and processor speed.

# How This Book Is Organized

*Fireworks 2 Bible* can take you from raw beginner to full-fledged professional if read cover-to-cover. However, you're more likely to read each section as needed, taking the necessary information and coming back later. To facilitate this approach, *Fireworks 2 Bible* is divided into seven major task-oriented parts. When you're familiar with Fireworks, feel free to skip around the book, using it as a reference guide as you build up your own knowledge base.

The early chapters present the basics, and all chapters contain clearly written steps for the tasks you need to perform. In later chapters, you encounter boxed sections labeled "Fireworks Techniques." Fireworks Techniques are step-by-step instructions for accomplishing specific Web designer tasks; for example, using mask groups to create three-dimensional images. Naturally, you can also use the Fireworks Techniques as stepping-stones for your own explorations into Web page creation.

If you're running Fireworks while reading this book, don't forget to use the CD-ROM. An integral element of the book, the CD-ROM offers a number of additional Fireworks textures, gradients, and HTML templates in addition to trial programs from major software vendors.

## Part I: Come See the Fireworks

Part I begins with an overview of Fireworks's philosophy and design. To get the most out of the program, you need to understand the key advantages it offers and the deficiencies it addresses. Part I takes you all the way from setting up documents to getting the most out of Fireworks.

The opening chapters give you a full reference to the Fireworks interface and all of its customizable features. Of special interest to Fireworks 1 users is a complete guide to all the newly added features (and there are a lot of them) in Chapter 1. Later chapters in this part provide an overview of everything that Fireworks can do — I'm sure you'll agree that this is one feature-rich program.

## Part II: Mastering the Tools

The Fireworks approach to graphics is fundamentally different from any other tool on the market. Consequently, you'll need to travel the short learning curve before you can get the most out of Fireworks. The early chapters in Part II cover all the essentials from basic object creation to full-blown photo manipulation.

Color is a key component of any graphic designer's toolkit, and color on the Web requires special attention as you'll see in Chapter 7. The object-oriented nature of Fireworks is explored in chapters on creating simple strokes and combining paths in a variety of ways to make more sophisticated graphics. Fireworks excels at creating graphical text for the Web — you'll see how in Chapter 10.

## Part III: Achieving Effects

Fireworks graphics really begin to gain depth in Part III. The variety of fills and textures available — as well as the ability to add your own — are critical for the wide range of image production a Web designer is responsible for. Chapter 12 explores the exciting world of Fireworks Live Effects; exciting not just because they're easy to create and they look great, but also because of the positive impact Live Effects will have on your workflow.

It's the rare graphic that consists of a single object or image. Chapter 13 explains the Fireworks methods for arranging and compositing multiple objects to achieve stunning results; the mask group feature is especially powerful. In addition to manipulating vector graphics, Fireworks is adept at handling bitmapped imagery. Check out Chapter 14 to learn all you need to know about applying Xtras and Filters.

## Part IV: Coordinating Workflow

Web design is an ongoing process, not a single event. Part IV is dedicated to helping you streamline your workflow efficiently as you acquire images via scanning or importing, manipulate them in Fireworks, and then optimize them on export. While it's true that Web graphic design is an art form, it's also a business — and Fireworks can make your business better.

One element of the business of Web graphics is enforcing a consistent look and feel on a client-by-client basis. Styles, new in Fireworks 2, are terrific for achieving this goal as well as representing an efficient means for applying multiple effects. The final chapter in Part IV describes how Fireworks 2 works to help you update and maintain your graphics through new features such as the URL Manager and Find and Replace.

## Part V: Entering the Web

As the first image editor to output HTML and JavaScript code, Fireworks has broken new ground. With its full-featured capabilities to create hotspots, image maps, and sliced images embedded in HTML tables, Fireworks is notably Web-savvy. Part V explains the basics of Web interactivity for those designers unfamiliar with the territory and also offers specific step-by-step instructions for linking JavaScript behaviors to graphics.

While you may think you know all that Fireworks can do, you haven't seen anything until you've explored its customizable features. Built into Fireworks is a full JavaScript language interpreter that allows you to batch process files, execute search-and-replace operations, and perform backups — all under script control; Chapter 21 has all the details. Finally, in Part V, if you work with Dreamweaver (or work with someone who does), you'll want to check out Chapter 22 to get the most out of the integration possibilities between Fireworks and Dreamweaver.

## Part VI: Animation

Animations have become very important to the Web. Not only do they offer an alternative to static displays, but GIF animations are used extensively in the creation of banner ads. Animation in Fireworks 2 is very full-featured with the addition of Onion Skinning for precise positioning and multiframe editing for overall adjustments. Moreover, Fireworks employs a feature called Symbols and Instances to achieve tweening effects for rapid production of movement and other effects.

## Appendixes

In a program as full-featured as Fireworks, your productivity gets a boost with every keyboard shortcut you can memorize. Appendix A is a handy reference guide to them all for both Macintosh and Windows systems, while Appendix B covers all the material available on the CD-ROM.

# Conventions Used in This Book

The following conventions are used throughout this book.

## Windows and Macintosh conventions

Because *Fireworks 2 Bible* is a cross-platform book, it gives instructions for both Windows and Macintosh users when keystrokes for a particular task differ. Throughout this book, the Windows keystrokes are given first; and the Macintosh are given second in parentheses, as follows:

> To undo an action, press Ctrl+Z (Command+Z).

The first action instructs Windows users to press the Ctrl and Z keys in combination, and the second action (in parentheses) instructs Macintosh users to press the Command and Z keys together.

## Key combinations

When you are instructed to press two or more keys simultaneously, each key in the combination is separated by a plus sign. For example:

> Ctrl+Alt+T (Command+Option+T)

The preceding line tells you to press the three listed keys for your system at the same time. You can also hold down one or more keys and then press the final key. Release all the keys at the same time.

## Mouse instructions

When instructed to *click* an item, you must move the mouse pointer to the specified item and click the mouse button once. Windows users use the left mouse button unless otherwise instructed. *Double-click* means clicking the mouse button twice in rapid succession.

When instructed to select an item, you may click it once as previously described. If you are selecting text or multiple objects, you must click the mouse button once, hold it down, and then move the mouse to a new location. The item or items selected invert color. To clear the selection, click once anywhere on the Web page.

## Menu commands

When instructed to select a command from a menu, you see the menu and the command separated by an arrow symbol. For example, when instructed to execute the Open command from the File menu, you see the notation File ⇨ Open. Some menus use submenus, in which case you see an arrow for each submenu, as follows: Insert ⇨ Form Object ⇨ Text Field.

## Typographical conventions

*Italic* type is used for new terms and for emphasis. **Boldface** type is used for text that you need to type directly from the computer keyboard.

## Code

A special typeface indicates HTML or other code, as demonstrated in the following example:

```
<html>
<head>
<title>Untitled Document</title>
</head>
<body bgcolor="#FFFFFF">
</body>
</html>
```

This code font is also used within paragraphs to designate HTML tags, attributes, and values such as <body>, bgcolor, and #FFFFFF.

The (¬) character at the end of a code line means you should type the next line of code before pressing the Enter (Return) key.

# Navigating Through This Book

Various signposts and icons are located throughout the *Fireworks 2 Bible* for your assistance. Each chapter begins with an overview of its information, and ends with a quick summary.

Icons are placed in the text to indicate important or especially helpful items. Here's a list of the icons and their functions:

 Tips provide you with extra knowledge that separates the novice from the pro.

 Notes provide additional or critical information and technical data on the current topic.

 Sections marked with a New Feature icon detail an innovation introduced in Fireworks 2.

 Cross-Reference icons indicate places where you can find more information on a particular topic.

 The Caution icon is your warning of a potential problem or pitfall.

 The On the CD-ROM icon indicates the CD-ROM contains a related file.

# Further Information

You can find more help for specific problems and questions by investigating several Web sites. Macromedia's own Fireworks Web site is the best place to start:

```
http://www.macromedia.com/products/fireworks
```

I heartily recommend that you visit and participate in the official Fireworks newsgroup:

```
news://forums.macromedia.com/macromedia.fireworks
```

You're also invited to visit my Web site for book updates and new developments:

```
http://www.idest.com/fireworks
```

You can also e-mail me:

```
jlowery@idest.com
```

I can't promise instantaneous turnaround, but I answer all my mail to the best of my ability.

# Acknowledgments

It may be my name on the cover, but it wouldn't be there if it weren't for the help of an awful lot of very generous people. Right off the bat, I really want to thank those supportive folks at IDG Books Worldwide who took a chance on a new title, Debra Williams Cauley and Kathy Yankton in particular. I know it's not easy getting the go-ahead for a book to be published, and I really appreciate their efforts.

Of course, getting the ball rolling is just the start of the game. I owe Laura Brown a huge debt of gratitude for all her work in keeping the momentum up — especially during those up-hill times. Special thanks to Laura for assembling such a capable team, including copy editors Timothy Borek, Jennifer Mario, and Bill McManus. Ram Ganesh, in addition to being a top-notch graphics designer and Web developer, revealed another talent by serving as my technical editor for this book who telecommuted to work from Singapore, no less. I'm especially grateful to Ram for his asides into technique and style as I am to fellow Fireworks author (not to mention New York City resident) Sandee Cohen. Sandee's work continues to inspire me and I wish her continued success.

Simon White, and his company MediaFear, is known among the Fireworks and Dreamweaver newsgroup regulars as one of the most knowledgeable and generous experts around. I'd especially like to thank Simon for his contributions to this book, not to mention his availability as a sounding board for some of my more off-the-wall concepts. It's always refreshing to me to find someone whose artistic vision is so well formed and energized. You'll find numerous examples of Simon's work throughout the book and especially in the color plate section. Several other top designers contributed work to demonstrate the power of Fireworks, including Lisa Lopuck, Donna Casey, and Ruth Peyser — warm hugs and great thanks all 'round.

Of course, I wouldn't be writing this book — and you certainly wouldn't be reading it — if it weren't for the fantastic vision of the Fireworks team. Fireworks is a marvelously complex program, and there is a true glory in bringing it to life. A hearty thank you and a round of applause to you all: Dennis Griffen, Doug Benson, David Morris, John Ahlquist, Jeff Ahlquist, Matt Bendicksen, Steven Johnson, Jeff Doar, and Eric Wolff. I'd also like to single out Mark Haynes for not only the specific questions he helped me with, but for all the users he's helped on board the Fireworks effort with his tireless answers in the newsgroup. Finally, let me offer a special thanks to Diana Smedley, Fireworks Product Manager, for her early support and encouragement as well as the openness and access she granted me.

# Contents at a Glance

# Contents

## Part II: Mastering the Tools    111

# Come See the Fireworks

# Welcome to Fireworks

E very Fourth of July, I sit with my friends and family on a neighbor's rooftop to watch the fireworks explode over Manhattan. Almost every apartment building roof around us holds a similar gathering. Everyone oohs and ahhs to their own view of the spectacular light show, some of the patterns and images familiar, while others have never been seen before.

The World Wide Web has become a global light show, running around the clock. The graphics that fill Web pages explode with brilliance, intensity, and meaning, and are viewed by millions, each from their own perspective. The Web is a new medium uniquely capable of both enlightening and entertaining; it's also an extremely voracious medium, as thousands upon thousands of new and updated Web sites emerge daily. In addition to content, the Web needs graphics: all manner of images, illustrations, logos, symbols, and icons. Some of the imagery is static, others animated, and still others are interactive. Design has definitely encountered a whole new frontier.

To contribute the most to this new medium, new tools are necessary. The Web is screen-, not print-based, and it has its own set of rules and guidelines. Though some print-oriented graphic tools have begun to extend themselves with the Internet in mind, a completely new tool was needed — a tool that did everything Web designers needed and did it efficiently but with flair. A tool capable of creating graphics light enough to soar, yet powerful enough to brighten the night.

Enter Fireworks.

# The New Generation of Web Graphic Tools

Fireworks is the premier Web graphics program from Macromedia. As a next-generation software package, Fireworks has definitely benefited from all the great computer graphics programs that came before it. But whereas much of Fireworks works in a similar way to other graphic tools — which significantly shortens the learning curve — the program is purely focused on the Web and offers many innovative Internet-only features, especially in version 2.

Fireworks was built from the ground up with the Web in mind. Macromedia examined the way graphic designers were creating their imagery and found that, before Fireworks, most designers used a wide variety of tools to achieve their goals. An initial design was usually laid out in a vector drawing program like FreeHand or Adobe Illustrator. But vectors aren't native to the Web, so the illustration was then ported to an image-editing program such as Photoshop or Paint Shop Pro. In these pixel-based programs, special effects like drop shadows or beveled edges were laboriously added and text was merged with the bitmap before it was exported to an optimizing program. An optimizer, such as Debabelizer, was necessary to ensure that Web-safe colors were used and the file size was the smallest possible for the bandwidth-limited Internet. Next came integration into the Web: linking URLs, image maps, rollovers, slices, and more. A slew of small specialty programs filled these needs. Moreover, many designers were forced to learn HTML and JavaScript; because no program did everything that was needed, many tasks had to be done manually. Adding to the intense difficulty of mastering all of the various programs was the problem of modifying an image. If a client wanted a change — and clients always want changes—the whole graphic had to be rebuilt from scratch.

Fireworks offered a revolutionary new way to create Web graphics. It combined the best features of all the various programs:

✦ Vector drawing tools for easy layout

✦ Sophisticated pixel-based image-editing tools for working with existing graphics and scanned imagery

✦ Live effects for straightforward but spectacular special effects

✦ An export engine for file optimization to Web standards, with onscreen comparison views so the Web designer could select the best image at the smallest size

✦ HTML and JavaScript output tied to the graphics themselves

Best of all, virtually every single aspect of a Fireworks graphic can be altered at any stage. In other words, in Fireworks everything is editable, all the time. Not only is this a tremendous time-saver, but it's also a major production enhancement — and the Web requires an extraordinary amount of material and maintenance. Not only are new sites and Web pages constantly going online, but existing pages need continual updating. The underlying philosophy of Fireworks — everything editable, all the time — reflects a deep awareness of the Web designer's real world situation.

If you're coming from a print background and you're used to working with tools like Photoshop, it's important to grasp certain Fireworks fundamentals. First, you should realize that Fireworks is not an image-editing program primarily, although it has excellent image-editing tools. Fireworks is basically a vector drawing program that outputs natural-looking bitmap images. Once you get the hang of drawing with vectors — also known as paths and far more flexible than bitmaps — and applying bitmapped strokes and fills, you'll never want to go back.

Second, Fireworks, as a Web graphics engine, is screen — not print — oriented. The resolution of an image on a monitor is typically far lower than the resolution of the same image in print. Images are generally worked on and saved in their actual size; the technique of working with a larger image for fine detail and then reducing it to enhance the resolution won't work with Fireworks — in fact, it will backfire and you'll lose the very detail you were trying to instill. However, you can zoom in (up to 6,400%) for detailed correction. Just keep in mind that ultimately, all images are viewed at 100% in the browser.

Which brings us to the final point for designers new to the Web: Fireworks is not just screen-based, it's Internet-based. Many Fireworks options are geared toward Web realities such as the importance of a minimum file size, the limitations of Web-safe colors, and capabilities of the majority of browsers. Fireworks is extremely respectful of the Web environment and, when properly used, will help you conserve production, browser, and Internet resources.

# Of Pixels and Paths: The Best of Both Worlds

Although the Web is ultimately a pixel-based medium, paths are much easier to control and edit. Fireworks bases most of its graphic creation power on vectors, while offering a complete range of image-editing options. By switching effortlessly between paths and pixels, Fireworks 2 very smoothly integrates them both.

Fireworks treats the separate graphic elements as independent objects that can be easily manipulated, arranged, and aligned. This object orientation is also extremely useful for production work. A single path object that defines the basic outline of a button, for example, can quickly be duplicated and positioned to build a navigation bar where each button is identical except for the identifying text, as shown in Figure 1-1.

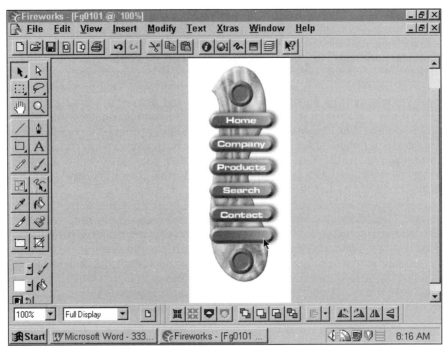

**Figure 1-1:** The basic shape for each of these buttons consists of one object, highlighted here.

## Vector tools with organic bitmaps

For ultimate flexibility, Fireworks separates the stroke, fill, and effects of an object from the object itself. This lets the Web designer create almost endless combinations for custom artwork while keeping each element individual and editable. If the client loves the orange glow around a button, but wants the text to be centered instead of flush right, it's no problem in Fireworks. Changing one aspect of a graphic — without having to rebuild the image from scratch — is one of Fireworks's key strengths.

While Fireworks depends on vector objects to create the underlying structure of its graphics, what goes on top of that structure (the stroke, fill, and effects) is displayed with pixels. Moreover, the bitmapped imagery is calculated with numerous variables to give an organic feel to the object. An object's bitmapped elements are recalculated and reapplied each time the path structure is changed, as shown in Figure 1-2. This procedure eliminates the distortion that occurs with other programs that just reshape the pixels.

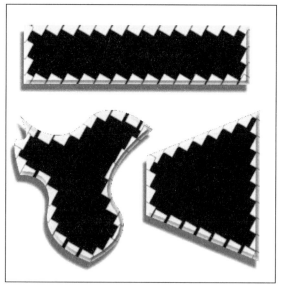

**Figure 1-2:** Change the shape of a Fireworks object and the bitmapped fill and stroke are recalculated and reapplied.

**Cross-Reference** To find out more about strokes, see Chapter 8. You can learn more about fills in Chapter 11.

## Bitmap compatibility

As a next-generation graphics tool, Fireworks gracefully respects much of the imagery that has been previously created. With a full range of import filters, Fireworks can open and edit files from Photoshop, CorelDraw, xRes, and many more tools. Fireworks offers a full complement of bitmap selection tools including Marquee, Lasso, and Magic Wand, as well as pixel-level drawing tools such as Pencil and Eraser.

Filters are a large aspect of an image-editing program's featureset, and Fireworks is no slouch in that respect, either. In addition to various built-in filters such as Gaussian Blur, Invert, and Sharpen, Fireworks is compatible with the Photoshop filter standard. Consequently it works with any third-party plug-in that adheres to the standard, including Eye Candy from Alien Skin Software (Figure 1-3), Kai's Power Tools from MetaCreations, and Intellihance from Extensis. Moreover, you can easily include all of the third-party plug-ins you use in Photoshop by just selecting a single preference.

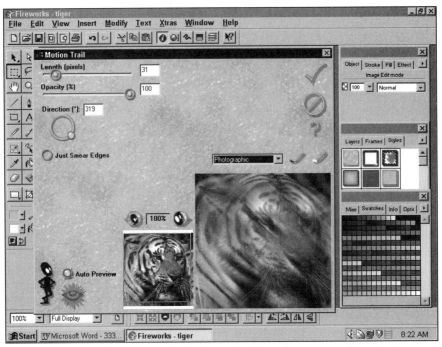

**Figure 1-3:** Fireworks works with all the major Photoshop-compatible plug-ins such as those from Alien Skin Software.

**Cross-Reference**    Want to know more about using third-party filters in Fireworks? Turn to Chapter 14.

## Live effects

One of the most challenging aspects of Web graphics used to be special effects, such as applying beveled edges and drop shadows. Fireworks takes all that complex, painstaking layer and mask manipulation previously required and replaces it with Live Effects. Live Effects provides almost one-step ease with sophisticated variations for such effects as Inner Bevel, Outer Bevel, Drop Shadow, Glow, and Emboss.

Not only are these effects very straightforward to create in Fireworks, but they adapt to any changes made to the object itself — hence, the name Live Effects. This feature is very important for modifying graphics and it speeds up production work tremendously. You can even batch process a group of files, reducing them in size, and the effects are scaled and reapplied automatically.

For detailed information on effects in Fireworks, see Chapter 12.

## Styles

Styles are a new method in Fireworks 2 of consistently applying the look and feel of a graphic. A Fireworks Style quickly replicates an object's stroke, fill, effect, and even text settings. Web designers can use Styles to keep a client's Web site consistent-looking across the board. Additionally, because Styles can be shared as files, a lead designer can create a base style for a Web graphic that can then be applied on a production basis to the rest of the site.

Fireworks 2 comes with a huge range of prebuilt Styles, available through the program itself and on its CD-ROM, a few of which are shown in Figure 1-4. It's also quite easy to define any combination of stroke, fill, and effect as its own style and always have it available.

**Figure 1-4:** The same geometric shape, created in Fireworks, with three different styles applied.

 Styles are emerging as a major time- and work-saver; to learn more about them, see Chapter 17.

## Animation

Before Fireworks, one of the bevy of tools in a Web designer's arsenal was often a package to create animated GIFs, especially with the increased use of banner ads. This type of separate program is no longer necessary: Fireworks enables Web designers to build, preview, and export animated GIFs in any size or shape. Naturally, you can take advantage of all Fireworks path and bitmap tools to create and edit your animation.

Fireworks also supports Symbols and Instances, as well as tweening. A Symbol is a defined graphic that is linked to its copies or Instances. If you change the Symbol, by altering its color for example, all of the Instances instantly change as well. Furthermore, Fireworks is capable of creating any specified number of tweened copies between a selected Symbol and Instance. You could, for example, create an animated fade by tweening a fully opaque Symbol and its transparent Instance.

**Cross-Reference** Animation is a specialized but integral aspect of Web graphics. To find out more about it, turn to Part VI, "Animation."

# Linking to the Web

What do you call a graphics program that doesn't just output graphics? In the case of Fireworks, I call it a major innovation. On the surface, a Web page appears to be composed of images and text, but underneath it's all code. Fireworks bridges the gap between the images of a Web page and its HTML and JavaScript code to create image maps, slices, rollovers, and much more. In Fireworks 2, you even have the option of choosing different styles of code, depending on your Web authoring tool.

Fireworks is fully integrated with the Web in mind. Every aspect of the program, from Web-safe color pickers to export optimization, keeps the Internet target clearly in focus. Even functions common to other programs have been given a special Web-oriented twist. For example, the capability to output a graphic to print is invaluable to Web designers as a way to present comps to clients; in Fireworks, you can print an image the way it will appear on the Web or at a higher print resolution — it's your choice.

## Hotspots and slices

*Hotspots* and *slices* are frequently used elements in Web page design. Until Fireworks came along, however, designers had to create them using a program outside their usual graphics tools or tediously handcraft them individually. A *hotspot* is used as part of a Web page image map and is made of a series of $x,y$ coordinates — elements definitely not in traditional visual artist vocabulary. Fireworks lets you draw out your hotspot, just as you would any other object, and handles all the math output for you.

*Slice* is a general term for the different parts of a larger image that has been carved into smaller pieces for faster loading or to incorporate a rollover. The separate parts of an image are then reassembled in an HTML table. If it sounds to you like an overwhelming amount of work, you're right — if you're not using Fireworks. However, Fireworks guides your slicing efforts, as shown in Figure 1-5, and then builds the HTML table for you. Additionally, Fireworks lets you optimize different slices, exporting one part as a GIF and another as a JPEG (or whatever configuration gives you the highest quality at the lowest file size).

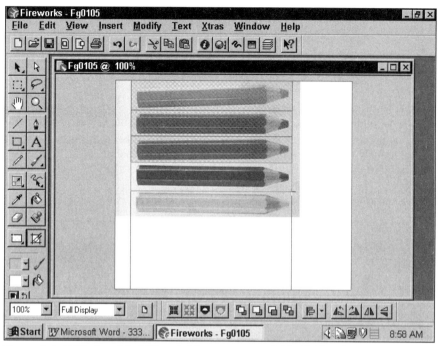

**Figure 1-5:** With the aid of Slice Guides, you can quickly divide a larger image into separate slices.

**Cross-Reference** Explore more of what's possible with Fireworks hotspots and slices in Chapter 19.

## Images with behaviors

Static images are no longer enough on the Web; interactive images — images that react in some way when selected by the user — are a requirement for any state-of-the-art Web page. Fireworks handles this interactivity through a technique known as *Behaviors*. A Behavior is a combination of image and code: quite complex HTML and JavaScript code, to be exact. But when you apply a Behavior in Fireworks, all the code writing is handled for you.

Fireworks Behaviors can display a message when users pass their pointers over a particular image, or it can swap one image for another. Fireworks 2 can even swap an image in one place when a graphic in another place is selected. Best of all, you can output code specific to your Web authoring tool as necessary. Fireworks includes code templates for Dreamweaver 2, Dreamweaver Libraries, and Microsoft FrontPage, as well as generic code that works with most tools. And, if you've got the need and the savvy, you can also create custom templates.

For more information about Behaviors, check out Chapter 20.

## Optimizing for the Web

An overriding concern of many Web designers is file optimization: how do you get the best-looking image possible at the smallest size? The Fireworks 2 Export module lets you compare the results of up to four different file compression views simultaneously to quickly pick the best Web candidate, as shown in Figure 1-6. Or, if you need to target a specific file size, choose the Export to Size wizard and have Fireworks make the selection for you.

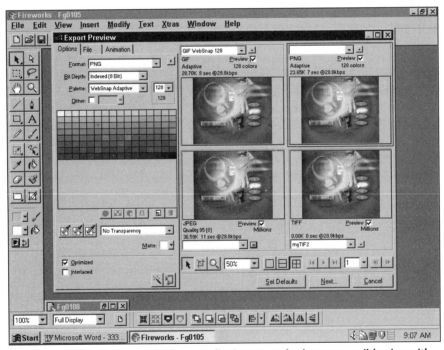

**Figure 1-6:** Quickly find the highest-quality image at the lowest possible size with Fireworks's Export Preview.

The Export Preview has been significantly enhanced for Fireworks 2. Color management is greatly improved: colors can be edited, locked, snapped to Web safe, or made transparent at the click of a mouse. You can now also visually crop an image directly at export or scale it proportionately.

**Cross-Reference** To get the most out of exporting in Fireworks, check out Chapter 16.

## Dreamweaver integration

Dreamweaver 2 is a top-of-the-line Web authoring tool, now made even better through a tighter integration with Fireworks 2 — and a tighter integration means enhanced productivity for both facets of Web creation. If you already have Dreamweaver 2 installed, when you install Fireworks, numerous new commands and options are added to Dreamweaver including the capability to optimize an inserted image directly in Dreamweaver with standard Fireworks controls.

The integration is not apparent just from the Dreamweaver side, either. Fireworks is now capable of outputting standard Dreamweaver code or Dreamweaver Library code, which creates reusable elements. The two programs are moving closer to each other from a usability viewpoint also; for example, Fireworks 2 now previews in a browser exactly the same way that Dreamweaver does.

**Cross-Reference** For all the details on maximizing the Fireworks 2/Dreamweaver 2 combination, see Chapter 22.

# Production Tools

Though the Web offers plenty of room for creative expression, creating Web graphics is, bottom-line, a business. To succeed at such a business you need a tool capable of high production output, and Fireworks 2 certainly fits the bill. In this version of Fireworks, you can insert whole pages of URLs at a time, rescale entire folders of images, or update all the text embedded in images in a Web site.

## URL Manager

To take the fullest advantage of Fireworks HTML and JavaScript output, you need to attach hyperlinks or URLs to your images. Previously, this operation was a fairly tedious process that involved entering each URL by hand. In Fireworks 2, you can import URLs from URL libraries, Bookmark files, or HTML pages through the new URL Manager, shown in Figure 1-7. Not only does this remove the drudgery of manually entering the links, but it also eliminates the errors that are so easy to make when inputting complex hyperlinks. Once these URLs are in the URL Manager, you can easily apply them to the buttons of a navigation bar or hotspots of an image map.

**Figure 1-7:** The new URL Manager instantly reads in URLs from almost any source: a Fireworks URL library, a browser Bookmark file, or a standard HTML page.

## Batch processing

The sheer volume of Web pages — and their included images — have made batch processing of images a virtual necessity. It's not at all uncommon for a client to request that thumbnail images of an entire product line be created for an online catalog. With Fireworks 2, just point to the folder of full-size images and tell Fireworks whether to scale them to a particular pixel size or a percentage, as was done for the six images in Figure 1-8. Best of all, you can easily save your script as a Fireworks Scriptlet to apply at a later date or customize.

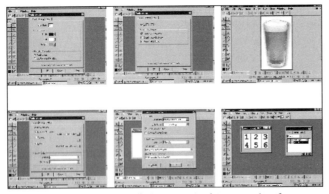

**Figure 1-8:** Using Fireworks's new Batch Processing feature, these images were automatically, consistently scaled.

Another new feature of Fireworks 2 is Find and Replace. Find and Replace in a graphics program? What use could that possibly have? Very far-reaching uses, to be frank. Fireworks can now search and replace text, fonts, color, and/or URLs in any Fireworks graphic. You can update the graphics — and the links — for an entire Web site in one fell swoop. Moreover, these Find and Replace operations can be part of a Batch Processing scriptlet and stored, reused, or customized as needed.

# What's New in Fireworks 2

Any way you look at it, the jump from the first version of Fireworks to Fireworks 2 was quite a leap. The Fireworks engineering team rethought major areas of the interface and added feature after feature to meet both customer needs and users' wishes in addition to stamping out bugs and tossing in some innovations of their own.

The following listing is fairly comprehensive, but I won't claim it's exhaustive. The Fireworks team packed this release to the rafters with Web graphic advances too numerous for anyone to keep track of.

## User interface

User interface enhancements may not seem to qualify as a "feature" to many people, but they definitely have one of the largest impacts. Significant enhancements, such as those implemented in Fireworks 2, greatly increase productivity and workflow. One of the biggest improvements was in the handling of bitmapped images. Previously, image edit mode was difficult to get into and somewhat frustrating to the user. Now, switching between image objects and path objects is almost effortless.

User interface enhancements include

- ✦ Draggable tabs
- ✦ Document Properties dialog
- ✦ Fewer disabled items
- ✦ Hide Panels command
- ✦ Icon buttons in Layers and Frames panels
- ✦ Image edit switching enhancements
- ✦ Info tabbed panel
- ✦ Object inspectors
- ✦ Pop-up color swatches
- ✦ Precise cursors

✦ Preview drag

✦ Saved export settings enhancements

✦ Slice guides in the workspace

✦ Styles panel

✦ Swatches tabbed panel for windows

✦ URL/slice inspectors

✦ URL/slice tools in the toolbox

**Cross-Reference** For details on all the user interface changes, see the rest of the chapters in Part I, "Come See the Fireworks."

## Graphic creation

The largest number of Fireworks additions falls under the category of graphic creation. Some program modifications were enhancements to existing features, but many new features were added in this area. Chief among them are a whole series of Path Operations that were only previously feasible in a dedicated vector drawing program such as FreeHand—now Fireworks can combine path objects in numerous ways that really open up the object creation techniques.

Graphic creation enhancements include

✦ Constrain Brush and Pencil tools

✦ Constrain proportions in numeric transform

✦ Crop tool enhancements

✦ Join paths

✦ JPEG enhancements

✦ Modify ➪ Document ➪ Image Size

✦ Modify ➪ Document ➪ Trim Canvas

✦ Multiple effects

✦ New masking model

✦ Onion skinning for animation

✦ Paint Bucket fills similar areas

✦ Path operations

✦ Photoshop plug-in enhancements

✦ Shared layers

✦ Slice along guides

✦ Text editor anti-alias

✦ Text editor auto apply

✦ Text editor color well

✦ Underlined text

✦ VCR-style animation controls

**Cross-Reference** To find out how to get the most from these new features, see Part II, "Mastering the Tools."

## Web connectivity

When Fireworks first came out, its capability to output HTML code was like a rocket taking off. Now the rocket has dropped its first stage and the booster has truly kicked in. Connectivity to the Web has been greatly enhanced in a myriad of ways: new behaviors have been added, along with a new, more extensible model for applying them; slices and hotspots are far more flexible and powerful than before, as well as easier to use; code can now be output to different types of tools, both standard and custom; and a tighter integration with Dreamweaver has been achieved. With all these improvements, Fireworks has brought the two worlds of Web designers — graphics and code — much closer together.

Web connectivity enhancements include

✦ Behaviors panel

✦ Customizable HTML and JavaScript

✦ Customized auto-naming

✦ Disjoint rollovers

✦ Export Dreamweaver Library

✦ External source rollovers

✦ Hotspot rollovers

✦ Insert Slice command

✦ Interactive swap image user interface

✦ Launch and optimize from Dreamweaver

✦ Preview in browser

✦ Streamlined export functions

✦ Toggle group behavior

✦ Web Dither Fill

✦ Web Layer

When you're ready to explore the new Web connectivity, see Part V, "Entering the Web."

## Image optimization

For many, image optimization is at the heart of Fireworks. Getting the best possible image with the smallest possible file size is what it's all about. Fireworks 2 offers much better control over the export process in general with numerous additions, especially in the area of color management to the Export Preview command.

Image optimization enhancements include

✦ Export images as CSS layers

✦ Export images as image wells

✦ Export Palette enhancements

✦ Export Preview enhancements

✦ Export to Size wizard

 To learn more about Fireworks as an optimizing engine, see Chapter 16.

## Workflow management

Almost every feature in the Workflow Management category is completely new in Fireworks 2. On the input side, there's the much-needed scanner and digital camera support, as well as the new option to open several files simultaneously — including the capability to combine those files as an animation. As part of the overall batch processing improvements in Fireworks 2, you can now edit files as a group with the very robust Find and Replace engine. Finally, one of my favorite new features, the URL Manager, greatly simplifies the process of linking graphics to the world outside.

Workflow management enhancements include

✦ Batch processing enhancements

✦ Find and Replace

✦ Open multiple files

✦ Scanning and digital camera support

✦ URL Manager

**Cross-Reference** To get the most out of the new Fireworks workflow improvements, see Part IV, "Coordinating Workflow."

# Summary

"Pick the right tool for the job," the saying goes — and Fireworks is definitely the right tool for the job of creating Web graphics. In many cases, it's the only tool you'll need to handle every aspect of this particular job: image creation, editing, optimization, and Web integration. It's no surprise that in the past, Web designers had to master many programs to even come close to what Fireworks can accomplish. When you're looking at Fireworks for the first time, keep these points in mind:

✦ Fireworks replaces an entire bookshelf of programs that Web designers had previously adapted for their use. With only one program to master, designers can work more efficiently and creatively.

✦ Fireworks is equally at home with vector-based objects and bitmapped-based images. Moreover, it combines vector structures with bitmapped surfaces to make editing easier and the results cleaner.

✦ Fireworks works with Photoshop and many other existing file types — and can even use Photoshop third-party filters to create special bitmap effects.

✦ One of Fireworks's key capabilities is to connect easily to the Web. To this end, Web-safe palettes are always available and HTML and JavaScript code — standard or custom — is just a click away.

✦ The more you work on the Web, the faster you realize just how much work there is to do. Fireworks is a terrific production tool and makes updating graphics, via search and replace operations or batch processing, an automated process instead of a manual drudge.

✦ Fireworks 2 improved upon almost every aspect of the initial version of Fireworks. More than 60 major enhancements were incorporated in Fireworks features such as the user interface, graphics creation, Web connectivity, image optimization, and workflow management.

In the next chapter, you'll take an extensive tour of Fireworks user interface and all of its commands.

✦　　✦　　✦

# Understanding the Interface

**F**ireworks was designed to meet a need among Web
graphics artists: to simplify the workflow. Before
Fireworks, designers typically used different programs for
object creation, optimization, and integration in the HTML
environment. Fireworks combines the best features of
several key tools — while offering numerous innovative
additions of its own — into a sophisticated interface that's
easy to use.

With Fireworks, the designer has tools for working with both
vector-based objects and pixel-based images. You'll even find
ways to combine the two different formats. When your image
is ready to make the move to the Web, Fireworks provides
various bridges to make a smooth transition to HTML. Best of
all, your graphics can be integrated with the necessary code
through a point-and-click environment.

Fireworks 2 continues the trend toward simplification with
several new features. First, you'll notice a much more fluid
transition between working with pixels and working with
vectors. Should you choose a pixel-oriented tool, Fireworks 2
automatically picks the pixel image in your graphic and not
the vector object. Fireworks 2 has also made the floating
panels both dockable and groupable to enable you to customize your workspace.

As with any truly powerful computer graphics program,
examining all the tools and options that Fireworks has to offer
at one time can be overwhelming. However, that's not how
most artists work. It's generally best to familiarize yourself with
a new tool by carrying out a specific task. Whereas it's fine to
go all the way through this chapter — which covers every
element of the Fireworks interface — you'll probably get the
most value when you use it as a reference guide. Once you've
discovered the power of Fireworks, it's hard to design Web
graphics any other way.

# Navigating the Drawing Area

Whether you start your graphics session by creating a new document or loading in an existing one, each file is opened into the *document window*. The document window, shown in Figure 2-1, can hold a single image, maximized to fill the space or a series of images, each in their own moveable, resizable window. You can even display multiple views of the same image at differing levels of magnification, if desired. The document window also holds all of Fireworks's various toolbars, floating panels, and the Toolbox.

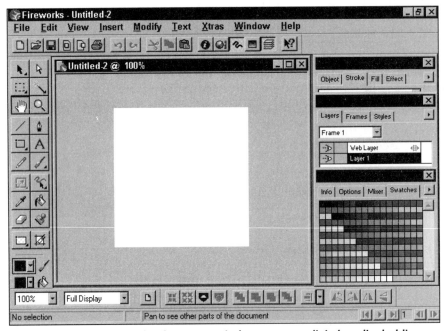

**Figure 2-1:** In Fireworks, the document window acts as a digital studio, holding any number of open images as well as the various tools and inspectors.

Think of the document window as your digital studio, not just a single canvas. Part of the power of computer graphics comes from the capability to cut-and-paste images, blending one into another. It's very easy in Fireworks to maintain and manage multiple images. Each image window has its own controls, according to the operating system in use. Window users have a drag bar, minimize, maximize and close buttons. All image windows on Macintosh systems also have a drag bar, maximize/resize, and close buttons. Both systems permit the image window — as well as the overall document window — to be moved, resized, and shifted from front to back with a single click.

**New Feature**

If an image window is expanded larger than the size of the canvas, a gray inactive region surrounds the canvas. With Fireworks 2, you can drag a corner of the image into the inactive area to resize it or expand the Crop tool beyond the canvas to enlarge the canvas size.

Should you shrink the size of the image window smaller than the current canvas — or magnify the image larger than the window — both horizontal and vertical scrollbars appear as needed.

You can select only one image window at a time. However, if you have several windows open, and your workspace is getting cluttered, you can organize all the windows in three different ways:

✦ Choose Window ➪ Cascade to stack your open images atop one another in a diagonal, so that the title bar for each is visible.

✦ Select Window ➪ Tile Horizontal to see all open images evenly distributed from top to bottom in the document window.

✦ Select Window ➪ Tile Vertical to view all open images evenly distributed from left to right in the document window.

As noted previously, not only can Fireworks display multiple images simultaneously, but it can also show multiple views of the same image, at various magnifications. To open a new view of a selected image, choose Window ➪ New Window. The new view opens at the same magnification as the previous image, but, as Figure 2-2 shows, you can easily zoom in for detail work on one view while displaying the overall effect in another.-

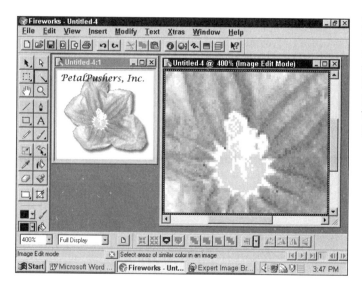

**Figure 2-2:** Use the New Window command to open a new view of the same image when both pixel-level modifications and the big picture are required.

## Working with Multiple Monitors

Fireworks 2 works with multiple monitors on both Macintosh and Windows 98 systems. Traditionally, the best strategy for using multiple monitors is to keep your graphic images on one monitor and all the floating panels and toolbars on the other. You can set up this arrangement through the Monitors tab of the Display Properties control panel in Windows and the Monitors & Sounds control panel in Macintosh systems.

With multiple monitors, you can also easily display the same graphic with different screen resolutions simultaneously. In general, you should view Web graphics under various resolutions to see what the Internet audience sees. If your monitors are set to two different resolutions—for example, one is at 640 × 480 and 256 colors, while the other is at 800 × 600 and 16 million colors—you can choose Window ➪ New Window to present a new view. Now, just drag one of the windows to the secondary monitor.

# Accessing Toolbars

In a computer graphics environment, toolbars are a major time saver. Although not as fast as keyboard shortcuts, onscreen toolbars with easily identifiable buttons make choosing a command very intuitive and drastically reduce the learning curve. In addition to numerous floating panels and inspectors (covered later in this chapter), Fireworks offers two toolbars—Toolbox and View Controls—common to both computer platforms and three toolbars—Main, Modify, and the Status bar—that are only available on Windows systems. Any functionality, however, found on the Windows toolbars, is also accessible through the menus for Macintosh users.

**Note**    Users of Fireworks version 1 will notice that Fireworks 2 has far fewer toolbars. The Info, Object, and URL toolbars have all been transformed into floating panels.

You can position the toolbars anywhere on the screen by clicking and dragging their title bar. Additionally, toolbars in Windows can be docked on any border of the document window; by default, the Main toolbar is docked on the top, the Toolbox is on the left, and the View Controls and Status bar toolbar are on the bottom. To detach a docked toolbar, click and drag the toolbar on any border. To dock a detached toolbar, drag the toolbar close to an edge of the document window until it snaps into position.

## Opening the Toolbox

The primary toolbar is called, appropriately enough, the Toolbox. All Fireworks drawing and editing tools can be found in the Toolbox. Most tools work with both pixel-based images and vector-based objects, although they occasionally do something different. In addition to the original 32 tools found in the first version of Fireworks, four tools for inserting Web objects such as hotspots and slices have been relocated to the Toolbox in Fireworks 2.

Tools that are similar — such as the Lasso, Polygon Lasso, and Magic Wand — are grouped together. Tool groups are recognizable by the small triangle in the right corner of the button. Clicking and holding any of these buttons causes the tool group to appear. Once the tool group is visible, you can select any of the tools in the group by moving the pointer over the tool and releasing the mouse; Figure 2-3 shows both the default toolbar and each of the tool groups.

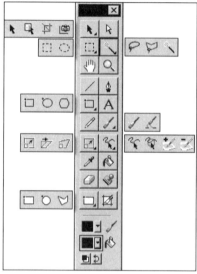

**Figure 2-3:** The Toolbox contains 36 different creation and editing tools for both graphics and Web objects.

All of the tools have keyboard shortcuts. As befits a program that incorporates both pixel- and vector-editing tools, these single-key shortcuts parallel pixel-based tools in Photoshop and vector-based ones in FreeHand. Where two or more tools share a keyboard shortcut (as with m for Marquee and Ellipse Marquee), the key acts as a toggle between the tools; the letter r toggles through six tools in all: the rectangle, the ellipse, and all the Web tools. You can find the button for each tool as well as its keyboard shortcut and a brief description in Table 2-1. More detailed information on each tool is presented throughout this book as the tool is used for various operations.

## Table 2-1
## Fireworks Toolbox Tools

| Button | Name | Shortcut | Description |
|---|---|---|---|
| | Pointer | v or 0 | Selects and moves objects |
| | Select Behind | v or 0 | Selects and moves objects behind other objects |
| | Crop | c | Decreases or increases canvas area |
| | Export Area | j | Exports a selected portion of an image |
| | Subselection | a | Selects points on a path or a member of a group |
| | Marquee | m | Selects a rectangular portion of a pixel image |
| | Ellipse Marquee | m | Selects an elliptical portion of a pixel image |
| | Lasso | l | Selects a freely drawn area of a pixel image |
| | Polygon Lasso | l | Selects a polygon-shaped area of a pixel image |
| | Magic Wand | w | Selects similar color areas of a pixel image |
| | Hand | h or spacebar (press and hold) | Pans the view of a document |
| | Zoom | z | Changes the magnification of the view |
| | Line | n | Draws straight lines |
| | Rectangle | r | Draws rectangles, rectangles with rounded corners, and squares |
| | Ellipse | r | Draws ellipses and circles |
| | Polygon | g | Draws polygons and stars |
| | Text | t | Inserts text objects |
| | Pencil | y | Draws single-pixel freeform strokes |
| | Brush | b | Draws strokes using the Stroke panel settings |
| | Redraw Path | b | Redraws a selected stroke |
| | Scale | q | Resizes and rotates objects |
| | Skew | q | Slants, rotates, and modifies the perspective of objects |
| | Distort | q | Reshapes and rotates objects |

| Button | Name | Shortcut | Description |
|--------|------|----------|-------------|
| | Freeform | f | Pulls or pushes a stroke segment with a variable-size cursor |
| | Reshape Area | f | Reshapes an object's area with a variable-size cursor |
| | Path Scrubber (+) | u | Increases stroke settings, controlled by cursor speed or stylus pressure |
| | Path Scrubber (-) | u | Decreases stroke settings, controlled by cursor speed or stylus pressure |
| | Eyedropper | i | Picks up color from any onscreen image to be applied to the active color well |
| | Paint Bucket | k | Fills the selected area with color, gradients, patterns, or textures and enables fills to be adjusted |
| | Eraser | e | Deletes pixels from pixel-based images and cuts the paths of vector-based objects |
| | Rubber Stamp | s | Repeats portion of pixel images |
| | Rectangle Hotspot | r | Draws an image map hotspot area in a rectangular shape |
| | Ellipse Hotspot | r | Draws an image map hotspot area in an elliptical shape |
| | Polygon Hotspot | r | Draws an image map hotspot area in a polygonal shape |
| | Slice | r | Draws a rectangular Slice object |
| | Swap Colors | x | Swaps the Stroke and Fill colors |
| | Reset Colors | d | Resets Stroke and Fill colors to black and white |

**Tip**      Certain tools have keyboard shortcuts that enable you to temporarily replace the active tool. Press Ctrl (Command) to switch to the Pointer temporarily, and Alt (Option) to switch to the Eyedropper. You can also quickly zoom in with Ctrl+spacebar (Command+spacebar) and zoom out with Ctrl+Alt+spacebar (Command+Option+spacebar).

## View controls

Although the final product of a Fireworks session is typically viewed at 100 percent of its size, the Web artist requires a wide range of views while creating a graphic.

Fireworks's different display methods are grouped on the View Controls toolbar found, by default, at the bottom left of the document window in Windows and along the bottom of each image window in Macintosh systems.

The View Controls toolbar, shown in Figure 2-4, features three items: the Magnification pop-up, the Display Modes pop-up, and the Page Preview button.

**Figure 2-4:** Use the View Controls toolbar to zoom in or out of your image and display it in Full or Draft mode.

**Tip**    Windows users: Like the Toolbox, Main, and Status Bar toolbars, you can position the View Controls toolbar freely in the document window or dock it on a border. Just drag the toolbar by any border to the desired position.

### Magnification settings

By far, the Magnification pop-up is the most useful — and most often used — of the View Controls. Whether you're working with pixels or vectors, a polished, finished graphic often demands close-up, meticulous work. Likewise, the designer often needs to be able to step back from an image to compare two or more large images for overall compatibility or to cut and paste sections of a graphic. Fireworks offers a fast zoom control with numerous keyboard shortcuts for rapid view changes.

Fireworks uses a series of magnification settings, from 6 percent to 6,400 percent, for its zoom control. Because Fireworks works with pixels as well as vectors (which are much more flexible from a zoom standpoint), the magnification settings are predefined to offer the best image pixel to screen pixel ratio. When an image is viewed at 100 percent magnification, one screen pixel is used for each image pixel. Should you zoom in to 200 percent, two screen pixels are used for each image pixel. Zooming out reverses the procedure: at 50 percent, each screen pixel represents two image pixels. Fireworks's preset zoom method offers a full range of settings while maintaining image fidelity.

Clicking the arrow button in the Magnification pop-up displays the available settings, as shown in Figure 2-5. Highlight the desired zoom setting and release the mouse button to change magnifications. Fireworks also offers a variety of keyboard shortcuts to change the zoom setting, as detailed in Table 2-2. In addition to specifying a magnification setting, you can also have Fireworks fit the image in the current window. With this command, Fireworks zooms in or out to the maximum magnification setting possible — and still displays the entire image.

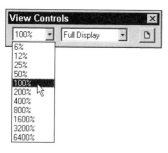

**Figure 2-5:** Choose from any one of 11 different zoom settings through the Magnification pop-up.

| Table 2-2 **Magnification Shortcuts** | | |
|---|---|---|
| *Magnification* | *Windows Keyboard Shortcut* | *Macintosh Keyboard Shortcut* |
| 100% | Ctrl+1 | Command+1 |
| 50% | Ctrl+5 | Command+5 |
| 200% | Ctrl+2 | Command+2 |
| 400% | Ctrl+4 | Command+4 |
| 800% | Ctrl+8 | Command+8 |
| 3200% | Ctrl+3 | Command+3 |
| 6400% | Ctrl+6 | Command+6 |
| Zoom In | Ctrl++ (plus) or Ctrl+spacebar | Command++ (plus) or Command+spacebar |
| Zoom Out | Ctrl+ – (minus) or Ctrl+Alt+spacebar | Command+ – (minus) or Command+Option+spacebar |
| Fit Selection in Window | Ctrl+0 (zero) | Command+0 (zero) |
| Fit All in Window | Ctrl+Alt+0 (zero) or Double-click Hand tool | Command+Option+0 (zero) or Double-click Hand tool |

## Display modes

Most of the time, Fireworks designers work in Full Display mode; in fact, it's so common many don't realize that another mode is even available. The Display Mode pop-up offers the two options: Full Display and Draft Display. Draft Display shows all vector-based objects with one-pixel-wide outlines and no fill; pixel-based images are shown as rectangles with an X in the middle.

What makes Draft Display so useful is that when a portion of a graphic is selected—either a pixel image or a vector object—that selection is rendered in Full Display mode while all the other parts of the picture are outlined, as shown in Figure 2-6. You can even select the entire image and then deselect sections, thus rendering them in Draft Display mode, so you can concentrate on particular areas of the image. The display mode can be toggled between Full and Draft Display with a keyboard shortcut, Ctrl+K (Command+K).

**Figure 2-6:** While you're in Draft Display mode, Fireworks renders any selected portion of your graphic in Full Display mode for editing.

## Page preview

I frequently need to check the overall size of an image I'm working on. Rather than open up the Image Size dialog box (by choosing Modify ⇨ Document ⇨ Image Size), I usually just click the Page Preview button on the View Controls toolbar. The Page Preview button offers a quick dimensional overview of the current document. When selected, the Page Preview button displays the width, height, and resolution of the selected graphic in a small pop-up window, shown in Figure 2-7.

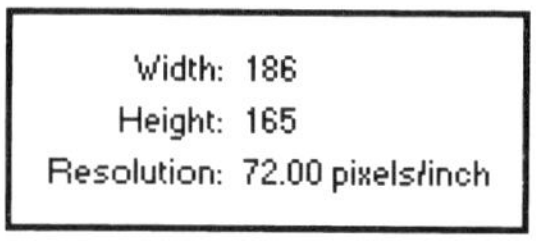

```
Width:  186
Height:  165
Resolution:  72.00 pixels/inch
```

**Figure 2-7:** When you need to verify a document's dimensions and resolution quickly, select the Page Preview button on the View Controls toolbar.

# Main toolbar (Windows only)

On Windows systems, the Main toolbar displays a row of buttons to access the most commonly used menu functions — 17 in all. The Main toolbar enables you to perform several key file operations, such as create a new document, open or save an existing one, and export or import an image, all with just one click. The most often-used editing features — Undo, Redo, Cut, Copy, and Paste — are also located on the Main toolbar. Finally, the Main toolbar brings five important floating panels into view or hides them. Like the other Windows toolbars, the Main toolbar can be positioned freely, as shown in Figure 2-8, or docked on the document window border. Table 2-3 describes each button in the Main toolbar.

**Figure 2-8:** The Main toolbar gives Window users one-click access to many commonly used commands.

## Table 2-3
## Main Toolbar

| Button | Name | Description |
|---|---|---|
| | New | Opens a blank document. |
| | Open | Loads an existing document. |
| | Save | Saves the current document in PNG format. |
| | Import | Imports an image into the current document. |
| | Export | Exports the current document. |
| | Print | Prints the current document. |
| | Undo | Undoes the last action. |
| | Redo | Redoes the last action that was undone |
| | Cut | Cuts the selected object to the clipboard. |

*Continued*

| | | |
|---|---|---|
| **Button** | **Name** | **Description** |

Table 2-3 (continued)

| Button | Name | Description |
|---|---|---|
| | Copy | Copies the selected object to the clipboard. |
| | Paste | Pastes an object on the clipboard into the current document. |
| | Object | Displays/hides the Object inspector. |
| | Color Mixer | Displays/hides the Color Mixer. |
| | Stroke | Displays/hides the Stroke panel. |
| | Fill | Displays/hides the Fill panel. |
| | Layers | Displays/hides the Layers panel. |
| | Help | Lets the user select an item to get help on and opens the Fireworks Help Pages for that item. If double-clicked, opens the index for the Help Pages. |

**Note**      Macintosh users should note that they can access all the commands available on the Main and Modify toolbars through the menus.

## Modify toolbar (Windows only)

The Modify toolbar, shown in Figure 2-9, offers single-click access to four primary types of modification:

✦ **Grouping:** Group or join two or more objects for easier manipulation. Buttons are also available for ungrouping and splitting combined objects.

✦ **Arranging:** Position objects in front of or behind other objects. Objects can also be moved on top of or underneath all other objects.

✦ **Aligning:** Align two or more objects in any of eight different ways, including centered vertically or horizontally.

✦ **Rotating:** Flip selected objects horizontally, vertically, or rotate them 90 degrees, either clockwise or counter-clockwise.

**Figure 2-9:** Group, arrange, align, or rotate selected objects with the Modify toolbar.

Unlike all the other buttons on the Modify toolbar, the Align option opens a pop-up. The Alignment option chosen from the pop-up uses the first object selected as the guide. For example, if you first choose a rectangle on the left and then a bitmapped image on the right, selecting the Align Left option causes both objects to align along the left edge of the rectangle — the first object selected. Table 2-4 details each button on the Modify toolbar.

## Table 2-4
## Modify Toolbar

| Button | Name | Description |
|---|---|---|
| | Group | Groups selected objects |
| | Ungroup | Separates previously grouped objects |
| | Join | Joins the paths of two vector objects |
| | Split | Separates previously joined objects |
| | Bring Front | Positions the selected object on top of all other objects |
| | Bring Forward | Moves the selected object one step closer to the top |
| | Send Backward | Moves the selected object one step closer to the bottom |
| | Send to Back | Positions the selected object underneath all other objects |
| | Align Left | Aligns the selected objects on the left edge |
| | Center Vertical Axis | Centers the selected objects vertically |
| | Align Right | Aligns the selected objects on the right edge |
| | Align Top | Aligns the selected objects along the top edge |
| | Center Horizontal Axis | Centers the selected objects horizontally |
| | Align Bottom | Aligns the selected objects along the bottom edge |
| | Distribute Widths | Evenly distributes the selected objects horizontally |

*Continued*

| Button | Name | Description |
|--------|------|-------------|
| Table 2-4 *(continued)* | | |
| ☐ | Distribute Heights | Evenly distributes the selected objects vertically |
| ◭ | Rotate 90° CCW | Rotates the selected object 90° counter-clockwise |
| ◮ | Rotate 90° CW | Rotates the selected object 90° clockwise |
| ◮ | Flip Horizontal | Flips the selected object horizontally |
| ◁ | Flip Vertical | Flips the selected object vertically |

## Status bar (Windows only)

The Status bar runs along the very bottom of Fireworks in Windows systems. The Status bar has three different sections:

✦ **Selection indicator**: Displays the type of object or objects selected.

✦ **Description**: Provides tooltips for each of the tools that are selected or moused over. If you're in Image Edit mode, a red circle with an X in the middle appears, which acts as an exit button from the mode.

✦ **Animation controls**: VCR-like controls for playing a frame-based animation.

The Status bar can be toggled on and off by choosing Window ➪ Status Bar.

**New Feature**  The Animation controls, shown in Figure 2-10, are new in Fireworks 2 and make it easy to preview any frame-based animation. With these new VCR-like buttons, you can play the animation straight through, using the timing established in Export Preview. You'll also find buttons to move through the animation a frame at a time or to go to the first or last frame. Note: Macintosh users have the same Animation controls at the bottom of each image window.

Selection indicator                    Description                    Animation Controls

**Figure 2-10:** The Status bar consists of three areas, including the new Animation controls.

# Managing the Floating Panels

Fireworks maintains a great deal of functionality in its floating panels. In all, the program offers 15 different panels for modifying everything from the stroke color to a JavaScript behavior. And even though you have a dazzling array of options to choose from, the effect is not overwhelming because various panels are grouped together. To choose a panel for use, simply click its tab.

 **New Feature** In Fireworks 2, the floating panels interface is now even more accessible because you can customize the groupings to fit the way you work. If you're working with dual monitors, you might very well want to display every panel separately, so that all 15 are instantly available. On the other hand, you could conserve maximum screen real estate by grouping all the panels into one supergroup with tabs visible for each individual panel. More likely, though, is the middle ground; by default, Fireworks combines the floating panels into four different groups. The next section describes how to customize your panel groupings.

The more you work in Fireworks, the sooner you'll arrive at an interface configuration best for you. I tend to group my floating panels on the right side of the screen and use the left area as my workspace. I've also found it useful to stack my three main groups of floating panels so that a bit of each one is always exposed, regardless of which group is in front. This arrangement lets me always bring a group forward by clicking part of its window. I also get tremendous mileage out of the new keyboard shortcut for hiding and revealing all the panels, the Tab key. Because I typically add and modify Web objects such as Slices and Behaviors after I've finished creating my graphics, I'll keep the floating panel group with Behaviors, URL Manager, Find & Replace, and the Project Log closed until I need it.

## Grouping and moving panels

Grouping and ungrouping floating panels is a very straightforward process. To separate a floating panel from its current group, click the panel's tab and drag it out into the inactive area of the document window. As you drag, you'll see an outline of the panel. Release the mouse button to place the panel onscreen.

Similarly, grouping one panel with another is also a drag-and-drop affair. Drag the panel's tab until the outline appears. When your pointer moves over a different panel, the outline snaps to that of the static panel. Release the mouse button and a tab, representing the panel being moved, is added to the right of the existing group.

**New Feature** In addition to the grouping feature, the floating panels in Fireworks 2 now snap to the borders of the document window or another floating panel. This snapping feature enables the designer to move panels out of the way quickly and align them in a visually pleasing manner. It may seem like a minor detail, but when snapped to an edge, the workspace appears less cluttered and more useable.

The floating panels are very easy to position around the screen. Just click on the panel's title bar and drag it to a new position. Likewise, you can easily resize and reshape any of the floating panels. Position your pointer over any border of the panel so that the cursor becomes a two-headed arrow. Then click and drag the border into a new size or shape. Each of the panels have a minimum size where the border stops resizing.

**Tip** Macintosh users can minimize any of the floating panels by double-clicking the panel's title bar. The panel will "roll up" like a window shade. To expand the panel, double-click the title bar.

## Hiding and revealing panels

The floating panels are extremely helpful for making all manner of alterations to your images, but they can also get in the way, visually as well as physically. When working on a large image at 100 percent magnification, I often hide all the panels, to better see and manipulate my image. As noted previously, Fireworks 2 has made hiding—and revealing—all the floating panels a one-key operation. With just a press of the Tab key, the floating panels all disappear, or, if they are already hidden, reappear.

Although the Tab key is extremely convenient, you can choose a number of other methods to hide and reveal panels:

✦ Choose View ➪ Hide Panels to toggle the panels off and on.

✦ Use the other keyboard shortcut, Ctrl+Shift+H (Command+Shift+H).

✦ On Windows systems, you can select one of the panel buttons on the Main toolbar—Object, Color Mixer, Stroke, Fill, or Layers. If all the chosen panels or all of the panels are hidden, selecting one of these buttons reveals them all again. If the panel is onscreen, but under another floating panel, selecting the panel's button once brings it to the front; selecting it again hides the panel.

## Examining common features

Although each floating panel does something different, they all share common interface elements. Many of the features will be familiar to users of other graphic software and computer programs in general, but one or two are uniquely Fireworks. Figure 2-11 displays several different floating panels with different interface features highlighted.

Here's an overview of the most common Fireworks interface elements:

✦ **Option lists:** For many selections, Fireworks uses option lists, also called options pop-ups. Click the arrow button of an option list to see the available choices. In some circumstances, as with Patterns and Textures, the option list displays a visual image as well as a text listing of the options. This feature makes it easy in Fireworks to find what you're looking for

**Tip** You can type the first letter of the entry in the option list you're looking for to jump to it. If multiple entries have the same first letter, pressing the letter again cycles through them.

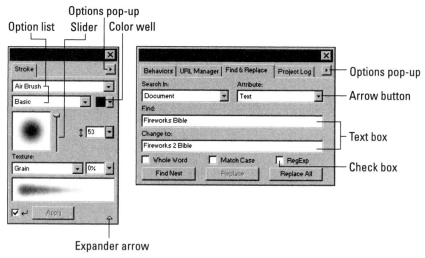

**Figure 2-11:** These floating panels exemplify many interface features found throughout Fireworks.

✦ **Color wells:** Any color selection in Fireworks is handled through a color well that displays the current color for a certain aspect of the image. Click the color well to pop up the color picker with the active swatch. In Fireworks 2, all color pickers have an Eyedropper tool for choosing onscreen colors and a Palette button for opening the system's color pickers. Most color pickers also have a No Color button for deselecting any color.

✦ **Sliders:** Any entry that requires a numeric value—whether it is a percentage, a hexadecimal value, or just a plain number—uses pop-up sliders. Selecting the arrow button next to a variable number, such as a stroke's tip size, pops up a sliding control. Drag the slider and the numbers in the text box increase or decrease in value. Release the mouse button when you've reached the desired value. You can also directly type a numeric value in the adjacent text box. Generally, sliders are shown vertically, but if the slider is too close to the top or bottom of the screen, it is displayed horizontally.

✦ **Options pop-ups:** All floating panels except for the Tool Options panel have a number of different options you can access by selecting the Options pop-up arrow button in the upper right of the panel. The Options pop-ups offer a different list of choices for each floating panel. Choose an option as you would with any drop-down menu.

✦ **Expander arrow:** Several floating panels—Stroke, Fill, and Effect—have an additional preview section that you can reveal by selecting the expander arrow. The expander arrow is a small white triangle in the lower right corner of a floating panel that acts as a toggle. Select it once and the floating panel expands to display the preview section; select it again and the panel returns to its previous size.

✦ **Text boxes:** Enter values directly into text boxes. All Fireworks sliders have text boxes next to them so you can quickly enter in a number instead of using the mouse to move the slider.

✦ **Check boxes:** You can enable an option by clicking the associated check box or disable it by clicking it again to remove the check mark.

## Object inspector

The Object inspector is primarily responsible for displaying and controlling how a selected object (or objects) interacts with the canvas and other objects in the graphic. This floating panel displays one of nine different interfaces, depending on what is selected. Figure 2-12 offers three examples of the Object inspector.

Path Object inspector

Text on a
Path Object inspector

Slice Object inspector

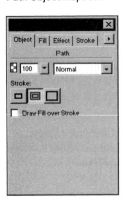
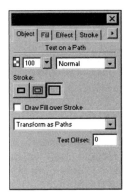

**Figure 2-12:** The Object inspector offers a variety of different options depending on the type of object selected.

**New Feature**

The Object inspector is new in Fireworks 2. Several features were moved from the previously used Object toolbar and combined with several new additions to create this floating palette. Both Opacity (how transparent an object is) and the Blending Mode (how an image's pixels blend with those underneath it) can be found on every Object inspector variation.

The type of object selected is identified at the top of the Object inspector. The possible selections are

✦ **No Selection:** No image or object is selected. The Opacity and Blending Mode of the last selection are displayed.

✦ **Path:** When a vector-based object is selected, the term *Path* is displayed in the Object inspector along with Opacity and Blending Mode controls. Two additional stroke options are available. One is Stroke Placement, which determines whether the stroke is drawn outside, inside, or centered in the Path; the other is the aptly named Draw Fill Over Stroke option.

✦ **Image:** If a pixel-based image is selected, the Object inspector lets you alter the Opacity and Blending Modes, but only if you are not in Image Edit mode.

✦ **Text:** In addition to the Opacity, Blending Modes, and Stroke options, the Object inspector for text enables you to change the Transformation method from Transform as Paths to Transform as Pixels. Text objects are explored in Chapter 10.

✦ **Text on a Path:** The Object inspector for Text on a Path is the same as that for Text with one addition: you can set the number of pixels by which the text is offset from the Path.

✦ **Mask Group:** A selected Mask Group can use the Object inspector to alter the Opacity, Blending Mode, type of group (regular or mask) and the clipping region (Top Object's Image or Top Object's Path). You'll learn more about Groups and Mask Groups in Chapter 13.

✦ **Symbol:** Only the Opacity and Blending Mode of a Symbol (or an Instance) can be altered through the Object inspector. Symbols and Instances are covered in Chapter 24.

✦ **Hotspot:** Much of the information necessary for a selected hotspot to function as a Web object is entered through the Object inspector: the URL, the ⟨alt⟩ tag, and the target. You can also set the color of the overlay and the hotspot's basic shape (Rectangle, Oval, or Polygon) here. Find out how to use hotspots in Chapter 19.

✦ **Slice:** In addition to the Web-specific information (URL, ⟨alt⟩ tag, and target), the selected Slice object can also choose export settings, the overlay color, and naming conventions. Turn to Chapter 19 to find out how to use this key Fireworks tool.

Most any selected object can be affected by the Options pop-up commands outlined in Table 2-5; you can even convert a Hotspot object to a Slice object and vice versa.

### Table 2-5
### Object Inspector Options Pop-up Commands

| Option | Description |
| --- | --- |
| Make Hotspot | Converts the selected object into a hotspot |
| Make Slice | Makes a slice based on the selected object |
| Behaviors | Opens the Behavior inspector for the selected Hotspot or Slice object |

## Stroke panel

Any object created using one of the vector drawing tools—Pen, Brush, Rectangle, Ellipse, Line, or Text tool—is initially constructed with a path, the outline of the object. When a path is visible, it is said to be *stroked*. In Fireworks, strokes can be as basic as the one-pixel Pencil outline or as complex as the multicolored Confetti. The Stroke panel controls all the possible path settings and is a key tool in the graphic artist's palette.

**Note**    Fireworks 1 users might be a little confused by the appearance of the Stroke panel and the disappearance of the Brush panel. Fireworks 2 now uses the industry-standard term *stroke* for what was previously called *brushes* in Version 1. The functionality is fundamentally the same, just the name has been changed.

Fireworks comes with a number of built-in stroke settings accessible through the Stroke panel, shown in Figure 2-13. You can also modify existing settings and save them as new strokes. Seven major options can affect the stroke:

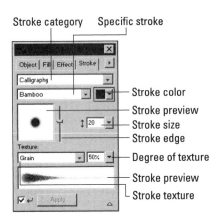

Stroke category    Specific stroke

Stroke color
Stroke preview
Stroke size
Stroke edge
Degree of texture
Stroke preview
Stroke texture

**Figure 2-13:** The Stroke panel controls the appearance of an object's outline or path.

✦ **Stroke category:** Fireworks provides 11 different stroke categories from which to choose: Pencil, Basic, Airbrush, Calligraphy, Charcoal, Crayon, Felt Tip, Oil, Watercolor, Random, and Unnatural. To hide the path entirely, choose None.

✦ **Specific stroke:** Once you've chosen a stroke category, a set of specific strokes, different for each category, is available. When you edit, rename, or save new strokes, the changes are reflected in the specific stroke option list.

✦ **Stroke color:** Selecting the arrow button next to the stroke color well displays the color picker pop-up from which you can select a color from one of the swatches, use the Eyedropper tool to select an onscreen color, or click the Palette button to open the system color picker.

✦ **Stroke edge:** Use the stroke edge slider to soften or harden the stroke. The higher the slider, the softer the stroke; when the slider is all the way to the bottom, the stroke has no softness.

✦ **Stroke size:** The stroke size slider determines the stroke size in pixels. You can increase the size by moving the slider up; you can also enter the value (from 1 to 100) directly in the stroke size text box. The size of the brush is previewed dynamically in the Stroke panel.

✦ **Stroke texture:** In addition to color, size, and softness, you can also apply a texture to the stroke. Fireworks comes with 26 different textures and you can also add your own.

✦ **Degree of stroke texture:** Once a texture has been selected, you must specify how intensely you want the texture applied by using the stroke texture slider or entering a percentage value in the appropriate text box. The degree of stroke texture basically controls the opacity of the texture as it overlays the stroke.

If an object is selected while Auto-Apply is enabled, any changes made on the Stroke panel are automatically applied. Otherwise, you'll need to click the Apply button to see the effect of any new settings on your selected object.

You can manage current strokes and create new ones through the tools available in the Options pop-up commands, detailed in Table 2-6.

| Table 2-6 | |
| :---: | :---: |
| **Stroke Panel Options Pop-up Commands** | |
| *Option* | *Description* |
| Save Stroke As | Saves the current stroke settings under a new name |
| Edit Stroke | Opens the Edit Stroke dialog box |
| Rename Stroke | Relabels the current stroke settings |
| Delete Stroke | Removes the current stroke from the menu |
| Auto Apply | Automatically applies the stroke settings as changes are made |

**Cross-Reference** Strokes are covered in detail in Chapter 8.

# Fill panel

Just as the Stroke panel controls the outline of a drawn shape, the Fill panel controls the inside. Fills can be a solid color, a gradient, a pattern, or — new in Fireworks 2 — a Web dither. All fills can have textures applied with a sliding scale of intensity; moreover, textured fills can even appear transparent.

**New Feature**

Fireworks 2 greatly increases the available Web-safe colors—from 216 to 46,656—that can be used for fills with the addition of the Web dither option. A dithered color is one that is made up of a pattern of two colors to depict a third color. Fireworks uses only the Web-safe colors (compatible with both major browsers) to create the dither pattern; hence the term *Web dither*.

Once you've chosen the type of fill from the Fill panel, shown in Figure 2-14, you can go on to pick a specific color, pattern, edge, or texture. The key options on the Fill panel are

Fill category ⌐

Specific patterns or preset gradients ⌐

Fill edge ⌐

Feather degree ⌐

Texture transparency ⌐

Fill preview ⌐

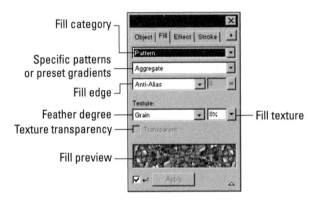

⌐ Fill texture

**Figure 2-14:** The Fill panel offers many options—including the new Web dither—to modify the interior of a drawn shape.

✦ **Fill category**: Select a fill category from these options: Solid (single color fill), Web dither (two-color pattern), Pattern, or Gradient. The available standard gradients are: Linear, Radial, Ellipse, Rectangle, Cone, Starburst, Bars, Ripple, Waves, Satin, and Folds.

✦ **Specific pattern or gradient color scheme**: If you choose Pattern or one of the gradient options, a second option list appears with choices for each type of fill.

✦ **Fill edge**: The fill itself can have a hard edge, an anti-aliased edge, or a feathered edge.

✦ **Degree of feathering**: If the fill is given a feathered edge, you can specify the degree of feathering (the number of pixels affected) with this slider control or by entering a value into the text box.

✦ **Fill texture**: The same textures available to the Stroke panel are available to a fill. You can save additional textures as PNG files; they're accessible once Fireworks is restarted.

✦ **Degree of texture**: To make a texture visible, you must increase the degree of the texture's intensity by using the appropriate slider or text box. The higher the value, the more visible the texture.

✦ **Transparency of texture**: If the Transparency check box is selected, the lighter parts of the texture can be seen through.

The gradient fill type offers a number of options for creating and modifying your own gradient patterns, as noted in Table 2-7.

| Table 2-7 | |
|---|---|
| **Fill Panel Options Pop-up Commands** | |
| **Option** | **Description** |
| Save Gradient As | Saves the current gradient settings under a new name |
| Edit Gradient | Opens the Edit Gradient dialog box |
| Rename Gradient | Relabels the current gradient settings |
| Delete Gradient | Removes the current gradient from the menu |
| Auto Apply | Automatically applies the gradient settings as changes are made |

**Cross-Reference**     To delve deeper into fills, see Chapter 11.

## Effects panel

In the early days of the Web, special graphic effects like drop shadows and beveled buttons required many tedious steps in programs such as Photoshop. Now, Fireworks enables you to apply wondrous effects in a single step through the Effect panel. More importantly, like everything else in Fireworks, the effects are "live" and adapt to any change in the object. And you can easily alter them by adjusting values in the Effects panel.

**New Feature**     Fireworks adds the capability to simply apply several effects in Version 2. Now, in addition to the standard five categories of effects (Drop Shadow, Inner Bevel, Outer Bevel, Glow, and Emboss), you can select Multiple from the Effects category option list. With Multiple selected, you can combine any or all of the standard effects, except Emboss.

Selecting an individual effect displays the specific panel for that effect. Each effect has a different set of options, although they all come with a number of preset options and the capability to set the effect color and its intensity. For example, the Drop Shadow Effects panel, shown in Figure 2-15, gives you control over the distance the shadow falls from the object, as well as its color, edge softness, opacity, and angle. You can even use the Knock Out option to erase the object fill and stroke and leave just the shadow.

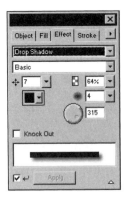

**Figure 2-15:** The various Effects panels — like this one for the Drop Shadow effect — offer a range of options to vary the look and feel of the standard effects.

As you develop specific effects, you can save them with each image by working with the Options pop-up commands listed in Table 2-8.

### Table 2-8
### Effects Panel Options Pop-up Commands

| Option | Description |
|---|---|
| Save Effect As | Saves the current effect settings under a new name |
| Rename Effect | Relabels the current effect settings |
| Delete Effect | Removes the current effect from the menu |

**Cross-Reference**   Effects can add serious pizzazz to your graphics in a hurry. Find out more about them — with details on how to get the most from each Effects panel — in Chapter 12.

## Info panel

Often it's necessary to check an object's size or position when you're creating an overall graphic. The Info panel not only provides you with that feedback, but it also enables you to modify those values numerically for precise adjustments. In addition, the Info panel, shown in Figure 2-16, also lists the current pointer coordinates and the color values of the pixel found under the pointer, updated in real time.

**Caution**   Usually with a series of text boxes, you can press the Tab key to simultaneously enter the input text and move to the next text box. However, with the Info panel, you must input your value and then press the Enter (Return) key to cause any change to take effect.

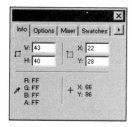

**Figure 2-16:** You can find any object's dimensions and position in the Info panel.

The color model and measurement system shown in the Info panel is user-definable. Choose the Options pop-up and select one of the options detailed in Table 2-9.

| Table 2-9 | |
|---|---|
| **Info Panel Options Pop-up Commands** | |
| *Option* | *Description* |
| Hexadecimal | Changes the color settings display to Hexadecimal |
| RGB | Changes the color settings display to Red, Green, and Blue |
| CMY | Changes the color settings display to Cyan, Magenta, and Yellow |
| HSB | Changes the color settings display to Hue, Saturation, and Balance |
| Pixels | Changes the measurement display to pixels |
| Inches | Changes the measurement display to inches |
| Centimeters | Changes the measurement display to centimeters |
| Scale Attributes | Enables attributes to be scaled with the object |

## Tool options panel

Many tools from the Fireworks Toolbox have configurable settings accessible through the Tool Options panel. You have two basic ways to expose the Tool Options panel for a specific tool:

✦ Display the panel (by choosing its tab or Window ➪ Tool Options) and then select the tool from the Toolbox.

✦ Double-click the tool in the Toolbox; this brings the Tool Options panel to the front.

Like Object panel, the Tool panel's options vary according to what is selected. Some tools, such as the Eraser shown in Figure 2-17, provide numerous choices. Several tools — including the Hand, Magnify, Line, Pen, Ellipse, Brush, and the Web tools — have no options at all. Each of the tool's options is covered in the section devoted to that tool.

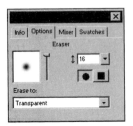

**Figure 2-17:** When the Eraser tool is double-clicked, several alternatives for its use become available through the Tool Options panel.

# Color mixer

Web designers come from a variety of backgrounds: some are well-rooted in computer graphics, others are more familiar with print publishing, while an increasing number know only Web imagery. The Color Mixer lets you opt for the color model that you're most familiar with and that is best suited to your work. The Color Mixer, shown in Figure 2-18, displays three different ways to choose colors:

✦ **Stroke and Fill color wells**: Select a color well to open the color picker pop-up and gain access to the system color pickers through the Palette button.

✦ **Color ramp**: The full-spectrum preview of the chosen color model is known as the color ramp. You can select any color visually by clicking it.

✦ **Color component sliders**: Like the color ramp, the color component sliders change according to the chosen color model. Four of the five color models — RGB, Hexadecimal, CMY, and HSB — display three different sliders, whereas Grayscale shows only one, K (Black).

Like the Toolbox, the Color Mixer also features a Default Colors button for restoring the preset stroke and fill colors and a Swap button for reversing the colors. Choose a color model by selecting the Options pop-up as listed in Table 2-10.

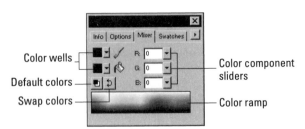

Color wells
Color component sliders
Default colors
Swap colors
Color ramp

**Figure 2-18:** Select your stroke and fill colors with any of five different color systems available through the Color Mixer.

**Table 2-10**
**Color Mixer Options Pop-up Commands**

| Option | Description |
|---|---|
| Hexadecimal | Changes the color mixer display to Hexadecimal |
| RGB | Changes the color mixer display to Red, Green, and Blue |
| CMY | Changes the color mixer display to Cyan, Magenta, and Yellow |
| HSB | Changes the color mixer display to Hue, Saturation, and Balance |
| Grayscale | Changes the color mixer display to Grayscale |

 **Cross-Reference** A full understanding of the color possibilities and pitfalls is a must for any Web designer. Learn more about using the Color Mixer in Chapter 7.

## Swatches panel

Whereas the Color Mixer defines the color universe, the Swatches panel identifies a more precise palette of colors to be used. As the name implies, the Swatches panel is made up of a series of color samples, as you can see in Figure 2-19. You select a color to use by clicking on the swatch.

 **Tip** To reset a swatch palette after you've modified it or sorted it by color, select the palette again from the Swatch Options pop-up.

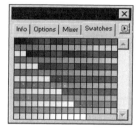

**Figure 2-19:** Palette management is coordinated through the Swatches panel.

A major feature of the Swatches panel is tucked away in its Options pop-up: palette management. With the commands in the Options pop-up, you can switch to standard palettes (such as the Web 216, Windows, or Macintosh system palettes), save and recall custom palettes, or access the current optimized export palette. The Add Swatches command is especially useful; with it, you can load palettes previously stored in the Photoshop .aco file format or pull the color information from a GIF file to use. Table 2-11 outlines all the Options pop-up commands.

**Table 2-11**
**Swatches Panel Options Pop-up Commands**

| Option | Description |
|---|---|
| Add Swatches | Imports previously saved palettes from .aco or GIF files |
| Replace Swatches | Exchanges the current palette set for a previously saved one |
| Save Swatches | Stores the current palette set |
| Clear Swatches | Removes all palettes from the panel |
| Web 216 Palette | Switches to the Web 216 palette |
| Windows System | Switches to the Windows system palette |
| Macintosh System | Switches to the Macintosh system palette |
| Grayscale | Switches to a grayscale palette |
| Current Export Palette | Switches to the custom Export Preview palette set |
| Sort by Color | Sorts the swatches by color |

## Layers panel

Layers in Fireworks enable the creation of extremely complicated graphics as well as compatibility with files stored in Photoshop format. Fireworks layers permit multiple images and objects — each with their own stacking order — to be treated as a group and, in turn, placed on top of, or beneath, other layers. Moreover, each layer can be hidden from view for easier editing of complex images or locked to prevent accidental editing.

**New Feature** Layers have undergone a significant overhaul for Fireworks 2. The Background layer is no longer standard and is only seen when opening Photoshop and older Fireworks files. Now, the canvas sits below all other layers and provides the background color, if any. All Web objects — such as slices and hotspots — are now stored in a Web Layer, which can be hidden or locked. Any layer can be shared across frames, which brings a new flexibility to GIF animation.

Furthermore, new controls have been added to the Layer panel, as shown in Figure 2-20. In addition to the layer list, with its Show/Hide and Lock/Unlock columns, you can now quickly add another layer by clicking on the New Layer button or remove a selected layer by choosing the Delete Layer button. The Distribute to Frames command—which places objects in the current layer on frames based on their stacking order—also has a button on the Layer panel. Much of layer management is coordinated through the Options pop-up commands, as described in Table 2-12.

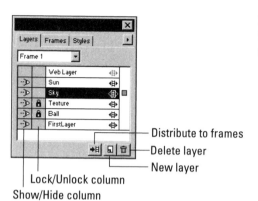

Lock/Unlock column
Show/Hide column

Distribute to frames
Delete layer
New layer

**Figure 2-20:** Objects on a layer can be hidden or locked with a single click on the Layers panel.

## Table 2-12
## Layers Panel Options Pop-up Commands

| Option | Description |
|--------|-------------|
| New Layer | Adds a new layer on top of all current image layers |
| Duplicate Layer | Clones the current layer |
| Layer Options | Opens the Layer Options dialog box to rename the layer and set the Share Across Frames option |
| Delete Layer | Removes the current layer |
| Hide All | Conceals all layers in the document |
| Show All | Reveals all layers in the document |
| Lock All | Prevents the selected layer from editing |
| Unlock All | Enables a locked layer to be edited |
| Share Layer | Enables all objects on the selected layer to be shared across all frames |
| Single Layer Editing | Restricts edits to the current layer |

## Frames panel

Frames have two primary uses in Fireworks: rollovers and animations. When used to create rollovers, each frame represents a different state of the user's mouse with up to four frames being used. To create an animated GIF, each frame in Fireworks corresponds to one frame of the animation. You can use as many frames for your animation as necessary (although file size often dictates that the fewest frames possible is best).

The Frames panel, shown in Figure 2-21, is laid out like the Layers panel, with a list of Frames featured prominently. In Fireworks 2, several new buttons have been added to the panel: New Frame, Delete Frame, and Distribute to Frames. Most of the functionality found in these buttons is duplicated in the Options pop-up, as listed in Table 2-13.

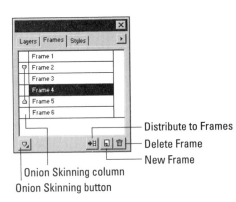

**Figure 2-21:** The Frames panel is Fireworks's center stage for creating rollovers and animated GIFs.

Distribute to Frames
Delete Frame
New Frame

Onion Skinning column
Onion Skinning button

## Table 2-13
## Frames Panel Options Pop-up Commands

| Option | Description |
| --- | --- |
| Add Frames | Opens the Add Frames dialog box |
| Duplicate Frame | Duplicates the current frame |
| Delete Frames | Deletes the current frame |
| Copy to Frames | Copies the selected object to a frame or range of frames |
| Distribute to Frames | Distributes each selected object to a different frame as determined by the stacking order of the objects |

New Feature

Fireworks 2 adds a significant enhancement to animation creation: Onion Skinning. Used by traditional animators, Onion Skinning enables you to see a series of frames simultaneously so that you can more accurately create your animation without flipping back and forth from frame to frame. Which frames are visible by onion skinning is noted in the new Onion Skinning column. Controls for this feature (described in Table 2-14) are available through the Onion Skinning button found on the lower left of the Frames panel.

| Table 2-14 |
| :-- |
| **Onion Skinning Options** |

| Option | Description |
| --- | --- |
| No Onion Skinning | Disables Onion Skinning |
| Show Next Frame | Shows the frame after the current one with a different opacity |
| Before and After | Shows the previous and next frame with a different opacity |
| Show All Frames | Shows all frames with varying opacity |
| Custom | Opens the Onion Skinning dialog box |
| Multi-Frame Editing | Enables edits on one frame to be reflected on all others |

## Styles panel

If you've ever spent hours getting just the right combination of stroke, fill, and effects for an image — and then find you need to apply the same combination to all the navigation buttons sitewide — you'll greatly appreciate Fireworks 2's new Styles feature.

New Feature

In Fireworks, a *style* is a collection of attributes that can be applied to any object. The Styles panel is preset with 50 such designs, which appear as graphical buttons and text, with 300 more available on the Fireworks CD-ROM. To apply a style, select the object and then select the style; you can even select multiple objects (such as a row of navigation buttons) and apply the same style to them all with one click. Styles are a terrific time-saver and a great way to maintain a consistent look and feel.

The Styles panel, shown in Figure 2-22, is composed of a series of icons, each representing a different style. A style can have the following attributes: fill type, fill color, stroke type, stroke color, effect, text font, text size, and text color. In addition to the preset styles, you can also save your own combinations. Just highlight the object with the desired attributes and select the New Style button on the Styles panel. You can also accomplish this by choosing New Style from the Options pop-up command. A full list of the Style Options pop-up commands appears in Table 2-15.

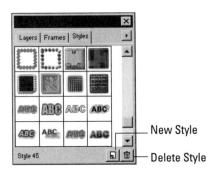

**Figure 2-22:** Automate applying a consistent look and feel to your objects through the new Styles panel.

— New Style

— Delete Style

### Table 2-15
### Styles Panel Options Pop-up Commands

| Option | Description |
| --- | --- |
| New Style | Creates a new style based on the current object |
| Edit Style | Opens the Edit Style dialog box |
| Delete Styles | Removes a selected style or styles |
| Import Styles | Loads a new set of styles after the currently selected one |
| Export Styles | Stores the currently selected style or styles |
| Reset Styles | Reloads the default configuration of styles |
| Large Icons | Displays the available styles with icons twice as large as normal |

Cross-Reference

Find out more about creating and applying styles in Chapter 17.

## Behaviors inspector

One of the key features of Fireworks that separates it from other graphics programs is its capability to output HTML and JavaScript code along with images. The code activates the image and makes it capable of doing something — such as changing color or shape when the user passes the mouse over it. The code is known in Fireworks as a *Behavior*. A Behavior is actually composed of two parts: an action that specifies what's to occur, and an event that triggers the action.

**New Feature** Fireworks extends its capacity to use Behaviors in Version 2 and adds the Behavior inspector as the primary tool for managing them. Behaviors require a Web object, such as a slice or a hotspot, to function. After you've selected the desired Web object, you assign a Behavior by choosing the Add Action button (the plus sign) from the Behavior inspector. Fireworks 2 comes with four Behaviors from which to choose: Simple Rollover, Display Status Message, Swap Image, and Toggle Group.

All assigned Behaviors for a given Web object are listed in the Behavior inspector, as shown in Figure 2-23. The events (such as OnMouseOver or OnClick) are listed in the first column and the actions in the second. The third column, Info, offers specifics identifying the Behavior. To remove a Behavior, select it and then choose the Remove Action button (the minus sign). You can also delete a Behavior — or all of the Behaviors for a Web object — through the Objects pop-up commands listed in Table 2-16.

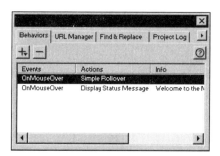

**Figure 2-23:** Use the Behavior inspector to generate HTML and JavaScript code at the click of a mouse.

Table 2-16
**Behaviors Inspector Options Pop-up Commands**

| Option | Description |
|---|---|
| Edit | Opens the dialog box for the selected Behavior |
| Delete | Removes the currently selected Behavior from its attached object |
| Delete All | Removes all Behaviors attached to the current object |

**Cross-Reference** Behaviors are a very rich feature in Fireworks 2. To find out more about them, see Chapter 20.

## URL Manager

URLs are the life-blood of the Web. When a URL (short for Uniform Resource Locator and also known as a *link*) is attached to an image on a Web page, the user need only click once to jump to another section of the document, another page on the Web site, or another computer halfway around the world. For all their power, URLs can be difficult to manage — one typo in the often-complex string of letters and symbols can break a link. Fireworks 2 greatly eases the pain of handling URLs with the introduction of the URL Manager.

**New Feature**

The URL Manager is a new panel, shown in Figure 2-24, that lists all the Internet addresses inserted in the current session (the URL History) or loaded from an external file (the URL Library). Now you can easily assign URLs with a click of a listed item; more importantly, you can maintain a list of links for a particular Web site so you don't have to re-enter them each time. To move an item from the History list to the Library, select the Add button (the plus sign).

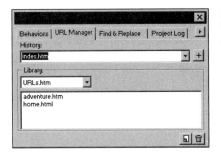

**Figure 2-24:** Adding links to your Web objects is easier than ever through the new URL Manager.

You can access most of Fireworks's URL management utilities through the panel's Options pop-up. The commands, detailed in Table 2-17, enable you to manipulate both the History and the Library features of the URL Manager.

## Table 2-17
## URL Manager Options Pop-up Commands

| Option | Description |
| --- | --- |
| Add History to Library | Adds the list of current URLs to the URL Library |
| Clear History | Removes all URLs from the current listing |
| Add URL | Adds a new URL to the URL Library |
| Edit URL | Opens the Edit URL dialog box |
| Delete URL | Removes the selected URL from the URL Library |
| New URL Library | Creates a new URL Library |
| Import URLs | Loads a new set of URLs from a previously stored URL Library, a bookmark file, or an HTML page |
| Export URLs | Stores the current URL Library |

## Find & Replace panel

Let's suppose you've just finished the graphics for a major Web site, chock-filled with corporate logos, and you receive *the call*. You know, the one from the client who informs you that the company has just been acquired and instead of NewCo, Inc., it's now New2Co, Inc. Could you please redo all the graphics — by tomorrow?

**New Feature**

What used to be an impossibility is now just another click of the mouse with Fireworks 2's new Find & Replace feature. Because text in Fireworks is always editable, Find & Replace makes updating a series of Web graphics a snap. You can change all the graphics in a selection, a file, a frame, or a series of files. Moreover, Find & Replace can handle more than just text; you can also alter fonts, colors, and URLs.

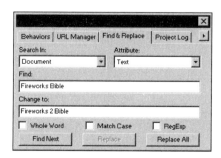

**Figure 2-25:** Need to make global changes in text, font, color, or URLs? Pull up the Find & Replace panel and get the job done fast.

The Find & Replace panel, shown in Figure 2-25, takes you step-by-step through the process:

1. Select the scope of the search from the Search In option list.

2. Set the type of search required by choosing an option from the Attribute option list.

3. Enter the criteria to search for in the Find area.

4. Choose your replacement options in the Change To section.

   Both the Find and the Replace sections change according to the Attribute you select. For text and URLs, you can input text directly. With a font selection, you can choose from any available system font, in any style. For replacing a color, use the available color picker pop-up.

5. Select your specific Attribute options.

   With text and URLs, you can search for the Whole Word or choose to Match Case. Selecting RegExp enables you to use a wildcard system known as Regular Expressions. When altering color, you can specify the range of applications — whether to apply just to an image's fill, strokes, effects or a combination of these settings. With fonts, you can search for a range of font sizes and choose a replacement size for them all.

The Find & Replace feature works well with the new Project Log panel, which tracks changes made to your images. You can enable Project Log tracking through the Options pop-up commands, listed in Table 2-18, as well as specify replacement options for multiple file operations.

| Table 2-18 | |
|---|---|
| **Find & Replace Options Pop-up Commands** | |
| *Option* | *Description* |
| Add Files to Project Log | Tracks changes made in a Find & Replace operation in the Project Log |
| Replace Options | Displays options for multiple-file Find & Replace operations |

**Cross-Reference**

Web graphics is often a production business and you can really ramp up your production level when you master the new Find & Replace feature. To learn more about it, see Chapter 18.

## Project log

With all the power inherent in Fireworks 2's new automation tools such as Find & Replace and Batch Processing, you need a way to keep track of what's happened. The new Project Log details each change that has taken place and enables you to not only receive confirmation of the change, but also easily open any file affected.

**New Feature**

Each change occurring through a Find & Replace or Batch Process operation is listed in the Project Log, shown in Figure 2-26. In addition to the name, the Project Log entry also shows the frame affected and the time and date of the alteration. Best of all, you can quickly open any altered image in Fireworks by selecting it and choosing the Project Log's Open button.

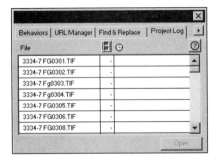

**Figure 2-26:** Use the Project Log to manage your Find & Replace and Batch Process operations.

In addition to listing images altered during an automated process, you can use the Project Log to keep a number of files close at hand, ready to be opened at will. Through the Add Files to Log command, one of the Options pop-ups listed in Table 2-19, files can be made accessible, but not immediately opened. The Options pop-up also enables you to quickly make changes to files in the Project Log and re-export them using their previous settings.

| | Table 2-19 | |
| :-- | :-: | --: |
| | **Project Log Options Pop-up Commands** | |
| **Option** | **Description** | |
| Export Again | Exports selected files in the Project Log using their previous settings | |
| Add Files to Log | Includes additional graphic files in the Project Log without initially opening them | |
| Clear Selection | Removes the selected files from the Project Log | |
| Clear All | Removes all files from the Project Log | |

**Cross-Reference** To find out more about the new capabilities made possible by the Project Log, turn to Chapter 18.

# Using the Menus

Many of the commands and options available in the various Fireworks panels can also be found in its menus. You'll also find, however, many features unavailable anywhere else but the menus. This section provides a reference to every menu item in Fireworks with its corresponding keyboard shortcut, if available.

## File menu

It's standard practice to place basic computer operations — creating, saving, and printing files — in the File menu. Fireworks follows this practice and adds some new commands, such as Open Multiple, Scanning, and Batch Process, for Version 2. All File menu commands are listed in Table 2-20.

**Note** As with many programs, you won't see all Fireworks menus until a document — new or existing — is open.

## Table 2-20
## File Menu Commands

| Command | Description | Windows Shortcut | Macintosh Shortcut |
| --- | --- | --- | --- |
| New | Creates a new file | Ctrl+N | Command+N |
| Open | Opens an existing file | Ctrl+O | Command+O |
| Open Multiple | Opens several files at the same time | Ctrl+Shift+O | Command+Shift+O |
| Scan ⇨ Twain Acquire | Scans in an image using the current Twain device | n/a | n/a |
| Scan ⇨ Twain Select | Selects a new Twain device | n/a | n/a |
| Close | Closes the current document | Ctrl+F4 or Ctrl+W | Command+F4 or Command+W |
| Save | Saves the current document in PNG format | Ctrl+S | Command+S |
| Save As | Saves the current document under a new name or location | Ctrl+Shift+S | Command+Shift+S |
| Save A Copy | Saves a copy of the current document under a new name or location | n/a | n/a |
| Revert | Replaces a modified, but not saved, file with its previously saved version | n/a | n/a |
| Import | Inserts a file into the current document | Ctrl+R | Command+R |
| Export | Exports the current document according to user-specified settings | Ctrl+Shift+R | Command+Shift+R |
| Export Special ⇨ Export As Files | Exports each layer, frame, or slice object as a separate file | n/a | n/a |
| Export Special ⇨ Export As CSS Layers | Exports each layer, frame, or slice object as a separate Cascading Style Sheet layer | n/a | n/a |
| Export Special ⇨ Export As Image Wells | Exports each layer, frame, or slice object in Image Well format to be used by Lotus Domino servers | n/a | n/a |

| Command | Description | Windows Shortcut | Macintosh Shortcut |
|---------|-------------|------------------|--------------------|
| Export Again | Exports the current document again using the same settings previously established | Ctrl+Shift+X | Command+Shift+X |
| Export Wizard | Opens the Export Wizard for step-by-step instructions and recommendations on exporting an image | n/a | n/a |
| Batch Process | Converts a group of files | n/a | n/a |
| Run Script | Executes a custom batch processing scriptlet | n/a | n/a |
| Preview in Browser ⇨ Your Browsers | Previews the current image in your set browsers | n/a | n/a |
| Preview in Browser ⇨ Set Primary [F12] Browser | Determines the primary browser to be used in previews | F12 | F12 |
| Preview in Browser ⇨ Set Secondary [Shift+F12] Browser | Determines the alternate browser to be used in previews | Shift+F12 | Shift+F12 |
| Print | Prints the current image | Ctrl+P | Command+P |
| Page Setup | Opens the Page Setup dialog box to set page margins, orientation, and paper size and source | n/a | n/a |
| Document Properties | Sets the slice and image map properties for a document | n/a | n/a |
| Preferences | Opens the Preferences dialog box | n/a | n/a |
| Your Last Four Opened Files | A dynamic list that provides access to the last four files opened | n/a | n/a |
| Exit | Quits Fireworks | Alt+F4 | Option+F4 |

# Edit menu

As evidenced by its name, the Edit menu holds the standard editing commands such as Undo, Cut, Copy, and Paste, as well as numerous commands specific to Fireworks graphics, such as Paste Inside and Crop Selected Image. Fireworks 1 users will find commands from the old Select menu, such as Select All, Subselect, and Select Inverse in Table 2-21 as well.

<table>
<tr><td colspan="4" align="center">Table 2-21<br>**Edit Menu Commands**</td></tr>
<tr><td>*Command*</td><td>*Description*</td><td>*Windows Shortcut*</td><td>*Macintosh Shortcut*</td></tr>
<tr><td>Undo</td><td>Undoes the last action</td><td>Ctrl+Z</td><td>Command+Z</td></tr>
<tr><td>Redo</td><td>Redoes the last undone action</td><td>Ctrl+Shift+Z</td><td>Command+Shift+Z</td></tr>
<tr><td>Cut</td><td>Cuts the selected object to the clipboard</td><td>Ctrl+X</td><td>Command+X</td></tr>
<tr><td>Copy</td><td>Copies the selected object to the clipboard</td><td>Ctrl+C</td><td>Command+C</td></tr>
<tr><td>Paste</td><td>Pastes the contents of the clipboard into the current document</td><td>Ctrl+V</td><td>Command+V</td></tr>
<tr><td>Clear</td><td>Deletes the selected</td><td>Backspace or Delete</td><td>Backspace or Delete</td></tr>
<tr><td>Paste Inside</td><td>Appears to paste the contents of the clipboard inside a selected object; actually creates a mask group clipped to the top object's path</td><td>Ctrl+Shift+V</td><td>Command+Shift+V</td></tr>
<tr><td>Paste Attributes</td><td>Pastes the attributes (stroke, fill, and effects settings) of an object on the clipboard to a selected object</td><td>Ctrl+Shift+ Alt+V</td><td>Command+Option+ Shift+V</td></tr>
<tr><td>Select All</td><td>Selects all objects in a document</td><td>Ctrl+A</td><td>Command+A</td></tr>
<tr><td>Deselect</td><td>Unselects any selected objects</td><td>Ctrl+D</td><td>Command+D</td></tr>
</table>

| Command | Description | Windows Shortcut | Macintosh Shortcut |
|---|---|---|---|
| Superselect | Selects an object's entire group, mask group, or symbol, if any | Ctrl+Up arrow | Command+ Up arrow |
| Subselect | Selects objects within the current selection | Ctrl+Down arrow | Command+ Down Command |
| Select Inverse | Selects pixels currently not selected and deselects those selected (Image Edit mode only) | Ctrl+Shift+I | Command+Shift+I |
| Feather | Blurs the edge of the selection's alpha channel (Image Edit mode only) | n/a | n/a |
| Select Similar | Selects colors in an image with colors already selected using the Magic Wand (Pixel-based images only) | n/a | n/a |
| Duplicate | Creates a copy of the selection and pastes it into the document offset to the left and down | Ctrl+Alt+D | Command+ Option+D |
| Clone | Creates a copy of the selection and pastes it into the document directly over the original | Ctrl+Shift+C | Command+Shift+C |
| Find & Replace | Opens the Find & Replace panel | n/a | n/a |
| Crop Selected Image | Places crop handles around the current selection (Pixel-based images only) | Ctrl+Alt+C | Command+ Option+C |

## View menu

The View menu commands, listed in Table 2-22, control the Web artist's views during the creation phase. In addition to numerous magnification commands, the View menu also contains helpful layout aids such as Rulers, Grids, and Guides. You'll also find several features to help you see just the graphic when you need to have a clear, uncluttered perspective.

### Table 2-22
### View Menu Commands

| Command | Description | Windows Shortcut | Macintosh Shortcut |
|---------|-------------|------------------|--------------------|
| Zoom In | Magnifies the view of the selected object by one preset level. | Ctrl++ | Command++ |
| Zoom Out | Reduces the magnification of the selected object by one preset level. | Ctrl+- | Command+- |
| Magnification ⇨ 6%–6400% | Selects a specific preset magnification. | Various. See the section "View Controls." | Various. See the section "View Controls." |
| Fit Selection | Changes the zoom level so that the entire selection can be seen at the highest possible magnification. | Ctrl+0 | Command+0 |
| Fit All | Changes the zoom level so that the entire image can be seen at the highest possible magnification. | Ctrl+Alt+0 | Command+ Option+0 |
| Full Display | Shows the document with all fills, strokes, and effects. Toggles with Draft Display. | Ctrl+K | Command+K |
| Hide Selection | Removes the selection from view. If selected again, the selection reappears. | Ctrl+M | Command+M |
| Show All | Displays all objects in an image. | Ctrl+Shift+M | Command+Shift+M |
| Hide Edges | Stops the marquee selection lines and selection highlight lines from displaying. | Ctrl+H | Command+H |
| Hide Panels | Removes all open floating panels from view. | Ctrl+Shift+H or Tab | Command+Shift+H or Tab |
| Rulers | Displays vertical and horizontal rulers in pixels. | Ctrl+Alt+R | Command+ Option+R |
| Grids | Displays the layout grid according to the Grid Options settings. | Ctrl+' | Command+' |

| Command | Description | Windows Shortcut | Macintosh Shortcut |
|---|---|---|---|
| Grid Options ⇨ Snap to Grid | Snaps objects to nearest grid intersection. | Ctrl+Shift+' | Command+Shift+' |
| Grid Options ⇨ Edit Grid | Displays the Edit Grid dialog box to set grid size and color. | Ctrl+Alt+G | Command+ Option+G |
| Guides | Toggles custom alignment lines. | Ctrl+; | Command+; |
| Slice Guides | Toggles custom alignment lines for slices. | Ctrl+Alt+Shift+; | Command+Option+ Shift+; |
| Glide Options ⇨ Lock Guides | Prevents set guides from being moved. | Ctrl+Alt+; | Command+Option+; |
| Glide Options ⇨ Snap to Guides | Snaps objects to nearest guide. | Ctrl+Shift+; | Command+Shift+; |
| Glide Options ⇨ Edit Guides | Displays the Edit Guides dialog box to color of guides, slices, and slice guides. | Ctrl+Alt+Shift+G | Command+Option+ Shift+G |
| Status Bar | Toggles the Status Bar. (Windows only.) | n/a | n/a |

## Insert menu

I've found the Insert menu commands, noted in Table 2-23, most useful when I'm converting an object to a hotspot or a slice Web object. Fireworks automatically handles what would normally be a very time-consuming procedure for me. If you do any work with Symbols and Instances — great for roughing out animations — you'll find the Insert menu indispensable.

| Table 2-23 Insert Menu Commands | | | |
|---|---|---|---|
| Command | Description | Windows Shortcut | Macintosh Shortcut |
| Hotspot | Converts the selected object into a hotspot | Ctrl+Shift+U | Command+Shift+U |
| Slice | Converts the selected object into a slice | n/a | n/a |
| Behaviors | Displays the Behaviors panel | n/a | n/a |

*Continued*

| | Table 2-23 *(continued)* | | |
|---|---|---|---|
| **Command** | **Description** | **Windows Shortcut** | **Macintosh Shortcut** |
| Image | Imports an image (pixel or vector) into the current document | Ctrl+R | Command+R |
| Empty Image | Creates a blank image object that enables you to use the pixel creation tools | Ctrl+Alt+Y | Command+ Option+Y |
| Symbol | Makes the current selection a Symbol | Ctrl+Alt+Shift+M | Command+Option+ Shift+M |
| Tween Instances | Creates interpolated differences between a Symbol and an Instance or two Instances | Ctrl+Alt+Shift+T | Command+Option+ Shift+T |
| Symbol Options ⇨ Break Link | Changes a Symbol and its instances into standard objects | n/a | n/a |
| Symbol Options ⇨ Add to Symbol | Groups a selection to a selected Symbol, causing all Instances to gain the selection as well | n/a | n/a |
| Symbol Options ⇨ Find Symbol | Selects the Symbol for a given Instance | n/a | n/a |
| Symbol Options ⇨ Delete Instances | Removes all Instances of a selected Symbol | n/a | n/a |
| Layer | Adds a new layer to the top of the layer list, underneath the Web Layer | n/a | n/a |
| Frame | Adds a new frame after the current frame | n/a | n/a |

## Modify menu

Once you've created your basic image, you'll undoubtedly spend as much, if not more time, tweaking and modifying your image to get it just right. The Modify menu commands, detailed in Table 2-24, are quite numerous and specific. Several very powerful path commands have been added in Fireworks 2 under the Combine and Alter Path headings.

### Table 2-24
### Modify Menu Commands

| Command | Description | Windows Shortcut | Macintosh Shortcut |
|---|---|---|---|
| Stroke | Opens the Stroke panel. | Ctrl+Alt+B | Command+Option+B |
| Fill | Opens the Fill panel. | Ctrl+Alt+F | Command+Option+F |
| Effect | Opens the Effect panel. | Ctrl+Alt+E | Command+Option+E |
| Image Object | Enters Image Edit mode. | Ctrl+E | Command+E |
| Exit Image Edit | Leaves Image Edit mode. | Ctrl+Shift+D | Command+Shift+D |
| Document ⇨ Image Size | Resizes the current document. | n/a | n/a |
| Document ⇨ Canvas Size | Opens the Canvas Size dialog box to increase or reduce the size of the canvas. | n/a | n/a |
| Document ⇨ Canvas Color | Changes the color of the canvas. | n/a | n/a |
| Document ⇨ Trim Canvas | Reduces the canvas size to the smallest size possible that includes all objects. | n/a | n/a |
| Edge ⇨ Hard Edge | Gives the selected object a hard edge. | n/a | n/a |
| Edge ⇨ Anti-Alias | Gives the selected object an anti-aliased edge. | n/a | n/a |
| Edge ⇨ Feather | Gives the selected object a feathered edge. The default feather size is 10 pixels. | n/a | n/a |
| Free Transform | Permits moving, resizing, and rotating through transformation handle around the selected object. | Ctrl+T | Command+T |
| Transform ⇨ Scale | Alters the size of the selected object. | n/a | n/a |
| Transform ⇨ Skew | Slants the selected object at an oblique (or non-right) angle. | n/a | n/a |
| Transform ⇨ Distort | Uses eight handles to enable reshaping of the selected object. | n/a | n/a |

*Continued*

## Table 2-24 *(continued)*

| Command | Description | Windows Shortcut | Macintosh Shortcut |
|---------|-------------|------------------|--------------------|
| Transform ⇨ Numeric Transform | Displays the Numeric Transform dialog box to alter scale by percentage, size by pixels, or rotation by angle. | Ctrl+Shift+T | Command+Shift+T |
| Transform ⇨ Rotate 180° | Rotates the selected object 180°, essentially turning it upside-down. | n/a | n/a |
| Transform ⇨ Rotate 90° CW | Rotates the selected object 90° clockwise. | n/a | n/a |
| Transform ⇨ Rotate 90° CCW | Rotates the selected object 90° counter-clockwise. | n/a | n/a |
| Transform ⇨ Flip Horizontal | Flips a selected object horizontally. | n/a | n/a |
| Transform ⇨ Flip Vertical | Flips a selected object vertically. | n/a | n/a |
| Transform ⇨ Remove Transformations | Removes transformations from a text block. | n/a | n/a |
| Arrange ⇨ Bring to Front | Moves the selected object all the way to the front. | Ctrl+F | Command+F |
| Arrange ⇨ Bring Forward | Moves the selected object on top of the object in front of it. | Ctrl+Shift+F | Command+Shift+F |
| Arrange ⇨ Send Backward | Moves the selected object all the way to the back. | Ctrl+B | Command+B |
| Arrange ⇨ Send to Back | Moves the selected object behind the object in back of it. | Ctrl+Shift+B | Command+Shift+B |
| Align ⇨ Left | Aligns the selected objects to the left edge of the object furthest left. | Ctrl+Alt+1 | Command+Option+1 |
| Align ⇨ Center Vertical | Aligns selected objects on the vertical center of all objects. | Ctrl+Alt+2 | Command+Option+2 |
| Align ⇨ Right | Aligns the selected objects to the right edge of the object furthest right. | Ctrl+Alt+3 | Command+Option+3 |

| Command | Description | Windows Shortcut | Macintosh Shortcut |
|---------|-------------|------------------|---------------------|
| Align ⇨ Top | Aligns the selected objects to the top edge of the highest object. | Ctrl+Alt+4 | Command+Option+4 |
| Align Center Horizontal | Aligns selected objects on the horizontal center of all objects. | Ctrl+Alt+5 | Command+Option+5 |
| Align ⇨ Bottom | Aligns the selected objects to the bottom edge of the lowest object. | Ctrl+Alt+6 | Command+Option+6 |
| Align ⇨ Distribute Widths | Moves selected objects so that there is an equal amount of space between each object, horizontally. | Ctrl+Alt+7 | Command+Option+7 |
| Align ⇨ Distribute Heights | Moves selected objects so that there is an equal amount of space between each object, vertically. | Ctrl+Alt+9 | Command+Option+9 |
| Join | Connects the two endpoints of two selected paths. | Ctrl+J | Command+J |
| Split | Divides paths at selected points. | Ctrl+Shift+J | Command+Shift+J |
| Combine ⇨ Union | Joins two or more closed paths into a single path enclosing the area of the original objects. The stroke and fill attributes of the object furthest back are applied to the resulting path. | n/a | n/a |
| Combine ⇨ Intersect | Joins two or more closed paths into a single path encompassing the overlapping area. The stroke and fill attributes of the object furthest back are applied to the resulting path. | n/a | n/a |
| Combine ⇨ Punch | With two or more closed paths, removes all of the object furthest back and any area it intersects with the other objects. | n/a | n/a |

*Continued*

## Table 2-24 *(continued)*

| Command | Description | Windows Shortcut | Macintosh Shortcut |
|---------|-------------|------------------|--------------------|
| Combine ⇨ Crop | With two or more closed paths, retains all of the object furthest back except any area it intersects with the other objects. | n/a | n/a |
| Alter Path ⇨ Simplify | Reduces the number of points in a path while keeping the same or similar shape. | n/a | n/a |
| Alter Path ⇨ Expand Stroke | Displays the Expand Stroke dialog box, which converts an open path to a closed path outlining the original shape. | n/a | n/a |
| Alter Path ⇨ Inset Path | Displays the Inset Path dialog box, which creates an object outlining of a closed path inside or outside of the original object. The original object is removed. | n/a | n/a |
| Merge Images | Changes one or more objects into a single pixel-based image. | Ctrl+Alt+Shift+Z | Command+Option+ Shift+Z |
| Merge Layers | Converts all objects on all visible layers to a single pixel-based image on one layer. | n/a | n/a |
| Group | Locks two or more objects together so that they can be moved or transformed to-gether while retaining their separate attributes. | Ctrl+G | Command+G |
| Mask Group | Crops selected objects to the shape of the topmost object and can also be used to filter the selected objects through the alpha channel of the topmost object. | Ctrl+Shift+G | Command+Shift+G |
| Ungroup | Separates previously grouped objects. | Ctrl+U | Command+U |

# Text menu

Text in a graphics program plays a relatively small, but key role. In a Web graphics program such as Fireworks, text becomes more important because words and phrases are often incorporated into buttons, navigation bars, and even full paragraphs of graphics. The Text menu commands, described in Table 2-25, offer many shortcuts that enable you to manipulate text objects without opening the Text Editor.

| | Table 2-25 | | |
|---|---|---|---|
| | **Text Menu Commands** | | |
| *Command* | *Description* | *Windows Shortcut* | *Macintosh Shortcut* |
| Font ⇨ Your Font List | Displays a subset of the fonts available on your system | n/a | n/a |
| Font ⇨ More Fonts | Opens the Select Font dialog box with an option list of all fonts installed on your system | n/a | n/a |
| Size ⇨ 8–120 | Enables 12 different font sizes from 8 to 120 points | n/a | n/a |
| Style ⇨ Plain | Changes the selected text object to a plain style | Ctrl+Alt+Shift+P | Command+Option+ Shift+P |
| Style ⇨ Bold | Changes the selected text object to a bold style | Ctrl+Alt+Shift+B | Command+Alt+ Shift+B |
| Style ⇨ Italic | Changes the selected text object to an italic style | Ctrl+Alt+Shift+I | Command+Alt+ Shift+I |
| Style ⇨ Underline | Changes the selected text object to an underline style | Ctrl+Alt+Shift+U | Command+Alt+ Shift+U |
| Align ⇨ Left | Aligns the text to the left edge of the bounding box | Ctrl+Alt+Shift+L | Command+Alt+ Shift+L |
| Align ⇨ Center | Centers the text between the left and right edges of the bounding box | Ctrl+Alt+Shift+C | Command+Alt+ Shift+C |
| Align ⇨ Right | Aligns the text to the right edge of the bounding box | Ctrl+Alt+Shift+R | Command+Alt+ Shift+R |
| Align ⇨ Justified | Aligns text to the left and right side of the bounding box with equal spaces between words | Ctrl+Alt+Shift+J | Command+Alt+ Shift+J |

*Continued*

| Table 2-25 *(continued)* | | | |
|---|---|---|---|
| *Command* | *Description* | *Windows Shortcut* | *Macintosh Shortcut* |
| Align ⇨ Stretched | Stretches text to fit the dimensions of the bounding box while maintaining a single space between words | Ctrl+Alt+Shift+S | Command+Alt+ Shift+S |
| Align ⇨ Top | Aligns vertically flowing text to the top of the bounding box | n/a | n/a |
| Align ⇨ Center | Centers vertically flowing text between the top and bottom of the bounding box | n/a | n/a |
| Align ⇨ Bottom | Aligns vertically flowing text to the bottom of the bounding box | n/a | n/a |
| Align ⇨ Justified | Aligns vertically flowing text to the top and bottom of the bounding box with equal spaces between lines | n/a | n/a |
| Align ⇨ Stretched | Stretches vertically flowing text to fit the dimensions of the bounding box while maintaining a single space between words | Ctrl+Alt+Shift+S | Command+Alt+ Shift+S |
| Editor | Opens the Text Editor | Ctrl+Shift+E | Command+Shift+E |
| Attach to Path | Attaches a selected text block to a selected path | Ctrl+Shift+Y | Command+Shift+Y |
| Detach from Path | Detaches a text block from its path | n/a | n/a |
| Orientation ⇨ Rotate Around Path | Sets the bottom of each letter in an attached text block to be closest to the path | n/a | n/a |
| Orientation ⇨ Vertical | Sets the side of each letter in an attached text block to be closest to the path | n/a | n/a |
| Orientation ⇨ Skew Vertical | Slants text to make each letter lean in relation to the path | n/a | n/a |

| Command | Description | Windows Shortcut | Macintosh Shortcut |
|---|---|---|---|
| Orientation ⇨ Skew Horizontal | Slants text to make each letter distort in relation to the path | n/a | n/a |
| Reverse Direction | Reverses the direction of the text attached to the path | n/a | n/a |
| Convert to Paths | Changes a text block to a series of vector objects | n/a | n/a |

## Xtras

In Macromedia parlance, an Xtra is a plug-in that extends the capabilities of a program. With Fireworks, Xtras are primarily image filters. As you can see in Table 2-26, the Xtras menu commands list, Fireworks comes with nine standard filters as well as a licensed version of the CSI PhotoOptics plug-ins. Because Fireworks can read most Photoshop filters and plug-ins, you can greatly extend the available Xtras, either by including them in Fireworks's Settings/Plug-ins folder or by assigning the proper folder in Preferences.

 **Caution** Because all Fireworks Xtras are pixel-based image filters, any Xtra applied to a vector-based object first converts that object to an image.

### Table 2-26
### Xtras Menu Commands

| Command | Description | Windows Shortcut | Macintosh Shortcut |
|---|---|---|---|
| Repeat Last Command | Repeats the last Xtra | Ctrl+Alt+Shift+X | Command+Option+Shift+X |
| Blur ⇨ Blur | Averages the pixel edges of a selection so that it appears to blur | n/a | n/a |
| Blur ⇨ Blur More | Like blur, but averages three times the number of pixels from the edge | n/a | n/a |
| Blur ⇨ Gaussian Blur | Opens the Gaussian Blur dialog box, which enables a user-definable blur setting | n/a | n/a |

*Continued*

## Table 2-26 *(continued)*

| Command | Description | Windows Shortcut | Macintosh Shortcut |
|---|---|---|---|
| Invert ⇨ Invert | Changes each color in a selection to its mathematical inverse according to the RGB settings | n/a | n/a |
| Other ⇨ Convert to Alpha | Changes any object into a grayscale image with transparency | n/a | n/a |
| Other ⇨ Find Edges | Marks the parts of an object that act as a transition from one color to another | n/a | n/a |
| Sharpen ⇨ Sharpen | Increases the contrast of adjacent pixels in a selected object. | n/a | n/a |
| Sharpen ⇨ Sharpen More | Like Sharpen, but increases adjacent pixels to a higher level of contrast | n/a | n/a |
| Sharpen ⇨ Unsharp Mask | Opens the Unsharp Mask dialog box, which permits you to control the increase of contrast for adjacent pixels | n/a | n/a |
| CSI Photo-Optics | A series of Photoshop-compatible filters; see Chapter 14 | n/a | n/a |
| Your Xtras | A list of your installed plug-ins | n/a | n/a |

## Window menu

The Window menu commands, listed in Table 2-27, give you menu — and keyboard shortcut — access to all of Fireworks's floating panels and toolbars. In addition, several commands help you work with multiple images or multiple views of the same image.

**Table 2-27**
**Window Menu Commands**

| Command | Description | Windows Shortcut | Macintosh Shortcut |
|---|---|---|---|
| New Window | Opens a new view of the selected document | Ctrl+Alt+N | Command+Option+N |
| Toolbars ➪ Main (Windows only) | Shows/Hides the Main toolbar | Ctrl+Alt+T | n/a |
| Toolbars ➪ Modify (Windows only) | Shows/Hides the Modify toolbar | n/a | n/a |
| Toolbars ➪ Modify (Windows only) | Shows/Hides the Modify toolbar (Windows only) | n/a | n/a |
| Toolbars ➪ View Controls (Windows only) | Shows/Hides the View Controls toolbar (Windows only) | n/a | n/a |
| Object | Shows/Hides the Object inspector | Ctrl+I | Command+I |
| Stroke | Shows/Hides the Stroke panel | Ctrl+Shift+B | Command+Shift+B |
| Fill | Shows/Hides the Fill panel | Ctrl+Shift+F | Command+Shift+F |
| Effect | Shows/Hides the Effect panel | Ctrl+Shift+E | Command+Shift+E |
| Info | Shows/Hides the Info panel | Ctrl+Shift+I | Command+Shift+I |
| Tool Options | Shows/Hides the Tool Options | Ctrl+Shift+O | Command+Shift+O |
| Styles | Shows/Hides the Styles panel | Ctrl+Shift+J | Command+Shift+J |
| Color Mixer | Shows/Hides the Color Mixer | Ctrl+Shift+M | Command+Shift+M |
| Swatches | Shows/Hides the Swatches panel | Ctrl+Shift+S | Command+Shift+S |

*Continued*

## Table 2-27 *(continued)*

| Command | Description | Windows Shortcut | Macintosh Shortcut |
|---|---|---|---|
| Layers | Shows/Hides the Layers panel | Ctrl+Shift+L | Command+Shift+L |
| Frames | Shows/Hides the Frames panel | Ctrl+Shift+K | Command+Shift+K |
| Behaviors | Shows/Hides the Behavior inspector | Ctrl+Shift+S | Command+Shift+S |
| URL Manager | Shows/Hides the URL Manager | Ctrl+Shift+U | Command+Shift+U |
| Find & Replace | Shows/Hides the Find & Replace panel | n/a | n/a |
| Project Log | Shows/Hides the Project Log panel | n/a | n/a |
| Cascade | Groups open windows so that the title bar and left edge are showing | n/a | n/a |
| Tile Horizontal | Positions open windows so that each window displays horizontally | n/a | n/a |
| Tile Vertical | Positions open windows so that each window displays vertically | n/a | n/a |
| Your Open Windows | Lists your open windows | n/a | n/a |

## Help menu (Windows only)

Everyone needs help now and then, especially when working with a program as rich and deep as Fireworks. The Help menu commands, detailed in Table 2-28, give you quick access to the Fireworks Help Pages, various online resources, and a number of key tutorials to explain the basics. There's even a special pop-up screen that explains how hotspots and slices work in Fireworks 2 for users of the previous version.

Table 2-28
**Help Menu Commands**

| Command | Description | Windows Shortcut | Macintosh Shortcut |
|---|---|---|---|
| Fireworks Help | Opens the Fireworks Help Pages in your primary browser | F1 | F1 |
| Help Index | Opens the Fireworks Help Pages pointing to the Index | n/a | n/a |
| Contacting Macromedia | Displays the Contacting Macromedia page in the Fireworks Help Pages | n/a | n/a |
| Using Hotspots and Slices | Displays the Web objects help screen | n/a | n/a |
| Register Fireworks | Goes to the Macromedia Web site to register the program online | n/a | n/a |
| Fireworks Web Site | Goes to www.getfireworks.com | n/a | n/a |
| About Fireworks | Displays the About Fireworks credit and serial number | n/a | n/a |
| Tutorials | Opens the Contents page for the Tutorials in your primary browser | n/a | n/a |
| Optimizing JPEGs | Describes how to use Export Preview to get the best-quality JPEG images at the smallest file size | n/a | n/a |
| Optimizing GIFs | Describes how to use Export Preview to get the best-quality GIF images using Web-safe colors and other features | n/a | n/a |

*Continued*

## Table 2-28 *(continued)*

| Command | Description | Windows Shortcut | Macintosh Shortcut |
|---|---|---|---|
| Animating | Details how to use Symbols and Instances to make an animated GIF | n/a | n/a |
| Creating an Image Map | Explains how to use hotspots to create an image map | n/a | n/a |
| Creating Slices | Explores using slices with custom export settings | n/a | n/a |
| Assigning Behaviors | Details how to attach behaviors to Slice objects and export the code | n/a | n/a |
| Creating Rollovers | Explains how to make a simple rollover | n/a | n/a |
| Exporting Rollovers and JavaScript | Describes how to build rollovers and export the code | n/a | n/a |
| Applying Live Effects | Details how to apply single and multiple effects | n/a | n/a |
| Batch Processing | Describes the steps involved in Batch Processing | n/a | n/a |

## Online Help

The Macromedia and Fireworks Web sites offer a tremendous range of support options. If you're troubleshooting a problem, you should start with the searchable TechNotes, which cover virtually every aspect of working with Fireworks. You'll also find links to useful tutorials, articles on Web graphics design, and interviews with industry leaders in Fireworks's main Support section.

One of the most important resources is the Fireworks newsgroup, hosted by Macromedia. This discussion group, found at `news://forums.macromedia.com/macromedia.fireworks`, is an essential source for contacting other users of Fireworks. Fireworks support staff, as well as expert and novice users alike, frequent the newsgroup. Need a quick answer to a perplexing graphics problem? Can't figure out the final step in a procedure? Looking to have users with different systems and browsers check your site for compatibility? The Fireworks newsgroup can help in all these areas and more.

# Summary

With a program as feature-laden as Fireworks, it's helpful to have an overview of what's possible. The Fireworks user interface is very flexible and, with the new groupable floating panels, customizable. The more familiar you become with the layout of the program, the smoother your workflow. When you're looking at the Fireworks interface, keep these points in mind:

✦ In some ways, Fireworks combines tools from several different types of applications: a bitmap graphic program, a vector drawing program, an image optimizer, and a Web code generator.

✦ All of the tools found in Fireworks's Toolbox have one-key shortcuts, such as **v** for the Select tool and **z** for the Zoom tool.

✦ Customize your workspace in Fireworks 2 by grouping the floating panels however you'd like.

✦ Many tools have special options you can access by double-clicking its Toolbox button — or by choosing the tool and then opening the Tool Options panel.

✦ Xtra commands are pixel-based commands. This doesn't mean you can apply them only to images, however. But keep in mind that if you do use an Xtra with a vector-based object, it will be converted to a bitmapped image.

In the next chapter, you'll see how you can set up the Fireworks environment to suit your work style.

✦     ✦     ✦

# Customizing Your Environment

**Y**ou'll never find any two artists' studios that are exactly alike. And why should you? Creating — whether it's fine art, print images, or Web graphics — is a highly personal experience that requires the artist to be in comfortable, personalized surroundings. Fireworks 2 reflects this attitude by enabling you to personalize numerous preferences to facilitate your workflow, from importing existing images through graphic editing all the way to exporting your final product. This chapter describes all the options Fireworks offers to custom-fit the program to your work style.

## Setting Preferences

Most, but not all, of Fireworks's customization options are handily grouped in the Preferences dialog box. Though you can adjust these preferences at any time, they are generally used to fine-tune the program's overall functions. Consequently, changes to a number of the options do not take effect until Fireworks is restarted.

To access these program-wide settings, choose File ➪ Preferences. The Preferences dialog box then opens with the first of its three tabbed panels displayed. The three panels — detailed in the following sections — are labeled General, Editing, and Folders.

**Cross-Reference**

Fireworks 2 now has an additional general preference: floating windows are now dockable. You can create your own combination of windows — Layers, Color Mixer, Frames, and so on — by dragging and dropping them on one another. For all the details on this aspect of customizing your workspace, see Chapter 2.

# General preferences

The General panel of the Preferences dialog box, shown in Figure 3-1, is divided into three sections: Undo Steps, Color Defaults, and Photoshop Conversion.

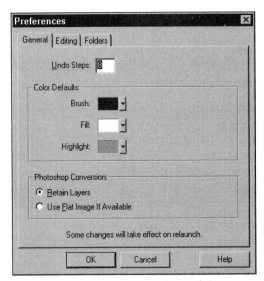

**Figure 3-1:** Reserve memory for undoing your actions, change the color defaults, and specify Photoshop import options in the General panel of the Preferences dialog box.

## Specifying undo levels

The capability to undo an action — whether it's a font color change, an image rotation, or an out-and-out deletion — is critical in computer graphics. Although some graphics programs only let you reverse or *undo* your last command, Fireworks gives you multiple undo levels. Fireworks requires a certain amount of memory to keep track of the changes to a graphic. Rather than grab all of your system's resources to use for an unlimited number of reversals, Fireworks lets you specify the number of undo levels — and thus the required amount of memory.

By default, Fireworks reserves enough memory for eight undo levels. You can change this by altering the Undo Steps value. The amount of memory needed to undo an operation depends on the type of operation. For example, rotating a 500 × 600 pixel photograph requires far more memory than changing the color of a straight line.

If you alter the number of Undo Steps, the new setting takes effect after Fireworks is restarted.

**Note** Macintosh users can specify how much memory is to be used by a particular program. Macromedia recommends that 24MB of RAM be dedicated to Fireworks, if possible.

## Color defaults

Although the Web designer has a full palette from which to choose, Fireworks starts with just three basic colors:

✦ **Brush:** The default Brush color is applied to any path that is drawn or *stroked* with any of the drawing tools, such as the Pencil, Pen, Brush, or Rectangle.

✦ **Fill:** The default Fill color is applied to any object when a Solid fill-type is selected in the Fill window.

✦ **Highlight:** To show a selected object, Fireworks temporarily changes the outline of the object to the Highlight color. When the object is deselected (or another object is selected), the Highlight color is removed.

You make all default color changes through the Default Colors section of the General panel in the Preferences dialog box. To alter any of the Brush, Fill, or Highlight colors, select the arrow button next to their respective color wells. The Fireworks color picker is displayed. Choose any of the Web-safe color swatches shown or use the Eyedropper tool to select an onscreen color. For a wider selection of colors, select the Palette icon to display the system color pickers.

**Tip** To turn off the automatic fill or stroke, select the No Color icon (the slash-in-circle symbol,(∅) from the pop-up color picker. Although a color is still displayed in the color well when No Color is selected, any objects created are drawn with Fill and/or Stroke option set to None.

You can alter both the Brush and Fill colors by choosing their respective color well on the Toolbox, the Color Mixer, or any number of other windows. The Highlight color can only be changed through Preferences. All color changes take place immediately after the Preferences dialog box closes.

**Tip** If you choose a gradient fill-type (such as Linear, Radial, or Cone) for an object, but no color combination, Fireworks uses the current Brush and Fill selections to create the gradient.

## Photoshop preferences

Photoshop is a well-established image editing program that gains much of its power from its capability to layer one image on top of another with varying degrees of opaqueness and transparency. Fireworks handles Photoshop files quite elegantly and can not only load the latest version, but also keep the layers separate for manipulation. Occasionally, however, the designer finds it easier to work with a single "flat" image, rather than a series of individual layers. Fireworks lets you load and import Photoshop files in whichever manner is best suited to your project. You can even change the preferences at any time before you open the next series of images.

By default, in Fireworks the Retain Layers option is selected and each layer of a Photoshop image is put in its own Fireworks layer. To load a flat, single-layer version of the graphic, choose the Use Flat Image If Available option.

**Note**    Not all Photoshop images can be displayed in flat versions. If the file was saved from an earlier version of Photoshop (3 or 4) where the Photoshop 2.5 compatibility option was not chosen, you'll get an image with the message that this file requires Photoshop 3.0 to open it when Fireworks has the Use Flat Image If Available option selected.

## Editing preferences

The Editing panel of Preferences, shown in Figure 3-2, offers some new options in Fireworks 2 to customize your image creation techniques. Most of the new options affect editing bitmapped pixel images, rather than vector objects; however, the Precise Cursors option is useful in both modes.

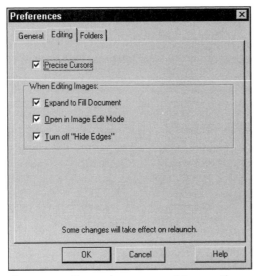

**Figure 3-2:** Customize your graphics creation style in the Editing panel of Fireworks Preferences.

**New Feature**    By default, when a particular drawing or selection tool is selected, the cursor changes into a representative shape. For example, select the Pencil tool and the cursor changes to a pencil shape. When enabled, the Precise Cursors option replaces all the affected individual cursor shapes with a cross-hair cursor.

## Using precise cursors

If the Precise Cursors option is selected, the following tools use the cross-hair cursor:

✦ All selection tools including the rectangular and elliptical Marquee, and the Lasso, Polygon Lasso, and Magic Wand

✦ Drawing tools such as the Line, Pen, Rectangle, Ellipse, Polygon, Pencil, and Brush

✦ Modification tools such as Eraser and Paint Bucket

✦ All Web objects tools, including Hotspot Rectangles, Circle and Polygons, and the Slice tool

The Precise Cursor is very useful for detail work where the tool-specific cursor might block the designer's view, as illustrated in Figure 3-3.

**Figure 3-3:** Use the new Precise Cursor feature for close-up work where a standard cursor might hamper pixel-level accuracy.

**Tip**    If you haven't enabled the Precise Cursors option in Preferences, the option can be toggled on or off with the Caps Lock key. This keyboard shortcut stays in effect until reselected. Unless you find the standard cursors distracting, I recommend keeping the Precise Cursors option disabled in Preferences and using the Caps Lock key whenever the cross-hair cursor is needed.

### Examining pixel-based image options

The three other choices on the Editing panel affect only pixel-based images. Because Fireworks creates and edits both pixel-based images and vector-based objects, a selected image is often just a portion of the overall graphic. Previously, when an image was selected for editing, the bounding box indicating the selection with the "barberpole" design was restricted to the image itself. This made edits that extended beyond the image difficult and setup required a multistep process. Fireworks 2 simplifies image editing.

**New Feature**    When you choose the Expand to Fill Document option, anytime you enter Image Edit mode, the entire document is selected and surrounded by the familiar barberpole stripes. This enables you to treat the entire canvas as a bitmapped surface, if necessary. For example, you can use the Rubber Stamp tool, which copies an image from one area to another, to repeat a portion of the bitmap in another section of the canvas.

In another enhancement, you can now open bitmapped images in either Image Edit or Object Edit mode. The Open in Image Edit Mode option, when enabled, causes Fireworks to allow immediate pixel editing on bitmapped images. If this option is not selected, you have to enter Image Edit mode by double-clicking the pixel-based image, choosing Modify ➪ Image Edit, or selecting and using one of the image-editing tools such as Marquee. In practice, I generally leave this option deselected because I find that Fireworks 2 makes entering Image Edit mode far easier than before.

The final Editing panel preference enables you to turn off the "Hide Edges" command when working with pixel-based images. Normally, Hide Edges, found under the View menu, makes all the selection outlines — both the barberpoles around the bitmapped images or the "marching ants" around a selection — vanish. When the Turn Off "Hide Edges" option is enabled (and the edges have been hidden), making any selection causes the edges to reappear; the Hide Edge command has to be reselected. When the option is disabled (and View ➪ Hide Edges is chosen), the edges stay hidden all the time. I've found that it's easy to lose track of selections if edges are hidden all the time, so I generally enable this option and either choose the menu command or, more often, the keyboard shortcut — Ctrl-H (Command-H) — when I want to see my graphic without additional outlines.

## Folder preferences

One of the features of a truly great software program is its capability to extend its functionality. This extensibility comes in many forms — Fireworks opens up three key areas for expansion:

✦ Fireworks enables you to include additional plug-ins or filters for applying effects to bitmapped images. Fireworks works with Photoshop-compatible plug-ins — and compatibility has been greatly enhanced for Fireworks 2.

✦ A second textures folder — images that can be merged with other images to give the appearance of different surfaces — can be referenced.

✦ Similarly, another patterns folder (a single image that repeats to fill a selected area) can be included.

All of these additions are specified on the Folders panel of the Preferences dialog box (Figure 3-4) in the same manner. Select the ... (Browse/Choose) button next to the Photoshop Plug-Ins, Textures, or Patterns checkboxes. A Browse for Folder dialog box opens; select the folder containing the extensions you want to use in Fireworks and click the OK button. After you've closed Preferences and restarted Fireworks, these options are available to you.

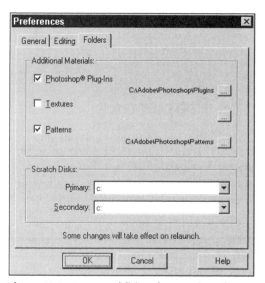

**Figure 3-4:** Access additional extensions for Fireworks through the Folders panel of Preferences.

Typically, designers use this feature to include extensions currently available to another program, such as Photoshop. Fireworks also has its own Plug-ins (called Xtras), Textures, and Pattern folders from which to pull resources.

Patterns and textures add a great deal of richness to your graphics. For more details on how to apply them in Fireworks, see Chapter 11. For details on how to incorporate plug-ins, turn to Chapter 14.

The final option in Preferences sets up an additional workspace for Fireworks called a *scratch disk*. Graphics manipulation requires a great deal of memory and, when Fireworks needs to perform an operation and not enough memory is available, the hard drive is used as a temporary workspace. By default, Fireworks uses the standard hard drive (c:) as both the primary and secondary scratch disks. If you have additional drives or partitions, you can establish them as the scratch disks.

Let's say I have one other hard drive available, labeled d:, other than my primary system drive. If I don't want Fireworks to use my system drive, where I store all my programs and operating system, I would set the Primary Scratch Disk option to d: by selecting the drive letter from the drop-down list. Because I don't want Fireworks to use the c: drive at all, I set the Secondary Scratch Disk option to None.

Although it's possible to use removable media (such as a SyQuest or Zip drive) as a scratch disk, it's not recommended. Removable media is notably slower than the standard fixed hard drive and somewhat less reliable. If you're doing a fair amount of extensive graphic editing, it's probably worthwhile to invest in another hard drive.

## Adjusting a Document's Properties

Fireworks files are similar to those from a page layout program in one important way: both are intended for publication. While the page layout program outputs files intended for a printer or service bureau, Fireworks generates files to be published on the Web. Because of the increased variations possible with its HTML output, Fireworks 2 now enables you to set a range of properties for each document.

The Document Properties command enables you to set options for both slicing and image map operations. Briefly, *slicing* cuts an image into smaller sections, which are placed in an HTML table, whereas an *image map* is a graphic with one or more hotspots. The parameters chosen through the Document Properties command can be used for a single graphic or designated as the current default settings. Choose File ➪ Document Properties to open the dialog box shown in Figure 3-5 and set these parameters.

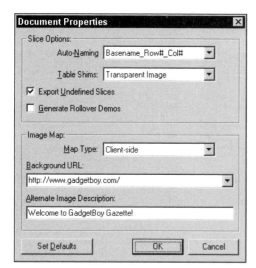

**Figure 3-5:** Control the HTML output of your document through the new Document Properties options.

## Slicing an image

When Fireworks slices an image, each sliced section must be stored using a unique name. Rather than asking the designer to name each section on export, Fireworks automatically generates a filename. The naming convention combines a *basename* — the name entered in the Export process — before or after one of three different extensions, to make six different combinations. The following combinations are available from the Auto-Naming drop-down list on the Document Properties dialog box:

✦ **Basename_Row#_Col#:** Combines the basename with the number of the row and column of the HTML table used to display the slices; row numbers are prefaced with an "r" and columns with a "c". Examples: welcome_r1_c1; welcome_r1_c2; welcome_ ; welcome_r2_c1.

✦ **Basename_Alphabetical:** Mixes the basename with an alphabetical suffix, in ascending order. For slices with many images, Fireworks uses a multiple letter combination, for example, AA, BB, CC, and so on, to name those images after the 26th one. Examples: welcome_A; welcome_B; welcome_C.

✦ **Basename_Numeric:** With this option, the unique name consists of the basename and an ascending number. Fireworks uses a smart-naming algorithm: if there are less than ten slices, the numbers 1 through 9 are used; however, if there are ten or more slices, a leading zero is used for the single digits. Examples: welcome_01; welcome_02; welcome_03.

✦ **Row#_Col#_Basename:** Uses the row and column numbers of the HTML table as described previously as a prefix to the basename. Examples: r1_c1_welcome; r1_c2_welcome; r2_c1_welcome.

✦ **Alphabetical_Basename:** Places the alphabetical reference before the basename. Examples: A_welcome; B_welcome; C_welcome.

✦ **Numeric_Basename:** Creates a unique name by combining the number of the slice with its basename. Examples: 01_welcome; 02_welcome; 03_welcome.

Both the numeric and alphabetical naming schemes follow the same pattern as they name objects in the HTML table. Objects are named row by row, left to right, as shown in Figure 3-6.

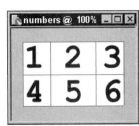

**Figure 3-6:** This figure depicts the slicing order for an object with six sections.

Slicing is one of Fireworks's richest features. For a complete discussion of slicing, see Chapter 19.

## Shim options

An unfortunate fact-of-Web-life has made a device known as the *table shim* pretty much a necessity for sliced images. When an image is sliced, each section is placed in a separate HTML table cell. Not all browsers handle tables in the same manner. Some browsers — notably versions of Netscape Navigator — collapse the tables unless some content is included in each cell, rendering the image unattractive. Fireworks solves this problem by placing a 1-pixel shim in each outside column and row, as shown in Figure 3-7. The shims serve to keep the graphic looking as-designed, no matter what browser is used.

With Fireworks 2, the range of possibilities has increased for using shims. Simply select the Table Shims arrow button and select one of the three options from the drop-down list. The default method is to use transparent shims around the outside of the image. Only one image is added — a 1-pixel ¥ 1-pixel GIF file — called shim.gif with a tiny file size of 43 bytes. The shim.gif file is used repeatedly and resized in the browser, if necessary.

The drawback to the transparent GIF shim is that images could not butt up against each other — because of the 1-pixel barrier. Now, through Document Properties, you can opt to have the shim cut out of the image itself, thus avoiding use of the transparent shim.gif file. This solution works for many sliced images where graphics must be positioned side-by-side.

Do not choose the Shims from Image option if your graphic has a rollover that extends to the edge. The shim cut from the image will not be affected by the rollover and, consequently, the effect is less than desirable.

Regular slice      Shim from image

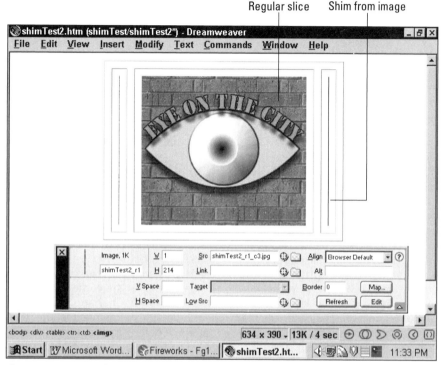

**Figure 3-7:** Fireworks 2 lets you choose transparent shims, no shims, or — as shown here in an exaggerated view from Dreamweaver — shims from the image itself.

The third shim option is to not use shims at all. The No Shims option should be used only after testing to make sure that the image is viewed as desired in all required browsers.

## Exporting undefined slices

When an image is sliced, every portion of the canvas doesn't have to be covered by a slice object. Although most of the time the entire graphic is translated into slices, the designer may occasionally need to store just the specifically sliced areas.

Let's look at an example. Let's say that a designer uses a single canvas to create multiple, similar buttons that will ultimately be used on separate pages. If the Export Undefined Slices option is left selected (it's the default), the entire graphic will be exported in a single table with the individual elements in the same relative position to each other — however, they could not be used on different Web pages. If, on the other hand, the Export Undefined Slices option is deselected, the sliced objects are exported as separate files, using the naming convention described in the previous section.

**New Feature**

In the first version of Fireworks, the only way to see the sliced rollovers in action was to select the Create Demo Rollover option when exporting. In Fireworks 2, you can preview your rollovers directly in the browser without saving a separate file, as well as choosing from a number of HTML output options when exporting. If you find it necessary to have an additional file to demonstrate the working rollovers, select the Generate HTML Demo option.

## Using image map options

Fireworks 2 offers three options for any image maps used in the current document. As noted earlier, an *image map* is a graphic that uses hotspots to denote different URLs on the same image. The hotspots are created with Fireworks tools capable of drawing rectangles, ellipses, or polygons.

Two types of image map technologies are used in HTML. The earliest versions of image maps were said to be *server-side* because the image map file resided on the host computer, which also handled all the click-detection. Almost all browsers, although not all servers, support some form of server-side image maps. Server-side image maps are quite processor-intensive and are generally regarded as a slower alternative to the more recent *client-side* image maps. As the name implies, the browser itself, also known as the *client* in networking jargon, handles all the processing in a client-side image map scheme. The only drawback to client-side image maps — and it's a minor one — is that a few older browsers (versions 2.0 and earlier) can't handle them. The vast majority of browsers in use today are capable of using client-side image maps.

Fireworks 2 lets you select one of three options for the type of image map used in a document: Client-Side, Server-Side (NCSA), and Both. You can select these choices from the Map Type option list.

**Note**

*NCSA* is an abbreviation for the National Center for Supercomputing Activities, one of the pioneers in early server-side Web technology. Fireworks uses the NCSA format for its server-side image map code. Several different server-side formats exist. Check with your Internet service provider (ISP) to find out if NCSA format is supported.

When a user clicks in a hotspot on an image map, the user's browser jumps to the associated Internet address or *URL*. Often, a designer wants to assign a general URL to the overall image, in case it is selected. This type of Internet address is known as the *background URL*, and you can enter either a relative or absolute URL in the Background URL text box on the Document Properties dialog box.

Similarly, when the user's pointer passes over a hotspot, a small bit of identifying text appears in a small box referred to as a *tooltip*. The information for the tooltip is set in the <alt> tag of the Object window in Fireworks. For a tooltip to appear when the user's pointer is over the general image map, but not any specific hotspot, that information should be entered into the Document Properties Alternate Image Description text box. This <alt> text will also appear briefly in the browser window as the image is being loaded.

**Cross-Reference** To better understand the potential for image maps, turn to Chapter 19.

# Selecting Print Options

Although Fireworks is by far a Web-oriented program, occasionally a printout of a graphic is useful. Quite often the designer is expected to present visual concepts to clients or other team members, occasionally in a printed format. To print graphics created in the first version of Fireworks, you had to insert the graphics in a Web page and then print them from a browser. Fireworks 2, however, simplifies the process and you can now print your images directly from within the program.

**New Feature** Fireworks's Print feature is very straightforward and uses standards set on both Macintosh and Windows operating systems. The File ⇨ Page Setup command opens a standard dialog box — the Windows version is shown in Figure 3-8 — which enables the user to determine the page size, paper source, orientation, and margins. Choosing the Printer button opens the standard dialog box with printer-specific options. When you're ready to print the selected image, just choose File ⇨ Print and select the number of copies and other choices.

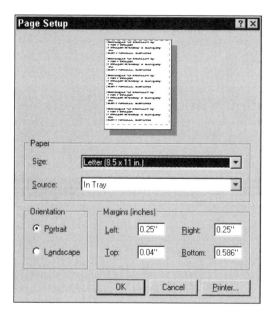

**Figure 3-8:** Use the Page Setup dialog box to establish your page size and orientation for printing graphics from within Fireworks 2.

When Fireworks prints a selected image, the graphic is positioned in the center of the page at the preset resolution. You can change the resolution and the print size by selecting Modify ➪ Document ➪ Image Size and entering new values in the appropriate text boxes in the Image Size dialog box.

# Summary

Setting your preferences not only lets you work more comfortably, but also more effectively. Fireworks 2 gives you control over many aspects of your graphics creation, output, and even printing. Here are a few key points to keep in mind about setting your Fireworks preferences:

✦ You can find most of the program's options by choosing File ➪ Preferences.

✦ Several preferences — such as including other Photoshop plug-ins, patterns, and texture filters — require you to restart Fireworks before they take effect.

✦ You can turn the cross-hair cursor on and off by pressing the Caps Lock key, but only if you do not choose the Precise Cursors option in the Editing panel of Preferences.

✦ Each document opened or created can have its own set of special properties that affect the HTML output for slices and image maps.

✦ You no longer have to export your image just to get a hard copy. With Fireworks 2's new Print command support, you can use system-standard Page Setup and Printer dialogs.

In the next chapter, you'll learn how to create new canvases for your Web graphic creations as well as how to open existing works for modification.

✦　　✦　　✦

# Setting Up Documents

**O**il painters have a fairly set ritual to complete before
they can begin to paint. Whereas Web artists don't have
to stretch or prime their canvases, choosing certain options
prior to undertaking a new work can save time down the line.
Of course, one of the major benefits of electronic illustration
in general, and Fireworks in particular, is that you can modify
virtually anything at any stage.

This chapter covers all you need to know about "prepping
your canvas" in Fireworks. In addition to the basics of page
opening, saving, and closing, you'll also find a complete
section on modifying your document for those inevitable
moments that planning did not prevent. In addition, this
chapter examines the significant features Fireworks 2 has
added for the power user who's looking to work with multiple
images at the same time.

## Creating New Pages

Quite often, you'll start a new graphic with a blank canvas. But
before you actually begin work, it's best to consider what you
are aiming to create. The better you can visualize the final result,
the fewer modifications you'll have to make along the way. This
is not to say that experimenting on a large canvas is out of the
question. However, if you know you need to build a horizontal
navigation strip that will be placed against a black background,
you'll want to avoid starting with a white vertical page.

Fireworks gives you control over four basic elements of the canvas:

✦ **Width:** The horizontal dimension of a document, available in pixels, inches, or centimeters.

✦ **Height:** The vertical dimension of a document, also available in pixels, inches, or centimeters.

✦ **Resolution:** The number of pixels per inch or pixels per centimeter.

✦ **Canvas color:** The color of the underlying layer for your work. A transparent option is also considered a valid "color."

## Width and height

Although it may appear otherwise sometimes, all Web graphic files are ultimately rectangular. A document's width and height determine not only a document's size, but also its shape. Whereas there are no theoretical limitations to the size of an image, the Web designer must always consider file size to be a vital factor and, everything else being equal, the larger the image, the bigger the file size. Typically, image dimensions are given in pixels, short for picture elements. Pixels are the red, green, and blue dots that make up a computer color monitor's screen. From time to time, it's helpful to switch to nonscreen-based measurement systems, like inches or centimeters, and Fireworks gives you that option. But Web design is a pixel-oriented world and you'll find yourself primarily using them for measuring.

## Resolution

In print, resolution refers to the number of dots per inch (dpi). The higher the resolution, the sharper the image. On the Web, resolution literally hits a glass ceiling—the monitor—with a comparatively low value. Most monitors, especially from an end-user perspective, have a screen resolution of 72 pixels per inch. By comparison, the lowest print resolution in general use today is around 300 dpi, whereas most printed images range anywhere from 2400 to 3600 dpi.

Fireworks uses a default resolution of 72 pixels per inch. Though you can increase the resolution to whatever value you like, chances are you won't achieve the effect you're trying for. On documents created from scratch, you won't see any noticeable benefit from the increased resolution. Moreover, if you open a high-resolution image, translating or *resampling* each dot to a pixel on a one-to-one basis, the image will be many times larger than the original. For example, an image with a print resolution of 300 dpi resampled for a screen resolution of 72 pixels per inch would end up more than four times the original size.

Bottom line on resolution: stick to Fireworks's default value of 72 pixels per inch.

**Caution** The resolution is pretty much the only facet of a document that can't be altered once the document is created. If you ever do need to change the resolution of an existing graphic, copy the entire image and paste it into a new document with the adjusted resolution. Fireworks will ask if you want to resample the graphic to match the new resolution; choose Don't Resample to keep the image the same size or Resample to match the new resolution.

## Canvas color

Canvas color is very important, but also very flexible in Fireworks 2. When you're creating Web graphics, the canvas color often needs to match the background color of a Web page. Whereas you don't have to match the colors when creating your new page, if you can, you should and it will save you a step or two in the near future. You can modify the canvas color at any point in Fireworks by choosing Modify ➪ Document ➪ Canvas Color.

Initially, you have three basic choices for a canvas color: white, transparent, or custom. Although white is not the default color for browsers, it is for many Web-authoring tools, including Dreamweaver, and is often a safe choice for a beginning canvas color. Naturally, transparent is not really a color — it's the absence of color. However, as many Web pages use an image or pattern for a background, designers often choose the transparent option to enable part of the background to be visible through their graphics. This enables graphics — which are always saved in a rectangular format — to appear nonrectangular. Fireworks 2 includes many techniques for outputting a graphic with a transparent background, but many artists like to work with a transparent canvas regardless.

The third choice, marked custom color, is really all the colors. Selecting the Custom Color radio button enables you to choose a color from 216 Web-safe colors displayed on the pop-up color picker or from the extended color palette. (A Web-safe color is one that displays the same in the major browsers on different computing plat-forms.) The Custom Color option is great when you're trying to match a Web page background.

**Cross-Reference** An understanding of color on the Internet is crucial for the Web graphics designer. See Chapter 7 for more information on using color in Fireworks.

To create a new page, follow these steps:

1. Choose File ➪ New or select the New button from the Main toolbar (Windows only). The New Document dialog box, shown in Figure 4-1, opens.

2. To change the horizontal measurement of the canvas, enter a new value in the Width text box. Press Tab when you're done.

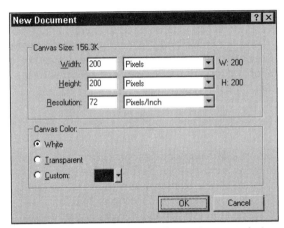

**Figure 4-1:** Set your graphics dimensions, resolution, and canvas color in the New Document dialog box.

3. To change the vertical measurement of the canvas, enter a new value in the Height text box. Press Tab.

4. To enter a new resolution for the canvas, enter a value in the Resolution text box. The default resolution in Fireworks is 72 pixels per inch.

5. To change the measurement system used for Width, Height, or Resolution, select the arrow button next to the corresponding list box. You can choose Pixels, Inches, or Centimeters for both Width and Height; with Resolution, you can select either Pixels/Inch or Pixels/cm (centimeter).

**Note**    Whenever you switch Width or Height measurement systems, Fireworks automatically converts the existing values to the new scale. For example, if the new canvas was originally 144 pixels wide at 72 pixels per inch resolution, and the Width measurement system was changed to inches, Fireworks converts the 144 pixels to 2 inches. No matter which system you choose, Fireworks always displays the dimensions in pixels on the right side of the dialog box as W (width) and H (height).

6. Select a Canvas Color: White, Transparent, or Custom Color.

7. To choose a Custom Color, select the arrow button next to the color swatch and pick the desired color from the pop-up color palette.

8. For a more extensive color choice (beyond the 216 Web-safe colors in the pop-up display), either select the painter's palette icon on the pop-up display or double-click the swatches to reveal the system color pickers.

9. Click OK when you're done.

**Tip**     The New Document dialog box remembers your last settings the next time you create a new file, with one exception. If you've cut or copied a graphic to your system's clipboard and you select File ➪ New, the dialog box contains the dimensions of the image on the clipboard. This makes it easy to paste an existing image into a new file.

# Opening Existing Images

Images worked on in Fireworks fall into two distinct categories: those created in Fireworks and those created in another program. Because Fireworks is terrific at optimizing images for the Web, you're just as likely to find yourself opening an existing file as creating a new one.

As probably anyone who's ever touched a computer graphic is aware, different computer programs, as well as platforms, store files in their own file format. Fireworks opens a wide range of these formats: a dozen, in addition to its own formats. With formats from advanced graphic applications, such as Photoshop, Fireworks retains as much of the individual components of the image like layers as possible. You can even open ASCII or RTF (Real Text Format) files to import text into Fireworks.

**Cross-Reference**     Opening files saved in vector graphics programs like Macromedia FreeHand, Adobe Illustrator, or CorelDraw causes Fireworks to display a dialog box for setting special options. The Vector File Options dialog box is described in Chapter 15.

Table 4-1 details formats supported by Fireworks.

| Table 4-1<br>**Supported File Formats** | | |
|---|---|---|
| *Format* | *File Extension* | *Notes* |
| Fireworks native (PNG) | .png | PNG (Portable Networks Graphics) capable of combining bitmapped and vector graphics with additional information |
| FreeHand version 7.x or 8.x | .fh* or .ft* | Vector graphics format |
| GIF | .gif | Bitmapped graphics format |
| JPEG | .jpg, .jpe, or .jpeg | Bitmapped graphics format |
| Photoshop | .psd | Bitmapped graphics format with layers |

*Continued*

| | | Table 4-1 *(continued)* |
|---|---|---|
| **Format** | **File Extension** | **Notes** |
| PICT | .pict | Macintosh-only format capable of supporting both vector and bitmapped graphics |
| xRes | .lrg | Bitmapped graphics format from Macromedia's xRes program |
| TIFF | .tif, .tiff | Tagged Image File Format, a bitmapped format |
| Targa | .tga | Bitmapped graphics format |
| Illustrator | .ai or .art | Vector graphics format |
| CorelDraw | .cdr | Vector graphics format |
| ASCII | .txt | Plain text |
| Real Text Format | .rtf | Formatted text |
| Batch Process Script | .jsf | Fireworks native batch processing instructions |

**Note**    Fireworks can open animated GIF files as well as standard ones. When opened, each frame of the animated GIF is placed on its own frame in Fireworks.

To open an existing file in Fireworks, follow these steps:

1. Choose File ➪ Open or use the keyboard shortcut, Ctrl+O (Command+O). Windows users can also select the Open button from the Main toolbar. The Open dialog box appears, as shown in Figure 4-2.

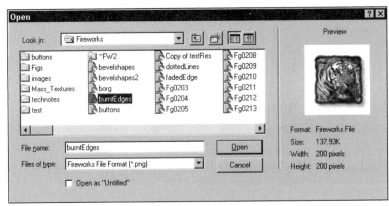

**Figure 4-2:** Preview files before opening them with the Fireworks Open dialog box.

2. Select the desired file in the Open dialog box. Fireworks identifies the file and displays a thumbnail of the image for certain file types in the Preview section of the dialog box. Previewable file types include: JPEG, GIF, FreeHand 7.x/8.x, and PNG.

3. To look for a different file format, click the arrow button next to the Files of Type drop-down list and select a format.

4. To choose from every file type, select All Files (*.*) from the Files of Type drop-down list or type an asterisk in the File Name text field.

5. To choose from Fireworks-compatible files, select All Readable Files from the Files of Type drop-down list.

6. To open a copy of the graphic, choose the Open as "Untitled" option.

7. Click OK when you're done. Fireworks opens the file, reducing the magnification, if necessary, so that the full image is displayed.

**Tip**
You can also open files in Fireworks with the drag-and-drop method. First position Fireworks and the desktop (or a program manager like Windows Explorer or Macintosh Finder) so that both windows are accessible. Then select a compatible graphic's icon or name and drag it into the Fireworks window. Releasing the icon on an open document copies the file into that document.

## Loading Photoshop Files

Fireworks makes it relatively easy to open and work with Photoshop images. By default, Fireworks retains the separate layer information — not only the object, but even the names of the layers. You can force Fireworks to flatten the Photoshop files it opens by selecting the Flatten Image if Possible option in Preferences. As a further enhancement, Photoshop masks created from grouped layers are converted to Mask Groups in Fireworks 2.

Perhaps the only remaining conversion issues are editable text. Photoshop added this feature in version 5, but Fireworks continues to bring in the text layer as a bitmap. If the text is quite substantial or otherwise difficult to reenter, you could save it as a separate text file and then import the file in either ASCII or RTF formats into Fireworks.

# Opening Multiple Images

It's the rare Web page that has but a single image on it. Most Web pages contain multiple graphics and, occasionally, a designer needs to work on several of them simultaneously. Though working on multiple images at the same time has never been an issue in Fireworks, each graphic did have to be opened separately. Now, however, you're saved from a minor bit of tedium with Fireworks 2's new Open Multiple command.

**New Feature** With the new Open Multiple command, you can select as many files as you want to load into Fireworks, all at the same time. The files can come from the same folder or each from a different folder, if necessary. Select a range of files to open or double-click each file to add it to the List Window. You can easily remove files from the List Window, and when you're ready, Fireworks opens and displays all the files in a series of cascading windows.

One significant advantage to the Open Multiple command: you can use it to create animated GIFs. In Fireworks, an animated GIF is a series of frames. When you choose the Open as Animation option in the Open Multiple dialog box, Fireworks inserts each chosen file in a single graphic, but on an individual frame. Then, preview the animation using Fireworks VCR controls or adjust the timing in the Export dialog box.

To open several files in one operation, follow these steps:

**1.** Choose File ➪ Open Multiple or use the keyboard shortcut Ctrl+Shift+O (Command+Shift+O). The Open Multiple dialog box displays, as shown in Figure 4-3.

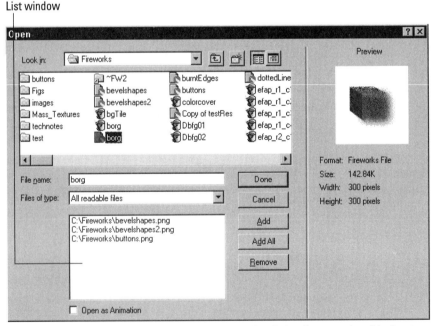

**Figure 4-3:** Select as many files as you'd like to load simultaneously with the Open Multiple command.

2. Navigate to the folder containing the images to open.

3. To add a single file to the list of files to be opened, double-click it. The full path of the image is displayed in the List Window.

4. To add a continuous range of files, select the first file, press and hold the Shift key, and then select the last file in the range. Select the Add button.

5. To select a number of files in the same folder that are not in a range, press and hold the Ctrl (Command) key. When you're ready, select the Add button.

6. To open an entire folder, select the Add All button.

 **Tip**     You can also open an entire folder of images by dragging and dropping the folder on the Fireworks icon. Fireworks will open all images in the selected folder and any existing subfolders.

7. To place the selected images in a series of frames, choose the Open as Animation option. Each image is placed in a separate frame of a single graphic, in the order listed.

8. To delete a file from the list, select it and choose the Remove button.

9. When you're ready, select the Done button.

# Storing Files

Every computer graphics professional has one — a nightmare story about the system crash that erased all the intense, meticulous, time-eating effort that went into an unsaved image. Saving your files is crucial in any graphics program, but it becomes even more important in Fireworks. To maintain the "everything's editable, all the time" capability, you must save your graphics in Fireworks's native format, PNG. Although the latest browser versions support PNG to a limited degree, most Web graphics are still in either GIF or JPEG format to ensure backwards-browser compatibility. Fireworks offers a very full-featured Export module to convert your graphics into whichever Web format you choose. However, a Fireworks file exported as a GIF or JPEG loses its all-encompassing editability — text can no longer be edited as text, vector-based objects are converted to bitmaps, effects are locked, and so on.

To keep the full range of Fireworks's features active then, it's essential that each file be saved as well as exported. Fireworks uses standard commands to save: File ⊏ Save, the keyboard shortcut Ctrl+S (Command+S), and, for Windows users, a Save button on the Main toolbar. When you select any of these methods to store your file the first time, the Save As dialog box (Figure 4-4) automatically opens. Although the program does offer a Save as Type drop-down list, it has only one option: Fireworks File Format (*.png).

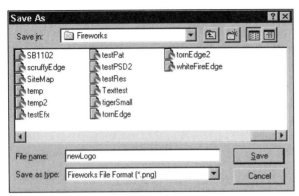

**Figure 4-4:** To maintain full editability, be sure to save every working graphic as a Fireworks file in addition to exporting it as a GIF or JPEG.

**Cross-Reference**  When you need to store your file in a format other than PNG, turn to the Export command. To get all the details on this powerful Fireworks function, see Chapter 16.

Saving a file after the initial save overwrites the existing file. If you would like to store multiple versions of the same file, Fireworks gives you two options: Save As and Save a Copy. Save As enables you to rename the file and Save a Copy enables you to store a backup file in another folder. Both function identically. Choose File ➪ Save As or File ➪ Save a Copy to open the Save As dialog box. Enter the new filename or navigate to a new folder in which to store the file (or both) and press the Save button.

## Closing a file

When you're finished with a graphic, but want to continue working in Fireworks, you can close the file in one of several ways:

✦ Choose File ➪ Close.

✦ Use one of the keyboard shortcuts, Ctrl+W (Command+W) or Ctrl+F4 (Command+F4).

✦ Select the window's Close button.

If the graphic has not been saved since the last modification, Fireworks prompts you to save the file before proceeding.

## Reverting to a saved file

Part of the joy of computer graphics is the capability to try different approaches without fear of losing your earlier work. I'm a big fan of the Revert command, which enables you to completely alter a graphic and then restore it to its last-saved condition with one command. Between Revert and Undo, you can experiment to your heart's content, safely.

The Revert command is very straightforward to use. After you've made some changes to your graphic and want to return to the original, choose File ⇨ Revert. Fireworks asks for confirmation to revert to the last saved version of the file, and, when confirmed, replaces the onscreen image with the stored version.

# Modifying Canvases

What do you mean, you want to change the size of your canvas? And its color, too? Are you saying you're not perfect and didn't predict needing these alterations? Don't worry, you're certainly not alone. In fact, very few of my images don't undergo some level of document surgery before they're done. It's the nature and the glory of computer graphics in general, and Fireworks in particular, to be very forgiving about changes.

In Fireworks, you can easily change the size of the complete image and its canvas, just the canvas dimensions, or the canvas color. It's very easy to expand the canvas in a particular direction, making it wider on the right, for example. Moreover, Fireworks 2 now adds the capability to visually enlarge the canvas, through an extended use of the Cropping tool.

## Changing image and canvas size

Many times you'll need to adjust the size of an entire completed image either up or down to make it fit properly in a Web page. Fireworks 2 lets you make your adjustments either through specifying absolute pixel values or relative percentages.

**New Feature**

With Fireworks 2, you can maintain the original proportions of your graphic or stretch it in one direction or another. The new Image Size command enables you to *resample* your image as well as resize it. Resampling refers to the process of adding or subtracting pixels when the image is resized. This interpolation works better with object-oriented (or vector-based) graphics than with bitmapped graphics, especially when you're enlarging an image. However, the Fireworks 2 algorithm is fairly sophisticated and the results are often on target.

Fireworks lets you independently alter the onscreen pixel dimensions and the print size by changing the resolution of the image. With this capability, you can print a higher or lower resolution of the image, at the original image size. It does, however, proportionately alter the pixel dimensions of the image for onscreen presentation. In Figure 4-5, for example, the original tiger image on the left is 256 × 256 pixels, with a print size of 3.5 inches square at 72 pixels per inch resolution. The smaller tiger on the right has half the resolution and, consequently, half the pixel dimensions (128 × 128), but keeps the same print size.

**Figure 4-5:** The original tiger on the left was resampled at one-half the resolution to create the tiger on the right.

To alter the image size, follow these steps:

1. Choose Modify ➪ Document ➪ Image Size. The Image Size dialog box opens, as shown in Figure 4-6.

2. To alter the dimensions of the onscreen image proportionately, enter a new value in width (the horizontal double-headed arrow) or height (the vertical double-headed arrow) text boxes.

   If the default option, Constrain Proportions, is selected, changing one value causes the other to change as well.

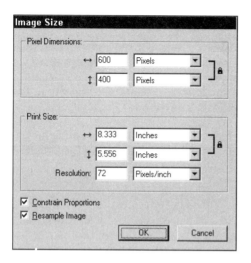

**Figure 4-6:** To proportionately enlarge or reduce your entire graphic, use the new Image Size command.

**Caution**    It's better to select the entire value in the text boxes first and then enter in your new number. If you try to backspace through each digit, you'll encounter an alert when you delete the final number. Fireworks warns you that you're entering an invalid number, as it sees you trying to reduce the dimensions below 1.

3. To alter the dimensions by percentage rather than by pixel measurement, select the arrow button next to the width or height drop-down lists and choose Percent.

4. To use the print size as a guide for adjusting the image size, enter a value in the Print Size width and height text boxes.

5. To alter the print size by percentage or centimeters rather than the default inches, select the arrow button next to the Print Size width and height drop-down lists and choose the desired alternative.

6. To change the number of pixels per inch, enter a new value in the Resolution text box.

7. To disable the proportional sizing, deselect the Constrain Proportions option.

8. To change the print size, but not the onscreen image, deselect the Resample Image option and choose new values for the Print Size width and height text boxes. When Resample Image is deselected, the Pixel Dimensions section becomes unavailable.

9. Click OK when you're done.

# Altering the canvas size only

You don't always want or need to alter the entire image. Sometimes, the existing image is the perfect size, but you need to add an effect or another graphic and there's no room on the canvas. Alternatively, very often you'll start out with a canvas larger than necessary and you'll need to trim the canvas to fit the image. Whatever the situation, Fireworks has you covered.

Fireworks 2 now offers three different methods for enlarging or reducing the canvas: numerically, using a menu command; visually, using the Crop tool; or according to the actual image by trimming the canvas.

## Specifying a new canvas size numerically

Quite often, I find myself needing to add a drop shadow and realize that I have to expand the canvas just a few pixels to the right and down for the effect to fit. With Fireworks, you can expand the canvas from the center out or in any of eight specific directions. Naturally, only the size of the canvas is modified; the image does not change at all, except in its placement on the canvas.

The key concept to understand when you're resizing the canvas numerically is the *anchor*. The placement of the anchor (handled through the Canvas Size dialog box) determines how the canvas changes to meet the newly input dimensions. By default, the anchor is placed in the center of the canvas. If, for example, the canvas dimensions were increased by 100 pixels horizontally and 100 pixels vertically with a center anchor, the canvas edge would increase by 50 on all four sides. However, if the upper-left anchor was chosen and the same increase in dimensions entered, the canvas would increase by 100 pixels on the right and bottom border; because the upper-left is the anchor, the canvas in that corner does not change.

To resize the canvas by the numbers, follow these steps:

1. Choose Modify ➪ Document ➪ Canvas Size. The Change Canvas Size dialog box opens, as shown in Figure 4-7.

2. To alter the dimensions of the canvas horizontally, enter a new value in the width (the horizontal double-headed arrow) text box.

3. To alter the dimensions of the canvas vertically, enter a new value in the height (the vertical double-headed arrow) text box.

 **Note**    Fireworks always displays the original image size in pixels in the Current Size section of the dialog box.

4. To alter the canvas size by inches or centimeters rather than the default pixels, select the arrow button next to the width and height drop-down lists and choose the desired alternative. The dimensions in pixels appear to the right of the height and width text boxes.

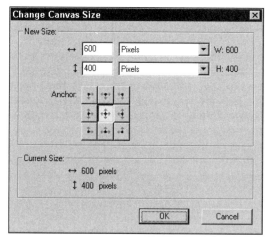

**Figure 4-7:** Enter new dimensions and select an anchor point to alter the canvas size.

**5.** Choose one of the buttons inside the Anchor grid to determine how the canvas will expand or contract.

**Tip** When one of the elements in the Anchor grid is selected, by tabbing through the dialog box, you can use the arrow keys to select a different anchor.

**6.** Click OK when you're done.

**Tip** Unlike the Image Size command, Canvas Size does not have a Constrain Proportions option. If you'd like to alter the canvas proportionately, but don't have a calculator handy to figure out the proper dimensions, open the Image Size command and enter a value with Constrain Proportions selected. You'll get the other dimension required. Jot that number down and cancel the Image Size command. Then, open the Canvas Size dialog box and enter your values.

## Using the Crop tool

Resizing the canvas numerically is great when you have to match a specific width or height for your image. Unfortunately, it can also take a lot of trial and error to get the tightest fit for an effect like a glow or a drop shadow. The Crop tool provides a much faster method. Cropping is a familiar concept to anyone who has ever worked with photographs and needs to eliminate extraneous imagery. To *crop* means to cut off the excess; however, in Fireworks 2, the Crop tool has some terrific new functionality.

**New Feature**

In addition to making the image smaller by cutting away the canvas and any unwanted imagery, the Crop tool can now expand the canvas as well. The Crop tool works by enabling you to draw a rectangle with numerous sizing handles around an image. You then use these sizing handles to adjust the dimensions and shape of the cropped area. When the cropped region looks right, a double-click in the defined area completes the operation. With Fireworks 2, the cropping border can stretch out past the edge of the canvas and, when double-clicked, the canvas is extended to the new cropped area.

To access the Crop tool, press and hold the Pointer tool in the Toolbox. Choose the Crop tool from the flyout menu. You can also use the keyboard shortcut by pressing the letter c.

For an example of the Crop tool being used to extend the canvas, take a look at Figure 4-8. The image on the right shows a very tight canvas, pressed right up against the objects. If glow effects were applied to the objects, much of the glow would be cut off. However, by using the Crop tool to draw a rectangle outside of the current canvas, you can incorporate the glow as shown in the image on the right.

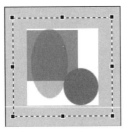 

**Figure 4-8:** The canvas of the figure on the left has no room to include effects, so the Crop tool is being used to expand the canvas, the results of which appear on the right.

In practice, using the Crop tool to extend the canvas actually requires an additional step. When you first use the Crop tool and try to draw on the outside of the current canvas, you'll find that Fireworks snaps the cropping border to the edge of the canvas. As most designers are familiar with using the Crop tool to cut excess canvas, this is a convenient starting point for most operations. To extend the cropping border, you then need to drag any of the sizing handles to a new position outside the canvas.

**Cross-Reference**

For more about using the Crop tool on images, see Chapter 5.

## Trimming the canvas

What's the fastest, most accurate way to reduce the canvas to just the essential images? Trim it, of course. If you've ever trimmed a canvas with a razor-sharp matte knife, you know it's a very dramatic, fast operation. However, Dreamweaver 2's new Trim Canvas command is even faster — it handles four edges at once and there's no need to keep a supply of bandages at the ready.

**New Feature**

The beauty of the Trim Canvas command is that it's all automatic — you don't even have to select any objects for Fireworks to trim to. Moreover, this feature even takes into account soft edges like glows or drop shadows, so you can't accidentally truncate your effect. In fact, it's a great command to use in combination with other canvas expanders, likethe Crop tool or Canvas Size. Just open up the canvas more than you think necessary, make the alterations, and then choose Modify ⇨ Document ⇨ Trim Canvas. Presto! All the canvas edges are hugging the graphics as tightly as possible.

Note: As the name indicates, Trim Canvas can only make your overall image size smaller; it can't expand it even if part of the image is moved off the canvas.

## Picking a new canvas color

Although you set the canvas color when you create the document, you're by no means stuck with it. You can adjust the color at any point by choosing Modify ⇨ Document ⇨ Canvas Color. Invoking this command opens the Canvas Color dialog box (Figure 4-9), which replicates the Canvas Color section of the New Document dialog box. Again, you have three choices: White, Transparent, and Custom Color. Of course, selecting the arrow button next to Custom Color opens the pop-up color picker with the palette of 216 Web-safe choices. For a wider color selection, choose the palette icon from the pop-up color picker to display the system color pickers.

**Tip**

All Photoshop images, when loaded into Fireworks, are placed against a transparent canvas. Whereas the Background layer may appear to be a specific flat color, if you move it, you'll see the transparent canvas underneath. After the image is loaded in Fireworks, choose Modify ⇨ Document ⇨ Canvas Color to change a Photoshop's actual canvas

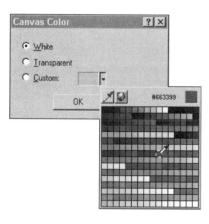

**Figure 4-9:** The pop-up color picker is useful for quickly picking a Web-safe color for the canvas.

# Summary

Setting up your document is the basis for all image creation in Fireworks. Whether you're starting with the fresh slate of a new document or opening an existing file, Fireworks gives you all the tools you need to build a solid foundation and modify it when necessary. When working with your images from an overall document perspective, keep these points in mind:

✦ The more you can visualize your graphics and thus design the canvas, the less time you'll spend making modifications.

✦ When you're creating a new document, Fireworks enables you to set the height, width, resolution, and color of the canvas.

✦ Fireworks can open more than a dozen different file formats, including Photoshop layers.

✦ With Fireworks 2, you can load a series of files simultaneously with the new Open Multiple command.

✦ To get the most out of Fireworks, always save at least one version of your graphic in the native PNG format.

✦ You can alter the canvas size using any of three different methods: Canvas Size, the Crop tool, or Trim Canvas.

✦ You can modify the canvas color at any time.

In the next chapter, you begin exploring the heart of Fireworks's graphics: objects.

✦     ✦     ✦

# Mastering
# the Tools

# Creating and Transforming Objects

**O**bjects are the foundation of Fireworks. Don't get me wrong: all the other elements — images, effects, Web objects — are vital, but objects are what gives Fireworks its flexibility, precise control, and editability.

As you might suspect, a great number of Fireworks tools and features focus on objects. This chapter covers the basic object operations — creation of the simple, geometric shapes and freeform lines and drawings — that draw special attention to one of the most difficult to master, but most rewarding concepts, Bézier curves.

## Understanding Objects in Fireworks

An object, in Fireworks lingo, is a path- or vector-based graphic. Unlike bitmapped graphics that use pixels to make mosaic-like images, objects use lines, or more accurately, the description of a line. Instead of plotting a series of pixels on the screen, a vector-based graphic basically says, "start a line at position X, Y and draw it to position A, B." Or "draw a circle with a midpoint at C, D and make it 1.5 inches in diameter." Of course, you don't see all these instructions on the screen — it's all under the hood of the graphics engine — but it's what enables drawing programs, such as FreeHand and Adobe Illustrator, to maintain a smooth line regardless of how the image is scaled.

Whereas Fireworks's objects maintain the underlying path structure, their surfaces are composed of pixels. Although this may seem to be a contradiction, it's really at the heart of Fireworks's brilliance as a graphics tool. Whenever you modify an object — slanting a rectangle, for example — the modification is applied first to the path structure and then the pixel surface is reapplied. It is as if an image of a ballerina in a magazine suddenly became alive, leaped across the stage, and then became an image again.

# Examining Paths

Objects begin as *paths*. Paths are lines with at least two points. Whether you draw a squiggly line with the Pencil tool or a multipointed star with the Polygon tool, the outline of your drawing is what is referred to as the path. By themselves, paths are invisible. Don't believe me? Try this:

1. Start up Fireworks and open a new document by choosing File ⇨ New.

2. Now select the Rectangle tool from the Toolbox.

3. Draw out a shape by clicking on the canvas and dragging the mouse out to form a rectangle.

4. Release the mouse when you have a visible shape. You'll see the path in the default highlight color, as shown in Figure 5-1.

5. Now, choose the Pointer tool from the Toolbox and click anywhere on the document, outside of the just-drawn rectangle. The highlight — and the rectangle's path — disappears.

6. If you pass your pointer over the existing rectangle, it will highlight temporarily so that you can select it again.

## Applying a stroke

To make a path visible, you have to apply a *stroke* to see the outline. In Fireworks 2, you can quickly apply a stroke to a selected object by choosing a color from the Stroke color well, located on the Toolbox or on the Color Mixer. This action applies a Pencil type stroke five pixels wide with a soft or *anti-aliased* edge. Strokes can vary in color, width, softness, texture, and type of brush to name a few characteristics; several examples of different strokes are shown in Figure 5-2. You'll notice in the figure how regardless of their different attributes, strokes always follow the path of an object.

Pointer tool        Rectangle tool    Stroke Color well

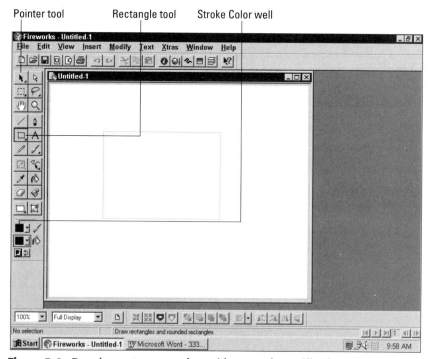

**Figure 5-1:** Drawing out a rectangle—with no stroke or fill selected—gives you just the path.

**Figure 5-2:** You can see the same selected path in each of these different strokes.

Cross-Reference

Part of Fireworks's power is derived from the wide range of strokes possible. To learn more about strokes, see Chapter 8.

## Open and closed paths

There are two types of paths: *open* and *closed*. The difference between the two is simple—a closed path connects its two endpoints (the start and finish of the line) and an open path doesn't. Closed paths define different shapes, whether standard, such as an ellipse, square, or polygon, or custom, such as a freeform drawing. Just as a stroke gives the outline of a path substance, a *fill* makes the interior of a path visible. Like strokes, fills come in different categories, colors, and textures. In addition, a *pattern*, created from a PNG file, can be used as a fill. You can even change the softness of a fill's edge. As Figure 5-3 shows, regardless of what the interior fill is, it always follows the established path.

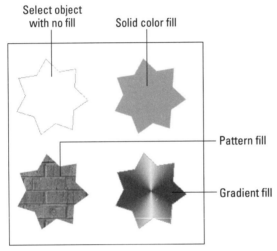

Select object
with no fill     Solid color fill

Pattern fill

Gradient fill

**Figure 5-3:** A path can be filled with a solid color,
a gradient, or a pattern.

**Note**    Whereas fills are by far most often applied to closed path objects, it's perfectly legal to apply a path to an open path object—although the results are not as predictable. But then, that's one of the beauties of computer graphics—try it and if you don't like it, undo it.

## Center point

One common feature that all objects in Fireworks share is a *center point*. A center point is an invisible point in the middle of any path; if the path is open, the center point is on the line. If the path is closed, it's inside the object. Center points are useful when you need to rotate an object. In Fireworks, you can adjust the center point so it's not in the absolute center of the object.

**Cross-Reference**    You'll see how to work with rotation in Chapter 9.

## Direction

The final point to keep in mind about objects is that their paths all have *direction*. Though it's more obvious with an object like a line that you start drawing at one point and finish at another, it's true even with rectangles and ellipses. Generally, Fireworks draws objects in a clockwise direction, starting at the upper left corner of rectangles or squares and the left center of an ellipse or circle, as shown in Figure 5-4. Path direction becomes important when you begin attaching text to a path — wrapping a slogan around a circle, for example. Fireworks includes several tools for adjusting the path's direction.

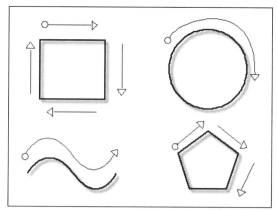

**Figure 5-4:** A path's direction determines how text is attached.

# Starting from Shapes

It's the rare graphic that's composed of only one object, no matter how elaborate. Most images are amalgams of many, many objects of different types, sizes, colors, and attributes. However, you must master the capabilities of each basic object to get the greatest effect in the shortest amount of time.

Fireworks provides tools for creating a series of basic geometric shapes — rectangles, ellipses, and polygons — as well as those for drawing structured and freeform lines. All of these tools will be familiar to anyone who has worked with a vector drawing program in the last few years. In fact, most of the shortcuts are industry-standard. This chapter, though, is written from a complete novice's point of view. Even if you've never used a computer to draw before, you'll have a full understanding of the basic tools in Fireworks after working your way through this chapter.

The quickest way to create a Web page image, particularly the often-required navigational buttons, is to use one of Fireworks's shape-building tools. Although at first glance there only seems to be three such tools — the Rectangle, Ellipse, and Polygon — these tool pack enough options to produce a wide range of graphics. Moreover, Fireworks offers a very straightforward method of specifying the exact pixel dimensions and placement of any geometric shape.

## Rectangles and squares

My dictionary defines a rectangle as "any four-sided figure with four right angles." A Web designer generally sees a rectangle as a basic building block for a button or a frame. The Rectangle tool from the Toolbox is very straightforward to use and offers a number of very useful options.

### Creating rectangles

Like almost every other computer drawing tool on the planet, Fireworks creates rectangles using the familiar click-and-drag method. To draw a rectangle in Fireworks, follow these steps:

1. Select the Rectangle tool from the Toolbox or use the keyboard shortcut, r.

2. Click once to select your originating corner and drag to the opposite corner to form the rectangle, as shown in Figure 5-5. As you drag your pointer, Fireworks draws a preview outline of the form.

3. Release the mouse button when the rectangle is the desired size and shape. If any stroke or fill has been set, these attributes are drawn when you release the mouse button.

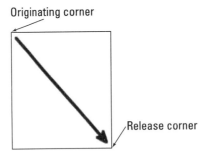

Originating corner

Release corner

**Figure 5-5:** Once you've selected your originating corner with the Rectangle tool, you can drag out a box shape in any direction, as indicated by the arrow.

### Using keyboard modifiers

You can use two keyboard modifiers with the Rectangle tool, Shift and Alt, for often-required effects.

✦ **To create a square:** You can easily make your rectangle into a square by pressing Shift while you drag out your shape. Unlike some other graphics programs, you don't have to press Shift before you begin drawing; pressing Shift at any time while you're drawing causes Fireworks to increase the shorter sides to match the longer sides of the rectangle to form a square.

✦ **To draw from the center:** To draw your rectangle from the center instead of from the corner, press Alt when dragging out the shape. When Alt is selected, Fireworks uses the distance from your originating point to the current pointer position as the radius rather than the diameter of the rectangle. As with Shift, you can press Alt at any time when drawing to change to a center origin.

Moreover, you can also use these two keys together to draw a square from the center, as shown in Figure 5-6.

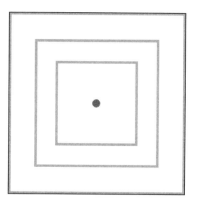

**Figure 5-6:** These three concentric squares were drawn by pressing Alt and Shift simultaneously while using the Rectangle tool; the center dot was used as the starting point for all squares.

Tip    You can use the Info panel to check the pixel placement of your rectangle as you are drawing. One section displays the Width and Height (marked with a W and H) dynamically, while another displays the upper-left point of the rectangle, even if it is being drawn from the center.

## Creating rounded corners

The standard rectangle and square, by definition, is composed of four right angles. However, Fireworks can create rectangles with rounded corners — and you can even set the degree of "roundness." The corner setting is visible on the Options panel when the Rectangle tool is selected. The quickest way to do both is to double-click the Rectangle tool; the Options panel will automatically open. You can also display the Options panel by choosing Window ➪ Tool Options or using the keyboard shortcut, Ctrl+Alt+O (Command+Option+O).

Once the Options panel is available, choose how rounded you want the corners of your rectangle to appear by entering a value in the Corner text box or by using the Corner slider. The Corner scale is percentage-based: 0 represents a standard rectangle and 100 creates a fully rounded rectangle — also known as a circle. As Figure 5-7 shows, the higher the Corner value, the more rounded the rectangle's corners become.

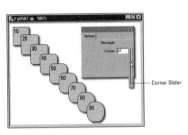

**Figure 5-7:** Use the Corner slider from the Rectangle Options panel to determine the degree of roundness for your rectangle's or square's corners.

Corner Slider

As mentioned previously, Fireworks calculates the roundness of the rectangle by using the specified Corner value as a percentage. Exactly how Fireworks applies the percentage is most easily explained with an example. Let's say you draw a rectangle 100 pixels wide by 50 pixels tall and choose a Corner value of 50 percent. As shown in Figure 5-8, Fireworks plots the points of the corner 50 pixels along the top edge (50 percent of 100 pixels = 50 pixels) and 25 pixels along the side edge (50 percent of 50 pixels = 25 pixels). The resulting arc makes the corner. If you created an ellipse with a horizontal diameter of 50 pixels and a vertical one of 25, it would fit right into a newly rounded corner.

Arc points for corner

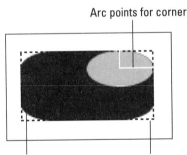

Rounded corner rectangle    Same size standard rectangle

**Figure 5-8:** Fireworks draws the rounded corner of a rectangle according to a percentage formula.

**Caution**    Be sure to set the desired corner percentage on the Options panel before you draw your rectangle. You can't convert a right-angle rectangle to a rounded-corner rectangle (or vice-versa) after it's been created.

## Ellipses and circles

In Fireworks, ellipses and circles are created in exactly the same manner as rectangles and squares. Clicking the mouse once sets the origin point and then the shape is drawn out as the pointer is dragged. Even the keyboard modifiers (Alt (Option) and Shift) function similarly. In fact, only two differences exist between the Rectangle and the Ellipse tool. First, it's pretty obvious that there's no need for an ellipse function equivalent to the Round Corners option for rectangles; ellipses are already rounded. Second — less apparent, but notable nonetheless — is the fact that the origin point of an ellipse or a circle never appears on the path of a drawn oval. This is particularly important for novice designers who are trying to place an ellipse correctly.

### Using an imaginary bounding box

When Fireworks draws an ellipse, an imaginary bounding box is used, as shown in Figure 5-9. The origin point of the bounding box acts as one corner, while the end point becomes the opposite corner. As with rectangles, if Alt (Option) is pressed, the center point is used as the origin. In either case, neither the origin nor the end point are located on the path of the ellipse.

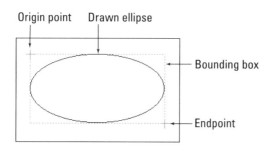

**Figure 5-9:** When you drag out a circle or oval using the Ellipse tool, Fireworks draws the shape using an imaginary bounding box, indicated by the dashed rectangle.

Tip

It's particularly helpful to keep the concept of the imaginary bounding box in mind when you are trying to align ellipses of different sizes. The Align commands work using an ellipse's bounding box rather than the drawn path of the shape.

### Drawing an ellipse or circle

To draw an ellipse or a circle, follow these steps:

1. Select the Ellipse tool from the Toolbox by clicking and holding the Rectangle tool until the flyout appears and then choosing the Ellipse button.

   You can also press r twice. The first time you choose the letter r, the Rectangle tool is selected; pressing it again selects the Ellipse tool.

2. Click once to select the origin point and drag to the opposite corner to create the ellipse. As you drag your pointer, Fireworks draws a preview outline of the form.

3. Release the mouse button when the ellipse is the desired size and shape. If any stroke or fill has been set, these attributes are drawn when you release the mouse button.

4. To draw a circle, press the Shift key while you are drawing the ellipse.

5. To draw an ellipse or circle that uses the center point of the shape as the origin, press the Alt (Option) key while you are drawing.

# Polygons and stars

In Fireworks, the Polygon tool creates many-sided objects where all the sides — and all the angles connecting the sides — are the same. The technical term for this type of geometric shape is an *equilateral polygon*. Fireworks permits the graphic designer to specify the number of sides, from 3 to 25. You can also use the Polygon tool to create a special type of polygon, a star. Star shapes can be drawn with anywhere from 3 to 25 points (and thus, 6 to 50 sides). Moreover, Fireworks gives you the option of either specifying the angles for the star points or having the program assign them automatically.

## A drag-and-draw affair

As with rectangles and ellipses, making polygons is a drag-and-draw affair. Click once to set the origin point and then drag out the shape. However, that's where the similarities end. With polygons, there's only one possible origin point, the center — there is no keyboard modifier to switch to an outside edge. You'll also immediately notice as you draw out your first polygon that you can quickly set both the size and the rotation. Dragging the pointer straight out from the origin increases the dimensions of the polygon; moving the pointer side to side rotates it around its midpoint.

## Drawing a polygon

To draw a polygon, follow these steps:

1. Select the Polygon tool from the Toolbox by clicking and holding the Rectangle tool until the flyout appears and then choosing the Polygon button.

   Alternatively, press the keyboard shortcut, g.

2. To set the number of sides for a polygon:

   • First, choose Window ➪ Tool Options or double-click the Polygon tool to open the Options panel shown in Figure 5-10.

   • In the Options panel, make sure the shape type is set to Polygon (instead of Star).

   • Next, enter a value in the Sides text box or use the Sides slider.

3. Click once where you want the center of the polygon to appear and drag out the polygon shape.

   Fireworks displays a preview of the polygon as you draw.

4. Rotate the polygon to the desired position by moving your pointer from side to side.

5. Release the mouse button when you're done. Fireworks draws the polygon with the current stroke and fill settings.

Fireworks interprets the distance from the origin point to the release point as the radius to each of the points on the polygon. As you can see in Figure 5-10, just changing the number of sides results in a wide range of basic shapes.

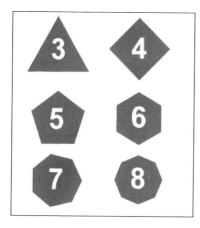

**Figure 5-10:** Polygons in Fireworks can have up to 25 sides — each creating a unique geometric shape.

Pressing the Shift key while drawing a polygon constrains a side's angle to a multiple of 45 degrees. Because, however, each shape as it is initially drawn is equilateral — with identical sides and angles — you'll only notice a couple of variations for each type of polygon. When drawing a hexagon and constraining the angle with the Shift key, you'll only notice three differently angled shapes, although you can actually draw eight (there are eight increments of 45 degrees in a full 360-degree circle).

Tip

For most polygons, you can draw it so that the bottom of the shape is parallel to the bottom of your canvas by either dragging straight up or straight to one side while holding down the Shift key.

### Automatic angles

Although you can specify up to 25 sides for a polygon, polygons with more than 10 sides look very much like a circle. Not so with Fireworks stars, which, with the proper angle setting, can create very distinctive graphics with any number of sides. Fireworks offers both automatic and customizable angle options. When Automatic Angles is selected (the default), Fireworks draws stars so that the opposite arms are automatically aligned. With a five-pointed star, such as the ones shown in Figure 5-11, the tops of the left and right arms are aligned.

As is readily apparent in Figure 5-11, the automatic angles on stars with higher number of sides tend to flatten out the sharpness of the points. These types of angles are known as *obtuse* angles. An obtuse angle is one over 90 degrees. The opposite of an obtuse angle is an *acute* angle. Acute angles create much sharper points on stars, as shown in Figure 5-12. To create an acute star in Fireworks, you need to enter a custom value in the Angle text box.

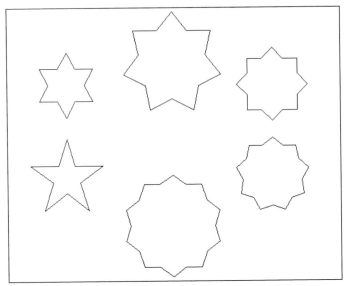

**Figure 5-11:** With the Automatic Angle option enabled, the stars' opposing arms are aligned.

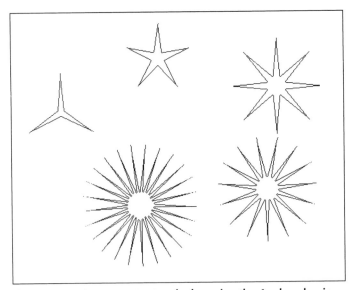

**Figure 5-12:** Create acute stars by lowering the Angle value in the Options panel and drawing with Star selected for the Polygon tool type.

### Creating a star

To create a star in Fireworks, follow these steps:

1. As with drawing a regular polygon, select the Polygon tool from the Toolbox by clicking and holding the Rectangle tool until the flyout appears and then choosing the Polygon button.

   Alternatively, press the keyboard shortcut, g.

2. Choose Window ⇨ Tool Options or double-click the Polygon tool to open the Options panel.

3. In the Options panel, change the shape type by selecting the option arrow and choosing Star.

4. To change the number of points, enter a value in the Sides text box or use the Sides slider.

5. To change the angle of the star arms, enter a value in the Angle text box or use the Angle slider.

**Tip** Use lower numbers for sharper points and higher numbers for blunter ones.

6. If you want to use the Fireworks predetermined angle for your star, choose the Automatic check box.

7. Click on the canvas to set the origin point for the center of the star and drag out to the desired size and rotation.

8. Release the mouse when you're done. As with any other shape, Fireworks applies the current stroke, fill, or effect setting, if any.

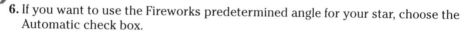

## Precisely Adjusting a Shape's Dimensions and Position

Like any graphic design, Web graphics are a blend of visual flair and precise placement. To many artists, an image isn't right until it's aligned just so. Whereas much of Fireworks's interface enables very intuitive drawing with a mouse or graphics pad, you can also position and size objects numerically through the Info panel.

Typically, I use the Info panel to get a general sense of the dimensions of an object or its X, Y coordinates. However, I occasionally need to render an exact rectangle, one that's exactly 205 pixels wide by 166 high, say, and starts at 20 pixels in from the left and 35 pixels down. With Fireworks, you can rough out your shape and placement and then numerically resize and reposition the object. Values can be entered into each of the four text boxes on the Info panel representing the dimensions and the position of the bounding box surrounding the object. If the object is a circle or a triangle, for example, the height and width displayed would be that of the invisible rectangle encompassing them.

To specify a new dimension or placement of an object, follow these steps:

1. Select the object you wish to alter.

*Continued*

*(continued)*

2. Double-click the value in the text box that you want to change. The four possibilities are

   - W (width)

   - H (height)

   - X (horizontal origin)

   - Y (vertical origin)

3. Enter a new value.

4. Confirm your entry by pressing Enter (Return) — not Tab. Fireworks changes the selected object.

5. To change another value, repeat steps 2–4.

Note that there are numerous types of alignment and transformation tools as well as those available through the Info panel.

# Drawing Lines and Freeform Paths

The path tools in Fireworks primarily vary according to how structured they are. At one end of the spectrum is the Line tool, which only draws single straight lines; at the other end you'll find the Pencil and Brush tools, both of which are completely freeform. In the middle (leaning more toward the Line tool) is the Pen tool, which draws mathematically accurate curves.

Like a geometric shape, a path is invisible unless a particular stroke is applied to it. All paths accept strokes, but only closed paths also accept fills. For a path to be closed, the two endpoints that define the line must be joined. Fireworks displays a special cursor when two endpoints are about to be joined.

## Straight lines

The Line tool is perhaps the simplest command in the entire Fireworks Toolbox. Click once to set the beginning of the line, drag in any direction, and release to set the end of the line. Two endpoints and a straight line in between; that's it and there's not a whole lot more to the tool. Straight lines are by definition open paths and thus can only display the stroke and not the fill settings; effects, however, can also be applied to Line-created paths, as shown in Figure 5-13.

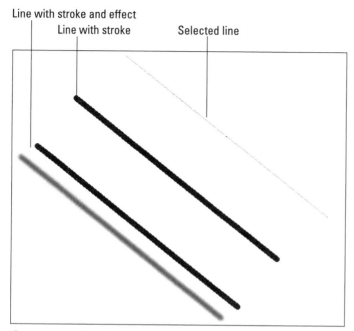

**Figure 5-13:** The Line tool draws straight-as-a-ruler lines that can take on a stroke setting and even an effect.

To use the Line tool, follow these steps:

1. Select the Line tool from the Toolbox or use the keyboard shortcut, n.

2. Position the pointer where you'd like the line to begin and click and hold the mouse button.

   Optionally, you can draw straight lines at a 45-degree angle if you press the Shift key while drawing the line.

3. When the line is at the desired size and angle, release the mouse button.

## Freeform Pencil and Brush

The Pencil and Brush are also drag-and-draw tools, but without any of the restraints imposed on all the other tools. Anything you can draw with a mouse or graphics tablet, you can draw with the Pencil or Brush. As you move your pointer on the screen, Fireworks tracks the movements and plots points to replicate your drawing. Remember, these are vector-based objects, not pixel, and if you draw a perfectly straight line, Fireworks only needs two points to depict the line. All of the points that make up the line can be edited — moved, deleted, or increased — and the line changes accordingly.

**Cross-Reference**

Fireworks not only tracks your pointer's movement across the screen, it also follows the speed with which you draw your lines. With certain strokes, such as Watercolor and Charcoal, the velocity is translated visually when the stroke is rendered. For more details on varying your strokes, see Chapter 8.

Freehand drawing with the mouse is particularly difficult and many artists use the tool sparingly. But for some images that require an unrestrained look — like the bomb in Figure 5-14 — the Pencil and Brush are ideal. Because of the limitations of the mouse as a drawing device, many artists use a graphic tablet and stylus, which emulate a pencil (or pen) and pad of paper.

**Figure 5-14:** Short curving strokes, such as those used in this graphic, are best created with the Pencil or Brush tools.

## Applying strokes automatically

The major difference between these two tools and all the other geometric shape tools (including Line) is that both Pencil and Brush automatically apply a particular stroke, even if none is selected. This feature enables you to see all paths completed with these tools instantly — instead of having to wait until a stroke is selected and applied.

The stroke setting also holds the sole difference between the Pencil and the Brush. Any path drawn with the Pencil tool is rendered with a Pencil category, single-pixel width stroke with a hard edge, as seen in the Stroke panel shown in Figure 5-15 — even if a different stroke has been predetermined.

**Note**

The only exception to the Pencil's adherence to these basic parameters is color. If you alter the stroke color, the Pencil tool draws with the new color.

The Brush tool also uses the same single-pixel Pencil type stroke, but only as a default, when otherwise no stroke is established. Once you select a different setting from the Stroke panel, that setting is used by the Brush until it is changed.

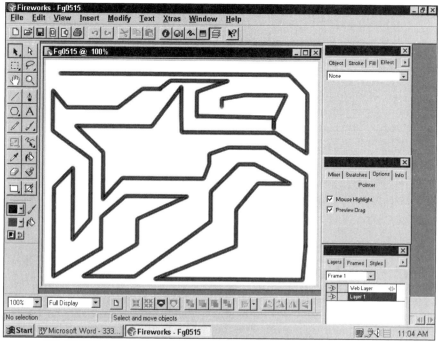

**Figure 5-15:** The Pencil enables you to draw freeform shapes that use the same settings from the Stroke panel.

As noted previously, both the Pencil and the Brush are capable of creating either open or closed paths. Remember, a closed path is one in which the beginning and final endpoints meet. With many graphic tools, this simple procedure becomes quite difficult, because it's often hard to position one pixel directly on top of another. Fireworks makes closing a path very straightforward. When you draw a path over the initial endpoint, a small black square appears on the lower right of the Pencil cursor, as shown in Figure 5-15. Releasing the mouse button when this cursor is displayed forces Fireworks to close the path.

## Using the Pencil or Brush

To use the Pencil or Brush, follow these steps:

1. To draw with the Pencil, select the Pencil tool from the Toolbox or press the keyboard shortcut, y.

2. To draw with the Brush, select the Brush tool from the Toolbox or press the keyboard shortcut, b.

3. Click and drag the pointer on the canvas. Fireworks renders the drawn path for a Pencil with a one-pixel width stroke and the Brush with the current settings of the Stroke panel.

4. To draw a perpendicular line, press the Shift key while you're dragging the pointer. If your movement is primarily left to right, a horizontal line is drawn; if it is up and down, a vertical line is drawn.

Here's a rather peculiar feature of the Brush tool. If you use the Shift key to constrain your Brush path to a perpendicular line and then release the mouse button — but not the Shift key — a small plus sign appears next to the Brush cursor. Draw another Brush stroke (still holding down the Shift key), and Fireworks connects the final point of your previous stroke with the beginning point of your new stroke. I used this technique to create the rather elaborate maze depicted in Figure 5-15.

**Cross-Reference**

The Pencil tool has one other use. If you are in Image Edit mode, modifying a pixel-based graphic, the Pencil changes any pixels it touches to the current Stroke color. You can find out more about editing pixel-based images in Chapter 6.

# Constructing Bézier Curves

Remember those plastic stencils you used in school to trace different size circles, stars, and other shapes? One of those "other shapes" was probably an asymmetrical, smoothly curving line that was referred to as a French curve. The Frenchman who invented this type of curve was a mathematician named Pierre Bézier. His theoretical work, collectively known as *Bézier curves*, forms the foundation for much of vector computer graphics, both in print through PostScript and on the screen through programs such as FreeHand, Illustrator, and, of course, Fireworks. The learning curve — pun definitely intended — for Bézier curves is a steep one, but it's one that every graphic designer using vectors must master. Bézier curves are amazingly flexible, often graceful to behold, and worth every bit of effort it takes to fully understand them. So let's get started.

Pierre Bézier's breakthrough was the realization that every line — whether it was straight or curved — could be mathematically described in the same way. Imagine a rainbow. The shape appears to start in one place, arch to the sky, and then land some distance away. The beginning and ending points of the rainbow are easily described; if we were plotting them on a piece of graph paper, we could set down their location as X and Y coordinates. But what about the arc itself? Consider an imaginary element in the sky that the rainbow is attracted to, almost magnetically, which causes the center to arch up, anchored by the beginning and ending points. Bézier postulated that every anchor point on a curve had two such magnetic elements, called *control points* — one that affects the curve going into the anchor point and one that affects it coming out of the anchor point, as shown in Figure 5-16. In the Bézier vernacular, an anchor point with curves on either side is called, naturally enough, a *curve point*. An anchor point with a curve on just one side is known as a *corner point*.

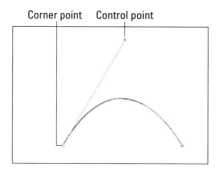

Corner point    Control point

**Figure 5-16:** Bézier curves use control points to alter the shape of a curve.

# Drawing lines with the Pen

Fireworks's primary tool for creating Bézier curves is the Pen, although all objects use Bézier curves. But how could a Bézier curve describe a straight line? When the control points are in the same location as the corner or curve points, the line is not pulled one way or the other; it remains straight. In fact, the Pen is terrific for creating connected straight lines. Unlike the Line tool, which draws a single straight line by clicking and dragging, the Pen draws a series of straight lines by plotting each point and letting Fireworks draw the connecting lines.

To draw a straight line with the Pen, follow these steps:

1. Select the Pen on the Toolbox or use its keyboard shortcut, p. The cursor changes to a cross with a small open box on the lower-right side.

2. Click once where you want the line to start.

3. Move your pointer to where you want the line to end. Fireworks draws a path from your starting point to the current cursor position, as shown in Figure 5-17.

4. Click once to set the next point. Fireworks draws a straight line path from the first point to the second and renders the stroke settings, if any.

5. Repeat Steps 3 and 4 to continue adding straight lines.

6. Double-click to end the series of straight lines.

**Figure 5-17:** Create a Z with the Pen tool much like Zorro carves one with his sword, moving from point to point.

As with the Brush and Pencil tools, you can close an open path created by the Pen by moving the pointer over the beginning point. The cursor adds a solid black square on the lower right to indicate a possible closed path. Click once when you see the black square to complete the shape.

## Creating smooth curves with the Pen

Laying out a series of straight lines is a fine feature, but the Pen tool really shines when it comes to drawing curves. The key difference between Pen-drawn lines and curves is that, with curves, you drag the pointer after you've set the anchor's position while, with lines, there is no dragging whatsoever, you are just plotting corner points.

One of the simplest types of Bézier curves to draw is an S-shaped curve. The reason for its simplicity is when you drag out the curve approaching an curve point, you're simultaneously dragging out the curve *leaving* the same curve point. Follow these steps for creating an S-curve, illustrated in Figure 5-18, and you'll see what I mean:

1. With the Pen tool, click once where you want the S-curve's top to start.

2. Move the pointer straight down so that you're at the middle of the S-curve, directly beneath your first point.

3. Click to set the curve point and then drag the pointer away from the point to the lower-right at about a 45-degree angle. As you drag in one direction, the upper part of the S-curve begins to form in the opposite direction.

4. Release the mouse button when the top of the S-curve looks the way you want it. Fireworks now displays the curve point just set and its two control points while previewing the next curve as you move your pointer.

5. Move the pointer to where you want the S-curve to end (roughly inline with the first two curve points) and double-click to complete the S-curve.

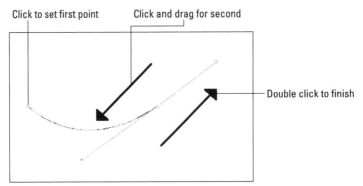

**Figure 5-18:** When you drag out one Bézier curve, you begin to create this curve.

## Mixing lines and curves

You can, of course, combine the straight and curved line techniques with the Pen by alternating just clicking with both clicking and dragging. However, because dragging a control point affects curves on either side of the curve point, it is often difficult to place a straight line directly next to a curve. Fireworks uses the Alt (Option) key to constrain the control point that affects the previous curve, while permitting you to manipulate the current curve. As an example of this option, follow these steps to create an arch, as shown in Figure 5-19:

1. Use the straight-line capability of the Pen to draw the outer edge of the arch by clicking once for each of the outside points, starting at the inside left corner and moving in a clockwise direction. After you've drawn all the straight lines, you'll have the outer shell of the arch, minus the inner arc, completed.

2. Move your pointer back over the beginning point. The closed path cursor is displayed.

3. Click and hold the mouse button as if you are going to drag it. Press the Alt (Option) key while continuing to hold down the mouse button.

4. Drag the control point in the direction of the arch. If Alt (Option) was not pressed, the connecting line (on the left side of the arch) would be affected by the control point drag.

5. Release the mouse button when the arch is in the desired shape.

You can also use this constraining property to draw uneven curves, where you drag a little bit before pressing Alt (Option) and effectively lock the previous curve.

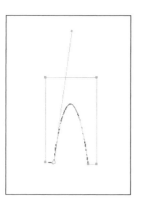

**Figure 5-19:** Use the Pen — in combination with the constraining Alt (Option) key — to draw straight and curved lines.

**Caution**  Be sure the mouse button is down before you press Alt (Option) to constrain the control points. Pressing Alt (Option) by itself temporarily activates the Eyedropper tool for sampling color. Should you accidentally sample a color, choose Edit ➪ Undo — or use the keyboard shortcut Ctrl+Z (Command+Z) — and then proceed as intended.

## Adjusting curves

The alternative name for the two control points in Bézier curves is *control handles*. As the name implies, control handles can be grabbed and manipulated. By changing the position of the control handle, you can adjust the shape of the curve. Here are a few guidelines for moving control handles:

✦ The closer the control handle is to its associated curve point, the flatter the curve.

✦ Alternatively, the further away the control handle is from its curve point, the steeper the curve.

✦ If a control handle overlaps its curve point, the curve becomes a straight line and the curve point becomes a corner point.

✦ You can convert straight lines into curves by pulling the control handle away from the corner point.

✦ After you've drawn a curve point, you can retract one of the control handles so that the next segment can either be a curve or a straight line.

All of the manipulations involving control handles can be accomplished after the fact using the Subselection tool; you'll find a discussion of how to use this point adjustment device in Chapter 9. However, you can perform a few of these operations while drawing with the Pen. The two key operations involve adding and removing a control handle.

### Adding a control handle to a corner point

To add a control handle to a corner point, follow these steps:

1. Use the Pen to draw a path with a curve point. Two control handles are visible.

2. Move the pointer over the last curve point set. A small arrow appears on the Pen cursor, as shown in Figure 5-20.

3. Click once. The control handle that affects the curve to be drawn is retracted into the curve point.

4. To draw a straight line from the curve point, move your pointer away and click once.

5. To draw a curve, move your pointer away and click and drag out the control handles.

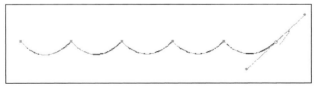

**Figure 5-20:** By retracting one control handle, you can continue the curve in the same direction.

This technique is very handy for drawing a series of scallop or wave shapes where the curves all go in the same direction.

### Extending a control handle from a corner point

The opposite of retracting a control handle is extending one. To extend a control handle from a corner point, you need to enlist the aid of a couple of keyboard modifiers: Ctrl+Alt (Command+Option) to be specific. When you extend a control handle while drawing, you are, in effect, changing your mind. Instead of proceeding with the straight line that you first indicated you want with the corner point, you can now draw a curve.

To extend a control handle from a corner point while drawing, follow these steps:

1. Draw a straight line segment with the Pen.

2. Move the pointer over the last point set. A small arrow appears on the Pen cursor.

3. Press Ctrl+Alt (Command+Option) and then click and drag a control handle out from the point. When you press the keyboard modifiers, the pointer changes to a white arrowhead.

4. Release the mouse button when you've positioned the control handle where desired.

5. Move the pointer to the position for the curve to end.

6. Continue drawing or double-click the final point to complete the shape.

In this technique, it's important that you press the keyboard modifiers before you drag the control handle. If you begin dragging before pressing the special keys, you'll move the anchor point instead of extending a control handle. This is actually a feature and enables you to move a previously set point by starting the drag and then pressing the Ctrl (Command) key — the Alt key has no effect on this sequence.

## Using the keyboard modifiers

Bézier curves in Fireworks use a fair number of keyboard modifiers to achieve various effects. While I've explained the use of these special keys throughout this section in context, I thought it would be useful to put them all in one place (Table 5-1) for easy reference.

**Cross-Reference**  There's a lot more to manipulating Bézier curves and other Fireworks objects, as you'll find in Chapter 9.

| | Table 5-1 | |
| --- | --- | --- |
| | **Bézier Curves Keyboard Modifiers** | |
| **Windows Keys** | **Macintosh Keys** | **How Used** |
| Shift | Shift | Constrains the straight line or control handle to a 45-degree angle |
| Ctrl | Command | Moves a set curve or corner point or a control handle to a new position |
| Ctrl and Double-click | Command and Double-click | Completes an open path without adding another point |
| Ctrl+Alt | Command+Option | Extends a control handle from a corner point |

# Summary

Recently, I had to indoctrinate a corporate design team in Fireworks in a two-day training session. When it came to objects, I described them as being the "skeleton" of Fireworks graphics. After the graphic is completed — with the body of fills and the clothing of strokes — you won't be able to see the underlying structure of the path object, but it is the basis of the image. As you begin to build your graphics with objects, keep these points in mind:

✦ Paths are the most basic element of Fireworks's vector-based objects. A path must be stroked and/or filled before it can be seen.

✦ The three basic geometric shape tools — Rectangle, Ellipse, and Polygon — can also create squares, rounded rectangles, circles, and stars.

✦ The Line tool creates one straight line at a time.

✦ Two freeform tools, Pencil and Brush, enable you to draw on the Fireworks canvas without restriction. The Pencil tool always defaults to a 1-pixel-wide stroke.

✦ The Pen draws Bézier curves, which use a series of corner and curve points in conjunction with control handles to make smooth curves and connected straight lines.

In the next chapter, you'll begin to learn about the other side of Fireworks graphics: bitmapped images.

✦     ✦     ✦

# Working with Images

**P**ath-based objects may form the backbone of Fireworks, but the Web is still a pixel-based medium. Even if you only used original artwork, straight from Fireworks, you'd still be faced one day with modifying the exported GIFs or JPEGs. Bitmapped images are altered in a far different manner than vector objects, and Fireworks has a full complement of tools and commands equal to the task.

Almost all work with images takes place in Fireworks's Image Edit mode, which, in Version 2, is much more accessible. Now, instead of having to enter Image Edit mode before being able to use a bitmap tool such as the Magic Wand, once you start to use an image-editing tool, you automatically enter the mode. It may seem like a small difference, but it's key. Image editing in Fireworks 2 is far more fluid and intuitive than it ever was in the previous version.

This chapter begins with a discussion of how images are generally handled in Fireworks. Even if you're familiar with the program, you may want to read through this section — numerous changes have been incorporated into the new version. Next, we'll delve into an exploration of the various tools available for bitmap editing: those dedicated to Image Edit mode, as well as the object tools that function slightly differently when applied to raster graphics. Finally, we'll cover how to change an object into an image and what benefits that might bring your design.

## Understanding Bitmapped Images in Fireworks

Here's a quick refresher course on bitmapped images — just in case you're coming from the world of vector graphics and can't tell a pixel from a pig in a poke. Bitmapped images are indeed made up of *pixels* (short for picture elem-ents). The term *bitmapped* refers to the fact that in any given image, each pixel is set or *mapped* to a color stored in a memory; it used to take one *bit*, equivalent to eight bytes, of memory to hold the color name. Editing a bitmapped image basically involves remapping the pixels to a different set of colors. Even when you erase part of an image, you're just setting the color of those excess pixels to "None."

The best way I can think to describe the difference between a bitmapped image (also called a *raster graphic*) and a path-based object is to ask you to think of a line, 100 pixels long and 1 pixel high. With vector graphics, all you need to make this line visible is two points and a stroke in between. With a bitmapped image, you need exactly 100 pixels. To move one end of the object version of this line up a notch, you just need to move one of the endpoints. With pixel-based images, however, you have to erase all of the pixels in the line and redraw them in another location.

# Examining Image Edit Mode

As you can see, manipulating path-based objects and pixel-based images are two completely different operations. For that reason, Fireworks has two different modes: an Object Edit mode for vector objects (discussed in Chapter 5) and an Image Edit mode for bitmapped images. Some tools work in one mode but not the other, whereas some tools seem to work the same, but actually return different results. It's not that one mode is better than the other, they are just used for different purposes.

**New Feature**
Frankly, in Fireworks 1, Image Edit mode was a bit of a pain. It was difficult to get into and difficult to get out of. Many tools were inaccessible — grayed out on the menus — if you weren't in the proper mode. As noted in the introduction to this chapter, that's all changed in Fireworks 2. Now, mode changes are tool-driven: start to use an image-editing tool and you automatically enter Image Edit mode. Pick an object-editing tool, start to work, and you're back in Object Edit mode. Tools are no longer designated as inactive for a particular mode; instead, you get an informative message from Fireworks if, for example, you try to use the Reshape Path tool in Image Edit mode.

All in all, switching between the two modes is much faster, and seems more natural, in the new version. Many images in Fireworks start out in one camp or the other — either they're all pixels or all paths. However, eventually the lines begin to blur (pun intended, maybe) and you find yourself moving back and forth between the two modes effortlessly and with no real conscious thought.

## Starting Image Edit mode

In addition to automatically invoking Image Edit mode by choosing a particular tool, you can also enter it explicitly in several ways:

✦ Double-click a bitmapped image with the Pointer or Subselection tool. This is probably my most commonly used technique for accessing Image Edit mode.

✦ Choose Modify ➪ Image Object.

✦ Use the keyboard shortcut, Ctrl+E (Command+E).

✦ Choose Insert ➪ Empty Image Object, which creates a new image object
to apply pixel-based tools.

It's easy to tell when you're in Image Edit mode; in fact, Fireworks offers multiple
different visual cues, as shown in Figure 6-1. First, a striped border surrounds the
image object or, if you have the proper option set in Preferences, the entire canvas.
Second, you'll notice the phrase "(Image Edit Mode)" in the Title Bar of the graphic
you're working on. Finally, along the bottom of the document window in the Status
bar on Windows systems and on the Status bar of the image window on Macintosh
systems, you'll see another note: "Press Stop to exit Image Edit mode" followed by
the Stop button itself, a white X in a red circle.

**Figure 6-1:** The signs indicating you're in Image Edit mode are very clearly marked.

## Leaving Image Edit mode

When you leave Image Edit mode, any bitmap image, if selected normally, has a bounding box around it. In Fireworks, images can also be manipulated — moved, resized, aligned, distorted — as image objects. You can even apply an effect, such as a drop shadow, to a selected image object.

The most obvious way to leave Image Edit mode and go to Object Edit mode is to select the Stop button. However, the Fireworks team created a number of other exits, as well. Here's a list of all the methods for leaving Image Edit mode:

✦ Choose Modify ➪ Exit Image Edit.

✦ Use the keyboard shortcut, Ctrl+Shift+D (Command+Shift+D).

✦ Press the Stop button on the Status bar.

✦ If the Image Edit border surrounds just the object, the cursor becomes a Stop button when not over the object itself and you can click the Stop button cursor once.

✦ If the Image Edit border surrounds the entire document, choose a selection tool (Marquee, Ellipse Marquee, Lasso, Polygon Lasso, or Magic Wand) and double-click any open area.

By default, the Image Edit border surrounds the entire document object. To cause it to encompass just the image, first choose File ➪ Preferences. In the Preferences dialog box, select the Editing tab. On the Editing tab, uncheck Expand to Fill Document under the When Editing Images option. After you click OK, the change takes place immediately.

**Tip**  Why would you want to have the Image Edit border surround more than just the image? Quite often, you need to expand the canvas of an inserted image — to blur the edges or make the shape nonrectangular, for example. If the Image Edit border tightly hugs the bitmapped graphic, there's no room for expansion. By enabling the Expand to Fill Document option, you have plenty of canvas in which to maneuver.

## Examining other Image Mode functions

The other two options — Open in Image Edit Mode and Turn Off "Hide Edges" — under the Editing tab in Preferences can also prove useful. If you're doing a lot of work with bitmaps, you might want to enable the Open in Image Edit Mode option. This preference won't take place until you close and relaunch Fireworks, but it effectively makes Image Editing mode the default.

As helpful as the striped — also known as the barberpole — border is in identifying Image Edit mode, it can be a bit of a visual nuisance. To temporarily view your image without the striped border, choose View ➪ Hide Edges; you can also use the keyboard shortcut, Ctrl+H (Command+H). The Hide Borders command is turned off when you exit Image Edit mode, so the next time you edit your bitmap, the striped border will return. If you want to work continually without the striped border appearing, deselect the Turn Off "Hide Edges" option found on the Editing tab in Preferences and then select View ➪ Hide Edges.

## Opening existing images

I'm sure you've heard the expression, "Success is 1 percent inspiration and 99 percent perspiration." In the Internet graphics field, the formula is a bit different: "Web design is 20 percent creation and 80 percent modification." Of course, this is just my rough estimate — but it definitely feels like I spend most of my day revising an image already created by myself or someone else.

Fireworks offers multiple ways to open existing images — and it supports a wide range of image formats as well. Increasingly, more of your work will be stored in Fireworks format, PNG, which enables both object and image editing. However, many times you'll find yourself forced to work with an exported GIF or JPEG, or a bitmapped file from another program such as Photoshop.

As with many computer programs, Fireworks loads images and other files through the File ➪ Open command. This displays the Open dialog box, which can preview various file types (JPEG, GIF, FreeHand 7.x/8.x, and PNG). In Fireworks 2, you have the option of opening several files at the same time through the Open Multiple command. Through the Open Multiple dialog box, as shown in Figure 6-2, you can select entire folders or selected files from one or several folders to load. The Open Multiple feature is extremely helpful when you're cutting and pasting from one image to another or modifying a series of rollover buttons and the Fireworks source file is not available. It also has a very useful option, Open as Animation, that creates a GIF animation from separate files.

 **Cross-Reference** For detailed information on how to use the Open and Open Multiple commands to load any type of file, see Chapter 4.

Fireworks 1 users will probably notice that the ever-present Background layer is gone in version 2. Previously, any imported bitmapped images were automatically placed on the Background. In Fireworks 2, the Background layer has been replaced by a shared layer referred to as the Canvas. The primary difference between the Background and the Canvas is that neither images nor objects can be placed on the Canvas, unlike the Background. Bitmapped images opened in Fireworks 2 are placed on a layer named Background above a transparent Canvas.

Pointer

**Figure 6-2:** Fireworks' new Open Multiple command loads any number of files from one or more folders.

# Inserting an Image into a Document

Collage—the mixing of various images and other graphics—is a very important design tool on or off the Web. Whether you're overlapping images or just laying them side-by-side, Fireworks's Insert Image command enables you to include an existing graphic wherever necessary in an open document.

To include an image in a document, follow these steps:

1. Choose Insert ➪ Image or use the keyboard shortcut, Ctrl+R (Command+R). Fireworks displays the standard Open dialog box.

2. In the Open dialog box, select your image and choose Open when you're done. The cursor changes to a corner bracket.

3. Position the Insert Image cursor wherever you'd like the upper-left corner of the image to be initially located and click once. The chosen image is inserted into the document as a new image object and selected.

If you need to adjust the position of the newly inserted image object, select the Pointer tool and click and drag it to a new place. For more precise placement, use the cursor keys to move the selected image object any direction, one pixel at a time.

**Tip**     When pressing Shift, the arrow keys move the selected image object in 10-pixel increments.

## Inserting an Empty Image

So far we've seen how Fireworks can open a wide range of file formats for bitmap editing. But what if you want to create a bitmapped image directly from within Fireworks? Whereas path-based objects are far more editable than bitmapped images, occasionally only a bitmap will do. For those times, you can use a Fireworks feature that creates an editable bitmap area by choosing Insert ⇨ Empty Image or by pressing Ctrl+Alt+Y (Command+Option+Y).

**Tip**     The Empty Image command is extremely helpful when you need to paint a fairly large background with a brush such as the Airbrush, and don't want to use the Fill tool. You can then modify the Airbrushed background with any of the pixel-based tools, such as the Eraser.

When you insert an empty image, Fireworks immediately goes into Image Edit mode and selects the Marquee tool. If you want to limit your drawing area, use the Marquee tool to draw out a rectangle. Any drawing will now be clipped to the selected region. Otherwise, use any of the available tools to draw straight to the bitmap. When you leave Image Edit mode, the image object just created is sized only to be as large as necessary to encompass all the applied pixels. This automatically trimmed image object can naturally be repositioned or manipulated like any other image object.

## Using Image Edit Mode Tools

The scoreboard shows a fairly equal number of Fireworks tools dedicated to working with images (five) as opposed to those that work only with objects (six). The vast majority of tools work in both modes, some in a different manner and others exactly the same. Naturally, the better you understand what a tool is intended for and how best it is used, the more fluid your workflow becomes. This section discusses those tools, which are intended for use in the Image Edit mode only.

Those tools that are exclusive to the Image Edit mode are primarily concerned with *selection* and there's a very good reason for this emphasis. It's much harder to select pixels than it is to select paths. To select the most complicated path possible takes just one click. Pixels are chosen either by their position by a tool such as the Lasso, or by their color by the Magic Wand. Quite often you need to use a combination of tools and methods to get the desired results.

Luckily, Fireworks offers a full range of selection tools: Pointer, Marquee, Elliptical Marquee, Lasso, Polygon Lasso, and Magic Wand. Each has its own way of working as well as a variety of user-definable options.

## Pointer

Though technically the Pointer should be listed as one of the tools capable of being used in both modes, I included it here for a simple reason. Double-clicking the pointer on an image is one of the fastest and most intuitive methods of entering Image Edit mode. Moreover, because this method is a holdover from Fireworks 1, it's likely to have many adherents who are not as accustomed to the other techniques. You can also use the Pointer to reposition the image once you're in Image Edit mode by clicking and dragging anywhere within the image object, as shown in Figure 6-2.

Pointer

**Figure 6-2:** The Pointer is used for selecting or repositioning objects.

**Tip**　It's not obvious, but you can also use the Pointer to resize an image object, whether you're in Image Edit or Object Edit mode. You can drag the border surrounding the image to a new position, resizing the graphic much like the Distortion tool. You can even obtain proportional resizing by pressing Shift while dragging a corner Image Edit or image object border. The image object, however, is a tad easier to use because the sizing handles are apparent.

# Marquee

The Marquee tool is one of the most frequently used selection tools and not only because it's the default tool after entering Image Edit mode. The Marquee selection tool is quite similar to the Rectangle drawing tool. Both are generally used by selecting a point for one corner of the rectangular shape and dragging diagonally to the opposite corner. However, the Marquee tool doesn't draw a shape on the image; it temporarily surrounds and selects an area of pixels for another operation to take place, such as a copy or a fill.

## Two types

There are actually two different Marquee tools. The first is the default rectangular Marquee, which is selected through its button on the toolbar or by pressing the keyboard shortcut, m. The second parallels the Ellipse drawing tool: the Ellipse Marquee selects an oval or circular area. The Marquee and Ellipse Marquee use the Shift keyboard modifier to make square and circular pixel regions.

**Caution**　Whereas Shift used with the Marquee and Ellipse Marquee selects square and circular areas, this keyboard modifier also has another function: it adds selected areas to those already selected. Say, for example, you've selected a rectangular region with the Marquee tool and realize you meant to make a square selection instead. If you press Shift while the first selection is still active, the newly drawn square selection will be added to the rectangular selection. To avoid this problem, choose Edit ⇨ Select None or use the keyboard shortcut, Ctrl+D (Command+D) before using Shift to select a square or circular area. You can also just click once outside the marquee to deselect it.

To use the Marquee or Ellipse Marquee, follow these steps:

1. To select a rectangular or square region, select the Marquee tool from the Toolbox or through its keyboard shortcut, m.

2. To select an elliptical or circular region, select the Ellipse Marquee tool from the Toolbox by clicking and holding the Marquee tool and choosing the button from the flyout menu. Alternatively, you can press the keyboard shortcut, m, twice.

3. Click where you want one corner of your selection to begin and drag to the opposite corner. Fireworks displays a moving dashed line, called a marquee or, more familiarly, as "the marching ants" shown in Figure 6-3.

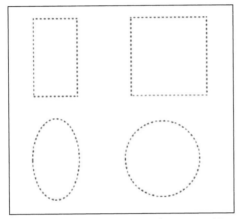

**Figure 6-3:** The Marquee tools are used for marking rectangular, square, elliptical, or circular areas for selection.

The two Marquee tools draw from the center, rather than a corner, if you press down and hold the Alt key while dragging out the marquee, like the Rectangle and Ellipse drawing tools.

## Tool Options panel

The two Marquee tools also share a set of options available from the Tool Options panel. You can display the Tool Options panel, as shown in Figure 6-4, by double-clicking either the Marquee or Ellipse Marquee tool, or by choosing one of the tools and then selecting Window ➪ Tool Options. The Marquee Tool Options affect two separate areas, Constraints and Edge.

**Figure 6-4:** Use the Tool Options panel to set the Marquee to a predetermined size or ratio; you can also change the edge of the selection from hard to feathered.

### Constraint portion

Normally, the Marquee tools are unrestrained, meaning the selection can be any size or shape drawn out. However, sometimes it's helpful to be able to specify the needed selection dimensions. The Constraint portion of the Marquee Tool Options panel has three possibilities:

✦ **Normal:** This default state enables you to drag out your rectangular or elliptical selections freely.

✦ **Fixed Ratio:** Sets the horizontal-to-vertical ratio for the Marquee selection tools. Enter horizontal values in the first text box (marked with the side-to-side double-headed arrow) and vertical values in the second (marked with the up-and-down double-headed arrow). This option is useful when you know that the selection must be a particular proportion. If, for example, you knew that the selection should be twice as wide as high, you would enter a 2 in the horizontal text box and a 1 in the vertical text box. When you use either Marquee tool with a Set Ratio option enabled, the selection size varies, but not the proportion.

✦ **Fixed Size:** Sets the dimensions to a particular pixel width and height. Enter the desired pixel values in the horizontal and vertical text boxes. When either Marquee tool is selected with this option enabled, a selection outlining the specified dimensions is attached to the pointer and can be easily repositioned on the screen. After you've located the area to be selected, clicking once drops the selection outline on the image. The Fixed Size option works well when you need to create a number of same-sized images or objects.

**Tip** If you enter a value in one of the Fixed Size text boxes, but leave the other blank, Fireworks creates a selection outline the width or height specified that spans the entire image. It's a great way to grab a slice of an image, one or two pixels wide or tall, and ensures that you get the full image without having to draw it. For this technique, it's best to use the Marquee tool rather than the Ellipse Marquee.

### Types of edges

The Tool Options panel also controls the type of edge that the selection uses. The default edge type is a hard-edged line — what you select is what you get. The other two types, Anti-Alias and Feather, act to soften the selection. Anti-Alias is the more subtle of the two options. When you choose the Anti-Alias option for your selection, any jagged edges caused by an elliptical or circular selection are blended into the background, much like bitmapped type is anti-aliased to make it appear less jagged.

**Tip** You can get a very smooth bitmapped crescent by making a circular selection using the Ellipse Marquee tool on a solid color. Set the Edge type on the Marquee Tool Options panel to Anti-Alias and make your selection. Then, use the arrow keys to move the selection one or two pixels vertically and the same distance horizontally. You'll be left with a crescent shape that blends smoothly into its points.

Feathering a selection is much more noticeable. Basically, think of feathering as blending. After selecting the Feather option, the value box becomes active with a default of 10 pixels. Any feathered selection is blended equally on either side of the selection outline. If, for example, you choose a small Feather value of 2 pixels for a rectangular selection, four rows of pixels will be altered — two inside the selection and two outside. If you delete a feathered selection, you'll be left with a hole in the image, blending smoothly into the canvas. If you cut and paste a feather selection, the selection will have a faded edge, as shown in Figure 6-5.

**Note**    Although it may appear to be blending the edges of a selection, feathering actually affects just its *alpha channel*. The alpha channel is the method used to define transparency in Fireworks. The feathering, then, is an increase in the transparency of the alpha channel over the specified number of pixels. Because the alpha channel can have 256 levels of transparency, from opaque to transparent, the Feather values go from 0 to 255.

**Figure 6-5:** Cutting and pasting a feathered selection from an image blends both the remaining image and the resulting selection.

## Lasso and Polygon Lasso

Not all regions to be selected are rectangular or elliptical. The Lasso tools select irregularly shaped areas of an image. As the name implies, the Lasso tools surround or lasso the desired pixels to select them. The standard Lasso tool is a click-and-drag type instrument that enables freeform selection, much like the Pencil or Brush is used for freeform drawing. The Polygon tool, on the other hand, is more like the Pen in its straight line mode, and makes selections through a series of connected straight lines.

All Lasso selections are by their very nature closed paths. As with the drawing tools, when you drag the pointer near the beginning of a Lasso selection, Fireworks displays a closed path cursor with a black square in the lower-right corner, as shown in

Figure 6-6. You can also close a Lasso tool selection by releasing the mouse button; Fireworks draws a line from the beginning point to the ending point, closing the shape. With the Polygon Lasso, double-click the last point to automatically close the shape in the same manner.

Polygon Lasso

**Figure 6-6:** The outline of the plane was selected using the Polygon Lasso; now that the object is selected, it can be copied and pasted in another document.

To make a freeform selection, follow these steps:

1. To use the Lasso, select it from the Toolbox or use the keyboard shortcut, l.

2. With the Lasso, click at the starting point for your selection and drag the mouse around the desired area, releasing the mouse when you're done.

3. To use the Polygon Lasso, select and hold the Lasso tool until the flyout appears and then choose the Polygon Lasso or press the keyboard shortcut, l, twice.

4. With the Polygon Lasso, click at the starting point for your selection and then move the mouse to the next point on the outline surrounding the desired area and click again. Fireworks connects each point that you set down with a straight line.

**5.** Repeat Step 4 until you've outlined the entire area and then close the selection by moving your pointer over the starting point and clicking once or double-clicking to permit Fireworks to connect the first and final points.

As a matter of personal preference, I get a lot more use out of the Polygon Lasso than I do the regular drawing Lasso. Selecting an area of pixels is often a painstaking chore and I find the Polygon Lasso to be far more precise. Generally, I use the Lasso to outline some stray pixels for deletion only when there's little chance that I'll select part of the main image.

**Tip**    As with many drawing tools, you can constrain the Polygon Lasso tool to increments of 45 degrees by using the Alt (Option) key.

You can determine the type of edge the Lasso tools use through the Tool Options panel. As with the Marquee tools, the three options are Hard Edge, Anti-Alias, and Feather, and they work in exactly the same manner as described in the previous Marquee section.

## Magic Wand

The Magic Wand is a completely different type of selection tool from those already discussed. Instead of encompassing an area of pixels, the Magic Wand selects adjacent pixels of similar color. This type of tool enables you to quickly select single-color backgrounds or other regions.

Using the Magic Wand is very straightforward. Choose the Magic Wand tool from the flyout that appears by clicking and holding the Lasso tool, or use the keyboard shortcut, w. Now select any pixel in the image and it, and all pixels of a similar color next to it, are selected.

**New Feature**    With both the Magic Wand and the Lasso, I find that the representational pointers sometimes get in the way. It's hard to see exactly which pixel you're pinpointing if there is a sparkly wand cursor obscuring the area. In Fireworks 2, you can toggle Precise Cursors — a cross-hair pointer — whenever you like by pressing the Caps Lock key.

The key phrase in the description of the Magic Wand is "pixels of a similar color." Many bitmapped images, especially photographic JPEGs, tend to use a range of colors even when depicting a seemingly monochromatic area. You control what Fireworks defines as a "similar color" through the Tolerance setting on the Tool Options panel. The Tolerance scale goes from 0 to 255; lower tolerance values select fewer colors and higher values select more.

Here's how the Magic Wand and the Tolerance work. By default, the initial Tolerance is set to 32. The Tolerance value is applied to the RGB values of the selected pixel — the exact one clicked on by the Magic Wand. If the Tolerance value is 50 and the selected pixel's RGB values are 200, 200, and 200, Fireworks judges any adjacent pixel with an RGB from 150, 150, 150 to 250, 250, 250 as being similar enough to select. Pixels within that color range but not in some way touching the originally selected pixel will not be chosen.

In addition to varying the Tolerance, you can also determine the type of edge for a Magic Wand selection. Edge options, like those for Marquee and Lasso tools, are Hard Edge, Anti-Alias (the default), or Feather. For a detailed explanation of how these tools work, see the "Marquee" section earlier in this chapter.

## Increasing and Reducing the Selection Area

Fireworks's selection tools are very full featured, but, for complex selections, you need more flexibility. With Fireworks, you can add several selections together, or you can use one selection tool to eliminate part of an existing selection. The key is to use the keyboard modifiers as you draw your selections: press Shift to add selections and Alt (Option) to remove them. You'll notice that the pointer indicates the operation; a plus sign appears when Shift is pressed and a minus sign appears when Alt (Option) is pressed.

For example, I often use Shift in combination with the Magic Wand to select additional areas of an image, rather than alter the Tolerance. This enables me to quickly Shift-click until I gather the necessary region. The added selections can either extend the existing selection or appear separately, as shown in the accompanying figure.

*Continued*

*(continued)*

Just as you can add onto selections, you can take away from them, too. Use the Alt (Option) key when applying any of the selection tools to reduce an existing selection. The basic technique is to "carve out" the undesired selection; in the following figure, the donut shape was created by first drawing a circular selection and then pressing Alt (Option) while drawing a smaller elliptical selection inside. Then the ragged bite was taken out of the side by using the Polygon Lasso again in combination with Alt (Option). The soft edge was achieved through use of the Feather edge option. Obviously, the selection reduction feature enables some very unusual shapes to be created.

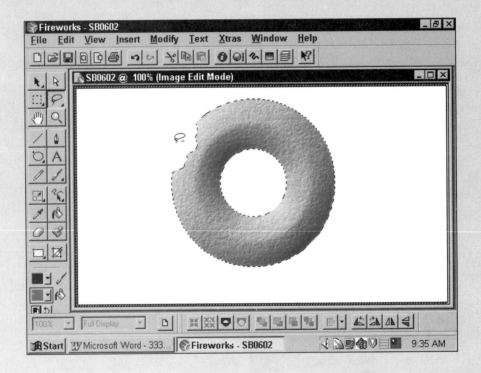

Using the keyboard modifiers to increase or reduce existing selections doesn't stop them from being used in their other functions. Pressing Shift while using the Polygon Lasso still constrains the angle of the new selection to increments of 45 degrees while adding to existing selection. Moreover, you can still use the Alt (Option) to draw from the center with either Marquee tool, while reducing a selection, but there is a small trick. Press Alt (Option) once to trigger the selection removal function and begin dragging out the rectangle or ellipse selection. Then press Alt (Option) again to trigger the draw from center command.

# Rubber Stamp

If you're looking for a cool tool, look no further than the Rubber Stamp. One of the few pixel-based drawing tools, Rubber Stamp copies sections of an image in another location in your document. Always wanted to give your favorite model a third eye, as I did in Figure 6-7? The Rubber Stamp tool makes it easy to pick up portions of an image and blend them in other areas of the graphic.

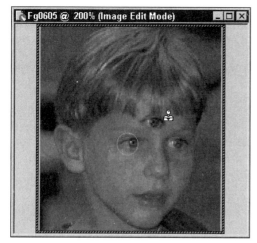

**Figure 6-7:** The Rubber Stamp tool was used here twice to pick up sections of each eye to make a third, unique eye.

The Rubber Stamp is a two-part tool with both source and destination pointers. The source, or origin, pointer is initially placed on the area of the document that you want to duplicate. The destination pointer draws the duplicated section in a different location on the image. While you are drawing, the two pointers maintain the same relationship to each other; if you move the destination pointer to the left, the source pointer moves to the left as well. It's a little tricky to get a handle on this tool, but well worth the time you spend mastering it.

To use the Rubber Stamp tool, follow these steps:

1. Select the Rubber Stamp tool from the Toolbox or use the keyboard shortcut, s.

2. Set the source pointer by clicking once on the image. If you attempt to set the source pointer on a path object, Fireworks tells you that the Rubber Stamp tool can only be used on floating image objects.

**3.** Move the destination pointer to where you want the copied image to appear and draw by clicking and dragging. As the source pointer moves over the image, following the movement of the mouse, the image is copied under the destination pointer.

## Two basic modes

You can use the Rubber Stamp in two basic modes, selectable from the Source options list found on the Rubber Stamp Tool Options panel. First, with the Aligned Source mode (default), you can always keep the relationship between the source and destination pointers constant, not just when you're drawing. This is useful if you want to copy different portions of the image to a remote area, but keep them proportionally spaced. For example, if I wanted to position two eyes as if they were floating in space above the subject's head, I would copy one eye using the Rubber Stamp tool, release the mouse button, and position the source pointer over the second eye and then begin dragging and drawing again until the second eye was completed.

The other Rubber Stamp mode is Fixed Source. In Fixed Source mode, whenever the mouse button is released, the source pointer snaps back to its original starting place. This mode enables you to copy the same image in several locations. If, for example, I wanted to place a series of floating eyes around my model's head, I would use Fixed Source mode.

**Tip**    Press Alt (Option) to reset the origin for the Rubber Stamp.

## Other options

Though the Rubber Stamp only draws pixels, you can use it to copy any part of your document, whether image or object. In the Sample option list, choose Image to copy only from the image and Document to copy from anywhere in the document. There is one small trick to using the Sample Document option, however. Because the Rubber Stamp tool is intended as a pixel-based tool, you can't start by clicking outside of the image—Fireworks won't permit it. You can, however, click once on the image to set the source pointer and then immediately move it by pressing Alt (Option) and resetting it on an area outside of the image. Then you can set the destination pointer normally and begin copying the image.

Two other controls are available on the Rubber Stamp Tool Options panel. The Edge Softness slider affects the hardness of the duplicated image's edge; the higher the slider, the softer the edge. To blend a copied image more (like the third eye from Figure 6-5), use a softer edge. You can also change the size of the source and destination pointers with the Stamp Size slider. The range of the Stamp Size slider is from 0 to 72 and the default is 16 pixels. The selected Stamp Size includes any feathering that may be required by the Edge Softness setting.

# Eraser

As you might suspect, the Eraser removes pixels from an image. What you might not guess, however, is that the Eraser tool has numerous options and can achieve a variety of effects. The Eraser, which works only on pixel-based images, shares a Toolbox spot with its path-oriented counterpart, the Knife. To see the Eraser button appear on the Toolbox, select a bitmapped image.

To use the Eraser, follow these steps:

1. Select the Eraser (or the Knife) from the Toolbox; alternatively, you can use the keyboard shortcut, e.

2. If necessary, select the image you want to work on.

3. Click and drag over the pixels you wish to remove. Fireworks deletes the pixels according to the preferences selected in the Tool Options panel, as shown in Figure 6-8.

**Figure 6-8:** The Eraser tool removes pixels from your image according to the settings established on the Tool Options panel.

In addition to being able to set the Edge Softness and Size of the Eraser on the Tool Options panel, as you can with the Rubber Stamp tool, you can also select its basic shape. By default, the Eraser is circular, but you can change it to a square by choosing the Square Eraser button.

The final set of choices on the Tool Options panel gives the Eraser a fair degree of power. With some graphics programs, you're always erasing to whatever the current background is or, in Fireworks jargon, the canvas color. In Fireworks, you can select what will replace the area erased from four different choices:

✦ Transparent

✦ Fill color

✦ Stroke color

✦ Canvas color

**Note** If the image is floating over the canvas and you choose the Erase To Transparent option, it will look like you're erasing to the canvas color. However, if you move the image over another object, you'll see that the area erased is indeed transparent.

# Fireworks Technique: Limiting Your Drawing Area

Not only can the selection tools modify your images after they're created, but they can also structure them before they're made. When you place a selection on an image canvas — whether it's an existing image or an inserted Empty Image — any subsequent drawing is limited to that selected area. The selected area can be any shape possible with any or all of the selection tools: Marquee, Ellipse Marquee, Lasso, Polygon Lasso, and Magic Wand. Figure 6-9 used both the Ellipse Marquee and the Polygon Lasso to predefine the possible drawing areas. As you can see, one of the benefits to this technique is that you don't have to fill the entire restricted area, thus creating the illusion of drawing behind parts of an image.

**Figure 6-9:** The flying saucer and tractor beam were added by first dragging out selections and then filling in the sections with the Brush and other drawing tools.

The only prerequisite for using this drawing technique is to make sure that the selection is active before you begin drawing. An active selected area is designated by the marquee or marching ants border.

# Selecting Images

The selection tools found in the Toolbox are handy, but they aren't the only selection options in Fireworks. The Edit menu holds seven commands pertinent to selecting objects. These commands moved from the Select menu in Fireworks 1 to the Edit menu in Fireworks 2.

## Selecting all

When you need to select all the objects — both images and paths — in the current document, choose Edit ➪ Select All. I find myself using the keyboard shortcut for this command, Ctrl+A (Command+A), in combination with the Delete key all the time when I want to erase all the work in a document and start over. Of course, any operation that needs to be applied universally to every portion of a document benefits from the Select All command.

If you are in Image Edit mode and issue the Select All command, just the image is selected. If, on the other hand, you're in Object Edit mode, all the path-based objects and the pixel-based images are selected. Keep in mind, though, that the image is selected as an image object and image tools such as the Rubber Stamp that work only in Image Edit mode will not function.

 **Cross-Reference** All but two of the select menu commands are covered here. Both Superselect and Subselect are concerned with groups and are therefore explained in Chapter 13.

## Selecting none

The opposite of Select All is Deselect. I use this command so frequently, it goes on my Top 10 Keyboard Shortcuts to Memorize list: Ctrl+D (Command+D). It's a very straightforward and extremely useful command. Choose Edit ➪ Deselect to remove all selections in the current document for any image, object, or text.

## Selecting inverse

Isolating a foreground figure from the background of an image is a common Web designer task. One of the standard techniques for accomplishing this is a three-step process in Fireworks:

1. First, select your foreground object through whatever tool or combination of tools are required.

2. Choose Edit ➪ Select Inverse or use the keyboard shortcut, Ctrl+Shift+I (Command+Shift+I). Fireworks selects everything in the image *except* your just-selected foreground image.

3. Press Delete to remove the background.

Because this command quite literally inverts the selection, it's often far easier to combine it with a selected object when all you want is the object. The difference between the two sets of marquees, one for the selected part of the image and one for the inverted selection, can often be quite similar, as shown in Figure 6-10.

**Figure 6-10:** Selecting a foreground figure and then using the Invert Selection command can quickly isolate the foreground.

## Feathering an existing selection

You've seen the Feather option for all the Toolbox selection tools. However, you may have noticed that in each case, feathering has to be established prior to the selection being made, whether through the Marquee or the Magic Wand. But what do you do when you want to feather an existing selection? Choose Edit ➪ Feather to open the Feather Selection dialog box, as shown in Figure 6-11. Whatever value is entered into the Radius text box is then applied to the current selection.

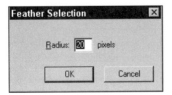

**Figure 6-11:** The Feather Selection dialog box permits you to feather the edges of the current selection.

Remember that the Feather command does not blur the selection's edges, but rather alters the selection's alpha channel, which controls transparency. To see the effect of a feathered selection, it's often necessary to move or cut and paste the selection. As with all the other feathering options, both the selection and the area adjacent to the selection are affected.

**Cross-Reference**    If you do just want to blur the edges of an image, you'll want to use one of the Blur commands found under the Xtras menu. Find out more about these commands in Chapter 14.

## Selecting similar

The Select Similar command is an extension of the Magic Wand selection tool. Whereas the Magic Wand selects pixels within a particular color range adjacent to the one initially chosen, Select Similar selects *all* the pixels in a document within that color range, whether they are adjacent to the original pixel or not. To use this command, choose Edit ➪ Select Similar after setting the Tolerance level on the Magic Wand Tool Options panel.

**Caution**　This is a very powerful command and one that should be used with care. It's often extremely difficult to predict all the areas of an image that will be affected. Keep your Undo button at the ready.

# Applying Object Tools to Images

Whether you're creating a bitmapped image from scratch or touching up an existing graphic, you'll need additional tools. In Fireworks, all of the geometric shapes — Rectangle, Ellipse, and Polygon — and most of the drawing tools, such as — Pencil and Brush — are applied in exactly the same way in Image Edit mode as in Object Edit mode. The primary difference is that what's drawn is easily editable when it's an object and not when it's an image. Sometimes, however, you don't have a choice and you have to work in Image Edit mode. Table 6-1 explains how the object tools are used in Image Edit mode.

| Table 6-1 Tools in Image Edit Mode | |
| --- | --- |
| **Tool** | **Effect** |
| Rectangle and Square | Works the same way in Image Edit mode as with objects and use the current Stroke and Fill settings. |
| Ellipse and Circle | Works the same way in Image Edit mode as with objects and use the current Stroke and Fill settings. |
| Polygon and Star | Works the same way in Image Edit mode as with objects and use the current Stroke and Fill settings. |
| Line | Works the same way in Image Edit mode as with objects and uses the current Stroke settings. |
| Pencil | Works the same way in Image Edit mode as with objects and uses the basic one-pixel stroke setting. |
| Brush | Works the same way in Image Edit mode as with objects and uses the current Stroke settings. |

*Continued*

| Table 6-1 *(continued)* | |
| --- | --- |
| *Tool* | *Effect* |
| Pen | Ends Image Edit mode; tool must be selected again to use in Object Edit mode. |
| Text | Ends Image Edit mode and opens Text Editor. |
| Transform, Skew, and Distort | No effect in Image Edit mode. You can, however, use these tools to modify a selected image object. |
| Freeform, Reshape Area, and Path Scrubber | No effect in Image Edit mode; Fireworks alerts the user that these tools can be used only with paths. |

# Converting an Object to an Image

Whereas it's best to keep as many parts of your graphic in an object form for easy modification, occasionally you need to convert the path-based objects to a bitmapped image. To convert an object to an image, select the object and then choose Modify ➪ Merge Images. As shown in Figure 6-12, Fireworks converts the path outline to a rectangular bounding box surrounding all the pixels from the object's fill, stroke, and effect settings.

If you have selected multiple objects, you can convert them all at one time with this command. However, you lose the capability to reposition them individually as they all become part of one image—as the command name implies, you are merging the images.

**Figure 6-12:** When you convert an object to an image through the Merge Images command, Fireworks puts a bounding box around the new image object.

**Caution** Once you've converted an object to an image, you can't go back without using the Undo feature. Converted objects that have been saved and reloaded cannot be returned to their object state under any circumstances.

# Summary

Images are used throughout the Web and Fireworks offers a robust set of tools for creating and manipulating them. Whereas images don't have the flexibility of objects, their editing is a large part of the Web designer's job. When it comes time to begin modifying an existing image in Fireworks, keep these points in mind:

✦ Images are composed of pixels and, to be visible, each pixel in an image is assigned a particular color. At the most basic level, editing images involves changing the colors of pixels.

✦ In Fireworks, images are modified primarily in Image Edit mode, which you can enter by double-clicking an image with the Pointer or working with any image-based tool such as the Marquee.

✦ All of the image selection tools in Fireworks — Marquee, Ellipse Marquee, Lasso, Polygon Lasso, and Magic Wand — have numerous options available through the Tool Options panel.

✦ By selecting an area of the image prior to drawing, you can limit your drawing area.

✦ One of the best techniques for separating a figure from the background is to select the figure and then choose Edit ➪ Select Inverse. Then you can delete or fill the background, as desired.

✦ Most of the primary object drawing tools, such as the Rectangle, Pen, and Brush, work in Image Edit mode as well.

In the next chapter, you'll see how to handle color in Fireworks.

✦    ✦    ✦

# Managing Color

**F**or any graphic designer, the importance of color is a given. Not only can color attract the eye and convey emotions, but it's also an important commercial consideration. On the Web, as with any mass medium, color also becomes a key factor in branding. After all, if you're working on a logo for the Coca-Cola Web site, you'd better make sure you're using genuine Coca-Cola red.

Fireworks 2 outputs graphics for a screen-based medium. You won't find complex color separation, halftone, or calibration tools in Fireworks; those are instruments for the world of print. Moreover, Fireworks is not just screen-based, it's Internet-based — a distinction that signifies an important balance of freedoms and restrictions.

This chapter covers color on the Web — both its basic theory with the various standards, and its actual practice with Fireworks. If you're familiar with how computers handle color in general, feel free to skip the initial part of the chapter and dive right into the more hands-on Fireworks sections. If, on the other hand, you think RGB is a one-hit wonder band from the '80s and hexadecimal is a library catalog system, the first section should be pixel-perfect for you.

## Working with Color on the Web

Color in the natural world comes at us full force, without any impediments. Color on the Web, however, passes through many filters. At the most basic level, the computer dictates how color is generated. Rather than using a system of blending inks as with print, the computer blends light — red, green, and blue light to be precise. Next, the color settings on a viewer's specific system determine the range of colors to be used; not very long ago, the vast number of systems in use were set for 256 colors, even though they were capable of displaying far more. The final filter for Web-based color is the browser in all of its varied configurations and versions. Necessary to visit any Web site, the browser limits the viewable color spectrum even more distinctly.

To get the most out of your Web graphics, you'll need a basic understanding of how computers create color. The smallest component of a computer screen you can see is the pixel, which, you'll remember, is short for *picture element*. Pixels are displayed by showing three colors in combination: red, green, and blue, often referred to by their initials, RGB. The blend of red, green, and blue, at full intensity, creates white, and when they're at their lowest level, black.

**Note**    If you're coming from a print background, you're going to be more familiar with the CMYK (cyan, yellow, magenta, and black) color model than the RGB model. It's generally not too difficult to make the transition; Fireworks offers ways to convert a color in one system to its equivalent in the other, as you'll see in the section, "Using the Color Mixer," later in this chapter.

If RGB on full makes white and off makes black, how are other colors made? The intensity of each of the key colors in a pixel — red, green, and blue — and their combination, can be varied. For example, if you have the red all the way up and both blue and green off, you'll get a pure red; if you add a full dose of blue to the red, you'll create a deep purple. However, having just the capability to turn a color on or off greatly limits the number of color combinations possible. What's needed is an increase in the number of steps or levels between on and off.

## Bit depth

The number of accessible RGB levels is called the *bit depth*. A bit is the smallest element of computer memory and each bit is basically an on-off switch. A computer display with a bit depth of 1 is capable of showing two colors — one color in the on position and another in the off. Now, if the bit depth is doubled, twice as many colors can be defined.

Each time you increase the bit depth, the number of colors increases exponentially. Here is a look at how bit depth affects the range of colors in Table 7-1.

| Table 7-1 | |
|:---:|:---:|
| **Bit Depth and Color Range** | |
| *Bit Depth* | *Number of Colors* |
| 1 | 2 |
| 2 | 4 |
| 3 | 8 |
| 4 | 16 |
| 5 | 32 |

| Bit Depth | Number of Colors |
|:---:|:---:|
| 6 | 64 |
| 7 | 128 |
| 8 | 256 |
| 15 | 32,768 |
| 16 | 65,536 |
| 24 | 16,777,216 |

In Table 7-1, I jumped from 8-bit depth to 15, 16, and 24 because those are the most commonly used color settings in monitors. One additional high-end setting is in use: 32-bit. Although with 32-bit color, you could potentially see more than 4 billion colors, the human eye can't differentiate that many colors. Thirty-two-bit color is therefore a combination of 24-bit color, with its 16.7 million colors, and an 8-bit grayscale overlay or *mask* that serves to sharpen the colors much the same way that black works with cyan, magenta, and yellow in the CMYK model. This grayscale mask is also known as the *alpha channel.*

Because bit depth is directly related to computer memory (remember that a bit is a chunk of memory), the higher the color range, the more memory is used. And not just any memory, but video memory. Until recently, video memory was fairly limited and most computer systems were shipped displaying only 256 colors (8 bit). Therefore, when designing for the Web, artists have been forced to work with the lowest common denominator and created work in 256 colors.

**Note**
Increasingly, computers surfing the Web have an increased bit-depth and can display more colors. A recent poll showed that out of 7 million Web visitors, less than 15 percent are using 256 color systems. However, this doesn't mean that all graphics can now be in 16.7 million colors — the more colors used, the larger the graphic files, and download speed over the Internet is a major consideration in Web design.

## Hexadecimal colors

In HTML, the language of the Web, RGB color values are given in *hexadecimal.* Hexadecimal is a base-16 number system, which means that instead of the numbers running from 0 to 9 and then beginning to repeat, there is an initial series of 16 number values:

```
0, 1, 2, 3, 4, 5, 6, 7, 8, 9, A, B, C, D, E, F
```

where the single letters are used to represent values that would normally take two digits, A is equal to 10, B to 11, C to 12, and so on. In our standard number system, two digits can be used to express any number up to 99; in the hexadecimal number system, a pair of values can express any number from zero (00) to 255 (FF) — 256 values, in other words. This is why RGB values in hexadecimal (or *Hex*, as it is more commonly called) are given in paired triplets with one pair each corresponding to red, green, and blue respectively.

For example, white in RGB values would be represented as 255, 255, 255 — each color being its most intense. The equivalent in Hex is FF, FF, FF, which in HTML is written all together, like this: FFFFFF. Black is 0, 0, 0 in RGB and 000000 in Hex, whereas a pure red would be 255, 0, 0 in RGB, and FF0000 in Hex.

Though it may seem completely foreign to you initially, hexadecimal colors quickly become very recognizable. You'll even start to notice patterns; for instance, any color where the Hex triplets are all the same represents a shade of gray — 111111 is the darkest gray, and EEEEEE is the lightest.

## Web-safe colors

As noted previously, the generally accepted lowest-common denominator in monitor displays is 8-bit, or 256 colors. Unfortunately, there's yet one more restriction on Web colors: the browser. Each of the major browsers, from Microsoft and Netscape, uses a fixed palette of 256 colors to render 8-bit images on both Windows and Macintosh operating systems. Once the 40 different colors used for system displays are subtracted — because you generally would like your Web graphics to look the same on both platforms — a common palette of 216 remains. Because any of these colors can safely be used by any system, they are collectively referred to as the *browser-safe* or *Web-safe* palette.

Because of its importance in Web design, Fireworks makes extensive use of the Web-safe palette. By default, the color picker pop-up accessible from every color well in the program is set to the Web-safe palette. You can even force a selected color outside of the palette to snap to its nearest Web-safe neighbor.

**Tip**    Interestingly enough, Web-safe colors are very easy to spot when given in hexadecimal. Any color composed of Hex value pairs evenly divisible by three falls into the Web-safe camp. In other words, if the color contains some combination of 00, 33, 66, 99, CC, or FF — such as 0000FF, 336699, or FFCC00 – it is Web safe.

## Platform differences

Not only does the Web designer have to contend with a limited palette and a host of issues with the wide variety of browsers in the market, but many differences worth noting exist between the Windows and Macintosh platforms. Chief among these is the *gamma* setting. The gamma setting, or more properly, the *gamma correction* setting, is designed to avoid having midtones onscreen appear too dark. The problem is that there are different gamma settings for different systems.

Apple systems (actually, their QuickDraw display elements) typically use a lower gamma than PCs; this setting works well to emulate LaserWriter printing output, but they also make the monitor display brighter than a PC. Consequently, the same graphic appears darker on a Windows machine than on a Macintosh.

There are two possible solutions to the gamma problem. One is compromise: make your images a little brighter on the PC side and a little darker on the Mac side. The other solution is still in the "coming soon" stage and can be found in Fireworks's native format, PNG. Images saved in a PNG format have built-in gamma correction so that they will be displayed correctly regardless of the user's system. Although both major 4.0+ browsers offer native display for PNG, only Internet Explorer offers full gamma support. Hopefully, the next generation of browsers will standardize this important feature.

# Mixing Colors

The general color mechanism in Fireworks is the Color Mixer. With the Color Mixer, you can select your Fill and Stroke colors from the entire spectrum available to you in any of five different color models. You can also directly determine a color by entering the appropriate values through the sliders or text boxes.

## Using the Color Mixer

To open the Color Mixer, choose Window ⇨ Color Mixer or, in Windows, select the Color Mixer button from the Main toolbar. The Color Mixer, shown in Figure 7-1, is divided into three main areas:

  ✦ **Color wells:** The Stroke and Fill color wells display the active color for the selected object stroke and fill, respectively. The color defaults can also be applied and swapped through buttons in this section.

  ✦ **Color sliders:** Use the color sliders to choose a color by altering its components.

  ✦ **Color ramp:** The color ramp displays all colors of a particular color model and enables you to select them with an Eyedropper tool.

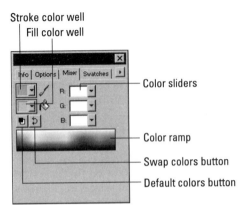

Stroke color well
Fill color well
Color sliders
Color ramp
Swap colors button
Default colors button

**Figure 7-1:** Open the Color Mixer to visually select your Stroke and Fill colors from the color ramp or set them with the color sliders.

## Choosing a color

The Web artist alternates between creating new graphics fresh from the mind's eye and matching or adapting existing imagery. Both situations are valid ways of working and Fireworks enables you to select the colors you need accordingly. Should you want to create visually, selecting your colors direct from the palette, you can sample colors either from a full-spectrum color ramp, the more limited showing of the active swatches, or directly off the screen from another image. If you'd prefer to work more formulaically, the color sliders enable you to enter a precise value in five different color models.

### Using the color ramp

To select a color from the color ramp, follow these steps:

1. Open the Color Mixer by choosing Window ⇨ Color Mixer. Windows users can also select the Color Mixer button in the Main toolbar.

2. Select either the Stroke or Fill color well. The selected color well is highlighted with a border around it.

3. Move your pointer over the color ramp. The pointer changes into one of two Eyedropper tools. The Eyedropper tool with the wavy line indicates that the Stroke color is to be selected, whereas the one with the solid block indicates the Fill color.

**Tip**

Initially, the color ramp display matches the chosen color model, like RGB, Hexadecimal, or Grayscale. You can change the color ramp, however, by Shift-clicking on it. With each Shift-click, the color ramp cycles through one of three displays: the Web-safe, full-color, and grayscale spectrums.

4. Choose any desired color in the color ramp by clicking on it once.

Tip
> If you click and drag your pointer across the color ramp, the wells and the slider settings update dynamically. This gives you a better idea of the actual color you're selecting — the swatch in the color well is bigger and the color values are easy to follow. If the color chosen is unsatisfactory, select Edit ⇨ Undo to return to your previous setting.

5. After you've released the mouse button to select the color, both the color well and sliders display the new color. If an object was selected when the new color was chosen, its Fill or Stroke color changes to match the new one.

### Using Color Mixer sliders

Another method of selecting a color uses the Color Mixer sliders. As with other Fireworks sliders, you can enter the values either directly in the text boxes or by dragging the slider handle up or down. Which sliders are available depends on the color model chosen. Sliders for RGB, CMY, and HSB all match their respective initials. Choosing the Hexadecimal model displays the R, G, and B color sliders, and selecting Grayscale shows just one slider, K, which represents the percentage of black.

If you're not trying to match a specific RGB or other value, you can visually mix your colors by moving the slider and watching the selected color well. If you have an object selected, its stroke or fill settings will update when you release the mouse button.

## Accessing the color models

Aside from the previously described RGB and Hexadecimal, Fireworks offers three other possible color models. The capability to switch between different color models is very important in Web design. Quite often the Web artist is asked to convert graphics from another medium, be it print or another computer-based medium. You can also switch from one system to another to take advantage of its special features. For example, switching the HSB enables you to select a tint of a particular color by reducing the saturation.

All color models are chosen by selecting the Option pop-ups button in the upper-right corner of the Color Mixer. Choose a color model from the list that appears, as shown in Figure 7-2.

### RGB

Choosing the RGB color models enables you to select a color from anywhere in the 24-bit color spectrum from any one of 16.7 million colors. Whereas not all of the colors are represented visually on the RGB color ramp (at a screen resolution of 72 pixels per inch, displaying all pixels would require over 19,000 square feet — that's a mighty big monitor), you can enter any required value in the color sliders shown in Figure 7-3. The color sliders use values from 0 to 255.

**Figure 7-2:** Choose from five different color models by selecting the Color Mixer's Options pop-up.

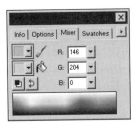

**Figure 7-3:** Work with the RGB color model to specify one of 16.7 million colors, such as the yellowish-green one here.

**Note**      If your computer display is not capable of showing as many colors as are viewable in the color model—for example, if your system is set on 256 colors and you choose RGB—you'll see some dithering in the color ramp. *Dithering* is the combination of two or more colors to simulate another color and appears as noticeable dots. However, although the display may dither, the colors the Eyedropper tool chooses are accurate RGB values.

## Hexadecimal

When you select the Hexadecimal color model, two things happen. The Color Mixer sliders translate their displayed values to hexadecimal values and the color ramp depicts a Web-safe spectrum, as shown in Figure 7-4. With a Web-safe color ramp (which is the default when Fireworks first starts up after installation), you'll notice what's referred to as *banding*. Banding occurs when the range of colors is not large enough to make a smooth gradation.

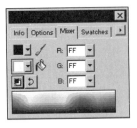

**Figure 7-4:** Although you can enter a valid RGB hexadecimal value in the color sliders with a Hexadecimal color model, only Web-safe colors are selectable in the default color ramp.

**Caution** All values entered manually in the slider text boxes must be in the proper hexadecimal pair format. If you try to enter a numeric value outside of hexadecimal range, such as 225, Fireworks just drops the first number without properly converting the value.

## CMY

As mentioned previously, most designers coming from a print background are used to expressing color as a mixture of cyan, magenta, yellow, and black: CMYK, also known as the four-color process. In theory, the color range should be representable with just the first three colors, but in printing practice, the fourth color, black, is necessary to produce the darker colors.

Fireworks presents CMY colors as a range of numbers from 0 to 255. In some ways, CMY can be considered the opposite of RGB. RGB is referred to as an *additive* process, because you add the colors together to reach white. CMY is a *subtractive* process, because you take colors away to make white. When you choose CMY from the Options pop-up of the Color Mixer, the panel displays a slider for C (Cyan), M (Magenta), and Y (Yellow), as shown in Figure 7-5.

**Figure 7-5:** Print designers new to the Web will find the CMY color model familiar.

Fireworks isn't concerned with output to a print medium, so it can express the color spectrum with just cyan, magenta, and yellow, without resorting to the addition of black. This, however, does make it difficult to translate a CMYK color to a CMY color. The best workaround I've found is to use a common third model, such as RGB or a specific Pantone color.

## HSB

HSB is short for Hue, Saturation, and Brightness and is a color model available on numerous graphics programs, including Photoshop. Hue represents the color family, as seen on a color wheel. Because of the circular model, Hue values are presented in degrees from 0 to 360. Saturation determines the purity of the color, in terms of a percentage. A 100 percent saturation is equal to the purest version of any hue. The Brightness value, also expressed as a percentage, is the amount of light or dark in a color—0 percent is black and 100 percent is brightness a color can appear. If the brightness is reduced to zero, both the Hue and Saturation values are also automatically reduced to zero as well. After choosing HSB from the Options pop-up on the Color Mixer panel, the three sliders change to H, S, and B (Figure 7-6).

**Figure 7-6:** Use the HSB color model to easily lighten or darken a particular hue.

Caution

Don't attempt to directly translate HSB values from the similarly named HLS color model. HLS (Hue, Luminosity, and Saturation), a color model used in FreeHand and other drawing programs as well as available in the Apple OS color picker, uses Luminosity rather than Brightness as its "light" component. The key difference between Luminosity and Brightness lies in how the color is affected at the higher end of the scale. In HSB, when full Brightness is combined with full Saturation, colors are at their most vivid. In HLS, full Luminosity, regardless of the Saturation level, makes colors white.

## Grayscale

Despite the richness of the realm of color—or maybe because of it—grayscale images have an undeniable power. Whether you're constructing graphics as an homage to black-and-white movies or blending black-and-white photographs in a full-color site, access to a grayscale palette is essential. Fireworks's grayscale palette is a full range of 256 tones from absolute white to absolute black.

When Grayscale is selected from the Color Mixer's Options pop-up, the three sliders of the other palette are reduced to one, marked K: for black. As shown in Figure 7-7, the black value is expressed as a percentage where 100 percent is black and 0 percent is white.

**Figure 7-7:** To access any one of 256 shades of gray, select the Grayscale color model.

# Selecting Swatches of Color

Quite often the graphics for a Web site are designed with a particular palette in mind. The most common palette contains the 216 Web-safe colors, which is used to keep images from shifting colors on different platforms. Palettes are also devised to match a particular color scheme—either for an entire Web site or for one particular area. Each palette can be saved as a separate swatch file.

Fireworks provides very full palette support through its Swatches panel. Swatches can be modified, stored, loaded, or completely scrapped to start fresh. You can even grab the palette from a sample image.

## Choosing from the color wells

In Fireworks 2, your working palette is accessible from any color well, thanks to the new color picker pop-up. Now you can immediately select any color you need without sacrificing any screen real estate to an additional toolbar.

**New Feature**

In addition to adding enhanced accessibility, the new color picker pop-up adds new functionality with several new tools. First, the Eyedropper tool enables you to select a color from any onscreen image—whether it's in Fireworks or part of another program entirely. Next, the Palette button gives you instant access to your system color pickers. Finally, the No Color button can quickly set a stroke or fill to None, without your having to open their respective panels.

To access the colors in the current swatch set, select the arrow button next to any color well. When the color picker pop-up appears, as shown in Figure 7-8, move your pointer over any of the color swatches. As you move your pointer, you'll notice that the color chip in the upper-right corner dynamically updates to show the color underneath the pointer; the color name in hexadecimal is also displayed. Click once to choose a color.

**Tip**

If you've selected a color for a stroke or fill where previously there was none, Fireworks 2 automatically enables the setting, turning the Stroke type to Pencil and the Fill type to Solid for the selected color.

Eyedropper button     Palette button

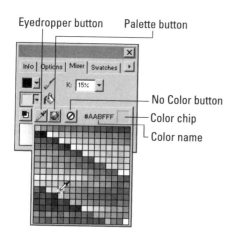

— No Color button
— Color chip
— Color name

**Figure 7-8:** You can open the color picker pop-up from any color well in Fireworks.

## Using the Eyedropper

The Eyedropper is a great tool for ensuring color fidelity across images. Need to match a particular shade of purple in the background graphic for the outline of the navigation bar you're building? Click once with the Eyedropper to grab that color; the selected color well is now filled with the chosen color.

The Eyedropper tool is very straightforward to use. Once you've displayed the color picker pop-up, click once on the Eyedropper button; the pointer changes to its namesake shape. Now you can easily select a color from anywhere on the Fireworks screen.

Moreover, the new Eyedropper tool is not limited to sampling colors from Fireworks. You can pick up a color from any application or graphic displayed on your computer. There are, however, different ways to enable this feature for each computing platform:

✦ With Macintosh systems (8.0 and higher), press the Option key to get an Eyedropper anywhere.

✦ With Windows systems (95/98 and NT), click and drag the Eyedropper tool from the color picker pop-up. The Eyedropper tool remains active as long as the mouse button is down.

**Tip**   It's possible — even likely — that the color you sample with the Eyedropper won't be Web-safe. To snap the sampled color to the closest Web-safe value, press the Shift key when you select your color.

### Accessing the system color pickers

If you work with a number of graphic applications, you may find it more convenient to work with your system's color pickers than with those in Fireworks. The Macintosh, especially, has a far more diverse series of color pickers. To open the system color pickers, select the Palette button.

The Mac system color picker version has several color schemes from which to choose: CMYK (for print-related colors), RGB (for screen-based colors), and HTML (for Web-based colors). The CMYK, HTML, and RGB systems offer you color swatches and three or four sliders with text entry boxes, and accept percentage values for RGB and CMYK and Hex values for HTML. Both RGB and HTML also have a "Snap to Web color" option for matching your chosen color to the closest browser-safe color. The Hue, Saturation, and Value (or Lightness) sliders also have color wheels. Depending on other software installed on the Macintosh, other color pickers might be available, as shown in Figure 7-9.

The Windows system color picker is split into two parts, as shown in Figure 7-10. On the left, you'll find 48 color chips featuring Windows standard colors. On the right is a full-color spectrum with a value bar, for mixing colors. Both RGB and Hue, Saturation, and Luminance text boxes are available below the spectrum. To choose a custom color, you must choose a color from both the main spectrum and the value bar.

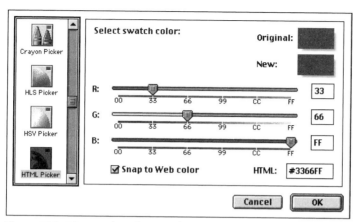

**Figure 7-9:** The Macintosh OS color picker offers numerous color models from which to choose.

With both system color pickers, closing them automatically assigns the last selected color to the Fireworks color well.

### Opting for no color

When it comes to stroke and fill colors, it's important to remember that "no color" is as valid an option as any color. Under the previous version of Fireworks, to turn off either the fill or stroke settings, you had to go to their respective panels and choose None from the category option list. To disable a fill or stroke in Fireworks 2, just select the arrow button next to the appropriate color well and choose the No Color button. When you select the No Color button, the color chip displays the checkerboard pattern used to depict transparency in Fireworks.

**Note** The No Color button is only available on the Fireworks color picker pop-ups called from the Stroke and Fill color wells found on the Toolbox and the Color Mixer.

## Using the Swatches panel

The Swatches panel is deceptively simple in appearance. Consisting of just colors (with the exception of the Options pop-up button), the Swatches panel enables you to choose a stroke, fill, or effect color from the active palette. Like all other Fireworks floating panels, the Swatches panel can be moved and resized — the latter feature is especially important to show a larger palette.

**Note** It's important to remember that the Swatches panel displays the current Fireworks palette, not the palette of the current document.

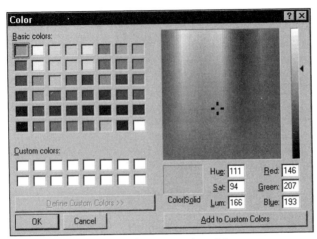

**Figure 7-10:** In the Windows OS color picker, you can either select from 48 standard colors or find your own from the available full spectrum.

The most basic use of the Swatches panel is similar to the Color Mixer and the color picker pop-up. Select the color well you want to alter and then choose a color by clicking any of the color chips in the Swatches panel, as shown in Figure 7-11. There's no real feedback on the Swatches panel to identify the color other than visually; you'd need to have the Info panel visible to see the RGB or other components.

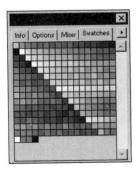

**Figure 7-11:** Pick a color, any color, from the Swatches panel.

As you'll see in the next section, you can choose from a number of preset color palettes. However, you can also add any custom mixed color — or color selected with the Eyedropper — to a swatch. This custom color then becomes available from anywhere in the program where you can click a color well or access the Swatch panel. New colors can either be added, extending an existing palette or replacing a color on the palette. You can also delete standard or custom colors from a palette.

To add, replace, or remove a color on the Swatches panel, follow these steps:

1. Mix or sample the color you want to add so that it appears in the active color well.

2. Display the Swatches panel by choosing Window ⇨ Swatches or clicking the Swatches tab if the panel is behind others in a group.

3. To add a new color to the current palette, position your pointer over an open area in the Swatches panel and click once. When over an open area, the Eyedropper pointer becomes a paint bucket.

4. To replace an existing color in the current palette, hold the Shift key while you position your pointer over the color to be replaced and click once. When you press the Shift key when the pointer is positioned over existing colors, the pointer becomes a paint bucket.

5. To remove a color from the current palette, hold the Ctrl (Command) key down, position the pointer over the color to be deleted, and click once. When you press the Ctrl (Command) key, the pointer becomes a pair of scissors. For best results, position the scissors so that the crossing of the blades — the middle of the X — is placed directly over the color you want to delete.

To reset any standard palette that has been modified, select that palette from the Options pop-up.

### Picking preset swatches

Fireworks has four standard palettes that you can select at any time:

✦ **Web 216 Palette:** Colors common between both major browsers, Netscape Navigator and Internet Explorer, on the various platforms

✦ **Windows System:** The colors palette used by Windows to display its system elements

✦ **Macintosh System:** The color palette used by the Macintosh operating system

✦ **Grayscale:** A monochrome palette from white to black

All palettes with the exception of Web 216 are composed of 256 colors.

To switch palettes, choose the Options pop-up from the Swatches panel. When the option list shown in Figure 7-12 appears, select one of the four palettes.

There's one additional palette available from the Options pop-up: the Current Export palette. When a graphic is exported, generally as a GIF or JPEG, you have an option to limit the number of colors used to reduce file size. Fireworks 2 offers a great number of special controls over colors at export time, including locking and transparency. Once you have completed any export operations — or saved any settings as defaults — the Current Export palette becomes available as an option. If selected, whatever colors were last used to export an image becomes the active palette.

**Figure 7-12:** The Options pop-up from the Swatches panel enables you to select different standard palettes or load your own.

## Managing swatches

The real power of Fireworks's swatches comes with its capability to load and store custom palettes. The remaining five commands on the Options pop-up are dedicated to managing swatches. Fireworks can load and save palettes in a format known as Active Color Table (ACT). Adobe Photoshop also can read and write ACT files. It's very easy to load Photoshop palettes in Fireworks.

However, you don't have to save your palettes as ACT files to work with them in the Swatch panel. Fireworks can also glean the palette from any GIF or other 8-bit indexed color file. Moreover, you have two different ways to access a previously stored palette. You can either append the saved palette to the current swatch or you can use just the saved palette.

To load palettes into the Swatches panel, follow these steps:

1. From the Swatches panel, select the Option pop-up button.

2. If you want to extend the existing palette with a new one, choose Add Swatches.

3. If you want to use the just saved palette, choose Replace Swatches.

   In either case, the Open dialog box appears for you to select a palette.

4. Choose the kind of palette you wish to load:

   - Color table (*.act)

   - GIF files (*.gif)

5. Locate the file and click Open when you're ready.

If you chose Add Swatches, the new palette is appended to the end of the existing Swatch. If Replace Swatches was added, the existing swatch is removed and the new palette is displayed in its place.

**Tip**

Although the feature is a bit hidden, you can also load Adobe Swatches in addition to Adobe Color Tables in Windows. Adobe Swatches have a file extension of .aco rather than the Color Tables extension of act. Fireworks only offers the ACT file type in its Open dialog boxes. However, you can, in Windows, enter **\*.aco** in the File Name text box and press Return. This forces the Open dialog box to list all the files with the desired extension, .aco.

In Fireworks, all palettes are saved in Active Color Table format. To save a current swatch, simply choose Save Swatches from the Options pop-up and name the file in the standard Save As dialog box.

If the Swatch panel is no longer desired, you can erase the entire palette by choosing Clear Swatches for the Options pop-up. This completely removes any palette displayed in the Swatches panel, but it doesn't affect the default palettes at all. If you do issue the Clear Swatches command, the color wells revert to using the default Web-safe palette in the color picker pop-ups.

The final Options pop-up command in the Swatches panel is Sort by Color. As the name implies, Sort by Color displays the active palette by color value rather than the default mathematical order. If new colors have been added — or a completely new palette loaded — those colors are sorted as well. Please note that there is no way to undo a Sort by Color command; to restore standard palette to their previous configuration, choose the particular palette from the Options pop-up.

# Fireworks Technique: Converting Pantone Colors to Web-Safe Colors

Many Web designers have clients with very specific concerns regarding the use of their logos, trademarks, and other brand identifiers. Many larger companies have spent large amounts of money to develop a distinct look in their print, television, and other media advertising and marketing — and they want to ensure that that look continues over the Internet. Most designers work with a set series of colors — Pantone colors are among the most popular — that can be specified for print work. It will come as no surprise to discover that many of these colors fall outside of the Web-safe palette of 216 colors.

There is a way, however, to bring the two seemingly divergent worlds together. In fact, there are several ways. Pantone makes a product called ColorWeb Pro that converts their colors so they are usable in computer graphics. ColorWeb Pro is a small utility that enables you to look up a Pantone color by number and then displays a color chip with the equivalent RGB and/or HTML color values.

**On the CD-ROM** If you don't have ColorWeb Pro, but want to try out this technique, there's a trial version of the software, for both Macs and PCs, on the CD-ROM that accompanies this book in the Additional Software folder.

ColorWeb Pro runs in two modes: the Pantone Matching System, which provides keys to 1,012 colors, and Pantone Internet Color System, which limits selection to the 216 Web-safe color palette. If your client's all-important colors fall in the Web-safe range, count yourself lucky; you can use the colors pretty much anywhere in Fireworks. However, Fireworks new Web Dither fill opens up many of the other Pantone colors for use on the Internet where it counts the most — in the fill areas.

To convert a Pantone color to a Web-safe color in Fireworks, follow these steps:

1. Start ColorWeb Pro.

2. If you haven't already done so, right-click (hold-click) the Pantone color chip and enable Stay on Top from the shortcut menu. Because you'll be working with both Fireworks and ColorWeb Pro, you need to be able to see both programs simultaneously.

3. Double-click the Pantone color chip to display the Color Picker.

4. Locate the desired color either by entering its number in the Find Color text box or by visually selecting it. Click OK when you're done to return to the color chip.

5. In Fireworks, select the object you want to fill with a Pantone color.

6. Display the Fill panel by choosing Window ➪ Fill or using one of the alternative methods previously described.

7. Select the Fill color well arrow to open the pop-up color picker and choose the Eyedropper tool. Be sure to pick the main color well (the first one) and not either of the two dither color wells.

8. Use the Eyedropper to sample the Pantone color chip. Windows users must click the Eyedropper and drag it off the pop-up to sample colors outside of Fireworks.

   Fireworks calculates the closest match using the Web Dither technique, as shown in Figure 7-13. If the Pantone color is Web safe, both dither color wells hold the same color.

Though this system is not absolutely perfect — I occasionally find Pantone colors that do not have an exact duplicate in the Web Dither mode — it's darn close. In those cases, where the Fireworks and Pantone RGB values did not match precisely, I couldn't visually tell the difference.

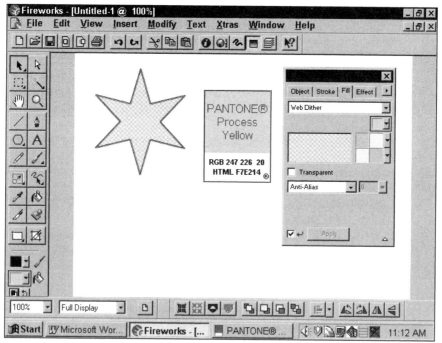

**Figure 7-13:** With ColorWeb Pro and Fireworks Web Dither fill, you can match Pantone colors for the Web.

# Summary

Fireworks offers very brisk color control, enabling the designer to select from the overall color model and specific palette that best serves. In Fireworks 2, color manipulation has been greatly simplified with the introduction of the pop-up color picker, available from any color well. As you begin to delve deeper into color with your Fireworks graphics, considers these points:

✦ RGB is the language of color for the screen. Pixels depend on a mixture of red, green, and blue to get their color variations.

✦ HTML uses hexadecimal notation to designate particular colors. Fireworks enables you to switch between several different color models, including Hexadecimal, RGB, and, from the realm of print, CMY.

✦ To ensure your colors appear the same regardless of which browser is used to view them, work with Web-safe colors. Fireworks enables you to choose a Web-safe palette to pick from or to snap selected colors to their nearest Web-safe equivalent.

✦ Fireworks uses two floating panels for color control: the Color Mixer and the Swatches panel. The Color Mixer enables the designer to specify a new custom color or modify an existing one. The Swatches panel displays a series of color chips that can come from a standard palette, like the Web 216 Palette or from a custom palette.

✦ The Eyedropper tool on the color picker pop-up can sample colors from any onscreen image, in Fireworks or another application.

✦ Fireworks lets you manage your palettes with commands to load, save, and clear swatches in the Options pop-up.

In the next chapter, you'll explore working with the fine lines of Fireworks graphics, strokes.

✦      ✦      ✦

# Choosing Strokes

✦ ✦ ✦ ✦

**In This Chapter**

Applying strokes

Mastering the Stroke panel

Working with the standard strokes

Creating custom strokes

Fireworks technique: building a dotted stroke

Working with graphic tablets

✦ ✦ ✦ ✦

**S**trokes are one of the three key features of a Fireworks graphic. Along with fills and effects, strokes can give each element of your graphic its own unique character. The stroke (known in Fireworks 1 as the brush) is what makes a path visible. It's far more than just "visibility," however — you can vary a stroke's width, color, softness, and shape, as well as control how it reacts to the speed, pressure, and direction of your drawing. Moreover, you can modify strokes already applied to any selected path and instantly see the results.

In addition to 48 built-in, standard strokes in Fireworks, you can customize your strokes with an almost infinite set of variations. Numerous options, such as color, stroke width, and edge softness, exist right on the Strokes panel for easy experimentation. Additionally, Fireworks enables you to completely custom build your own stroke from the ground up. You'll find explanations of all the controls in this chapter, as well as step-by-step instructions for developing special strokes such as dotted lines.

## Using the Stroke Panel

The Stroke panel is your control center for all stroke settings. Though you can set the stroke color in two other places, the Toolbox and the Color Mixer, the Stroke panel is the only place to select all the options.

Here's the typical process for setting up or modifying an existing stroke that uses all the options available on the Stroke panel:

1. Choose Window ➪ Stroke to open the Stroke panel (Figure 8-1). Alternatively, you can use the keyboard shortcut, Ctrl+Alt+B (Command+Option+B) or choose the Stroke tab, if it's onscreen.

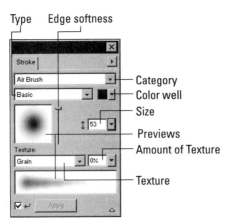

Type    Edge softness

Category
Color well
Size
Previews
Amount of Texture
Texture

**Figure 8-1:** Use the Stroke panel controls to modify the stroke for an existing path or establish one before you begin drawing.

2. Select one of the 11 categories from the Category option list. To turn off the stroke, select None from the Category option list.

3. Choose any of the available types listed for each category from the Type option list. When you choose a type, the default settings for that type's size, edge softness, and texture are also selected.

4. If desired, select a new color from the stroke color well.

5. To change how the stroke blends, use the Edge Softness slider.

6. Alter the size of the stroke by using the Size slider or entering a value directly in the Size text box. As you move the Edge Softness or Size slider, Fireworks previews the stroke. If the Apply check box is selected, any changes are instantly reflected on a selected path.

7. Add a texture by choosing one from the Texture option list and setting its opacity through the Amount of Texture slider.

As noted previously, you can either modify the stroke for an existing, selected path or you can set up the stroke before you draw. To select a path, with or without a stroke already applied, first move the Pointer tool over the desired path and click once on the highlighted path. The path displays a red highlight when it is capable of being selected and, by default, a light blue highlight when selected.

Tip

If your work uses the same or similar color that Fireworks uses for highlighting a chosen path, you can change it. Choose File ➪ Preferences and, on the General tab, select the Highlight color well to pick a different hue or shade.

Sometimes it's easier to select the path for stroke modification by using the marquee feature of the Pointer tool. If you click and drag the Pointer, a temporary rectangle is drawn out. Any paths touched by this rectangle are selected. The Pointer marquee is a great way to select multiple paths when you want to change the stroke settings for several paths simultaneously. Alternatively, pressing Shift enables you to select multiple paths, one at a time, with the Pointer tool.

**Tip** You can quickly switch to the Pointer tool from any other tool, by pressing and holding Ctrl (Command). When you release this keyboard shortcut, the previously selected tool returns.

When you're setting up your next stroke, be sure that no path or object is selected — otherwise, that path will be modified as well if AutoApply is enabled. Use the Pointer to click on an empty canvas area or choose Edit ⇨ Select None — or its keyboard equivalent, Ctrl+D (Command+D) — to clear any previous selections.

## Stroke categories and types

With the None option, Fireworks 2 offers an even dozen different stroke categories. From the simplest, Pencil and Basic, to the most outrageous, Random and Unnatural, the stroke categories run the gamut, as evident in Figure 8-2. When you select a category, that category's types become available, with the first one in an alphabetical list chosen.

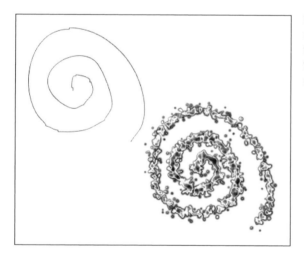

**Figure 8-2:** Choose any of the preset stroke types — from the most basic Pencil to the farthest out Unnatural Fluid Splatter.

The standard strokes are covered in detail later in this chapter, but two primary factors apply to all the basic strokes. First, when a particular stroke category and type are selected, the default settings for that stroke are selected — even if you just modified it seconds ago and are returning from trying out another stroke. Second, every facet of all of the standard strokes can be modified, altered, and adjusted.

Later in this chapter, in the section "Creating New Strokes," you'll see how to store and re-use a modified stroke.

## Stroke edge and size

If you're reading this book in sequence, you've already discovered the concept of feathering as it relates to bitmapped images in Chapter 6. As you'll remember, a feathered edge is one that blends into the background. Strokes can be "feathered" as well as images through the Edge Softness slider found on the Stroke panel. Moving the slider all the way to the bottom creates the hardest edge, with no blending, whereas sliding it all the way to the top creates the softest edge, with maximum blending for the current stroke size.

As in feathering, the edge softness is actually an application of the alpha channel, which controls transparency. There are 256 degrees of transparency in the alpha channel and only 100 degrees of edge softness, but the overall control is similar. Although you can select any degree of softness from the full range for any stroke, you won't see much of a difference if the stroke is thin. The thicker the stroke, the more softness variations are apparent. At the softest setting, Fireworks maintains roughly two-thirds of the stroke size the object's opacity and the other one-third is blended into transparency equally on either side of the stroke.

You change the thickness of a stroke either by using the Size slider or by entering a value in the Size text box; the range of possible values extends from 1 to 100 pixels wide. The thickness of the stroke is previewed in the Stroke panel. The top preview panel is not big enough to show stroke widths over 53 pixels; you'll notice a value appears indicating the actual width for strokes between 54 and 100 pixels, as shown in Figure 8-3.

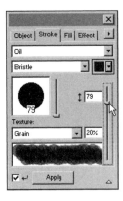

**Figure 8-3:** When you select a stroke size larger than 53 pixels, Fireworks displays a numeric reminder.

## Stroke texture

Applying texture to a stroke can give a line true character and depth. Fireworks 2 comes with 26 standard textures built-in and a library of 21 more on the CD-ROM. Each of these textures can be applied to any stroke with a variable degree of intensity. Some of the preset strokes, such as the Textured Airbrush or the Basic Crayon, use a texture.

To apply a texture to a stroke, follow these steps:

1. On the Stroke panel, select the category and type of stroke to which you want to apply the texture.

2. If necessary, set the size, color, and edge softness for the stroke. Note: Many textures will not be apparent if the stroke width is too small.

3. Choose a texture from the Texture option list.

4. Set a degree of intensity for the Texture from the Amount of Texture slider. You can also enter a percentage value (with or without the  percent sign) into the Amount of Texture text box. Please note: you must enter a percentage value greater than 0 percent or no texture will be visible.

Textures, in effect, are image patterns that are overlaid on top of the stroke. The Amount of Texture controls how transparent or opaque those textures become. At 0 percent, the texture is completely transparent and, for all intents and purposes, off; at 100 percent, the texture is as visible as possible. Figure 8-4 displays the same stroke with several variations of a single texture. As a general rule, textures containing highly contrasting elements show up better, whereas those with less contrast are more subtle.

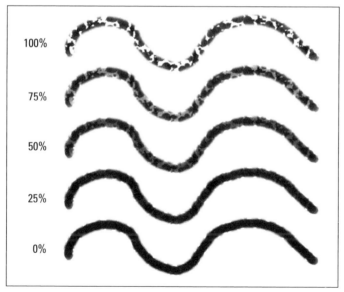

**Figure 8-4:** The higher the amount of texture, the more visible the texture becomes.

Can't get enough of those fabulous textures? You'll find another 50 courtesy of Massimo Foti and the Fantastic Corporation on this book's CD-ROM, in the Textures folder.

# Working with the Built-in Strokes

One of the key advantages of Fireworks's preset strokes is speed—just pick one and go. The other main advantage is consistency. You can use the Textured Airbrush time and again and you'll always get the same effect. Even if you prefer to work only with custom strokes, you generally begin the creation process with one of the standard ones.

This section explores each of the stroke categories and the different presets each one offers. Fireworks starts the stroke categories with two of the simplest, Pencil and Basic. After these, the list proceeds alphabetically from Airbrush to Unnatural. The overall impression, however, is that the more often-used standard strokes are found at the top of the list, and the more elaborate decorative strokes at the end.

## Pencil

When you start to draw with the Pencil tool, the path is rendered in the Pencil 1-Pixel Hard stroke, regardless of any previous stroke settings for other tools. If fact, if you use the Brush and no stroke settings have been established, you get the same Pencil stroke. You might say that the Pencil is one of the real workhorses of the preset strokes.

The Pencil is a fairly generic stroke, intended to give a simple representation to any path without any embellishments. You can see the differences between its four presets, listed in Table 8-1, in Figure 8-5. The 1-Pixel Soft Pencil stroke anti-aliases the path to avoid the jaggies that may be apparent with the 1-Pixel Hard setting. The Colored Pencil, at four pixels, is slightly wider and is designed to lighten with increased pressure and speed. The final preset, Graphite, is also affected by the pressure and speed at which the paths are drawn; in addition, a high degree of texture is added to further break up the stroke.

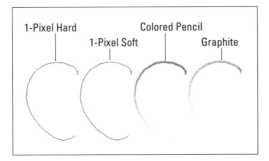

**Figure 8-5:** The 1-Pixel Hard and 1-Pixel Soft strokes remain constant when drawn, but the Colored Pencil and Graphite strokes are affected by pressure and speed.

| Table 8-1 Pencil Type Attributes | | | | |
|---|---|---|---|---|
| **Name** | **Size** | **Edge Softness** | **Texture** | **Amount of Texture** |
| 1-Pixel Hard | 1 | 0 percent | None | n/a |
| 1-Pixel Soft | 1 | 0 percent | None | n/a |
| Colored Pencil | 4 | 0 percent | None | n/a |
| Graphite | 4 | 0 percent | Grain | 80 percent |

## Basic

Another, slightly heavier variation of the simple path is the appropriately named Basic stroke. All of the Basic presets, detailed in Table 8-2, are 4 pixels wide and vary only with the basic shape of the line (square or round) and its anti-alias setting. Hard Line and Hard Line Rounded are not anti-aliased, whereas both Soft Line and Soft Line Rounded are. The variations are subtle, but easier to see in the magnified comparison shown in Figure 8-6.

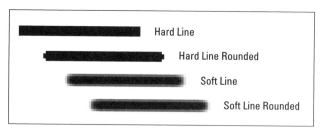

**Figure 8-6:** You can see the differences between the four Basic stroke types far easier in this 400 percent view.

| Table 8-2 Basic Type Attributes | | | | |
|---|---|---|---|---|
| **Name** | **Size** | **Edge Softness** | **Texture** | **Amount of Texture** |
| Hard Line | 4 | 0 percent | None | n/a |
| Hard Line Rounded | 4 | 0 percent | None | n/a |
| Soft Line | 4 | 0 percent | None | n/a |
| Soft Line Rounded | 4 | 0 percent | None | n/a |

## Airbrush

I'll fess up—I'm an airbrush addict. I can't get enough of the variations that Fireworks's Airbrush offers. Both presets (Table 8-3) are very sensitive to changes in speed and pressure, plus—like a real airbrush—the ink builds up if you stay in one spot, as seen in Figure 8-7. The Textured Airbrush is significantly different from the Basic Airbrush and offers a good example of what's possible when applying a texture to a stroke.

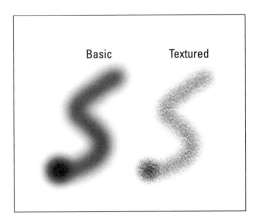

**Figure 8-7:** The difference between the two Airbrush presets is quite noticeable, as is the build-up on each at the end of the two strokes.

| Table 8-3 | | | | |
|---|---|---|---|---|
| **Airbrush Type Attributes** | | | | |
| *Name* | *Size* | *Edge Softness* | *Texture* | *Amount of Texture* |
| Basic | 60 | 100 percent | None | n/a |
| Textured | 50 | 100 percent | Grain | 80 percent |

## Calligraphy

Calligraphy is an elegant handwriting art where the thickness of the stroke varies as the line curves. The Calligraphy stroke in Fireworks offers five variations on this theme, as detailed in Table 8-4 and shown in Figure 8-8. Only the Bamboo preset does not create distinct thick-and-thin curved lines—that's because all the others use a slanted brush, whereas Bamboo's brush is circular, like a bamboo stalk. The Quill preset is pressure- and speed-sensitive and, along with the Ribbon and Wet presets, builds up the ink as it rounds a curve, emphasizing the angles.

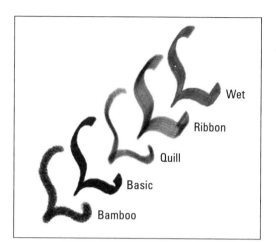

**Figure 8-8:** Great lettering possibilities is a hallmark of the Calligraphy stroke.

Wet

Ribbon

Quill

Basic

Bamboo

Table 8-4
**Calligraphy Type Attributes**

| Name | Size | Edge Softness | Texture | Amount of Texture |
|------|------|---------------|---------|-------------------|
| Bamboo | 20 | 0 percent | Grain | 50 percent |
| Basic | 14 | 0 percent | None | n/a |
| Quill | 20 | 20 percent | Grain | 25 percent |
| Ribbon | 25 | 0 percent | None | n/a |
| Wet | 20 | 0 percent | None | n/a |

# Charcoal

The Charcoal strokes are notable for their texture, both within the stroke itself and on its edges. As you can see in Table 8-5, each preset uses some degree of Grain texture. The Creamy and Pastel presets vary according to a stroke's pressure and speed — Creamy more so than Pastel. The key difference with the Soft preset is that the size of the brush changes randomly as you draw — the width fluctuates from a maximum of 20 to a minimum of 5 pixels. Figure 8-9 shows a side-by-side comparison of the Charcoal presets.

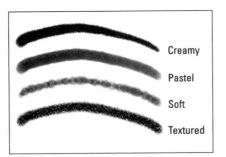

**Figure 8-9:** The Charcoal strokes offer a range of rough textures.

Creamy

Pastel

Soft

Textured

Table 8-5
**Charcoal Type Attributes**

| Name | Size | Edge Softness | Texture | Amount of Texture |
|------|------|---------------|---------|-------------------|
| Creamy | 20 | 0 percent | Grain | 16 percent |
| Pastel | 20 | 0 percent | Grain | 24 percent |
| Soft | 20 | 20 percent | Grain | 30 percent |
| Textured | 20 | 60 percent | Grain | 85 percent |

# Crayon

Kids can never understand why their parents like to draw with crayons as much as they do. The Crayon stroke in Fireworks captures that broken edge that gives real-world crayons character. The three Crayon presets are interesting to compare; if you look at the samples in Figure 8-10 and their details in Table 8-6, you'll see an obvious anomaly. The Rake preset has the smallest stroke size, but actually appears slightly thicker than both the Basic and Thick preset. This difference is because the Rake preset uses multiple tips — four to be precise; it's as if you were drawing with four crayons at the same time. This is what combines the overlapping lines with one tip extending on the end.

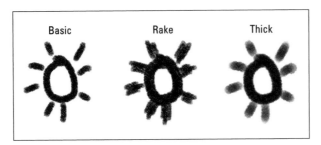

Basic        Rake        Thick

**Figure 8-10:** Return to your childhood — this time with scientific precision — through the Crayon strokes.

| Table 8-6 Crayon Type Attributes | | | | |
|---|---|---|---|---|
| **Name** | **Size** | **Edge Softness** | **Texture** | **Amount of Texture** |
| Basic | 12 | 0 percent | Grain | 65 percent |
| Rake | 8 | 0 percent | Grain | 65 percent |
| Thick | 20 | 0 percent | Grain | 20 percent |

## Felt Tip

I've placed the four presets for the Felt Tip stroke over a photograph in Figure 8-11 so you can see the different degrees of transparency that they offer. Both the Highlighter and the Light Marker presets are largely transparent, whereas the Dark Marker and Thin presets are not. The Light Marker also uses a slightly softer edge than the other presets, as noted in Table 8-7.

**Figure 8-11:** The various Felt Tip strokes over other graphics or images achieve transparent and opaque effects.

| | | Table 8-7 | | |
| | | **Felt Tip Type Attributes** | | |
| *Name* | *Size* | *Edge Softness* | *Texture* | *Amount of Texture* |
| --- | --- | --- | --- | --- |
| Dark Marker | 8 | 0 percent | None | n/a |
| Highlighter | 16 | 0 percent | None | n/a |
| Light Marker | 12 | 5 percent | None | n/a |
| Thin | 4 | 0 percent | None | n/a |

# Oil

When you look at the comparison of the five Oil stroke presets in Figure 8-12, it's hard to believe that the second one, Broad Splatter, is a single stroke. Although the size for the Broad Splatter is only ten pixels — the same as the Bristle and Splatter presets as shown in Table 8-8 — the larger width is because it uses two tips instead of one and they're spaced 500 percent apart. In other words, the Broad Splatter preset can be five times the width of its pixel size. All but the Splatter preset use multiple tips as well, but because they're set to be less than 100 percent apart, the stroke appears as a single line.

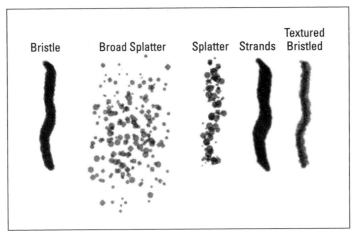

**Figure 8-12:** Looking for a stroke that doesn't look like a line? Try the Oil Splatter and Oil Broad Splatter presets.

| Name | Size | Edge Softness | Texture | Amount of Texture |
|------|------|---------------|---------|-------------------|
| **Table 8-8** | | | | |
| **Oil Type Attributes** | | | | |
| Bristle | 10 | 0 percent | Grain | 20 percent |
| Broad Splatter | 10 | 0 percent | Grain | 30 percent |
| Splatter | 10 | 0 percent | Grain | 30 percent |
| Strands | 8 | 43 percent | None | n/a |
| Textured Bristles | 7 | 0 percent | Grain | 50 percent |

## Watercolor

Like any of the pressure- and speed-sensitive strokes, you can't get a true Watercolor feel if you draw using one of the geometric shapes or the Pen. You have to use a freeform tool such as the Brush to achieve the more realistic look apparent in Figure 8-13. The Thin preset especially appears to run out of ink when completing a stroke. Both the Heavy and Thick presets are quite transparent and blend well when applied over an image because of their relatively soft edge (Table 8-9).

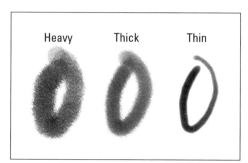

**Figure 8-13:** Watercolor strokes blend well and fade naturally due to the pressure and speed sensitivity.

| Table 8-9<br>**Watercolor Type Attributes** | | | | |
|---|---|---|---|---|
| *Name* | *Size* | *Edge Softness* | *Texture* | *Amount of Texture* |
| Heavy | 50 | 50 percent | Grain | 30 percent |
| Thick | 40 | 70 percent | Grain | 5 percent |
| Thin | 15 | 25 percent | None | n/a |

# Random

So much for natural media—it's time to create strokes that only a computer can create. In addition to the varying sizes, edge softness, and textures shown in Table 8-10, the Random strokes also change the shape of the brush and the color of the resulting stroke. The basic brush shape is evident in both the Random preset names—Dots, Fur, Squares, and Yarn—and in the sample strokes shown in Figure 8-14, but you'll have to turn to Color Plate 8-1 to really see the color variations. The Confetti preset is the most colorful and Dots is the least, but all the Random strokes exhibit some changing hues.

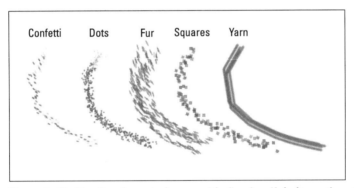

**Figure 8-14:** The Random strokes provide five fanciful alternatives to natural media strokes.

| Table 8-10<br>**Random Type Attributes** | | | | |
|---|---|---|---|---|
| *Name* | *Size* | *Edge Softness* | *Texture* | *Amount of Texture* |
| Confetti | 6 | 25 percent | None | n/a |
| Dots | 3 | 20 percent | None | n/a |

| Name | Size | Edge Softness | Texture | Amount of Texture |
|------|------|---------------|---------|-------------------|
| Fur | 10 | 0 percent | None | n/a |
| Squares | 5 | 0 percent | Grain | 20 percent |
| Yarn | 8 | 0 percent | None | n/a |

# Unnatural

I think it's a pretty safe bet that the Unnatural strokes were developed in a, shall we say, party-like atmosphere. How else do you explain the messiness of Fluid Splatter or the glow-in-the-dark feel to Toxic Waste — not to mention the otherworldliness of Viscous Alien Paint? No matter how they were developed, I find myself returning to them time and again when I need a unique and distinctive look for my graphics. As you can see in Table 8-11, all the presets are roughly the same size with the exception of Chameleon. Several of the strokes have a transparent area: 3D Glow, Fluid Splatter, Outline, Paint Splatter, and Toxic Waste. Although you can get a sense of the preset variations from Figure 8-15, you'll have to turn to Color Plate 8-2 to see the Unnatural strokes in all their glory.

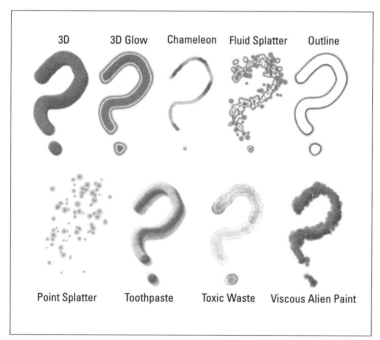

**Figure 8-15:** The Unnatural strokes provide an offbeat alternative to Fireworks's natural media strokes.

Table 8-11
**Unnatural Type Attributes**

| Name | Size | Edge Softness | Texture | Amount of Texture |
|------|------|---------------|---------|-------------------|
| 3D | 20 | 12 percent | None | n/a |
| 3D Glow | 19 | 100 percent | None | n/a |
| Chameleon | 6 | 0 percent | Grain | 31 percent |
| Fluid Splatter | 12 | 100 percent | None | n/a |
| Outline | 19 | 100 percent | None | n/a |
| Paint Splatter | 12 | 100 percent | None | n/a |
| Toothpaste | 18 | 50 percent | None | n/a |
| Toxic Waste | 18 | 100 percent | None | n/a |
| Viscous Alien Paint | 12 | 30 percent | None | n/a |

# Creating New Strokes

What, the standard 48 strokes aren't enough? You need a slightly smaller Airbrush or a Calligraphy stroke with more texture? What about a dashed or dotted line instead of a solid one? Fear not, in Fireworks 2, custom strokes are just a click or two away. Not only can you store your minor adjustments as new strokes, you can completely alter existing strokes and save them as well, either with the document or through Fireworks 2's new Styles feature.

This section is divided into two parts. The first explains how to manage your strokes so that you always have the ones you need available. The second part delves into the somewhat complex, but altogether addictive, option of editing your strokes.

## Managing your strokes

Stroke management is handled through the Stroke panel Options pop-up shown in Figure 8-16. When you choose this arrow button, five menu commands appear:

✦ **Save Stroke As:** Stores the current stroke under a new name within the active document

✦ **Edit Stroke:** Displays the Edit Stroke dialog box, covered in detail later in this chapter

✦ **Delete Stroke:** Removes the current stroke, custom or standard, from the Stroke panel

**Caution**  Use the Delete Stroke command carefully—although Fireworks asks for confirmation, you can't undo removing a stroke.

✦ **Rename Stroke:** Relabels the current stroke

✦ **Auto Apply:** Automatically applies changes made in the Stroke panel to any selected stroke

To store a modified stroke, follow these steps:

1. Modify any existing stroke by changing the Edge Softness, Size, Texture, and/or Amount of Texture. The stroke color is not stored as part of the stroke.

2. Choose the Options pop-up and select Save Stroke As. The Save Brush As dialog box appears. Fireworks 1 users will remember that strokes were previously known as brushes.

3. Enter a unique name for the stroke. If you choose a name already in use, Fireworks asks if you want to replace the existing brush.

4. After entering a new name, choose Save. The new stroke name is displayed alphabetically in the Type list options of the active Stroke category.

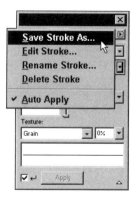

**Figure 8-16:** Manage your strokes through the Strokes panel Options pop-up.

It's important to understand that any new or modified strokes are stored within the document in which they're used. The newly defined stroke will always be available for use in the document in which it was stored, even if no paths currently employ it. To use the stroke in another document, follow these steps:

1. Open the document containing the stroke you want to use.

2. Select a path using the new stroke. If no path currently uses the stroke, draw a temporary one and select it.

3. Open the new document in which you want to use the new stroke.

4. Copy the selected path to the new document either by using the Edit ➪ Copy and Edit ➪ Paste or by dragging and dropping the path from one document to the other while pressing Alt (Option). The new stroke setting is added to the Strokes panel when the path containing the stroke is pasted into the document.

5. If desired, delete the copied path from the new document.

You can achieve the same effect of transferring strokes from one document to another several other ways:

✦ Use Insert ➪ Image to insert a document containing one or more custom strokes. After you've clicked once to place the document, choose Undo. The graphics will vanish, but all custom strokes will be incorporated into the Strokes panel. With this technique, only custom strokes actually applied to paths are transferred.

✦ Copy the path with the custom stroke in one document and just paste the attributes to a path in the new document by selecting that path and choosing Edit ➪ Paste Attributes.

Perhaps the best way to always be sure your custom strokes are available is to use the Styles feature, new in Fireworks 2. To create a new style using a custom stroke, follow these steps:

1. Select a path that uses the custom stroke.

2. If necessary, choose Window ➪ Styles, use the keyboard shortcut, Ctrl+Alt+J (Command+Option+J), or click the Style tab, if visible. The Style panel displays.

3. On the Style panel, select the New Style button. The Edit Style dialog box displays, as shown in Figure 8-17.

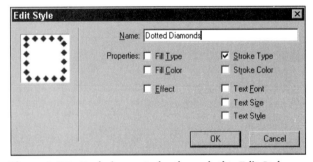

**Figure 8-17:** Declaring a stroke through the Edit Style dialog box stores the stroke definition for easy access from all Fireworks documents.

4. In the Edit Style dialog box, enter a descriptive name for your stroke in the Name text box and deselect all checkboxes except Stroke Type.

5. Click OK when you're done. A new style is entered in the Style panel.

Any style added in the fashion just described is always available for any Fireworks document. To apply the stroke, just highlight any Fireworks path object and select the new style. Your custom stroke is then added to the Stroke panel.

 **Cross-Reference** To find out more about the powerful Styles feature, see Chapter 17.

## Editing the stroke

Whereas you can make certain modifications through the Strokes panel, if you really want to customize your strokes, you have to use the Edit Strokes dialog box. Although the array of choices the dialog box offers can be a bit overwhelming, once you understand how to achieve certain effects, creating new strokes becomes easy, fun, and very compelling.

You can access the Edit Strokes dialog box one of two ways:

✦ Choose the Options pop-up button from the Strokes panel and then select Edit Strokes from the menu.

✦ Double-click the Strokes panel top preview where the stroke shape is displayed.

The Edit Strokes panel is divided into three tabs: Options, Shape, and Sensitivity. Each of the tabs contains a preview panel that updates after every change is made. If you have selected a stroke prior to opening the Edit Strokes panel, you can see the effect by using its Apply button.

 **Caution** In my explorations of the Edit Strokes dialog box, I uncovered one technique that worked differently than I expected. First, if you make a change to a stroke without selecting a path, the change does not register. Always select a path, even a temporary one, before you create a custom stroke.

### The Options tab

The Options tab hosts a number of general, but very important, attributes. In addition to providing controls for familiar parameters such as the stroke's degree of texture and opacity, the Options tab, as shown in Figure 8-18, also holds the key to affecting the tightness of the stroke, how it reacts over time, and what, if any, edge effect is employed.

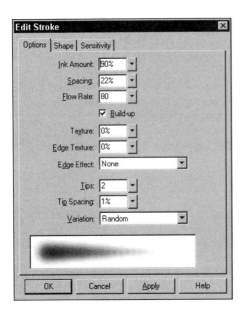

**Figure 8-18:** The Options tab of the Edit Strokes dialog box contains many key controls.

### Ink Amount

The first stroke attribute on the Option tab is Ink Amount. Generally this parameter is set at 100 percent, but lowering it is a possibility for any stroke. The Ink Amount value is responsible for a stroke's opacity: 100 percent is completely opaque, and 0 percent is completely transparent.  Figure 8-19 shows how a standard stroke such as the Calligraphy Quill is affected when the Ink Amount is reduced to 50 percent.

**Figure 8-19:** Reducing the Ink Amount of a stroke reduces its opacity.

You can also alter an object's overall opacity through the Object panel, but changing just the Ink Amount value alters just the stroke. Combine the two and the effect is additive; if, for example, you see a stroke's Ink Amount at 50 percent and you reduce the opacity of the path object to 50 percent, the stroke would appear to be 25 percent opaque (as half of 50 percent is 25 percent). The Felt Tip Highlighter preset is a good example of a stroke that uses a reduced Ink Amount to obtain transparency.

### Spacing

Technically, each stroke is made up of a long series of *stroke stamps*. A *stamp* is the smallest unit of a stroke; you can see it by selecting a stroke and the Brush tool and then clicking the mouse once, without moving. As you draw with the Brush or other tool, one stamp after another is laid down. How close those stamps are to each other is determined by the Spacing attribute. As detailed later in this chapter, you can create dotted lines by changing the Spacing value.

**Note**    If you try to modify the Pencil 1-Pixel strokes or any of the Basic strokes, you'll find that no matter what you do, you won't be able to enable the Spacing or Flow Rate options. These strokes actually use a different rendering engine than all the other strokes, which sacrifices spacing and flow control to gain pinpoint pixel accuracy. To see the effects of changing either the Spacing or Flow Rate options, edit any other brush.

The Spacing value ranges from 0 percent to 1000 percent. When the Spacing attribute is set at 100 percent, stroke stamps in a straight line are positioned directly next to each other. If the Spacing is less than 100 percent, the stamps are overlaid on top of one another; if the Spacing is greater than 100 percent, the stamps are separated from one another. Strokes with a soft edge, like the Airbrush, appear to be separated even when the Spacing is set to less than 100 percent, but this is only because the soft edge is incorporated into the stroke stamp. The effect in Figure 8-20 is achieved by applying a standard Airbrush stroke where the Spacing is adjusted from 20 percent to 50 percent to a spiral.

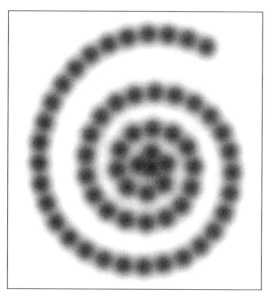

**Figure 8-20:** Create dotted line patterns by increasing the Spacing value.

**Caution** There's a known problem with the Spacing slider on the Edit Stroke dialog box. If you choose the slider arrow, the Spacing value jumps to almost ten times its current setting; for example if the Spacing is set to 50 percent and you select the slider arrow, Spacing changes to 485 percent. Though you can pull the slider back down, I always find it easier to enter the Spacing value manually in the appropriate text box.

### Flow Rate and Build-up

Most stroke settings alter how the stroke changes as it's drawn across the screen — distance, in other words. The Flow Rate value, however, affects the stroke over time and not distance. The Airbrush category is the best example of the use of Flow Rate, and is, in fact, the only type of stroke that can take advantage of this attribute. The Flow Rate percentage value represents how fast the ink sprays; the higher the number, the faster the spray. Both preset Airbrushes, Basic and Textured, use a fairly high percentage, 80 percent.

 **Caution** At present, the Flow Rate value cannot be changed for any stroke, even the Airbrush.

The Build-up option is another way of affecting a stroke's opacity. If Build-up is enabled, as with the Felt Tip Highlighter preset, for example, and the stroke crosses itself as in Figure 8-21, you'll notice a darker area at the overlap of the stroke. If you disable the Build-up option, the Highlighter has a much flatter, monochrome appearance.

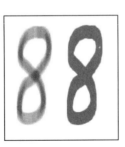

**Figure 8-21:** The normal Felt Tip Highlighter stroke on the left has the Build-up feature enabled; the stroke on the right does not.

### Texture, Edge Texture, and Edge Effect

The Texture setting in the Edit Stroke dialog box is reflected on the Stroke panel as the Amount of Texture value. Increase the Texture value to make the chosen texture more visible on the opaque portion of the stroke; a value of 0 percent effectively turns off the texture.

 **Caution** The type of texture cannot be specified from within the Edit Stroke dialog box; but must be set through the Stroke panel. Whereas the texture type is saved with the stroke when the Save Stroke As command is selected, if another texture type is chosen temporarily, the original texture does not reappear when the custom stroke is reselected. Reload the document with the saved stroke to establish the custom texture settings again.

Just as the Texture value causes the chosen texture to appear over the opaque portion of the stroke, the Edge Texture setting causes the texture to appear over the transparent portion. Remember that in Fireworks, edge softness is created by affecting the stroke's alpha channels or transparency. By increasing the Edge Texture and lowering the Texture value, as with the lower stroke in Figure 8-22, the soft edge of the stroke is textured more noticeably than the center.

**Figure 8-22:** The top path was stroked with a standard Textured Charcoal stroke where the Texture is set at 85 percent and the Edge Texture at 35 percent; the bottom stroke reversed the texture settings so that the edge is more textured.

**Note**     Edge Texture values, no matter how high, won't be effectively visible if the Edge Softness is at 0 percent.

In addition to altering an edge's texture, you can also create a different Edge Effect. Technically speaking, the five Edge Effects are created by applying an algorithm affecting the alpha channel for both the stroke and its edge. In this case, descriptions are a poor second to a visual representation of the intriguingly named Edge Effects shown in Figure 8-23. Because Edge Effects rely on the transparency of the stroke's edge, you can't apply an Edge Effect to a stroke with a 0 percent Edge Softness value.

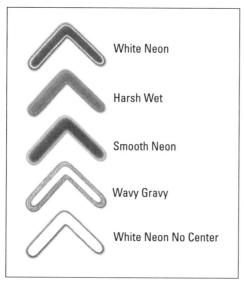

White Neon

Harsh Wet

Smooth Neon

Wavy Gravy

White Neon No Center

**Figure 8-23:** The five preset Edge Effects combine both stroke and edge transparency.

### Tips, Tip Spacing, and Variations

Have you ever drawn with a fistful of colored pencils or noticed, too late, that your paint brush has dried with the bristles separated? In each case, the result is a series of separate strokes that curve and move together. In Fireworks jargon, each pencil or separate bristle is referred to as a *tip* and is determined by the Tips attribute. Every stroke must have at least one and can have as many as ten tips.

**Note**   For either the Tip Spacing or Variations attribute to become active, you must have more than one Tip.

Whether the number of tips is apparent or not is determined primarily by the Tip Spacing attribute. Similar to the Spacing parameter, Tip Spacing is set in a range from 0 percent (where each tip is drawn on top of one another) to 1000 percent (where each tip is as far apart as possible). You can see the results of an extreme experiment in Figure 8-24, where the Unnatural 3D stroke is set to use both five and ten Tips with a Tip Spacing of 1000 percent and a single star was drawn for each graphic.

**Figure 8-24:** Although it looks like these groups of stars were cloned, only a single star was used for each image; multiple tips and a wide Tip Spacing is the key to drawing many identical images with one stroke.

Variations are the final elements on the Options tab. When multiple tips are used, how the different tips are depicted is determined by which of the Variations are selected. Each of the Variations alter the color of the additional tips. The five Variations are

✦ **Random:** A new color is selected at random for each tip with each new stroke.

✦ **Uniform:** All tips use the base color selected in the Stroke color well.

✦ **Complimentary:** If the stroke uses two tips, one tip is displayed in the complimentary color (on the opposite side of an HLS (Hue, Lightness, Saturation) color wheel) of the base color. If more than two tips are specified, the additional tips are selected from evenly spaced hues between the initial complimentary colors.

✦ **Hue:** Multiple tips are presented in hues similar (plus or minus 5 percent on an HLS color wheel) to the stroke color.

✦ **Shadow:** Additional tips are shown in alternating lighter and darker shades of the stroke color (the Lightness).

## The Shape tab

Compared to the Object tab, the Shape tab of the Edit Strokes dialog box (Figure 8-25) is almost self-explanatory. Like the Strokes panel, it has two preview panes; the upper pane shows the stroke stamp and the lower pane shows a representation of the stroke over distance.

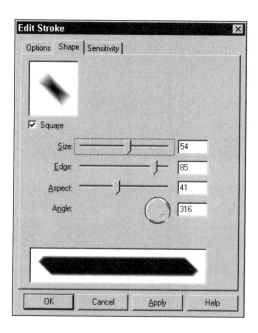

**Figure 8-25:** The look of the stroke stamp, and ultimately the stroke itself, is influenced by the attributes of the Shape tab.

In all, there are five parameters on the Shape tab:

✦ **Square:** When enabled, the Square option makes the stroke stamp square or rectangular according to the Aspect setting. If Square is disabled, the stroke stamp is circular or elliptical.

✦ **Size:** Sets the initial stroke width, in pixels, from 1 to 100. The value set here is displayed in Stroke panel.

✦ **Edge:** Determines the softness of the stroke's edge. This value is also reflected in the Stroke panel.

✦ **Aspect:** Sets the height to width aspect ratio. Values 0 and 100 make circles or squares — any other value creates rectangles or ellipses.

✦ **Angle:** Determines the angle of the stroke stamp. Values can be entered directly by hand or by dragging the dial in a circle.

You can achieve a wide range of different shapes by combining different parameters from the Shape tab. I've found the Aspect and Angle controls to be especially useful. For example, I was able to use them to create a diamond dotted stroke, as detailed later in this chapter.

## The Sensitivity tab

The Sensitivity tab of the Edit Strokes dialog box, shown in Figure 8-26, permits you to establish somewhat interactive controls for custom strokes. By altering your drawing pressure, speed, or direction, your strokes can assume different sizes, angles, opacities, or colors. You can even set up the stroke to alter any of its properties randomly.

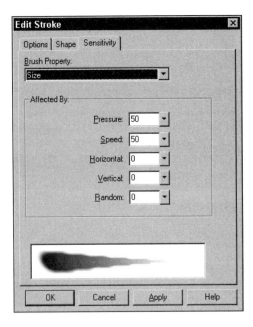

**Figure 8-26:** Create interactive strokes through the Sensitivity tab of the Edit Strokes dialog box.

The basic procedure for working in the Sensitivity tab is to select one of the stroke attributes from the Brush Properties option list and then setting the desired control found in the Affected By area. For example, if you wanted your stroke to shift colors when drawn across the document but not down it, you would choose Hue from the Brush Properties option list and set the Affected By Horizontal value to a high percentage value. The higher the value, the more impact the condition (Pressure, Speed, and so on) will have.

The seven stroke attributes are

✦ **Size:** When the Size property is affected, the stroke always gets smaller than the initial width, never larger. If the setting is at 50 percent, the stroke loses, at most, one-half of its size.

✦ **Angle:** The angle of the stroke stamp can be affected by as much as 90( when Angle property is selected and an Affected By value is set to its maximum, 100 percent.

✦ **Ink Amount:** As on the Options tab, Ink Amount refers to opacity. At the highest setting, the affecting condition can make the stroke completely transparent.

✦ **Scatter:** The amount of variance that stroke stamps are drawn away from the path. Scatter is really only effective with the Random condition.

✦ **Hue:** The color of the stroke. Multicolored strokes such as those in the Random category make great use of this property.

✦ **Lightness:** The amount of white in a color. To make a stroke fade the faster you draw, choose the Lightness property and increase the Speed condition.

✦ **Saturation:** The intensity of the color. The higher the value set in the condition, the more the Saturation is affected — actually lessened. A stroke with a high Speed setting for Saturation becomes grayer the faster the path is drawn.

The conditions that affect these properties each have a separate slider and text box for entering values directly:

✦ **Pressure:** The degree of pressure applied by a stylus used with a pressure-sensitive graphic tablet.

✦ **Speed:** The amount of speed used when the path is drawn either with a graphic tablet or the mouse.

✦ **Horizontal:** Drawing paths from left to right or vice versa.

✦ **Vertical:** Drawing paths from top to bottom or vice versa.

✦ **Random:** The selected property is affected without any additional input from the user.

The Affected By conditions can be used together. For example, setting Angle to be equally affected by both the Horizontal and Vertical conditions causes a stroke, such as Random Fur, to change direction as the path is drawn.

Generally, the Sensitivity tab settings tend to react more predictably with hand-drawn paths such as those created with the Brush tool than paths constructed with one of the geometric shapes, such as the Rectangle or Ellipse. However, experimentation is the key to uncovering unique effects with almost all of the Edit Stroke parameters and you have nothing to lose by trying a particular setting.

# Fireworks Technique: Making Dotted Lines

All the strokes in Fireworks's standard arsenal are more or less solid lines and nothing that can be used as a dotted line. Although there are a few exceptions — such as most of the Random presets — these tend to be too unconventional to use for a basic dotted line. As you've seen in the previous section, however, Fireworks offers you a tremendous degree of control in customizing your own strokes. The procedure for creating a dotted line is a fairly straightforward one and a good introduction to the world of custom stroke creation.

The key to creating a dotted line is in the Spacing control found on the Options tab of the Edit Stroke dialog box. When the Spacing value is 100 percent, each stroke stamp (the smallest component of a stroke) is right next to the one following it. If the value is less than 100 percent, the stroke stamps overlap and — here's the heart of the dotted line — when the value is greater than 100 percent, the stroke stamps are separated.

When creating any custom stroke, you want to start with one that's closest to your goal. Though either of the Basic or Pencil 1-Pixel strokes would be ideal, they are not useable for this modification. The key attribute necessary to creating the dotted line, Spacing, is not available for these strokes. As explained earlier in this chapter, these strokes are rendered with an eye toward pixel precision that is incompatible with the Spacing and Flow attributes. However, one of the other Pencil presets, Colored Pencil, works quite well as a stroke on which to build the custom dotted line, with a minimum of adjustments required.

To create a simple dotted line, follow these steps:

1. Display the Stroke panel by choosing Window ➪ Strokes or selecting its tab, if visible.

2. Choose Pencil from the Category option list.

3. Choose Colored Pencil from the Type option list.

4. Open the Edit Stroke dialog box by selecting the Options pop-up button and choosing Edit Stroke or by double-clicking the top stroke preview pane.

5. On the Options tab of the Edit Stroke dialog box, change the Spacing value from 15 percent to 200 percent.

   You'll notice in the preview pane that the line is now dotted, as shown in Figure 8-27.

6. Click OK when you're done.

7. From the Options pop-up menu, choose Save Stroke As.

8. In the Save Stroke As dialog box, enter a unique name for the custom stroke.

Test out your new dotted line by using almost any of the path drawing tools — the Rectangle, Ellipse, Polygon, Brush, or Pen.

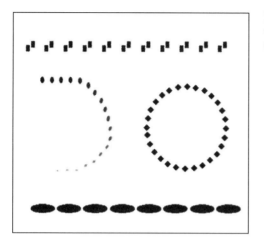

**Figure 8-27:** You can easily create a wide variety of dotted lines by modifying the Edit Stroke settings.

Now that you've seen how easy it is to customize a brush stroke, here are a few variations you can try. Each set of instructions assumes that you're working in the Edit Strokes dialog box.

To give the dotted line a harder, more consistent edge, make these changes:

✦ Change the Edge Texture value on the Options tab to 0 percent.

✦ On the Shape tab, change the Edge value to 0 percent.

✦ On the Sensitivity tab, change the Size Speed setting to 0, the Ink Amount Pressure and Speed settings to 0, and the Lightness Pressure and Speed settings to 0.

To create a dotted line with circles instead of squares:

✦ On the Shape tab, deselect the Square option.

✦ Also on the Shape tab, change the Aspect value to 100.

To create a horizontal line with dashes:

✦ From the Shape tab, change the Aspect value to 50.

✦ Also on the Shape tab, change the Angle to 0.

To create a vertical line with dashes:

✦ From the Shape tab, change the Aspect value to 50.

✦ Also on the Shape tab, change the Angle to 270.

To create a dotted line with diamonds:

✦ From the Shape tab, make sure the Square option is selected.

✦ Also on the Shape tab, change the Aspect value to 100.

✦ Change the Angle to 45.

# Orienting the Stroke

Strokes are useful whether they are intended for an open path, such as a line, or a closed path, such as a circle or rectangle. When a stroke is applied to a closed path, however, Fireworks offers an additional set of options. By default, strokes are rendered centered on a path. Select any closed path object and you'll see the stroke rendered on either side of the actual path. The orientation of stroke to path can be changed: the stroke can also be drawn completely inside the path or outside the path. As you can see from Figure 8-28, wildly different effects are possible with this option.

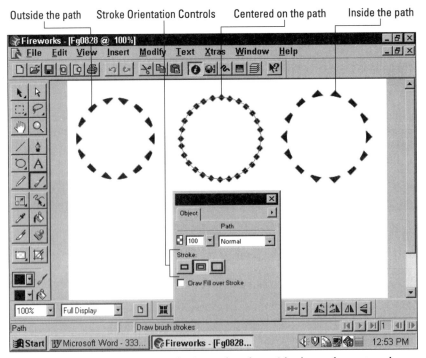

**Figure 8-28:** Here, the same stroke is rendered outside the path, centered on the path, and inside the path.

The controls for orienting the stroke to the path are found on the Object panel. The three buttons, from left to right, place the stroke inside the path, centered on the path, or outside the path. There is also another option below the stroke orientation controls: Draw Fill over Stroke. By default, the stroke always appears on top of the fill color, pattern, or gradient. However, by enabling the Draw Fill over Stroke option, you can reverse this preference.

**Tip** By combining the Draw Fill over Stroke option with a stroke rendered on the center of the path and a fill with a feathered edge, the stroke appears to blend into the fill while retaining a hard outer edge.

# Using Pressure-Sensitive Tablets

I came to computer graphics through the computer side rather than the artistic side, so for the longest time, I created all my graphics with a mouse. Often derided as "drawing with a bar of soap," I found workarounds and techniques to make it work for me. When graphic tablets — a flat panel that you draw on with a pen-like stylus — arrived, they were too expensive, too sensitive, and too unwieldy. But like most other technology, graphic tablets became faster, cheaper, and better — so much so that I could no longer ignore them and now I'm a shameless, zealous convert to their use, especially with Fireworks.

There's really almost no learning curve to using a graphic tablet with Fireworks. Everything works as with the mouse, you just have far more control. In addition to providing an easier method of drawing (the classic test is a signature — try signing your name with a mouse and then with a graphic tablet — it's a world of difference), numerous strokes take advantage of the tablet's additional abilities. Most graphic tablets today offer some degree of pressure-sensitivity; as with a real-world brush or pen, press down harder and you'll get a heavier line, or use a lighter touch for a softer line. Many of Fireworks's standard strokes are sensitive to pressure, including all of the Airbrush, Calligraphy, Charcoal, Oil, and Watercolor presets.

**Tip** If you don't have a tablet, you can simulate increased or decreased pressure with your keyboard. Press 1 to decrease the pressure and 2 to increase it. Be aware, however, that unlike with a graphic tablet, the pressure doesn't even out when you stop drawing. If you press 1 three times to decrease the pressure, the pressure will continue to be light until you press 2 three times to restore it to its default state or until you relaunch Fireworks.

# Summary

In many ways, the stroke is the defining surface of a graphic. Fireworks offers a superb catalog of standard strokes and even more flexibility to create your own. As you begin to work with strokes, use these guidelines:

✦ Strokes make paths visible. An unstroked line cannot be seen unless the path is closed and a fill added.

✦ The Stroke panel offers immediate control over a stroke's color, size, edge, and texture. Two previews show the stroke stamp — the smallest unit of a stroke — and the stroke over distance.

✦ Fireworks includes 48 different preset strokes spread over 11 categories. Many of the stroke presets are interactive and vary according to the speed and pressure with which you draw.

✦ Fireworks strokes can be customized with a great number of variations through the Edit Strokes dialog box.

✦ After you've customized your stroke, you can save it with the document using the Stroke panel Options pop-up commands. You can also store your custom strokes within a Style, new in Fireworks 2.

✦ Although Fireworks doesn't come with a preset dotted line pattern, it's very easy to create one.

✦ Fireworks works well with graphic tablets and takes great advantage of their pressure sensitivity.

In the next chapter, you'll see how you can employ advanced path techniques in Fireworks.

✦        ✦        ✦

# Structuring Paths

**In This Chapter**

Transforming paths

Fireworks technique:
creating perspective

Working at the point
level on a path

Editing existing paths

Using the new path
power tools

**E**ven with the coolest stroke, the snazziest fill, and the wildest effect, you rarely get exactly the graphic you need the first time you draw an object. Maybe it needs to be a little bigger, smaller, taller, or wider, or maybe it's perfect — but it's facing the wrong way and it's upside down. Whatever the problem, Fireworks 2 has the tools to fix it and, because Fireworks blends pixel surfaces with vector skeletons, you'll get amazingly sharp results.

**New Feature** Fireworks 2 introduces a new series of commands to manipulate two or more path objects. Now you can combine several paths in any number of ways with evocatively named tools such as Union, Intersect, Punch, and Crop. Naturally, what you have joined together can be split apart and regrouped as needed. Additionally, any path can now be simplified, expanded, or inset with Fireworks 2 commands.

This chapter covers all the tools and techniques you'll find in Fireworks for transforming and combining objects. You'll also find a section that describes how you can use Fireworks to create perspectives in your imagery.

You really begin to appreciate the power of Fireworks's vector-bitmap combination when you start transforming your objects. In a bitmapped graphics application, if you increase the size of an image, you have to add pixels, whereas shrinking an image causes the program to throw away pixels — you rarely achieve ideal results in either situation. However, in Fireworks, when you rescale an object, the path is altered (a snap for vector graphics) and the pixels are reapplied to the new path, just as if you had drawn it that way to begin with.

# Transforming Objects Visually

Fireworks 2 includes methods for transforming objects both visually and numerically. The visual method relies on three key tools found in the Toolbox: Scale, Skew, and Distort.

**Note**   Although I primarily use path objects as examples in this section, all of the transformation tools work with image objects as well.

## Scaling

In Web design, the size of an object frequently needs to be adjusted. Sometimes a button is too large for the current navigation bar or the client wants the "on sale" notice to be much bigger. Other times a graphic just looks better at a particular size. Regardless of the reason, Fireworks gives you a quick way to resize an object — either up or down — through the Scale tool.

The Scale tool is the first of three transformation tools on the Toolbox that become active when an object is selected. Choose the Scale tool (or use the keyboard shortcut, q) and the standard selection highlight is replaced with a transforming highlight, as shown in Figure 9-1. There are eight sizing handles — one on each corner and one in the middle of each side — and a centerpoint on the transforming highlight. You can drag any of the sizing handles to a new position to resize the selected object. Dragging any corner handle scales the object proportionately.

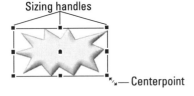

**Figure 9-1:** When any transform tool is chosen, sizing handles and a centerpoint appear on the selected object.

To resize an object using the Scale tool, follow these steps:

1. Select the object you want to resize.

2. Choose the Scale tool from the Toolbox or use the keyboard shortcut, q. You can also use the menu command, Modify ➪ Transform ➪ Scale. Sizing handles and a centerpoint appear on the highlight for the selected object.

3. Position your pointer over any sizing handle until it changes into a two-headed arrow.

4. Click and drag the sizing handle in the direction you want the object to grow or shrink.

5. To scale an object while maintaining the current proportions, click and drag a corner sizing handle.

6. To accept a rescaled object, double-click anywhere on the document. You can also complete the resizing by selecting the Transform button on the Options panel, if it's visible.

7. To cancel a resizing operation and return the object to its original dimensions, press Esc.

You can also move or rotate an object when any of the transform tools are selected. When the pointer is positioned within the selected object and becomes a four-headed arrow, click and drag the object to a new position. If the pointer is outside of the selected object's bounding box, the pointer turns into a rotate symbol; clicking and dragging when this occurs rotates the object around its centerpoint.

The transform tools all have two options available through the Options panel. By default, when you resize an object, the stroke, fill, and effect settings are resized as well. If you disable the Scale Attributes option, these settings are reapplied without being recalculated. Why might you want to do this? Although the results can be unpredictable, interesting variations can occur, as noticeable in Figure 9-2.

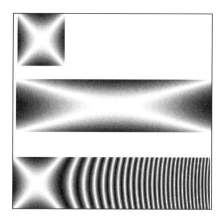

**Figure 9-2:** Most of the time you want your stroke, fill, and effects to rescale along with your image, but turning off the Scale Attributes option can lead to some interesting effects.

**Tip**

In my experimentation with the Scale Attributes option, I found that I got the most interesting effects when my object was filled with a gradient and the Scale Attributes option was turned off.

The other option in the transform tools Options panel is Auto-crop Images. If this option is turned off, transparent rows and columns that can be applied to a transformed image object will not be automatically deleted.

# Changing scaling options

Shortly after Fireworks 2 was released, several users noticed that certain kinds of files — screen shots with lots of text, for instance — became blurry when scaled down. The Fireworks engineers responded by releasing an update (Fireworks 2.02) which, among other things, incorporated four different scaling options:

✦ **Bicubic Interpolation:** With bicubic interpolation, Fireworks averages every pixel with all eight pixels surrounding it — above, below, left, right, and all four corners. The default scaling algorithm in Fireworks 2, bicubic interpolation, has been enhanced for the 2.02 update. This scaling option gives the sharpest results under the most conditions and is recommended for most graphics.

✦ **Bilinear Interpolation:** Bilinear interpolation is similar to bicubic, but only uses four neighboring pixels (above, below, left, and right), instead of eight.

✦ **Nearest Neighbor:** The Nearest Neighbor algorithm causes Fireworks to copy neighboring pixels whenever a new pixel must be interpolated. Consequently, the Nearest Neighbor scaling option creates very pixelated, stairstep-like images.

✦ **Soft Interpolation:** Soft Interpolation was the original scaling option used in Fireworks 1 and it offers a smoothing blur to the scaled-down images. The Soft Interpolation scaling option is a good choice if your images are producing unwanted artifacts using the other scaling images.

As you can see from Figure 9-3, the different scaling options do indeed present different results. I've found that although I tend to use Bicubic Interpolation most of the time, I do turn to Bilinear and Soft Interpolation in some cases, usually when small text is involved. I haven't found much use for the blockiness produced by the Nearest Neighbor scaling option.

The scaling options are presented as Fireworks scriptlets. To implement a new scaling option at any time, you must run the scriptlet in any of the following ways:

✦ Double-click the scriptlet icon.

✦ Choose File ➪ Run Script and select the scriptlet found in the Scaling Options folder of Fireworks.

✦ Drag the scriptlet icon onto the Fireworks application icon.

✦ Windows only: drag the scriptlet icon into the Fireworks window.

There's no need to relaunch Fireworks — the scaling changes are immediate. The new scaling option is then used in every scaling operation, including

✦ Choosing Modify ➪ Transform to select Scale, Skew, Slant, or Numeric Transform

✦ Accessing any of the transform tools from the Toolbox

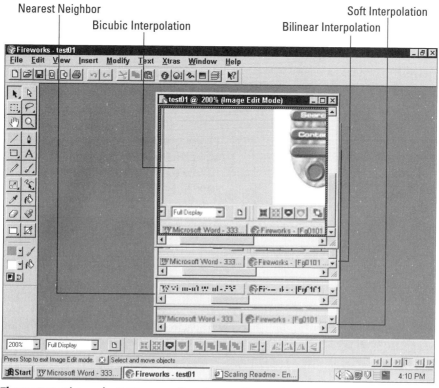

Nearest Neighbor

Bicubic Interpolation

Soft Interpolation

Bilinear Interpolation

**Figure 9-3:** Fireworks 2.02 now offers four scaling options.

+ Dragging an object's corner handles to resize it

+ Choosing Modify ⇨ Document ⇨ Image Size and using the resize or rescale options

+ Scaling an exported file through the File tab of the Export Preview dialog box

+ Scaling an imported vector file, such as one from FreeHand or Illustrator

A new scaling option stays in effect — even after Fireworks has quit and been relaunched — until you run another scaling option scriptlet.

## Skewing

The Skew tool is used to slant one side of an object while the opposing side remains stationary. Selecting the Skew tool, either by clicking and holding the Scale tool until you can select the second tool of the flyout or by pressing the keyboard shortcut (q) twice, causes transform handles to appear on the selected object as with Scale. The Skew handles work somewhat differently, however:

✦ Drag any middle Skew handle to slant that side of the object.

✦ Drag any corner Skew handle to slant that side and the opposing side in the opposite direction.

Skewing a corner is a useful technique for making your image appear in perspective, as can be seen in Figure 9-4. You'll find other useful perspective techniques described later in this chapter.

**Figure 9-4:** You can skew an object along one side by dragging the middle handle or two sides with a corner handle, as in the top logo.

Completing a Skew operation is handled the same way as resizing: double-click anywhere to accept the new shape or press Esc to revert to the original image.

## Distorting

With both the Scale and Skew tool, entire sides move when one of the transform handles is adjusted. The Distort tool (the third button on the transform flyout) removes those restrictions. When the Distort tool is selected, you can adjust the bounding box surrounding the selected object by dragging the handles in any direction. The object is then redrawn to fit within the confines of the new bounding box shape.

The Distort tool is very useful for warping flat objects — especially images — into novel shapes. The kites in Figure 9-5 were each created by applying the Distort tool to a rectangular image.

**Tip** You can use the Distort tool to flip an image horizontally or vertically by dragging a middle handle across the opposite side. This technique won't automatically size the image to match the original as the Flip Horizontal or Flip Vertical commands do; instead, you can control the sizing.

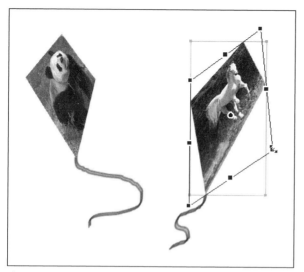

**Figure 9-5:** Use the Distort tool to reshape an image or an object by altering its bounding box.

## Rotating

Rotating is available with any of the transform tools: Scale, Skew, or Distort. As you can see in Figure 9-6, you can rotate an object to any angle. Additionally, you can move the centerpoint to rotate around a different axis.

To rotate any object, follow these steps:

1. Select any one of the transform tools from the Toolbox or choose the equivalent tool from the Modify ➪ Transform menu.

2. Move your pointer outside of the bounding box. The pointer turns into a rotation symbol.

3. Click and drag in any direction to rotate the object.

4. Double-click to accept the new angle or, from the Options panel, click the Transform button.

5. To cancel the rotation and return to the original object, press Esc.

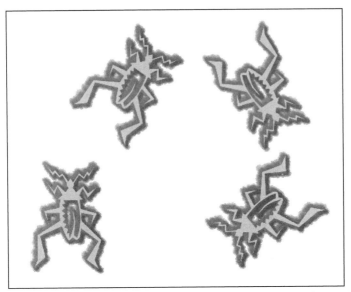

**Figure 9-6:** The original image in the lower left is shown after copies of the object have been rotated and placed around the screen.

An object rotates around the centerpoint which, by default, is placed in the middle of the transform highlight. To change the rotation axis, click and drag the centerpoint to a new location—the centerpoint can remain within the object's bounding box or be placed outside of it. If the centerpoint is placed outside of the object, the radius used connects the centerpoint and the nearest corner handle, as shown in Figure 9-7.

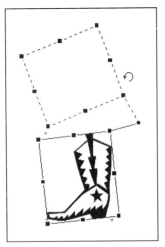

**Figure 9-7:** Rotate an object around a central axis by dragging the centerpoint away from the object's bounding box.

**Tip** Pressing the Shift key while you rotate an object constrains the rotation to 15-degree increments.

# Transforming Objects Numerically

Transforming an object interactively by clicking and dragging works well for many situations, but sometimes it's preferable to specify your new measurement or rotation precisely. For those exacting occasions, turn to Fireworks's Numeric Transform feature. With Numeric Transform, you can scale any object up or down by a percentage, set a specific pixel size, or rotate to an exact degree.

To use Numeric Transform, follow these steps:

1. Select the object you want to change.

2. Choose Modify ⇨ Transform ⇨ Numeric Transform or use the keyboard shortcut, Ctrl+Shift+T (Command+Shift+T). The Numeric Transform dialog box, shown in Figure 9-8, appears.

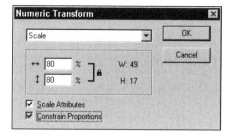

**Figure 9-8:** The Numeric Transform command gives you precise control over an object's size and angle.

3. To rescale an object proportionately:

   • Choose Scale from the Option list.

   • Enter a new percentage value in either the height or width text boxes.

   • Press Tab.

4. To resize an object to a specific pixel size:

   • Choose Resize from the Option list.

   • Enter the pixel dimensions in either the width or height text boxes.

   • Press Tab.

5. To rotate an object to a specific degree:

   • Choose Rotate from the Option list.

   • Enter a degree value in the text box or drag the knob to select a rotation degree.

6. To rescale or resize an object in different proportions than the original, deselect the Constrain Proportions option.

7. To modify an object without recalculating the attributes, deselect the Scale Attributes option.

# Fireworks Technique: Creating Perspective

Though Fireworks is not a 3D modeling program, you can quickly generate perspective views using several of its transform and other tools. If you've ever taken Drawing 101, you understand the basic principles of perspective: the particular view you're illustrating has a *vanishing point* where the imaginary lines of the drawing meet on the horizon. The vanishing point concept is most simply applied by using a special property of the Skew tool.

 The techniques described in this section encompass some features of Fireworks discussed elsewhere in this book, including Texture fills (Chapter 11), Live Effects (Chapter 12), and Mask Groups (Chapter 13).

Take a look at Figure 9-9. On the left, you see a standard rectangular image, inserted into a Fireworks document. On the right, you see the same image, transformed by the Skew tool. Two lines have been added to illustrate the perspective vanishing point.

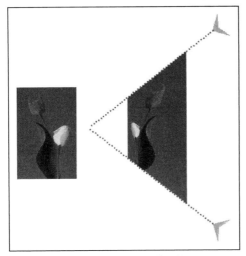

**Figure 9-9:** You can make a flat figure appear to have perspective by using the Skew tool.

**Tip** One of the most common — and effective — ways to add to the depth of illusion is by using a drop shadow effect. Fireworks has a very effective drop shadow that is easily applied to most any object.

To convert a flat image to a perspective image, follow these steps:

**1.** Select the image you wish to convert.

**2.** Choose the Skew tool from the toolbox or press the keyboard shortcut, q, twice.

**3.** Choose the direction of perspective:

- To make the image appear as if it is along on a left wall, drag the left corner away from the image, vertically.

- To make the image appear as if it is along a right wall, drag the right corner away from the image, vertically.

- To make the image appear as if it is on the floor, drag a bottom corner away from the image, horizontally.

- To make the image appear as if it is on the ceiling, drag a top corner away from the image, horizontally.

**4.** To intensify the perspective, repeat Step 3 with the opposite corner, dragging in the opposite direction. For example, in Figure 9-9, I dragged the right bottom corner away from the image and the left bottom corner into the image to exaggerate the effect.

Applying textures to a rectangle fill is a good way to start building a perspective background. I've found it's better to break up the textures into small rectangles, rather than use one large rectangle. The room depicted in Figure 9-10 uses a series of rectangles with a Wood-Light pattern fill, which are then grouped and skewed together to gain the perspective feel. By duplicating and flipping this skewed group, I'm able to quickly build the other sides of the room.

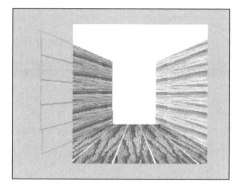

**Figure 9-10:** When using a pattern for perspective, try smaller rectangles of the same pattern, grouped and skewed together.

Tip     Dragging the corner with the Skew tool always moves the top opposite sides equally. This operation makes an object's vanishing point appear to be evenly spaced between the sides of an image, which is not always the case. You can also use the Distort tool to drag one corner unevenly. But use the Distort tool with caution — or perhaps with the Grid visible; there's no way to snap a dragged corner when using the Distort tool, and straight lines are often difficult to maintain.

## Altering the opacity

One key to enhancing the illusion of perspective is providing a light source — or, at least, a simulated one. Two basic techniques give a perspective object the appearance of light and shadow. First, you can alter the object's opacity through the Object panel. Reducing an object's opacity makes it appear lighter, whereas higher opacity makes it appear darker. To best take advantage of this technique, set the opacity for the "normal" condition lower than its normal 100 percent; this enables you to have both lighter and darker ranges. For example, in Figure 9-11, each wooden plank in the perspective room is given a slightly different opacity to create a range of light to dark areas.

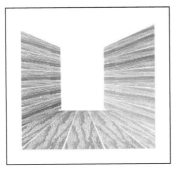

**Figure 9-11:** You can enhance the perspective illusion by using different opacities to lighten or darken objects.

## Using Mask Groups

The second technique for adding a light source to an image is a bit more complex than the opacity technique, but it's also much more flexible. In Fireworks, you can make any object appear to have its own shading of light and dark by using a special *Mask Group*. A Mask Group is a combination of objects where one object is viewed through another. When the masking object uses a black-and-white gradient fill, the Mask Group takes on alpha channel transparency characteristics. In other words, the image has a controllable light to dark range added. This enables you to adjust the "lighting" so that it looks appropriate with your particular graphic.

To use Mask Groups to simulate light and shadow in perspective, follow these steps, shown in Figure 9-12:

1. Using one of the geometric drawing tools (Rectangle, Ellipse, or Polygon), draw a masking object over your primary graphic.

2. From the Fill panel, choose a Linear gradient fill with the White, Black color preset.

3. Create a Mask Group of the gradient fill object and the original object by selecting both and choosing Modify ➪ Mask Group or pressing Ctrl+Shift+G (Command+Shift+G). The image fades in from the white portion of the gradient to the black portion.

4. If desired, select the Paint Bucket tool to adjust the gradient.

5. Drag the round starting handle of the gradient fill to reposition the gradient.

6. Drag the square ending handle to adjust the angle of the gradient.

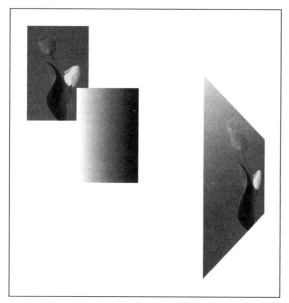

**Figure 9-12:** A Mask Group with a gradient fill enables you to adjust the simulated lighting of an image.

I used the Linear gradient in the previous example, but you can get some really great effects (such as a starburst of light) by applying different gradient types. Moreover, you can adjust the subtlety of the lighting by editing the gradient and toning down the pure white to a more muted gray.

**Cross-Reference**   For more about gradients, see Chapter 11.

# Managing Points and Paths

Sometimes transforming a object in its entirety is more than you really want or
need to do. Fireworks offers numerous options for adjusting paths on a point-by-
point basis. You can easily move, add, or delete points. In addition, paths can be
joined, either to itself, changing an open path to a closed path, or to another path.
Naturally, joined paths can also be split at any point.

## Moving points with the Subselection tool

Much of path work on the point level is handled through the Subselection tool.
Similar to the Pointer tool in that it is used for selecting and dragging, the Subselection tool works on the components of the path rather than on the path itself.

The Subselection tool is located directly across from the Pointer on the Toolbox; it
can also be chosen through its keyboard shortcut, a. When you select a path with
the Subselection tool, all the points that create the path appear, not just the path
that becomes visible when the Pointer is used. Each point on a path initially resembles a small filled-in square. When you approach a point with the Subselection tool,
the white pointer changes into a single white arrowhead indicating a point is available for selection, as shown in Figure 9-13. Clicking on that point changes the solid
square to a hollow square and the Bézier control handles appear, if any.

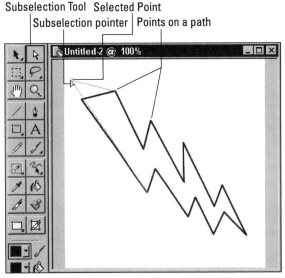

**Figure 9-13:** Adjust paths on the point level by using
the Subselection tool.

**Tip** If no Bézier control handles are visible from a point on a path, you can use the Subselection tool, in combination with the Alt (Option) key, to drag them out.

Clicking and dragging any point causes the path to move along with it. You can completely reshape any path by using the Subselection tool.

## Adding and removing points

It's very easy to add or delete points on a path. Why would you want to increase the number of points? Most commonly, the object you're working on has a line that you need to extend in a different direction—and the Bézier curves create too smooth a transition. The reasoning behind removing points is just the reverse: you have a sharp break where you'd prefer a smooth curve. You'll also find that drawing any path with a freeform tool such as the Brush or Pencil creates lots of points. Not that there is really any increased overhead, such as file size, associated with additional points—it's just easier to work with an object with fewer ones.

To add a point on a path, follow these steps:

1. Choose the Pen tool from the toolbox or use its keyboard shortcut, p.
2. Press and hold Ctrl (Command) to temporarily switch to the Subselection tool.
3. Select the path to work on.
4. Release Ctrl (Command).
5. Position your pointer over the area on the path where you want to add a point. A small caret (^) is added to the Pen tool pointer, as shown in Figure 9-14.

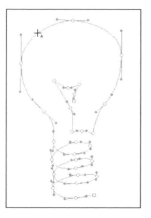

**Figure 9-14:** Add points with the Pen tool when it's over a selected line.

6. To add a single point, click once.

7. To add a point with Bézier curves, click and drag.

8. Continue adding points by repeating Steps 5-7.

9. When you're finished adding points, select another tool.

To delete points from a path, follow these steps:

1. Choose the Subselection tool from the Toolbox.

2. Select the path from which you want to delete points.

3. Move the pointer over the point you want to delete. A small X is added to the pointer when you are over a point on the path.

4. Click once to select the point.

5. Press Delete or Backspace to remove the point.

 **Tip**

To delete multiple points, press Ctrl (Command) to temporarily use the Pointer tool and drag a selection rectangle around the points you want to remove. Press Delete or Backspace to remove the points.

## Closing an open path

Whether by accident ("Drat, I thought I closed that path") or design ("I like the simpleness of the open path"), sometimes you need to convert an open path to a closed one. Luckily, the Pen tool makes it a very simple operation.

To close an open path, follow these steps:

1. Select the path you need to close.

2. Choose the Pen tool from the toolbox.

3. Position your pointer over one endpoint of the path. An X is added to the lower right of the Pen cursor when it is over an existing endpoint, as shown in Figure 9-15.

4. Click once on the endpoint.

5. Continue the path with the Pen. With each plotted point, any stroke or effects attributes are applied to the extended path.

6. To close the path, position the Pen over the remaining endpoint. A solid square appears on the lower right of the Pen cursor.

7. Click once to close the path.

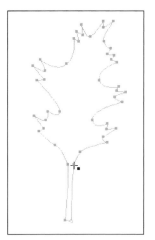

**Figure 9-15:** Use the Pen tool to close any open path.

**Tip**     If your stroke varies its thickness or opacity by speed or pressure, the Pen-completed section of the path may look off. This is because the Pen recognizes neither speed nor pressure. However, you can use the Path Scrubber tools, discussed later in this chapter, to increase or reduce these types of effects.

## Working with multiple paths

Joined paths share the same stroke, fill, and effects settings — just as if they were the same stroke. Initially, this capability may appear to fall into the "yeah, so what?" category. However, once you realize that the paths don't have to overlap, touch, or even be near each other, the design possibilities open up considerably. For example, take a look at Figure 9-16, where two paths are joined and a radial gradient fill is applied.

To join two or more paths, follow these steps:

1. Select each path you'd like to join with the Pointer tool.

2. Choose Modify ➪ Join or Ctrl+J (Command-J).

   Windows users can also select the Join button on the Modify toolbar.

Once you've joined paths, they will stay that way until they are split. To split joined paths, choose Modify ➪ Split or use the keyboard shortcut, Ctrl+Shift+J (Command+Shift+J). In Windows, you can also select the Split button on the Modify toolbar.

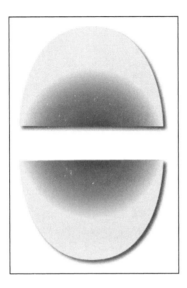

**Figure 9-16:** When two or more paths are joins, all their attributes — such as a gradient fill — are shared.

# Editing Paths

So far in this chapter, most of the path editing tools have been fairly extreme; delete, distort, rescale, rotate — these terms don't promise much degree of subtlety. Fireworks does offer several other tools, however, that can redraw portions of a path or reshape an area with a varying amount of pressure. And for those times that require a precise, almost surgical removal of path segments, Fireworks offers a Knife tool that performs as sharply as any blade.

## Redrawing a path

If you've ever drawn a perfect shape — except for one little area — you'll greatly appreciate the Redraw Path tool. As the name implies, this tool enables you to redraw any portion of a completed path, in effect throwing away the portion of original path you're replacing.

The Redraw Path tool, found on the flyout under the Brush, is a freehand drawing tool. When you're redoing a segment of a path, you initially select any part of the path to start redrawing and then reconnect to the original path. Fireworks erases the portion of the original path that is in between the beginning and the ending points of your redrawn section and connects your new path to the old.

To redraw a portion of a path, follow these steps:

1. Select the path you want to redraw.

2. Choose the Redraw Path tool from the flyout under the Brush tool. Alternatively, you can press the keyboard shortcut, b, twice.

3. Move the pointer over the area of the path where you want to start redrawing. Fireworks displays a small caret (^) in the lower right of the pointer when you are in position over the path.

4. Click and drag out your new path.

5. Position your pointer over the original path where you want to connect the new and old paths and release the mouse button. Fireworks removes the old path segment and connects the new path segment.

The Redraw Path tool isn't just for correcting mistakes, though. Figure 9-17 shows how the Redraw Path tool can be used to make a portion of a geometric shape more organic.

**Figure 9-17:** The Redraw Path tool can easily alter a standard shape into something unique.

Tip    Pressing Shift while using the Redraw Path tool constrains your replacement path to lines in increments of 45 degrees.

## Freeform and Reshape Area

Looking for a cool tool to give your objects that unique twist? Look no further than Freeform and Reshape Area. Rather than add or delete points like other tools, these reshaping features let you sculpt the path, pulling and pushing the line like so much stretchable clay.

Although similar, there are a couple of key differences between the two tools:

✦ **Freeform:** Both pushes and pulls a segment of a selected path.

✦ **Reshape Area :** Only pushes a path, but controls the degree it pushes through the strength field on the Tool Options. Moreover, this tool can reshape an entire object as well as just a segment.

### Pulling a path segment into a new shape

To pull a segment of a path into a new shape, follow these steps:

1. Select the path you want to alter.

2. Choose the Freeform tool from the Toolbox or use its keyboard shortcut, f.

3. Position your cursor directly over the segment of the path you want to pull. An S-curve is added to the lower-right of the Freeform cursor, as shown in Figure 9-18.

4. Click and drag in the direction you want to pull the segment. You can pull the path away from or into the object.

5. Release the mouse button to complete the pull.

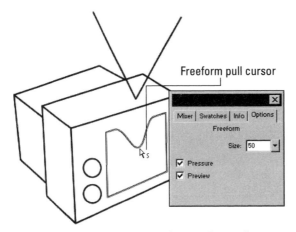

**Figure 9-18:** The Freeform tool is used to pull out a segment of a path.

Fireworks adds as few pixels as possible when you are pulling with the Freeform tool. When you use the pull mode of the Freeform tool, it's like you're pinching just the one point of the path and dragging it away from the rest of the shape. By contrast, the push mode of the Freeform tool is more like using a ball to reshape the path. The size of the ball with which you push is determined through the Freeform Tool Options panel, shown in Figure 9-19.

### Pushing a path into a new shape

To push a path into a new shape with the Freeform tool, follow these steps:

1. Select the path you want to alter.

2. Choose the Freeform tool from the Toolbox or use it's keyboard shortcut, f.

Freeform push cursor

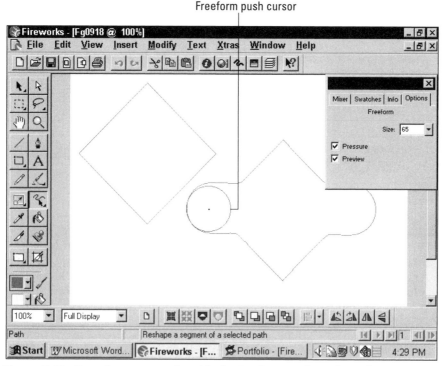

**Figure 9-19:** Round out your paths with the Freeform tool's push mode.

3. Position your cursor directly over the segment of the path you want to pull.

A small open circle is added to the lower-right of the Freeform cursor, as shown in Figure 9-18.

4. Click and drag the ball cursor into the path, pushing it into a new shape.

5. Release the mouse button when you're satisfied with the shape.

## Freeform tool's Options panel

To alter the size of the ball used with Freeform push mode, double-click the Freeform tool to open the Options panel and enter a new value in the Size text box or use its slider to choose a new pixel size. The Size option ranges from 1 to 500 pixels.

**Caution**

Don't push with the Freeform tool too fast or too far or you'll get an overlapping path line with unpredictable results.

There are two other options on the Options panel for the Freeform tool. The Preview option draws the stroke and fill, if any, as you use the tool. Although this can be a bit processor-intensive, I enable it whenever I'm using Freeform on an object with a wide stroke, such as an Airbrush, because the final effect can be so different from just the path. When the Preview option is not on, you'll see both the old outline and the new one while you are using the tool; when you stop drawing, the old outline vanishes.

The other option, Pressure, is generally useful only if you're using a pressure-sensitive graphic tablet. When enabled, a medium amount of pressure uses a push cursor the size set in the Options panel; lighter amounts of pressure reduce the size and greater amounts increase it.

**Caution**    I've found this Pressure option of the Freeform tool very useful, but extremely pro-cessor-intensive on my Windows machine. I often need to disable the Preview option to use it successfully.

### Altering a path object with one operation

Though the Reshape Area tool, when set to a small size, achieves similar effects to the Freeform tool, that's not what makes it special. The Reshape Area tool is best when used to warp or reshape an entire image. Take Figure 9-20, for example. I start with a star created with the Polygon tool, and then apply the Reshape Area tool, set to a size on the Options panel larger than the star. By dragging the Reshape Area tool over the star, I transform the entire standard shape — not just one segment — into something more unique.

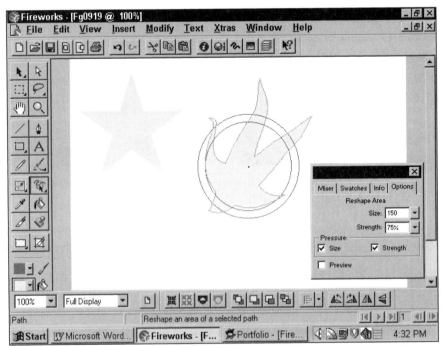

**Figure 9-20:** The Reshape Area tool can alter an entire path object with one operation.

### Using the Reshape Area tool

To use the Reshape Area tool, follow these steps:

1. Select the path you want to alter.

2. Choose the Reshape Area tool from the flyout underneath the Freeform tool, or press the keyboard shortcut, f, twice.

3. Position your pointer over the object you want to reshape.

4. Click and drag in the desired direction.

5. Release the mouse button when you're satisfied with the resulting object.

Like the Freeform tool, the Size is set on the Options panel; you'll also find Pressure and Preview options that function in the same manner as those for the Freeform tool. In addition, the Reshape Area tool has a Strength option. The Strength value determines how strong the gravitational-like pull of the Reshape Area tool is to be. Strength is percentage-based; at 100 percent, you'll get the maximum effect from the tool. If you're using a pressure-sensitive graphic tablet, you can alter both the size and the strength of the Reshape Area tool while drawing with your stylus.

**Tip**    Don't have a graphic tablet yet? To simulate a lighter stylus touch, use either 1 or the left arrow key; pressing 2 or the right arrow key simulates increasing the pressure on a graphics pad.

## Path Scrubber

The Path Scrubber tools are fairly subtle compared to the others covered in this chapter. If you've experimented with strokes such as Airbrush, you've noticed how the stroke can change according to how fast or, with a graphic tablet, how much pressure you use when you draw. The Path Scrubber tools alter those variables, after you've completed the path. One Path Scrubber tool increases the interactive effect and one lessens it, as shown in Figure 9-21.

### Using the Path Scrubber tools

To use the Path Scrubber tools, follow these steps:

1. Select a path that uses speed- or pressure-sensitive effects, such as the Airbrush stroke.

2. Choose the Path Scrubber Minus tool from the flyout underneath the Freeform tool or use the keyboard shortcut, u, twice.

3. Trace over that portion of the path where you want to lessen the speed or pressure effect.

4. If you find you've reduced the effect on the stroke too much, choose the Path Scrubber Plus tool and trace over that area of the path to increase or restore the effect completely.

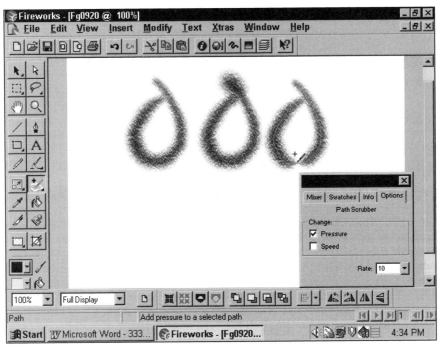

**Figure 9-21:** The same path is altered by the Path Scrubber Plus tool and the Path Scrubber Minus tool.

### Options panel

When Fireworks draws a path, both speed and pressure data are gathered. The Path Scrubber tools can work with either the speed or pressure information or both; moreover, it can do it at a variable rate. The Options panel for this tool have all the controls you'll need:

✦ **Rate:** The relative strength of the tool. Pick a value from 10 (the most effect) to 1 (the least effect).

✦ **Pressure:** Enabling this option directs the Path Scrubber tools to adjust the path according to the simulated pressure of the stroke.

✦ **Speed:** Enabling this option directs the Path Scrubber tools to adjust the path according to the simulated speed of the stroke.

## Knife

One of my favorite—and most useful—design tools is my X-acto knife. Being able to finely trim the tightest curves has saved me many times. The computer equivalent to this excellent implement is the Knife tool. The Knife tool is used only with paths, as its partner the Eraser is only used with bitmapped images. Basically, the Knife tool divides one path into two separate paths.

The Knife cuts paths by drawing a line where you want the separation to take place. You can use the Knife tool on open or closed paths or any path-based object. With an open path, you need only intersect the path once to make the cut once—with a closed path, you have to draw a line with the Knife all the way across the object, as shown in Figure 9-22.

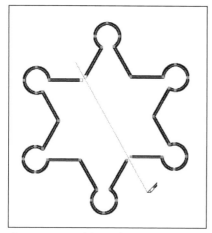

**Figure 9-22:** This path object was cut across the middle with the Knife tool.

To use the Knife, follow these steps:

1. Select the path you plan to divide.

2. Choose the Knife tool from the Toolbox or use the keyboard shortcut, e.

3. Draw a line through the path with the Knife tool. Fireworks separates the path, although because both parts of the path are still selected, it is not immediately obvious.

4. To move one of the newly divided paths, choose the Pointer tool and click once on the canvas, away from any object. The split paths are deselected.

5. Select either portion of the original path. Only one part is now selected and can be deleted, moved, or otherwise modified.

The Knife tool is also great for making specific shapes, such as arcs. Just draw a standard circle and then use the Knife to slice off a portion of it. Like many tools, pressing Shift constrains the Knife to angles with increments of 45 degrees.

**Note** Although the Options panel shows various selections for the Knife tool, all the parameters are only useful for the bitmap-oriented Eraser. Changing the options has no effect on the Knife tool.

# Path Operations

The more you work in vector-based drawing programs such as Fireworks, the sooner you begin to look for new and novel shapes. Face it, no matter how many points you put on that star, it's still a star. Whereas you can warp and reshape any existing object using the various tools described elsewhere in this chapter, sometimes it's far easier to create a compound shape composed of two or more basic shapes.

**New Feature**

Until Fireworks 2, the only compound shape option was the Join command. This is a good starting point, but there are so many more ways that two or more objects can be combined than just a simple join — and now many of those options are available in Fireworks 2. In addition to four new commands that enable you to combine paths in novel ways, three new stroke commands have been added to expand Fireworks's path vocabulary.

You can find all the new commands that merge paths — Union, Intersect, Punch, and Crop — under the Modify ⇨ Combine menu option. You'll find the stroke commands — Simplify, Expand Stroke, and Inset Path — under Modify ⇨ Alter Path.

**Note**

When you combine multiple paths, the stroke, fill, and effects setting of the rearmost object — the one furthest to the back — is applied to the new combination.

## Union

The Union command enables you to combine basic shapes — and toss away the overlap. One technique that helps me decide whether Union is the proper command to use is that time-honored artist's tool, squinting. After I've positioned the objects to form my new shape, I lean back from the monitor and squint, so I can see just the outline. That's precisely what Union does — it combines the shapes into an overall outline and removes any overlapping areas.

The technique for using Union, like all of the Combine commands, is very straightforward. Just position your objects, select them all, and then choose Modify ⇨ Combine ⇨ Union. Occasionally, you'll have to adjust the individual paths to get them just right. For example, when making the martini glass in Figure 9-23, I united three objects: a triangle, a rectangle, and a custom Pen-drawn shape for the base. After my first attempt I realized that the rectangle and the base didn't quite match, so I chose Edit ⇨ Undo — okay, I actually used the shortcut, Ctrl+Z (Command+Z) — and adjusted the base. Then after reselecting them and reissuing the command, I was ready to pour.

**Figure 9-23:** The three separate figures on the left were combined with the Union command to form the new object on the right.

## Intersect

Whereas Union throws away the overlapping parts of combined paths, Intersect keeps only the overlapping areas from all selected paths. Believe it or not, the key word in the previous sentence is *all* — if even one object doesn't overlap at least some part of all of the other selected objects, the Intersect operation erases all of your objects. That caveat out of the way, you'll find Intersect to be a very useful command. I mean, what other graphics tool could you use to create the perfect pizza slice, as I did in Figure 9-24? After the two objects on the left were selected, I chose Modify ➪ Combine ➪ Intersect. Pizza's ready!

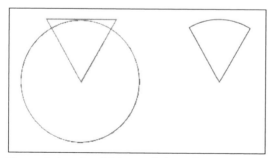

**Figure 9-24:** Combining a circle and a triangle with the Intersect command creates the perfect pizza slice.

# Punch

Remember the paper punch you had in school? That little handheld device that took a round bite out of whatever you could get between its jaws? The Punch command is the same concept, except you define the punch shape to be anything you want. When two path objects are overlapped, the shape on top is punched out of the shape on the bottom. You can see the Punch command illustrated in Figure 9-25, as I continue the food metaphors with the creation of a pie shape, minus one piece. After making sure that my triangle was on top of the circle, I selected them both and chose Modify ⇨ Combine ⇨ Punch.

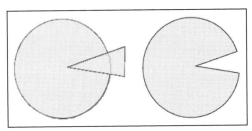

**Figure 9-25:** The Punch command removes the shape of the top object from the bottom path.

**Note** What happens when you apply the Punch command to more than two selected objects? The top object is still used as the punch pattern — and all of the objects are affected, but not joined.

# Crop

Plainly put, Crop is the opposite of Punch. Whereas with Punch, the top object is cut out of any other selected object, with Crop, it's the bottom object that forms the clipping path for the top object. To round out our food-like illustrations of the Combine commands, Figure 9-26 makes a quick fortune cookie by creating a small circle and then putting a wedge shape on top of it. The two objects are then selected and Modify ⇨ Combine ⇨ Crop is chosen. Add a little inner bevel effect with a touch of patterned filling and voilá, dessert is served.

# Simplify

Freeform drawing tools are terrific for quickly sketching out a specific shape. But, quite often, the computer representation of your flowing strokes turns out pretty blocky. The new Simplify command is designed to reduce the number of points used in a path while maintaining the overall shape of the object.

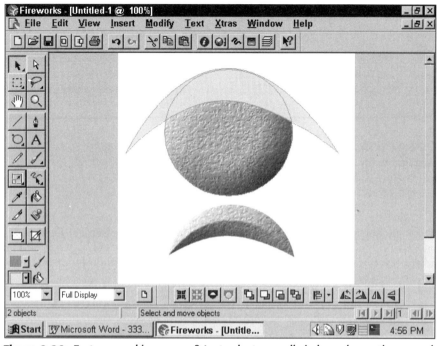

**Figure 9-26:** Fortune cookie, anyone? Just select a small circle underneath an overlapping arc and use the Combine Crop command to finish it off.

When you choose Modify ➪ Alter Path ➪ Simplify, the Simplify dialog box opens and enables you to specify the number of pixels affected — the range is from 1 to 24. As you can see from Figure 9-27, even the default value of 10 can have a dramatic effect. The original hand-drawn G on the left has too many points to even begin to count; I wouldn't know where to begin if I wanted to tweak it. After I selected its path and applied the Simplify command, the path on the left resulted. Once my overly complex path has been simplified, I can choose specific points and adjust their Bézier handles as needed.

## Expand Stroke

Though you can do a lot with an open path through the Stroke panel, sometimes you need the Fill as well. The Expand Stroke command is an easy way to convert any path — open or closed — to a closed path. This feature works by completely enclosing the existing path, and then deleting it.

**Figure 9-27:** After the Simplify command is applied to the original path on the left, the resulting path on the right is much easier to adjust.

When you apply this command by choosing Modify ➪ Alter Paths ➪ Expand Stroke, the Expand dialog box appears, as shown in Figure 9-28. As you can see, it offers quite a few options to enable you to control exactly what kind of path to use to expand the stroke. The options include:

✦ **Width:** Determines the final width of the expanded stroke. The range is from 1 to 99 pixels.

✦ **Corners:** Choose from three types of corners. From left to right, the buttons represent:

• **Miter:** With a miter corner, the outside edges of the path extend until they touch in a sharp corner. Because miter corners can become quite long, you can limit their length with the Miter Limit option, explained below.

• **Round:** The corner is rounded equally from both sides of the path approaching the corner. Round corners and round end caps are often used together.

• **Bevel:** The corner is cut off at the center of the meeting paths rather than on the outside edge, as with the miter corner. This results in a truncated corner.

✦ **Miter Limit:** The number of pixels the miter corner can extend before being cut off. The Miter Limit works only with miter corners.

✦ **End Caps:** Choose between three different end cap types to close off the expanded path:

• **Butt Cap:** The Butt Cap creates a right-angle end cap where the end is perpendicular to the last point of the stroke.

• **Round Cap:** A Round Cap attaches a semicircle to the end of the path, extending it the same radius as half the set width.

• **Square Cap:** Similar to the Round Cap, the Square Cap attaches a square to the end of the path, again extending it the same radius as half the set width.

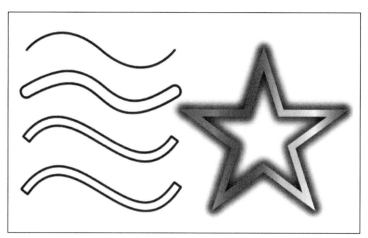

**Figure 9-28:** Choose your options to make a wide range of Expanded strokes.

Also shown in Figure 9-28 is one of the possible effects you can achieve by applying Expand Stroke to a closed path, a star. This star initially has no fill, but once Expand Stroke has been used, a fill can be given to the border of the star. An Airbrush stroke was used to make the star stand out, inside and out.

## Inset path

Where Expand Stroke applies strokes on either side of a selected path, Inset Path only does it on one side. The Inset dialog box is identical to the one for the Expand Stroke command except for the addition of Inside and Outside options. You'll get the most predictable results with Inset Path when you apply it to closed paths, but you can use it with any kind of path, with one exception: the straight line.

One of my favorite uses for the Inset Path command is to create concentric shapes. Though it does take a step or two longer, the results as seen in Figure 9-29 are quite worthwhile.

**Figure 9-29:** Create concentric shapes by applying the Inset Path command to clones of your original object.

To use the Inset Path command to create concentric shapes, follow these steps:

1. Select the closed path to which you want to add concentric shapes.

2. Choose Edit ➪ Clone. Because Inset Path erases the original path, you have to apply the command to a clone of the original.

3. Choose Modify ➪ Alter Path ➪ Inset Path. The Inset dialog box appears.

4. Choose the Direction, Width, and Corner option. If you choose the Miter Corner, you can enter a Miter Limit. Click OK when you're done. The new path is drawn and the old path deleted.

5. Repeat Steps 2–4 for as many concentric shapes as desired, keeping the same values in the Inset dialog box to create equidistant shapes.

After you've created your basic shapes, you can go in and vary the stroke width or other settings to create interesting effects.

# Summary

Mastering the manipulation of paths is essential to getting the most out of Fireworks. Path objects can be distorted, resized, rotated, and adjusted in many more subtle ways to get the basic shapes you need for unique Web graphics. When altering Fireworks objects, keep these points in mind:

✦ Objects can be manipulated as a whole by using the transform tools: Scale, Skew, and Distort.

✦ You can rotate an object using any one of the transform tools.

✦ For precise sizing or rotation, use the Numeric Transform feature.

✦ The Skew tool is great for simulating perspective views — especially of image objects. You can enhance the illusion by adding simulated light and shadow effects.

✦ Whereas the Pointer is used to move an entire path, the Subselection tool is used to maneuver individual points — and their Bézier control handles.

✦ Once you draw a path, you can edit it in numerous ways by using tools such as Freeform, Redraw Path, Redraw Area, and Path Scrubber.

✦ Fireworks 2 added some real power tools for working with paths: Union, Intersect, Punch, Crop, Simplify, Expand Path, and Inset Path.

In the next chapter, you'll see how to add text to your Web graphics in Fireworks.

✦        ✦        ✦

# Composing with Text

T ext has a special place in Web graphics. Though the
vast majority of text — paragraphs, lists, and tables of
information — is a product of the HTML page viewed through
a browser, graphic-based text is generally used to create
logos, fancy headings, and other decorative elements. In
addition, text is an integral part of a key Web element:
navigation. Many navigation buttons use text, either alone or
in combination with symbols, to quickly convey meaning.

Before Fireworks, a recurring nightmare for Web designers
involved modifying a text graphic. Whether it was a typo or
a client change-of-mind that forced the revision, the designer
was stuck having to redo an entire graphic because any text,
once applied, was just another bunch of pixels. Fireworks
changed all that with the introduction of editable text. Now,
if a client's logo changes because of a $7 billion merger or
you just forgot to put the period at the end of "Inc.," text
modifications are just a double-click away.

A few programs have since followed Macromedia's lead, but
Fireworks 2 continues to improve its text-handling abilities.
This chapter covers all the previous text features, as well as
introduces you to the new ones, such as multicolored text and
instant preview. You'll also explore a technique that enables
you to blend images and text so that the graphic conveys both
emotion and information.

## Using the Text Editor

In Fireworks, all text creation and most modification takes
place in the Text Editor. The Text Editor, shown in Figure 10-1,
is a separate window with a full range of text controls and its
own preview pane. After the text is created, a *text object*
appears in the current Fireworks document, surrounded

by a bounding box. The text object has many, but not all of the properties of a path object — you can, for example, use the transform tools such as Skew, but you can't use Reshape Area to warp the text as you can a path. On the other hand, text objects have features unlike any other object, such as the capability to be aligned to a circle or any path. If necessary, it's possible to convert a text object to either an image object or a path object, but the text can no longer be edited.

Text Control          Preview Pane

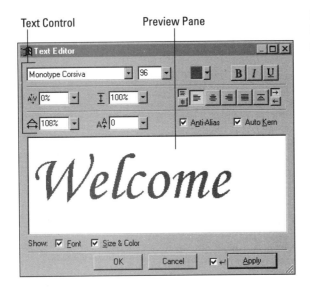

**Figure 10-1:** The Text Editor is used to compose and edit text in Fireworks.

The Text tool in the Toolbox is your initial gateway into the Text Editor. The Text tool can be used two ways:

✦ Click once with the Text tool to set a starting point for your text. If necessary, the text flows to the edge of the current document and expands downward toward the bottom of the document.

✦ Drag out a rectangular text region with the Text tool. The text created in the Text Editor wraps on the horizontal boundaries of the established region and, if necessary, expands downward.

The general steps for inserting text into a Fireworks document are

1. Select the Text tool from the Toolbox or use the keyboard shortcut, t.

2. Set the text area by

   • Clicking once on the document where you'd like the text to start

   • Dragging out a text area for the text to fit into

   Either method opens the Text Editor.

**3.** From the Text Editor, choose the text characteristic such as font, size, color, and alignment.

**4.** Click in the Preview pane and input the text. If Auto-Apply is enabled, Fireworks 2 updates the text object in the document after each keystroke.

**5.** Click OK when you're done.

Once the text object is onscreen, you move it as you would any other Fireworks object, by clicking and dragging with the Pointer tool. To adjust the shape of the text object, drag any of the six handles that become available when the object is selected.

**Note**    A text object can be increased in size horizontally at any time and the text will automatically reflow to fit the new dimensions. However, text objects can only be increased in size vertically to permit more text already inserted through the Text Editor to be visible.

When you need to edit an existing text object, there are several ways to open the Text Editor. You can select the text object as you would any other Fireworks object and then choose Text ⇨ Editor. Alternatively, once the text object is selected, you can press the keyboard shortcut, Ctrl+Shift+E (Command+Shift+E). Perhaps the most efficient method (and certainly my most often-used one) is to double-click the text object with the Pointer or Subselection tool. If the Text tool is active, you'll see the I-beam cursor with a small right-pointing triangle when you move over a text object; at this point, a single click on any text object opens the Text Editor.

## Previewing on the fly

In the previous version of Fireworks, the chasm between the text object and the Text Editor was quite wide. Perhaps the biggest problem was that you couldn't see the results of your editing until the Text Editor was closed. If the resulting object didn't fit just right or was an inappropriate font, the Text Editor had to be reopened and the text adjusted. This process made for a lot of back-and-forth between the two modes. Now, however, thanks to the efforts of the Macromedia engineers, your trial-and-error days are at an end.

**New Feature**    Fireworks 2 features real-time text updating in the document for each change made in the Text Editor. Any edit — either to the text itself in the Preview pane or through the text controls — is instantly reflected in the text object, as shown in Figure 10-2. This enhancement greatly simplifies both the creation phase, when you're trying to find the right overall look, and the tweaking phase, as you make incremental adjustments.

Fireworks also offers an augmented preview, right in the Text Editor. Fireworks 1 let you see the typeface and its size applied to the text through the Font and Size options. Fireworks 2 adds color to this preview feature and even enables you to create multicolored text.

**Figure 10-2:** Updates in the Text Editor are instantly applied to the text object in the document in Fireworks 2.

## Choosing basic font characteristics

Within the Text Editor, you have full control over the look and style of your text. The Text Editor offers two methods of working, just like a word-processing program. To set your options, use either one of the following techniques:

✦ Set the font attributes prior to entering text into the Preview pane.

✦ Select the text you want to modify in the Preview pane — all or a portion — and then alter the attributes.

The core characteristics are all found at the top of the Text Editor, as shown in Figure 10-3. The basic attributes are very straightforward to establish:

✦ **Font:** To choose a typeface, select a name from the Font option list. The Font option list displays all the available fonts on your system. You can scroll down the list or, if you know the name of the font you wish to use, select the Font option list and begin typing the first letters of the name. The Font option list jumps to the typeface with the matching letters.

✦ **Size:** Choose the text size using the Size slider or by entering a value directly in the Size text box. Size is the height of a font, and is given in points, where 72 points equals one inch. Fireworks accepts sizes from 4 to 1,000 points, although the slider only goes from 8 to 96.

✦ **Color:** Initially, the Text Editor applies the color specified in the Fill color well. However, you can easily choose a new text fill color by selecting the option arrow next to the color well in the Text Editor. The standard color picker pop-up is displayed with the current swatch set. In Fireworks 2, each letter or symbol can have its own color.

✦ **Style:** Choose from Bold, Italic, and—new in Fireworks 2—Underline styles for your text; each style button is a toggle and any one can be mixed with any other. The Underline option is especially useful for displaying hyperlinks in a comp artwork.

Font option list    Size slider  Font color well  Style buttons

**Figure 10-3:** Select your font typeface, size, color, and style from the top of the Text Editor.

All of the basic attributes are applicable on a letter-by-letter basis. You can, although you're not advised to, change every letter's font, size, color, or style. Ransom notes were never easier.

**Tip**    Need to try out a bunch of different fonts? If you're on a Windows system, here's a quick way to run through your font list. Highlight the text in the Preview pane and then select your first typeface from the Font option list. When both your text and the Font option list are highlighted, you can use the arrow keys to scroll through the different fonts and instantly see the results in the Preview pane and in the document.

## Adjusting text spacing

All adjustments to how text is located within the text object occurs in the Text Editor. Fireworks includes five text spacing controls, as shown in Figure 10-4.

Baseline shift
Kerning
Horizontal scale
Leading
Auto-kerning option

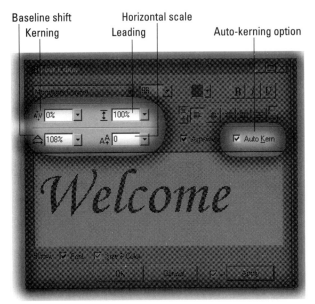

**Figure 10-4:** Control your text character and line positioning through Fireworks's text spacing controls.

### Kerning

Kerning determines how close letters appear to each other. The default value of 0 percent uses the standard font spacing. Increasing the Kerning slider (1 percent to 100 percent) moves letters further apart, whereas decreasing it (–1 percent to –99 percent) moves letters closer together, or overlapping. The kerning can be altered between two letters by placing the cursor between the letters in the Preview pane of the Text Editor and moving the Kerning slider or entering a new value. To change the kerning for a range of letters or the entire text in the Preview pane, select the letters before changing the kerning value.

**Note**  Changes in the kerning are not shown in the Preview pane. However, if you have the Apply option checked, you can see the effect of kerning on your text object in the document itself after each change.

### Auto Kerning

Many fonts define the spacing for *kerning pairs*, like the letters "WA" or "ov," which fit together to make text more legible. Some fonts come with as many as 500 kerning pairs defined. Fireworks applies the kerning pair information whenever the Auto Kerning option is enabled. The Auto Kerning option affects the entire text object.

The effect of kerning pairs is most noticeable in the larger font sizes. Figure 10-5 displays an unkerned word above a kerned version. Note the differences in the overall length of the word as well as how the first A is closer to its neighbors in the Auto Kerned text.

**Figure 10-5:** Use the Auto Kerning option, as with the text on the bottom line, to create a more readable headline.

### Leading

Leading (pronounced *ledding*) is the printer's term for line spacing. In Fireworks, leading is expressed as a percentage of the font size and only affects text with multiple lines. Single-spaced lines use the default 100 percent; a double-spaced paragraph would use 200 percent. Leading values less than 100 percent cause lines to overlap. Unless you're creating a special effect, it's best to keep your leading 90 percent or higher.

Tip

Although the range of the Leading slider is from 50 percent to 250 percent, you can enter most any value you want directly into the Leading text box.

### Horizontal Scale

You can alter the relative width of any text through the Horizontal Scale control. The range of the Horizontal Scale slider is from 10 percent to 200 percent; unlike several other controls, you cannot specify a value outside of the Horizontal Scale range through the text box. The effect of the Horizontal Scale can be seen in Figure 10-6 where the same text is presented at 200 percent, 100 percent, and 25 percent. Horizontal Scale does not display in the Preview pane.

**Figure 10-6:** Change the width of text by adjusting the Horizontal Scale slider in the Text Editor.

**Tip**     Want to make your text really wide? To circumvent the Horizontal Scale limitations, use the Scale tool on the text object. Best of all, you retain editability in Fireworks.

### Baseline Shift

If you're building a Web site where chemical formulas are a key element, you'll be happy to discover the Baseline Shift control. Normally, all text is rendered along the same baseline so that the bottoms of most letters are aligned. The Baseline Shift control enables you to place letters or words above or below the normal baseline. Fireworks specifies the Baseline Shift value in points: negative values go below the baseline, and positive values go above. For a standard subscript letter, such as the 2 in $H_2O$, use a negative value half the size of the current font. Likewise, for a superscript, choose a positive value, half the current font size. I followed these guidelines to create the example found in Figure 10-7, and I also decreased the size of the TM by half to make it more proportional.

**Figure 10-7:** Specify a new Baseline Shift value for special subscript and superscript characters.

## Aligning Text

All text objects, when selected in the Fireworks document, are surrounded by a bounding box. The bounding box sets the position of the text through its upper-left corner coordinates, but it also determines the limits for the text block. Most importantly, all alignment for the text is relative to the bounding box.

Fireworks 2 includes a very robust set of alignment options within the Text Editor, shown in Figure 10-8. First, text can be either Horizontal (the default) or Vertical. Depending on which of the two options you choose, the remaining alignment buttons change. When Horizontal is selected, the available buttons are

✦ **Left Alignment:** Text is aligned to the left edge of the bounding box.

✦ **Right Alignment:** Text is aligned to the right edge of the bounding box.

✦ **Center Alignment:** Text is centered between the left and right edges of the bounding box.

✦ **Justified Alignment:** Text is evenly spaced so that the letters of each line touch both the left and right edges of the bounding box; the letters, however, remain the size specified in the Font size.

✦ **Stretched Alignment:** Text is expanded horizontally so that the letters of each line touch both the left and right edges of the bounding box.

✦ **Text Flows Left to Right:** Text is rendered across the screen, from left to right.

✦ **Text Flows Right to Left:** Text is rendered across the screen, from right to left.

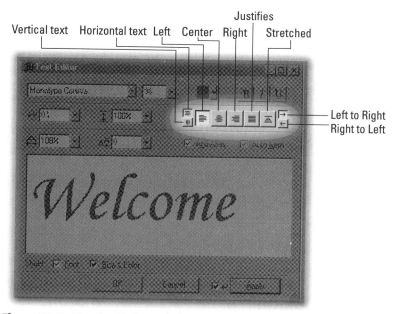

**Figure 10-8:** Use the Horizontal Alignment controls to align text left, center, right, justified, or stretched.

**Tip**

The middle sizing handles on a text object's bounding box are always adjustable. This is a very useful feature, because you can quickly center text in a document by dragging the middle sizing handles to either edge of the canvas and choosing the Center alignment option in the Text Editor.

Different alignment options can be applied to different text in the same text object, as long as each piece of text is on its own line. Figure 10-9 illustrates this capability with each of the five horizontal alignment options displayed in text object.

Navigation
Navigation
Navigation
N a v i g a t i o n
**Navigation**

**Figure 10-9:** You can apply different alignments to separate lines of text in a single text object.

When Vertical Text is chosen, the alignment options change to

✦ **Top Alignment:** Text is aligned to the top of the bounding box.

✦ **Center Alignment:** Text is centered between the top and bottom of the bounding box.

✦ **Bottom Alignment:** Text is aligned to the bottom of the bounding box.

✦ **Justified Alignment:** Text is evenly spaced so that the letters of each line touch both the top and bottom edges of the bounding box; however, the letters remain the size specified in the Font size.

✦ **Stretched Alignment:** Text is expanded vertically so that the letters of each line touch both the top and bottom edges of the bounding box.

✦ **Text Flows Down and Up:** Text is rendered down the screen, starting from the top of the bounding box.

✦ **Text Flows Up and Down:** Text is rendered up the screen, starting from the bottom of the bounding box.

## Enabling Text Editor options

The final element found in the Text Editor are the options: two for the Text Editor itself and three for the final product. To get the closest approximation possible in the Preview pane, enable both the Font and Font Size & Color options. The Font option displays the text in the current selected typeface; when the Font option is turned off, the Preview pane shows text in a sans-serif font, such as Arial or Helvetica. The Size & Color option — no surprises here — let you see your text in the current size and color. Without this option enabled, you'll see text at approximately 24 points and black.

The three other options, Anti-Alias, Auto-Kern, and Apply, are applicable to the text object. The Anti-Alias option smoothes the text by providing an anti-aliased edge to the fill for the text object. Auto-Kern, as discussed in the previous section on text spacing, uses a font's kerning pairs. Apply enables any changes made in the Text Editor to be automatically updated and viewed in the document's text object.

In my way of working, only occasionally do these features actually become optional. If I have a large block of text in the Preview pane, I might disable the Size & Color option, but I almost never turn off the Font option. Only when I'm trying to achieve a special effect would I even consider disabling either Anti-Alias or Auto-Kern. And I've noticed that I'm totally dependent on the Apply function for constant feedback as I work.

# Re-Editing Text

The Text Editor is perhaps the most commonly used method for editing text in Fireworks, but it's not the only one. To make a global change to a text object, such as altering the typeface or size, you can use a menu command. Although you do sacrifice the full range of features, menus can be much faster than using the Text Editor, especially if you take advantage of the keyboard shortcuts.

In all, five menu items under the Text heading can be applied to a selected text object:

✦ **Font:** Lists the fonts available on your system, in alphabetical order. To access a font not shown in the list for lack of room, choose Text ⇨ Fonts ⇨ More Fonts to open a small dialog box that enables you to access all of the fonts in your system.

✦ **Size:** To quickly change your selected text object to a set size, choose Text ⇨ Size and then one of the dozen point sizes: 8, 9, 10, 12, 14, 18, 24, 36, 48, 72, 96, and 120.

✦ **Style:** In addition to the options available through the Text Editor (Bold, Italic, and Underline), the Text ⇨ Style menu enables you to remove all styles with one command, Text ⇨ Style ⇨ Plain. You can also use the keyboard shortcut, Ctrl+Alt+Shift+P (Command+Option+Shift+P).

✦ **Align:** The Text ⇨ Align menu is broken up into two groups, one for horizontal text and one for vertical text. Choosing an alignment from one group automatically alters the orientation of the text, if necessary. For example, if you apply Text ⇨ Align ⇨ Bottom to a horizontal text object, the text object converts to a vertical text object and aligns the text to the bottom, simultaneously.

To be completely thorough, there is one other Text command that could be listed in this category, Text ⇨ Editor, which opens the Text Editor for the selected text object. Alternatively, you can use the keyboard shortcut, Ctrl+Shift+E (Command+Shift+E).

# Importing Text

As noted in the introduction to this chapter, almost all text used in Web graphics is relatively short and the longer paragraphs are part of the HTML file rendered by the browser. There are numerous reasons why text on the Web is generally not in graphic form, although first and foremost — as with many aspects of the Web — is file size. Download times for a page of graphic text is considerably longer than for that of HTML text.

However, in the for-every-rule-there's-an-exception category, occasionally blocks of text have to be rendered as a graphic. Some clients insist on an absolute fidelity to their traditional printed material across all platforms. The only way to keep these types of clients happy — even at the expense of a longer download — is to render the text as a graphic. In these cases, you'll have the potential for taking advantage of one of Fireworks's least-known features: text import.

In addition to the numerous graphic file types supported by Fireworks, you can also open ASCII and Rich Text Format (RTF) files. ASCII files are the lowest common denominator of all text files and contain no formatting whatsoever. RTF files, on the other hand, convey a good deal of basic formatting, such as typeface, size, styles (bold, italic, and underline), and alignment.

Although you can copy text from another program and paste it in Fireworks's Text Editor, for a large block of text, you're better off importing it. The key method for inserting text in Fireworks is the somewhat hidden command, Insert ⇨ Image. Though used primarily for importing images, it works just fine for text as well.

To insert a text file, follow these steps:

1. Be sure the file you want to import is saved in either ASCII or RTF format.

2. Choose Insert ⇨ Image or use the keyboard shortcut, Ctrl+R (Command+R). The Import dialog box displays.

3. From the Files of Type option list, choose either ASCII Text (*.txt) or RTF Text (*.rtf).

4. Select your file and click OK when you're ready. After the Import dialog box closes, the Insert cursor appears.

5. Place the imported text in your document in one of two ways:

   • Position the cursor where you'd like the upper-left corner of the text object to start and click once.

   • Click and drag out the bounding box for the text file.

   The text flows into the new text object.

**Note**    The click-and-drag method for creating a text object is currently somewhat limited. Rather than have the full freedom to draw whatever shape you desire, the rectangle is constrained to a 4:1 ratio of vertical to horizontal space. In other words, the initial text object will always be four times as wide as it is tall. More importantly, Fireworks renders the text to fit within this bounding box, regardless of its previous font size.

# Transforming Text

You really start to feel the power of Fireworks once you begin adding strokes, textured gradient fills, and multiple effects to a block of text—and you're still able to edit it. You can even use any of the transform tools—Scale, Skew, or Distort—to completely warp the text, and it's still editable.

There's no real shortcut to mastering text in your images. You really can only get a sense of what's possible by working, experimenting, trying—in essence, playing. In the following sections, you'll find some avenues to begin your text explorations.

## Adding strokes

When you first create a text object, only the basic fill color is applied. However, this doesn't mean you can't add a stroke to your text—any combination of stroke settings is fair game. You do have to be a bit careful, though. Some of the preset strokes, such as Basic Airbrush, are quite hefty and can completely obscure all but text in the larger font sizes. However, modifying a stroke size (or color, softness, or texture) is quite easy and you can generally adjust the presets to find a workable setting.

One use for text with an added stroke is to create outlined text. Almost all fonts—with a few decorative exceptions like Desdemona—are presented with solid, filled-in letters. In Fireworks 2, however, you can make almost any font an outline font, such as the one shown in Figure 10-10, with a fairly straightforward procedure:

1. Select a text object.

2. Open the Stroke panel by choosing Window ⇨ Stroke or clicking the Stroke tab.

3. Change the stroke category from None to any of those available in the Category option list.

**Tip**   Not all strokes are suitable for outlining text. Try to choose those categories of fonts that have anti-aliased presets, such as Basic Soft or Pencil 1-Pixel Soft.

4. Select any desired preset from the Type option list and modify its settings as needed.

5. Open the Fill panel by choosing Window ⇨ Fill or clicking the Fill tab.

6. Set the fill category to None in the Category option list. The solid fill disappears and the remaining stroke outlines the text.

**Figure 10-10:** The top text object uses a standard Goudy Stout typeface; the bottom one uses the same typeface, but is outlined by Fireworks strokes.

Another technique for adjusting the look of a stroke on text is to alter the stroke's orientation. With most path objects, an applied stroke is centered on the path. With text objects, however, the default is to place the stroke on the outside of the path. The orientation of the stroke is changed on the Object panel with the text object selected. When the stroke orientation is altered, you can get three completely different graphic looks, as shown in Figure 10-11.

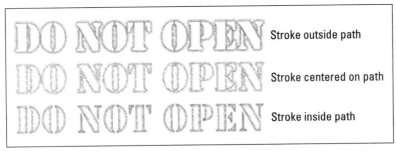

Stroke outside path

Stroke centered on path

Stroke inside path

**Figure 10-11:** The only difference between these three variations is the orientation of the stroke.

**Cross-Reference**    To find out more about strokes, turn to Chapter 8.

## Enhancing fills

Although the default method of displaying text already uses a colored fill, it's just the tip of what's possible with Fireworks text. Any type of fill that can be devised — solid color, Web dither, gradient, or textured — is applicable to text objects. More-over, you can alter the edges of a fill to give either a softer or harder textual appearance.

Applying a fill to text is very straightforward. Just select the text object and choose your fill from the Fill panel. Fireworks treats the entire text object as a single unit so gradients and patterns flow across all the separate letters and words. You can, however, adjust the way the fill is distributed by adjusting the gradient and pattern controls, as described in these steps:

1. Select your text object.

2. Choose Window ➪ Fill or click on the Fill tab, if visible. The Fill panel opens.

3. Choose a gradient or pattern fill.

4. If Auto-Apply is not enabled, select Apply. The gradient or pattern fill is applied to the text object.

5. Select the Paint Bucket tool. The gradient editing handles appear on the filled text object, as shown in Figure 10-12.

6. To adjust the centerpoint of the gradient, click and drag the round starting handle.

7. To adjust the direction of the gradient, click and drag the square ending handle. Some gradients, such as Ellipse, Rectangle, and Starburst, have a third handle, which can be moved to adjust the width and skew of the gradient.

8. Click any tool other than the Paint Bucket to leave the Edit Gradient mode.

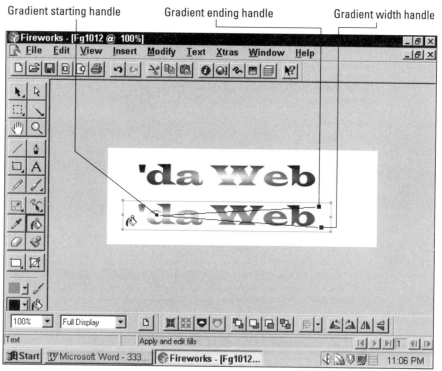

**Figure 10-12:** Alter the way a gradient moves across your text by moving the Gradient Fill handles.

It's also possible to apply the gradient individually to each letter of the text object rather than the entire text object at one time, as can be seen in Figure 10-13. The downside of this technique is that you lose editability of the text. To assign gradients to individual letters, follow these steps:

1. Select your text object.

2. Choose Text ➪ Convert to Paths. After the text is converted to paths, it can no longer be re-edited.

3. Choose Window ➪ Fill or click on the Fill tab to open the Fill panel. Make sure that all the letters in the former text block are still selected.

4. Select any gradient or pattern fill.

**Figure 10-13:** Though you can cause a gradient fill to work separately on each letter, you lose editability of the text when you do so.

The Fill panel can also be a tool for blurring text. The standard edge for a text fill is Anti-Alias to remove any jaggies that might be apparent in text. Though this is useful for the vast majority of cases, it's good to know you can achieve special effects such as those seen in Figure 10-14 by changing the fill edge type to Feather. From left to right, each number uses an increasingly larger Feather type fill, starting with 1 pixel for the slightly fuzzy number 9 and ending with 8 pixels for very blurry number 6.

10... 9... 8... 7... 6...
How Many Bottles of Beer on the Wall?

**Figure 10-14:** I caused the numbers in this graphic to achieve their fuzziness by applying a Feathered edge to an increasing degree.

**Cross-Reference**    Want to know more about fills? Turn to Chapter 11.

## Using the transform tools

Each of the three transform tools — Scale, Skew, and Distort — can be applied to any text object. This means that text can be resized, rotated, slanted, and even pulled out of shape and still be edited in the Text Editor. In this regard, text objects act just like path objects: the same sizing handles appear and even the Numeric Transform command can be used. Nonetheless, you should keep a few points in mind about transforming text:

✦ Before using the Skew tool on a text object, narrow the bounding box on either side of the text object as much as possible. Skew affects all portions of a text object and excess area will probably give you an undesirable effect.

✦ As with a regular path object, both Skew and Distort are useful for providing perspective effects with text, as shown in Figure 10-15. Adding an effect to text, such as inner bevel or drop shadow, also helps the effect.

✦ Text can be transformed in one of two ways: as a path object or as a pixel image. These options are available on the Object panel when the text object is selected. The Transform as Path option (the default) results in smoother, less jagged text than the Transform as Pixels option; however, in some instances, you may prefer the more ragged look.

**Figure 10-15:** The Skew tool is great for text perspective — particularly when combined with effects like a drop shadow and inner bevel.

## Converting text to paths

So if editability of text is such a big deal, why would you ever want to give it up? There are certain effects — such as Reshape Area — that cannot be applied to a standard text object, but can be applied to a text object converted to paths. Moreover, if you want to alter a letter's shape, you need to gain access to its underlying points. To do any of these operations, your first step is to choose Text ➪ Convert to Paths.

Fireworks gives you the option to create new graphics based on typography. To modify the paths of any of the letters of a text object, follow these steps:

1. Select your text object.

2. Choose Text ➪ Convert to Paths or use the keyboard shortcut, Ctrl+Shift+P (Command+Shift+P). Each letter in the text object is converted to a path or composite path object.

3. To work on one or more letters, choose Modify ➪ Ungroup.

4. Choose the Subselection or another path tool. The pull mode of the Reshape Path tool was used to create the example shown in Figure 10-16.

**5.** Select the path object letter to modify and begin work.

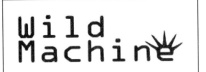

**Figure 10-16:** Once the text was converted to paths, the Reshape Path tool could be used to create the special letter.

**Tip**

Not only can you convert text to paths, you can also convert it to an image. Just select the text object and choose Modify ➪ Merge Images. As with the path conversion, text converted to pixels is no longer editable through the Text Editor.

Because each letter in a text object is grouped together after the text object is converted to a path, you often have to ungroup them to work on the separate parts. Sometimes, however, a tool requires that you ungroup *and* join them as a composite path to function correctly. Reshape Area is such a tool and here are the steps necessary for prepping your text for use:

1. Select your text object.

2. Choose Text ➪ Convert to Paths. Each letter in the text object is converted to a path or composite path object.

3. Choose Modify ➪ Ungroup.

4. Choose Modify ➪ Join.

5. Select the Reshape area tool and, in the Options panel, set the Size large enough to cover multiple letters, if not the whole object. In the example (Figure 10-17), the Reshape Area tool was approximately half the size of the original text block so it could be shaped in two directions.

6. Apply the tool to the text.

**Figure 10-17:** After converting the text to paths, the paths were ungrouped and then joined before being molded with the Reshape Area tool.

**Caution**

Once you've converted text to a path and saved the results, you won't be able to open the text. If possible, save a master file with all changes except for the final text-to-path step. Then, if edits to the text are required, you won't have to rebuild everything. Another way to keep a master version is to put a copy of the text object on a hidden layer.

# Text on a Path

For the most part, text is either strictly horizontal or vertical. The Text on a Path command, however, enables you flow text in the shape of any path — whether the path is a circle, rectangle, or freeform shape.

The basic procedure is pretty simple: first, create each part — a text object and a path — and then combine them. Because paths can come in so many shapes, Fireworks offers a number of different controls and options to help you get what you want. Amazingly enough, text remains editable even after it's been attached to a path.

To align text on a path, follow these steps:

1. Draw or create any path object.

2. If necessary, create a text object.

3. Select both the path and text object.

4. Choose Text ➪ Attach to Path or use the keyboard shortcut, Ctrl+Shift+Y (Command+Shift+Y). The text flows along the path and the attributes of the path (stroke, fill, and effect) disappear, as shown in Figure 10-18.

5. To edit the text, double-click it to open the Text Editor.

6. To separate the text from the path, choose Text ➪ Detach from Path.

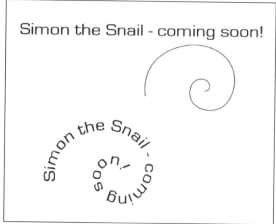

**Figure 10-18:** The two separate objects — text and path — are combined in one with the Attach to Path command.

Several variables affect exactly how the text flows along the path. First, the alignment of the text itself can have an effect:

✦ **Left Aligned:** The text starts at the beginning of the path.

✦ **Centered:** The text is centered between the beginning and end of the path.

✦ **Right Aligned:** The text ends at the end of the path.

✦ **Justified:** All the characters are evenly spaced along the path with additional spacing, if necessary.

✦ **Stretched:** All the characters are stretched to fit along the path with standard spacing.

It's pretty easy to guess where a linear path starts and ends, but how about a circle? If you remember the discussion on using the Ellipse tool in Chapter 5, you might recall I mentioned that circle paths generally start at about 9 o'clock and travel in a clockwise direction, around the outside of the circle. To cause the text to begin its flow in a different area, you have three options:

✦ Rotate the text attached to the path using one of the transform tools.

✦ Choose Modify ⇨ Transform ⇨ Numeric Transform and select Rotate from the option list before choosing the angle of rotation.

✦ Enter an Offset value in the Objects panel.

The Offset value moves the text the specified number of pixels in the direction of the path. Because circle diameters vary, trial and error is the best method for using the Offset value. The Offset option also accepts negative numbers to move the text in the opposite direction of the path.

To flow the text along the inside of the circle, choose Text ⇨ Reverse Direction. With an Offset value at 0, the text will begin at 6 o'clock and flow counter-clockwise. In order for the lower circle to wrap correctly in Figure 10-19, I had to use the Reverse Direction command and set the Offset to -125.

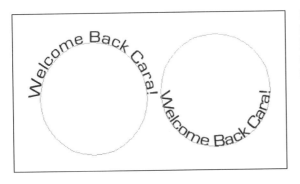

**Figure 10-19:** Use the Reverse Direction command in combination with Offset to properly place your text in a circle.

The final aspect that you can control with regard to attaching text to a path is the text's orientation to the path. You can find the options, shown in Figure 10-20, under Text ⇨ Orientation:

✦ **Rotate around Path:** Each letter in the text object is positioned perpendicularly to its place on the path (the default).

✦ **Vertical:** Each letter of the text object remains straight relative to the document, as it travels along the path.

✦ **Skew Vertical:** Rotates the letters along the path, but slants them vertically.

✦ **Skew Horizontal:** Keeps the letters straight on the path and slants them horizontally according to the angle of the curve.

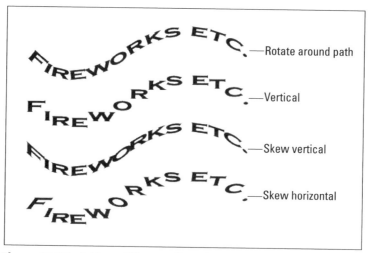

**Figure 10-20:** Achieve different effects by changing the orientation of the text to its attached path.

After looking at the Skew Horizontal example in Figure 10-20, you might be wondering why this option was included. One of the reasons why it looks so unappealing is that the skew changes when the underlying path changes its angles. When Skew Horizontal is applied to a path with no or fewer curves, you can achieve a more pleasing effect, as shown in Figure 10-21.

**Figure 10-21:** The Horizontal Skew orientation looks best when it's applied to a path with few or no curves.

# Fireworks Technique: Masking Images with Text

What do you get when you combine images and text so that the text becomes the image? A graphic worth a thousand and one words? Actually, I think the technique of masking images is often worth far more. Moreover, its relative ease of creation in Fireworks makes it especially valuable.

A *mask group* is two or more objects grouped together where the bottom object is visible only through the top object. Take a look at Figure 10-22 and you'll see immediately what I mean. Because color is often so vital to a mask group's effect — and because I think it's cool — I've also included the image in the color section as Color Plate 10-1.

**Figure 10-22:** Combine imagery and text through a mask group.

To mask an image with text, follow these steps:

1. Create your image and text object and move them into the same document with the text object in front of the image.

2. Position the text object over the image in its approximate final place.

3. Select both objects.

4. Choose Modify ⇨ Mask Group. The image is now only visible through the text.

5. Use the Subselection tool if you need to slightly modify the placement of the image.

**Tip**    You can still edit the text used in a Mask Group — you just have to ungroup it and select it by itself. When you're finished with your edits, apply the Mask Group command again.

The basic technique for masking an image with text is the same as using any other object as a mask. I've found, however, that manipulating the text into the proper shape beforehand creates a more successful mask. I try to start with a fairly wide font so that much of the image comes through and then apply the Horizontal Scale and/or Kerning controls in the Text Editor to get the largest possible type. For example, the font used in Figure 10-22 is Wide Latin at 96 points and a –29 percent Kerning value.

Often you also need to massage the imagery to take the most advantage of the type placement. In this example, I flipped the original photograph horizontally, cut out about half of the sunset, moved the sun a few degrees to the right, and transferred the camel from the middle of the desert to a silhouette. And, of course, I did it all in Fireworks.

# Summary

Text and images are codependents on the Web. It's nearly impossible to have one without the other, but the text-handling features of Fireworks make for a smooth integration. Gaining a complete understanding of creating and editing Fireworks's text objects is essential for strong Web design. Keep these considerations in mind as you work with text in Fireworks:

✦ Text is always editable for files saved in Fireworks native format. You can apply a stroke, fill, effect, or transform text repeatedly — and you'll still be able to edit all the text, all the time.

✦ Text in Fireworks is represented in the document as a text object. Text objects are created through the Text Editor or can be imported from ASCII or RTF files.

✦ The Text Editor is the major text interface and contains all the controls necessary for assigning attributes such as typeface, size, color, spacing, and alignment to text.

✦ In Fireworks 2, alterations made in the Text Editor are instantly visible in the document.

✦ Text can accept the full range of strokes, fills, and effects available in Fireworks. The transform tools — Scale, Skew, and Distort — also work with text objects.

✦ Some operations, such as Reshape Path, require that you convert a text object into a series of paths; such converted text is no longer editable through the Text Editor.

✦ Fireworks has a very full-featured Align Text with Path command that enables you to flow text around a circle, down a curving slope, or tracing any path you desire. Moreover, you can adjust the spacing of the text through the Alignment and Offset features.

✦ You can easily combine text and images by using the Fireworks Mask Group command.

In the next chapter, you'll get into the center of Fireworks objects as we examine fills and textures.

✦     ✦     ✦

# Achieving Effects

# Fills and Textures

Fills and strokes are pretty much equal partners in Fireworks graphics. A fill gives substance to the inside of an object, just as a stroke does the outside. Fills in Fireworks come in many flavors — solid colors, gradations of color, and image patterns — and, like strokes, they are astoundingly flexible and almost infinitely variable. Moreover, fills in objects are always editable, which means changing from a flat color to a repeating pattern takes only a click or two.

After touring the standard fills included with Fireworks — including the new Web Dither option — this chapter begins to explore all the many ways you can customize and enhance fills. In addition to the techniques for editing gradients and patterns and the many variations obtainable through the addition of textures, you'll see how you can add custom gradients, patterns, and textures.

## Using Built-in Fills

As with strokes and the Stroke panel, fills are generally applied and modified from the Fill panel, shown in Figure 11-1. You can display the Fill panel by choosing Window ➪ Fill, clicking on the Fill tab if visible, or using the keyboard shortcut, Ctrl+Alt+F (Command+Option+F).

There are four primary fill categories:

- ✦ **Solid:** Specifies a flat color fill, selectable from the color picker pop-up or by using the Eyedropper.

- ✦ **Gradient:** Inserts one of 11 gradient patterns blending two or more colors. The Gradient category is not separately listed, but implied through the listing of the gradient patterns.

✦ **Web Dither:** Extends the Web-safe color range by using two Web-safe colors to create a pattern that simulates a third Web-safe color.

✦ **Pattern:** Applies a full-color image as a repeating pattern.

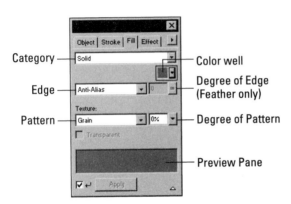

**Figure 11-1:** The Fill panel is your command center for applying and modifying any type of fill.

Each of the different categories offers a slightly different Fill panel. If you choose Solid, for example, no additional presets are presented, whereas if you select Pattern, an option list with all the available patterns appears. There are some similarities for all fill types, however. The Fill color well (also available on the Toolbox and Mixer) are present for all categories, as is the Edge option list.

The Edge option acts exactly like the one found in the Stroke panel with three choices: Hard Edge, Anti-Alias, and Feather. Choosing a Hard Edge fill uses just the fill specified with no enhancements; Anti-Alias blends the edge a bit, softening away the jaggies, if any; and Feather blends the edge the number of pixels specified through the Amount of Feather slider.

Textures work with fills in the same fashion as they do with strokes, but because they're so much more visible, you'll find a special section later in this chapter that delves deeper into their use.

## Turning off an object's fill

Just as important as adding a fill is knowing how to remove the fill. In Fireworks 2, there are two methods you can use. The first technique is to choose None from the Category option list on the Fill panel.

**New Feature**

A second technique for removing the fill has been added in Fireworks 2. When you select the Fill color well in either the Toolbox or the Mixer, the color picker pop-up now has a No Color button next to the Palette button. Selecting the No Color button eliminates any type of fill, regardless of whether it's a solid, gradient, or pattern type.

# Solid

A Solid fill is a basic, monochrome fill, sometimes called a *flat fill*. The color used in the Solid fill type is selected from the Fill color well — whether it's the one on the Fill panel, the Toolbox, or the Mixer. The Fill color well uses the standard Fireworks color picker pop-up, shown in Figure 11-2. The color picker displays the swatches active in the Swatches panel, which, by default, is the Web 216 palette.

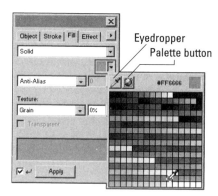

Eyedropper
Palette button

**Figure 11-2:** Assign a solid color fill through the Fill color well.

To apply a solid color to an object, follow these steps:

1. Select the object.

2. Access the Fill color well in one of these three ways:

    • Choose Window ➪ Fill to open the Fill panel and select the color well.

    • Select the Fill color well, as marked by the Paint Bucket, in the Toolbox.

    • Choose Window ➪ Mixer to display the Mixer and select the Fill color well, as marked by the Paint Bucket.

    Any of the above methods causes the color picker pop-up to display.

3. To choose a color from the current swatch set, select any of the visible swatches.

4. To choose a color found onscreen, select the Eyedropper tool and click that color.

5. To access the operating system color picker, select the Palette button and select one of the colors in that dialog box.

Solid fills can be adjusted in several ways. You can select different edge options (Hard, Anti-Aliased, or Feather) from the Edge option list on the Fill panel; if you choose Feather, the Amount of Feather slider becomes available. In addition, a texture chosen from the Texture option list on the Fill panel may be applied. Remember, though, for a texture to be visible, you have to increase the Amount of Texture past 0 percent.

# Web Dither

Color is one of the most frustrating elements of Internet design. Because of the restrictions of older color displays, most Web designers use a palette of 216 Web-safe colors that the major browsers display correctly. The most obvious limitation is the relatively small number of colors: 216 out of a visible palette of millions of colors. This limitation becomes particularly acute when a client's logo contains colors not in the Web-safe palette. Luckily, Fireworks 2 offers you a way to increase the Web-safe color variations to over 45,000: the Web Dither fill.

To understand how to use the Web Dither fill, you'll need a little more background in computer color. *Dithering* refers to the process where two or more pixels of different colors are positioned to create a pattern which, to the human eye, appears to be a third color. This technique works because a small pattern of pixels tends to blend visually; the grouping of pixels is too difficult for the eye to separate the individual pixels. Dithering was originally developed by computer graphics programs to overcome the 256 color restriction of early computer monitors. If you convert a photograph with millions of colors in JPEG format to a GIF with only 256 colors, you'll notice dithered areas where the computer graphics program is attempting to simulate the unavailable colors. In cases like these, dithering is considered undesirable and should be avoided.

**New Feature**

However, a positive capability of dithering called Hybrid-Safe Colors was recognized initially by Don Barnett and Bruce Heavin and later popularized by Web designer Lynda Weinman. A Hybrid-Safe color consists of two Web-safe colors in an alternating 2 × 2 pattern. Fireworks 2 has adopted this technique, renamed it Web Safe, and made it available as a Fill category. Not only does this feature now give you a total of 46,656 (216 × 216) Web-safe colors, but it also enables you to make any Solid fill semitransparent, opening up a whole new area of graphic design.

When you choose the Web Dither category from the Fill panel, you'll notice a new set of options becomes available, as shown in Figure 11-3. Instead of one color well, there are now three. The top color well represents the current Fill color, whereas the other two color wells are used to create the dither pattern. If the current Fill color is already Web safe, both dither colors will be identical. If the Fill color is not Web safe, Fireworks creates the closest match possible by dithering two Web-safe colors.

To apply a Web Dither fill, follow these steps:

1. Select your object.

2. Choose Window ➪ Fill or click on the Fill tab, if visible.

3. Select the option arrow next to the topmost color well. The Fireworks color picker pop-up displays.

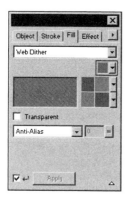

**Figure 11-3:** The new Web Dither fill greatly expands the range of possible Web-safe colors that can be used.

4. Pick a color that is not Web-safe in one of these ways:

   - To select a color from the swatch in your active palette, choose the color from the pop-up color picker. The active color must not be the Web 216 Palette for this method.

   - To select a color from an image onscreen, choose the Eyedropper from the pop-up color picker and sample the desired color.

   - To select a color using your system's color picker, choose the Palette button from the pop-up color picker.

**Tip**     If you can't find a non–Web-safe color, try entering the hexadecimal values 00-00-83 (a deep blue) directly in the RGB text boxes on the Mixer panel when the Fill color well is selected.

Fireworks creates the closest color match possible by dithering your original color.

The Web Dither fill is terrific for finding absolute must-have colors — like those used for a logo — in a Web environment. With Fireworks's new scanning capability, you could scan in the logo and then sample the color for the Web Dither fill.

**Caution**     Though the Web Dither fill appears to give you a huge range of colors to choose from, some combination may be less than optimum. If you choose two highly contrasting colors for the dither color wells, the dithered pattern appears to be dotted. It's always best to select the desired color for the Fill color well by using the Eyedropper or any other method and let Fireworks create the dither pattern for you.

Fireworks 2 takes the Web Dither fill further by including a Transparent option. When you enable the Transparent option, Fireworks sets the first dither color well to None while snapping the second dither color well to the nearest Web-safe color.

The dither pattern now alternates a transparent pixel with a Web-safe colored pixel and the resulting fill pattern is semitransparent. If you fill an object with a Web Dither fill with the Transparent option enabled, you'll get an effect much like the one I achieved in Figure 11-4, where the text maintains its basic color, but permits the background to show through.

**Figure 11-4:** The text here takes advantage of the new Web Dither fill with the Transparent option turned on, so that it can be both seen and seen through.

**Tip**    When you export a figure using a Transparent Web Dither fill, be sure to select either the Index or Alpha Transparency option.

# Managing Gradients

A *gradient* is a blend of two or more colors. Gradients are used to add a touch of three-dimensionality or provide a unique coloration to a graphic. A gradient is composed of two parts: a *color ramp*, which defines the colors used and their relative positioning, and a *gradient pattern*, which describes the shape of the gradient.

Fireworks includes 11 different types of gradient patterns and 13 preset color combinations. As you may have guessed, that's just scratching the surface of what's possible with gradients because, like many features in Fireworks, gradients are completely editable.

## Applying a Gradient fill

A Gradient fill is applied in a slightly different manner than a Solid or Pattern fill. To apply a Gradient fill, follow these steps:

1. Select your object.

2. Choose Window ➪ Fill or click the Fill tab to bring the Fill panel to the front.

**3.** From the Category option list, choose one of the gradient options below the divider. When the selected gradient is initially applied, the current Brush and the Fill colors are used to create the blend and a Preset option list appears in the Fill panel, as shown in Figure 11-5.

**4.** Choose a color combination from the Preset option list.

**5.** Change the fill edge or add a texture, if desired.

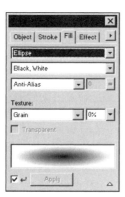

**Figure 11-5:** Select a gradient pattern and preset color combination from the Fill panel.

Rather than describe the standard gradients in words, it's much easier to grasp the differences visually, as demonstrated in Figure 11-6. The colored gradients are such a treat, it's only right to present them in full color. They can be seen in Color Plate 11-1.

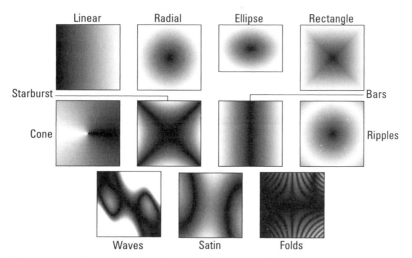

**Figure 11-6:** Fireworks provides 11 different gradient patterns.

## Altering gradients

Fireworks's built-in gradient patterns and preset colors offer a good number of possibilities, but the real power of gradients comes in its customizability. Gradients can be modified two major ways:

✦ Every gradient pattern's center, width, and skew (if any) are all adjustable. With this facility, you can reshape the gradient's appearance with any object.

✦ The color ramp used to create the progression of colors in a gradient is completely flexible. Existing colors can be changed, deleted, or moved, and new colors can be added anywhere in the gradation.

The custom color ramp information can be saved as a new preset, much like a custom stroke. However, a modified gradient pattern cannot be saved, either as a gradient or style. Unfortunately, there's no way to transfer a modified gradient pattern other than copying and pasting the actual object.

### Modifying the gradient pattern

The key to unlocking—and customizing—the gradient pattern is the Paint Bucket tool. The Paint Bucket is generally used to fill any selected areas of an image object or any path objects with the current Fill panel settings. However, if the Paint Bucket is chosen when a Gradient or Pattern fill is in use, the gradient controls appear. As noted earlier, all gradients have a starting point and an ending point, and four (Ellipse, Rectangle, Starburst, and Ripples) use two controls to adjust the size and skew of the pattern. The gradient controls are placed differently for each gradient pattern, as is evident in Figure 11-7.

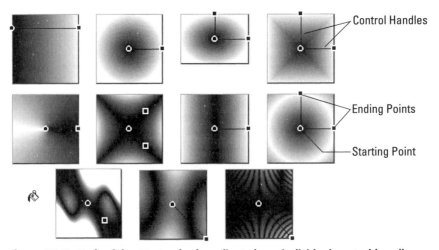

**Figure 11-7:** Each of the 11 standard gradients have individual control handles.

To modify a gradient pattern, follow these steps:

1. Select the image with the Gradient fill.

2. Select the Paint Bucket tool from the Toolbox, or use the keyboard shortcut, Ctrl+K (Command+K). The gradient controls appear.

3. To move the starting point for the gradient, drag the circular handle to another position.

4. To rotate the direction of the gradient, move the cursor over the length of any control handle until the Rotate cursor appears and then drag the handles to a new location. As you rotate the gradient, Fireworks uses the gradient's starting point as a center axis.

5. To change the size of any gradient, drag the square handle straight to another position.

6. To alter the skew of an Ellipse, Rectangle, Starburst, or Ripples gradient, drag either square handle in the desired direction.

You're not limited to keeping the gradient controls within the selected object. Any gradient control — beginning, ending, or sizing/skewing handle — can be moved away from the object. In fact, some of my nicest gradient patterns resulted from placing the controls completely outside of the object. Experiment and think "outside the box."

**Caution**    Remember, there's no way to copy a modified gradient pattern from one object to another — much less one image to another — outside of copying and pasting the object itself. To mimic an effect on two widely different objects, you have to duplicate the placement of the gradient controls by hand.

## Editing gradient colors

If you cycle through the preset gradient color combinations, you'll notice that some presets have as few as two colors and others have as many as six. To see how the color preset is structured, click the Fill panel Options pop-up and then choose the Edit Gradient command. The Edit Gradient dialog box, shown in Figure 11-8, is divided into three main areas: the color ramp, the color wells, and the preview pane.

The color ramp shows the current color combination as it blends from one key color to another. The key colors are displayed in the color wells, located beneath the color ramp. The preview pane shows how the color combination would be applied to the active gradient pattern. You can either modify a preset gradient or adjust a gradient created from the Fill and Brush colors.

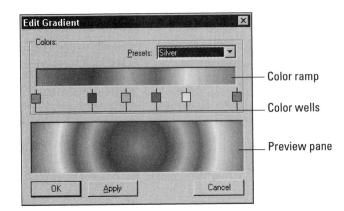

**Figure 11-8:** Modify the colors used in a gradient through the Edit Gradient dialog box.

Color ramp

Color wells

Preview pane

To edit a gradient, follow these steps:

1. Select the Fill panel Options pop-up.

2. Choose Edit Gradient. The Edit Gradient dialog box appears.

3. If you'd like to modify a preset gradient, choose one from the Preset option list.

4. To adjust the rate of change between colors, drag the color wells into new positions. One color well can be dragged on the far side of another color well.

5. To remove a color well completely, drag the color well away from the color ramp toward the preview pane.

6. To add a new color well, click anywhere directly below the color ramp. The added color well displays the color directly above it in the color ramp.

7. To select a new color for a color well, double-click the color well. The standard color picker pop-up appears. Select any of the available swatches or use the Eyedropper tool to sample an onscreen color, including one from another color well. The Palette button on the color picker pop-up can be used to access the system color picker.

8. Click OK when you're done.

Although there's no real limit to the number of colors you can add to an edited gradient, it's not practical to add more than two dozen or so. With so many colors, the color wells begin to overlap and it becomes increasingly difficult to select the correct one to modify.

# Saving and renaming

Once you've modified an existing gradient, you need to save it in order to recall it. In Fireworks 2, you can store an altered gradient two ways:

✦ Use the Save Gradient command, found on the Fill panel Options pop-up, to store the gradient color combination in the current document.

✦ Create a new Style and save just the Fill type.

## Examining Fill panel options

The Fill panel Options pop-up offers several gradient management options:

✦ **Save Gradient As:** Stores the current gradient under a new name within the active document

✦ **Edit Gradient:** Displays the Edit Gradient dialog box

✦ **Delete Gradient:** Removes the current gradient, custom or standard, from the Gradient panel

✦ **Rename Gradient:** Relabels the current gradient

✦ **Auto Apply:** Automatically applies changes made in the Fill panel to any selected object

## Storing a modified gradient

To store a modified gradient, follow these steps:

1. Choose the Options pop-up and select Save Stroke As. The Save Gradient As dialog box appears.

2. Enter a unique name for the gradient. If you choose a name already in use, Fireworks asks if you want to replace the existing gradient.

3. After entering a new name, choose Save. The new gradient name is displayed alphabetically in the Preset option list of any gradient.

## Using the gradient in another document

It's important to understand that any new or modified gradients are stored only within the document in which they're used. To use the gradient in another document, follow these steps:

1. Open the document containing the gradient you want to use.

2. Select an object using the new gradient.

3. Open the new document in which you want to use the new gradient.

4. Copy the selected object to the new document either by using Edit ⇨ Copy and Edit ⇨ Paste or by dragging and dropping the object from one document to the other while pressing Alt (Option). The new gradient setting is added to the Fill panel when the object containing the gradient is pasted into the document.

5. If desired, delete the copied object from the new document.

There are several other ways to achieve the same effect of transferring gradients from one document to another:

✦ Use Insert ⇨ Image to insert a document containing one or more custom gradients. After you've clicked once to place the document, choose Undo. The graphics will vanish, but all custom gradients will be incorporated into the Gradients panel.

✦ Copy the path with the custom gradient in one document and just paste the attributes to a path in the new document by selecting that path and choosing Edit ⇨ Paste Attributes.

## Using the Styles feature

Perhaps the best way to always be sure your custom gradients are available is to use the Styles feature, new in Fireworks 2. To create a new style using a custom gradient, follow these steps:

1. Select an object that uses the custom gradient.

2. If necessary, choose Window ⇨ Styles, use the keyboard shortcut, Ctrl+Alt+J (Command+Option+J), or click the Style tab, if visible. The Style panel displays.

3. On the Style panel, select the New Style button.

4. In the Edit Style dialog box, enter a descriptive name for your gradient in the Name text box and deselect all checkboxes except Fill Type.

5. Click OK when you're done. A new style is entered in the Style panel.

Any style added in the just-described fashion is always available for any Fireworks document. To apply the gradient, just highlight any Fireworks object and select the new style. Your custom gradient is then added to the Fill panel.

**Cross-Reference**    To find out more about the powerful Styles feature, see Chapter 17.

# Fireworks Technique: Making Transparent Gradients

Although you can pick any available color in the spectrum for a gradient color well, you can't pick "no color." In other words, there's no way to create a gradient that uses transparency in the Edit Gradient dialog box. However, there is a fairly straightforward and flexible technique you can apply to get the desired effect of having any Fireworks object — path or image — fade away.

Almost all of Fireworks's transparency effects take advantage of the Mask Group feature — and the transparent gradient is no exception. A Mask Group combines a regular object with an object with a black-to-white Gradient fill and makes the black parts transparent and the white, opaque. Because there is a gradual blend from black to white, you get a smooth transition from transparent to opaque.

**Note**

Technically speaking, a Mask Group uses the alpha channel of the top object as a transparency mask for the other objects.

To create a transparent gradient, follow these steps:

1. Create or insert an object or image that you want to make partially transparent.

2. Draw a second masking object that completely encompasses the original object. If you are masking a path object, rather than an image object, you can clone the original.

3. Open the Fill panel.

4. With the masking object selected, choose a gradient pattern, such as Linear or Radial.

5. From the Preset option list, choose Black, White.

6. If necessary, reposition the masking object over the original object, making sure that the masking object is in front of the original object.

7. Select both objects.

8. Choose Modify ⇨ Mask Group or use the keyboard shortcut, Ctrl+Shift+G (Command+Shift+G).

As you can see in Figure 11-9, where I've taken a red square with a star and combined it with a Radial gradient, the transparent background shows through quite well. In fact, it may show through a bit too well. I often find that I need to adjust the standard Black and White gradient preset so that there is more black than white. I do this by choosing Edit Gradient in the Fill panel Options pop-up and sliding the black color well closer to the white one. To edit the gradient in this fashion, it's best to first select the Mask Group and then choose the Paint Bucket tool to expose the gradient control handles. When the gradient controls are active, you can use the Edit Gradient feature and immediately apply it—otherwise, you must first ungroup the Mask Group and reselect just the Gradient fill.

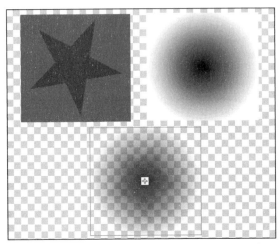

**Figure 11-9:** A gradient-filled object is combined with another object to make a Mask Group that enables a fade to transparency.

As you may have guessed, you can also alter the gradient controls by selecting the Mask Group and then choosing the Paint Bucket. Moreover, you can also change the gradient pattern from a Radial to a Rectangle for a different effect. Once you get the initial hang of using Mask Groups to create a gradient transparency, you can achieve a wide range of effects.

## Using Patterns

Simply put, a Pattern fill uses a repeating image to fill an object. Patterns are often used to provide a real-world surface, such as bricks or wood paneling, to a computer-generated drawing. More abstract patterns are also used to vary the look of a graphic. Fireworks 2 includes 14 standard patterns with an additional 70 available in the Goodies\Patterns folder of the Fireworks CD-ROM. Not surprisingly, you can also add your own images to be used as a pattern.

The Pattern fill is one of the primary categories found on the Fill panel. When you select the Pattern option, a second option list, Fill Name, appears with all the available patterns. As you move down the Fill Name option list, a small preview of the pattern is displayed next to each highlighted file, as shown in Figure 11-10.

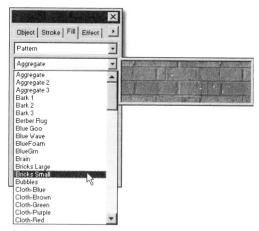

**Figure 11-10:** Choose your pattern file from the Pattern Fill Name option list.

The only Fireworks requirement for a Pattern fill image is that the image be in PNG format. However, not all images are well suited to making patterns; the best patterns are those that repeat seamlessly so that the original file cannot be detected. All of the standard Fireworks files fill this requirement, as is clearly visible in Color Plate 11-2.

Like any other fill, Pattern fills can be applied to any shape object. The other fill attributes — edge and texture — are also applicable.

## Adding new patterns

There are two ways to add new patterns to the standard list:

✦ Save or export a file in PNG format to the Fireworks\Settings\Patterns folder.

✦ Through the Preferences dialog box, assign an additional folder for patterns.

As PNG is Fireworks's native format, it's quite easy to store any file as a pattern just by saving it. Pattern images are usually full-color (whereas texture files must be grayscale), but that's not a hard-and-fast rule. Likewise, patterns are generally 128 pixels square, but that's just a convention, not a requirement; one of the patterns found on the Fireworks CD, Light Panel, is 12 pixels wide by 334 pixels high.

Once you've saved a file in your Patterns folder and restarted Fireworks, the new pattern is listed along with the other patterns. As shown with my new pattern in Figure 11-11, they even preview the same.

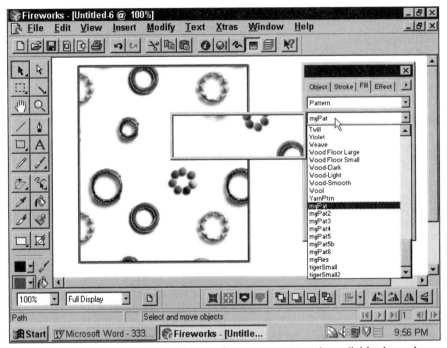

**Figure 11-11:** A 200 × 200 PNG file saved as a new pattern is available through the Fill panel.

Assigning an external Patterns folder is a very easy way to add a whole group of folders at one time, as well as a good way to share resources in a networked environment. To assign an additional Patterns folder, follow these steps:

1. Choose File ➪ Preferences. The Preferences dialog box opens.

2. Select the Folders tab.

3. In the Additional Material section, choose the browse button marked with an ellipse (...) next to the Patterns option. The Browser for Folder dialog box appears.

4. Locate the external folder that contains the PNG files you want to access as patterns. Click OK when you've selected the folder. The path to the folder appears next to the browse button and the Patterns checkbox is now enabled on the Preferences dialog box.

5. Click OK to accept the changes and close Preferences.

6. Relaunch Fireworks. The additional patterns will not be available until Fireworks is restarted.

**Tip** Want quick access to the 70 patterns on the Fireworks CD? Assign your external Patterns folder in Preferences to the Goodies\Patterns folder and restart Fireworks. When Fireworks opens, if the CD is present, the additional patterns are integrated into the Fill panel list — and you can remove the CD after Fireworks has finished loading and the patterns will still be available. If the CD is not available, Fireworks loads normally, but the additional patterns are not incorporated.

## Altering patterns

Patterns can be adjusted in the same manner as gradients. After a Pattern fill has been applied to an object, selecting the Paint Bucket tool causes the control handles to appear, as shown in Figure 11-12. The same types of vector controls are available:

✦ Adjust the center of the Pattern fill by dragging the round starting point.

✦ Rotate the Pattern fill by moving the cursor over the length of any control handle until the Rotate cursor appears, then drag the handles to a new angle.

✦ Change the size of any pattern by dragging either square handle straight to another position.

✦ Alter the skew of any pattern by dragging either square handle in the desired direction.

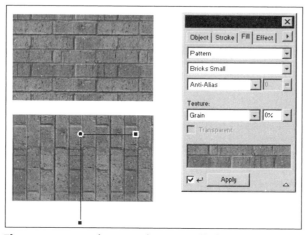

**Figure 11-12:** Both rectangles were filled with the standard Bricks Small pattern and then the control handles of the bottom rectangle were rotated 90 degrees to change the pattern direction.

Unlike gradients, all patterns have two control handles in addition to the starting point of the fill. The handles are always perpendicular to one another and presented in the same ratio as the height to the width.

**Tip**    When rotating an object, the pattern or Gradient fill does not rotate with it. Instead, you'll need to use the pattern or gradient control handles to change the angle of the fill.

# Fireworks Technique: Creating Seamless Patterns

The biggest problem with creating new Pattern fills is making them appear seamless. When Fireworks tries to fill an object larger than the size of the pattern file, it repeats or *tiles* the image until the object is completely filled. If an image is used with even the smallest border, the repeating pattern is immediately noticeable; in most cases, this is not the desired effect. Several methods eliminate the appearance of seams.

The first, and simplest, technique is to avoid placing graphic elements near the edge of your pattern image. This enables the canvas — or background color — to blend smoothly from one instance of a pattern into another. As shown in Figure 11-13, this technique works best when the graphics are placed to avoid any appearance of a repeating pattern.

**Figure 11-13:** The original image keeps all graphics away from the edges so that the pattern can repeat seamlessly.

Many images, of course, rely on a visually full background where the canvas color is completely covered. For this type of graphic to be converted to a pattern, a fair amount of image editing is necessary to make the edges disappear. Luckily, Fireworks contains enough graphic editing power to make this procedure feasible.

A tiled pattern places images next to every side of the original image. To remove any indication of a boundary, you need to simulate a tiled pattern and then blend the images so that no edges show. The following steps detail the procedure I use to smooth pattern edges in Fireworks.

**Note** Throughout this technique, I refer to the menu syntax for the command, like Edit ⇨ Copy. Naturally, you should feel free to use whatever keyboard shortcuts you're familiar with.

1. Open the image you'd like to convert to a pattern.

2. Select a portion of the image to use as the basis for your pattern.

   It's quite common to use just a part of a scanned image or other graphic as a pattern. The best technique I've found for this is to determine how large you want your pattern to be (128 × 128 is a good size) and then use the Fixed Size feature of the Marquee tool available through the Options panel to set those dimensions. This lets you work with a preset Marquee and move it into position more easily.

3. Choose Edit ⇨ Copy to copy the selected area.

4. Choose File ⇨ New to create a new document. The document should be at least three times the size of your selected image. Because mine is 128 square, 384 × 384 would be my minimum size.

5. To guide placement, choose View ⇨ Grid Options ⇨ Edit Grid to set thesize of the grid the same as your image, and enable the Show Grid and Snapto Grid options.

6. Choose Edit ⇨ Paste to paste the copied area in the upper-left corner of the document, as shown in Figure 11-14.

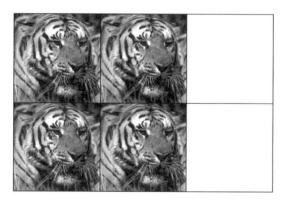

**Figure 11-14:** After setting the grid to help with alignment, the first image is pasted down.

**7.** Copy the image with the Alt+drag (Option+drag) method. Place the copy of the image to the right of the original.

**8.** Repeat Step 7 twice more, but place the two new image copies below the two already in place, as shown in Figure 11-15.

**Figure 11-15:** With all four copies in place, the edges are plainly visible.

**9.** Turn off both the grid (choose View ➪ Grid) and the Snap to Grid options (choose View ➪ Grid Options ➪ Snap to Grid).

**10.** Select all four copies of the image and choose Modify ➪ Merge Images. This step is necessary because the core of this technique uses the Rubber Stamp tool, which only works with image objects. By selecting all copies, the four separate image objects have been merged into one.

**11.** Select the Rubber Stamp tool from the Toolbox.

The next step is the core of this procedure and, as such, requires a bit of finesse and trial-and-error to get it right. You might want to save the document at this stage just so you can restart the process without having to start completely over.

**12.** Working on the vertical seam between the copies on the left and the right, click the Rubber Stamp origin point down one side a few pixels to the side, near the edge. Drag over the edge in a left-to-right motion (or from right to left, depending on which side the Rubber Stamp origin is located), extending the side of one image into the side of another.

Follow this procedure down the vertical seam. Occasionally you might need to switch directions and origin point to vary the blurring. Press Alt to reset the origin point of the Rubber Stamp tool. If necessary, set the Rubber Stamp options to the softest possible edge on the Options panel.

**13.** After you've blurred the vertical seam, repeat the process for the horizontal seam, changing the direction of the Rubber Stamp as needed.

When you're done blurring both the vertical and horizontal edges, the resulting image should appear to be a seamless pattern, as shown in Figure 11-16. After this step, it's time to copy the portion of the image used to make the pattern.

**Figure 11-16:** After the edges are blurred, it's hard to tell where one image stops and the other starts.

14. Choose View ➪ Grid Options ➪ Edit Grid and reset the grid to half of its former size, enabling both the view and the snap options as well. Using a half-sized grid lets you easily grab the center of the current image. My original grid was 128 × 128, so my new one for this step is 64 × 64.

15. Choose the Marquee tool from the Toolbox. The Marquee's Options should still be set to the Fixed Size option, using your original dimensions.

16. Use the Marquee to select the central portion of the overall image.

17. Choose Edit ➪ Copy to copy the selection. Notice that the selection takes a part of all four images, previously separate, as shown in Figure 11-17.

**Figure 11-17:** The final pattern image uses the center of four adjacent images.

18. Choose File ➪ New to create a new document. Fireworks automatically sizes the new document to match the graphic on the Clipboard.

19. Choose Edit ➪ Paste to paste the selection.

20. Choose File ➪ Save and store the image in the Fireworks\Settings\ Patterns folder.

21. Quit and restart Fireworks.

22. Test your pattern by drawing out a closed path and filling it with your new pattern.

23. If necessary, open the just-saved Pattern file and edit to remove any noticeable edges.

There are numerous other ways to blur the line between your edges, but the Rubber Stamp tool works in many situations. Although it does take a bit of practice to get the hang of the tool and this technique, the results are definitely worth it.

 **Cross-Reference**    For more information on the Rubber Stamp tool and its options, see Chapter 6.

# Adding Texture to Your Fills

A common complaint about computer graphics in general is that their appearance is too artificial. If you take a quick look around the real world, very few surfaces are a flat color—most have some degree of texture. Fireworks simulates this reality by enabling any fill (or stroke, for that matter) to combine with a *texture*. In Fireworks, a texture is a repeating image that can be applied on a percentage basis.

Like Fireworks patterns, textures are PNG images designed to be repeated, which are stored in a specific folder. But that's pretty much where the similarity with patterns ends. Whereas a pattern replaces any other fill, a texture is used in addition to the chosen fill. A texture is, in effect, another object, which is blended on top of the original object. As you increase the degree of a texture through the Fill panel slider, you are actually increasing the opacity of the texture. When the amount of texture is at 100 percent, the texture is totally opaque and the textured effect is at its maximum.

Another difference between pattern and texture is color: patterns can be any range of color, whereas textures must be grayscale images. The reason for this is purely functional: if textures included color, the color of the original fill or stroke would be altered. One consequence of the grayscale property is that flat white fills are almost totally unaffected by textures.

 **Tip**    Generally, textures work better with darker colors, which permit more range of contrast.

Fireworks provides a wide range of textures: 26 included with the program and 21 more on the Fireworks CD-ROM. Each texture is chosen from an option list on the Fill panel and, like patterns, a preview is displayed for each texture. Next to the Texture option list is a slider that controls the chosen texture's degree of intensity. The higher the amount of texture, the more pronounced the texture's effect on the fill, as shown in Figure 11-18.

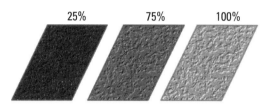

25%   75%   100%

**Figure 11-18:** Increasing the amount of texture on the Fill panel makes the texture more visible.

There's one other property of textures: transparency. If your textured object is on top of other objects, enabling the Transparent option lets the background objects show through the light portions of the texture. The higher the degree of texture, the more transparent an object becomes.

## Extending Textures to Strokes and Images

Textures aren't limited to enhancing fills. You can just as easily apply them to strokes and, with just a little more work, images as well. Sometimes a stroke is used to define a filled object and it's best not to extend the texture onto the stroke. Certain images, however, benefit from a continuation of the texture from fill to stroke.

Take, for example, this image of the glowing X. I created a very simple texture to simulate video scan lines. If the texture is applied to just the fill, the stroke breaks the flow of the texture and ruins the illusion. Because the same set of textures are available from both the Fill and Stroke panel, it's easy to duplicate settings from one panel to the other. In the case of the pictured X, both stroke and fill use my custom texture at 20 percent.

*Continued*

*(continued)*

Applying a texture to an image requires an additional step. Currently, image objects in Fireworks are compatible only with effects—strokes and fills cannot be applied directly to an image. The technique then is to create a path object that completely covers the image and apply the texture to that path object. When you first try this, however, you'll notice that the texture doesn't blend as evenly with the image as it does with regular objects. To accomplish the smooth effect achieved in the image of the monitor with the lips, I reduced the opacity of the textured path object to the same level as I would a built-in texture. Essentially you use the Opacity slider, found on the Object panel, in the same manner as you do the Amount of Texture slider.

## Adding new textures

New textures are accessed exactly the same way that new patterns are added:

✦ Save or export a file in PNG format to the Fireworks\Settings\Textures folder.

✦ Through the Preferences dialog box, assign an additional folder for textures.

Textures files work best when they enable a repeating pattern without visible edges and, as mentioned previously, all textures must be a grayscale image.

### Converting a color image to grayscale

There are a couple of ways to convert a color image in Fireworks to grayscale—one converts the file to a bitmapped image and the other uses a grayscale palette on export. To use the bitmapped-image method of creating a grayscale and saving it as a texture, follow these steps:

1. Select the entire graphic by choosing Edit ⇨ Select All.

2. Choose Modify ⇨ Merge Images to convert all path objects to image objects.

3. Choose Xtras ⇨ PhotoOptics ⇨ CSI MonoChrome to access one of the filters that come bundled with Fireworks. The CSI MonoChrome dialog box, shown in Figure 11-19, is displayed.

4. Choose the Default Settings, where Hue, Saturation, and Exposure are all set to 0 percent.

5. Click OK to accept these changes.

6. Choose File ➪ Save to store the converted file in PNG format.

7. In the Save dialog box, browse to the Fireworks\Settings\Textures folder.

### Using a grayscale palette on export

While fairly straightforward, the disadvantage to the method just described is the loss of editability. To keep your texture file in Fireworks native format and export it as grayscale, follow these steps.

1. If you haven't yet, save your document by choosing File ➪ Save. Although you don't have to, it might be best to store the master file in a different location than the Textures folder.

2. Choose File ➪ Export to open the Export dialog box.

3. From the Options tab of the Export Preview dialog box, choose PNG from the Format option list.

4. From the Bit Depth option list, choose Indexed (8 Bit).

5. From the Palette option list, select Grayscale.

6. Click the Next button.

7. From the Export dialog box, browse to the Fireworks\Settings\Textures folder.

8. Enter a unique name for the texture in the File Name text box and click Save.

9. Quit and restart Fireworks to see the new texture listed.

## Assigning an additional Textures folder

If you have an entire group of textures you want to add at one time, you can assign an additional folder for Fireworks to include in the texture list. To assign an additional Textures folder, follow these steps:

1. Choose File ➪ Preferences. The Preferences dialog box opens.

2. Select the Folders tab.

3. In the Additional Material section, choose the browse button marked with an ellipse (...) next to the Textures option. The Browser for Folder dialog box appears.

4. Locate the external folder that contains the PNG files you want to access as patterns. Click OK when you've selected the folder. The path to the folder appears next to the browse button and the Patterns checkbox is now enabled on the Preferences dialog box.

**5.** Click OK to accept the changes and close Preferences.

**6.** Relaunch Fireworks. The additional patterns will not be available until Fireworks is restarted.

**On the CD-ROM** Can't get enough textures? You'll find 50 additional ones in the CD-ROM of this book in the Textures folder.

# Filling with the Paint Bucket

The Paint Bucket tool is used to fill a selected area with the current Fill panel settings — whether those settings involve a solid color, a gradient, or a pattern. The Paint Bucket can be used to fill both path objects and image objects. There is a difference, however; the Paint Bucket fills all of a path object completely, whereas it only fills the selected portion of an image object, as shown in Figure 11-19. The Paint Bucket has an additional property with regard to the image objects — it can either fill a range of like, adjacent colors within a selection or the entire selection.

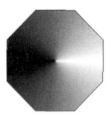

**Figure 11-19:** The path object on the left is filled completely by the Paint Bucket, whereas the image object on the right fills only the selected area.

With path objects, nothing is simpler than using the Paint Bucket. Just choose the Paint Bucket tool (or use the keyboard shortcut, k) and then click the object once to apply the current Fill panel settings. If Fill is set to None, the current fill color — seen on the Toolbox and Mixer — is used to give the object a Solid fill.

**Caution** Fireworks doesn't distinguish between open and closed paths when the Paint Bucket is used. If the Paint Bucket is used on an open path, such as an S-curve, an invisible line is drawn from the beginning to the ending point and the fill is applied.

Image objects are a different story with regard to the Paint Bucket. If you click an image object with the Paint Bucket without selecting an area using one of the selection tools (Marquee, Ellipse Marquee, Lasso, Polygon Lasso, or Magic Wand), one of three things will happen:

✦ The current Fill settings will be applied to the selected pixel and the neighboring pixels that fall within the Tolerance range set in the Options panel.

✦ The entire image object will be filled with the current Fill settings, if the Fill Selection Only object is selected from the Options panel and the Expand to Fill Document option from Preferences is not enabled.

✦ The entire document will be filled with the current Fill settings, if the Fill Selection Only object is selected from the Options panel and the Expand to Fill Document option from Preferences is enabled.

As you can see, the Options panel, shown in Figure 11-20, becomes very important when you apply the Paint Bucket tool to image objects. The available options are

✦ **Mouse Highlight:** Highlights a selectable area when passed over with the pointer.

✦ **Fill Selection Only:** Disregards color tolerance settings and fills a selected area, or if no area is selected, either the image object or document according to the Expand to Fill Document setting.

✦ **Tolerance:** Sets the range of colors to be filled when Fill Selection Only is not enabled. The Tolerance slider accepts values from 0 (where no additional colors are filled) to 255 (where all additional colors are filled).

✦ **Edge:** Determines the type of edge on the fill — Hard, Anti-Aliased, or Feather. If Feather is selected, the Amount of Feather slider becomes available, which sets the degree to which the fill is blended into surrounding pixels.

**Figure 11-20:** The Options panel for the Paint Bucket tool has a major effect on how image objects are filled.

**Tip**

Once you've made a selection in an image object, you don't have to click in the selected area with the Paint Bucket to change it. Clicking anywhere in the document automatically fills the selected area.

# Summary

Fills are one of Fireworks's basic building blocks. Without fills, objects would appear to have outlines only and it would be difficult, if not impossible, to arrange objects on top of one another. As you begin to work with fills, keep these points in mind:

✦ Fills can be applied to any Fireworks object: path or image.

✦ Access all the fill settings through the Fill panel. The Fill color well can also be found on the Toolbox and the Mixer.

✦ There are four major types of fills: Solid, Gradient, Pattern, and the new Web Dither.

✦ The Web Dither fill visually blends two Web-safe colors to make a third color outside the limited Web-safe palette.

✦ You can modify a Gradient or Pattern fill by selecting the filled object with the Paint Bucket tool and adjusting the control handles.

✦ New gradient color combinations can be saved in each document and reused or stored in a style.

✦ A Pattern fill can be made from any repeating image, stored in PNG format.

✦ Textures can bring a touch of realism to an otherwise flat graphic.

✦ The Paint Bucket options control whether the entire image object is filled or just a selection is filled.

In the next chapter, you'll learn about the razzle-dazzle side of Fireworks: Live Effects.

✦ ✦ ✦

# Live Effects

**M**any Fireworks graphics are based on three separate but interlocking features: strokes, fills, and effects. Not everyone would put effects — the capability to quickly add a drop shadow or bevel a button — on the same level as strokes and fills, but most Web designers would. Effects are pretty close to essential on the Internet. Not only is the look-and-feel of many Web sites dependent on various effects, but much of the functionality, especially where such techniques as button rollovers are concerned, demands it.

Live Effects were a Fireworks innovation. For the first time, designers could edit common effects without having to build the graphic from the ground up. But what makes Live Effects truly "Live" is Fireworks's capability to automatically reapply the effects to any altered graphic — whether the image was reshaped, resized, or whatever. Fireworks 2 continues the innovative trend by introducing multiple effects. Now, any or all of the effects can be combined in a far more user-friendly fashion than before.

After touring the standard Fireworks effects — with a very in-depth look at their options — you'll see how you can begin to apply multiple effects. Later in the chapter, you'll see how you can store your most commonly used effects and even take a look at some special techniques for using Fireworks Live Effects.

## Working with Predesigned Effects

Fireworks ships with the five most-requested effects built-in:

- ✦ **Inner Bevel:** Adds a three-dimensional look to an object by beveling its inside edge
- ✦ **Outer Bevel:** Frames the selected object with a three-dimensional rounded rectangle

✦ **Drop shadow:** Shadows the object against the background to make it stand out more effectively

✦ **Emboss:** Simulates an object in relief against its background

✦ **Glow:** Puts a halo or soft glow all around the selected object

All five effects are definable from the Effect panel. Although basically the same, each effect has its own particular attributes and thus, its own Effect panel configuration. They are, however, all applied in basically the same fashion:

1. Select the object or objects. Fireworks can apply the same effect to multiple objects, simultaneously.

2. Choose Window ➪ Effects to open the Effect panel. Alternatively, you could use the keyboard shortcut, Ctrl+Alt+E (Command+Option+E) or click the Effects tab, if visible.

3. Select your effect from the Effect category option list.

4. Choose the preset effect from the Effect Name option list, if desired.

5. Alter the parameters of the effect.

If you have the Auto-Apply feature turned on — either by choosing Auto-Apply from the Effect panel Options pop-up or by selecting the Apply check box — the selected object is updated for every change that is applied.

Once an effect is applied, Fireworks keeps it alive throughout any other changes the object undergoes. Fireworks actually recalculates the required pixel effects and reapplies the effect after the change is made for path, image, or text objects. To my mind, the capability to attach a live effect to a bitmapped image, as shown in Figure 12-1, is a superb addition to the Web designer's toolbox.

**Figure 12-1:** Fireworks effects are "live" — so that if you apply an effect such as the drop shadow to the image on the left and then cut out the primary figure, the drop shadow follows the changes.

As good as Fireworks effects look, sometimes your objects look better with none at all. To remove an effect, first select the object and then, from the Effect panel, choose None from the Category option list.

# Inner and Outer Bevel

The two bevel effects, Inner Bevel and Outer Bevel, are Fireworks's key to 3D. Both simulate light coming from a specific direction, illuminating a graphic that seems to be raised out of or sunken into the background. The bevel effects are very similar in terms of user interface, available attributes, and preset options. In fact, they only differ in two key areas:

✦ As the names imply, the Inner Bevel creates its edges inside the selected object, whereas the Outer Bevel makes its edges around the outside the selected object.

✦ The Outer Bevel effect has one attribute that the Inner Bevel does not: color. The Inner Bevel uses the object's color to convert the inside of the graphic to a bevel, whereas the Outer Bevel applies the chosen color to the new outside edge.

When you select either Inner Bevel or Outer Bevel from the Effect category option list, the Effect panel interface displays the available parameters, as shown in Figure 12-2.

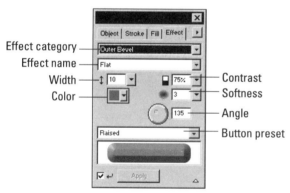

**Figure 12-2:** The Outer Bevel's Effect panel is the same as the Inner Bevel's except for the additional color well.

## Effect panel options

The Effect panel options include:

✦ **Effect name:** Seven different types of bevel effects are accessible through the Effect name option list. Each type of effect alters the number, shape, or degree of the bevel.

✦ **Width:** Sets the thickness of the beveled side. The Width slider has a range from 0 to 10 pixels, although you can enter a higher number directly in the text box.

✦ **Contrast:** Determines the difference in relative brightness of the lit and shadowed sides where 100 percent provides the greatest contrast and 0 percent provides no contrast.

✦ **Softness:** Sets the sharpness of the edges used to create the bevel where 0 is the sharpest and 10 is the softest. Values above 10 have no effect.

✦ **Angle:** Provides the angle for the simulated light on the beveled surface. Drag the knob control to a new angle or enter it directly in the text box.

✦ **Button Preset:** Offers four preset configurations, primarily used for creating rollover buttons.

✦ **Color:** Available for Outer Bevel, this standard color well is used to determine the color of the surrounding border.

Caution    Though the bevel effects can be applied to any object, if the object's edge is feathered too much, you won't be able to see the effect. To combine a feathered edge with a bevel, set the Amount of Feather to less than the width of the bevel.

Each of the bevel effects have the same types of edges. Compare the Inner Bevel effects (Figure 12-3) to those for the Outer Bevel (Figure 12-4) and you'll see the similarities of the seven types for both effects. Found under the Effect name option list, these types vary primarily in the shape of the bevel itself.

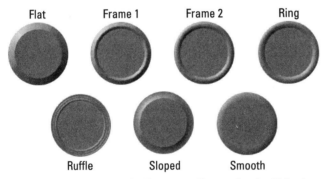

**Figure 12-3:** Inner Bevel effects are all contained within the original path of the object.

Looking at each of the bevel shapes from the side, as in Figure 12-5, makes it easier to differentiate between the possible shapes.

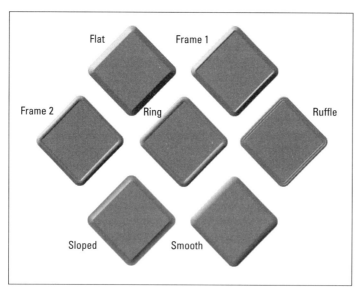

**Figure 12-4:** Outer Bevel effects create edges outside the original path.

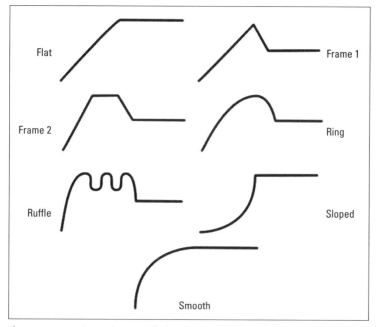

**Figure 12-5:** It's easier to tell the types of effects apart by looking at their side views.

### Bevel effect Button presets

Bevel effects are terrific for creating buttons for all purposes: navigation, forms, links, and so on. One of the most common applications of such buttons involves *rollovers*. Rollover is the generally used name (another is *mouseover*) for the effect where a user moves the pointer over a button and it changes in some way. Both bevel effects provide four presets under the Button preset option list — Raised, Highlight, Inset, and Inverted — which can be employed for rollovers.

Unlike Stroke or Fill panel presets, the bevel Button presets do not actually change the panel attributes, but rather internally change the lighting angle and lighten the object (Figure 12-6). The Raised and Highlight presets use the same lighting angle, derived from the Angle value, but Highlight is about 25 percent lighter. The Inset and Inverted presets, on the other hand, reverse the angle of the lighting — and, of this pair, Inverted is the lighter one.

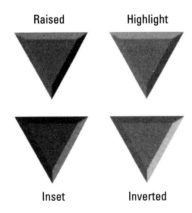

Raised      Highlight

Inset      Inverted

**Figure 12-6:** Both the bevel effects offer four Button presets: Raised, Highlight, Inset, and Inverted.

**Tip**    To take the fullest advantage of the bevel effect Button presets in creating rollovers, set your lighting angle first with the Effect panel Angle knob. Then duplicate the image and apply the different Button presets to each copy.

## Drop shadows

I remember the overwhelming sense of pride I felt after I made my first drop-shadow in an early version of Photoshop. Of course, it had taken me all afternoon to follow two different sets of instructions and involved masking layers, Gaussian blurs, nudged layers, and who-remembers-what-else. My pride was quickly deflated when I tried out my new drop shadowed image against a color background — and found a completely undesired halo of white pixels around my graphic.

All of that effort and anxiety is out the window with Fireworks. Applying a drop shadow to an object can be a simple two-step process: select the object and then choose Drop Shadow from the Effect panel. Just as vital as its ease of use is its editability. Feel free to change the color, softness, distance, or opacity of the shadow — there's no problem in Fireworks, because the Drop Shadow is a Live Effect. Best of all, you can position the drop shadow against any colored background; Fireworks adjusts the blending of shadow to background, eliminating the unwanted halo effect.

**Note**     Not to defame Photoshop, a fine imaging program, it's only fair to acknowledge that the latest version of that program now also has a Drop Shadow effect that's easily applied.

A drop shadow is a monochrome copy of an image, offset so that it appears behind the image to one side. Drop shadows are usually presented in a shade of gray (although they can be any color) and can be either faded on the edge or hard-edged. Drop shadows are used extensively on the Web — some would say that they're overused. However, the effect of giving flat images dimension by adding a shadow behind it is so compelling and downright useful that I think drop shadows will be around for a long time.

### Applying a drop shadow

To apply a drop shadow to any object in Fireworks, follow these steps:

1. Select the object. Drop shadows can be applied to most any object: open or closed paths, geometric shapes, image objects, text objects, and more.

2. Choose Window ➪ Effect or click the Effect tab, if visible. The Effect panel opens.

3. Choose Drop Shadow from the Effect Category option list. The initial Drop Shadow parameters are displayed in the Effect panel, as shown in Figure 12-7.

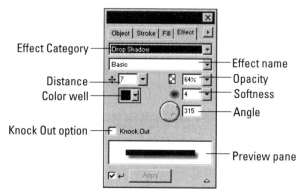

**Figure 12-7:** The default Drop Shadow effect offers a classic soft shadow, slightly cast to the right.

4. To use one of the preset drop shadow configurations, choose either Basic or Soft from the Effect name option list. The differences are

- **Basic:** A 7-pixel-wide drop shadow, set to 64 percent opacity, with an edge softness of 4 pixels that uses a light angle of 315 degrees. This creates a dark centered shadow that fades slightly on the edges.

- **Soft:** A 12-pixel-wide drop shadow, set to 40 percent opacity, with an edge softness of 8 pixels that uses a light angle of 315 degrees. This preset makes a larger, lighter drop shadow where more of the edge is transparent.

5. To make the shadow appear further or closer, change the Distance slider or enter a value directly in the associated text box.

**Tip**     The Distance slider has a range from 0 to 100 pixels, but you can enter a higher number in the text box to make the shadow appear even further away if you like. The text box also accepts negative numbers, which cause the shadow to be cast in the opposite direction of the Angle setting.

6. To change the shadow color from the default black, pick a color from the Color well.

7. To change the transparency of the shadow, alter the Opacity slider or text box. Opacity is given in a percentage value; 100 percent is completely opaque and 0 percent is completely transparent (and therefore invisible).

8. To make the edge of the shadow softer or harder, move the Softness slider or enter a value in its text box. The Softness slider goes from 0 to 30, but you can enter a higher value directly in the text box.

9. To change the direction of the shadow, drag the Angle knob to a new location or enter a degree (0 to 360) directly in the text box.

10. To display just the shadow and make the object disappear, choose the Knock Out option.

I find myself using a hard-edged shadow almost as much as I do the soft-edge versions, particularly in graphics, where file size is paramount. Any image with a blended edge is larger than the same image with a solid edge because more pixels are necessary to create the faded look — typically half again as many. When file size is key — and you like the look of a solid drop shadow — bring the Softness slider all the way down to zero.

I do find softer shadows particularly effective, however, when one shadow overlaps another. A good way to enhance the three dimensionality of your Web graphics is to place one object with a shadow over another object, also with a shadow. As long as you keep the Angle the same for both objects, and the Opacity relatively low (around 50 percent or less), you'll get an effect like the one seen in Figure 12-8.

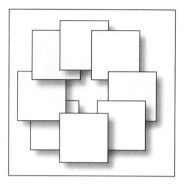

**Figure 12-8:** Placing figures with soft drop shadows on top of one another adds an extra dimension to your graphics.

## Using the Knock Out option

The Knock Out option offered on the Drop Shadow effect deserves special mention. The phrase *knock out* is an old printer's term referring to the practice of dropping the color out of certain type to let background show through. Obviously if you eliminated the color from an ordinary bit of type—without an outline or other surrounding element—the type would seem to disappear. A shadow is perfect for surrounding knocked out type because of the way the mind has of filling in the details that are missing from the actual image. Selecting the Knock Out option removes both the fill and stroke color of the object and leaves just the shadow. Knock Out works for both type and other objects, as shown in Figure 12-9, where a crescent moon was made from a knocked out circle.

**Figure 12-9:** Use Knock Out to highlight text or object with just the shadow.

**Tip**

In the introduction to this section, I noted how it's easy in Fireworks to avoid the so-called halo effect that occurs when you move a drop shadow built against one background to another. In Fireworks, there are really two ways to do this. If you don't need for the object or its shadow to be transparent, change the canvas color to the background color of your Web page and export the image normally. To avoid the halo effect, but maintain a transparent image, make the background color transparent during export.

## Emboss

If you've ever seen a company's Articles of Incorporation or other official papers, you've probably encountered embossing. An embossing seal is used to press the company name right into the paper — so that it can be both read and felt. Fireworks's Emboss effect provides a similar service, with a great deal more flexibility, of course.

Like the Knock Out option of the Drop Shadow effect, Emboss removes the object's fill with the canvas or color of background objects, but it also adds highlights and shadows. The Emboss presets, Inset and Raised, reverse the placement of these highlights and effects to make the embossed object appear to be pushed into or out of the background, respectively, as shown in Figure 12-10.

Inset Emboss preset       Raised Emboss preset

**Figure 12-10:** The Emboss effect makes an object appear to be part of the background — either pushed out or into it.

Applying an Emboss effect is very similar to applying the other effects. The Emboss options available on the Effect panel, shown in Figure 12-11, are

- ✦ **Effect name:** As noted previously, Emboss has two presets, Inset and Raised.
- ✦ **Width:** Determines the thickness of the embossed edges. As with other effects, the slider's range is from 0 to 30, but higher values can be entered directly into the associated text box.
- ✦ **Contrast:** Contrast controls the relative lightness of the highlights to the darkness of the shadows.
- ✦ **Softness:** Sets the sharpness of the embossed edges; higher numbers make the edges fuzzier.
- ✦ **Angle:** Establishes the direction of the embossed edges.

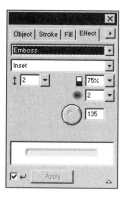

**Figure 12-11:** Set the degree of the Emboss effect through the Effect panel.

# Glow

Whereas a drop shadow is only visible at the side of an object, the Glow effect creates a border all around the object. By default, the border fades into the background, creating a glowing effect. The glow's color is user-selectable, as is its width, opacity, and softness. Moreover, Fireworks offers two different types of glows (Figure 12-12), selected from the Effect name option list:

✦ **Basic:** The soft colored border is directly outside of the object path or stroke, if any.

✦ **Halo:** The border is separated from the object's path (or stroke, if any) by a transparent boundary approximately 8 pixels wide.

**Figure 12-12:** While they're both positively radiant thanks to the Glow effect, she's the one with a Halo.

**Tip** Although the distance between the halo and the object cannot be conventionally changed, there is a workaround: stroke the object with a brush the same color as the canvas or background. Because the halo is drawn a set distance from the stroke, and not the path, increasing the size of the stroke will increase the apparent space between the object and the halo.

To apply a glow, follow these steps:

1. Select the desired object.

2. Choose Window ⇨ Effect or click the Effect tab, if visible. The Effect panel opens.

3. Choose Glow from the Effect Category option list. The initial Glow parameters are displayed in the Effect panel, as shown in Figure 12-13.

**Figure 12-13:** Choose Glow effect attributes through the Effect panel.

4. Choose either Basic or Halo from the Effect name option list.

5. Set the other options — Width, Color, Opacity, and Softness — if desired.

All of the Glow effect parameters are the same as those found on the Drop Shadow Effect panel.

**Tip** You can use the Glow effect to create a rounded-edge frame around any bitmap image by applying the Glow with the Softness set to 0 to the image object. For a three-dimensional effect, use the Outer Bevel effect the same way.

# Fireworks Technique: Making Perspective Shadows

With the current version, the five Live Effects are the only effects directly supported. However, Fireworks is flexible enough to enable you to create many of your own effects. One such possibility is perspective shadows. Unlike drop shadows, perspective shadows are not flat carbon-copies of the selected object, but rather shadows that appear to exist in a three-dimensional world. In addition, perspective shadows can appear in front, behind, or to the side of the object.

This perspective shadow technique takes advantage of Fireworks's facility with path objects and its capability to adjust gradients and edges. With this technique, you can add perspective shadows to text, image, or path objects, as shown in Figure 12-14.

**Figure 12-14:** Create perspective shadows in Fireworks by combining gradient fills to distorted copies of an object.

To create a perspective shadow, follow these steps:

1. Duplicate the outline of the original object to create a new shadow object. Depending on the type of object, this first step is either very simple, very time-consuming, or something in-between. Here are techniques for working with the three basic types of objects:

   • **Path objects:** By far the easiest of the three, simply choose Edit ➪ Clone to copy any path object. Cloning is a better choice than Duplicating, because it's easier to align the shadow and its source later.

   • **Text objects:** Although it's not absolutely necessary, I've found it sometimes easier to work with text as a path for my shadow object than with regular text. In my experience, distorting path objects gets more predictable results than distorting text. Therefore, I first Clone the text and then choose Text ➪ Convert to Paths. Finally, to reduce the gradients of the separate letters to one, choose Modify ➪ Combine ➪ Union.

- **Image objects:** Image objects can be simple rectangles or — as in the previous Figure 12-14 — cut-outs of images. If your object is rectangular or another geometric shape, use the Rectangle, Ellipse, or Polygon to create a same-size copy of the object. Otherwise, the best tool I found for this particular job is the Pen. For outlining an image, I use the Pen primarily in its straight-line mode, clicking from one point to the next, although occasionally when I need to copy a curve, I can with the Pen's Bézier curve feature. The outline doesn't have to be exact, although the more details you include, the more realistic your shadow will be.

2. If necessary, flip the shadow object. Depending on your hypothetical light source, you'll want to flip the shadow object vertically so that the perspective shadow falls in front of the original object.

3. If necessary, move the shadow object into position.

   You won't need to move the shadow object if the perspective shadow falls behind the original object. However, for perspective shadows in front, you do need to move the shadow object so that the bases of each object meet. While it's entirely possible to use the mouse to drag the shadow object into position, I often find myself using the cursor keys to move the selected shadow object in one direction. Pressing Shift+Arrow key moves the object in ten-pixel increments and the regular arrow keys, one pixel.

4. Send the shadow object behind the original object.

   Whether you choose Modify ⇨ Arrange ⇨ Send Backward, or Modify ⇨ Arrange ⇨ Send to the Back, depends on what other objects are in the document and how you want the shadow to relate to them. But even if the perspective shadow falls in front of the source object, you'll want to put it behind to mask the meeting point.

5. Distort the shadow object.

   Here's where the real artistry — and numerous attempts — enter the picture. Select the shadow object and choose the Skew tool from the Toolbox to slant the shadow in one direction; again, the direction depends on where the apparent "light" for the shadow is coming from. Next, while the Skew tool is still active, switch to the Scale tool. (By pressing the keyboard shortcut, q, twice, you don't have to move the mouse.) You can now easily resize the same bounding box. Choose the middle horizontal sizing handle on the edge furthest away from the original object. Now you can drag that handle to either shorten or lengthen the shadow.

6. Optionally, fill the shadow object with a gradient.

   You may be satisfied with the shadow as it stands now, but adding and adjusting a gradient will add more depth and realism to the image. From the Fill panel, choose the Linear gradient with a Black, White preset color combination.

7. Adjust the gradient of the shadow object.

As applied, the Linear gradient just goes left-to-right. If you need it to flow at a different angle (and you probably will), choose the Paint Bucket tool while the shadow object is selected to activate the gradient controls. Reposition and angle the gradient so that the starting point is at the juncture of the source and shadow object and the ending point is just beyond the end of the shadow. This permits the shadow to gently fade away.

8. If desired, feather the edge of the shadow object slightly.

To my eye, shadows look a bit more realistic if they're not so hard-edged. I like to set my Fill panel Edge option list to Feather and set the Amount of Feather relatively low, about three or four pixels. You may have to adjust the shadow object a bit to hide the feathered edge where it touches the original object.

Many enhancements can be added to this technique. For example, you could add an object for the shadow to fall over by bending or pulling the shadow object with the Reshape Path or Reshape Area tools or the shadow itself could be not so realistic to make a point. Computer graphics make it oh-so-tempting to turn anyone's shadow into a horned devil or winged angel. Play with perspective — you'll be glad you did.

# Applying Multiple Effects

Each of the individual effects is quite special by itself, but what if you want to combine them? How about a beveled button with a drop shadow or a two-tiered, inner and outer bevel shape with a glow? This was all doable since the first version of Fireworks, but, to tell the truth, it was as the programmers say, a kludge. In order to add one effect to another, you had to group the object with itself. And if you wanted to add a third object, you had to group it again. Naturally, this meant that if you wanted to edit the original object you had to ungroup it several times — and then regroup it to restore it. Workable, but definitely a kludge.

**New Feature**

Well, kludge no more! In Fireworks 2, multiple effects can be added, edited, and removed as easily as — maybe even easier than — single effects. Choosing the Multiple option under the Effects Category option list presents you with an Effect panel displaying the available effects complete with check boxes to show their status, as shown in Figure 12-15. You can tell at a glance which effects are active and which are not. Moreover, their attributes are just a single click away.

Four out of the five general effects are available to be applied together. The Emboss effect, because it eliminates the fill, is not compatible with the other four. Don't worry, though — you can achieve a very wide range of effects with the remaining combinations. With multiple effects, all the attributes for each effect are set on a separate dialog box than the Effect panel. The interface for these dialog boxes are quite similar to the Effect panel and each is similar to each other as well, so the learning curve is close to nonexistent. The only minor difference is that the Presets can now be found under a button on the upper right of the dialog box.

**Figure 12-15:** Select one or all four available effects with the new Multiple Effects option.

To apply more than one effect, follow these steps:

1. From the Effect panel, choose Multiple from the Effects Category option list. The Effect panel displays the Multiple interface.

2. To select an individual effect, choose the check box next to the effect's name. The dialog box for that effect is displayed, like the one for the Inner Bevel effect shown in Figure 12-16.

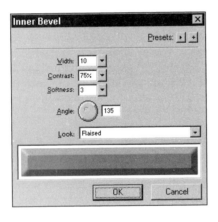

**Figure 12-16:** Once you choose a Multiple effect, a dialog box for that effect appears, like this one for the Inner Bevel effect.

3. Set the effect attributes as you would on the Effect panel.

4. Click OK to accept your choices.

5. To edit an existing Multiple effect, select the Edit Effect button next to the name of the effect.

6. To remove a Multiple effect from an object, uncheck the corresponding check box.

The Multiple Effects option is quite handy for mixing glows or drop shadows with beveled effects, but you can also make unlikely combinations that work quite well. Take a look at Figure 12-17 as an example. By making similar color choices, I was able to combine Inner Bevel, Outer Bevel, and Glow effects to fashion an unusual but effective logo. Best of all, the text — and all effects — remain editable at every point.

**Figure 12-17:** This logo mixed both Inner and Outer Bevel with a Glow effect through Fireworks 2's new Multiple Effects option.

**Caution** If you open a Fireworks 2 object with multiple effects in Fireworks 1, only the first effect in the effect list is saved. Should you then save the same object in Fireworks 1 and open it in version 2, only the first effect is accessible, until you clear multiple effects by selecting None from the Effect panel Category option list. You'll then need to reapply the multiple effects.

## Managing Live Effects

Like strokes and fills, custom configurations of Live Effects can be saved with each document. These custom effects can then later be applied to other objects in the same document or, if the object is copied to another document, other graphics. As with strokes and fills, all such management of custom effects is handled through the Options pop-up menu.

The Effect panel Options pop-up commands are

✦ **Save Effect As:** Stores the current effect settings under a unique name in the Effect name option list.

✦ **Rename Effect:** Renames any custom or standard effect.

✦ **Delete Effect:** Removes any custom or standard effect. If you remove a standard effect, it will be restored when Fireworks is restarted or when you access another document.

✦ **Auto Apply:** Automatically applies each change in the Effect panel to the selected object.

## Storing a customized effect

To store a customized effect, follow these steps:

1. Choose the Options pop-up and select Save Effect As. The Save Effect As dialog box appears.

2. Enter a unique name for the effect. If you choose a name already in use, Fireworks asks if you want to replace the existing effect.

3. After entering a new name, choose Save. The new effect name is displayed alphabetically in the Effect name option list of any effect.

## Using the effect in another document

It's important to understand that any new or modified effects are stored only within the document in which they're used. To use the effect in another document, follow these steps:

1. Open the document containing the effect you want to use.

2. Select an object using the new effect.

3. Open the new document in which you want to use the new effect.

4. Copy the selected object to the new document either by using Edit ➪ Copy and Edit ➪ Paste or by dragging and dropping the object from one document to the other while pressing Alt (Option). The new effect setting is added to the Effect panel when the object containing the effect is pasted into the document.

5. If desired, delete the copied object from the new document.

You can achieve the same effect of transferring effects from one document to another several other ways:

✦ Use Insert ➪ Image to insert a document containing one or more custom effects. After you've clicked once to place the document, choose Undo. The graphics will vanish, but all custom effects will be incorporated into the Effect panel.

✦ Copy the path with the custom effect in one document and just paste the attributes to a path in the new document by selecting that path and choosing Edit ➪ Paste Attributes.

## Using the Styles ffeature

Perhaps the best way to always be sure your custom effects are available is to use the Styles feature, new in Fireworks 2. To create a new style using a custom effect, follow these steps:

1. Select an object that uses the custom effect.

2. If necessary, choose Window ➪ Styles, use the keyboard shortcut, Ctrl+Alt+J (Command+Option+J), or click the Style tab, if visible. The Style panel displays.

3. On the Style panel, select the New Style button.

4. In the Edit Style dialog box, enter a descriptive name for your effect in the Name text box and deselect all checkboxes except Effect.

5. Click OK when you're done. A new style is entered in the Style panel.

Any style added in the just-described fashion is always available for any Fireworks document. To apply the effect, just highlight any Fireworks object and select the new style. Your custom effect is then added to the Fill panel.

**Cross-Reference** To find out more about the powerful Styles feature, see Chapter 17.

# Summary

Effects may be the icing on the cake, but then what's cake without icing? Seriously, effects play a very important role in Web graphics, particularly when it comes to creating button with variations that can be used for rollovers. Fireworks makes the hardest effect easy by providing five standard effects and numerous preset looks. When you first begin applying effects to your graphics, consider these points:

◆ Fireworks applies Live Effects, which are recalculated every time a graphic is altered.

◆ All Fireworks effects are specified through the Effect panel, which changes to offer different attributes according to the effect chosen.

◆ The Inner and Outer Bevel effects are similar but result in completely different looks. The Inner Bevel effect uses the object's color to create an edge within the object itself, whereas the Outer Bevel effect uses a separate color chosen by the designer to make a border around the outside of the object.

◆ The Drop Shadow sets off any path, text, or image object with a shadow behind the figure—large or small, subtle or bold, your choice.

◆ Emboss removes the fill and stroke from any selected object and builds edges from the underlying canvas or objects to make it appear as if the object is emerging from the background, or sinking into it.

✦ Fireworks offers two types of Glow effects: Basic and Halo. Basic forms a soft colored border around any object, whereas Halo offsets that border with a fixed-width gutter.

✦ Using a combination of other Fireworks tools and commands, any object can have a perspective shadow.

✦ In Fireworks 2, you can easily apply and edit multiple effects without having to group them.

✦ Custom effects can be stored with any graphic and applied to any other graphic.

In the next chapter, you'll learn how Fireworks is used to arrange and compose different objects.

✦    ✦    ✦

# Arranging and Compositing Objects

**F**ireworks differs dramatically from other bitmap-editing applications in that the parts of your Fireworks document are always independent objects and are always editable. When you are ready to combine those objects, their independence enables you to group or composite them in a variety of ways. Even advanced operations, such as alpha masking, leave the masked image — and the mask itself — intact and editable.

**Tip**     *Compositing* is the process of combining multiple images into one image, usually by feathering, blending, and altering the transparency of the images.

This chapter looks at the various ways to combine, group, arrange, align, blend, and generally lay out multiple objects within Fireworks.

## Using Layers

Using layers is a powerful Fireworks feature that enables you to organize your document into separate divisions that you can work with individually, or hide from view when convenient. Think of an artist drawing on separate transparencies instead of one sheet of paper. The artist could take one transparency out of the stack and draw only the background elements of the drawing, and then take another transparency and put related foreground elements on that. The artist could then restack the transparencies to produce a finished drawing.

**Caution**   The concept of "layers" can differ from program to program. Layers in Fireworks may not work exactly as you expect if you're used to another application. Layers in Fireworks, for example, work more like the layers in most vector drawing programs than like the layers in Photoshop.

The Layers panel (see Figure 13-1) is the central control center for using layers. To show or hide the Layers panel, choose Window ⇨ Layers. The Layers panel enables you to see at a glance how many layers you have in your document, which ones are locked or hidden, and even whether a selection exists on the current layer.

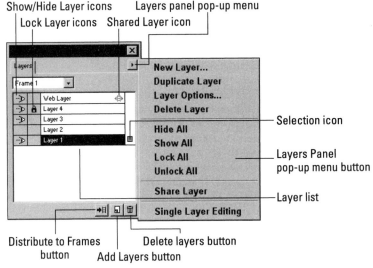

**Figure 13-1:** The Layers panel packs many layer-manipulation options into a small, convenient space.

## Working with layers

When you create a new document in Fireworks, it initially has two layers:

✦ **Web Layer:** A special layer just for hotspots and slices

✦ **Layer 1:** A regular layer on which you create objects when you start drawing, until you create another layer

### Adding a layer

Each new layer that you add to your document is named "Layer," by default, and is given the next available number. You can change the names of layers, however, to help you remember what sort of objects are on each layer. For example, you might name a layer with background elements "Background," or name a layer with text elements "Text."

To add a new layer to your document, do one of the following:

✦ Click the Add Layer button on the Layers panel.

✦ Hold down the Alt (Option) key and click the layer list in the Layers panel.

✦ Choose New Layer from the Layers panel pop-up menu.

✦ Choose Insert ➪ Layer.

The new layer appears at the top of the layers list (but underneath the Web Layer). To change the name of a layer, double-click its name in the layer list and type a new name in the Layer Options dialog box.

You can also add a new layer by duplicating one that already exists. When you duplicate a layer, all the objects on that layer are also duplicated.

**Tip** Duplicating a layer and then hiding the duplicate is a quick way to make a backup of all the objects on a layer before you perform extensive edits. If the edits don't go well, you can always delete them and show the "backup" layer, taking you back to square one.

To duplicate a layer, drag the layer to the New Layer button (blank piece of paper) in the Layers panel, or select a layer and choose Duplicate Layer from the Layers panel pop-up menu.

## Deleting a layer

When you delete a layer, all the objects on that layer are also deleted. If you delete a layer accidentally, choose Edit ➪ Undo right away to get it back.

To delete a layer, do one of the following:

✦ Drag a layer from the layer list in the Layers panel to the Delete Layer button (trash can) on the Layers panel.

✦ Select a layer from the layer list in the Layers panel and click the Delete Layer button.

✦ Select a layer from the layer list in the Layers panel and choose Delete Layer from the Layers panel pop-up menu.

## Changing stacking order

After you have more than one layer in your document, you may want to change their stacking order at some point. To change the stacking order of layers in your document, you simply have to click and drag a layer higher or lower in the layer list in the Layers panel. This moves all the objects on that layer either ahead or behind objects on other layers.

## Moving objects between layers

When you want to move objects from one layer to another, you might be inclined to cut them to the Clipboard, change the current layer, and then paste the objects into the new layer. That works fine, but the Layers panel provides you with a quicker method.

Whenever you select an object or objects on the canvas, a small blue box appears in the layer list next to the layer the selected objects are on. Drag this box up or down to another layer, and the objects are moved there.

To move objects to another layer, follow these steps:

1. Select the objects. Fireworks displays a selection icon (blue square) next to the current layer's name in the layer list of the Layers panel.

2. Drag the selection icon to the target layer.

## Layer-by-layer editing

To work on one layer at a time, you can lock or hide the layers that you don't want to affect, or you can choose Single Layer Editing from the Layers panel pop-up menu. In Fireworks, working on all the layers simultaneously is the default. You have to ask specifically to work on only one layer at a time. This is the opposite of the way that Photoshop and some other applications handle layers.

To show or hide a layer, click within the leftmost column of the Layers panel, next to the layer that you want to show or hide. When the eye icon is visible, the layer is visible. When the eye icon is not showing, the layer is hidden and all the objects on that layer are invisible in the document window.

**Tip**      When a layer is hidden, it also is locked, and the objects on that layer cannot be selected, edited, or changed. After you hide a layer, you don't need to lock it as well.

To lock a layer, click within the second column of the Layers panel, next to the layer you want to lock. When a layer is locked, a padlock icon appears in that column, and none of the objects on that layer can be selected or edited in the document window, although they are still visible.

The Layers panel pop-up menu features shortcut commands for hiding or showing all layers simultaneously, or locking or unlocking all layers simultaneously.

To enter Single Layer Editing mode, choose Single Layer Editing from the Layers panel pop-up menu. When you're in Single Layer Editing mode, you can select or edit only the objects on the current layer, although you can still see objects on other layers. As you select each layer from the layers list in the Layers panel, the other layers automatically act as if they are locked. When working with a complex document, this is a very easy way to limit the scope of your edits.

Giving your layers descriptive names before using Single Layer Editing mode really speeds up your editing. If your layers are named Background, Text, and so forth, you can quickly select a layer, based on which objects you want to edit, without worrying about accidentally altering objects on other layers.

### The Web Layer

All Fireworks documents have a Web Layer, on which you can draw "Web objects," such as hotspots and slice guides. You can move the Web Layer in the stacking order by dragging it up or down the layer list in the Layers panel, but you can't delete the Web Layer. The Web Layer is always shared across all frames.

 For more information about using the Web Layer, see Chapter 21 and Chapter 22. For more details about sharing layers across frames, and about frames in general, see Chapter 25.

In addition to creating hotspots in the traditional way, with the hotspot tool, you can create hotspots out of regular objects by using the Layers panel. This is a handy way to quickly add hotspots to objects if you want the hotspots to be the same size as the objects.

To create hotspots out of objects, follow these steps:

1. Select in the document window the object or objects that you want to make into hotspots.

   Fireworks displays a selection icon (a blue box) in the rightmost column of the Layers panel, next to the layer the selected objects are on.

2. Drag the selection icon and drop it in the same column, next to the Web Layer.

   If you have multiple objects selected, Fireworks asks whether you want to create one hotspot or multiple hotspots. Choosing to create one hotspot combines the shapes into one.

The hotspots are created on the Web Layer, and your original objects are unaffected.

## Hiding selected objects

You not only can hide layers, but you also can hide selected objects within a layer, to get them out of the way. You can even close a document and then reopen it, and the objects will remain hidden.

To hide one or more objects, select them and choose View ⇨ Hide Selection. To show the objects again, choose View ⇨ Show All.

# Aligning and Distributing Objects

One of the most basic layout techniques is aligning and distributing objects. If you've ever used any kind of drawing or publishing application, then you're familiar with the concept. When you're not in Image Edit mode in Fireworks, every object on the canvas "floats" and can be easily aligned with another.

When you're aligning a selection, imagine a rectangle around your selection (see Figure 13-2). The rectangle is described by the objects themselves. The top of the rectangle is the topmost point on the topmost object, the left side of the rectangle is the leftmost point on the leftmost object in the selection, and so on. This theoretical rectangle is what you align objects to, and what you distribute them across.

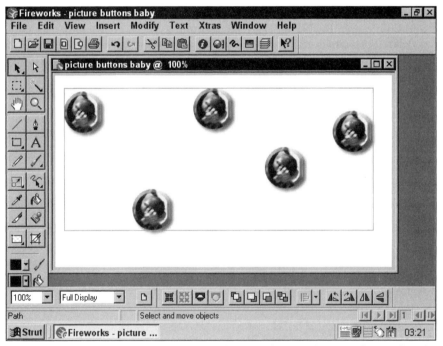

**Figure 13-2:** Imagine a theoretical rectangle around your selection. This is what the objects are aligned to.

When you left-align the objects, all the objects move left until they bump into the left border of the theoretical rectangle. Similarly, if you align to the bottom, all the objects move down until they hit the bottom border of the rectangle.

**Note**  Alignment in Fireworks has nothing to do with aligning to a page, or to the canvas, as in many other applications. In Fireworks, objects are aligned and distributed within a selection. If you try to align only one object, the alignment commands are unavailable. If you want to align one object to the canvas, draw a rectangle the size of the canvas and align the object to that rectangle. If you want to make the canvas quickly fit around the rectangle, choose Modify ➪ Document ➪ Trim Canvas.

To align a selection of objects to the selection's left, right, top, or bottom, select the objects that you want to align and choose the appropriate alignment command:

✦ Choose either Modify ➪ Align ➪ Align Left or the keyboard shortcut Ctrl+Alt+1 (Command+Option+1) to align all objects to the leftmost point of the leftmost object.

✦ Choose either Modify ➪ Align ➪ Align Right or the keyboard shortcut Ctrl+Alt+3 (Command+Option+3) to align all objects to the rightmost point of the rightmost object.

✦ Choose either Modify ➪ Align ➪ Align Top or the keyboard shortcut Ctrl+Alt+4 (Command+Option+4) to align all objects to the topmost point of the topmost object (see Figure 13-3).

✦ Choose either Modify ➪ Align ➪ Align Bottom or the keyboard shortcut Ctrl+Alt+6 (Command+Option+6) to align all objects to the bottommost point of the bottommost object.

In addition to the traditional left, right, top, and bottom alignment, Fireworks has two special alignment commands:

✦ Choose either Modify ➪ Align ➪ Center Vertical or the keyboard shortcut Ctrl+Alt+2 (Command+Option+2) to align all objects to a theoretical vertical center line.

**Tip**  Remember that the "center" is not the center of the canvas, but the center of the selection.

✦ Choose either Modify ➪ Align ➪ Center Horizontal or the keyboard shortcut Ctrl+Alt+5 (Command+Option+5) to align all objects to a theoretical horizontal center line.

Before  After

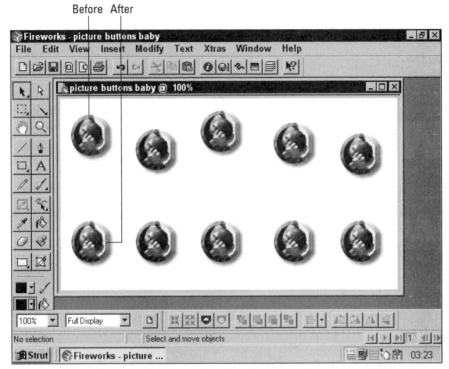

**Figure 13-3:** A selection of objects aligned to the top of the topmost object with the Align Top command

You can also distribute objects across the selection, which is handy when you have a few objects, such as a row of buttons, that you want to space evenly. To distribute a selection of objects across the selection, select the objects that you want to distribute and choose the appropriate distribute command:

✦ Choose either Modify ⇨ Align ⇨ Distribute Widths or the keyboard shortcut Ctrl+Alt+7 (Command+Option+7) to space your objects evenly from left to right (see Figure 13-4).

Choose either Modify ⇨ Align ⇨ Distribute Heights or the keyboard shortcut Ctrl+Alt+9 (Command+Option+9) to space your objects evenly from top to bottom.

Before    After

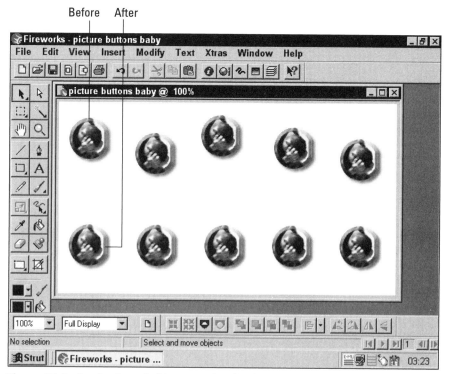

**Figure 13-4:** A selection of objects can be distributed from left to right with the Distribute Widths command.

# Getting Layout Assistance

Fireworks provides a variety of ways to precisely lay out objects on the canvas. Rulers enable you to place guides at precise locations and "snap" objects to those guides as you move them around. Or, you can choose to lay a grid over your document, to help you align things correctly.

## Using rulers

Rulers are a standard feature of pretty much every drawing or graphics application. In fact, rulers (the kind that you hold in your hand) are a standard feature of traditional, paper-based layouts, as well. Rulers enable you to keep track of the size of your objects and their placement on the canvas.

To toggle the visibility of the rulers, choose either View➪Rulers orthe keyboard shortcut Ctrl+Alt+R (Command+Option+R). The rulers +appear within your document, running along the top and left borders (see Figure 13-5).

Zero-Point marker

Selection height    Selection width    Horizontal ruler    Vertical ruler

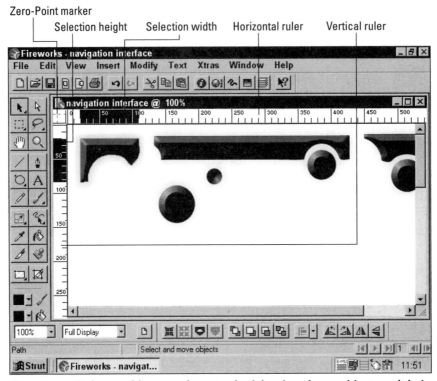

**Figure 13-5:** Rulers enable you to keep track of the size of your objects and their relationship to each other.

When you select an object, its width and height are displayed in the rulers, enabling you to arrange that object easier. If you want to place an object 20 pixels from the top and 20 pixels from the left, like the selected object in Figure 13-5, the rulers themselves tell you all that you need to know.

**Tip**    When you don't have an object selected, you can see your mouse pointer's position on the canvas, because the rulers tracks your mouse. This is helpful when you want to draw a new object at a precise position on the canvas.

By default, the ruler's *zero-point*—the point where the horizontal and vertical rulers meet—is set to 0 pixels, but you can set it to another location in your document by dragging the zero-point marker to a new location and releasing it. The zero-point marker is in the upper-left corner of the document window when the rulers are visible. If all objects in your document are going to be at least 20 pixels from the top and 20 pixels from the left, moving the zero-point to 20 × 20 (see Figure 13-6) simplifies the math that you do later as you align objects. To set the zero-point back to zero again, double-click the zero-point marker.

Zero-Point

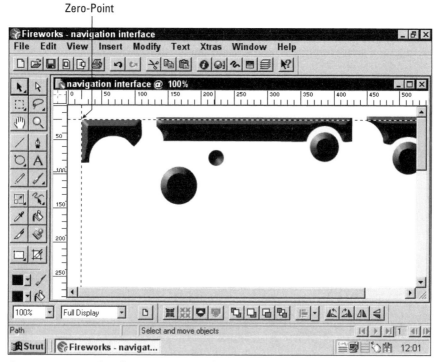

**Figure 13-6:** Moving the zero-point to the top and left of the topmost and leftmost object in your document can simplify the math that you have to do later when you align objects.

## Working with guides

Guides are simply lines that you can position to mark important points in your documents, such as a margin or center point. Guides don't print or export, and they exist above the layers of your document. They are a design-time tool intended to make laying out objects easier. For example, if your layout calls for many objects to be placed at 20 pixels from the top, then creating a horizontal guide at that position enables you easily to see where that point is, so that you can place objects there.

### Creating guides

Adding a new guide to your document is a simple, mouse-only affair. Simply clicking and dragging the horizontal ruler into your document creates a new horizontal guide that you can drop anywhere.

**Tip**

A horizontal guide runs parallel to the horizontal ruler, so you drag from the horizontal ruler to make a horizontal guide. Sometimes, this can be a bit confusing, because you'll tend to drop a horizontal guide after checking its position on the vertical ruler. In other words, you might place a horizontal guide at 20 pixels from the top according to the vertical ruler. If you find yourself trying to create horizontal guides by dragging from the vertical ruler, think of the guides as clones of the rulers from which you drag them. Horizontal for horizontal, vertical for vertical.

To add a new guide to your document, follow these steps:

1. If the rulers aren't visible, choose either View ➪ Rulers or the keyboard shortcut Ctrl+Alt+R (Command+Option+R) to show them.

2. Drag from the horizontal ruler to create a new horizontal guide. Drag from the vertical ruler to create a new vertical guide (see Figure 13-7). When you reach the position where you want to place your guide, simply drop it in place by releasing the mouse button.

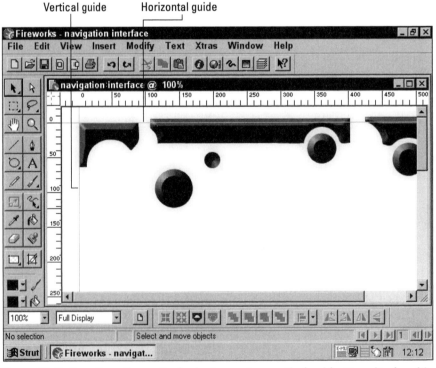

**Figure 13-7:** Drag from the vertical ruler to create a vertical guide. Drop it when it's in the right place.

## Locking or hiding guides

After you create quite a few guides, you may find that they get in the way. Because they aren't on a layer, you can't just lock or hide their layer to make them invisible or not editable. Carefully placing a guide in the correct spot and then dragging it somewhere else accidentally goes a long way toward negating the primary time-saving aspect of using guides.

To show or hide guides, choose either View ➪ Guides or the keyboard shortcut Ctrl+; (Command+;). Hiding guides periodically gives you a better sense of what your final image will look like.

To lock all of your guides so that they can't be moved, choose either View ➪ Guide Options ➪ Lock Guides or the keyboard shortcut Ctrl+Alt+; (Command+Option+;).

## Snapping to guides

Snapping objects to guides really uses guides to their full potential. With a little planning, you can create guides at important points in your document so that your layout comes together almost automatically as you move objects around the canvas.

To toggle whether objects snap to the nearest guide, choose either View ➪ Guide Options ➪ Snap to Guides or the keyboard shortcut Ctrl+Shift+; (Command+Shift+;).

## Guide colors

If your document contains a lot of yellow objects, the default yellow color of the guides will be hard to see. Guides can be any color. Choosing a color that contrasts sharply with the color scheme of your document makes guides easier to see and also has the effect of separating them from your document so that you can see your layout "through" the guides without having to hide the guides all the time.

To change the color that guides are displayed in, follow these steps:

1. Choose either View ➪ Guide Options ➪ Edit Guides or the keyboard shortcut Ctrl+Alt+Shift+G (Command+Option+Shift+G).

   Fireworks displays the Guides dialog box (see Figure 13-8).

2. Use the guides color picker to specify the color you'd like the guides to be displayedin, and then click OK.

**Tip**　For convenience, all the guide options have been collected into the Guides dialog box. You can check or uncheck Show Guides to toggle the visibility of the guides; check Snap to Guides to cause objects to snap to the guides; or check Lock Guides to lock them. Options for slice guides are also available here.

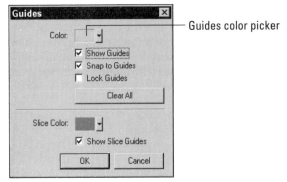

Guides color picker

**Figure 13-8:** Change the color that guides
are displayed in (and other options)
by using the Guides dialog box.

### Clearing guides

Removing a single guide from your document is a drag-and-drop affair, just as
adding one is. Simply "grab" the guide with your mouse and drag it out of your
document. You can drag it out to the left, right, top, or bottom and it will disappear
from you document.

You can also clear all the guides out of your document simultaneously by using the
Guides dialog box. To clear all guides, follow these steps:

1. Choose either View ➪ Guide Options ➪ Edit Guides or the keyboard shortcut
   Ctrl+Alt+Shift+G (Command+Option+Shift+G).

   Fireworks displays the Guides dialog box (refer to Figure 13-8).

2. Click the Clear All button to remove all the guides from your document. Click
   OK when you're done.

**Note**       The Clear All button removes ruler guides, but not slice guides.

## The grid

The *grid* is a quick way to achieve more precise layouts. Usually, you'll want objects
to align in a fairly regular pattern. The grid makes it easy to see the relationship
between the elements of your layout, by splitting the document into smaller, more
manageable sections. Grid lines don't export or print, and they aren't on a layer.
They're simply a visual aid at design time.

To show or hide the grid, choose either View ➪ Grid or the keyboard shortcut Ctrl+'
(Command+').

**Tip**    The apostrophe, or single quote, is the same key that you use for double quotes, next to the Enter (Return) key.

## Snap to Grid

You can choose to have objects snap to the grid automatically, just like you did earlier with guides. When this feature is enabled, you'll notice that objects are attracted to the grid lines like magnets. Because all of your objects are snapping to the same grid, you can get more precise layouts without any extra effort.

To make objects snap to the grid, choose either View ➪ Grid Options ➪ Snap to Grid or the keyboard shortcut Ctrl+Shift+' (Command+Shift+').

## Grid color and frequency

Again, just like guides, you can change the color of the grid to make it stand out from your document. The default color for each new document is black.

If you're creating a navigation bar with numerous buttons that are 100 pixels wide and 50 pixels tall, set the grid so that it also is 100 pixels wide and 50 pixels tall, so that you can easily see where each button should sit. Enable Snap to Grid, and your layout will come together automatically. The default grid frequency for new documents is 36x36.

To modify the grid, follow these steps:

1. Choose either View ➪ Grid Options ➪ Edit Grid or the keyboard shortcut Ctrl+Alt+G (Command+Option+G).

   Fireworks displays the Edit Grid dialog box (see Figure 13-9).

2. Use the grid color picker to specify the color in which you want the grid to be displayed.

 **Tip**    For convenience, you can also toggle the visibility of the grid or enable Snap to Grid while you're in the Edit Grid dialog box.

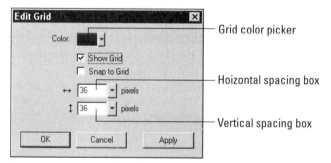

**Figure 13-9:** Set grid options in the Edit Grid dialog box.

3. Enter in the horizontal spacing box the horizontal spacing that you want the grid to have. This is the space, in pixels, between vertical grid lines.

4. Enter in the vertical spacing box the vertical spacing that you want the grid to have. This is the space, in pixels, between horizontal grid lines.

5. Click Apply to see the results of your modifications without exiting the Edit Grid dialog box. Click OK when you're done.

# Grouping Objects

When you group objects, you basically create an object that consists of other objects. You can treat a group as if it's a single object, and apply Live Effects, alter blending modes, and more.

Objects in a group maintain their positions and stacking order relative to each other. They retain their effects settings until you modify the whole group. If half the objects in a group have a drop shadow, and you apply a drop shadow to the whole group, than all the objects will have a drop shadow. Fireworks is smart enough to apply that drop shadow to the whole group as if all members were one object. You can also select and modify the component objects of a group individually, without ungrouping them.

Grouping objects is a good way to keep a complex drawing under control. For example, you might build a logo out of path and text objects, and then group together the objects so that you can manipulate and lay out the logo as one object. Group together any objects that you don't need to manipulate individually, so that you can manipulate them all at the same time.

To group two or more objects, select them and choose either Modify ➪ Group or the keyboard shortcut Ctrl+G (Command+G). Your grouped objects now behave as if they are one object. A Live Effect or opacity setting applied to a group affects the whole group as if it were one object (see Figure 13-10).

After you make a group, you can ungroup it at any time. To ungroup a group, select it and choose either Modify ➪ Ungroup or the keyboard shortcut Ctrl+U (Command+U).

## Subselecting and superselecting

To modify individual objects within a group, you can either ungroup them, or use the Subselection tool to subselect only the objects you want to work with. If you move a subselected object to another layer, it is removed from the group. To select all the component objects within a group, choose Edit ➪ Subselect. To select the parent group of an object, choose Edit ➪ Superselect.

**Cross-Reference**

Fireworks actually has three types of groups: the plain groups discussed here; mask groups, which are discussed next; and Symbols, which are covered in Chapter 24. You can use all the techniques, such as subselecting and superselecting, on any kind of group.

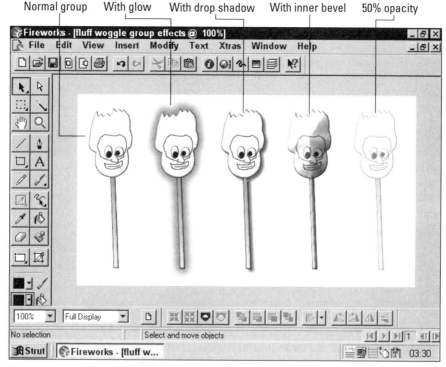

**Figure 13-10:** Applying a Live Effect or opacity setting to a group shows how it acts like one object.

## Mask groups

In a nutshell, *mask groups* are groups in which the luminance of the topmost object is used as an alpha mask for the entire group. The group then has the size and shape of the mask, and the advanced alpha transparency of a 32-bit PNG image.

**New Feature**

In Fireworks 1, the top object of a mask group had to be a grayscale image. With Fireworks 2, the luminance of any top object in a mask group is used as the mask. This object can even be a path object. Fireworks 2 saves you the bother of converting images, and the mask stays editable all the time.

If you've ever created a transparent GIF with a light-colored background and then placed that GIF in a Web page with a dark background, you've seen a graphic (no pun intended) example of the challenges of compositing transparent images. The edges of your image, where they meet the transparent color, are antialiased to either a light color or a dark color. Artifacts are visible when the image is placed over the opposite-colored background.

The 8-bit alpha mask used in Fireworks and the PNG image format solves this problem, enabling you to composite transparent objects without worrying about the color of the objects on which you're placing them, because transparency is specified for each and every pixel (see Figure 13-11).

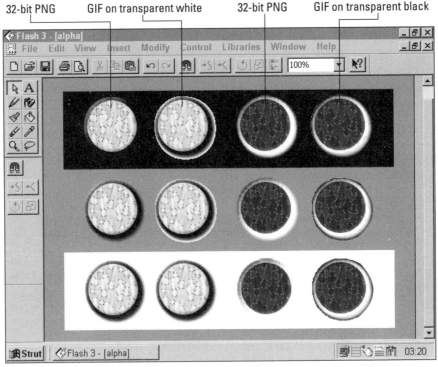

**Figure 13-11:** The 32-bit PNG images in the first and third column can be placed against any background color. The second column is a GIF, with white transparent. A GIF with black transparent is in the final column. White or black rings become apparent as the GIF is moved onto a background other than the one it was created for.

Typically, your Fireworks images have three 8-bit channels — one for red, one for green, and one for blue — resulting in a 24-bit RGB image. When you add one more 8-bit grayscale channels to describe the levels of transparency, you get a 32-bit image (see Table 13-1).

## Table 13-1
## Channels and Bit Depth

| Image | Channels | Bit Depth |
|---|---|---|
| Grayscale | 1 grayscale | 8-bit |
| True color (RGB) | 1 red, 1 green, 1 blue | 24-bit |
| True color with alpha mask | 1 red, 1 green, 1 blue, 1 grayscale (as mask) | 32-bit |

Each pixel of the alpha mask has a value between 0 and 255, to indicate the amount of transparency, which ranges from completely opaque (black, or 0) to completely transparent (white, or 255). The grays in between can be thought of as shades of transparency. Fireworks uses the value of each pixel of the mask to determine the transparency level for the underlying pixel of the mask group, which in turn determines how to blend that pixel with the background pixel it sits on.

If you haven't worked with 32-bit PNG images yet and are used to the limited transparency options inherent in the GIF format, the ease with which you can composite transparent objects by using alpha transparency will thrill you with.

**Caution** Currently, no Web browsers support the PNG alpha channel. Alpha transparency is still useful for working within Fireworks and exporting transparency to other applications, such as Macromedia Director and Flash. Incidentally, both Director and Flash can import your Fireworks PNG files — no need exists to export as a regular PNG.

To create a mask group, select two or more objects and choose either Modify ➪ Mask Group or the keyboard shortcut Ctrl+Shift+G (Command+Shift+G).

**Tip** If you use an image as a mask and the transparency is the inverse of what you want, the Invert Xtra can quickly invert your mask and set things straight. (See Chapter 2 for details about Xtras.)

Your objects are grouped, with the top object converted to grayscale and used as an alpha mask. If the top object is white, the group is transparent; if the top object is black, the group is opaque. Shades in between black and white vary in transparency from opaque to transparent, respectively (see Figure 13-12).

**Tip** You can convert a mask group into a regular group, and vice versa, by selecting the group and choosing the appropriate radio button from the Object inspector.

Image       Image with mask on top       Mask group

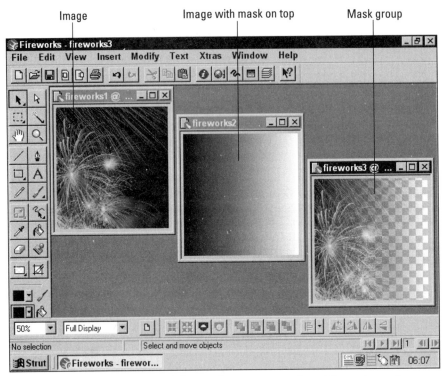

**Figure 13-12:** The black parts of the mask are opaque, the white parts are transparent, and every shade in between is transparent to some degree within this range. This mask group is ready to be placed on top of other objects.

## Mask group image cropping

Often, when you are working with an image object in Fireworks, you'll want to crop the image to a smaller size. Although you could use the crop tool to crop out a section, or make a pixel selection and copy out that area, those techniques are destructive. You alter the image object permanently. Later, if you want to add back 100 pixels, or add 10 pixels all around the image so that you can feather the edges, for example, you're out of luck. That information has been thrown away.

Mask groups provide a way around this, though. To crop an image nondestructively with mask groups, follow these steps:

1. To enter Object mode (if you aren't there already), either choose Modify ⇨ Exit Image Edit, use the keyboard shortcut Ctrl+Shift+D (Command+Shift+D), or click the stop button in the status bar.

2. Draw a shape (not a selection, but an actual shape in Object mode) on top of the image that you're going to crop. This can be a rectangle, circle, or polygon. Anything inside the shape will be kept, and anything outside the shape will be hidden.

3. Fill the shape with black.

4. Select the shape and your image by holding down the Shift key and clicking one after the other with the mouse. Choose Modify ➪ Mask Group.

A mask group is created, and your image is now the same size and shape as the black shape that you drew on top of it. Click the mask group handle in the center of your mask group and drag it to move the underlying image around without affecting the mask. Once again, an object remains editable in Fireworks. Double-click the handle to select the image, so that you can alter its properties. Apply an Xtra to it, if you like.

Now, select the entire mask group again by deselecting it and clicking it again, but not on its handle. You can alter the mask's fill, stroke, or Live Effects. Apply an inner bevel, change its color (which also changes the transparency of the whole group), or apply an interesting stroke to affect the edges of the group.

## Mask group suggestions

Mask groups are a very creative and powerful tool that you can experiment with again and again. Some suggestions for things to try:

✦ Apply Live Effects or Styles to path objects and then use them as masks.

✦ Make a mask group that includes another mask group.

✦ Alter the Stroke settings of a mask.

✦ Use a text object as a mask.

✦ Apply texture fills to masks.

✦ Apply Xtras to masks.

# Fireworks technique: quick photo edges

Fireworks Live Effects can create some nice border effects when applied to an image object in Object mode, but modifying a path object and using it as an alpha mask for an image gives you fine-control over your image's shape and transparency.

One application of alpha masks in Fireworks is to quickly give an image any one of an almost unlimited supply of interesting borders. Remember that the group will also be cropped to the size of the visible elements — although they won't actually be altered and remain editable — so this is a great way to bring together a group of differently sized objects.

To create an image border, open an image in Fireworks and follow these steps:

1. To enter Object mode (if you aren't there already), either choose Modify ➪ Exit Image Edit, use the keyboard shortcut Ctrl+Shift+D (Command+Shift+D), or click the stop button in the status bar.

2. Use the drawing tools to draw a rectangle on top of your image, but make the rectangle a bit smaller than the image itself (see Figure 13-13). The area outside the rectangle will be thrown away.

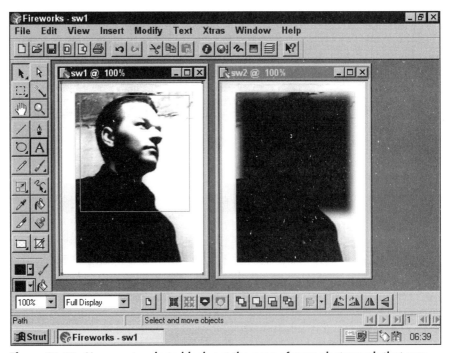

**Figure 13-13:** Use a rectangle to block out the area of your photograph that you want to keep.

3. Color the rectangle black by selecting it and choosing black from the fill color well at the bottom of the toolbox.

**Tip**    The next time that you use this technique, experiment by giving your shape various gradient fills or textures. Remember, any black area will be completely visible in your final image, whereas any white area will be thrown away. The darker the areas in between these extremes are the more transparent they become.

4. Select the rectangle and feather its edges by choosing Modify ➪ Edge ➪ Feather.

**Tip** The next time that you use this technique, stop at this point to experiment with applying Live Effects, Styles, Xtras, or various strokes to your shape, instead of feathering it. If you have Photoshop 5's filters installed, the Distort, Brush Strokes, Sketch, and Stylize filters are good choices. If you use Alien Skin's Eye Candy, the Jiggle feature is a great choice, too.

5. Select both the object and your image by holding down the Shift key and clicking each one with the mouse. If they are the only two objects in the document, you can quickly select them both by choosing either Edit ➪ Select All or the keyboard shortcut Ctrl+A (Command+A).

6. Choose either Modify ➪ Mask Group or the keyboard shortcut Ctrl+Shift+G (Command+Shift+G) to make them into a mask group.

Your image now has a feathered edge (see Figure 13-14). Many different photo edge effects can be created with this technique simply by modifying the mask in different ways. You can use a circle instead of a rectangle, or combine shapes to create complex masks.

**Figure 13-14:** A photo edge effect created by applying Live Effects to a path object and using it as an alpha mask for an image. The image on the left was created with this technique.

# Opacity and Blending

The primary tools in compositing images are opacity and blending. Altering these properties can literally merge two images together. You can make one image show through the other by giving the first image a lower opacity setting, or you can use a blend mode to make them steal colors from each other. An image object or pixel selection that appears to float above a background can be seamlessly integrated in just a few short steps.

**Tip**    Feathering objects before compositing them often provides good results. With a softer edge, removing the borderline between the two images is easier. Experiment with blending Fireworks Strokes, texture fills, and effects.

After you select an object in Fireworks, you can use the Object inspector (see Figure 13-15) to control various aspects of that object's properties. Opacity and blending modes are front and center.

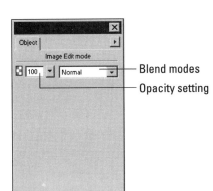

**Figure 13-15:** The Object inspector contains the opacity and blending settings for a selected object.

— Blend modes
— Opacity setting

## Controlling opacity

As you make an object more transparent, more of the background shows through. This can go a long way toward integrating two images.

Controlling opacity in Fireworks is very easy. Select an object, open the Object inspector by choosing either Window ➪ Object or the keyboard shortcut Ctrl+I (Command+I), and then slide the opacity slider. A setting of 100 is no transparency, or completely opaque. A setting of 1, with the slider all the way down, gives you the closest thing to invisible (see Figure 13-16). If you do want to make an image completely invisible, you can type a zero in the opacity box and press Enter (Return).

**Note**    If you specify an opacity setting without an object selected, you will set a default opacity for objects that you create from that point on. If you accidentally set it to 10% or less, you might not even be able to see some of the objects that you draw. If this happens to you, you'll know where to go to change it back. Deselect all objects with Edit ➪ Deselect and move the opacity slider in the Object inspector back to 100.

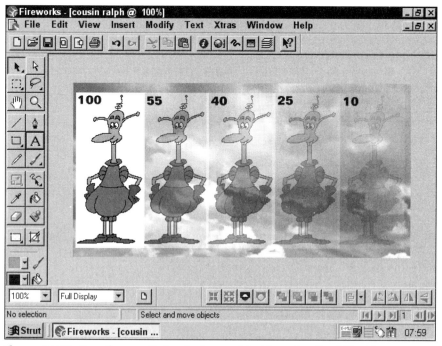

**Figure 13-16:** Vary the opacity level of your object by using the Object inspector. The fellow on the left is 100% opaque. On the extreme right, he's 10% opaque.

## Using blending modes

Blending modes manipulate the color of pixels in a foreground image and the color of pixels beneath them in the background image in a variety of ways to blend the two together. Before you start using blending modes, here's the terminology that you need to know:

✦ **Blend color:** The color of the selected object, typically a foreground object

✦ **Base color:** The color beneath the selected object, typically a background object

✦ **Result color:** The color resulting from the blend of the blend color and base color

For the sake of simplicity, this discussion uses *foreground, background,* and *result,* for the most part.

As you've seen already, Fireworks enables you to alter the opacity of an object at any time with the opacity menu in the Object inspector. The opacity of an object also effects the way it is blended.

A blend mode applies to an object or to an entire group. If you give an object a certain blend mode and then group it, the blend mode disappears, because the object is given the group's blending mode instead (although ungrouping will restore the individual object's blending mode). If you're working extensively with blending modes, instead of grouping your objects, you might want to use layers to separate and organize your objects. This also enables you to stack blending modes for interesting effects, as objects on each layer blend into ones on the layer below.

Depending on what kind of object you have selected, the blending modes work in one of the following ways:

✦ **Object mode:** The blending mode affects the selected object.

✦ **Image Edit mode:** If you have a marquee selection drawn, the blending mode affects the selection of pixels. If you don't have a marquee selection drawn, the blending mode affects the strokes and fills that you draw from then on. You draw with blending modes.

Select an object and modify its blending mode setting in the Object inspector. If no object is selected, modifying the blending mode creates a new default blending mode for objects that you create from that point on.

## The modes themselves

Blending modes can be confusing and strangely mathematical. The best way to start understanding them is to compare their results, which is what Figure 13-17 does.

Twelve mysterious blending modes can seem like a lot at first, but most modes have an opposite partner or other related modes. After you understand one mode of a group, you're well on your way to understanding them all.

**Note**    References to the foreground or background color refer to the color at the pixel level, not at the object level. Individual pixels of the foreground and background objects are compared.

### Multiply and Screen

*Multiply* mode multiplies the foreground color with the background color. It can give your blended image a deeper, richer tone. The result color is always darker. If the foreground or background color is black, the result will be black; if one of them is white, Multiply has no effect.

*Screen* mode is basically the opposite of Multiply. The result color is a ghostly, faded blend. It works by inverting the foreground color and then multiplying it with the background color. Whereas Multiply always results in a darker color, Screen always results in a lighter one. If either the foreground or background is white, the result color will be white. If either is black, Screen has no effect.

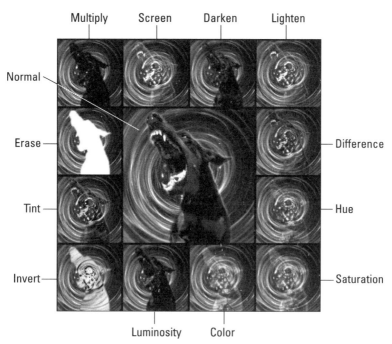

**Figure 13-17:** Comparing the 12 blending modes that Fireworks offers, with the unaltered image in the center

## Darken, Lighten, and Difference

*Darken* compares the foreground and background colors and keeps the darkest one, whereas *Lighten* does the opposite; the foreground and background color is compared and only the lightest is kept.

*Difference* compares the foreground color and the background color and subtracts the darker color from the lighter color. It can result in some surprising color choices.

## Hue, Saturation, Color, and Luminosity

*Hue* combines the hue value of the foreground color with the luminance and saturation of the background color. Essentially, you get the foreground color, but as dark or light as the background.

*Saturation* combines the saturation of the foreground color with the luminance and hue of the background color.

*Color* combines the hue and saturation of the foreground color with the luminance of the background color. Grays are preserved, so this is a good way to add color to a black-and-white photograph, or tint color photographs.

*Luminosity* combines the luminance of the foreground color with the hue and saturation of the background color.

### Invert and Tint

Invert and Tint don't bother with the foreground color at all. With *Invert*, the foreground object's colors are replaced with inverted background colors. With *Tint*, gray is added to the background color to create the result.

### Erase

Removes all background color pixels, leaving the canvas color.

## Fireworks technique: copy, paste, and blend

Suppose that you want a particular foreground element to create a strong impact and a feeling of motion. It might be a fast car, a martial artist, or a savage canine. You can use blending to accomplish this, by blending copies of your subject into the background. The blended versions typically aren't perceived as separate subjects when people view the image, but the blended versions create a dynamic impression.

To copy a foreground image from one document and blend it into another, follow these steps:

1. Open your source and target documents in Fireworks. The source document should have a foreground element, such as a dog. The target document should contain a suitable background.

2. In the source document, select the foreground image object or make a pixel selection (see Figure 13-18), if necessary, using the lasso or magic wand tool. Either way, you want to copy just the foreground element and not parts of the background from the source document. If you made a pixel selection, choose Edit ➪ Feather, enter 10 in the Feather Selection dialog box, and then click OK. Feathering your selection helps to clean up any rough edges.

3. Choose either Edit ➪ Copy or the keyboard shortcut Ctrl+C (Command+C) to copy the pixel selection to the Clipboard.

4. To enter Object mode (if you aren't there already) in your target document, either choose Modify ➪ Exit Image Edit, use the keyboard shortcut Ctrl+Shift+D (Command+Shift+D), or click the stop button in the status bar.

5. Choose either Edit ➪ Paste or the keyboard shortcut Ctrl+V (Command+V) to paste the pixel selection from the Clipboard into your document as a new image object.

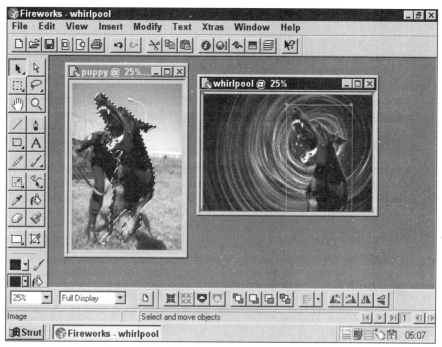

**Figure 13-18:** Copying a pixel selection into another document

6. Move the subject around until it's placed where you want it to be located.

7. Select the subject and choose either Edit ➪ Duplicate or the keyboard shortcut Ctrl+Alt+D (Command+Option+D). Do this a few times until you have a few copies of your foreground image.

8. Select the original subject and choose either Modify ➪ Arrange ➪ Bring to Front or the keyboard shortcut Ctrl+F (Command+F) to bring the original in front of the copies.

9. Choose either Window ➪ Object or the keyboard shortcut Ctrl+I (Command+I) to show the Object inspector.

10. Select each duplicate in turn and apply the Screen blending mode, by choosing it from the blending modes list.

11. Select each duplicate in turn and arrange them in an aesthetically pleasing manner (see Figure 13-19).

**Figure 13-19:** Using blending modes for effect

## Summary

Fireworks gives you lots of options for combining any types of objects to create more complex objects or special effects. When you are arranging or compositing objects in Fireworks, keep these points in mind:

✦ Layers can be used to organize objects in your document into separate groups, for easier selection and editing.

✦ The Layers panel is your control center for working with layers.

✦ You can choose to work with individual layers in a variety of ways, including hiding, showing, and locking layers.

✦ The ruler, grid, and guides are all available to help you precisely position objects on the canvas.

## Color Plate 1-1:

Fireworks 2 is capable of graphics ranging from the simple, clear navigation system to the wonderfully layered and sophisticated graphic shown here in a site design by Lisa Lopuck. And, as Lisa points out, everything is always editable in Fireworks.

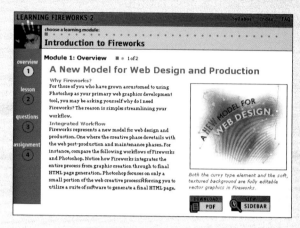

(Courtesy Lopuck Design, *www.lopuck.com*)

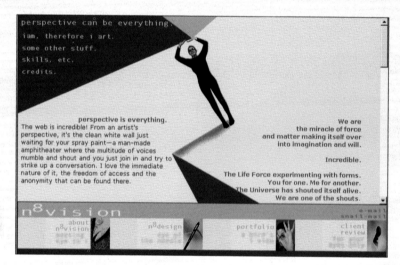

(Courtesy N8Vision, *www.n8vision.com*)

## Color Plate 1-2:

Fireworks handles object-oriented shapes, photorealistic graphics, and straightforward text with equal ease, as illustrated in this Web page by Donna Casey for N8Vision. Each of the navigation elements swaps a monochromatic image with a full-color image when a mouse passes over it, while the blurred text becomes crystal clear.

**Color Plate 1-3:**

Fireworks gives you the power to integrate many different types of images and objects. In this example, the flower (32-bit PNG with full alpha transparency) overlays a feather-edged JPEG file. The shooting star was created in Fireworks and then multiplied by using the Symbol and Instances feature. The type was grouped with a gradient to form a mask group.

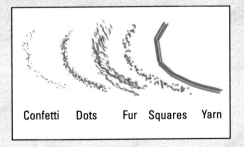

**Color Plate 8-1:**

The Random Strokes category takes advantage of Fireworks's stroke capability by randomizing the size, opacity, hue, and other characteristics.

**Color Plate 8-2:**

Wild color variations are the norm with the Unnatural category of Fireworks strokes.

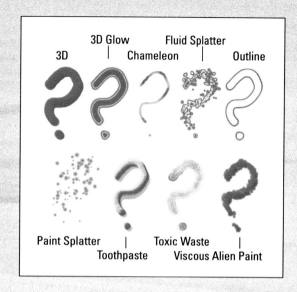

**Color Plate 9-1:**

The Distort tool is used to give a patterned wood rectangle some perspective, while group masks add light and shadow effects for enhanced depth.

**Color Plate 10-1:**

To place the camel and the sun in this image in the appropriate spots, the sun was moved down and to the right and the camel was cut and pasted on the horizon. Then, a group mask was applied to the text and image.

**Color Plate 11-1:**

These standard Fireworks patterns are always available—and more patterns can be added by creating a seamless image and saving it as a PNG file in the Patterns folder.

**Color Plate 11-2:**

When the Transparent option is used in Fireworks 2's new Web Dither fill, any filled object becomes semitransparent, like the text in this image.

**Color Plate 11-3:**

Textures can add significant depth to an image. Here, a custom texture (included on the CD-ROM) is used to create TV-like scan lines.

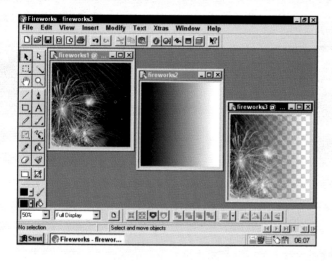

**Color Plate 13-1:**

A background can be blended into transparency through Fireworks's group mask feature where the initial image is grouped with a gradation, as shown here. The gradation is fully editable.

Multiply    Screen    Darken    Lighten

Erase

Tint

Invert

Difference

Hue

Saturation

Luminosity    Color

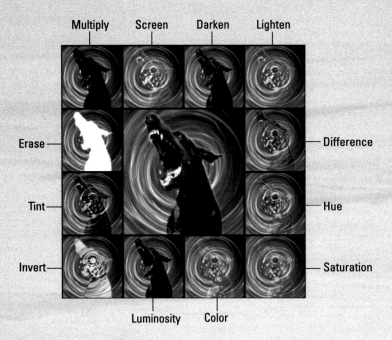

**Color Plate 13-2:**

The blending modes are best understood by comparing the various effects. Here, the dog is blended against the whirlpool pattern; the Normal blending mode is shown in the center image.

**Color Plate 13-3:**

With full opacity control, you can easily fade any object against any other object or image.

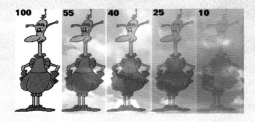

100    55    40    25    10

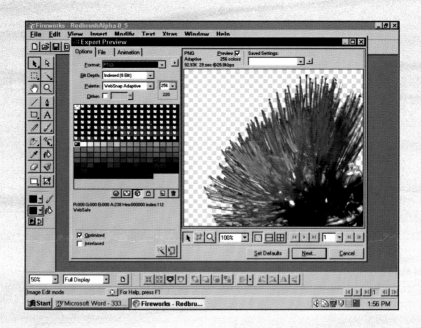

**Color Plate 16-1:**

With Fireworks's advanced PNG transparency control, you can set up to 256 levels of transparency. Images exported as 32-bit PNG files can be used directly in Flash, and all transparency is preserved.

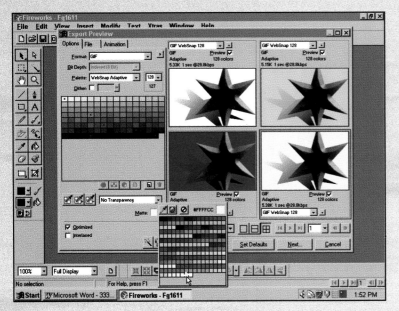

**Color Plate 16-2:**

With the new Matte feature, you can export the same image for use in different backgrounds without having to change the canvas color. Notice how the perspective shadow (created with group masks) blends perfectly in every background.

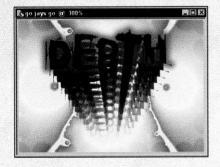

**Color Plate 24-1:**

Symbols and Instances are used here to give the image a sense of motion and depth.

✦ Objects can be grouped, and a group behaves as if its one object.

✦ Mask groups give you amazing control over alpha transparency.

✦ Blending modes enable you to composite objects quickly and easily.

The next chapter looks at using Xtras and Filters in Fireworks.

✦     ✦     ✦

# Xtras and Filters

## CHAPTER 14

O ne of the themes of Macromedia applications is extensibility, and Fireworks is no exception. The entire Xtras menu contains commands that refer to external applications that are added to Fireworks by placing them in Fireworks's Xtras folder. These Xtras "filter" images to create a particular effect, such as blurring or inverting colors. Many filters have options that allow you to specify such things as the intensity of the effect or what parts of the image are to be affected. Every pixel in the image is evaluated — filtered — and either modified or not according to the settings and the effect that's being applied.

**Note**

> The terms "Xtras" and "filters" are used interchangeably throughout this chapter. Xtras is what Macromedia calls application add-ons. With Fireworks, the application add-ons just happen to be image filters. Because most people either already have some third-party filters or are planning to get some, the discussion won't be limited to the Xtras that come with Fireworks, although this chapter certainly looks closely at them.

This chapter looks at how you can apply Xtras and what you can apply them to. You'll work with the Xtras that are included with Fireworks and examine some of the techniques that you can use to apply them creatively. You'll also see how you can add more Xtras to Fireworks, including ones that you may already have as part of another application. Finally, this chapter reviews two very popular third-party image filter packages: Alien Skin Eye Candy 3.0 and MetaCreation's Kai Power Tools 5.

## Apply an Xtra to. . . What?

Before you choose an Xtra from the Xtras menu, you have to decide what you want to modify with that Xtra, and select it in the appropriate way. All the Xtras that are included with Fireworks will work on any type of selection, but some third-party Xtras work better on selections within images, or even require such a selection to run. This section takes a look at the types of selections you can apply Xtras to (see Figure 14-1) and the issues involved with each.

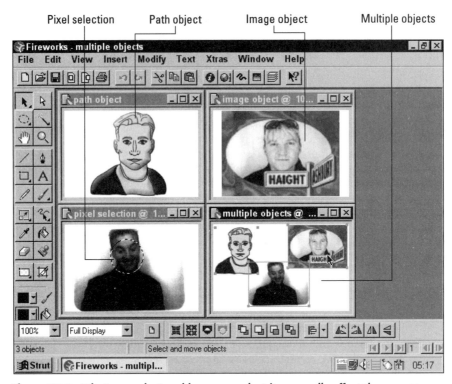

**Figure 14-1:** What you select and how you select it can really affect the way an Xtra works.

## Path objects

Applying an Xtra to a path object or path object group "flattens" it into an image object. The vector information is thrown away and you lose the advantages, such as scalability and editability, that path objects provide. Try using Live Effects on your path objects to achieve the look that you want, before you apply Xtras. After your path object becomes an image object, there's no going back.

**Tip**

Sometimes, though, you can get the best of both worlds. If you're using an Xtra that draws outside the selection (for example, the Eye Candy 3.0 Fire, which draws flames around your image), you can apply the Xtra to a copy of your object and then place the resulting, filtered image behind your original object and group them. Later, you can still color and use Live Effects on your path object. If you resize it, you should throw away the filtered image and reapply the saved settings of the filter to a new copy of your object. If you're applying an Xtra that alters within the selection, try applying the Xtra to a copy of your object, and then using the copy as an alpha mask for your original. Some interesting effects can be created this way, without being stuck in Image Edit mode.

When you do apply an Xtra to a path object, Fireworks warns you that doing so will convert it to an image object. You can disable this warning by checking the "don't show again" check box. I recommend that you leave it unchecked for a little while, until you get used to this conversion. If you accidentally convert a path object to an image object and then save your file, your vector information may be gone for good.

To apply an Xtra to a path object, select it with the mouse in Object mode and choose the Xtra from the Xtras menu.

## Image objects

Applying an Xtra to an image object couldn't be easier. The only thing to keep in mind is that some Xtras draw outside the selection, to create effects such as motion trails and drop shadows. If your image object is the same size as the canvas, the effect will either be invisible, because it's off the canvas, or, with some Xtras, won't even be drawn. Before applying one of these filters, resize the canvas to give them a little room.

To apply an Xtra to an image object, select it with the mouse in Object mode and choose the Xtra from the Xtras menu.

## Pixel selections in an image object

Many filters work best when applied to a pixel selection within an image object, because they create a difference between the area inside the selection and the area outside the selection. Often, complex pixel selections, such as those made with the Magic Wand or the Polygon Lasso, work better than simple rectangular or circular selections. The extra complexity creates areas where some filters create things such as bevels, shadows, or textures.

**Note**     Creating a pixel selection doesn't necessarily mean that you've limited an Xtra to drawing only inside the selection. Although most will stay inside, some draw outside the selection to create their effect. Your selection marks a focal point for whatever filter you're applying.

To apply an Xtra to a pixel selection within an image object, use one of the Marquee selection tools from the Toolbox to draw your selection in Image Edit mode, and then choose an Xtra from the Xtras menu.

**Cross-Reference**     For more on creating selections within image objects, see Chapter 6.

## False pixel selections

Some filters will ignore your pixel selections and apply their effect to an entire image object. If you find that a particular filter exhibits this behavior, you can work around it by creating a "false pixel selection," by copying your pixel selection to the Clipboard and pasting it as a new image object.

**Tip**    All the filters in Kai Power Tools 5, detailed later in this chapter, apply their effects to your entire image object and require that you use a false pixel selection to limit them to a portion of your image.

To create a false pixel selection, follow these steps:

1. Choose Modify ➪ Image Object or the key shortcut Ctrl+E (Command+E) to enter Image Edit mode.

2. Create a selection around the area to which you want to apply the Xtra by using one of the Marquee selection tools from the Toolbox.

3. Copy the selection to the Clipboard by choosing either Edit ➪ Copy or the keyboard shortcut Ctrl+C (Command+C).

4. Paste the selection back into the document by choosing either Edit ➪ Paste or the keyboard shortcut Ctrl+V (Command+V).

   The selection is pasted as a new image object, on top of the area it was copied from. Even though it now has a square marquee selection, the image object is, in fact, the same size and shape as what you originally copied to the Clipboard.

5. Apply an Xtra to the new image object by choosing the Xtra from the Xtras menu.

   The filter affects only the new image object.

6. Either choose Modify ➪ Exit Image Edit, use the keyboard shortcut Ctrl+Shift+D (Command+Shift+D), or press the stop button in the status bar to return to Object mode.

The original image object and the new one that you created and then filtered are merged into one. The net result is that only the area of your original pixel selection is modified.

## Multiple objects

In addition to individual objects, you can apply Xtras to a selection or group of multiple objects. If your selection or group contains any path objects, they will be converted to image objects, just as they would be if you were applying the Xtra to them individually. When applying Xtras to multiple objects, keep this in mind:

✦ If you apply an Xtra to a selection of objects in Object mode, the Xtra runs multiple times, applying to each object in turn. If you select three objects, for example, the Xtra runs three times in a row, once on each object. If you select Cancel in any of the filter's dialog boxes, it cancels the entire operation, and none of your objects will be altered.

✦ If you apply an Xtra to a group of objects, they will act as if they are one object. After you apply the Xtra, the objects actually are one image object, and you can't separate them. To make a selection of objects into a group, select multiple objects and choose Modify ➪ Group or use the keyboard shortcut Ctrl+G (Command+G).

**Caution** The exceptions to the preceding list are the Blur, Invert, Other, and Sharpen Xtras that come with Fireworks (all of those above the line in the Xtras menu). They act on a selection of objects as if they are already grouped.

The differences in the way groups and selections are handled by Xtras is actually quite handy. Imagine that you have created five objects that are going to be five buttons in a navigation interface. If you want to apply an Xtra with the exact same settings to all of them, group them and apply the Xtra. If, however, you want to apply the same Xtra to all of them, but tweak the settings for each—to add a slightly different texture to each one, for example—just select them and apply the Xtra.

 **Tip** Many Xtras start with the same settings as when you last used them. When applying an extra to a selection of objects, the second time the Xtra starts, it will have the same settings that you used on the first object, making it easier to apply a similar effect across a selection of objects. You can also save settings in some Xtras.

## Xtras That Aren't Extras

The Xtras that ship with Fireworks enable you to apply simple effects, such as blurring and sharpening, or convert a selection into an alpha mask to create advanced transparency effects. For the most part, these are pretty basic examples of what image filters can do, although the PhotoOptics package, which we'll look at later in this chapter, can create some very advanced effects.

Table 14-1 details the Xtras that are included with Fireworks, and what each one does:

| Table 14-1 Fireworks Xtras | |
| --- | --- |
| **Filter** | **Description** |
| Blur | Blurs pixels together to create an unfocused effect. |
| Blur More | Same as Blur, but across a slightly larger radius, for a more pronounced blur. |
| Gaussian Blur | Same as Blur More, but with a Gaussian bell curve and a dialog box that enables you to specify the blur radius. |
| Invert | Changes the color of each pixel to its mathematical inverse. Creates a photo-negative-type effect. |
| Convert to Alpha | Converts an image into a grayscale image that's suitable for use as an alpha mask. White pixels are colored transparent. |
| Find Edges | Detects the outlines of forms and converts them to solid lines. |

*Continued*

| Filter | Description |
|---|---|
| Table 14-1 *(continued)* | |
| Sharpen | Sharpens by finding edges and increasing the contrast between adjacent pixels. |
| Sharpen More | Same as Sharpen, but across a larger radius. |
| Unsharp Mask | Same as Sharpen More, but with control over which pixels are sharpened (and which are left "unsharp") according to the image's grayscale mask. |

**New Feature** The Convert to Alpha Xtra is obsoleted in Fireworks 2, because the luminance value of any object can now be used as an alpha mask just by making it the top object of a mask group. You might still use the Convert to Alpha Xtra to create an alpha mask for export, though.

**Cross-Reference** For more about mask groups, see Chapter 13.

## Sharpening to bring out detail

Sharpening an image can bring out depth that's not there, by finding the edges of objects and creating more contrast between pixels on either side of that edge. It can especially help to fix a bad scan, or bring out detail after you go overboard with special effects Xtras.

To sharpen an image a little bit, select it and choose Xtras ➪ Sharpen ➪ Sharpen or Xtras ➪ Sharpen ➪ Sharpen More.

To sharpen an image with control over settings, select it and follow these steps:

1. Choose Xtras ➪ Sharpen ➪ Unsharp Mask.

   Fireworks displays the Unsharp Mask dialog box.

**Note** Some Xtras have an ellipsis after their menu command, which indicates that choosing that command will open a dialog box in which you can specify settings. Xtras without the ellipsis after their commands don't have any options for you to change, and perform their function without asking for confirmation. If you choose one of these and don't like the resulting effect, choose Edit ➪ Undo or the keyboard shortcut Ctrl+Z (Command+Z).

2. Moving the Sharpen Amount slider specifies the intensity of the effect. You might start with this slider at about midway and increase or decrease it later after setting other options.

3. Move the Pixel Radius slider to control how many pixels are evaluated simultaneously. A larger radius value results in a more pronounced effect, because the differences among a larger group of pixels typically is greater.

**4.** Move the Threshold slider to determine which pixels are affected. Only pixels that have a grayscale value higher than the threshold value are affected. A lower threshold affects more pixels. Click OK when you're done.

Your image should now have a crisper, sharper look (see Figure 14-2).

Original image   Simulated bad scan   Sharpened image

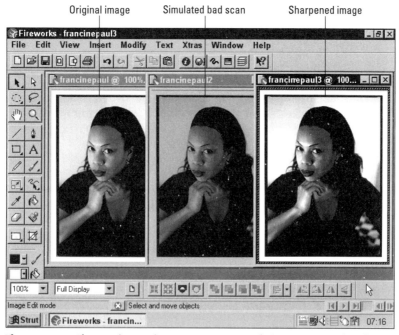

**Figure 14-2:** Sharpening an image may seem to bring out extra detail.

 **Tip**     Sometimes, a sharpened image will seem too harsh. Adding a little bit of noise with the PhotoOptics CSI Noise filter or a touch of blur with the Blur filter can sometimes help to remove this harshness.

## Adding depth with blurring

Sometimes, what should be the focal point of your image can get lost among other elements of the composition. This is especially true when you're compositing multiple objects or really laying the filters on thick. Adding a little blur to the background area of an image can cause the foreground to stand out, immediately drawing the viewer's eye to it.

To add depth to the background area of an image, follow these steps:

**1.** Use one of the Marquee selection tools to create a pixel selection around the part of your image that you want to remain in the foreground. You might create a circle to focus attention within that circle, or use the Magic Wand to create a complex selection, such as around a person's head or face.

**Note**    Fireworks automatically enters Image Edit mode when you use one of the Marquee selection tools.

2. Select the background area of your image by choosing either Edit ➪ Select Inverse or the keyboard shortcut Ctrl+Shift+I (Command+Shift+I).

   Fireworks creates a new selection. What was previously inside the selection is now outside, and vice versa.

3. Choose Xtras ➪ Blur ➪ Gaussian Blur.

   Fireworks displays the Gaussian Blur dialog box.

4. Adjust the Blur Radius slider to specify the intensity of the effect. The more blur you add, the more depth you add to your image. Generally, a blur radius of between 1 or 2 creates a depth effect without destroying the edges of the elements in the background area of your image. Click OK when you're done.

5. Choose Edit ➪ Deselect or the keyboard shortcut Ctrl+D (Command+D) to remove the pixel selection from your image.

The area that was within your original pixel selection now seems to stand out and draws the eye at first glance (see Figure 14-3). In addition, an overall feeling of depth has been created. Elements in the background seem to be a little further away.

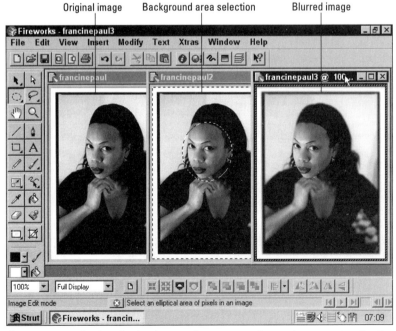

**Figure 14-3:** Blurring the background seems to give an image extra depth and makes the foreground stand out.Notice how your eye is immediately drawn to the subject's face.

# Working with the PhotoOptics Filters

The PhotoOptics filters, a third-party package from Cytopia Software, are included with Fireworks. They differ from many other filters in that they're based on photographic methods for contrast, exposure, and color correction. The effects that they simulate are the types of things that photographers achieve with camera or darkroom techniques.

After you learn how to use one of the filters, you're well on your way to learning the other ones, because they all share a similar interface, with these common elements (see Figure 14-4):

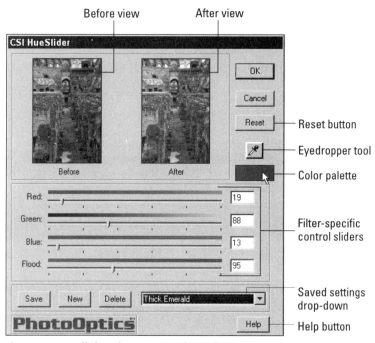

**Figure 14-4:** All the PhotoOptics filters share a similar interface dialog box. The CSI HueSlider dialog box is pictured here. Note that even though this is a third-party application, it opens directly within Fireworks.

✦ **Before and after views:** The image on the left is a thumbnail of your unaltered image. The one on the right is a dynamic preview of the changes you're making with the filter's controls.

✦ **Reset button**. Clicking the Reset button sets all the filter's controls to the default settings, usually 0.

✦ **Eyedropper tool and Color Palette:** Enable you to specify colors just as you do within Fireworks itself.

✦ **Control sliders:** Each filter has its own types of settings, although some, such as Exposure, appear in multiple filters where appropriate.

✦ **Saved settings:** A drop-down list enables you to access preset settings and settings that you've saved.

✦ **Help button:** The Help screen explains the controls and settings of the particular filter you're working in, not just general help that applies to all the filters. It might be a good idea to look at the Help screen the first few times that you use each filter, to remind you of what that filter does.

Table 14-2 details the PhotoOptics filters and what each one does:

| Table 14-2 | |
|:---:|:---:|
| **PhotoOptics Filters** | |
| **Filter** | **Description** |
| CSI GradTone | Colorizes an image. Luminance values are replaced with color hues. Use it to add color into an image before applying special effects Xtras, or just to spice up a grayscale image. |
| CSI HueSlider | Moves an image toward a target color. Pick the color with the RGB sliders and control the amount of color mixing and saturation with the other slider. Use this filter to introduce a subtle tint or to match the coloring of another image. |
| CSI Levels | Increases or reduces contrast. Use this filter to balance the range of light and dark tones in an image, or to flatten an image into black and white areas, for masking effects. Images that seem dull or too dark or light can benefit greatly from a subtle application of this filter. |
| CSI MonoChrome | Converts an image to monochrome. Convert a color photograph to black and white or another monochromatic combination. |
| CSI Negative | Unlike Fireworks's Invert command, this filter is designed to process scans of color negative film, which has an orange mask in the base of the film stock. |
| CSI Noise | Applies color noise or brightness noise to an image. Use it to rough up an image a bit, simulate film grain, or cover the blocky effect of an image that's been scaled up past its resolution. |
| CSI PhotoFilter | Modifies the color of the entire image as if the original photographer had used a lens filter. Add or subtract specific colors, just as you might swap specific lens filters. The presets are even numbered, using standard lens filter numbers. |
| CSI PseudoColor | Distorts the colors in a file. Simulate infrared film or use it to create special effects. |

**Tip**

You can use multiple Xtras on the same image, one after the other, to achieve certain effects.

## Saving PhotoOptics settings

You can save the settings of any PhotoOptics filter for reuse later.

**Caution**

Don't attempt to save your settings by clicking Save in a filter dialog box. Save will save your settings over the saved setting that is showing in the drop-down list. Instead, create a new setting by clicking New.

To save a setting, follow these steps:

1. Click the New button.

   Fireworks displays the New Settings dialog box.

2. Enter a name to save the setting under. Click the Save button in the New Settings dialog box when you're done.

Your new setting is added to the drop-down list in that filter. You can also modify previously saved settings by following these steps:

1. Recall a saved setting by choosing it from the drop-down list.

2. Modify it by using the controls. Click Save when you're done.

Your new settings are saved under the name showing in the drop-down list, overwriting the previously saved setting.

## Color correction

Color correction is a complex and involved topic that can mean slightly different things to different people depending on whether they're focused on print graphics, online graphics, or photography. With Fireworks, we work directly with online images and the Web, so we avoid the color correction concerns that go along with accurately reproducing color on paper. For the most part, color correction within Fireworks usually means removing an unwanted tint or color cast in an image.

**Tip**

If you open an image in Fireworks that was saved by a print application such as Photoshop that uses ICC profiles to match colors between scanners, printers, and displays, you might find that Fireworks displays the colors differently. If it's an option, return to the original application, turn off the ICC profiling, and export again. If that's not an option, the PhotoOptics CSI PhotoFilter or CSI HueSlider can be used to help adjust the colors.

## Color cast correction

A photographic image can end up with unnatural colors in many ways before it arrives in Fireworks and starts to be your problem. Incorrect colors can be introduced when the original photograph is taken. Photographs taken under fluorescent lighting often have a green cast, or ones taken in low light might have a blue cast. In addition, when an image is printed, white areas may end up with a touch of unwanted color. Finally, scans of photographic images may not be as accurate as you'd like them to be.

The CSI PhotoFilter Xtra allows you to correct an image's color cast quickly and easily.

 **Tip**    You might also want to introduce a color cast to an image deliberately, such as a photographer might do when working with an optical lens filter. CSI PhotoFilter is also suitable for doing that.

To correct the color cast of an image, select the image and follow these steps:

1. Choose Xtras ➪ PhotoOptics ➪ CSI PhotoFilter.

   Fireworks displays the CSI PhotoFilter dialog box (see Figure 14-5).

2. Click the Reset button to change the values of the PhotoFilter controls to 0.

   Your Before and After images should now match.

3. Click the eyedropper icon to pick up the Eyedropper tool, just as you do within Fireworks proper. Hover the Eyedropper tool over the unwanted color in the Before image. If your image has a blue cast that you want to remove, hover over the bluest area. Look at the Color Palette box to see a larger version of the color you're hovering over, and fine-tune your choice. Click to select the color when you're ready.

 **Tip**    If your image has a border of photographic paper around it, that might be a good place to select your color. You know that this border should be white, so if it has a blue cast, for example, that is your unwanted color. As you adjust the brightness of that color later, you can try to achieve a pure-white border.

   The color that you clicked is selected as the active color in the Color Palette. This is the color that you'll be modifying from now on.

4. Subtract your selected color by slowly reducing its brightness with the Brightness slider. Watch the After image carefully. Usually, you will find a midpoint between your original, unwanted color cast — where you started — and a similar cast of its complementary color. For example, if you're removing blue, removing too much will make the image appear orange. Stop adjusting when you have removed enough of the color to be satisfied with the result.

**5.** PhotoFilter automatically adjusts the exposure as you adjust brightness, but you may want to adjust the Exposure slider slightly. Correcting an exposure problem now will save time and reduce the number of separate changes you make to the image. Click OK when you're done.

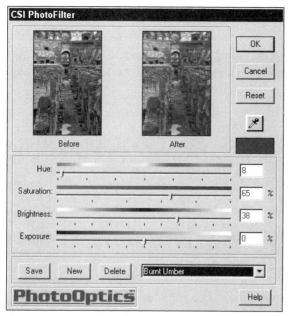

**Figure 14-5:** Use the PhotoOptics CSI PhotoFilter Xtra to remove an unwanted color cast, or to add one for a special effect.

Your image's color cast has now been corrected.

Tip    You can also use the preceding technique on a portion of an image, to correct "red-eye," for example. Before you use the Xtra, create a pixel selection by using one of the Marquee selection tools around the area you want to modify.

## Scans of color negatives

Scans of color negatives have an orange cast that is the result of features that are intended to create better color prints. You could correct this with PhotoFilter, just as you would any other unwanted color cast, but PhotoOptics has another filter, CSI Invert, that is specially designed to remedy this common problem.

To invert and color-correct a scan of a color negative, open the image in Fireworks and follow these steps:

1. Choose Xtras ⇨ PhotoOptics ⇨ CSI Invert.

   Fireworks displays the CSI Invert dialog box.

2. Check the Reversal Film check box. This enables color correction and tonal decompression. Basically, you're telling PhotoOptics that this is a scan of color negative film.

3. Adjust the Shadow, Highlight, and Exposure controls to compensate for the variation in your photographs. Click OK when you're done.

Your negative is now a usable image.

# Fireworks Technique: The Fireworks Photocopier

The following technique uses Xtras to modify an image to make it seem as if it had been photocopied. It's a good example of how you can use various Xtras, one after the other, each building on the work of the previous one. We're going to use the PhotoOptics CSI MonoChrome, CSI Noise, and CSI Levels filters, and also the Blur and Convert to Alpha Xtras. Optionally, if you want a really bad photocopier, we'll also use the Find Edges and Invert Xtras. A few quick steps, and you'll do a pretty good job of simulating the latest in document duplication technology, circa 1972.

To create the photocopier effect, open an image in Fireworks and follow these steps:

1. If your image is a black-and-white photograph, go to step 2. If it isn't, then convert it to a black-and-white photograph by choosing Xtras ⇨ PhotoOptics ⇨ CSI MonoChrome. Remove the colors from your image by setting Hue and Saturation to 0. Move their sliders all the way to the left. Set the Exposure slider to 0 by centering it. Click OK when you're done.

**Tip**    If you ever want to convert a color image to black and white, step 1 is one way to do it. The Convert to Alpha Xtra is another way, although it colors white pixels transparent at the same time. In this case, you don't want any transparency until at least after you add noise in the next step, because you want the noise to affect every pixel.

2. Choose Xtras ⇨ PhotoOptics ⇨ CSI Noise.

   Fireworks displays the CSI Noise dialog box.

3. Set the Hue slider to 0, so that you add only gray noise. Set the Saturation slider to 20 percent and the Brightness slider to 0. Set the density of the noise to 100 percent with the Coverage slider and check the Luminance check box.

If your image doesn't have any grays in it (for example, a line of black text on a white background), set the Saturation to 50 percent to create a more noticeable effect. Click OK when you're done.

**Note** Most PhotoOptics sliders only have positive values, so moving the slider all the way to the left is a setting of 0. However, some of them, such as the CSI Noise Brightness slider, have both positive and negative values, so a setting of 0 is in the center of the slider. Always take a look at the values in the fields to the right of the sliders.

4. Photocopiers don't actually produce any grays, just patches of black on white, so you need to increase the contrast of the image so that dark grays become black, and light grays become white. Choose Xtras ⇨ PhotoOptics ⇨ CSI Levels.

   Fireworks displays the CSI Levels dialog box.

5. Move the Shadow slider all the way to the left, and the High Light slider all the way to the right. Set Exposure to 0 percent by clicking Equalize. Click OK when you're done.

6. Repeat steps 4 and 5 to increase the contrast further, by choosing either Xtras ⇨ Repeat CSI Levels or the keyboard shortcut Ctrl+Alt+Shift+X (Command+Option+Shift+X).

   Fireworks displays the CSI Levels dialog box with the same settings as when you last used it. If you want to simulate a photocopier that is running out of toner, change the Exposure setting to 100 percent. Click OK to apply the filter again.

**Tip** Use the Xtras ⇨ Repeat Xtra command any time that you want to repeat quickly the last Xtra you used. The menu option always changes to show the name of that Xtra.

7. If you want to simulate a photocopier that's seen better days, choose Xtras ⇨ Other ⇨ Find Edges and then choose Xtras ⇨ Invert ⇨ Invert, to do some real damage to your image.

8. Choose Xtras ⇨ Blur ⇨ Blur to soften the detail.

9. Choose Xtras ⇨ Other ⇨ Convert to Alpha. The white areas of your document are made transparent. This allows you to change the color of the paper you're "photocopying" on.

10. Choose Modify ⇨ Document ⇨ Canvas Color.

    Fireworks displays the Canvas Color dialog box.

11. Select Custom and choose a new background color. Click OK when you're done.

    Your image now has a photocopied look (see Figure 14-6).

Original image                              "Photocopied" image

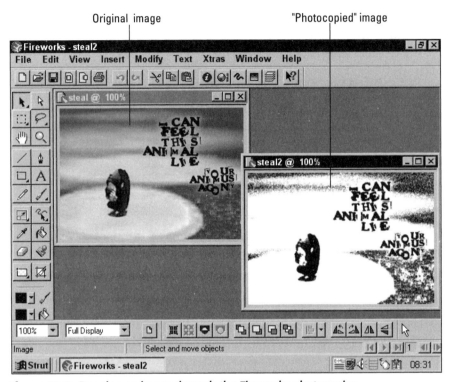

**Figure 14-6:** Running an image through the Fireworks photocopier.

# Using Photoshop-Compatible Filters

So far, you've seen what you can do with the Xtras that are included with Fireworks, but that's just the tip of the iceberg. Like most modern image-editing software, Fireworks uses standard Photoshop-compatible plug-in filters as Xtras, which enables you to choose from an almost unlimited range of image filters and effects.

**New Feature**

Fireworks 2 has much better support for standard filters than Fireworks 1. Many popular filters that could not previously be used now work perfectly. As improved as this support is, though, that doesn't mean that every filter will work.

## Installing third-party filter packages

Before you purchase third-party filters, check the Disabled plugins file in your Fireworks Xtras folder for a list of filters that are known to be incompatible with Fireworks. Just because a filter is not on that list doesn't mean that it's guaranteed to work with Fireworks. If you find a package that you like, ask the retailer or manufacturer whether it's been tested with Fireworks 2. Don't forget to also check the system requirements for the filter package.

**Tip**

Where can you get more filters? A good place to start is Adobe Plug-in Source's Photoshop Plug-ins page, at `www.pluginsource.com/photoshop/`, where you can find a variety of offerings available for purchase and download. Another site I like is PlugIn Com HQ, at `pico.i-us.com`, where you can find filter enthusiasts and lots of free filters and links.

Most filter packages come with installers that are just like the installers provided with full applications, such as Fireworks. Before you install a package, close Fireworks. You have to restart Fireworks before you use the filters, anyway. When the installer's instructions ask for you to locate your plugins folder, specify your Fireworks Xtras folder. If the package did not come with an installer, you have to copy the filters to your Xtras folder yourself.

**Note**

On Windows machines, the Fireworks Xtras folder is usually at C:\Program Files\Macromedia\Fireworks 2\Settings\Xtras. On Macintosh machines, it is usually located at Hard Drive:Applications:Macromedia:Fireworks 2:Settings:Xtras.

After the installation is complete, start Fireworks. You should see a new option under the Xtras menu. Usually, this will be a whole new submenu with multiple filters available (see Figure 14-7).

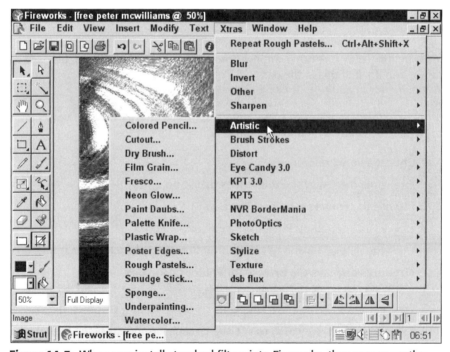

**Figure 14-7:** When you install standard filters into Fireworks, they appear on the Xtras menu. This copy of Fireworks has a few third-party packages installed, as well as Photoshop 5's filters.

## Using filters with multiple applications

If you use another image-editing application in addition to Fireworks, you may have a whole host of filters on your computer that can also be used in Fireworks. Sharing filters among numerous applications can instantly add many features to all of them, and can also speed up your workflow, because you don't have to leave an application to apply an effect.

Aside from Fireworks, here are some other applications that use filters:

✦ Adobe Photoshop and Illustrator

✦ Macromedia Freehand and Director

✦ Corel Photo-Paint and CorelDRAW

✦ JASC Paint Shop Pro

✦ MetaCreations Painter

I have about six or seven applications that use filters, so I keep all of my filters in one folder, independent of all the applications, and then have all the applications use that folder as their plugins folder. The alternative would be to install filters numerous times into the plugins folder of each and every application. If you have multiple applications that use standard filters, you might want to do the same thing.

You may have only one other application that uses standard filters, perhaps Photoshop itself. If this is the case, you can tell Fireworks to use that application's plugins folder in addition to using Fireworks's own Xtras folder.

Either way, Fireworks can use one other folder, besides its own, on your computer for Xtras. To specify which folder to use, follow these steps:

1. Choose File ➪ Preferences.

   Fireworks displays the Preferences dialog box.

2. Choose the Folders tab (see Figure 14-8).

3. Check the Photoshop Plug-Ins check box.

4. Click the ellipsis button to the right of the Photoshop Plug-Ins check box.

   Fireworks displays the Browse for Folder dialog box.

5. Select the folder that contains the filters you want to use. Click OK when you're done.

6. Exit and restart Fireworks to see the changes to the Xtras menu and to use your newly available filters.

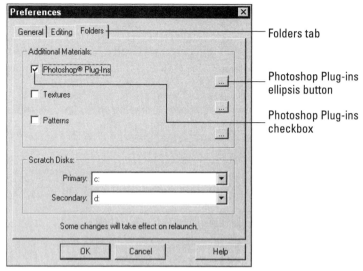

**Figure 14-8:** Fireworks can use Xtras from another folder on your computer, such as Photoshop's Plug-Ins folder.

## Alien Skin Eye Candy 3.0

Eye Candy is a popular filter collection that you can purchase and install as Xtras in Fireworks. Even if you don't (yet) have Eye Candy 3.0, this section introduces you to the kinds of things that are possible with filters in general, and may help you to evaluate other, similar packages for their quality and creative potential.

Tip      You can visit Alien Skin on the Web at www.alienskin.com.

The theme here is classic effects done right: beveling, drop shadows, smoke, motion trails, distortion. The Eye Candy filters are a great foundation for any filter collection, because they're the kind of blue-collar, hard-working, tried-and-true effects that are used again and again in the tips, tutorials, and techniques that you find in books, magazines, and on the Web.

Some of the features you'll find in Eye Candy 3.0 include

✦ All the filters share common interface features, to cut down the learning curve (see Figure 14-9).

✦ Lots of presets for each filter that allow you to start using them quickly. In addition, you can save your own settings to the preset list for later recall.

✦ A very dynamic preview capability that allows you to zoom in or out on your image for precise, detailed modifications.

Table 14-3 details each of the filters that make up Eye Candy 3.0 and explains what it does.

**Note**    Many of the Eye Candy filters draw outside the selection, and thus rely heavily on having a pixel selection within an image object, or having space around an image object against the canvas.

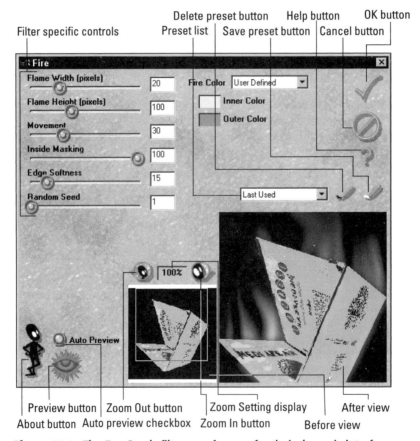

**Figure 14-9:** The Eye Candy filters are famous for their dynamic interface and easy-to-use presets. The Fire filter is shown here igniting a pixel selection.

## Table 14-3
## Alien Skin Eye Candy 3.0

| Filter | Description |
|---|---|
| Antimatter | Inverts brightness without affecting hue and saturation values. For example, dark red becomes light red, but is still red. |
| Carve | Makes a pixel selection appear carved or chiseled into the image. |
| Chrome | Applies a metallic effect that can be used to simulate chrome, silver, gold, and other metals. |
| Cutout | Makes a pixel selection appear as a hole in the image, including a shadow, so that it appears recessed. |
| Drop Shadow | Adds a drop shadow to a pixel selection or an object. |
| Fire | Creates a realistic flame effect rising from a pixel selection or object. |
| Fur | Applies randomly placed clumps of fur. |
| Glass | Superimposes a sheet of colored glass. |
| Glow | Adds a semitransparent glow around the outside edge of a pixel selection or object. |
| HSB Noise | Adds noise by varying hue, saturation, brightness, and transparency. |
| Inner Bevel | Makes a pixel selection or object appear embossed, or raised up from the background. The effect is placed within the pixel selection or object. |
| Jiggle | Creates a bubbling, gelatinous, or shattered effect. |
| Motion Trail | Creates the illusion of motion by smearing a pixel selection or object outward in one direction. |
| Outer Bevel | Makes a pixel selection or object appear embossed, or raised up from the background. The effect is placed outside the pixel selection or object. |
| Perspective Shadow | Adds a shadow to a pixel selection or object so that the light appears to come from above and in front, like standing in sunlight. |
| Smoke | Creates smoke coming from a pixel selection or object. |
| Squint | Unfocuses a pixel selection or object in a way similar to bad eyesight. |
| Star | Creates stars and other polygon shapes. |
| Swirl | Adds randomly placed whirlpools. |
| Water Drops | Adds randomly placed water drops. |
| Weave | Applies a woven effect. |

## Jiggle

Jiggle produces a unique distortion based on randomly placed bubbling. The patterns that it produces seem more random and organic — less computerized — than many distortion filters. A selection can seem like it's bubbling, gelatinous, or shattered.

To use Jiggle, select an image and follow these steps:

1. Choose Xtras ➪ Eye Candy 3.0 ➪ Jiggle.

   The Jiggle dialog box is displayed (see Figure 14-10).

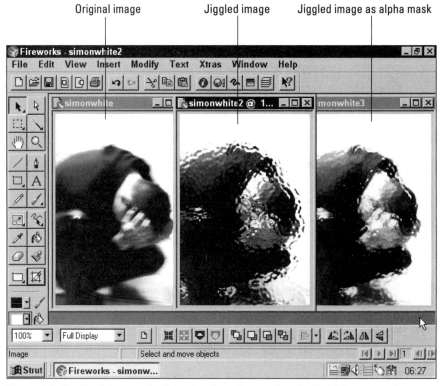

**Figure 14-10:** Jiggle's organic distortion in action, using the Bubbles type of movement. The third image (right) is the original image with the jiggled image as its alpha mask, and the canvas color changed to show through.

2. Adjust the controls to achieve the effect you desire:

   • **Bubble Size slider:** Controls the frequency of the distortion. The lower the value, the more closely spaced the distortion.

   • **Warp Amount:** Controls how much your selection is stretched.

- **Twist:** Controls the amount of twisting that occurs, measured in degrees.

- **Movement Type drop-down list:** Use to select the way you want the image jiggled. The three types of jiggling are Bubbles, which is a smooth, even distortion; Brownian Motion, which is a more ragged effect; and Turbulence, which creates sharper breaks in the image.

3. If you like, you can save your settings by using the Save Preset button. Click OK (the check mark) when you're done.

   The effect is applied to your image.

## Perspective Shadow

The ubiquitous drop shadow has its place, but a more realistic shadow that mimics the effects of the sun can be applied with Eye Candy's Perspective Shadow. The effect makes your selection appear to be standing up as the light comes from above and in front. The shadow is attached to the object rather than floating, which creates the 3D perspective.

To use Perspective Shadow, select an image and follow these steps:

1. Choose Xtras ⇨ Eye Candy 3.0 ⇨ Perspective Shadow.

   The Perspective Shadow dialog box is displayed (see Figure 14-11).

2. Select a preset effect and/or adjust the controls, if necessary, to achieve the effect you desire:

   - **Vanishing Point Direction:** Controls the direction in which the shadow falls behind your selection. The shadow always falls behind your selection.

   - **Vanishing Point Distance:** Controls how far the vanishing point on the horizon is from your selection. Lower values are closer.

   - **Shadow Length:** Controls the length of the shadow without affecting the tapering very much. Lower values produce a shorter shadow.

   - **Blur:** Controls how blurred the edges of the shadow will be. Higher values make the shadow blurrier and create the effect of a faraway light source.

   - **Opacity:** Adjusts the overall transparency of the shadow.

   - **Color:** Changes the color of the shadow.

3. If you like, you can save your settings, using the Save Preset button. Click OK (the check mark) when you're done.

   The effect is applied to your image.

**Cross-Reference**

To see how to build a perspective shadow totally in Fireworks, turn to Chapter 9.

Original part object          Perspective Shadows image object

**Figure 14-11:** Perspective Shadow puts a realistic 3D shadow at your disposal. The original is a path object. The Perspective Shadowed one is an image object.

## MetaCreations Kai's Power Tools 5

Kai's Power Tools 5 (KPT 5) stands out from the crowd with the extremity of the modifications you can make to your images. It's very easy to end up with a completely unrecognizable image after applying just one Xtra. In fact, it takes some work to make sure your image stays recognizable.

**Tip**    The Kai in Kai's Power Tools is Kai Krause, who became a legend among graphic artists when he introduced the original Kai Power Tools. He is now Chief Technology Officer at MetaCreations, which you can visit on the Web at `http://www.metacreations.com`.

Some of the highlights of KPT 5 include

✦ Common interface elements shared by the entire set of filters (see Figure 14-12)

✦ Complex masking and transparency options

✦ Complex 3D lighting and environment options

✦ Interactive Preview windows

✦ Presets with thumbnail views

Table 14-4 details the Kai Power Tools 5 filters:

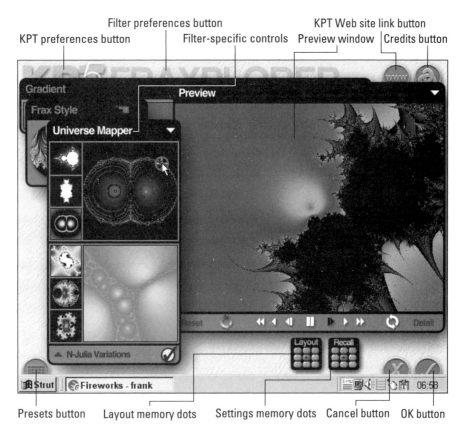

**Figure 14-12:** The KPT 5 interface is a bit tricky at first, but contains a lot of functionality. This is FraxPlorer.

**Tip**  The Kai Power Tools 5 package also includes Kai Power Tools 3, with 19 completely separate and useful plug-ins, making the KPT 5 package an excellent value.

| | Table 14-4<br>**Kai Power Tools 5** |
|---|---|
| **Filter** | **Description** |
| Blurrrr | All the blur effects you could ever need, including spins, zooms, spirals, and motion blurs. |
| Noize | Typical and unusual noise effects, including transparent noise. |
| RadWarp | Creates or corrects a fish-eye lens effect. Sort of like a fun-house mirror on steroids. |
| Smoothie | Multiple ways to clean up dirty, jagged edges, quickly and easily. |
| Frax4D | Creates 3D or 4D fractal sculptures. The 4D ones look like really chewed-up versions of the 3D ones. |
| FraxFlame | Fractal effects that look like fire. Reminiscent of long-exposure photographs of fireworks. |
| FraxPlorer | An incredible Fractal Explorer with real-time fly-throughs, which are like fractal movies. Create amazing textures or backgrounds, or just have fun playing. |
| FiberOptix | Adds true 3D fibers onto images, including masks. You can make something hairy and then composite it easily. |
| Orb-It | Creates very detailed 3D spheres. Make bubbles, raindrops, lenses, and distortions. |
| ShapeShifter | Makes 3D shapes from masks, including environment maps and textures. |

## RadWarp

KPT RadWarp simulates a photographic effect called *barrel roll*. You can either add the fish-eye effect to create fantastic variations on an image or use the filter to "unfish-eye" an image with a slight, unwanted barrel roll.

**Caution**    All the KPT 5 filters will affect your entire image object, even if you have created a selection. If you want to affect just a portion of an image object, see the work-around under "False pixel selections," earlier in this chapter.

To use RadWarp, select an image object and follow these steps:

1. Choose Xtras ⇨ KPT 5 ⇨ RadWarp.

   The RadWarp dialog box is displayed (see Figure 14-13).

**Tip**    By default, Kai Power Tools 5 dialog boxes open up full screen. If you want to change this behavior, hold down Ctrl (Command) and press 1 for 640 x 480, 2 for 800 x 600, 3 for 1024 x 768, 4 for 1152 x 870, 5 for 1280 x 1024, and 0 for full screen. The panels are also set to Panel Auto Popup, which I found distracting. Click the name of the filter at the top of its dialog box to select the panel options. If your display has a low resolution, Panel Solo mode will save the day.

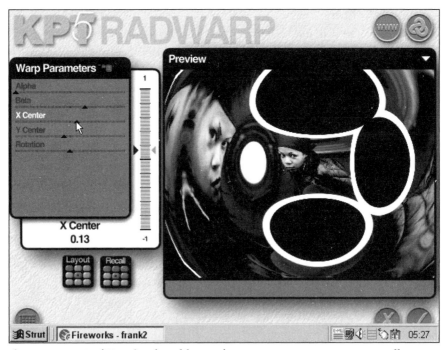

**Figure 14-13:** RadWarp is a lot of fun and can create some very extreme effects, including especially strange-looking faces.

2. Adjust the controls to achieve the effect you desire:

- **Alpha slider:** Controls how much of a rounded distortion is added

- **Beta slider:** Controls how much of another type of slightly squarer distortion is added

- **X Center:** Controls where the horizontal center of the warping effect is

- **Y Center:** Controls where the vertical center of the warping effect is

Tip

You can also modify X and Y Center by dragging your mouse in the real-time Preview window.

Rotation rotates the image.

3. Click OK (the check mark) to apply the effect.

The effect is applied to your image.

## ShapeShifter

When you're working with path objects in Fireworks, you can use Live Effects to apply amazing 3D effects. If you've ever tried to get the same effect with an image object using Live Effects, you were probably quite disappointed. KPT 5's ShapeShifter filter enables you to make those image objects compete with your path objects.

To use ShapeShifter, select an image and follow these steps:

1. Choose Xtras ➪ KPT 5 ➪ ShapeShifter.

   The ShapeShifter dialog box is displayed (see Figure 14-14).

**Figure 14-14:** Give your image objects that 3D look so that they can compete with the Live Effects on path objects.

2. In the Main Shape panel, click the thumbnail preview to import a mask. The mask specifies how the 3D shape is added to your image. Adjust the Bevel Scale and Height to determine how much of a 3D effect you're going to create. Select from the three bevel modes.

**Note**     Unfortunately, PNG images are not among the types that KPT 5 can use as masks. When you create a mask for KPT 5, export it from Fireworks as a TIFF image.

3. In the 3D Lighting panel, add light sources by clicking the + button. Drag light sources to different locations to affect the highlights and shadows on your image.

4. In the Bump Map panel, add a 3D texture to your image and set the scale and height. Scale zooms in on the texture. Height specifies how 3D the bump map will be.

5. In the Glow panel, add a colored glow to your image, if you want to. You can choose to offset it from the image and also vary the transparency.

**Tip**    Click the eye icon on the Glow panel to show or hide the glow, just like the eye icons in the Fireworks Layers panel.

6. In the Shadow panel, add a shadow to your image, if you want to. Just like glow, you can offset the shadow by varying degrees, choose colors, and specify transparency.

7. In the Top Mask panel, you can import another mask to create an emboss effect on top of your 3D object, as if you had stamped out a shape in the top.

8. In the Environment Map panel, load an image to be used as an environment map. This image will be reflected by your 3D shape like the sky on a quiet lake. This adds a lot of depth and character to your image.

**Tip**    You can also alter the settings by dragging your mouse across the Preview window.

9. Click OK (the check mark) to apply the effect. The effect is applied to your image.

# Summary

Fireworks Xtras allow you to modify images in a variety of ways. When working with Xtras, keep these points in mind:

✦ Xtras work on images only. Path objects are flattened when you apply Xtras to them.

✦ You can correct unwanted color casts quickly and easily with the CSI PhotoFilter Xtra.

✦ Fireworks includes simple Xtras and an advanced third-party filter collection called PhotoOptics, but other filters can also be plugged in.

✦ You can share filters among multiple, compatible applications, to have access to them wherever you're working.

✦ An amazing array of effects can be created with Xtras.

The next chapter looks at coordinating workflow in Fireworks.

✦        ✦        ✦

# Coordinating Workflow

# Scanning and Importing

**H**ow easily you can move information from one application to another has a great effect on your workflow and productivity. In addition to objects created from scratch in Fireworks, you can include elements created in a traditional drawing program, such as Macromedia Freehand, stock photos from a clip-art collection, or photographic prints directly from a page scanner.

**New Feature**

Fireworks 1 couldn't scan at all. Now, with Fireworks 2, you can select from multiple sources and acquire an image directly from a scanner or digital camera quickly and easily.

From a design perspective, incorporating elements from a wide variety of sources can give your documents depth and contrast and make them more interesting and pleasing to the eye. Simple vector shapes can be combined and contrasted with detailed photographs and organic bitmap textures. After these elements are incorporated into Fireworks, they're fair game for Fireworks's unique drawing tools and comprehensive export features.

This chapter begins with a discussion of using Fireworks with your page scanner or digital camera. Then, it explores how you can drag and drop or copy and paste from other applications. We'll look at importing bitmap and vector art files. Finally, we'll examine some of the issues involved in importing animations.

## Scanning and Resolution Basics

A page scanner enables you to capture printed documents — from drawings to artwork to photographs. You can scan an image and use it in your Fireworks document unaltered, or you can transform it a little or a lot with Fireworks's drawing tools, effects, and Xtras and then export it for publishing on the Web.

**Note**    Scanning for print publishing requires a different approach than scanning for online publishing. For the print publisher, the online image is part of the process and not an end in itself. Because Fireworks is almost exclusively a Web-publishing tool, we'll look at things from the perspective of the online publisher.

*Scanning* an image is the procedure of literally converting it from a printed image to an online image (one that's viewed on a computer). Most of the confusion in scanning comes from mixing up print and online concepts, especially when it comes to resolution. *Resolution* basically means "the number of dots," which is important to scanning, because print and online images all consist entirely of dots.

Resolution is measured differently for printed images than it is for online images. Printed resolution is a measure of how many dots are in an inch of the image, which is expressed as *dots-per-inch*, or *dpi*. An example is 300 dpi. Online resolution is a measure of how many dots are in the entire image, measured in $X$ pixels by $Y$ pixels. An example is 640 × 480. When you select an image in Fireworks and choose Modify ➪ Document ➪ Image Size, Fireworks displays the Image Size dialog box (see Figure 15-1), which clearly shows the relationship between online and printed resolution.

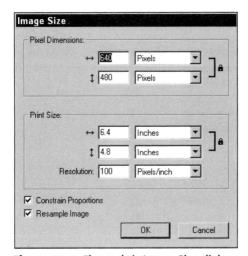

**Figure 15-1:** Fireworks's Image Size dialog box shows the relationship between an image's online and print resolution.

The following list describes some of the resolutions that you'll encounter as you scan:

✦ **The resolution of the printed image, in dpi.** The upper limit of detail that the printed image contains.

✦ **The scan resolution, in dpi.** Before you scan an image, you specify a *scan resolution,* which specifies how the scanner should translate the printed image, measured in inches, into an online image, measured in pixels. A scan resolution of 100 dpi tells the scanner to split each inch of the printed image into 100 parts, and make those 100 parts into 100 pixels of online image. We'll look more closely at scan resolution later in the chapter.

✦ **The scanner's maximum optical resolution, in dpi.** The upper limit of the scanner's ability to look at something it's scanning. A scanner with a maximum optical resolution of 300 dpi can split an inch of your printed image into 300 parts. Detail finer than that cannot be captured with that scanner.

✦ **The scanner's interpolated resolution, in dpi.** The upper limit of the scanner's ability to guess at details it can't see. A 300-dpi scanner that is asked to scan at a resolution of 600 dpi will guess at what the missing pixels should be. This is similar to *resampling* an online image to a higher resolution, and generally should be avoided.

✦ **The online image's resolution, in pixels.** Because each pixel of an online image is represented by one screen-pixel location, an online image's resolution is the same as its size. A 640 × 480-pixel image has a resolution of 640 × 480 pixels.

✦ **The display resolution, in pixels.** A computer display might have a resolution of 800 × 600 pixels, or 1024 × 768 pixels. How big the display is in inches is unknown and therefore unimportant.

**Note**
A common misconception is that computer displays have a standard "resolution" of 72 dpi. Early Macintosh displays did have a 72-dpi resolution, and it became a standard because all Mac displays had the same size and type of display. These days, computer displays come in a wide variety of sizes and resolutions. A 19-inch display with a resolution of 640 × 480 pixels has a drastically different number of dots per inch than a 14-inch display with a resolution of 1024 × 768 pixels.

# Fireworks, Meet Scanner

Acquiring an image from a hardware device such as a page scanner or digital camera is an almost magical process, unless your hardware and software aren't talking to each other. In Fireworks, getting this conversation started involves an industry standard protocol called *TWAIN*. On the Macintosh, Fireworks also supports Photoshop Acquire plug-ins. If your scanner or digital camera uses a Photoshop Acquire plug-in, see "Installing Photoshop Acquire plug-ins" later in this chapter.

**Note** If you haven't yet used your scanner or digital camera, verify that it is correctly connected to your computer and that its software is current and correctly installed. Consult the documentation that was included with the device for details.

## TWAIN-compliant devices

When you start Fireworks, if a TWAIN module is available, a Scan command will be added to the menus. If you have multiple TWAIN-compliant devices connected to your computer, you can select any one of them from within Fireworks.

**Note** What does TWAIN stand for? It's rumored to be an acronym for "Technology Without An Interesting Name." It might also have started as a play on bringing software and hardware together, as in "ne'er the twain shall meet." For its part, the TWAIN Working Group that created the standard claims that it's just a name and has no meaning at all. For more information about TWAIN, visit the TWAIN Working Group on the Web at www.twain.org.

To select a TWAIN source, follow these steps:

1. Choose File ➪ Scan ➪ Twain Select.

   Fireworks displays the Select Source dialog box (see Figure 15-2).

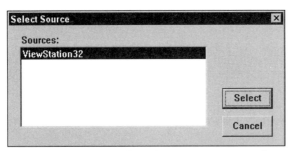

**Figure 15-2:** In Fireworks, select a TWAIN source from which to scan in the Select Source dialog box.

2. Choose the TWAIN-compliant device from which you want Fireworks to acquire an image. Click OK when you're done.

**Note** If you have a TWAIN-compliant hardware device and the Scan option is not present in the File menu, or your scanner is not listed in the Select Source dialog box, you will not be able to scan directly into Fireworks. Verify that the device is correctly installed and that you have the latest drivers. Macromedia cautions, however, that some TWAIN modules may not work with Fireworks.

**Tip**

If you haven't purchased a scanner or digital camera yet, but are planning to do so, visit the Fireworks Web site by choosing Help ➪ Fireworks Web Site and refer to the "Fireworks TechNotes" for a list of hardware that has been tested and found to work well with Fireworks.

## Installing Photoshop Acquire plug-ins (Macintosh)

On the Macintosh, Photoshop Acquire plug-ins provide another way to interface with a scanner or digital camera. Scanners that aren't TWAIN-compliant generally come with a Photoshop Acquire plug-in. To use one in Fireworks, you must do one of the following:

✦ Install the Photoshop Acquire plug-in in your Fireworks 2/Settings/Xtras folder.

✦ Install the Photoshop Acquire plug-in in your Photoshop Plug-Ins folder or another folder on your computer. Then, in Fireworks, choose File ➪ Preferences, select the Folders tab, check Photoshop Plug-Ins, and then browse to and select the folder that contains the Acquire plug-in.

After follow either of these methods, Fireworks adds a Scan command to the File menu. Select your Photoshop Acquire plug-in from that menu to initiate a scan.

**Note**

Some Photoshop Acquire plug-ins do not function correctly with Fireworks. If your Acquire plug-in doesn't work, check the manufacturer's Web site for an updated version that may be compatible with Fireworks, or investigate whether your hardware device is also TWAIN-compliant.

# The Scanning Process

When you initiate a scan in Fireworks, a dialog box specific to your scanner or Acquire plug-in is displayed so that you can specify the settings you want for this particular scan. The most important of these settings are the scan resolution and the color depth. We'll look at those closely, and then look briefly at some of the other options you might be presented with.

## Selecting a scan resolution

In simple terms, the scan resolution that you choose determines the size of the resulting online image — and that's all. Table 15-1 shows the relationship between the size of the original, printed image and the size of the resulting online image at various scan resolutions.

| Table 15-1 Scan Results at Various Scan Resolutions | | |
|---|---|---|
| Printed Image Size (inches) | Scan Resolution (dpi) | Online Image Size (pixels) |
| 5 × 7 | 10 dpi | 50 × 70 |
| 5 × 7 | 20 dpi | 100 × 140 |
| 5 × 7 | 50 dpi | 250 × 350 |
| 5 × 7 | 100 dpi | 500 × 700 |
| 5 × 7 | 150 dpi | 750 × 1050 |
| 5 × 7 | 200 dpi | 1000 × 1400 |
| 5 × 7 | 300 dpi | 1500 × 2100 |

Note that each of these three important pieces of information are measured in different ways:

✦ **Printed image:** Measured in inches. In print publishing, the inch is the constant. If you create an 8.5 × 11-inch page layout and print it at different print resolutions, it will still be an 8.5 × 11-inch page layout, but it will have a different number of dots on each page.

✦ **Scan resolution:** Measured in dots per inch. This is the translation of the printed image (in inches) to the online image (in dots, or pixels). How many pixels of online image do you want for each inch of printed image? Fifty? That's a scan resolution of 50 dpi.

✦ **Online image:** Measured in pixels. In online publishing, the pixel, or dot, is the constant. If you create a 640 × 480-pixel image and view it at different screen resolutions, it will still be a 640 × 480-pixel image, but it will be a different size in inches on each screen.

## Determining the ideal resolution

To determine an ideal scan resolution, follow these steps:

1. Decide how wide you want your online image to be, in pixels.

2. Divide that number by the width of the printed image, in inches.

   The result is your scan resolution in dots per inch.

Tip

If you're not sure how big you want the final image to be, overestimate rather than underestimate. Making an image smaller later is not as detrimental to its quality as trying to make it larger. A scan resolution of 100 dpi is a good place to start, because it makes the translation from inches to pixels easy to calculate. A 3 × 5-inch printed image will be 300 × 500 pixels after scanning. If 300 × 500 is too big or too small, adjust the scan resolution from there.

### Running out of printed resolution

When selecting a scan resolution, keep in mind the resolution of the printed image that you're scanning. At some point, increasing the scan resolution stops capturing more detail, when the scan resolution is equal to either the resolution of the printed image or the maximum optical resolution of your scanner. For example

✦ If your printed image was printed at 200 dpi, a scan resolution of 300 dpi will not add detail that isn't already there. Scan the image at 200 dpi and resample it to a larger size in Fireworks, if necessary.

✦ If your scanner's best optical resolution is 300 dpi, you won't be able to capture more than 300 dots for each inch of the printed image. Many scanners allow you to choose a higher scan resolution than they can really achieve, and then the scanner "interpolates" or fills in the missing information with a best guess. This is equivalent to scanning the image at your scanner's maximum optical resolution and resampling it in Fireworks if necessary.

## Choosing a color depth

Choose a color depth based on the type of document you are scanning. Typically, a scanner has three main color settings for you to choose from: line art, grayscale, and color. You may also be able to specify bit depth for grayscale and color scans. Higher bit depths scan a higher number of colors and are more accurate, but also result in a larger file size.

### Line art

*Line art* refers to black-and-white images that don't contain any shades of gray. This might include cartoons, blueprints, or diagrams. Line art is scanned with 1-bit color depth. In other words, each pixel is either on or off; black or white.

### Grayscale images

Grayscale images include actual shades of gray. Typically, a grayscale setting will also be 8-bit, meaning that your image will have 256 different shades of gray. This is the best setting for black-and-white photographs.

### Color images

The color setting is obviously used for scanning any sort of color image. Typically, this is 24-bit color, but some scanners have a 36-bit setting. Twenty-four bit color means that each pixel can be any one of 16.7 million colors. A 36-bit scanner can record 68.7 billion colors. Scan at your scanner's best setting and then remove extra colors when you export your image as a GIF, JPEG, or PNG for use on the Web.

**Cross-Reference**

For more about color depth, see Chapter 7.

## Setting other options

Consult the documentation that came with your scanner for specific information on other options or features that your scanner has.

Here are some of the options that you might be presented with (see Figure 15-3):

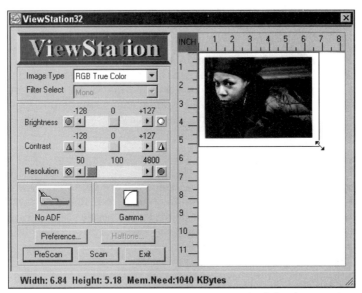

**Figure 15-3:** Setting options in a page scanner's dialog box. Each scanner or digital camera has its own unique interface. Note the size cursor outlining the area that we want to scan.

✦ A preview window in which you can see a thumbnail of the original before you perform the actual scan. You can usually draw a border in this window to limit the scan to the portion of the scanner window.

✦ Brightness and Contrast. Adjust these only if your original is exceptionally bright or dark or lacking in contrast.

✦ Image enhancements, such as dust and scratch removal or moiré removal.

✦ Orientation. You may be able to specify for the scanner to flip the image vertically or horizontally.

✦ Settings for different types of original documents, such as transparencies and slides.

To scan directly into Fireworks, follow these steps:

**1.** Place the original document onto your scanner or prepare your digital camera.

2. If you have multiple TWAIN-compliant devices, choose File ➪ Scan ➪ Twain Select and select the appropriate device.

3. Choose File ➪ Scan ➪ TWAIN Acquire. If you are using a Photoshop Acquire plug-in, choose File ➪ Scan and the name of that plug-in, instead.

    Your scanner's options dialog box appears.

4. In the scanner's options dialog box, adjust the settings for this scan, specifying resolution, color depth, and other settings, as required. Consult your scanner's documentation for specific information about the options you're presented with. Click OK when you're done.

    The device begins scanning and then sends the image to Fireworks. When the scan is complete, the image appears as a new document in Fireworks.

# Inserting Objects from Other Applications

So far, we've covered how you can import a document from external hardware. But, what if the elements that you want to include are sitting right there on your computer screen, but within another application? What's the use of multitasking if you can't apply multiple applications to a task?

Fireworks has two methods for directly inserting elements from other applications: copy and paste, and drag and drop.

## Copy and paste

The simplest and most widely used method for moving information from one application to another is the Clipboard and the commands Cut, Copy, and Paste.

You can paste the following formats into Fireworks:

✦ Bitmap images

✦ Vector art from Macromedia Freehand or Adobe Illustrator

✦ ASCII text

**Caution**  To retain vector information, CorelDRAW users should save their work in CorelDRAW as a file and then import that file into Fireworks. Copying and pasting or dragging and dropping from CorelDRAW to Fireworks changes vector art into image objects.

To copy from another application and paste into Fireworks, follow these steps:

1. In the source application, select the object(s) that you want to copy.

2. Choose either Edit ➪ Copy or the keyboard shortcut Ctrl+C (Command+C).

Your object(s) are copied to the Clipboard.

3. In Fireworks, choose either Edit ➪ Paste or the keyboard shortcut Ctrl+V (Command+V).

4. If your source object has a different resolution than your Fireworks document, Fireworks offers to resample the pasted image to match the target document. Choose Resample to maintain the pasted object's original width and height, adding or subtracting pixels as necessary. Choose Don't Resample to keep all the original pixels, which may make the relative size of the pasted image larger or smaller than expected.

Your object(s) are inserted and then centered into the active document.

**Tip**　　If you're pasting a bitmap image into Fireworks and you want it to fill a new, empty canvas, copy the image from the source application and then create a new Fireworks document. Fireworks will offer to make the new document the same dimensions as the image on the Clipboard. Note that this is not the case for vector art.

## Drag and drop

You can drag and drop objects into Fireworks from any application that supports OLE drag and drop on Windows, or Macintosh drag and drop on the Macintosh. Dropped objects are rendered as images, unless they're vector art from Macromedia Freehand or Adobe Illustrator. Some other applications that support drag and drop:

✦ Macromedia Flash

✦ Netscape Navigator

✦ Adobe Photoshop

✦ Microsoft Word

If you're not sure whether a specific application supports drag and drop, try it to find out. As you drag and drop, watch for your mouse cursor to change, as an indication of whether or not it's working.

To drag and drop an object into Fireworks from another application, follow these steps:

1. Make sure that you have a Fireworks document open to drop objects into.

2. Position the source application and Fireworks side by side so that you have a clear path to drag between them (see Figure 15-4).

3. In the source application, select the object(s) that you want to drag and drop into Fireworks.

4. Click the selected object(s) and hold down the mouse button to "pick up" the objects.

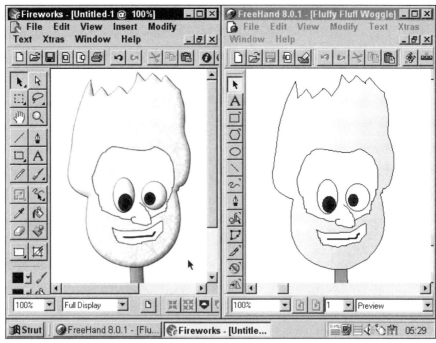

**Figure 15-4:** Drag and drop objects from other applications into Fireworks. This Freehand vector group (right panel) instantly became a Fireworks vector group and quickly fell victim to the Inner Bevel Live Effect and a Fiber texture fill.

5. While keeping the mouse button down, position the mouse cursor over the target Fireworks document.

6. Release the mouse button to drop the object(s) into Fireworks.

   The object(s) appear centered on your Fireworks canvas and are now part of your Fireworks document.

# Importing External Files

Sharing objects between applications on your computer is fine, but sometimes you'll want to import whole files into Fireworks. This is as easy as opening Fireworks' own PNG files. The process is slightly different depending on whether you're importing bitmap image files or vector art.

**Tip**    As well as using File ➪ Import, you can quickly import entire files into Fireworks by dragging and dropping them.

## Bitmap image files

Imported bitmap image files appear as image objects in Fireworks. Table 15-2 details the bitmap image file formats that Fireworks understands.

| Table 15-2 Bitmap Image Files Fireworks Can Import | | |
|---|---|---|
| **File Type** | **Extension(s)** | **Notes** |
| Portable Network Graphic | .png | Standard and Fireworks |
| Graphics Interchange Format | .gif | Static only. Animated GIF files must be opened instead of imported |
| Joint Photographic Expert Group | .jpeg, .jpg | Try to avoid importing JPEGs due to their lossy compression |
| Tag Image File Format | .tiff, .tif | Uncompressed and LZW compressed |
| Targa | .tga | Common UNIX format |
| Adobe Photoshop Document | .psd | Layer information is maintained, but not alpha channels and Photoshop 5's Layer Effects |
| Macromedia xRes | .lrg | The native format of Macromedia xRes |
| Windows Bitmap | .bmp | Windows only |
| Windows Device Independent Bitmap | .dib | Windows only |
| Windows Compressed Bitmap | .rle | Windows only |
| PICT | .pict | Macintosh only |

**Tip**    If your clip-art or stock-photo collection contains files in a format that Fireworks can't import — PCX, for example — you're not completely out of luck. Many clip-art browsers or image viewers can copy images to the Clipboard, ready to paste into Fireworks. If you copy the image before you create your Fireworks document, Fireworks will create the appropriately sized canvas.

### Importing a bitmap image into an existing document

To import a bitmap image into an existing Fireworks document, follow these steps:

1. Choose either Insert ➪ Image or use the keyboard shortcut Ctrl+R (Command+R).

   Fireworks displays the standard Open dialog box.

2. In the Open dialog box, select your image and click Open when you're done.

3. Hover your mouse cursor over the Fireworks document window that you would like to import to.

   The cursor changes to the import cursor, which looks like a right-angle.

4. Position the import cursor where you want the upper-left corner of the imported image to be located, and then do one of the following:

   • If you want to insert the image at its original size, click once.

   • If you want to insert the image so that it fits a specific area in your document, click and drag a box describing that specific area. Fireworks will resize the image to fit that area while maintaining the image's aspect ratio.

   The chosen image is inserted into the document as a new image object.

## Bringing in Photoshop files

Most of the bitmap files that Fireworks can import are fairly interchangeable. Importing a PNG or TIFF image results in a single image object inside Fireworks. Photoshop documents are a bit different, though, because they contain layer information, and thus can contain multiple image objects.

If your image Photoshop document has an alpha channel, it must be removed before importing into Fireworks. In Photoshop, use the Duplicate Channel command to copy the alpha channel to a separate file, and then remove the alpha channel from your file.

### Photoshop 5 Layer Effects

Photoshop 5 includes a new feature called Layer Effects. Unfortunately, Adobe has not publicly documented this feature, and Layer Effects cannot be transferred from Photoshop to other, non-Adobe applications, including Fireworks.

One workaround is to choose Layer ⇨ Effects ⇨ Create Layer(s) in Photoshop 5 as the last step before saving your document. All the effects are rendered as independent layers, and the document can then be imported into Fireworks successfully.

**Caution** Applying the preceding workaround to a text layer in Photoshop will flatten the text into a bitmap. Retain a backup copy of your document with Layer Effects and layers intact, for future editing.

Another, more Fireworks-centric workaround is to avoid using Layer Effects in Photoshop and instead use Fireworks Styles after the image objects are imported into Fireworks. Instead of using a drop shadow Layer Effect in Photoshop, for example, create a Fireworks Style that incorporates a suitable drop shadow, and apply it to objects after the document is in Fireworks.

**Cross-Reference** For detailed information on how to use Fireworks's new Styles feature, see Chapter 17.

### Photoshop documents from other bitmap-editing applications

Photoshop is certainly a popular bitmap-editing application, but other common bitmap-editing applications are available, too. Many of them can save or export their documents as Photoshop documents, which can then be imported into Fireworks with layers intact.

**Caution**
Corel Photo-Paint is a popular Photoshop alternative that can save images as Photoshop documents and retain layer information. Unfortunately, Fireworks imports Photo-Paint-created Photoshop documents as flat images.

## Vector art files

If you prefer to do your drawing in a traditional vector graphics drawing program, Fireworks is the ideal place to finish up your work and prepare it for the Web. Vector objects remain vector objects, just as if you had created them in Fireworks itself.

**Caution**
Even though Fireworks uses vector drawing tools and vector shapes and curves, it is not a traditional vector drawing program. The vector objects in Fireworks are rich pixel renderings and cannot be exported, except as bitmaps. For this reason, Fireworks should be the last step in your vector art workflow.

Table 15-3 details the vector file types that Fireworks can import.

| Table 15-3 Vector Graphics File Types Fireworks Can Import | | |
| --- | --- | --- |
| **File Type** | **Extension(s)** | **Notes** |
| Macromedia Freehand | .fh*, .ft* | Versions 7 and 8 only. |
| Adobe Illustrator | .ai, .art | Illustrator version 7 or better is recommended. Files from previous versions sometimes shift slightly off the canvas when imported into Fireworks. |
| CorelDRAW | .cdr | Files must be saved in CorelDRAW without bitmap or graphic compression. CorelDRAW 7 is supported, but 8 works as well. |

These file types cover the most common vector drawing tools. One vector art file format that is notable for its absence is Macromedia's own open vector standard, Shockwave Flash (.swf). Fireworks also can't import Windows Meta File (.wmf), which is commonly used for vector graphics clip-art collections. To open these files, first open them in another application and export them as one of the file types in Table 15-3.

## Understanding common translation problems

Just because Fireworks can import a file type, that doesn't mean that the transition from the original file to the Fireworks document will be completely seamless. In general, you can expect many of the very print-related features of your vector documents to be unsatisfactorily translated. These include

✦ Postscript strokes, fills, and effects

✦ Fine letter spacing, leading, and kerning

Rendering text as paths before saving a vector document for Fireworks import generally leads to better results, although the text will not be editable in Fireworks. If you want to keep text editable throughout your workflow, leave any fine text positioning or even text creation until you're in Fireworks.

## Importing a vector art file

To import a vector art file from Macromedia Freehand, Adobe Illustrator, or CorelDRAW into an existing Fireworks document, follow these steps:

1. Choose either File ➪ Import or use the keyboard shortcut Ctrl+R (Command+R).

   Fireworks displays the standard Import dialog box.

2. In the Import dialog box, select your CorelDRAW document and click Open when you're done.

   Fireworks displays the Vector File Options dialog box (see Figure 15-5), with suggested settings appropriate to the document you are importing.

3. In the Vector File Options dialog box, change the dimensions and/or resolution of the vector art, if necessary. Change the dimensions with the Scale box or the Width and/or Height boxes. Change the resolution with the Resolution box.

4. Under File Conversion, select what to do with pages from the Page Import drop-down list. You can choose to open a single page by choosing Open a Page and putting the page number in the Page box. You can also choose Open Pages as Frames to distribute all the pages in the file to frames in Fireworks.

5. Under File Conversion, select what to do with layers from the Layers Import drop-down list. Choose Ignore Layers to flatten the layers. Choose Remember Layers to keep them as they are. Choose Open Layers as Frames to distribute all the layers in the file to frames in Fireworks.

6. To include invisible and background layers, select the appropriate check boxes.

7. Under Render as Images, select how you want to handle complex vector objects. Deselect all the boxes to maintain vector information under all circumstances.

8. Select Anti-Aliased to apply antialiasing to your imported vector art. Click OK when you're done.

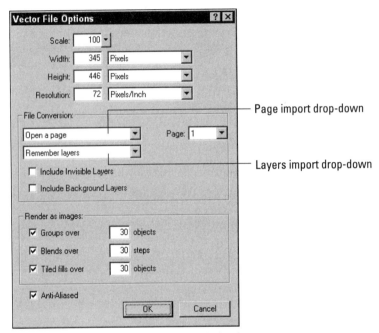

Page import drop-down

Layers import drop-down

**Figure 15-5:** The Vector File Options dialog box

9. Hover your mouse cursor over the Fireworks document window that you would like to import to.

The cursor changes to the import cursor, which looks like a right-angle.

10. Position the import cursor where you want the upper-left corner of the imported vector art to be located, and then do one of the following:

   • If you want to insert the vector art at its original size, click once.

   • If you want to insert the vector art so that it fits a specific area in your document, click and drag a box describing that specific area. Fireworks will resize the image to fit that area while maintaining the image's aspect ratio.

The vector information is inserted into the document as a new vector object.

# Importing Text

As well as importing bitmap and vector graphics, Fireworks can import two types of text files: Rich Text Format (RTF) and ASCII. RTF files contain formatting such as typefaces and italic or bold text. Most word-processing applications can save RTF files. ASCII text files are plain text with no formatting at all.

For more about importing and using text in Fireworks, see Chapter 10.

# Opening Animations

Opening an animated GIF by choosing File ➪ Open works just as you might expect: the animated GIF is opened, and the individual frames are available on — what else — Fireworks frames. You can then modify the GIF, if you like, and optimize and export it for the Web.

For more information about animation in Fireworks, see Chapter 25. For more information on exporting and optimizing images, see Chapter 16.

However, if you import an animated GIF into an existing animation, you may be in for a surprise. Only the first frame of the animated GIF will be imported. If you want to import one animation into another, the workaround is to open both animations in Fireworks and then copy and paste objects from one to the other until you have the combined animation that you require.

## Importing multiple files as a new animation

Most animation programs can export their animations as a series of individual documents, one frame of animation to one document. If your animation is ten frames long, you get ten files, each with a similar filename and numbered 1-10. You can open these files as an animation in Fireworks by using the Open Multiple command with Open as Animation checked. Each document becomes a frame in Fireworks, and you have an animation again.

Fireworks can now open multiple documents with File ➪ Open Multiple. Choose files from one or more folders on your computer and add them to the Open list.

Imagine that you've created an exciting, full-color animation with your favorite 3D animation program, and you want to make it into an animated GIF for use on the Web. Unfortunately, this 3D animation program is not very Web-savvy, and the GIFs it creates are always dithered and contain a full 256-color palette. You could create a much more optimized GIF if you could only create it in Fireworks. The way to achieve this is to export your animation as a series of high-quality PNG or TIFF bitmaps and then import that series into Fireworks.

Importing a group of files as a new animation will render them as images, even if they are vector art documents or Fireworks PNG files with vector information. For a workaround using Macromedia Flash as an example, see "Opening Flash Animations," later in this chapter.

To open a group of independent documents as one animation, follow these steps:

1. Choose either File ➪ Open Multiple or the keyboard shortcut Ctrl+Shift+O (Command+Shift+O).

   Fireworks displays the Open Multiple dialog box (see Figure 15-6).

Open list

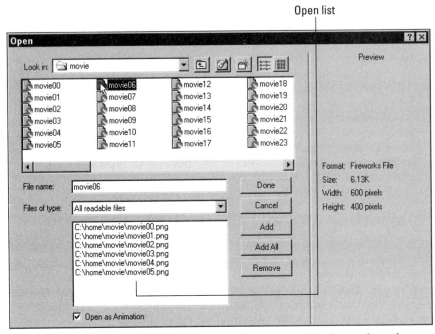

**Figure 15-6:** Files become frames when you import an animation series using File ➪ Open Multiple with Open as Animation checked.

2. In the Files of Type drop-down list, choose the type of files you will be opening.

3. Choose each of the files in your animation series in turn and click the Add button to add them to the Open list, or click the Add All button to add all the files in a particular folder.

**Tip** If the files you are importing are numbered — movie01.png, movie02.png, for example — Fireworks will distribute them to frames in the correct order. If the files are not numbered, Add each one to the list of files to be opened in the correct order.

4. Select the Open as Animation check box. Click Done.

   A new Fireworks document is created, and your files are now frames in that document.

**Tip**

Test your animation by setting it to play with the VCR-style controls in the Fireworks status bar. If the status bar is not visible, show it by choosing View⇨ Status Bar.

## Importing Flash animations

Macromedia Flash has more sophisticated animation tools than Fireworks, but its animated GIF export features pale in comparison.

If you want to use Fireworks tools on the vector elements of your Flash animation, you have to go a little further to import your Flash animation as vectors, because Fireworks's Open as Animation feature always renders vectors as image objects. The basic idea is to turn your Flash movie into a multilayer Adobe Illustrator document, where each layer is actually a frame of your movie, and then convert the layers to frames while importing into Fireworks. While this example uses Flash, if you use another vector animation application, the principles might still apply.

**Tip**

If you're not worried about retaining vector information, you can also export from Flash as a PNG sequence and then import that file into Fireworks by using Open Multiple with Open as Animation checked.

To import a Flash animation into Fireworks while retaining vector information, follow these steps:

1. Export your movie from Flash as a Shockwave Flash (SWF) file.

2. Create a new Flash document and import the Shockwave Flash file into it.

   You have effectively flattened the layers of your Flash movie, leaving you with a single-layer, frame-by-frame animation.

3. Export your movie from Flash as an Adobe Illustrator Sequence (AI).

4. Create a new Flash document and import the Adobe Illustrator Sequence into it. Select all the files in the sequence by Ctrl+clicking (Command+clicking) each file in turn until they are all selected. Click OK when you're done.

   You have effectively converted the frames of your Flash movie to layers. Frame 1 is now Layer 1, Frame 2 is Layer 2, and so on.

5. Export your movie from Flash as an Adobe Illustrator (AI) file.

   This is the file you will import into Fireworks. Flash can export seven different vector file types, and Fireworks can import three vector file types, but this is the only one they have in common.

**Note**

Choose Adobe Illustrator, not Adobe Illustrator Sequence.

**6.** In Fireworks, choose either File ➪ Open or the keyboard shortcut Ctrl+O (Command+O).

Fireworks displays the Open dialog box.

**7.** Choose the Adobe Illustrator file that you created in Step 5. Click OK when you're done.

Fireworks displays the Vector File Options dialog box.

**8.** Under File Conversion, select Convert Layers to Frames in the Layers Import drop-down list box, so that each layer of your Adobe Illustrator file is placed in a frame in Fireworks.

**9.** Under Render as Images, deselect Groups Over and Tiled Fills Over. Click OK when you're done.

Fireworks imports the file (see Figure 15-7). Your Flash animation is now a Fireworks animation, complete with vector information. Objects are editable and are ready to be manipulated with Fireworks's tools and exported as an animated GIF.

**Figure 15-7:** Animation series created in other applications can be imported into Fireworks, although maintaining vector information requires extra steps. Here, a former Flash animation, with vector information retained, is being modified with Fireworks's tools.

# Summary

Elements can be incorporated into Fireworks documents from external sources. When you're importing elements into Fireworks, keep these points in mind:

✦ You can acquire images directly into Fireworks from TWAIN-compliant hardware devices, such as page scanners and digital cameras. On the Macintosh, you can also use Photoshop Acquire plug-ins.

✦ Resolution — the number of dots — is the most important thing to understand about scanning.

✦ You can copy and paste or drag and drop elements from other applications into Fireworks.

✦ Photoshop 5 files that contain Layer Effects have to have the Layer Effects rendered as layers before saving in Photoshop and importing into Fireworks.

✦ A vector graphic that you import into Fireworks cannot be modified and then exported as a vector graphic. Fireworks is the final step for your vector art.

✦ Animated GIFs should be opened instead of imported. Opening them gets you an animated GIF, whereas importing them gets you only the first frame of the animation.

✦ A series of files can be imported as an animation. Extra steps are necessary to maintain vector information.

In the next chapter, we'll look at exporting your images from Fireworks 2.

✦    ✦    ✦

# Exporting and Optimizing

**T**he cross-platform, almost universal access of the Web is achieved with limitations. Browsers are currently limited to displaying only three file formats (GIF, JPEG, and PNG) out of the hundreds in use — and really only the first two are widely accepted. Bandwidth is severely limited for the mass market: while a lucky few enjoy the speed of a cable modem or T1 line, the vast majority of Web surfers still view the Internet through a 28.8Kbps dial-up modem.

These limitations make optimizing and exporting graphics a necessity and not just a nicety. Macromedia realized the importance of these features when it created Fireworks: much of the program is centered around making the best-looking graphic, with the smallest file size, in an accepted format. The export features covered in this chapter rank among the best available with advanced controls, such as color locking. Fireworks takes the limitations of the Web and turns them into an art form.

**Cross-Reference**

This chapter covers the fundamentals of exporting and optimizing your graphics. For more specific information on exporting graphics with hotspots and slices, see Part V, "Entering the Web." You'll find details on exporting animations in Chapter 25.

## Exporting for the Web

Although it's possible to use a graphic stored in Fireworks native format, PNG, in a Web page, this really isn't practical, nor is it the intention of the program for you to do so. Every graphic produced in Fireworks should really be stored in two files: a Fireworks format PNG master file, and an exported format to be published on the Web. Working hand-in-hand with selecting an appropriate file type is the other main goal of exporting: *optimization*. Optimization is the process of producing the best-looking, smallest possible file. An optimized image loads faster, without sacrificing its quality.

The following is an overview of the typical procedure to use when optimizing a file:

1. Select a file format based on the type of image you are exporting.

2. If the format uses a set number of colors, as does GIF, choose the number of colors. The fewer colors used the smaller the file.

3. If the format uses a compression scheme, as does JPEG, choose the highest degree of compression possible that is not detrimental to the image.

4. Select any additional options specific to the format, such as GIF Interlace or JPEG Smoothing.

5. If possible, crop or scale down the file, to further reduce the file size.

6. Export the file in its optimized form.

The hardest part of optimizing is finding a balance between image quality and file size. Fireworks takes a lot of the guesswork out of this task by providing up to four comparison views of different formats at various color resolutions or compressions. Optimizing every image that goes out on your Web page is important, because the smaller your files, the shorter the loading time of your Web pages — and the quicker visitors can view your work.

## Working with Export Preview

The main export engine in Fireworks is the Export Preview dialog box, shown in Figure 16-1. The Export Preview dialog box is displayed when you either choose File ➪ Export, press the keyboard shortcut Ctrl+Shift+R (Command+Shift+R), or — in Windows — click the Export button from the main toolbar. The dialog box itself is divided into two areas: on the left are three tabbed panels for setting various options, and on the right is the main Preview area.

The three tabbed panels in the Export Preview dialog box are the following:

✦ **Options:** The primary panel for optimizing your image. The file format, bit-depth, compression, transparency, and other preferences are selected here. All color control — such as locking, editing, and deleting colors — is handled here, as well.

Tabbed panels          Preview area

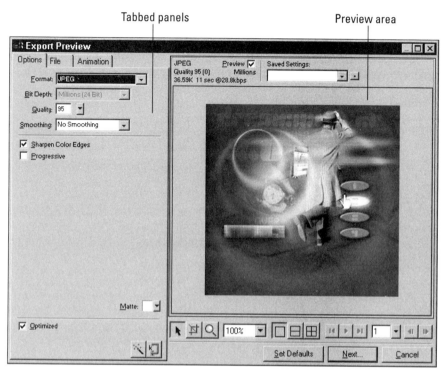

**Figure 16-1:** Virtually all export decisions are set in the Export Preview dialog box.

✦ **File:** Controls two aspects of an exported file: scale and numeric cropping. The exported image can be resized either by a percentage or to a precise pixel measurement. The image can be cropped by entering $X$ and $Y$ coordinates for the upper-left corner, and width and height dimensions of the new area. In Fireworks 2, the exported image can also be cropped visually in the Preview area.

✦ **Animation:** Contains all the settings for running an animated GIF, including the frame delay, disposal method, and looping preferences.

**New Feature**

The always-visible Preview area has been enhanced for Fireworks 2. In addition to providing a visual reference to compare different settings, you can now visually crop the image. I find this to be a major feature improvement and one that I use all the time. Also included are a panning tool (the Pointer), a Zoom tool (the magnifying glass), and a VCR-like control for playing an animation or other multi-frame file.

# Previewing

The main attraction for most exporting operations, however, is the Preview area, shown in Figure 16-2. Capable of comparing up to four export settings at the same time, the Preview area shows you both sides of the export equation: how the image looks, and the file size. The file size is given in both kilobytes and its approximate download time with a 28.8 Kbps modem.

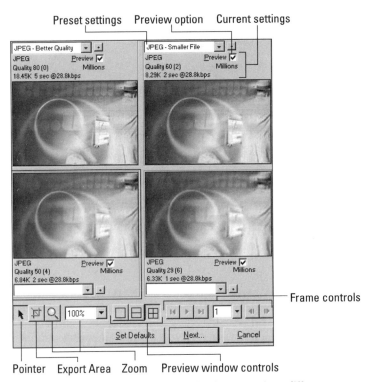

**Figure 16-2:** The Preview area can display up to four different views of different export settings.

**Tip**    When you first begin exporting, Fireworks greets you with an alert that informs you that the display is faster if you turn off Preview. You can disable this message by selecting the Don't Tell Me Again option.

To allow the preview to be generated whenever a change is made to the export, the Preview option at the top of the Export Preview dialog box must be enabled. With the Preview option turned on, Fireworks preliminarily completes the entire export process, short of storing the file or writing any code. Consequently, the Preview operation can sometimes take a moment or two. You can interrupt a Preview from rendering by pressing Esc on Windows and Command+. (period) on Macintosh systems. This is especially beneficial if the image is quite large and you want to change several Export parameters; if Preview is disabled, you can select all the necessary options and then re-enable the Preview option to see the results of your changes.

**Caution** Certain GIF palettes—Adaptive, WebSnap Adaptive, and Exact—are generated only when the Preview option is enabled. If Preview is deselected and one of these palettes is chosen, the swatches from the previous palette will still be displayed in the Options panel.

## Panning

If the image is too big to view all at once in the Preview area, you can use the Pointer tool to pan the image. When you select an image in the Preview area with the Pointer, the cursor becomes a hand, and you can drag the other parts of the image into view. The panning capability of the Pointer is especially valuable when viewing multiple settings. Panning one of the multiple views causes all the other views to be panned, as well, as shown in Figure 16-3, to make direct comparison very straightforward.

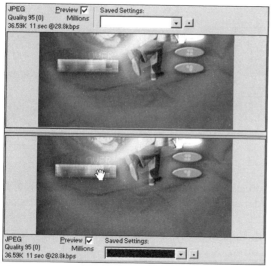

**Figure 16-3:** With multiple views, if you pan in one view, the other view pans, too.

## Cropping

In the first version of Fireworks, the only way to crop during an export operation was to use the numeric Export Area feature found on the File panel. The Export Area tool found on the Toolbox as part of the Pointer flyout also enabled you to crop an area visually, but you had to know ahead of time that you needed to crop an exported image. Both of these methods are still active in Fireworks 2, and a third one — visual cropping in the Export Preview — has been added.

When you initiate a cropping session during export by clicking the Export Area button in the Preview area, the familiar dashed cropping outline surrounds the image, as shown in Figure 16-4. The eight handles are used to narrow the exported area. The original image is not permanently cropped or altered in any way.

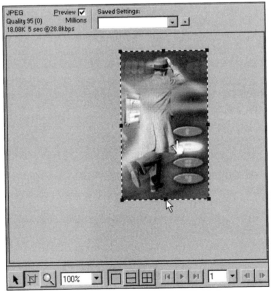

**Figure 16-4:** In Fireworks 2, you can now crop visually right in the Export Preview.

**Note**     Unlike the regular Crop tool in the document window, the Export Area tool can't be used to expand the boundaries of the canvas.

If the File panel is displayed in the Export Preview while you're cropping, the $X$ and $Y$ coordinates of the upper-left corner of your exported area, as well as the width and height dimensions, are visible. The numeric cropping information is updated each time after a cropping handle is dragged to a new position. Alternatively, you can adjust the visual cropping precisely by entering values in the appropriate Export Area text boxes.

## Zooming

One of the new features in Fireworks 2 is *color locking*; you can lock the color of any pixel on the screen simply by clicking it. But, how do you identify just the right pixel — you Zoom in, naturally. The Zoom tool and accompanying option list work exactly the same way in the Export Preview dialog box as they do in the document window. To magnify a view, either select the Zoom tool and click the image, or choose a magnification from the option list. To reduce the magnification of the view, press Alt while clicking with the Zoom tool — or choose a lower magnification.

**Tip** Keep in mind that your Web graphics will *always* be viewed at 100 percent. Although you might be tempted to make a decision on which file format to use based on a magnified view, the magnified view is largely irrelevant to how the graphics are ultimately viewed.

If you have two or four multiple views enabled, changing the magnification of one view changes the magnification for all of them, as shown in Figure 16-5.

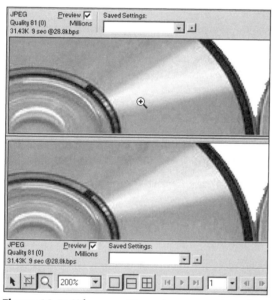

**Figure 16-5:** When you Zoom in on one view, the accompanying views also Zoom in.

**Tip** To pan in for a close-up view, without clicking the Pointer tool, press Ctrl (Command) to temporarily switch to the Pointer/Hand.

## Multiple windows

Fireworks's ability to offer side-by-side comparisons of the effects of different export settings on an image is crucial to optimizing a graphic. This chapter has noted several times that an "optimized graphic" is one that strikes a balance between the best appearance and the smallest file size. That balance can be directly judged through Fireworks's multiple windows. The Export Preview dialog box offers three types of views:

✦ **1 Preview Window:** A single view, approximately 384 × 325 pixels

✦ **2 Preview Windows:** Two views, each approximately 382 × 136 pixels, split horizontally

✦ **4 Preview Windows:** Four views, each approximately 185 × 118 pixels, arranged in a square

While the visual comparison very obviously is a benefit, the file size information that accompanies each view is just as important. If the Preview option is selected for the Preview window, every time that a change is made to the settings, the file size is recalculated and updated. The file size is shown in both kilobytes and the approximate length of time the exported image will take to download.

**Note**

If your image contains multiple frames, the file size shown is for the current single frame only, unless the chosen format is Animated GIF. Images with rollovers, for example, use multiple frames, and each frame is exported as a separate image. To find the total "weight" of a multiple-framed image, all frames must be added together.

To use the multiple windows, follow these steps:

1. From the Export Preview dialog box, click the button for the number of Preview windows that you want: 1, 2, or 4.

   All Previews initially display the current export settings.

2. Select one of the Preview windows.

   A selected Preview window can be identified by an additional frame around the window, as shown in Figure 16-6.

3. Change the export settings on the Options panel.

   The selected Preview window updates after every change if the Preview option is checked.

4. Compare the multiple views of the image and their file sizes to select the optimized image.

5. To pan the image, select the Pointer tool and drag the image in any view.

   All the other views pan to the new location.

6. To increase the magnification of an image, choose the Zoom tool and click any view; Alt+click (Option+click) to reduce the magnification.

   All other views reflect the new magnification settings.

7. Complete the export operation by choosing the Next button while the window with the optimized image is selected.

Preview window button | Preview windows button
Preview windows button

**Figure 16-6:** In multiple-window mode, the current window—here, the lower-right window—has an extra frame around it.

## Frame controls

The VCR-like controls are used to display different frames of a multiframed image in a manner similar to an animation or a rollover. The frame controls can be used to go quickly to a frame, for optimization, or to play the frames in sequence. The controls, left to right, are as follows:

✦ **Go to First Frame:** Displays the first frame of the image.

✦ **Play/Stop:** Plays all the frames in sequence. When the frames are playing, the button image changes to a square and, if pressed, stops the playback.

✦ **Go to Last Frame:** Displays the last frame of the image.

✦ **Frame Counter:** Displays the current frame number of the image. The frame can be changed by using the Frame Counter slider.

**Caution** Although Windows users can manually highlight and change the frame number in the Frame Counter field, the frame itself does not change unless you use the Frame Counter slider. On the Macintosh, be sure to press Tab for Fireworks to accept the change.

✦ **Previous Frame:** Displays the frame before the current one.

✦ **Next Frame:** Displays the frame after the current one.

In addition to being useful for viewing frames, I often use the Frame controls to step through the rollover frames. Remember that each frame in an image is a separate file and thus can be optimized individually.

## Export formats and palettes

Many factors contribute to image optimization, but the format of an image plays perhaps the most important role. In Fireworks, all format selections are made in the Options panel. Selecting a particular format displays the available options, such as Bit Depth or Quality, for that format.

Three formats currently are feasible to use in Web pages, without resorting to plug-ins: GIF, JPEG, and PNG.

### GIF

Typically, images that have large areas of flat color (that is, without gradients or continuous tones) and that require a limited number of colors are saved in GIF format. GIF (short for *Graphics Interchange Format*) files have several important characteristics:

✦ The GIF format is capable of displaying a maximum of 256 colors. These colors are maintained in a color index, so GIF is also called an *indexed format*.

✦ GIFs can be reduced to only the number of colors actually used in an image. Reducing the number of colors has a major impact on file size.

✦ If a GIF needs to represent more than 256 colors, the additional colors are created by *dithering*. A dithered color is made from a pattern of two or more colored pixels that, because the eye cannot differentiate the individual pixels, blend into the new color. Excessive dithering makes your graphic appear very dotty.

✦ Colors in a GIF can be made to appear transparent. This feature is extremely valuable on the Web, because it enables you to create graphics that appear nonrectangular, and enables you to create the illusion that one image is in front of another.

✦ Optionally, GIF files can be *interlaced*. An interlaced image appears to be developing on the page as it is downloaded.

Two types of GIF formats are available in Fireworks: GIF and Animated GIF. As the name implies, *Animated GIF* is used only to create animations in which each frame in an image is shown one after the other, usually rapidly, like a film or flipbook. The options for GIF and Animated GIF are identical, except for those additional options found on the Animation panel.

## Palette

A *palette* in the Export Preview dialog box is the group of colors actually used in the image. Fireworks offers nine preset palettes to choose from, plus the ability to create a custom palette. After you customize a palette, you can store it as a preset and access it from the Saved Settings option list.

> **Note**
>
> The Bit Depth field remains inactive for GIFs and Animated GIFs, because this format really only has one possible bit depth, 8, which allows 256 colors.

Each of the nine different palettes (available to all indexed formats, not just GIF) accesses a different group of colors. The WebSnap Adaptive and Web 216 palettes are the choices generally made for Internet graphics, although other palettes are appropriate in some situations. The following are the nine preset palettes:

✦ **Adaptive:** Looks at all the colors in the image and finds a maximum of 256 of the most suitable colors; it's called an *adaptive* palette because, instead of a fixed set of colors, it is the best 256 colors adapted to the image. If possible, Fireworks assigns Web-safe colors initially and then assigns any remaining non-Web-safe colors. The Adaptive palette can contain a mixture of Web-safe and non-Web-safe colors.

✦ **WebSnap Adaptive:** Similar to the Adaptive palette insofar as both are custom palettes in which colors are chosen to match the originals as closely as possible. After selecting the initial matching Web-safe colors, all remaining colors are examined according to their hexadecimal values. Any colors close to a Web-safe color (plus or minus seven values from a Web-safe color) are "snapped to" that color. Although this palette does not ensure that all colors are Web-safe, a greater percentage of colors will be.

> **Note**
>
> Exactly how does Fireworks decide which colors are within range for the use of WebSnap Adaptive? The plus or minus seven value range is calculated by using the RGB model. For example, suppose that one of the colors is R-100, G-100, B-105 — a medium gray. With the WebSnap Adaptive palette, that color snaps to the R-102, G-102, B-102, because the difference between the two colors is seven or less (R-2, G-2, B-3 = 7). If, however, the color was just slightly different, say R-99, G-100, B-105, the difference would be outside the WebSnap range and the actual color would be used.

✦ **Web 216:** All colors in the image are converted to their nearest equivalent in the Web-safe range.

✦ **Exact:** Uses colors that match the exact original RGB values. Useful only for images with less than 256 colors; for images with more colors, Fireworks alerts you that you should use the Adaptive palette.

✦ **Windows:** Matches the system palette used by the Windows operating system with a maximum of 256 colors.

✦ **Macintosh:** Matches the system palette used by the Macintosh operating system with a maximum of 256 colors.

✦ **Grayscale:** Converts the image to a grayscale graphic with a maximum of 256 colors.

✦ **Black & White:** Reduces the image to a two-color image; the Dither option is automatically selected when you choose this palette, but it can be deselected.

✦ **Uniform:** A mathematical progression of colors across the spectrum are chosen. This palette has little application on the Web, although I have been able to get the occasional posterization effect out of it by reducing the number of colors severely and turning off the Dither option that automatically is enabled..

✦ **Custom:** Whenever a stored palette is loaded or a modification is made to one of the standard palettes, Fireworks labels the palette Custom. Such changes are made through the Options pop-up menu found on the Options panel.

Given all of these options, what's the recommended path to take? Probably the best course is to build your graphic in Fireworks by using the Web Safe palette, and then export them by using the WebSnap Adaptive palette. This choice ensures that your image remains the truest to its original colors while looking the best for Web viewers whose color depth is set to 16-bit or higher, and still looking good on lower-end systems that are capable of showing only 256 colors. A Web-safe color is noted in the Options panel with a diamond in the center of the swatch, as shown in Figure 16-7.

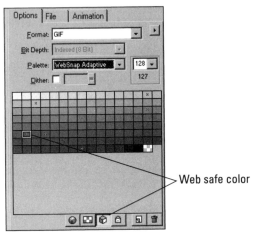

Web safe color

**Figure 16-7:** Choosing the GIF format allows you to choose between Adaptive, WebSnap Adaptive, Web 216, and six other palettes.

Keep in mind that even if you use all Web-safe colors in your graphic, the final result won't necessarily be completely within that palette. Fireworks generates other colors to antialias, to create drop shadows, and to produce glows, and the colors generated may not be Web-safe. This is why either the Adaptive palette or WebSnap Adaptive palette often offers the truest representation of your image across browsers.

**Cross-Reference**    Describing how the different palettes affect your images is helpful, but actually seeing the final results is much more informative. For a comparison view of the various palettes, in full color, turn to Color Plate 16-1 in the color insert.

## Number of colors

One of the quickest ways to cut down an image's file size is to reduce the number of colors. Recall that GIF is referred to as an *8-bit format*; this means that the maximum number of colors is 256, or 8 bit planes of information — higher-math lovers will remember that 256 is equal to $2^8$ (2 raised to the 8th power). Each bit plane used permits exponentially more colors and reserves a certain amount of memory (but also increases the file size). This is why the Number of Colors option list contains powers of 2, 4, 8, 16, 32, 64, 128, and 256.

To alter the bit depth for an exported image, choose a value from the Number of Colors option list. The value chosen then becomes the maximum number of colors that Fireworks uses to export the image. The colors are reduced by discarding those used the least amount. Pixels with a discarded color are converted to the remaining closest-color neighbor. Consequently, the further that you reduce the colors, the more regions of broad, flat color that appear.

## Dither

One way — although not necessarily the best way — to break up areas of flat color caused by the lower color capabilities of GIF is to use the Dither option. When the Dither option is enabled, Fireworks simulates new colors by using a pattern of existing colors — exactly how the Web Dither fill is created. However, because dithering is not restricted to a single area, but instead is spread throughout the graphic, the dithering can be significantly more noticeable — dithering makes the image appear "dotty," as shown in Figure 16-8, and usually increases your file size. The degree of dithering is set by changing the Dither Amount slider or by entering the amount directly in the text box.

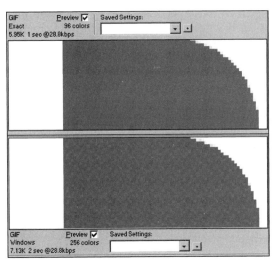

**Figure 16-8:** The image on the bottom was produced with dithering at 100 percent, causing the solid color to be heavily dotted.

### Transparency

One of the main reasons GIF is often selected as a format over JPEG is GIF's ability to make certain colors — and thus certain apparent areas — of the graphic transparent. As mentioned previously, transparency is the key to making nonrectangular-shaped graphics. The Fireworks transparency controls, listed next, are found on the Options tab, below the swatches and color controls, when either GIF, Animated GIF, or PNG (Indexed - 8 bit) is chosen:

✦ **Select Transparency button:** Select to choose a single color to be transparent, either from the swatch set or sampled directly from the previewed image.

✦ **Add to Transparency button:** Enables you to choose additional colors to make transparent, either from the swatch set or sampled directly from the previewed image.

✦ **Subtract from Transparency button:** Converts transparent colors to their original color, either from the swatch set or sampled directly from the previewed image.

✦ **Transparency option list:** Choose the transparency type: No Transparency, Index Transparency, or Alpha Transparency. By default, the canvas color is initially made transparent.

When a color is made transparent, its swatch and pixels in the Preview image are replaced with a gray-and-white checkerboard pattern, as shown in Figure 16-9. You can choose as many colors as you'd like to make transparent.

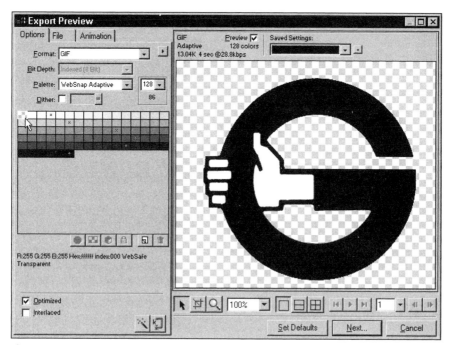

**Figure 16-9:** Part of the power of the GIF format is the ability to make any color transparent.

To make portions of your GIF image transparent, follow these steps:

1. Choose File ➪ Export to open the Export Preview dialog box.

2. If necessary, select GIF from the Format option list.

3. To make the canvas color transparent, select Index Transparency from the Transparency option list.

4. To make a color other than the canvas transparent, click the Select Transparency button and sample a color either from the swatch or from the Preview image.

**Tip**    If you want to select a small area in your image for transparency, use the Zoom tool to magnify that selection before choosing the color.

5. To make more colors transparent, click the Add to Transparency button and sample the colors either from the swatch or from the Preview image.

6. To restore a transparent color to its original color, click the Select from Transparency button and select the color either from the swatch or from the Preview image.

As noted in the Transparency option list description, two different types are available: Index and Alpha Transparency. Index Transparency allows you to make any color totally transparent—think of it as an On/Off switch; the color is either transparent or it isn't. Alpha Transparency, on the other hand, allows degrees of transparency—you can create tints and shades of a color. You'll find out more details about Alpha Transparency in the PNG section, later in this chapter.

Index Transparency is generally used for the GIF format, because, technically, only the PNG format truly supports Alpha Transparency. However, the Fireworks engineers have left Alpha Transparency enabled for GIFs, to achieve a slightly different effect. When Alpha Transparency is chosen, a new color register is created for the canvas and then made transparent. How is this different from converting the canvas color to transparent, as occurs with Index Transparency? If you've ever created an image where part of the graphic is the same color as the background— the white of a person's eyes is also the white of a canvas—you'll quickly understand and appreciate this feature. Basically, Alpha Transparency, as applied in Fireworks's GIF format, leaves your palette alone and just makes the canvas transparent, as shown in Figure 16-10.

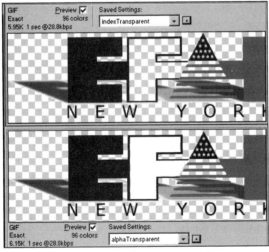

**Figure 16-10:** The upper image uses Index Transparency, which converts the canvas color to transparent; the lower image uses Alpha Transparency, which adds a new transparent color register for the canvas, leaving the original color scheme intact.

**Note**     If you don't notice a new color register being added when you select Alpha Transparency, check to see whether the Optimized option is enabled. If it is, Fireworks may combine other colors to keep the same number of colors.

## Additional options

Fireworks offers two additional options for the GIF format: Optimized and Interlaced. The Optimized option is a Fireworks-only feature that causes the program to discard duplicate and unused colors from a palette. Choosing the Optimized option can seriously reduce your file size, automatically, particularly when choosing one of the fixed palettes, such as Web 216 or either of the system palettes.

The Interlaced option enables a GIF property that allows a file to be displayed as it is being downloaded. The file is shown in progressively finer detail as more information is transferred from the server to the browser. Although a graphic exported with the Interlaced option won't download any faster, it provides a visual cue to Web page visitors that something is happening. Interlacing graphics is a matter of taste; some Web designers don't design a page without them; others are vehemently opposed to their use.

## JPEG

Besides GIF, the other major Web graphics file format is JPEG, an acronym for *Joint Photographic Experts Group*, the organization that developed the standard. As you might expect from its roots, the JPEG format is intended for photographic images or graphics that incorporate gradations or continuous tones. Whereas GIFs generally are made smaller by lowering the number of colors used, JPEGs use a sliding scale that creates smaller file sizes by eliminating pixels. This sliding scale is built on a *lossy* algorithm, so-called because the lower the scale, the more pixels that are lost. The JPEG algorithm is a very good one and you can significantly reduce the file size by lowering the JPEG quality, as shown in Figure 16-11. Other characteristics of the JPEG format include:

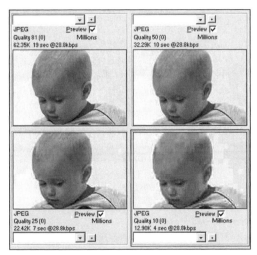

**Figure 16-11:** Each of these four images was compressed using a different JPEG quality value; only when the quality is lowered to 10 does the image become unacceptable.

✦ JPEG images are capable of displaying over 16 million colors. This wide color range, also referred to as *24-bit*, enables the subtle shades of a photograph to be depicted easily.

✦ Although JPEG images can display almost any color, none of the colors can be made transparent. Consequently, any image that requires transparency must be stored as a GIF.

✦ The JPEG format is a compressed format; thus, for a JPEG image to be viewed through a browser, it must be both downloaded and uncompressed. Browsers handle the decompression quickly, but it still takes time; given an equivalent file size, a file saved as a GIF displays quicker than a file saved as a JPEG.

✦ For JPEG images to be viewed as they are downloaded, they must be stored as Progressive JPEGs, which appear to develop onscreen, like an interlaced GIF; however, not all browsers (particularly Internet Explorer 3 and below) support Progressive JPEGs. Progressive JPEGs have a slightly better compression engine and can produce smaller file sizes.

**Note**    With the JPEG image-compression algorithm, the initial elements of an image that are "compressed away" are least noticeable. Subtle variations in brightness and hue are the first to disappear. With additional compression, the image grows darker and less varied in its color range.

### Quality

The major method for altering a JPEG's file size is by changing the Quality value. In Fireworks, the Quality value is gauged as a percentage, and the slider goes from 0% to 100%. Higher values mean less compression, and lower values mean that more pixels are discarded. Trying to reduce a JPEG's file size by lowering the Quality slider is always worthwhile — you can also enter a value directly in the text box. The JPEG compression algorithm is so good that almost every continuous tone image can be reduced in file size without significant loss of quality. On the other hand, increasing a JPEG's Quality value from its initial setting is never helpful. Whereas JPEG is very good at *losing* pixels to reduce file size, adding pixels to increase quality never works — you'll only increase the file's size and download time.

A good technique for comparing JPEG images in Fireworks is to use the four Preview windows option. Keep one view at your original setting, so that you always have an image on which to base your comparisons. In another view, reduce the Quality setting by half, approximately. If that image is acceptable, reduce the Quality setting by half again in another view. By then, you'll probably start to get some unwanted artifacts, so use the fourth window to try a setting midway between the last acceptable and the unacceptable Quality settings. Be sure to view your images at 100% magnification — that's how your Web audience will see them, so you should too.

**Note**   When switching from the 2 or 4 Preview window to the 1 Preview window, Fireworks does not automatically display the last selected window. Rather, it displays the top window from a 2 Preview window view or the upper-left window from a 4 Preview window view. To view a single screen with another setting, you need to reset the Quality and any other options.

### Smoothing

The more that a JPEG file is compressed, the "blockier" it becomes. As the compression increases, the JPEG algorithm throws out more and more similar pixels — after a certain point, the transitions from gradations are lost and areas become flat color blocks. Although nothing can be done to recover an image with a JPEG Quality setting of 1 percent or 2 percent, more-borderline cases can be helped significantly by using Fireworks's Smoothing feature.

Smoothing slightly blurs the overall image so that any stray pixels resulting from the compression are less noticeable. The Smoothing scale in the Options panel of the Export Preview dialog box runs from No Smoothing to 8 Maximum Smoothing. As Figure 16-12 shows, Smoothing offers two benefits. Not only does the blockiness largely disappear, but the file size also is somewhat reduced: the image with the lowest JPEG Quality setting and the highest Smoothing is also the smallest file. The Smoothing setting is displayed in each Preview window as the number in the parentheses, following the Quality setting; for example, a Smoothing setting of 2 is represented as Quality 30 (2). Whereas an extreme Smoothing setting tends to soften many images too much, a low Smoothing setting often enhances any JPEG compression — both visually and file-wise.

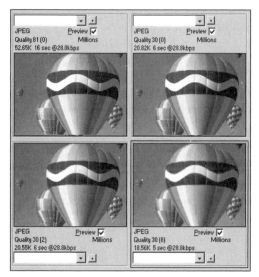

**Figure 16-12:** Smoothing blends away blockiness from heavily compressed JPEG files; the lower-right Preview window has the highest Smoothing and the lowest file size.

### Sharpen

Graphics on the Web are often a montage of photographs, illustrations, and text. Although JPEG is the right choice for a continuous tone image, such as a photograph, it can make text that overlays a photograph appear fuzzy, because JPEG is far better at compressing gradations than it is at compressing images with hard edges and abrupt color changes. To overcome these obstacles, use Fireworks's Sharpen option.

As the name implies, *Sharpen* restores some of the hard-edge transitions that are lost during JPEG compression. This is especially noticeable on text and simple graphics, such as rectangles, superimposed on photographs. For an example, take a look at Figure 16-13, in which both images are compressed with a JPEG Quality setting of 60, but only the upper image has the Sharpen option enabled. Without the Sharpen option, both the text and the surrounding rectangle appear a bit blurry; they're both much clearer with Sharpen selected. The other point to notice about Sharpen is that it can significantly increase your file size: in the example, the unsharpened image was 7.82K, whereas the Sharpen-enabled version grew to 11.81K. The Sharpen option is another tool whose use requires that you always keep an eye on the balance between image quality and file size.

### Progressive

To most, Progressive is known as an incremental display option for JPEGs, much like Interlaced for the GIF format. The Progressive option actually enables a different compression algorithm — a second generation one — that many times offers lower file sizes at the equivalent quality of the original JPEG compression. The Progressive JPEG format was developed by Netscape, but has won the support of recent browser versions from Microsoft, as well.

In practice, I find that enabling the Progressive option often gives me a smaller file size, but not always. For me, choosing this option generally depends on whether the client prefers to see the images slowly develop as they download or prefers them to download completely and appear as a finished image.

## PNG

The third Web format, PNG (*Portable Network Graphics*), is still in its infancy — well, maybe early childhood — as far as general browser acceptance is concerned. The PNG format holds great promise for Web graphics. Combining the best of both worlds, PNG has lossless compression, like GIF, and is capable of millions of colors, like JPEG. Moreover, PNG offers an interlace scheme that appears much more quickly than either GIF or JPEG, as well as transparency support that is far superior to both other formats.

One valuable aspect of the PNG format makes the display of PNG pictures appear more uniform across various computer platforms. Generally, graphics made on a PC look brighter on a Macintosh, and Mac-made images seem darker on a PC. PNG includes *gamma correction* capabilities that alter the image depending on the computer used by the viewer.

Until recently, the various browsers supported PNG only through plug-ins. After PNG was endorsed as a new Web graphic format by the World Wide Web Consortium (W3C), both Netscape and the Microsoft 4.0 browser versions added native, inline support of the new format. Perhaps most importantly, however, Macromedia's Dreamweaver was among the first Web-authoring tools to offer native PNG support. Inserted PNG images preview in the document window just like GIFs and JPEGs do. Then, Fireworks was introduced, which uses PNG as its own format.

Although support for PNG is growing steadily, browser support currently is not widespread enough to warrant a total switch-over to the PNG format. PNG is capable of many more features, such as Alpha Transparency, that are not fully in use by any major browser. Interestingly enough, Fireworks is way ahead of most other graphic programs in its support of PNG. One of the developers of the PNG format and the keeper of the PNG home page (`www.cdrom.com/pub/png`), Greg Roelofs, calls Fireworks, "the best PNG-supporting image editor available."

For an example of the type of imagery that Fireworks is capable of today, take a look at Color Plate 16-1. The flower images, overlaid on top of the photograph, are taken from an 8-bit PNG (256 colors), by Pieter S. van der Meulen, in which Alpha Transparency is turned on. The flower on the right uses a standard Fireworks drop shadow effect, but neither flower required any special handling to get the seamless blend onto the background photograph — that's the true power of Alpha Transparency.

When you export a PNG file with Alpha Transparency enabled in the Indexed (8-bit) mode, you'll notice a different type of symbol in the swatches. Instead of the full swatch displaying the checkerboard background that indicates transparency, certain colors have a checkerboard in the upper-left corner, as shown in Figure 16-13. These are the Alpha Transparent colors. Unlike an Index Transparency color, which is either completely transparent or completely opaque, an Alpha Transparent color can be partially transparent — in fact, the transparency can use as many as 256 gradations.

**Note**    The Fireworks native PNG format is considered an extended PNG format, because of the additional effects, text, and other data included in each file. Other programs capable of generally displaying PNG files may show the basic Fireworks image, but won't be able to edit it in the same way. To display a file in PNG format on a Web page, it's best to specify PNG as the format when you export.

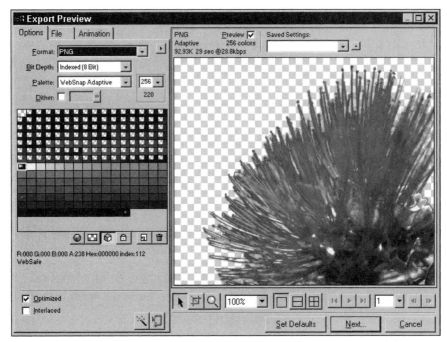

**Figure 16-13:** This PNG image by Pieter S. van der Meulen uses a true Alpha Transparency feature, as noted by the semitransparent swatches.

## Other formats

GIF, JPEG, and PNG are the primary formats used on the Web, but the world doesn't run on the Web alone. Fireworks can also export to three different formats for other purposes:

✦ **TIFF:** TIFF (Tag Image File Format) was developed by Aldus Corporation to support print graphics on both Macintosh and PC systems. TIFF handles photographs very well.

✦ **xRes LRG:** Used by Macromedia's discontinued graphics program, xRes.

✦ **BMP and PICT:** These formats were once the standard graphics file formats for Windows (BMP) and Macintosh (PICT). Fireworks supports only one of these formats for each operating system; in other words, you can't export a PICT file from a Windows system or export a BMP from a Macintosh.

All of these formats indicate that they are capable of exporting at Indexed (8 Bit), Millions (24 Bit), and Millions + Alpha (32 Bit); however, none of them can really handle transparency, so you'll see no difference if you choose the 32 bit option. The Matte feature, however, is active and available in both the 8 bit and 24 bit modes.

## Scaling and cropping exported images

It might seem like a cliché to note that "Web graphics come in all shapes and sizes" — except, it's also true to say that the *same* Web graphic often comes in different shapes and sizes. Reusing graphic elements is a very key design strategy in product branding in most media, and the technique is especially useful on the Web. Fireworks makes it very easy to export resized or cropped graphics from a master file, through the Export Preview dialog box.

As noted previously, in addition to the always-available visual cropping tool, the scaling and cropping controls are found on the File panel, as shown in Figure 16-14. You can resize a graphic by specifying either a percentage or an exact pixel size. By default, all rescaling is constrained to the original height-to-width ratio — however, you can disable the Constrain option to alter one dimension separately from the other.

### Resizing an image

To resize an image, follow these steps:

1. From the Export Preview dialog box, select the File panel.

2. To rescale an image by percentage, use the % slider or enter a value directly into the % text box.

   The % slider's range is from 1% to 200%, but you can enter any value in the text box.

3. To resize an image to an exact dimension, enter a figure in the *W* (Width) and/or *H* (Height) text box.

   If the Constrain option is selected, enter a value in just one of the dimension text boxes and press Tab. The other dimension will be calculated for you according to the image's original height-to-width ratio.

4. To alter the height-to-width ratio, deselect Constrain and perform Step 3.

**Cross-Reference**    The Fireworks 2.02 update enables you to use different scaling algorithms, depending on the type of image. For all the details on using these new scaling options, see Chapter 9.

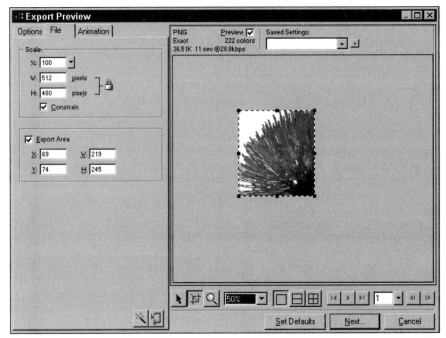

**Figure 16-14:** The File panel contains controls for numerically rescaling or cropping any exported graphic.

## Visually cropping an image

To crop an image visually, follow these steps:

1. Choose either the Export Area tool beneath the Preview window(s) or the Export Area option on the File panel.

   An outline with cropping handles appears around the image.

2. Drag the handles to a new position so that only the area you want to export is displayed.

3. Choose any other tool (Pointer or Zoom), or either the Set Defaults or the Next button to accept the new cropped area.

## Numerically cropping an image

To crop an image numerically, follow these steps:

1. From the File panel, select the Export Area option.

**2.** Select a new upper-left coordinate by entering new values in the *X* and/or *Y* text boxes, and press Tab to accept the changed value.

**3.** Select a new image size by entering new values in the *W* (Width) and *H* (Height) text boxes, and press Tab to accept the changed value.

Both cropping methods — visual and numeric — work together as well as separately. While viewing the File panel, select the Export Area tool and crop the image visually. When you release the mouse button, the numeric values automatically update. Similarly, change the numeric values, and the visual display is redrawn.

After you painstakingly find exactly the right format to use for a series of images, do you have to re-create it every time? Certainly not. Fireworks enables you to save any settings as a preset and recall it at any time, along with six other, standard presets. The export settings are available through the Saved Settings option list found at the top of the Preview window. If multiple views are used, a Saved Settings option list is available for each window.

The following are the six standard preset Saved Settings options:

✦ **GIF Web 216:** Sets the GIF format using the Web 216 palette. The Optimized and Dither options are enabled.

✦ **GIF WebSnap 256:** Sets the GIF format using the WebSnap Adaptive palette and a maximum of 256 colors. The Optimized option is enabled.

✦ **GIF WebSnap 128:** Sets the GIF format using the WebSnap Adaptive palette and a maximum of 128 colors. The Optimized option is enabled.

✦ **GIF Adaptive 256:** Sets the GIF format using the Adaptive palette and a maximum of 256 colors. The Optimized option is enabled.

✦ **JPEG – Better Quality:** Sets the JPEG format with a Quality setting of 80. The Optimized and Sharpen Color Edges options are enabled.

✦ **JPEG – Smaller File:** Sets the JPEG format with a Quality setting of 60. The Optimized option is enabled and Smoothing is set to 2.

Adjusting any preset export setting (except Matte) creates a custom setting. To save a custom export setting, click the Save Current Settings button (the plus sign) next to the Saved Settings option list. A simple Preset Name dialog box (Figure 16-15) appears for you to enter a unique name for the setting. After you enter the name and click OK, the setting is added to the preset list and is always available.

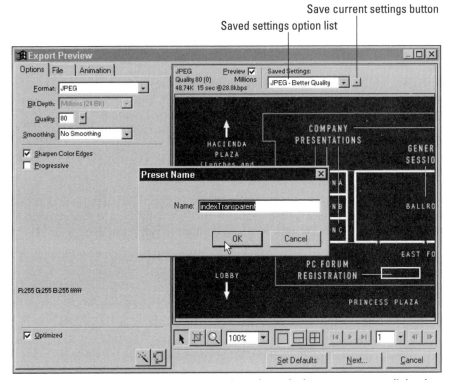

**Figure 16-15:** Save any custom export settings through the Preset Name dialog box.

# Export Color Options

Macromedia seriously upgraded the color command set in the Export Preview dialog box for Fireworks 2. In addition to the ability to add, edit, and delete individual colors, as well as store and load palettes, Fireworks 2 enables you to lock a color, snap it to its closest Web-safe neighbor, convert it to transparent, and even undo any changes to a color.

**New Feature**  As you can see in the command list shown in Figure 16-16, the Options panel pop-up menu now includes 16 color commands. All of these commands pertain only to the Indexed (8 Bit) Bit Depth setting, because that is the only mode in which swatches are available. One of the more important additions is the ability to lock one or more colors in your graphic. This capability ensures that the most important colors — whether they're important for branding, a visual design, or both — can be maintained, regardless of the palette chosen. After a color is locked, it does not change, regardless of the palette chosen. For example, you could preview your image by using the Web 216 palette, lock all the colors, and then switch to an Adaptive palette to broaden the color range, but keep the basic colors Web-safe. A locked color is identified by a square in the lower-right corner of the swatch.

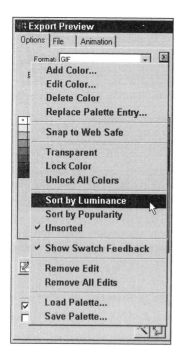

**Figure 16-16:** The Color commands in the Export Preview dialog box have become quite extensive in Fireworks 2

## Sort by Popularity

Sort by Popularity is another new, worthy feature. This command is very helpful when it's time to trim the file size by cutting colors. By default, the swatches are displayed in an unsorted order. After you choose Sort by Popularity from the Options panel pop-up menu, the most-used color is displayed first, in the upper-left corner, and the least-used color is shown last, in the lower-right corner. This makes it easy to select for deletion the colors that are least likely to be missed. You can Shift+select to choose a range of colors, or Ctrl+select (Command+select) to select multiple swatches that are not adjacent to each other.

As noted in Table 16-1, many of the commands, such as Lock Color, have button equivalents. These toolbar-like buttons can be found between the swatch set and the Transparency controls.

### Table 16-1
### Export Preview Option Pop-Up Commands

| Command | Button | Description |
| --- | --- | --- |
| Add Color | Yes | Allows you to insert an additional color into the current palette by using the system color picker. |

*Continued*

| | | |
|---|---|---|
| **Table 16-1** *(continued)* | | |

| *Command* | *Button* | *Description* |
|---|---|---|
| Edit Color | Yes | Opens the system color picker to permit a new color to be chosen or the selected color to be modified. |
| Delete Color | Yes | Removes the selected color(s). |
| Replace Palette Entry | No | Swaps the selected color for the color chosen through the system color picker. |
| Snap to Web Safe | Yes | Converts the selected color(s) to the closest color in the Web-safe palette. |
| Transparent | Yes | Makes the selected color(s) transparent. |
| Lock Color | Yes | Maintains the current color during any overall palette transformations, such as bit-depth reduction or palette changes. The color, however, can still be edited directly. |
| Unlock Color | Yes | Allows the color to be changed. |
| Sort by Luminance | No | Sorts the current palette swatch set from brightest to darkest. |
| Sort by Popularity | No | Sorts the current palette swatch set from most pixels used to least pixels used. |
| Unsorted | No | Restores the default swatch arrangement. |
| Remove Edit | No | Reverts the swatch to its original color. |
| Remove All Edits | No | Restores the current palette to its original state. |
| Load Palette | No | Allows a palette to be loaded from a Adobe Color Table (ACT) file or from a GIF. |
| Save Palette | No | Stores the current palette as a Color Table file. |

Tip
All of these commands are also available from the shortcut menu that appears when you right-click (hold-click) an individual swatch.

## Matte

Fireworks 2 introduces the concept of the canvas as a new tool for controlling an image's background. The power of the canvas, as a production tool, really comes into its own when you begin to use the Matte feature of the Export Preview dialog box.

The Matte feature is available for all the Fireworks export formats: GIF, Animated GIF, JPEG, PNG, TIFF, xRes LRG, and BMP.

**New Feature**

When a photograph is framed, the framer often mounts the image on a *matte,* which provides a different, contrasting background to make the photograph stand out. Fireworks 2 uses the matte idea to allow the Web designer to export images with varying canvas colors—without changing the canvas. One of the biggest problems with GIF transparency are the unwanted "halos" that result from creating a drop shadow or other gradation against a different background. The traditional method of handling this problem is to change your canvas color in the graphics program to match the background color on the Web page. This solution works well for one-off-type graphics, but many Web designers find that they need to use the same graphic in many different situations, against many different backgrounds. The Matte feature enables you to keep one master graphic and export as many specific instances—against as many different mattes or canvases—as necessary.

Choosing a Matte color is very straightforward: Simply click the Matte arrow button to display the standard color picker pop-up menu. From there, choose one of the swatches or sample a color by using the Eyedropper tool. To return a Matte color to transparent, click the No Color button in the color picker pop-up menu. You can even preview different Matte colors, as shown in Figure 16-17.

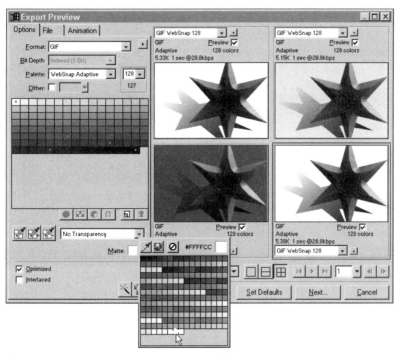

**Figure 16-17:** The new Matte feature enables you to export your image by using different canvas colors, without having to modify the original image.

# Using the Export Wizards

Fireworks's export options are very full-featured and can certainly be overwhelming if you're new to Web graphics. If you're not even sure how best to begin optimizing your image, let one of Fireworks's Export Wizards guide you. In addition to the original Export Wizard, which is very helpful for selecting the appropriate file format, Fireworks 2 introduces the Export to Size Wizard, to meet those absolute file-size limits.

If you are ready to export but don't know where to start, bring up Fireworks's Export Wizard, which not only helps you to determine the correct file format best suited to the graphic's purpose, but it also provides you with an alternative in certain cases. For this reason, seasoned Web designers can also use the Export Wizard to get quickly to a jumping-off place for further optimization.

Regardless of the selection that the Export Wizard makes for you, it always presents you with a visual display through the Export Preview dialog box, covered extensively earlier in this chapter. Feel free to either accept the recommendations of the Export Wizard as is — and click the Next button to complete the operation — or tweak the settings first before you proceed.

The Export Wizard has three primary uses:

✦ To help you select an export format.

✦ To offer suggestions to optimize your image after you select an export format.

✦ To recommend export modes that will reduce a graphic to a specified file size.

To use the Export Wizard to select an export format, follow these steps:

1. Choose File ➪ Export Wizard.

   The initial screen of the Export Wizard appears, as shown in Figure 16-18.

2. With the Select an Export Format option selected, click Continue.

3. The next screen of the Export Wizard appears and offers four choices for the graphic's ultimate destination:

   • **The Web**: Restricts the export options to the most popular Web formats, GIF and JPEG.

   • **An image-editing application:** Selects the best format for continuing to edit the image in another program, such as Photoshop. Generally, Fireworks selects the TIFF format.

   • **Desktop publishing application**: Selects the best print format, typically TIFF.

   • **Dreamweaver**: The same as The Web option, restricts the export options to the most popular Web formats, GIF and JPEG.

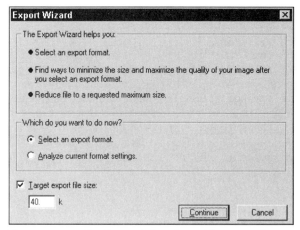

**Figure 16-18:** The Export Wizard provides a good aunch pad for export selections.

**Note**

If your graphic uses frames, the Export Wizard asks instead whether your file is to be exported as an Animated GIF, a JavaScript button rollover, or a single image file.

4. Click Continue after you make your choice.

   Fireworks presents its analysis of your image, with suggestions on how to narrow the selection further, if more than one export choice is recommended.

**Caution**

If you select Animated GIF as your destination for your multiframe image, you must select the resulting Preview window to display the details in the Options panel.

5. Click Exit to open the Export Preview dialog box and complete the export operation.

If you choose either The Web or Dreamweaver for your graphic's export destination, Fireworks presents you with two options for comparison: a GIF and a JPEG. The file in the upper Preview window is the smallest file size. Fireworks is fairly conservative in this aspect of the Export Wizard and does not attempt to seriously reduce the file size at the cost of image quality.

If you'd like to limit the file size while selecting an export format, select the Target Export File Size option on the Export Wizard's first screen. After you enable this option, you need to enter a file size value in the adjacent text box. File size is always measured in kilobytes. After you enter a file size, click Continue for Fireworks to calculate the results.

When Fireworks attempts to fit a graphic into a particular file size, it exports the image up to 12 times to find the best size with the least compression. Although it's usually very fast, this process can take several minutes to complete with a large graphic. Again, for graphics intended for the Web, Fireworks presents two choices — both at, or under, your specified target size.

**New Feature**    In addition to specifying a file size through the Export Wizard, you can choose the new Export to File Size Wizard by clicking the button on the Options panel of the Export Preview dialog box. The Export to File Size Wizard opens a simple dialog box that asks for the specified file size. The major difference between this wizard and the Export File Size option on the Export Wizard is that the Export to File Size Wizard works only with the current format — no alternative choices are offered. Consequently, the Export to File Size Wizard is faster, but it's intended more for the intermediate-to-advanced user who understands the differences between file formats.

## Additional Export Options

The vast majority of the time graphics are exported from Fireworks by using the Export Preview dialog box. However, Fireworks also offers several extra export options, including

✦ Export all layers separately.

✦ Export all frames separately.

✦ Export all slice objects separately.

✦ All the preceding items can be exported as either of the following:

　• A separate graphics file

　• A Cascading Style Sheet (CSS) layer for use in Dynamic HTML-capable browsers

　• In Image Well format, used in Lotus Domino documents

All of these additional export methods are grouped under the File ➪ Export Special menu. In fact, even though three separate commands exist (Export as Files, Export as CSS Layers, and Export as Image Well), each command displays the same dialog box (Figure 16-19) with different options set.

**Tip**    Regardless of which Export Special operation you undertake, the current settings in the Export Preview dialog box determine the file format and other settings. To establish new settings without actually exporting any files, choose the Set Defaults button in the Export Preview dialog box.

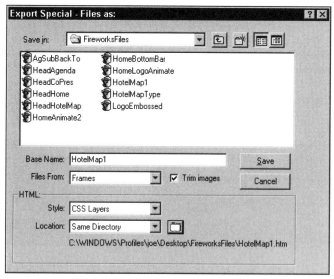

**Figure 16-19:** The Export Special dialog box handles a variety of individual export situations.

## Exporting files

Occasionally, you need to break up the component parts of your graphic — layers, frames, and slice objects — for use as a separate file. Perhaps you need to reuse some of these elements in another part of the Web site, or maybe you want to process the files in another application before reintegrating them in Fireworks. Whatever the reason, Fireworks provides a fairly straightforward method for generating separate graphic files for almost any situation.

Because each component is potentially stored as a individual file, Fireworks must assign a unique filename for each file. Each of the components uses a slightly different naming scheme. Both frames and slice objects combine a *base name*, selected in the Export Special dialog box, with a generated extension. Frames add _F*nn* as a suffix, where *nn* is number starting with 01 and incrementing for each frame. For example, exporting separate files from a graphic with three frames with the Base Name of myFrame would result in three files: myFrame01, myFrame02, and myFrame03.

Files created from slice objects, on the other hand, are named according to the current Auto-Naming scheme found in the Document Properties dialog box. By default, slice objects use an extension based on their row and column position in a completed table, such as mySlice_r1_c1 for a slice with the base name of mySlice found in row 1, column 1 of a table. You can override these automatic names by deselecting the Auto-Name Slices option in the Objects panel and entering a unique slice name. The Export Special command then uses those unique names.

Fireworks layers do not require a base name and suffix combination — instead, each file created from a layer takes its filename from the actual layer names used in Fireworks. By default, Fireworks names new layers sequentially (Layer 1, Layer 2, Layer 3, and so on). However, you can personalize a layer by double-clicking its name or by choosing the Layer Options command from the Layers panel Options pop-up menu.

To export a Fireworks element as a separate file, follow these steps:

1. Make sure that the format and settings that you want to use are the ones last used or saved in the Export Preview dialog box.

2. Choose File ⇨ Export Special ⇨ Export as Files.

   The Export Special dialog box appears.

3. Select the Fireworks component (Layers, Frames, or Slice Objects) to export from the Files From option list.

4. Select the Trim Images option to export the individual components on the smallest-sized canvas necessary.

   If Trim Images is not selected, each exported file will be the same dimensions as the original image.

5. For frames and slice objects, select a new Base Name, if desired.

6. Make sure that the HTML Style option is set to None.

7. Browse to the desired folder to store the images.

8. Click Save when you're ready.

**Tip**     You can control which frames or layers are exported by turning off their visibility in their respective panels. The visibility is controlled by the Eye symbol in the far-left column, next to each item name. If the frame or layer is not visible when the Export Special command is run, it's not exported.

## Exporting as CSS layers

The term *layers* is used quite often in the Web graphics field. To the Photoshop user, a "layer" is a division capable of holding a single graphic element. In Fireworks, a layer can hold any number of objects and is a useful organizational tool. In Dynamic HTML and in Web-authoring tools such as Dreamweaver, a "layer" is a type of container that can be precisely positioned, hidden, or displayed — or flown across the screen. These types of layers are created by using a standard known as Cascading Style Sheets (CSS). Fireworks enables you to save any of its components while generating the HTML required for putting those components in a separate CSS layer. This facility enables you to achieve effects such as parts of a graphic coming from different areas of a screen until they meet as one complete image, as shown in Figure 16-20.

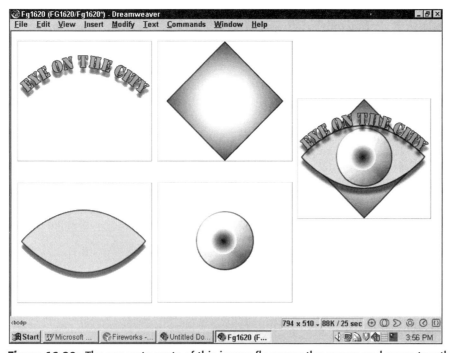

**Figure 16-20:** The separate parts of this image fly across the screen and come together to form the complete image shown on the right; this effect is made possible by Fireworks 2's new Export as CSS Layers command.

To export Fireworks components as CSS layers, follow these steps:

1. Make sure that the format and settings that you want to use are the ones last used or saved in the Export Preview dialog box.

2. Choose File ➪ Export Special ➪ Export as CSS Layers.

   The Export Special dialog box appears.

3. Select the Fireworks component (Layers, Frames, or Slice Objects) to export from the Files From option list.

4. Select the Trim Images option to export the individual components on the smallest-sized canvas necessary.

   If Trim Images is not selected, each exported file will be the same dimensions as the original image.

5. For frames and slice objects, select a new Base Name, if desired.

6. Make sure that the HTML Style option is set to CSS Layers.

**7.** Determine where the HTML file should be stored by selecting an option from the Location option list: Same Directory, One Level Up or Custom.

Selecting Custom (or clicking the Browse button) opens the standard Save As dialog box, which can be used for selecting a new folder and filename.

**8.** Browse to the desired folder to store the images.

**9.** Click Save when you're ready.

After you complete the export process, you'll have both the separate images and the HTML necessary to place each image in its own CSS layer. To use the layers on your Web page, you need to incorporate the generated code into your own Web page. You can accomplish this with any Web-authoring tool that allows you to access the HTML directly. When you display the generated HTML in a browser, you'll see your graphic appear one element at a time. If you look at the HTML in an application such as Dreamweaver's HTML Inspector, the code looks like this in the <body> section of the document:

```
<! -- BEGIN COPYING THE CODE HERE -->

<div id="Layer1" style="position:absolute; left:5px;
top:6px;width:80px; height:72px;z-index:1;"><img name="Layer_1"
src="Layer_1.gif" width="80" height="72" border="0"></div>

<div id="Layer2" style="position:absolute; left:109px;
top:96px;width:91px; height:100px;z-index:2;"><img
name="Layer_2" src="Layer_2.gif" width="91" height="100"
border="0"></div>

<div id="Layer3" style="position:absolute; left:37px;
top:34px;width:126px; height:128px;z-index:3;"><img
name="Layer_3" src="Layer_3.gif" width="126" height="128"
border="0"></div>

<! -- STOP COPYING THE CODE HERE -->
```

Although the code can appear quite overwhelming initially, only the plain-English phrases that bracket it are important for incorporating the code. In your favorite HTML or text editor, select the code from the line

```
<! -- BEGIN COPYING THE CODE HERE -->
```

and end your selection with the line

```
<! -- STOP COPYING THE CODE HERE -->
```

After you select the code, copy it and then open your working HTML page and paste the Clipboard contents anywhere in the <body> section. Now, you can continue to manipulate the layers however you like in your Web-authoring program.

**Note**

Dreamweaver users don't have to use the HTML Inspector or any other text tool to copy and paste the Fireworks code. In Dreamweaver, just find the Invisible Element symbols that enclose the layer code — you'll see a Dreamweaver HTML comment symbol on either side of the layer symbols. Select all of these symbols and then copy and paste into your working document. You must have Invisible Elements enabled for this technique to work.

## Exporting as Image Wells

Image Wells are used by Lotus Domino Designer R5 to create rollover effects. Just as Fireworks uses frames to separate the different rollover states — up, over, down, and overdown — Domino Designer uses Image Wells. If it were viewed separately, an Image Well would appear to be the frames of an image, side by side, separated by a single pixel, as the example in Figure 16-21 shows.

**Figure 16-21:** The final output of an Image Well export is used in Lotus Domino Designer R5.

**Note**

Image Wells are similar to the four state rollovers in Fireworks, but not exactly the same. The last two states — over and overdown — are reversed. Fireworks, however, understands this difference and exports your Image Well in the correct format.

This new feature is best used to convert to Image Wells your existing multiframe images used for rollovers. To export a graphic as an Image Well, follow these steps:

1. Make sure that the format and settings that you want to use are the ones last used or saved in the Export Preview dialog box.

2. Choose File ➪ Export Special ➪ Export as Image Well.

   The Export Special dialog box appears.

3. Select Slice Objects to export from the Files From option list.

   Trim Images is not relevant for Image Wells and is ignored.

4. Select a new Base Name, if desired.

5. Make sure that the HTML Style is set to Image Well.

6. Browse to the desired folder to store the images.

7. Click Save when you're ready.

Fireworks saves the Image Well as either a GIF or a JPEG, depending on the current Export Preview settings.

## Exporting single slices

Whereas the Export Special command is useful for exporting *all* the slices as separate files or in CSS layers, you can also export a single slice, if necessary. To export a single slice, follow these steps:

1. Select the slice that you want to export.

2. Choose either Window ➪ Object or the keyboard shortcut Ctrl+I (Command+I) to display the Object panel, as shown in Figure 16-22.

**Figure 16-22:** Click the Export button on the Object panel to export a single selected slice.

3. Click the Export button next to the Export settings.

   A restricted Export Preview dialog box with only the Options panel is displayed.

4. Set the desired export options.

5. Click the Export button.

   The Export dialog box appears.

6. Enter the filename and select the directory.

7. Click Save when you're done.

**Caution**   Exporting from the Object inspector on Macintosh systems has a known problem. When exporting a slice in this manner, the extension added to the filename is incorrectly taken from the default export format for the document rather than from the export format chosen for that slice. To work around this problem, you can either rename the file after it is exported or set the default export format to the same as the exported slice before beginning the procedure.

## Exporting Again

The Export Again command is a great time-saver. As its name implies, when File ⇨ Export Again is selected — or the keyboard shortcut, Ctrl+Shift+X (Command+Shift+X) — the current file is re-exported according to the last settings. This feature enables you to make any necessary changes to the file that don't significantly affect the file size or color, and then simply reapply the last settings.

When you invoke the Export Again command, the Export dialog box is displayed, enabling you to rename the exported image or alter the HTML output, if necessary. The Export Preview dialog box is not displayed.

# Summary

Exporting is a key facet of Fireworks. Every graphic created or edited in Fireworks is best optimized for the Web through the export process. Consequently, Fireworks 2 offers a wide variety of export options. Keep the following points in mind as you begin to explore the export options:

✦ Maintaining at least two versions of any file is considered a best practice: one version in the Fireworks PNG format and a second version in whatever format you've exported for use on the Web.

✦ Almost all the export operations are handled through the Export Preview dialog box, which is opened by choosing Window ⇨ Export.

✦ The primary goal of an export operation is to create the best-looking image with the smallest file size. This is called *optimizing* a graphic.

✦ Fireworks offers up to four comparison views of an image being exported, so that you can quickly judge appearance alongside the displayed file size and approximate download time.

✦ The two major formats for the Web — GIF and JPEG — are each best used for different types of images. The GIF format is good for graphics with flat color, for which transparency is important, such as logos. The JPEG format works best with continuous-tone images, such as photographs.

✦ Another format, PNG, is gaining acceptance on the Web, but still doesn't have enough support to warrant widespread usage. The PNG format has many advantages, such as full alpha transparency and gamma correction, to ameliorate image differences on different platforms.

✦ Images can be easily — and precisely — scaled and cropped during the export operation. Fireworks 2 now offers visual cropping right in the Export Preview dialog box.

✦ With Fireworks 2's new advanced color control, you can lock or replace any color in an indexed palette.

✦ Fireworks offers expert export guidance in the form of Wizards: the Export Wizard and the new Export to Size Wizard.

✦ In addition to the standard image export, Fireworks can also export components of an image, such as layers, frames, or slice objects, in several different ways.

In the next chapter, you'll see how to maintain a consistent look and feel for your Web graphics through Fireworks 2 Styles.

✦    ✦    ✦

# Working with Fireworks Styles

**A**lthough not obvious to the beginning designer, Web graphics is as much repetition as it is creation. After you establish a particular look and feel, that theme—the palette, fonts, effects, and more—often is carried through Web page after Web page. Several reasons exist for this repetition:

✦ It's a good design practice, because consistency of approach is one of the fundamental tenets of graphics.

✦ For commercial sites, a consistent look and feel often ties in with the particular marketing message or branding that is being pursued.

✦ With regard to the Internet, repetition of graphic elements aids visitors in the navigation of a Web site: if the link for the home page is always represented by a dark-blue house (or some other graphic), visitors stand a better chance of finding their way around the site— whether they've been there before or not.

However, no matter how many reasons exist declaring that repetition is good, it can also be mind-numbing drudgery. Fireworks 2 has come to every Web designer's rescue with a marvelous time- and work-saver known as *styles*. By using styles, you can easily apply the overall look and feel to any selected object. A single style can contain a variety of user-definable settings, and styles are always available as you move from document to document. Moreover, Macromedia designed styles to be very portable—you can import and export them as a group. This facility enables you, as a working Web designer, to keep different style files for different clients. Styles are, without a doubt, a major boost in Web productivity.

# Understanding Styles

A Fireworks object is potentially composed of several separate elements: a path, a stroke, a fill, and one or more effects. Each of those elements can be broken down further; for example, a stroke consists of a particular stroke type set to a specific color. Duplicating all the individual settings, one by one, that are necessary to establish a custom look would be extremely time-intensive and error-prone. The first version of Fireworks enabled you to copy an object and just paste its attributes. Although this was, and remains, a decent method of duplicating an object's look, it requires that the object always be available to copy.

**New Feature**

Fireworks 2 succeeds in separating the appearance of an object from the object itself, by offering styles. A Fireworks *style* is a collection of attributes — the stroke, fill, effects, and/or font settings — that exist independently of any object. Fireworks 2 provides a very novel, graphical method of maintaining and presenting styles: the Styles panel, shown in Figure 17-1. Acting like a library, the Styles panel allows styles to be imported, exported, deleted, and otherwise managed.

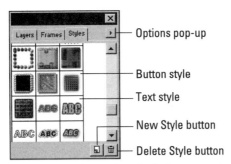

— Options pop-up

— Button style

— Text style

— New Style button

— Delete Style button

**Figure 17-1:** Fireworks 2 includes a standard palette of 52 styles, available through the Styles panel.

Styles are visually divided in the Styles panel into two different icons: button styles and text styles. The only difference between the two is that text styles retain some font information — font name, size, or color — and button styles do not. Button styles are depicted as squares (filled or unfilled, depending on the style settings), and text styles display a styled ABC. Fireworks comes with 40 button styles and 12 text styles built-in, and over 300 new styles are available on the Fireworks CD-ROM.

Even though the Styles panel is divided between the button and text style types, both can be applied to any Fireworks object. In other words, button styles can be applied to text objects, and text styles can be applied to path objects. Any unusable style information (such as font color, with a path object) is disregarded.

**Caution** The term *styles* is an often-used one in computer programs. Unlike word-processing styles or Freehand styles, Fireworks styles maintain no link between the original style and the applied objects.

# Applying Styles

To apply a style, you must first access the Styles panel, which can be opened in any one of several ways:

✦ Choose Window ⇨ Styles

✦ Use the keyboard shortcut, Ctrl+Alt+J (Command+Option+J)

✦ Click the Styles tab, if visible

After the Styles panel is available, actually applying the style is very straightforward: simply select the object and then choose a style from the Styles panel. If you don't like the results, you can select another style. You can even duplicate the object and apply several styles, to select the best option, as shown in Figure 17-2.

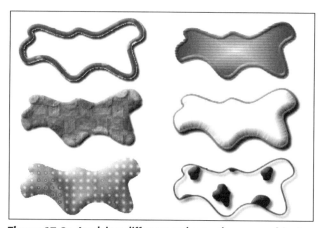

**Figure 17-2:** Applying different styles to the same object gives you a wide range of choices.

**Caution** Applying one style overrides another style only if both styles affect the same settings. However, if the two styles affect different settings, you could have portions of the old style mixed in with the new style on the object. For example, suppose that you apply a style that has a green-to-white gradient fill and a bright-pink Charcoal stroke. If you switch to another style that consists of a dark-blue Oil stroke and a Drop Shadow effect, the gradient fill from the first style will still be present.

After you apply a style, the object remains completely independent of the style, and all the settings on the various panels — Stroke, Fill, Effects, and Text — can be adjusted to customize the object. Regardless of what changes you make to a styled object, the style itself is unaltered.

# Creating New Styles

Although using the standard styles — or any of those included on the Fireworks CD-ROM — is a good way to establish a consistent look and feel quickly, you may not be able to find the exact style that you want. The real power from Fireworks 2 styles comes from the ability to create, save, and use your own styles. The look of any object — the stroke, fill, effect, or text settings — can be converted to a style.

To create a new style, follow these steps:

1. Select the object upon which you want to base the style.

2. Reveal the Styles panel either by choosing Window ⇨ Styles or by using one of the alternative methods.

3. Click the New Styles button at the bottom of the Styles panel.

   The Edit Style dialog box appears, as shown in Figure 17-3.

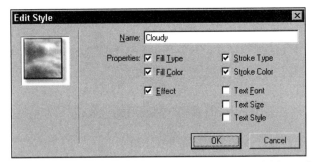

**Figure 17-3:** Create a new style by selecting available options in the Edit Style dialog box.

4. Enter a unique name for your new style in the Name text box.

**Caution**    Fireworks automatically names the new style with a unique numbered name, such as Style 53. You can rename the style by deleting the suggested name and entering your own choice. However, be aware that Fireworks does not check for conflicting names, which means that you could end up with two or more styles with the same name.

5. Select which of the available style settings should be saved with your style. Available styles settings are the following:

- **Fill Type:** Stores the Fill category (Solid, Gradient, Web Dither, or Pattern), the name of the gradient or pattern, the edge settings (including the Amount of Feather, if applicable), and all the texture settings (name, degree, and transparency)

- **Fill Color:** Stores the Fill colors for Solid fills. For Gradient, Web Dither, and Pattern fills, the colors are stored with the Fill Type option

- **Stroke Type:** Stores the category, name of stroke, all stroke stamp information (even if customized through the Edit Stroke command), the edge softness, the stroke size, and the texture settings (name and amount of texture)

- **Stroke Color:** Stores the selection in the current object's Stroke color well

- **Effect:** Stores all the settings for an object's effect, whether single (Inner Bevel, Outer Bevel, Drop Shadow, Glow, or Emboss) or multiple

- **Text Font:** Stores the name of the current font for a text object

- **Text Size:** Stores the size of the current font for a text object

- **Text Style:** Stores the style (bold, italic, and/or underline) for a text object

6. Click OK when you're done.

For all the information that styles are capable of retaining, you should note the following few items that are *not* stored (although you might expect them to be):

- ✦ While a style remembers gradients, Fireworks styles do not retain any gradient settings pertaining to modified Gradient Control handles, accessed through the Paint Bucket tool.

- ✦ None of the Text Style settings store any information on text spacing (kerning, leading, horizontal scale, or baseline shift), text alignment (horizontal, vertical, left, center, right, stretched, or direction), or anti-alias.

You should remember two points when you are creating and applying new styles. First, if a style does not affect a particular setting, that setting is left as is on the selected object. Second, a Stroke, Fill, or Effect set to None is as valid a setting as any other. For example, if the object on which you base your new style does not include a fill, but you've selected Fill Type on the Edit Style dialog box, any object to which this style is applied — whether it has a fill or not — will have the fill removed.

# Managing Styles

Every time that you add a style, it stays available for every document opened in Fireworks. If you really become adept at using styles, you'll quickly begin to have a massive collection of styles — truly too much of a good thing. Fireworks offers several commands, mostly grouped under the Styles panel's Options pop-up menu, for managing your styles and incorporating them into your workflow.

You've seen how you can create a style by selecting the New Style button from the bottom of the Styles panel. Its obvious companion is the Delete Style button right next to it. To remove any unwanted style, select its icon in the Styles panel and choose the Delete Style button.

**Tip**   You can select multiple styles to remove by pressing either Shift, to choose adjacent styles, or Ctrl (Command), to select styles one at a time. One brief note about using Shift: in the Styles panel, Fireworks links adjacent icons by the shortest route between the starting and ending icons. For example, if you want to select two rows of styles plus the first one on the following row, you can't select the first icon in the first row and the first icon in the third row: this selects only the first icons in each row. You have to use Shift to select the first two rows, using the last icon in the second row as your final icon, and then use Ctrl (Command) to select the remaining icon in the third row.

A total of seven commands are available in the Styles panel's Options pop-up menu, shown in Figure 17-4:

**Figure 17-4:** Manage your styles through the Styles panel's Options pop-up commands.

✦ **New Style:** Creates a new style based on the selected object. This command is identical to the New Style button.

✦ **Edit Style:** Opens the Edit Style dialog box, enabling you to select or deselect the setting options.

✦ **Delete Styles:** Removes a selected style or styles.

✦ **Import Styles:** Loads a new set of styles after the currently selected one. Styles must be stored in the Fireworks Styles format.

✦ **Export Styles:** Stores the currently selected style or styles in the Fireworks Styles format.

✦ **Resets Styles:** Reloads the default configuration of styles.

✦ **Large Icons:** Displays the available styles with icons twice as large as normal.

You've seen earlier in this chapter how to create and delete styles; the New Style and Delete Styles commands work identically as their respective buttons. Editing an existing style is also a familiar process. Choose Edit Style, and you are presented with the same options in the Edit Styles dialog box as when you create a new one. Just make any changes, click OK, and your revised style is ready to use.

The Import Styles and Export Styles commands open standard dialog boxes: the Open dialog box for Import Styles, and the Save As dialog box, shown in Figure 17-5, for Export Styles. Both commands initially limit the file type to Fireworks Styles, with a file extension in Windows of .stl. Fireworks Styles files don't have to be stored in a special folder when exported or imported.

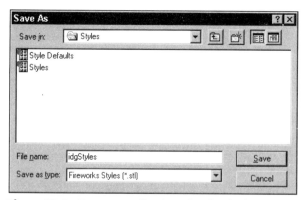

**Figure 17-5:** To save a collection of styles for later use, choose Export Styles from the Styles panel's Options pop-up menu.

**Tip**　　As noted previously, when you import a set of Fireworks Styles, all styles are inserted after the currently selected style. For this reason, I typically find it best to select the last standard style before importing. You also can create a spacer or two — create a style from a plain object with no fill, stroke, or effects. The style icon will appear blank and acts to separate your imported styles from the standard ones.

The final two Styles panel commands, Reset Styles and Large Icons, are fairly self-explanatory. Reset Styles removes all styles currently in the Styles panel and reloads the standard set of Styles in their place. Because this is a fairly drastic measure, Fireworks asks for confirmation before proceeding. Selecting Large Icons displays the style icons at twice their standard size — they enlarge from 36-pixels square to 72. This feature sometimes is useful when trying to differentiate between two similar styles.

# Fireworks Technique: Isolating Patterns and Textures from Styles

A close look at some of the styles that come with Fireworks — both the standards and the extras found on the Fireworks CD-ROM — reveals several new patterns and textures. For example, the last standard style, Style 51, has an intriguing spotted pattern, as shown in Figure 17-6. A quick check of the Fill panel reveals that a new texture, called (appropriately) cow, is in use as part of the style. However, no such file exists in the Textures folder; so, where did it come from? The texture is actually embedded in the style.

**Figure 17-6:** Examining the cow texture

Donna Casey, a Web designer whose work can be seen at www.n8vision.com, uncovered a technique for extracting the embedded textures and patterns that you may find in a style. Why would you do this? You might find that the pattern and/or texture is, to your eye, better when combined with a different stroke or effects setting — or you might want to incorporate just the pattern or texture in an image. Two methods are available to approach this problem. First, you could edit the style, removing all the options except for Fill Type. This is, at best, a partial solution. The pattern/texture is still encased in the other pertinent settings; textures, for example, could be part of a Solid, Pattern, or Gradient Fill. To separate completely the texture or pattern and then save it, follow these steps:

1. Draw a fairly large rectangle or square, approximately 500 × 500 pixels.

   The goal is to make the object large enough so that the pattern clearly repeats.

**2.** From the Styles panel, select the style whose texture or fill you want to isolate.

The style is applied to the object.

**3.** From the Stroke panel, choose None in the Stroke category.

**4.** In the Effect panel, select None in the Effect category.

**5.** To retrieve a texture, make the following changes to the Fill panel:

- Set the Fill category to Solid.

- Set the Fill color to black.

- Set the Amount of Texture to 100%.

**6.** To retrieve a pattern, set the Amount of Texture to 0%.

**7.** Choose the Crop tool from the Toolbox.

**8.** Crop the object to encompass the repeating pattern.

This is, by far, the hardest part; you might take several attempts to get it just right. A good idea is to save the file before you begin to crop the object.

**9.** When you finish cropping, save the file either in the Settings\Patterns or Settings\Textures folder.

**10.** Quit and restart Fireworks.

Your new extricated pattern or texture should now be available to you in the Stroke and Fill panels.

# Summary

Styles are a major production boost, new in Fireworks 2. Using Fireworks Styles, you can add a consistent look and feel to all of your graphics on a client-by-client or even site-by-site basis. Styles are also a significant work-saver — rather than having to add individually all the characteristics that compose a particular graphic, you can add them all with one click of the Styles panel. The main points regarding styles are as follows:

✦ A style, in Fireworks, may contain all the information for reproducing a graphic's stroke, fill, effect, and text settings.

✦ Unlike some other programs, such as Freehand, Fireworks styles do not retain a link or tag to images that use them.

✦ Styles are accessible through the Styles panel.

✦ Any newly created style is available to all documents until the style is removed from the Styles panel.

✦ Styles can be edited, imported, exported, and otherwise managed through the commands found in the Styles panel's Options pop-up menu.

✦ A style can be "reverse engineered" to isolate the pattern or texture used.

In the next chapter, you find out how to update and maintain your graphics in Fireworks 2.

✦    ✦    ✦

# Updating and Maintaining Web Graphics

I'm sure you've heard the expression, "1 percent inspiration and 99 percent perspiration." In my experience, Web graphics is more balanced — half the time you're creating a new work, and the other half you're revising something that you've already done. Updating Web pages is a continual, seemingly never-ending process, and although some of the work involves importing new text, quite often the graphics need to be altered, as well. No product can completely turn such a chore into a joyful, creative pleasure, but at least Fireworks helps you to get the job done in the most efficient manner possible.

Web-graphic maintenance is at the core of Fireworks's "everything editable, all the time" philosophy. When Fireworks first arrived, Web designers everywhere were thrilled with the ease with which changes could be made. Fireworks 2 extends that ease-of-use philosophy to include graphic production. Now, more than ever, Web graphics can be created, edited, and optimized with techniques that simplify your workflow and increase your production. The key to Fireworks productivity is its close ties to the Web. This chapter explores all the production enhancement techniques — from previewing your graphics directly in a browser to optimizing entire folders of images at a time.

# Preview in Browser

It's amazing to me how many so-called Web-graphics programs don't let you easily see your work through its intended medium: the browser. Fireworks 2 allows you to preview in not one, but two browsers at the press of a keyboard shortcut. Not only do you quickly get to see how the browsers are interpreting your graphics, but you can also test any rollovers or other behaviors you may have included in Fireworks.

Web designers, like most Internet users, tend to work with a particular version of Navigator or Internet Explorer most of the time. But, unlike ordinary Web surfers, Web designers must be able to view work under various conditions, to ensure consistency across platforms and browser versions. As of this writing, Netscape and Microsoft share the browser market fairly evenly. One company is usually ahead of the other in terms of new versions — and with them, new features — so the ability to preview in more than one browser is essential.

**New Feature**

Fireworks 2 has met the Web designer's browser needs head-on by permitting work to be previewed in both a primary and secondary browser. This makes quickly viewing your graphics — and even comparing their appearance in two different browsers — very straightforward. I even use the Preview in Browser feature to display different versions of the same graphic side by side, without having to make additional copies in Fireworks.

Before you can use the Preview in Browser feature, you have to tell Fireworks which two browsers you'd like to use. Although you don't *have* to define both a primary and a secondary browser, it's a good idea (if you have two browsers on your system). To set the browsers, follow these steps:

1. Choose File ➪ Preview in Browser ➪ Set Primary (F12) Browser.

   The Locate Browser dialog box appears, as shown in Figure 18-1.

2. In the Locate Browser dialog box, navigate to the browser directory to locate the primary program (also known as the *executable*) for the desired browser.

   Although the location of your browser depends entirely on its installation, by default the browsers are located as follows:

   - **Netscape Navigator (netscape.exe):** Found in the C:\Program Files\Netscape\Programs\ folder on Windows systems, and in the *System Disk*: Applications: Netscape Communicator: Netscape Communicator on Macintosh systems.

   - **Internet Explorer (Iexplore.exe):** Found in the C:\Program Files\ Internet Explorer folder on Windows systems, and in the *System Disk*: Applications: Microsoft Internet Applications: Internet Explorer on Macintosh systems.

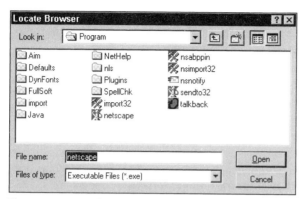

**Figure 18-1:** Declare your primary and secondary browsers through the Locate Browser dialog box.

3. Click Open after you locate the browser.

4. To define the secondary browser, choose File ➪ Preview in Browser ➪ Set Secondary (Shift+F12) Browser and repeat Steps 2 and 3.

After you define your browsers, they're immediately available for use. To view a graphic in a browser, select it and then choose File ➪ Preview in Browser ➪ Preview in *yourBrowser* (where *yourBrowser* is the filename of the browser executable). I heartily recommend memorizing the keyboard shortcuts for this command: to preview in your primary browser, press F12; to preview in your secondary browser, press Shift+F12.

**Caution**      Each time you preview a graphic, a new browser window opens. With Navigator, another browser window simply opens within the currently running Navigator program; however, Internet Explorer starts a whole new copy of the program. If you have numerous open Internet Explorer copies running, your system resources could be heavily taxed. Whenever possible, always close the browser before previewing again.

Working with a client who depends on a different browser or browser version than the one you normally use isn't an unusual circumstance. Thus, I find that keeping as many older versions of browsers around as possible is very helpful. Netscape allows you to have multiple versions of its browser, as does Microsoft, starting with Internet Explorer 5. However, to take advantage of Microsoft's feature, you have to have Internet Explorer 4 already on your system and select the multiple browser option during installation of Internet Explorer 5.

# Managing Links with the URL Manager

To me, links are the lifeblood of the Web. Without the ability to jump from one section, page, or site to another, the Internet would be a very linear medium — and nowhere near as popular. Before Fireworks, the normal course of Web graphics production kept the images and the links completely separate until the final Web page was assembled. However, because Fireworks extends its graphic capabilities into HTML and JavaScript code through behaviors and hotspots, links can actually be incorporated during the creation phase.

A link is more technically known as a URL (generally pronounced as if it were spelled out, U-R-L). URL is short for *Uniform Resource Locator* and is best thought of as the Web's address system. Every Web page on the Internet has a URL. Web design deals with two different kinds of URLs: absolute and relative. An *absolute URL* is the exact address that allows a Web page to be accessed from anywhere on the Internet, such as `http://www.idest.com/fireworks/index.htm#book`.

In this example, the URL is divided into five main parts:

✦ **Method:** The method specifies the protocol used to address the server. Web servers use HTTP (Hypertext Transport Protocol). Other methods include FTP (File Transfer Protocol), for transmitting files; News, for accessing newsgroup servers; and Mailto, for sending e-mail.

✦ **Domain:** The domain name (in this example, `www.idest.com`) is registered with an Internet authority, such as Network Solutions, so that the server to which the domain name refers can be found. The IP (Internet Protocol) number (for example, 199.227.52.143) can be used in place of a domain name.

✦ **Path:** Depending on exactly where on the server the Web page is located, the path can be a single folder, as it is in this example (*fireworks*), or many folders, in which case each folder is separated by a forward slash, /.

✦ **Page:** The name of the Web page itself is the name under which it is stored — in the example it's *index.htm*. The file extension used depends on the type of server and the authoring system. Most typically, Web pages end in either .html or .htm; however, you'll also see extensions such as .shtml, .asp, .cfm, and .taf, just to mention a few.

✦ **Named anchor:** A portion of the page marked with an HTML tag, called an *anchor* (in the example URL it's *#book*). With named anchors, you can quickly move from one section of a long document to another, all on a single page.

All but the target portion is mandatory for an absolute URL. The other type of URL, a *relative URL*, however, can use as little as just the page, or even just the named anchor. Whatever the link is, its location is relative to the current page. For example, if you need to link to another Web page in the same folder as the current one, the link would look something like this example:

```
contact.html
```

On the other hand, if you need to link to a page that is stored in a subfolder of the current page, the relative link would resemble the following:

```
old_news/pr98.htm
```

The more that your site structure is developed — blank Web pages and empty folders created — before working in Fireworks, the more you can take advantage of the program's URL tools, including the new URL Manager.

## Accessing the URL History list

In Fireworks, links are attached to either of the two types of Web object: a hotspot or a slice. You can assign a link to a selected Web object either through the Object panel or the URL Manager. The Object panel, shown in Figure 18-2, allows you to assign a link in one of two ways:

✦ Enter it directly into the Current URL text box.

**Caution**   If you choose to type your new link into the Current URL text box, double-check your text to avoid any mistakes. Computers are very literal when it comes to URLs, and thus every element — names, punctuation, and even case (upper- or lower-case) on some servers — must match.

✦ Select it from the Current URL option list.

Current URL text box

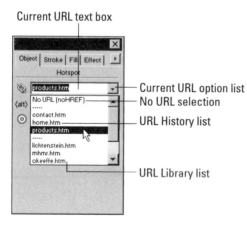

**Figure 18-2:** Enter a new URL or select one from the Current URL option list on the Object panel.

Current URL option list
No URL selection
URL History list
URL Library list

The Current URL option list is divided into three parts: the No URL selection, the URL History list, and the URL Library list. Choose the No URL (noHREF) selection when your slice or hotspot does not have a link assigned; this is the default selection for Web objects. The URL History is a list of links that have been added to the current document. Every time that you manually enter a new link in the Current URL text box, it is stored as part of the URL History.

**Tip**   Links are maintained in the URL History for a document only if they are actually assigned to a Web object in that document. For example, if you assign a link to a hotspot and then later delete that hotspot, the link in the URL History list is also deleted.

If your URL History list is filled with links that are no longer used, a command that is available through the URL Manager Options pop-up menu, Clear History, can remove all but the links actually used in the document. Another command, Add History to Library, can move your document links so that they can be retrieved independently of the document.

## Adding URLs to the URL Library

The URL Library represents a more permanent list of links than those found in the URL History. URL Libraries can be stored, edited, and reloaded to work with any graphic. This facility makes building all the graphics involving rollovers and image maps — anything that needs a URL — far easier on the site level. From a Web graphics production perspective, a different URL Library can be maintained for each client, which further simplifies your workflow.

Although you can access what's in the URL Library from the Object panel for a selected Web object, all management of the Library is handled through the URL Manager, shown in Figure 18-3. To open the URL Manager, choose Window ⇨ URL Manager or press the keyboard shortcut, Ctrl+Alt+U (Command+Option+U). Alternatively, if the tab for the URL Manager is showing, clicking it brings the panel forward.

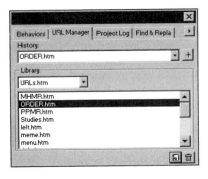

**Figure 18-3:** Use the URL Manager to build, access, and store URL Libraries.

The URL Library is stored in an HTML file format used for browser bookmark files; the default Library is called URLs.htm. However, you can add URLs to the Library in several ways, listed next, almost all of which are commands available in the Options pop-up menu, shown in Figure 18-4:

✦ **Add History to Library:** Allows you to incorporate URLs from the temporary, document-oriented History feature to the more permanent, cross-document Library feature

✦ **Add URL:** Adds a single URL directly to the Library

✦ **Import URLs:** Inserts URLs found within any HTML file, including Bookmark pages

✦ **Add to Library button:** Adds the URL in the History text box of the URL Manager to the Library

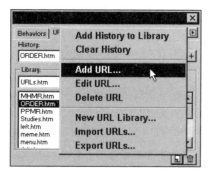

**Figure 18-4:** Most of the URL Library commands are accessible through the URL Manager's Options pop-up menu.

Combining the document's URL History with the current URL Library is a one-step process — just choose the Add History to Library command from the Options pop-up menu. Fireworks automatically integrates the two lists of links, alphabetically. If any links appear in both lists, the duplicates are eliminated.

To add a single URL to the Library, choose the Add URL command from the Options pop-up menu. The New URL dialog box appears, as shown in Figure 18-5. Enter the new link directly in the large text area and click OK when you're done. The new link is added to the Library list.

**Tip**

You can also click the New URL button located at the bottom of the URL Manager to add a new link.

The Import URLs command is a wonderful work-saver and is extremely flexible. Because you can import the links from any HTML file, you can quickly bring in all the links from a site just by loading a Web site's home page. Moreover, because Netscape Navigator Bookmark files are just a special type of HTML page, Fireworks can import these, as well.

To import links from an HTML page, follow these steps:

1. From the Options pop-up menu of the URL Manager, choose Import URLs.

   The standard Open dialog box appears.

2. Locate the HTML page containing the links you want to incorporate into a Library; click Open after you find it.

   Any links, relative or absolute, found on the selected HTML page are integrated with the current URL Library.

As you'll see in the next section, you can also create, edit, delete, store, and load URL Libraries through the URL Manager.

## Managing URL Libraries

URL Libraries are extremely flexible in Fireworks 2. New Libraries can be created with a single command and existing Libraries can be edited, deleted, loaded, or stored.

To edit an existing URL in the Library, follow these steps:

1. From the URL Manager's Options pop-up menu, choose Edit URL.

   The Edit URL dialog box, shown in Figure 18-5, appears.

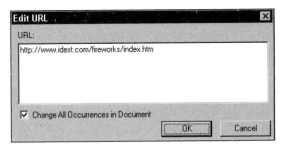

**Figure 18-5:** Update your URL Library links through the Edit URL command.

2. Enter the new URL in the text area and click OK.

   The URL is modified in the Library.

3. To update any existing links in the current graphic, select the Change All Occurrences in Document option.

**Caution**    There's a known problem with the Change All Occurrences in Document option not functioning correctly. To work around this problem, select all Web objects using the edited URL and select the URL from the Library.

The following are the two ways to remove a URL from the Library:

✦ Select the unwanted URL and then click the Delete URL button in the lower-right corner of the URL Manager.

✦ Select the URL and then select Delete URL from the Options pop-up menu.

By default, Fireworks starts with one URL Library, URLs.htm. You can add others by following these steps:

1. Choose the New URL Library command from the Options pop-up menu of the URL Manager.

   The New URL Library dialog box, shown in Figure 18-6, appears.

**Figure 18-6:** Organize a new Library for each client through the New URL Library command.

2. Enter a unique name for the new library.

   If you don't include an .htm or .html file extension, Fireworks automatically appends one.

Fireworks creates a new file in the Settings/URL Libraries folder. This file is updated when Fireworks closes; you don't need to save your URL Library in a separate operation.

 **Note**    While Fireworks makes creating a new Library a breeze, removing an unwanted Library is a little more hands-on. No command is available to delete a Library, so you have to delete the HTML file through a file manager or other means. The deleted Library will disappear from the URL Manager's list when Fireworks is restarted.

If Fireworks "automagically" stores your Libraries each time, why would you need an Export command? The Export URLs command, found in the Options pop-up menu, enables you to save the URL Library as an HTML file in another directory. The HTML file, as shown in Figure 18-7, is a very straightforward list of links. If your URL Library is complete, you could use the exported Library file as the basis for a site map or other navigational aid.

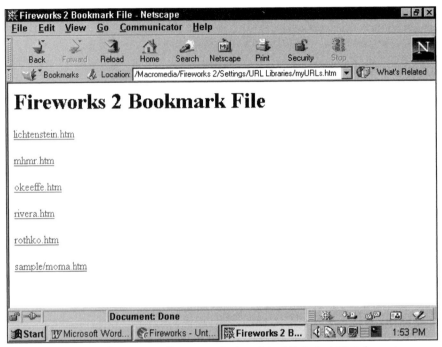

**Figure 18-7:** Exporting a URL Library results in a list of links in HTML format.

# Updating Graphics with Find & Replace

Fireworks has always been great about allowing you to alter any aspect of your graphic at any time. But, before Fireworks 2, that still meant you had to make every change by hand. Graphics for a Web site often have a great deal of overlap — a consistent color scheme, the same typeface, even the same URLs embedded in image maps and buttons. Replacing a misspelled client name in one graphic is one thing, replacing them in all the graphics, site-wide, is another.

**New Feature**    Fireworks 2 offers a robust Find & Replace feature that automates the onerous chore of modifying text, fonts, colors, and URLs. Through the new Find & Replace panel, you can direct your updates to the current selection, frame, document, or to a selection of documents. The Find & Replace options for text and URLs include a powerful wildcard capability known as Regular Expressions. Moreover, you can track your changes through Fireworks 2's new Project Log. Web graphics maintenance just got a whole lot easier.

Outside of batch processing and Scriptlets, all automated modifications in Fireworks are handled through the Find & Replace panel, shown in Figure 18-8, which displays different options depending on which attribute is being altered. The four attributes and their options are the following:

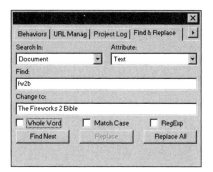

**Figure 18-8:** Use the Find & Replace panel to automate changes to text, fonts, URLs, and even color.

✦ **Text:** Any text object in a Fireworks file can be modified under Find & Replace. The text search can include anything from a single character to full sentences. Options include Whole Word, which ensures that the text to be found is not within another word; Match Case, which seeks out the exact text entered and replaces it verbatim; and RegExp, a system of wildcard matching more fully known as Regular Expressions, discussed in detail later in this chapter.

✦ **Font:** Every text object must use a particular font with a set style (or lack of one), in a particular size. Fireworks's Find & Replace feature enables you to update all of these characteristics, either separately or combined. You can even search for a font in a range of sizes and convert them all to one size.

✦ **Color:** In a Fireworks object, color is just another attribute that can be searched for and replaced, if necessary. You can find and replace a specific color from the pop-up color picker displaying the current swatch set (which can be selected in the Mixer panel) or from any system color picker. You can also use the Eyedropper tool to sample a color. Color can be altered in strokes, fills, effects, strokes and fills, or all four.

**Caution**     Some restrictions apply to replacing color by using the Find & Replace command. Bitmap or text objects can't be accessed. You can, however, replace the colors of any part of a graphic by using the Edit Color command in the Export Preview dialog box.

✦ **URL:** The URL Find & Replace panel is similar to the one for text. Any link can be altered in any way; you can even use the Find & Replace feature to remove all links. The Whole Word, Match Case, and RegExp options are available for the URL attribute just as they are for the Text attribute of Find & Replace.

Regardless of the specific attribute, with each Find & Replace operation, you have the option of making changes on a case-by-case basis or all at once. Click Find Next to locate the next item fulfilling the search criteria, and then click either Replace, to make a change to the selected item, or Find Next, to locate the next item without making a change. You can also click Replace All at any time to make the alterations within your search scope to all matches in the document(s).

**Tip**

What if you're running a Find & Replace operation and you make a mistake, such as clicking Replace All instead of Replace? If you're working within a single document, you can use Edit ➪ Undo to reverse all the changes and start over. Undo has no effect on Find & Replace actions applied to multiple files.

With all attributes, the scope of the search is defined by the value set in the Search In option list, which includes the following possible options:

✦ **Selection:** You can select any appropriate object (or objects), to narrow a search.

✦ **Frame:** Limits the search to the current frame of the active document.

✦ **Document:** Allows the search to be applied to any part of the current document.

✦ **Project Log:** Limits the search to files listed in the Project Log. Use of the Project Log is covered in detail later in this chapter.

✦ **Files:** Opens Fireworks Find & Replace operations to any accessible file. Replacements can be made globally or on a file-by-file basis. Selecting the Files option displays the Open Multiple dialog box, in which files are added to the selection list either individually or by the folder.

**Tip**

If you need to adjust the selected files for a Multi-File Find & Replace operation, getting the Open Multiple dialog box to reappear involves a small trick. Temporarily choose a different Search In option, such as Document or Frame, and then select Files again. The Open Multiple dialog box will reopen.

While all the Search In options have their place, Fireworks's Multi-File capability really gives the Find & Replace feature its power. Naturally, such increased power also brings increased risk for making a mistake. To offset that risk, Fireworks 2 offers two different backup options. To set the backup options, choose Replace Options from the Options pop-up menu on the Find & Replace panel. The Replace Options dialog box (Figure 18-9) appears. If the first option, Save and Close Files, is selected, Fireworks closes each file after it makes a replacement; if the option is not selected, the files are left open. The Backup Original Files drop-down list box includes three choices:

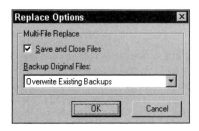

**Figure 18-9:** Choose your backup options from the Replace Options dialog box.

✦ **No Backups:** The source files are overwritten and no backups are saved.

✦ **Overwrite Existing Backups:** The source files are moved to a subfolder called Original Files, and retain their original names; copies of the original files, with the changes, are saved in the original folder. If additional changes are applied to these copies, they are copied to the Original Files folder, overwriting the first set of source files.

✦ **Incremental Backups:** If you don't want to risk losing any changes, choose this option, which also moves the source files to the Original Files subfolder, but each time that a change is made to the same file, the new source file is stored as well. To keep each of the files, they are renamed incrementally. For example, the first time a file named Star.png is changed, the source file is saved in the Original File subfolder as Star.png and the modified file is saved with the same name in the originating folder. The next time a change is applied to this new source file, it is stored in the Original File subfolder as Star.png and the first Star.png is renamed Star-1.png. The most recent version always retains the original name, and the oldest version ends with the highest number.

You could use the Incremental Backups option as a type of version control, but the downside is that this choice stores *all* the files. As a personal preference, I tend to use the Overwrite Existing Backups option, which allows me to experiment with graphics without fear of losing my last major revision, but does not create an overabundance of files.

## Searching and replacing text

I recently had a client come to me with every Web designer's major nightmare — a name change. Not only did every logo need to be altered, but much of the Web site incorporated the name as a graphic background. I was faced with days upon days of pure drudgery — until I realized with unbridled joy that this was the first site I built with Fireworks. Using Fireworks 2's advanced Find & Replace feature, I was able to make the revisions in a few short hours, much of the time spent amazed at how quickly the job was getting done.

To find and replace text, follow these steps:

1. If the Find & Replace panel is not showing, choose Window ➪ Find & Replace or, if visible, click its tab to bring the panel forward.

2. Choose the scope of the search operation by selecting one of the choices from the Search In option list.

3. Make sure that the Attribute selection is set to Text.

4. Enter in the Find text box the text to be found.

5. If you intend to change the text, enter its replacement in the Change To text box.

6. Select any options desired: Whole Word, Match Case, or RegExp.

7. To make changes on a case-by-case basis, first click Find Next and then click either Replace, to change the text, or Find Next again, to move to the next matched text.

8. To change all the text at once, click Replace All.

If no changes are made, Fireworks reports that the search is complete. Otherwise, Fireworks informs you of how many occurrences were changed.

Although the Find & Replace Text operation may be the most straightforward of all the attributes, you still need to be aware of some issues:

✦ Text objects do not automatically expand horizontally to make room for new words; if necessary, the text object automatically expands vertically. You may have to adjust the width of the text object after a Find & Replace operation.

✦ You can alter text (as well as font and URLs) in other vector-based file formats, such as Freehand, Illustrator, and CorelDRAW. However, all modified files are saved in Fireworks format.

✦ During Multi-File Find & Replace operations, if one of the selected documents is open in Fireworks, the document must be activated before any changes can be made.

## Searching with regular expressions

Fireworks 2 seriously enhances the Find & Replace engine with the addition of the RegExp, or Regular Expressions, option. I've referred to Regular Expressions as being similar to wildcards in other programs, but the Fireworks capabilities are really far, far more extensive.

*Regular Expressions* is best described as a text pattern-matching system. If you can identify any pattern in your text, you can manipulate it with Regular Expressions. For example, suppose that you're building a navigation bar in which the buttons are all contact names that are listed in a *Lastname, Firstname* format. With Regular Expressions, you could match the pattern and reformat the entire list, placing the Firstname before the Lastname, without the comma — all in one Find & Replace operation.

You can apply Regular Expressions to either the text or URL attributes by selecting the RegExp option. When you enable this option, Fireworks processes the text entered in both the Find and Change To text boxes differently, looking for special key characters, such as the backslash and asterisk.

The most basic Regular Expression is the text itself. If you enable the RegExp option and then enter "th" in the Find What text box, Fireworks will locate every example of "th" in the text and/or source. Although this capability by itself has little use, it's important to remember this functionality as you begin to build your patterns.

### Wildcard characters

Initially, it's helpful to be able to use what traditionally are known as *wildcards* — characters that match different types of characters. The wildcards in Regular Expressions represent single characters, as described in Table 18-1. In other words, no single Regular Expression represents all the characters, like the asterisk does when used in PC file searches (such as *.*). However, such a condition can be represented with a slightly more complex Regular Expression (described later in this section).

### Table 18-1
### Regular Expressions Wildcard Characters

| Character | Matches | Example |
|---|---|---|
| . | Any single character | **w.d** matches **wid**e but not world. |
| \w | Any alphanumeric character, including the underscore | **w\wd** matches **wid**e and **world**. |
| \W | Any nonalphanumeric character | **jboy\Widest.com** matches `jboy@idest.com`. |
| \d | Any numeric character, 0-9 | **y\dk** matches **Y2K**. |
| \D | Any nonnumeric character | **\D2\D** matches **Y2K** and **H$_2$0**. |
| \s | Any whitespace character, including space, tab, form feed, or line feed | **\smedia** matches **media** but not Macromedia. |
| \S | Any non-whitespace character | **\Smedia** matches Macro**media** but not media. |

**Caution**     Be careful with the \S wildcard. In Fireworks, it actually matches one more character than it should; for instance \Sworks actually matches Fir**eworks** instead of just Fire**works**.

The backslash character, \, is used to escape special characters so that they can be included in a search. For example, if you want to look for an asterisk, you need to specify it like this: \*. Likewise, when trying to find the backslash character, precede it with another backslash character: \\.

### Matching character positions and repeating characters

With Regular Expressions, you not only can match the type of character, but also match its position in the text. This feature enables you to perform operations on characters at the beginning, end, or middle of the word or line. Using Regular Expressions also enables you to find instances in which a character is repeated either an unspecified or specified number of times. Combined, these features broaden the scope of the patterns that can be found.

Table 18-2 details the options available for matching by text placement and character repetition.

| | Table 18-2 Regular Expressions Character Positions and Repeating Characters | |
|---|---|---|
| *Character* | *Matches* | *Example* |
| ^ | Beginning of a line | **^c** matches "**C**all me Ishmael". |
| $ | End of a line | **d$** matches the final *d* in "Be afraid. Be very afrai**d**". |
| \b | A word boundary, such as a space or carriage return | **\btext** matches **text**book but not SimpleText. |
| \B | A nonword boundary inside a word | **\Btext** matches Simple**Text** but not textbook. |
| * | The preceding character zero or more times | **b\*c** matches **BB**C and **c**old. |
| + | The preceding character one or more times | **b+c** matches **BB**C but not cold. |
| ? | The preceding character zero or one time | **st?un** matches **stun** and **sun** but not strung. |
| {n} | Exactly *n* instances of the preceding character | **e{2}** matches r**ee**d and each pair of two *e*'s in Ai**ee**eeeee!, but nothing in Fireworks. |
| {n,m} | At least *n* and at most *m* instances of the preceding character | **C{2,4}** matches #**CC**00FF and #**CCCC**00, but not the full string #CCCCCC. |

## Matching character ranges

Beyond single characters or repetitions of single characters, Regular Expressions incorporates the ability to find or exclude ranges of characters. This feature is particularly useful when you're working with groups of names or titles. Ranges are specified in *set brackets*. A match is made when any one of the characters within the set brackets is found, not necessarily all of the characters.

Table 18-3 describes how to match character ranges with Regular Expressions.

### Table 18-3
### Regular Expressions Character Ranges

| Character | Matches | Example |
|---|---|---|
| [abc] | Any one of the characters a, b, or c | **[lmrt]** matches the *l* and *ms* in **lemm**ings and the *r*'s and *t* in **r**oad**tr**ip. |
| [^abc] | Any character except a, b, or c | **[^etc]** matches each of the letters in **GIFs**, but not etc in the phrase "GIFs etc". |
| [a-z] | Any character in the range from a to z | **[l-p]** matches *l* and *o* in **lo**wery and *m, n, o,* and *p* in **p**oint**m**an. |
| x\|y | Either x or y | **boy\|girl** matches both **boy** and **girl**. |

## Using grouping with regular expressions

Grouping is perhaps the single most powerful concept in Regular Expressions. With it, any matched text pattern is easily manipulated—for example, a list of names like this:

```
Schmidt, John Jacob Jingleheimer
Kirk, James T.
Fishman, Cara
```

could be rearranged so that the last name comes last and the comma is removed, like this:

```
John Jacob Jingleheimer Schmidt
James T. Kirk
Cara Fishman
```

Grouping is handled primarily with parentheses. To indicate a group, enclose it in parentheses in the Find text field. Regular Expressions can manage up to nine grouped patterns. Each grouped patterned is designated by a dollar sign ($) in front of a number, (1 to 9) in the Change To text field, like this: $3.

To switch the series of names as previously described, enter the following in the Find text box:

```
(\w+),\s(.+)
```

In Regular Expressions speak, this translates into "(Pattern 1 matches any alphanumeric character, one or more times) followed by a comma, a space, and (Pattern 2 matches any character—including whitespaces—one or more times)." In the Change To text field, enter

```
$2 $1
```

This configuration places the second matching pattern before the first, with just a space in between.

**Caution** Remember that the dollar sign is also used after a character or pattern to indicate the last character in a line.

Table 18-4 shows how Regular Expressions uses grouping.

| | Table 18-4 | |
|---|---|---|
| | **Regular Expressions Grouping** | |
| **Character** | **Matches** | **Example** |
| (p) | Any pattern p | (\d).(\d) matches two patterns, the first before a period and the second after a period, such as in a filename with an extension. |
| $1, $2...$9 | The nth pattern noted with parentheses | The replacement pattern **$1's extension is ".$2"** would manipulate the pattern described in the preceding example so that Chapter07.txt and Image12.gif would become **Chapter07's extension is .txt** and **Image12's extension is .gif**. |

## Altering font characteristics

Choosing the Font attribute in the Find & Replace panel enables you to alter any or all of three different font characteristics:

✦ **Font name:** Selects the name of the typeface to be searched and/or replaced

✦ **Style:** Determines the style of the typeface: plain, bold, italic, underline, or any combination of these styles, such as bold italic

✦ **Size:** Searches a range of font sizes and, optionally, sets the text to a specific font size

The real power of the Font attribute is that you can search on one criteria, such as font size, and if a match exists, you can change another criteria, such as font name. This flexibility enables you to, for example, search all graphics in a site and, if the font size is between 8 and 10, change the font from Eras Light to Eras Medium, without changing the original size.

To change the font characteristic with Find & Replace, follow these steps:

**1.** If the Find & Replace panel is not showing, choose Window ➪ Find & Replace or, if visible, click its tab to bring the panel forward.

**2.** Choose the scope of the search operation by selecting one of the choices from the Search In option list.

**3.** From the Attribute option list, select Font.

The Find & Replace panel displays the Font options, as shown in Figure 18-10.

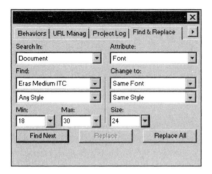

**Figure 18-10:** Change font size, typeface, or style when the Font attribute is selected from the Find & Replace panel.

**4.** To search for a specific typeface, choose one of the available fonts from the upper Find option list; to leave the font search criteria open, select Any Font.

**5.** To change to a specific typeface, choose one of the available fonts from the upper Change To option list; to avoid replacing the font, select Same Font.

**6.** To search for a specific font style, choose an option from the lower Find option list; to leave the style criteria open, select Any Style.

**7.** To change to a specific font style, choose an option from the lower Change To option list; to avoid replacing the style, select Same Style.

**8.** To search for a specific range of font sizes, set the minimum point size in the Min text box and the maximum point size in the Max text box; to search for a single point size, set the Min and Max text boxes to the same value.

The Min and Max sliders can also be used.

**9.** To change to a specific font size, enter a value in the Size text box or use the slider to select a value.

**10.** Click the Find Next and Replace buttons to make changes on a case-by-case basis, or click the Replace All button to make global changes.

## Changing colors throughout a site

A color can be as important to a brand as a logo — for example, IBM blue. Web graphics often use a specific color scheme to make a marketing point or to assist with navigation. Previously, updating graphics to incorporate a color change could be an extraordinarily tedious chore. In Fireworks 2, you can search for and replace colors just as easily as you can text — and, in some cases, even easier.

Fireworks applies color to its path objects via three primary components: strokes, fills, and effects. When the Color attribute is selected in the Find & Replace panel, you can change colors associated with any single one of these components, associated with both strokes and fills, or associated with all four. To search and replace a color, follow these steps:

1. If the Find & Replace panel is not showing, choose Window ➪ Find & Replace or, if visible, click its tab to bring the panel forward.

2. Choose the scope of the search operation by selecting one of the choices from the Search In option list.

3. From the Attribute option list, select Color.

   The Find & Replace panel displays the Color options, as shown in Figure 18-11.

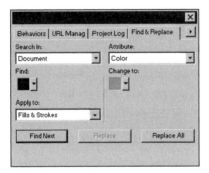

**Figure 18-11:** Update all the colors across a site with the Find & Replace panel's Color attribute.

4. In the Find pop-up color picker, select the color to search for.

   You can select one of the available swatches, use the Eyedropper tool, or select the Palette icon to open the system color pickers.

5. From the Apply To option list, set which component of Fireworks the search should be limited to.

6. In the Change To pop-up color picker, select the color to replace the color being searched for.

7. Click the Find Next and Replace buttons to make changes on a case-by-case basis, or click the Replace All button to make global changes.

## Updating URLs

After you spend any amount of time designing for the Web, you'll appreciate how active the Web is. Sites are constantly in motion, with new pages being added and old ones deleted or moved. Because Fireworks graphics are tied so directly to the

Web through the URLs embedded in hotspots and slices that Fireworks creates, you need a way to modify the links quickly, if necessary. The URL attribute of the Find & Replace panel fulfills that need.

The URL attribute works much the same way that the Text attribute does — in fact, the interfaces for the two are identical, as you can see in Figure 18-12. A link to be searched for is entered in the Find text box and the new link is entered in the Change To text box. The same three options (Whole Word, Match Case, and RegExp) apply. With URLs, however, a whole word is not designated by a space, but rather by a separator — either a period, a forward slash, or a colon.

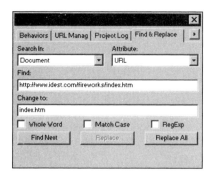

**Figure 18-12:** Update your links with the URL attribute of the Find & Replace panel.

To search and replace links embedded in Fireworks graphics, follow these steps:

1. If the Find & Replace panel is not showing, choose Window ⇨ Find & Replace or, if visible, click its tab to bring the panel forward.

2. Choose the scope of the search operation by selecting one of the choices from the Search In option list.

3. From the Attribute option list, select URL.

   The Find & Replace panel displays the URL options.

4. Enter the link to be found in the Find text box.

5. If you intend to change the link, enter its replacement in the Change To text box.

6. Select any options desired: Whole Word, Match Case, or RegExp.

7. To make changes on a case-by-case basis, first click Find Next and then click either Replace, to change the link, or Find Next again, to move to the next matched URL.

8. To change all the URLs at once, click Replace All.

As noted earlier in the chapter, the URL attribute can take advantage of Fireworks's new Regular Expressions features by selecting the RegExp option. The pattern-matching features of Regular Expressions goes far beyond any simple wildcard character. For example, suppose that you have to convert from absolute to relative an entire site's worth of links inside of graphics, where all the links are within the same folder. This would require changing files from `http://www.idest.com/fireworks/main.htm` to just `main.htm`. Moreover, suppose that you have links to files from both Windows and Macintosh designers, so that some files end in `.htm` and others in `.html`. With Fireworks's RegExp option enabled, here's what you'd enter in the Find text box:

```
(.+)/(\b.*\.html?)
```

which, translated from Regular Expressions language, means "(Pattern 1 contains all characters) before a forward slash and (Pattern 2, which can be any single word followed by a period and then either htm or html)."

To change these pattern to just the filename, enter **$2** by itself into the Change To text box. This returns just the results of pattern 2, without any other characters.

# Working with the Project Log

One of the dangers of working with a find-and-replace feature as powerful as Fireworks's Find & Replace is that unwanted changes can be made inadvertently and unknowingly. This is especially true when the Multi-File Search & Replace option is used — Fireworks can open, modify, and close a file so quickly that you won't know what happened. You won't know, that is, unless you enable the Project Log option to track all changes.

**New Feature**

With the Project Log option turned on, all Multi File changes are noted. The Project Log, shown in Figure 18-13, lists the filename, the frame in which the change was made, and the date and time the modification took place. Moreover, you can immediately check the alteration by double-clicking the filename in the Project Log to open the file in Fireworks.

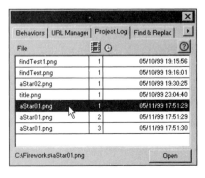

**Figure 18-13:** Keep track of all your Multi-File Find & Replace operations through the Project Log.

You enable the Project Log to note search-and-replace changes by selecting the Add Files to Project Log command found in the Options pop-up menu of the Find & Replace panel. Once selected, any file altered when the search scope is set to Files is listed by name, frame number, and date and time. To verify a change — or to reverse it — open the file from the Project Log by double-clicking its name or selecting it and then clicking the Open button.

The Project Log Options pop-up menu offers some additional functionality. The four commands are as follows:

✦ **Export Again:** Because all Find & Replace operations are conducted only on Fireworks format files, after you alter a file, you usually need to re-export it. The Export Again command repeats the last export setting and overwrites the previously exported file.

✦ **Add Files to Log:** You don't have run a Find & Replace procedure on a file to include it in the Project Log. By selecting the Add Files to Log command, you can select which additional files are listed in the Project Log. This is a very handy way of having your working files close at hand, but not opened until they're necessary.

✦ **Clear Selection:** Removes the currently selected listing from the Project Log.

✦ **Clear All:** Removes all entries from the Project Log.

The Project Log has yet another use: all files or selected files in the Project Log can be processed together with Fireworks Batch Processing feature, discussed in the next section.

 **Tip**    To get a separate hard copy of the Project Log, detailing all the changes in a session, open the Project_Log.htm file found in the Fireworks Settings folder and then print the page from your browser. The Project_Log.htm file is updated with every change.

# Batch Processing Graphics Files

The unfortunate truth is that producing graphics for the Web involves about as much mindless repetition as it does creative expression. The more you can automate the processes, the more time you'll have to experiment and create. Fireworks 2 has seriously enhanced its batch-processing capabilities, making it easier than ever to optimize, scale, and export large numbers of images.

The Batch Process dialog box, shown in Figure 18-14, is the automation control center.

**Figure 18-14:** Select your automation options from the Batch Process dialog box.

## Basic procedure

The basic procedure for running an automated session goes like this:

1. Choose File ➪ Batch Process to open the Batch Process dialog box.

2. Determine which files are to be affected by choosing from the Files to Process option list:

    • **Current Open Files:** All the files currently open in Fireworks, whether active or not, are processed.

    • **Project Log (All Files):** All the files listed in the Project Log, whether open or not, are processed.

    • **Project Log (Selected Files):** Only the selected files in the Project Log are processed. Multiple individual files can be selected by Ctrl+clicking (Command+clicking), and a range of files can be selected by Shift+clicking.

    • **Custom:** A selection of files chosen through the Open Multiple dialog box is processed. The Custom option can also be selected by clicking the ellipsis (...) button next to the Files to Process option list.

3. If you want a Find & Replace operation to be part of the batch process, click the Find & Replace ellipsis (...) button.

    This opens the Batch Replace dialog box (Figure 18-15), with options similar to the Find & Replace panel. Selecting the Update Project Log option adds to the Project Log any files that are processed.

4. If you want to include an Export operation, click the Export ellipsis (...) button, which displays the Batch Export dialog box (Figure 18-16), with the following options:

    • Select a preset setting from the Export Settings drop-down list or click the ellipsis button to access the Export Preview dialog box, which offers additional Export options.

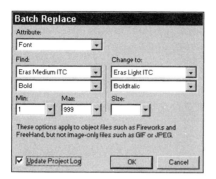

**Figure 18-15:** The Batch Replace dialog box changes according to the Attribute – Text, Font, Color, or URL – chosen. Here, the Font attribute is selected.

- To differentiate your exported files from the originals, you can add a custom prefix or suffix from the File Name option list.

- The Scaling options are No Scaling, Scale to Size (specific pixel measurements), Scale to Fit Area (while maintaining the proper aspect ratio within a maximum width and height), and Scale to Percentage. A common use of this Batch Process feature is to create thumbnails.

**Figure 18-16:** The Batch Export dialog box optimizes, scales, and renames groups of files with ease.

5. Select the backup options from the Save Backups dialog box (Figure 18-17). If used, backups can overwrite existing files or save each one incrementally, as described earlier in the "Updating Graphics with Find & Replace" section.

6. After setting all other criteria, you can save the Batch Process operation as a Scriptlet (discussed next) by clicking the Script button.

7. Clicking OK in the Batch Process dialog box initiates the procedure. A Batch Progress dialog box reports how many files have been processed and how many are remaining. When finished, the total number of affected files is displayed.

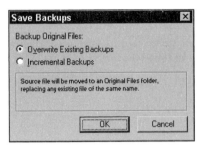

**Figure 18-17:** Fireworks offers two different types of backup options: Overwrite Existing Backups and Incremental Backups.

## Running Scriptlets

One of the significant enhancements to Fireworks 2 is the addition of *Scriptlets*. A Scriptlet is a Fireworks batch file, written in JavaScript. You can generate Scriptlets by using the Batch Processing dialog box, by hand-coding them, or by using a combination of both options. The simple, yet powerful, idea behind Scriptlets is that they are reusable.

After you save a Scriptlet, with an identifying .jsf file extension, you can run it in several ways from the Batch Process dialog box:

✦ Double-click the Scriptlet icon.

✦ Choose File ⇨ Run Script and select the Scriptlet from the Scaling Options folder of Fireworks.

✦ Drag the Scriptlet icon onto the Fireworks application icon.

✦ Drag the Scriptlet icon into the Fireworks window (in Windows only).

All Scriptlets run immediately. Fireworks includes many custom JavaScript "hooks" so that you can take advantage of the programs that are accessible through Scriptlets. For an example of Scriptlet power, you need look no further than the 2.02 update with its increased scaling options. These scaling options, capable of fundamentally changing Fireworks's output, are enabled by running a Scriptlet.

**Cross-Reference**    For more detailed information on coding your own Scriptlets, see Chapter 21.

# Summary

The term *production* can't be overemphasized in Web graphics production. Much of a Web designer's job is devoted to updating and editing existing graphics. Fireworks 2 offers a number of workflow solutions to reduce the workload:

✦ Graphics can be previewed immediately — with or without rollovers — directly in the primary and secondary browsers of your choice.

✦ Links used in Fireworks Web objects, such as rollovers and hotspots, are coordinated through the URL Manager, which maintains both the current document's links (URL History) and an independently stored set of links (URL Library).

✦ The links from any HTML file can be imported into a separate URL Library.

✦ The new Find & Replace feature allows you to update text, font attributes, colors, and URLs in the current document, frame, selection, or a series of selected documents.

✦ Export operations — including optimization and scaling of images — can be automated through Fireworks' expanded Batch Processing features. Moreover, Find & Replace operations and automatic backups can be batch processed as well.

✦ A batch processing session can be saved as a JavaScript file known as a Scriptlet. Scriptlets can be customized or run, as-is, any time they are needed.

In the next chapter, you'll learn more about working with Fireworks Web objects: hotspots and slices.

✦　　✦　　✦

# Entering
# the Web

# Mastering Image Maps and Slices

◆ ◆ ◆ ◆

**In This Chapter**

Working with Web objects

Assigning hotspots in image maps

Inserting exported code into a Web page

Dividing an image with slices

Exporting slices to HTML

Fireworks technique: animating a slice

◆ ◆ ◆ ◆

**H**ave you ever encountered a Web page in which all the image links are broken? All you see amidst the text is a bunch of rectangles with the browser's icon for "No graphic found." That's what a Web page really is to a browser: text and rectangles. You can use GIF transparency to disguise the box-like shape of an image file, but you can't intertwine graphics, like a yin-yang symbol. You can't, that is, without image maps or slices.

Fireworks excels in its support of image maps and slices. Collectively known as *Web objects* in Fireworks, both slices and image maps (or their individual parts, referred to as *hotspots*), serve several functions. In addition to helping designers break out of the rectangularity of the Web, Web objects add interactivity through links and a bit of flair through rollovers and other Behaviors. Although you could design a site full of Web graphics without ever coming near hotspots or slices, fully understanding their uses and limitations will significantly increase your Web design repertoire.

**Cross-Reference**
This chapter covers the basics of setting up hotspots and slices, and includes some techniques for incorporating them into your Web pages. For detailed information on building rollovers and using other Fireworks Behaviors, see Chapter 20.

## Understanding Image Maps and Hotspots

To understand how an image map works, you need go no further than an actual map of almost any country in the world. Divisions between regions, territories, or states are usually geographic and rarely rectangular. To best translate any such map to the Web, you'd want to make each irregular region (or territory or state) a separate clickable area. This is exactly the type of job for which an image map is intended.

Each separately defined area of an image map is referred to as a *hotspot,* as illustrated in Figure 19-1. Hotspots come in three basic shapes: rectangles, ovals, and polygons. Rectangles and ovals can be squares and circles, respectively, and every other shape is a polygon. After you define an area of an image map, you can name it and assign a URL to it. Hotspots can also be used to trigger other events, such as rollovers or the display of messages. Hotspots are not visible on the graphic when viewed through the browser; to be used, the hotspot information is translated into HTML code, which is embedded in the Web page.

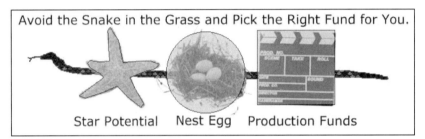

**Figure 19-1:** A separate hotspot for each region of this map was created in Fireworks.

The following are the two different kinds of image maps:

✦ **Server-side:** All the map data is kept in a file on the server. When the user clicks a particular hotspot on the image, the server compares the coordinates of the clicked spot with its image-map data. If the coordinates match, the server loads the corresponding link. The key advantage to a server-side image map is that it works with any image-capable browser. One disadvantage is that it consumes more of the server's processing resources and tends to be slower than the client-side version. Another problem is that various different server-side image map implementations exist. Probably the most popular one was developed by the National Center for Supercomputing Activities, and is known as the NCSA protocol; Fireworks outputs NCSA server-side image-map code.

✦ **Client-side:** All the map data that is downloaded to the browser is kept in the Web page. The comparison process is the same as with server-side image maps, but it requires a browser that is image-map savvy. Originally, only server-side image maps were possible. Not until Netscape Navigator 2 was released did the client-side version even become an option. Microsoft began supporting client-side image maps in Internet Explorer 3.

You can pretty safely assume that most users visiting your site can handle client-side image maps. That widespread availability plus the ease of access from the designer's point of view — no need to transfer files to the server simply to test the image map—has made server-side image maps all but obsolete. Nonetheless, it's good to know that Fireworks can output either (or both) varieties, should the need arise.

To set the type of code that Fireworks outputs, choose File ➪ Document Properties to open the Document Properties dialog box, shown in Figure 19-2. Choose the image map type through the Map Type option list: Client-side, Server-side (NCSA), or Both. Client-side is the default choice. Additionally, you can set the Background URL—the link used for an image if an area outside of any defined hotspots is selected—and the Alternate Image Description. Text entered in the Alternate Image Description text box appears while the image is loading or if the image is not available.

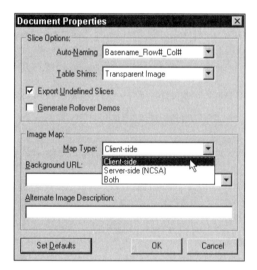

**Figure 19-2:** Select the image map server type and more through the Document Properties dialog box.

**Caution**    Any text entered in the Alternate Image Description text box is used for every Web object in the document—hotspots and slices alike. Use the Alt tag text box in the Object panel to set the alternate text for individual Web objects.

Because image maps and hotspots are HTML constructs and not data embedded in your graphics file, you need to export both the image and the code from Fireworks—and insert them both in your Web page. As you'll see later in this chapter, Fireworks handles this dual export quite effortlessly and gives you many options for incorporating graphics and code however you like.

# Using the Hotspot Tools

In Fireworks 2, the Hotspot tools are immediately accessible in the bottom-left area of the Toolbox. The following are the three basic Hotspot tools, corresponding to the three basic hotspot shapes:

✦ **Rectangle:** Use to draw rectangular or square hotspots. You can't round the corner of a rectangle, as you can with the standard Rectangle tool, although the keyboard modifiers work the same.

✦ **Oval:** Use to draw elliptical or circular hotspots. Again, the keyboard modifiers, Ctrl (Command) and Shift, function the same as they do with the regular Ellipse tool.

✦ **Polygon:** Use to draw irregular-shaped hotspots. It functions similarly to the Polygon Lasso and uses a series of points, plotted one at a time, to make the hotspot shape.

When drawn, the hotspot appears as a shape overlaying the other graphics, as shown in Figure 19-3. Fireworks 2 keeps all hotspots — and slices, for that matter — on the *Web Layer,* which is always shared across all frames and can be both hidden and locked, like other layers. Hotspots are displayed initially with the same color (actually, a Web dither fill with Transparency enabled), but each hotspot can be assigned its own color, if desired, through the Object panel.

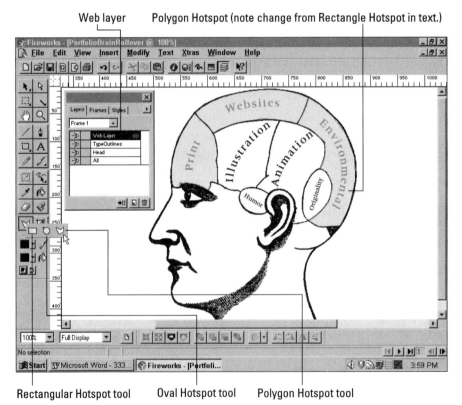

**Figure 19-3:** The Polygon Hotspot tool is used to outline each of these different brain regions. (Image courtesy of Ruth Peyser.)

## Rectangular hotspot

As noted previously, all the Hotspot tools work in a similar fashion to corresponding standard tools. However, a few key differences exist. To create a rectangular hotspot, follow these steps:

1. Select the Rectangular Hotspot tool from the Toolbox.

2. Click once to select your originating corner and drag to the opposite corner to form the rectangle.

   As you drag your pointer, Fireworks draws a preview outline of the hotspot.

3. Release the mouse button when the rectangle is the desired size and shape.

   Fireworks creates the hotspot with a colored, transparent fill, as shown in Figure 19-4.

**Figure 19-4:** Square or rectangular hotspots are created with the Rectangular Hotspot tool.

4. To create a square hotspot, press Shift while you drag out your shape.

5. To draw your hotspot from the center instead of from the corner, press Alt (Option) when dragging out the shape.

   The Object panel changes to display the Hotspot options and, if necessary, comes to the front of all the other floating panels.

**Tip** As with Shift, you can press Alt (Option) at any point when drawing to change to a center origin. You can also use Shift and Alt (Option) together to create a square hotspot, drawn from the center.

## Oval hotspot

To draw an elliptical or circular hotspot, follow these steps:

1. Select the Oval Hotspot tool from the Toolbox—click and hold down the Rectangular Hotspot tool until the flyout appears, and then click the Oval Hotspot button.

2. Click once to select the origin point and then drag to the opposite corner to create the oval.

   As you drag your pointer, Fireworks draws a preview outline of the form.

3. Release the mouse button when the oval is the desired size and shape.

Fireworks creates the oval hotspot, as shown in Figure 19-5.

**Figure 19-5:** Circular and oval hotspots can be created using the Oval Hotspot tool.

4. To draw a circle, press the Shift key while you are drawing the ellipse.

5. To draw an ellipse or circle that uses the center point of the shape as the origin, press the Alt (Option) key while you are drawing.

Tip

Precisely matching the size and shape of an elliptical object with a corresponding hotspot is fairly difficult. After you create hotspot objects, however, you can move them with the pointer, resize them with the transform tools, or adjust them numerically through the Info panel. If the oval you're creating a hotspot for is a separate object, the easiest method by far is to select the object and choose Insert ➪ Hotspot, which commands Fireworks to make the hotspot for you.

## Polygon hotspot

To draw a polygon hotspot, follow these steps:

1. Select the Polygon Hotspot tool from the Toolbox — click and hold down the Rectangular Hotspot tool until the flyout appears, and then click the Polygon Hotspot button.

2. Click at the starting point for your hotspot and move the mouse to the next point on the outline surrounding the desired area, and then click again.

   Fireworks connects each point that you set down with a straight line, as shown in Figure 19-6.

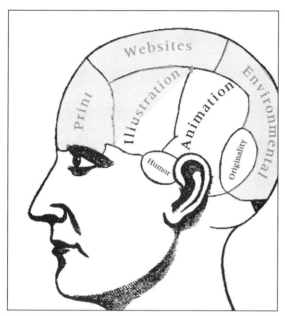

**Figure 19-6:** Fireworks fills in the polygon hotspot as you select each point.

3. Repeat Step 2 until you've outlined the entire area.

   As you create more points, Fireworks fills in the polygon with the default hotspot color.

4. To end the session, select another tool, such as the Pointer.

**Caution**     If you begin making another polygon hotspot immediately after creating one, Fireworks connects your old polygon with the new point. To avoid this problem, deselect the just created polygon hotspot before beginning a new object.

## Assigning links to hotspots

The Object panel does much more for hotspots than choose their color. In fact, the Object panel (Figure 19-7) could easily be regarded as the fourth Hotspot tool. To be truly useful, hotspots must be assigned a link and other HTML options — all of which is handled, in Fireworks 2, through the Object panel.

**Figure 19-7:** Use the Object panel for a selected hotspot to enter essential Web data, such as the linked URL.

The Object panel options for a hotspot include

✦ **Current URL:** Use this text box to both assign and display the link associated with the selected hotspot. You can either enter a new link by typing directly into the text field or choose an existing link by selecting one from the option drop-down list. The option list can be divided into as many as three parts: the No URL (noHREF) choice; the URL History list for the current document; and the current URL Library.

**Cross-Reference**  For more information on using the URL History and URL Library to manage your links as well as links in general, see Chapter 18.

✦ **Alt tag:** Alternate image text entered here is shown when either the image can't be found by the server or the user's mouse is hovering over the image. In the latter case, the text appears in a tooltip attached to the pointer. Fireworks includes both the standard alt attribute and Internet Explorer's title attribute in the generated HTML.

✦ **Link Target:** The target defines where the Web page requested by a link appears. Targets are commonly used with HTML framesets. You can enter a named frame directly in the Target text box or choose one of the following target keywords:

   • **_blank** opens the link into a new browser window and keeps the current window available.

   • **_parent** opens the link into the parent frameset of the current frame, if any.

   • **_self** opens the link into the current frame, replacing its contents (this is the default).

   • **_top** opens the link into the outermost frameset of the current Web page, replacing all frames.

✦ **Color:** When created, all hotspots are filled with the same semitransparent color. You can, however, alter an individual hotspot's color by selecting a new one from the color picker pop-up menu.

✦ **Shape:** Displays the current hotspot shape. This is initially derived from the tool used to create the hotspot, and is used to determine a portion of the HTML code. You can change the shape by selecting a different one from the option drop-down list, although this can radically alter your hotspot.

**Tip**

If you're entering links directly into the Current URL text box, be careful of your spelling. Web servers are very sensitive to typos — even the case of letters in some instances. You can save yourself a great deal of painstaking typing by using Fireworks Import URL feature, located in the URL Manager, to import links from any HTML file.

## Converting an object to a hotspot

As one who has played connect-the-dots one too many times while trying to create a star-shaped hotspot, I heartily embrace Fireworks's object-to-hotspot converter. Instead of attempting to outline an object with any of the hotspot drawing tools, select the object and choose Insert ➪ Hotspot. A hotspot precisely matching the shape of the object is created and ready for linking. This command works for rectangular, elliptical, and irregular shapes, whether they are path, image, or text objects.

**Note**

If you select multiple objects before using the Insert ➪ Hotspot command, Fireworks asks whether you want to create one hotspot or multiple hotspots. Choosing to create one hotspot will combine the Web Layer shapes into one rectangular hotspot encompassing all the selections.

In addition to creating hotspots in the standard methods with the Hotspot tools or the Insert ➪ Hotspot command, you can create hotspots by using the Layers panel. This is a handy way to quickly add hotspots to objects visually with a drag-and-drop technique.

To create hotspots out of objects, follow these steps:

1. Make sure the Layers panel is displayed, either by choosing Window ➪ Layers, by using the keyboard shortcut Ctrl+Alt+K (Command+Option+K), or by clicking its tab, if visible.

2. Select in the document window the object or objects that you want to make into hotspots.

   Fireworks displays a selection icon (the blue box) in the rightmost column of the Layers panel, next to the layer the selected objects are on.

3. Drag and drop the selection icon in the same column, next to the Web Layer.

The hotspots are created on the Web Layer, and your original objects are unaffected.

# Exporting Image Map Code

When an image map is translated into HTML, it appears in two key parts. The first part is the image tag, <img>, which holds the information for the overall graphic. The <img> attributes include src (the filename of the graphic), the dimensions of the image, and a connection to the map data, usemap. The usemap attribute is set to the name of the second image map element, the <map> tag. For every hotspot in the image map, a corresponding <area> tag exists within the <map>...</map> tag pair. The following code is for an image map with three hotspots — a polygon, a circle, and a rectangle:

```
<img src="images/imagemap.jpg" width="640" height="480"
usemap="#navbar"></p>
<map name="navbar">
  <area shape="poly"
coords="166,131,165,131,160,143,164,179,127,180,143,200,156,203
,118,229,119,236,158,229,177,217,199,238,212,247,220,242,196,20
3,232,190,241,189,241,182,223,177,185,182,175,134,166,132"
href="/starpro.html" alt="High Risk Funds">
  <area shape="circle" coords="312,202,56" href="/nestegg.html"
alt="Mutual Funds">
  <area shape="rect" coords="389,138,497,244"
href="/prodfunds.html" alt="Money Markets">
</map>
```

Fireworks handles outputting all of this code for you — and in several different styles for various authoring tools, as well. All that you're responsible for is incorporating the code in your Web page.

## Choosing an HTML style

The HTML code for an image map is generated by Fireworks when you export your image. During the export process, you can select from various HTML styles that dictate how the code is output. Choosing an HTML style that matches your Web-authoring program makes incorporating the Fireworks-generated code easier. The standard HTML styles included in Fireworks 2 are as follows:

✦ **Generic:** The basic code, useful in hand-coded Web pages and the majority of Web-authoring tools that work with standard HTML.

✦ **Dreamweaver 2:** Code stylized for Dreamweaver 2. For image maps, no real difference exists between the Generic and the Dreamweaver 2 code.

✦ **Dreamweaver 2 Library:** HTML to be used in a Dreamweaver 2 Library has additional code marking it as a Library item. This code must be saved in the site's Library folder.

✦ **FrontPage:** FrontPage uses a series of *webbots* to format its code; Fireworks includes the code necessary for an image map webbot, as well as instructional code that displays when the document is opened in FrontPage.

You'll find additional HTML templates on the CD-ROM accompanying this book, including templates for Adobe GoLive, as well as a series of standard templates reconfigured to output files with lowercase names. Some servers require lowercase filenames to function correctly. The additional templates can be found in the HTML Templates folder. To use, just copy the desired folder, with its files, to the Fireworks/Settings/HTML Settings directory—you don't need to relaunch Fireworks.

To export an image map, follow these steps:

1. Choose File ⇨ Export to begin the exporting process.

   The Export Preview dialog box appears.

2. Optimize your image as needed.

3. When you're satisfied with your image optimization, click Next from the Export Preview dialog box.

   The Export dialog box, shown in Figure 19-8 is displayed.

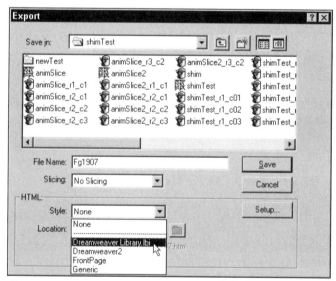

**Figure 19-8:** Choose the type of image map output from the HTML Style option list.

4. Set the filename and path of the Export in the upper part of the dialog box.

   To select a new path, use the system path option list and various navigation buttons, such as the Up One Level button in Windows or the New Folder button in Macintosh.

5. For image maps that do not use slices, make sure the Slicing option list is set to No Slicing.

6. In the HTML area of the Export dialog box, select the desired type of HTML output from the Style option list.

**Tip**

Fireworks remembers your last Style setting.

7. If you've chosen the Dreamweaver 2 Library HTML style, the Locate Site Library Directory opens for you to identify the Library folder of your site.

8. Choose the desired location for your HTML code:

- To output the code to the same folder as the images, select Same Directory from the Location option list.

- To output the code in the parent folder of the images, select One Level Up from the Location option list.

- To place the code in another folder, click the folder icon and select the path from the standard dialog box. Alternatively, you can open the dialog box by selecting Custom from the Location option list.

**Note**

Although the dialog box for the custom folder is titled Locate Site Library Directory, you don't have to choose the Library template to use the dialog box.

9. To alter any of the image map settings previously set, click Setup to reopen the Document Properties dialog box and adjust your settings.

10. After you make your selections, click Save to complete the export.

## Inserting image map code in a Web page

After you create the graphic, link the hotspots, and generate the code, how do you integrate all of that material within an existing Web page? Although the thought of touching code may be just this side of horrifying for many graphic designers, for most situations, it's really not that bad — and for some, it's an absolute breeze. Bottom line? If you can cut and paste in a word processor, you can insert an image map in your Web page.

Although the process is largely the same for most of the different style outputs, some variations exist in the procedure. The following sections detail how to integrate the Fireworks-generated code for each of the standard HTML styles.

### Generic

The Generic HTML code is, as the name implies, used in most general situations. If you're building Web pages by hand — using Notepad in Windows or SimpleText on the Macintosh — the Generic HTML style is for you. Likewise, if you're using a Web-authoring program, but not one for which Fireworks has a specific template, such as Dreamweaver or FrontPage, you should use Generic HTML.

The general procedure for incorporating a Generic image map is fairly straightforward:

1. Open the Generic code in a text editor, or in the text editor portion of your Web-authoring tool.

2. Select and copy to the Clipboard the section in the `<body>` tag that starts with

   ```
   <!———— BEGIN COPYING HERE ————>
   ```

   and ends with

   ```
   <!———— STOP COPYING HERE ————>
   ```

3. Open your existing Web page in a text editor, or in the text editor portion of your Web-authoring tool.

4. In the `<body>` section of your Web page, insert the code where you want the image to appear.

**Caution**    Be sure that you insert the code between the `<body>` and `</body>` tags, and not between the `<head>` and `</head>` tags.

5. Preview the page in a browser and adjust the placement of the `<img>` tag, if necessary.

It's not essential that the `<img>` part of the image map code and the `<map>` section appear side by side, as long as they are in the same document.

**Note**    If the image map is to form the basis of your document — and you don't have another existing page to use — you don't have to delete or move any code whatsoever. Just add HTML elements around the image map as you build your new page. If you'd like, you can remove the HTML comments, but, frankly, they don't add much weight to a page, so removing them really isn't necessary.

## Dreamweaver 2

Two ways exist to incorporate the standard Dreamweaver 2 HTML code into a Web page. The first is identical to the procedure used for including Generic code: cut the code from the Fireworks-generated page and paste it into the Dreamweaver page through the HTML inspector. As long as you make sure to insert the code in the `<body>` section of the document, and not the `<head>` section, you won't have any problems.

The other method takes advantage of Dreamweaver's Invisible Elements to completely avoid opening the HTML inspector. To incorporate Dreamweaver-style HTML visually, follow these steps:

1. In Dreamweaver, open the Fireworks-generated HTML page which was created with the Dreamweaver style option.

2. Make sure that View ⇨ Invisible Elements is enabled.

   You'll notice a series of three Comment symbols on one side of the image, followed by a Map symbol and two more Comment symbols on the other side, as shown in Figure 19-9.

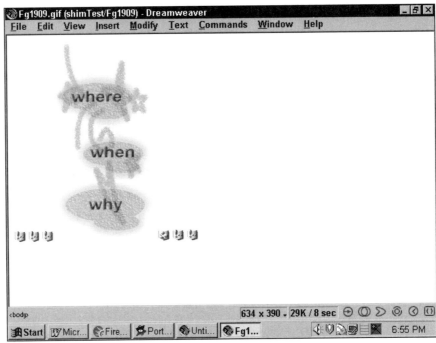

**Figure 19-9:** With Dreamweaver's Invisible Elements feature, you don't have to use the HTML inspector to copy and paste the image map code.

3. Select the image, press Shift, and click the Map symbol on the right of the image.

If you want to transfer all the comments, as well, click the first Comment symbol, press Shift, and then click the last Comment symbol.

4. Choose either Edit ➪ Copy or the keyboard shortcut Ctrl+C (Command+C).

5. Open the existing Web page to which you want to add the image map.

6. Place the cursor where you want the image map to appear.

7. Choose either Edit ➪ Paste or the keyboard shortcut Ctrl+V (Command+V).

The image map—and its code—is inserted into the Dreamweaver document.

If for some reason you don't see either the Comment symbols or the Map symbol, select Edit ➪ Preferences in Dreamweaver and, from the Invisible Elements panel, make sure that the Comments and Client-side Image Map options are selected.

## Dreamweaver 2 Library

Libraries are a very powerful Dreamweaver feature that allows a section of a Web page to be updated once, after which Dreamweaver automatically updates all pages on which the section appears. Originally intended to replace page elements that are often repeated, such as a copyright line or logo, Dreamweaver Library items are very useful, because each item is regarded as a single unit, no matter how much code is included. If, as a designer, you're familiar with Encapsulated PostScript, think of Dreamweaver Libraries as Encapsulated HTML.

For a Library item to be recognized as such, it must be stored in a special folder for each local site. When you choose the Dreamweaver 2 Library option from the HTML Style list during export, Fireworks prompts you to locate your site's Library folder. If you've never created a Library item for the current site before, you need to make a new folder. The folder must be placed in the local site root and must be named, appropriately enough, Library. For example, if your local site root is located at c:\dba\, the Library folder must be created at c:\dba\Library.

After you export the HTML file as a Dreamweaver Library item, follow these steps to incorporate the image map:

1. In Dreamweaver, choose Window ➪ Library or click the Library button from the Launcher palette. Alternatively, you can use the keyboard shortcut, F6.

The current site's Library palette is displayed, as shown in Figure 19-10.

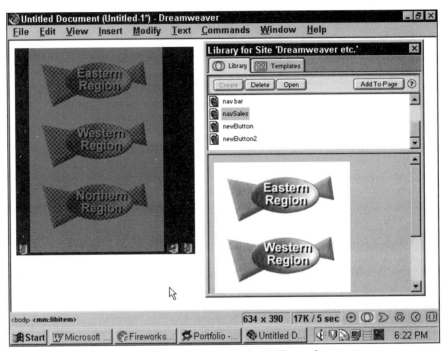

**Figure 19-10:** After you export an image map from Fireworks as a Dreamweaver Library item, it is available from Dreamweaver's Library palette.

2. Place your cursor in the document window where you want the image map to appear.

3. In the Library palette, select your exported image map from the list window.

The preview pane of the Library palette displays the selected list items.

4. Click the Add To Page button or, alternatively, drag and drop the item from either the preview pane or the list window.

The image map, and all the necessary code, are inserted into the Dreamweaver page.

If you ever need to edit the image map, you first need to select it and then click Open from Dreamweaver's Property inspector. A new HTML page appears with just the Library item on it. From there, you can choose the image and select either Edit from the Property inspector or Optimize in Fireworks from the Command menu. After you edit the image, closing the Library document window prompts Dreamweaver to ask whether you'd like to update the Library. Click Yes to update the Library items; click No to postpone the update.

## FrontPage

Microsoft's FrontPage is an introductory Web-authoring tool that uses proprietary code for many of its special effects, including image maps. Fireworks outputs code to match the FrontPage format by selecting FrontPage from the HTML Style option list during export. The exported image map is inserted into an HTML page (Figure 19-11) that instructs the FrontPage user how to incorporate the code.

**Figure 19-11:** With FrontPage-style code generated from Fireworks, you also get instructions on how to proceed.

To insert an image map from Fireworks into a FrontPage document, follow these steps:

1. Open the Fireworks-generated page in FrontPage.

**Caution** Both the FrontPage document and the Fireworks-generated document must be in the same folder.

2. Select the HTML View.

3. Select the code starting with

   ```
   [!——— BEGIN COPYING HERE ————]
   ```

   and ending with

   ```
   [!——— STOP COPYING HERE ————]
   ```

4. Choose Edit ⇨ Copy.

5. Open the document in which the image map is to be inserted.

6. While still in HTML View, choose Edit ⇨ Paste to insert the code into the document.

# Understanding Slices

If image maps allow you to target areas of a graphic for links, why not use them for everything? The primary drawback to an image map is also one of its key characteristics: an image map is a single file. As such, image maps of any size — and they tend to be sizable, to take advantage of multiple hotspots — take a long time to download and can be frustrating for the Web page visitor. Moreover, with one file, you're locked into one graphic format with a single palette. What if your image map contains a photographic image in one color with lots of flat color in the rest of the graphic? You'd be forced to export the entire file as a JPEG, to make the photo look good, and the file size would be much higher than if you exported the image as a GIF. And forget about including animations or special effects such as rollovers — duplicating frames of a large graphic would make the file huge.

An alternative approach to image maps is a technique known as *slicing*. Slicing takes a large image and literally carves it into multiple smaller graphics, which are reassembled in an HTML table for viewing. Each separate image is referred to as a *slice* and the whole process is often just called *slices*. Here are some of the key features of slices:

> ✦ **Incremental download:** On most servers, each slice appears as it's downloaded, which makes the whole image appear to be loading faster.
>
> ✦ **Linking without image maps:** Each slice can have its own link, although all such links are rectangular.
>
> ✦ **Mixed file formats:** Each slice can be optimized separately, reducing the overall file size of the image while enhancing the quality. This means that you not only can have a JPEG and GIF side by side, but can also export one slice as a JPEG at 100 percent and another slice as a JPEG at 30 percent.
>
> ✦ **Update image areas:** If your graphic includes an area that must be updated frequently, such as a headline or a date, you can simply alter the single image in the slice and leave the rest of the image untouched.
>
> ✦ **Embedded rollovers:** One of the chief uses of slices, especially in Fireworks, is to create rollovers (also known as *mouseovers*). With slices, you can have a series of rollovers, as with a navigation bar, that is all tied together in one graphic. You can also use one slice to trigger a rollover in another part of the image.
>
> ✦ **Embedded animation:** With a GIF animation in one slice, you can achieve special effects, such as a flashing neon sign in a large graphic, without doubling or tripling your file size.

The key, fact-of-life, limitation to slices is their shape: all slices are rectangular. Not only are images that make up each individual slice always rectangular, but the table cells into which the slices must fit are too. To create any illusion of nonrectangular shapes, you must use GIF or PNG files with transparency. An additional restriction is that slices cannot overlap.

When deciding whether or not to slice an image, keep in mind that slices depend on HTML tables to hold them together in the browser. Tables, in turn, have some of their own limitations. For example, you can't place two tables side by side on a Web page; the code won't allow it. However, you can nest one table inside another, to achieve a similar effect.

Because slices are tied to HTML tables, special care must be taken to ensure that all browsers treat the tables identically. Under some situations, tables viewed in some browsers (Netscape Navigator is a key offender) can "collapse" and lose all their width and height information that is necessary to appear as a single graphic. The workaround for this problem is to use very small (one pixel) transparent images called *shims*. Fireworks 2 automatically generates the shims if you like, or outputs the code for the sliced image without them. Shims are covered in detail later in this chapter.

**Cross-Reference**   This chapter covers the basics of creating slices. For information on how to use slices to build rollovers, see Chapter 20.

# Slicing Images in Fireworks

Slices and hotspots are created in a similar manner — generally, you draw a slice area on top of an image. However, because slices are only rectangular in shape, only one Slice tool is available, located on the lower right of the Toolbox, instead of three, as with hotspots. Fireworks supports the Slice tool with *slice guides*, which help you to keep the number of files exported to a minimum by aligning the slices. To slice an image in Fireworks, follow these steps:

1. Select the Slice tool from the Toolbox.

2. Click the image and draw out a rectangle the size and shape of the desired slice.

**Tip**   As with the regular Rectangle tool, the Alt key causes the Slice tool to draw from the center rather than from a corner, and the Shift key constrains the slice to a square.

3. Release the mouse when you're satisfied with the initial shape.

   Fireworks creates the slice object and fills in the rectangle with the default, semitransparent slice color. If enabled, the slice guides appear, as shown in Figure 19-12.

Slice tool          Slice guides          Slice objects

**Figure 19-12:** Slicing up an image allows different parts to be exported with different formats.

After you draw the slice object, you can manipulate it largely like any other object in Fireworks. You can use the four handles on the slice object to resize it — just drag one corner in the desired direction. Because slices are constrained to rectangles, moving just one point moves the entire side. In fact, you don't have to select the corner; it's just as effective to click and drag a slice object's side.

You can also use the transform tools, such as Scale, although any resulting nonrectangular shape is converted back into an encompassing rectangle. To move the slice object one pixel at a time, use the arrow keys.

An alternative to the Slice tool is to use the standard guides. In this technique, guides are dragged from the horizontal and vertical rulers to form the slicing grid. Then, during export, choose the Slice Along Guides option. This technique works well when your goal in slicing an image is to allow smaller portions of the image to appear quicker than a single large image could load.

# Working with slice guides

Before Fireworks, creating a sliced image by hand was very meticulous, eye-straining work. Each slice had to be measured and cut precisely to the pixel — if you were off even one pixel, the resulting image would either have gaps or over-lapping areas. You can approximate this level of frustration by disabling the slice guide features in Fireworks.

Unlike regular guides, you don't position slice guides by hand; they are auto-matically created as you draw out your slices. The slice guides effectively show you the table layout that would result from the existing slices. More importantly, the slice guides take advantage of the Snap to Guide feature and help you to avoid overlapping slices or sliced images with gaps.

Personally speaking, I find the slice guides very useful and highly recommend using them. Choose View ➪ Slice Guides to enable this feature. Slices automatically snap to the edge of a document, but to snap to the guides themselves, choose View ➪ Guide Options ➪ Snap to Guides.

The standard guides and the slice guides are drawn in two different colors. Occasionally, the slice guide color is too similar to that of the current image and you can't see where the guides are. To change the color of the slice guides, select View ➪ Guide Options ➪ Edit Guides to see the Guides dialog box, shown in Figure 19-13. Select a new color from the Slice Color pop-up menu.

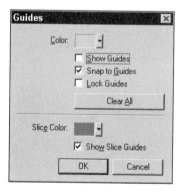

**Figure 19-13:** Choose a new slice guide color from the Guides dialog box.

You can also enable the slice guide feature from the Guides dialog box, by choosing Show Slice Guides, or turn on the Snap feature, by selecting Snap to Guides.

**Note**      Unlike the regular guides, the slice guides can't be dragged to a new location; their position is controlled by the slices themselves. Therefore, the Lock Guides option on the Guides dialog box applies only to standard guides.

## Copying an image to a slice

Sometimes, making sure that you have all of a particular object can be very tricky—especially if that object has a drop shadow or glow effect. Incorrect placement of a slice could lead to part of the image being cut off. To avoid these problems, you can have Fireworks do all the work for you. Just as Fireworks can convert any object to a hotspot, any object can also be made into a slice.

To make an object into a slice, select the object and choose Insert ⇨ Slice. Fireworks draws the slice completely encompassing the selected object—special effects and all. If you select multiple objects, Fireworks asks whether you want to create slices for all the items together or separately.

## Setting URLs in slices

To use a slice as a link, the slice must be assigned a URL. You can assign URLs to slices in two different locations: the Object panel or the URL Manager. The same options covered earlier in this chapter for Hotspots exist for slices on both panels, with one very important addition in the Object panel. With slices, you can set a specific export setting for each slice. Fireworks allows you to use any existing preset export settings—whether standard or custom—or to open the Export Preview dialog box to optimize the selected slice.

To assign a link to a slice by using the Object panel, follow these steps:

1. Select the slice to which you want to assign a link.

2. Choose either Window ⇨ Objects or the keyboard shortcut Ctrl+I (Command+I).

   The Object panel, shown in Figure 19-14, appears.

**Figure 19-14:** The Object panel allows you to assign both link and export settings to any slice.

3. If you want to use a different export setting than the current one, either choose a preset from the Slice Export Settings option list or click the ellipse (...) button to open the Export Preview dialog box.

**Note** You can also use the Export Preview dialog box to check the current settings or immediately export the current slice. Only the selected slice is displayed in the preview window of the Export Preview dialog box. Click OK to return to the Object panel, or click Export to save the slice.

4. Enter a link directly in the Current URL text box or select one from the option list. The option list shows both the URL History and the URL Library.

5. If desired, enter any alternative text in the Alt text field.

6. To set the target for the linked page to load into, choose one of the presets from the Target option list or enter a frame name.

7. To change the color of the selected slice object, pick a new one from the color picker pop-up menu.

8. To assign a custom name for the slice, deselect the Auto-Name Slices option and enter a new name in the Custom Base Name text box.

You can also set a different pattern for the Auto-Naming scheme in the Document Properties dialog box, as described later in this chapter.

## Text Slices

One little known, but useful feature of slices is the ability to create a *Text Slice*. A Text Slice displays HTML text in your image instead of part of the image, as shown in Figure 19-15.

**Figure 19-15:** Setting a slice's export type as Text allows you to incorporate HTML text inside a sliced graphic.

To make a Text Slice, follow these steps:

1. Select the slice and display the Object panel.

2. From the Slice Export Settings option list, choose Text (No Image).

The Object panel displays a text area.

3. Enter the desired text and/or HTML directly in the text area of the Object panel.

4. Select any other tool or object when you're done.

5. To edit the text, select the slice object and make your changes in the Object panel.

**Tip**

HTML tables used for slices typically have no borders or additional cell spacing or padding, so that all the images will fit snugly next to each other. However, if you are using a Text Slice, this can be a problem, because the text fits too snugly to the image, with no surrounding margin. You can work around this problem by creating a slightly larger, but empty, Text Slice in front of the Text Slice with the content.

## Slice options

Fireworks enables you to set several slice-specific options through the Document Properties dialog box. The four options are as follows:

✦ **Auto-Naming:** Choose from six options to set the Auto-Naming scheme for exported slices. The Auto-Naming choices are described next in this section.

✦ **Table Shims:** Fireworks 2 allows you to use transparent shims, shims from the image itself, or no shims at all. A detailed discussion of shims follows later in this chapter.

✦ **Export Undefined Slices:** If this option is not selected, only those areas of the image explicitly covered by a slice are exported. For most situations, this option should remain selected.

✦ **Generate Rollover Demos:** If selected, this option creates an additional HTML file entitled *filename*_Demo (where *filename* is the basename selected during export), which runs the rollover but does not link to any other page.

### Naming slices

Even with only two slices explicitly defined — depending on their placement — you can generate many slices for an image. For the slices to be inserted into a table, each slice has to have a unique filename. To save you the work of entering in name after name, Fireworks automatically names the slices. If desired, you can override the automatic naming on a slice-by-slice basis by unchecking the Auto-Name Slices option and entering a unique name in the associated text box. Although I like to name slices individually in a navigation bar, so that I can easily find the image reference in the HTML code, I tend to let Fireworks automatically name most of my slices.

**New Feature**

In Fireworks 2, you can choose from six different Auto-Naming schemes. For each pattern, a user-supplied basename is combined with a suffix or a prefix. The suffixes and prefixes are automatically generated according to the position of the slice in the table.

The Auto-Naming options and their examples are listed in Table 19-1, where the basename `logo` is used.

**Table 19-1**
**Auto-Naming Options**

| Option | Example |
| --- | --- |
| Basename_Row#_Col# | logo_r01_c01 <br> logo_r01_c02 <br> logo_r02_c01 |
| Basename_Alphabetical | logo_a <br> logo_b <br> logo_c |
| Basename_Numeric | logo_01 <br> logo_02 <br> logo_03 |
| Row#_Col#_Basename | r01_c01_logo <br> r01_c02_logo <br> r02_c01_logo |
| Alphabetical_Basename | a_logo <br> b_logo <br> c_logo |
| Numeric_Basename | 01_logo <br> 02_logo <br> 03_logo |

### Shims

Fireworks can create some extremely complex tables as a result of slicing; multiple column and row spans are quite normal. In some ways, such complex tables are like a house of cards — and certain browsers are a big wind, ready to knock them down. In some circumstances, the table cells appear to lose their carefully calculated widths and heights, and the table literally breaks apart to display the separate images.

To support such tables, Fireworks uses a series of *shims*. A shim is a very small (one pixel by one pixel) transparent GIF image placed along the top-right cells of the HTML table. Fireworks takes advantage of how HTML works, to use just one image, shim.gif, which weighs just 43 bytes — or, in other words, .04K. The same image is used in each shim cell and sized appropriately in the code. HTML enables you to specify a different height and width for an image and then allow the browsers to handle the scale. Although this is generally a bad idea for most images — browsers don't use very sophisticated scaling algorithms — it works perfectly well for shims. The shims are almost invisible: those along the top row remain one pixel in height and those on the side remain one pixel in width. But, most importantly, shims do the job for which they were intended — a sliced table with shims maintains its shape and integrity regardless of the browser.

**New Feature**

Despite all their intended good, the transparent shims introduced in the first version of Fireworks are not for every situation. Therefore, Fireworks 2 offers a degree of user control over shim creation, through the Table Shims option of the Document Properties dialog box. Now, the Web designer can choose to use transparent shims, shims taken from the image itself, or no shims at all.

Why might you prefer shims from the image rather than transparent shims? Occasionally, a sliced table must be placed directly next to the top or side of the Web page or below another table or image. Even with just a one-pixel shim, the gap is noticeable. To avoid this problem, choose the Shims from Image option of the Table Shims option list. With this option selected, Fireworks uses a very thin slice of the image — again, a single pixel — along the top and right of the table. Then, any perceived gap is gone, as shown in Figure 19-16. Using the Shims from Image option does have one downside: if a rollover or other effect where the image is swapped is applied to those shim edges, the shim does not get swapped as well.

**Figure 19-16:** If your sliced table needs to abut another image exactly, don't use Transparent Shims, like the left example — use Shims from Images, instead, like the example on the right.

If you're dead-set against using shims of any kind, in Fireworks 2, you can select No Shims from the Table Shims option list. Use this feature only with caution and an awful lot of testing in various browsers.

## Exporting Slices

When exporting an image map, you end up with an image and a snippet of HTML code. When exporting slices, you could get a whole lot of images and a bit more HTML. You need to realize that each sliced image ultimately means numerous files that must all be stored together. Fireworks offers two different slicing techniques and a variety of HTML styles from which to choose. The options you select are determined by how your slices were created and which Web-authoring tool you are using.

# Setting the Export options

After deciding on a path and filename for your images, you must select which slicing technique to use. In the Export dialog box, the options under Slicing are as follows:

✦ **No Slicing:** When this option is chosen, the image is exported in one piece, regardless of the number of slice objects.

✦ **Use Slice Objects:** The exported slices are created from the slice objects on the image.

✦ **Slice Along Guides:** The standard guides are used to determine the slices.

For most situations, Use Slice Objects is the best choice. Slice objects are required for rollovers or any other Behavior, and they are very easy to create. The only reason to choose Slice Along Guides is to carve a large image into numerous smaller ones, without any attached Behaviors. To use Slice Along Guides, you must have set the standard guides into place, as detailed earlier in this chapter.

To export an image in slices, follow these steps:

1. Choose File ⇨ Export and optimize your image in the Export Preview dialog box. Click Next when you're ready to export.

   The Export dialog box appears.

2. Set the filename and path of the Export in the upper part of the dialog box.

3. Choose either Use Slice Objects or Slice Along Guides from the Slicing option list.

4. In the HTML area of the Export dialog box, select the desired type of HTML output from the Style option list.

5. If you chose the Dreamweaver 2 Library HTML style, the Locate Site Library Directory opens for you to identify the Library folder of your site.

6. Choose the desired location for your HTML code:

   • To output the code to the same folder as the images, select Same Directory from the Location option list.

   • To output the code in the parent folder of the images, select One Level Up from the Location option list.

   • To place the code in another folder, click the folder icon and select the path from the standard dialog box. Alternatively, you can open the dialog box by selecting Custom from the Location option list.

7. To alter any of the slice settings previously set, click Setup to reopen the Document Properties dialog box, and adjust your settings.

8. After you make your selections, click Save to complete the export.

# Inserting slices in a Web page

As with image maps, Fireworks provides four HTML templates to choose from: Generic, Dreamweaver 2, Dreamweaver 2 Library, and FrontPage. Each template generates an HTML file with the same name as set in the Base Name text box of the Export dialog box.

Inserting code from a simple sliced image is very straightforward. From an HTML perspective, all the code is contained within one tag, `<table>`. Remember, in HTML, tags containing data use both a starting and ending tag; in the case of the tags for an HTML table, the starting tag is `<table>` and the ending tag is `</table>`. So, all the necessary code will be between `<table>` and `</table>`, inclusive. Fireworks plainly marks this code with HTML comments showing where to begin copying and where to stop.

**Cross-Reference**
The techniques provided in this chapter for integrating slices in your Web pages are for simple sliced images, without rollovers or other Behaviors. To learn how to export slices with Behaviors, see Chapter 20.

## Generic

The Generic template is used when you are hand coding your pages in a text editor or using a Web-authoring tool without a specific template.

Follow these steps to incorporate a Generic sliced image:

1. Open the Generic code in a text editor or in the text editor portion of your Web-authoring tool.

2. Select and copy to the Clipboard the section in the `<body>` tag that starts with

   ```
   <!———— BEGIN COPYING HERE ————>
   ```

   and ends with

   ```
   <!———— STOP COPYING HERE ————>
   ```

3. Open your existing Web page in a text editor or in the text editor portion of your Web-authoring tool.

4. In the `<body>` section of your Web page, insert the code where you want the image to appear.

5. Preview the page in a browser and adjust the placement of the `<img>` tag, if necessary.

## Dreamweaver 2

Although you can use Dreamweaver's HTML inspector to integrate the Fireworks-generated code, you can also do it visually, thanks to Dreamweaver's Tag Selector.

To insert Fireworks-generated code for a sliced image into Dreamweaver, follow these steps:

1. In Dreamweaver, open the HTML page generated in Fireworks.

2. Click once on the exported image.

   Because the image is now sliced into different sections, the entire image will not be selected, just one slice.

3. On the bottom left of the document window, select the `<table>` tag from the Tag Selector, as shown in Figure 19-17.

   The entire sliced image and all the code is selected.

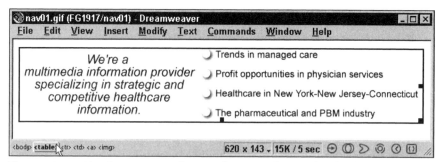

**Figure 19-17:** Use Dreamweaver's Tag Selector to choose the sliced image for cutting and pasting.

4. Choose either Edit ➪ Copy or the keyboard shortcut Ctrl+C (Command+C).

5. Open the existing Web page to which you want to add the sliced image.

6. Place the cursor where you want the sliced image to appear.

7. Choose either Edit ➪ Paste or the keyboard shortcut Ctrl+V (Command+V).

   The sliced image and corresponding code is inserted into the document.

## Dreamweaver 2 Library

The Dreamweaver 2 Library code template builds the same table as the Dreamweaver 2 template does, but it also marks the table as a Library item that can be inserted over and over again. As with the image map code, the sliced image code must be stored in a special folder called Library for each local site. If you've never created a Library item for the current site, you need to make a new folder in the local site root.

After you export the HTML file as a Dreamweaver Library item, follow these steps to incorporate the sliced image:

1. In Dreamweaver, choose Window ➪ Library or click the Library button from the Launcher. Alternatively, you can use the keyboard shortcut, F6.

   The current site's Library palette is displayed.

2. Place your cursor in the document window where you want the sliced image to appear.

3. In the Library palette, select your exported sliced image from the list window.

    The preview pane of the Library palette displays the selected list items.

4. Click the Add to Page button or, alternatively, drag and drop the item from either the preview pane or the list window.

    The sliced image, and all the necessary code, is inserted into the Dreamweaver page.

### FrontPage

Microsoft's FrontPage stores external code — including any JavaScript — in a structure (or *webbot* in FrontPage jargon) called HTMLmarkup. Fireworks produces the proper structure through the FrontPage template so that the code can be seamlessly integrated.

To insert an image map from Fireworks into a FrontPage document, follow these steps:

1. Open the Fireworks-generated page in FrontPage.

Caution    Both the FrontPage document and the Fireworks-generated document must be in the same folder.

2. Select the HTML View.

3. Select the code starting with [!——— BEGIN COPYING HERE ———-]

    and ending with

    [!——— STOP COPYING HERE ———-]

4. Choose Edit ➪ Copy.

5. Open the document in which the sliced image is to be inserted.

6. While still in HTML View, choose Edit ➪ Paste to insert the code into the document.

# Fireworks Technique: Animating a Slice

Fireworks is capable of building terrific animations — and with just a little technique, you can integrate any animation into a larger image through slices. Animations can be fairly heavy in terms of file size. If only a small section of an overall image is moving — such as a radar screen on a control panel — converting the entire image to an animation is prohibitive, due to the file size that would result. However, with slices, you can animate just the area that you need to animate, and keep the rest of the image static, thus dropping the size of the file dramatically.

To include an animation in Fireworks, follow these steps:

1. Build your animation in Fireworks as you would normally.

2. If the animation is already not part of a larger image, go to Frame 1 in the Frame panel, choose Modify ➪ Document ➪ Canvas Size, and enlarge the canvas as desired.

3. Complete the graphics surrounding the animation.

4. Choose File ➪ Export to open the Export Preview dialog box.

5. From the Animation tab, set the frame timing, disposal method, looping, and other options.

6. Click Set Defaults to store the settings and return to the document window.

7. Make a slice object from the animation either by choosing the animation and selecting Insert ➪ Slice or by using the Slice tool to draw a rectangle around the entire animation.

8. If it's not already visible, display the Object panel.

9. In the Object panel, set the link and any other desired options.

10. Click the ellipse button next to the Export preset option list.

    A special version of the Export Preview dialog box opens, in which only the Options tab is available, as shown in Figure 19-18.

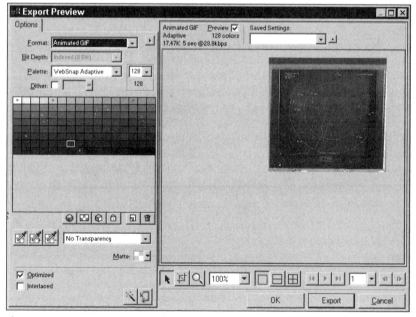

**Figure 19-18:** To export an animation as part of a slice, you have to set the slice explicitly to Animated GIF.

11. From the Format option list, choose Animated GIF.

12. Optimize the animation, if necessary.

13. Click OK when you're done.

14. Choose File ➪ Export.

    The full Export Preview dialog box appears.

**Note**    Although you can now access the Animation tab, changing these settings won't affect your animated slice.

15. Optimize the static image however you want. Make sure that the Format is not set to Animated GIF.

16. Click Next to continue.

    The Export dialog box opens.

17. Set your path and filename in the upper portion of the dialog box.

18. Choose Use Slice Objects from the Slicing option list, and choose the desired HTML template from the Style option list.

19. Click Save when you're ready to export.

    Your animation is exported as part of the overall image, as shown in the example in Figure 19-19.

**Figure 19-19:** In this image, the radar screen is animated, and the rest of the graphic is static.

# Summary

Fireworks Web objects — hotspots and slices — provide a gateway from graphic imagery to the Internet. By integrating Web objects with other graphic elements, the Web designer can seamlessly migrate from one medium to another, all the while maintaining editability. When beginning to work with Web objects, keep these points in mind:

✦ Fireworks supports two types of Web objects: hotspots and slices. A hotspot marks part of a larger graphic through code, whereas slices actually divide the larger image into smaller files.

✦ Hotspots come in three basic shapes: rectangle, oval, and polygon. Fireworks has a different tool for each type of hotspot. The term "hotspot" denotes an area of the overall image, called an image map.*   Any Fireworks object can be easily converted into a hotspot by selecting the image and choosing Insert ➪ Hotspot.

✦ When exporting image maps, be sure to get both parts of the code: the ⟨img⟩ tag containing the link to the source image, and the ⟨map⟩ code with the hotspot data.

✦ Fireworks makes slices in three ways: with the Slice tool, with the Insert ➪ Slice command, and with the standard guides.

✦ Enabling the Slice Guide option helps to reduce the number of slices to a bare minimum.

✦ To set a slice as an animation, select it and then, from the Object panel, click the ellipse button to open the Export Preview dialog box.

In the next chapter, you'll see how to assign Behaviors for interactive effects.

✦　　　✦　　　✦

# Activating Fireworks with Behaviors

**F**rom a user's perspective, the Web includes two types of images: graphics that you look at, and graphics that you interact with. You can create the "look, but don't touch" variety of graphics with most any graphics program — Fireworks is among the few that can output interactive graphics.

Although the result may be a complex combination of images and code, Fireworks uses *Behaviors* to simplify the process. With Fireworks Behaviors, you can create everything from simple rollovers, which exchange one image for another, to more complicated interactions, in which selecting a hotspot in one area may trigger a rollover in another — while simultaneously displaying a message in the status bar. And you can do it all in Fireworks without writing a line of code.

This chapter covers all the intricacies of using Behaviors and demonstrates some techniques that combine several Behaviors. You may never use all the Behaviors that Fireworks is capable of, but once you start to use them, your Web pages will never be the same again.

## Understanding Behaviors

Before Fireworks, making your Web pages responsive to Web page visitors required in-depth programming skills or a Web-authoring program (such as Dreamweaver) that automated the process for you. The basic Web page, scripted in HTML, is fairly static; only forms allow any degree of user interaction. To activate your page, you have to use a more advanced language. Because of its integration into both major browsers, JavaScript is the language of choice for this task for most Web programmers. Although JavaScript is not as difficult to use as, say, C++, the majority of Web designers don't have the time or the inclination to master it. Now that Fireworks permits Behaviors to be integrated into the graphics, they don't have to.

A Behavior consists of two parts: an *event* and an *action*. An event is a trigger that starts an action, like pushing Play on a VCR starts a videotape. Events on the Web are either user-driven, such as moving a pointer over an image, or automatic, such as when a page finishes loading. Several other products in the Macromedia family, including Dreamweaver and Director, use Behaviors in much the same way. Generally speaking, actions range from displaying a message to launching a whole new browser window. Behaviors are said to be "attached" to a specific element on the Web page, such as a text link or an image; Behaviors in Fireworks are always attached to Web objects, such as slices or hotspots.

In one sense, Behaviors can be thought of as Encapsulated JavaScript. As a designer, you need only make a few key decisions, such as which two images to swap, and Fireworks handles the rest. Then, the code is written for you, in the HTML style of your choice. With Fireworks, you can output code for various Web-authoring programs, including Dreamweaver. Before you can export your images and associated Behavior code, however, you must assign the Behavior through the Behaviors panel.

# Using the Behaviors Panel

The Behaviors panel, new in Fireworks 2, is used to add and remove Behaviors from images. Although each Behavior has its own dialog box for selecting options and entering parameters, the Behaviors panel lists basic information for every Behavior assigned. You can assign multiple Behaviors — either the same Behavior or different ones — to any slice or hotspot; the number of Behaviors that can be attached to a single Web object has no limits.

Currently, Fireworks supports four different Behaviors:

- ✦ **Simple Rollover:** Automatically swaps the image on the second frame with the first when the user's mouse rolls over the image. Optionally, the third and fourth frames can be swapped as well.

- ✦ **Display Status Message:** Shows a message in the browser's status bar.

- ✦ **Swap Image:** Displays one image in place of another. The swapped image can be located on a different frame, in a different slice, or both. An external image can also be exchanged for the current or any other slice in the document.

- ✦ **Toggle Group:** Allows a user-defined group of slices to react when just one slice is triggered. This most often is used in navigation bars, so that only one button appears selected at any time.

The Behaviors panel (see Figure 20-1) is the central control center for using Behaviors. To show or hide the Behaviors panel, choose Window ➪ Behaviors.

The Behaviors panel enables you to select a hotspot or slice object and add or remove Behaviors. It also shows any Behaviors that have been previously added to the selected object. After you add a Behavior to a hotspot or slice object, selecting it again enables you to remove the Behavior or change its settings.

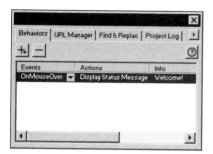

**Figure 20-1:** The Behaviors panel is the command center for attaching and deleting Behaviors from hotspots and slices.

## Adding new Behaviors

As noted previously, Behaviors are attached either to slices or hotspots. You need to understand that hotspots are only capable of triggering events, and are incapable of performing any actions. Slices, on the other hand, can both trigger and receive events.

Practically, this means that hotspots, by themselves, can be used only in conjunction with the Display Status Message Behavior; all other Behaviors require slices to work. However, you can use hotspots to trigger an action that occurs in a slice, as explained later, in the section "Working with hotspot rollovers."

The general procedure for adding a Behavior to an image is as follows:

1. Select the hotspot or slice for the Behavior to be attached.

2. Choose either Window ➪ Behaviors or the keyboard shortcut Ctrl+Alt+H (Command+Option+H) to open the Behaviors panel.

**Note**

If you have anything other than a Web object selected, Fireworks alerts you to this fact and gives you the option to create a Web object from the selected object. If nothing is selected when you try to add a Behavior, Fireworks asks you to choose a hotspot or slice first.

3. Click the Add Action button (the plus sign) and choose a Behavior from the drop-down list.

A dialog box specific to the chosen Behavior opens.

4. Enter the desired options for the Behavior and click OK when you're done.

The Behaviors panel displays the newly attached Behavior in the list window.

## Modifying a Behavior

To modify a Behavior that you've already added to a hotspot or slice object, select the hotspot or slice object and double-click the Behavior's entry on the Behaviors list in the Behaviors panel. Fireworks displays the Behavior's dialog box, in which you can adjust the settings you made when you added the Behavior.

In addition to modifying the Behavior's settings, you can select another event to trigger the Behavior. By default, Fireworks initially assigns the onMouseOver event for all events. The available events are as follows:

✦ **onMouseOver:** The user's mouse cursor hovers over the image and triggers the Behavior.

✦ **onMouseOut:** When the user's mouse cursor moves away from the image, the Behavior is triggered.

✦ **onClick:** When the user clicks the image, the Behavior is triggered.

When the Behavior is selected, the Event pop-up menu button (a down-pointing arrow) appears just to the right of the event in the Behaviors list (see Figure 20-2). Click this button to choose a new event from the Event pop-up menu.

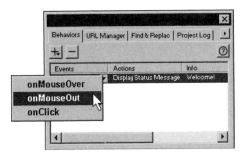

**Figure 20-2:** Click the Event pop-up button to choose another trigger for any selected Behavior.

## Deleting a Behavior

When you delete a Behavior, all the settings that you have created are lost.

To delete a Behavior, follow these steps:

1. Select the hotspot or slice object from which you want to remove the Behavior.

2. Choose the Behavior that you want to remove from the Behaviors list in the Behaviors panel.

   The Behavior's event, action, and information are highlighted.

**3.** Click the Remove Action button (the minus sign) on the Behaviors panel.

The Behavior is removed from your hotspot or slice object and its entry disappears from the Behaviors list.

# Creating Rollovers

Perhaps the most common use of JavaScript on the Web is the rollover. *Rollovers* are images in a Web page that change appearance when the user rolls the mouse over an image.

Rollovers are popular because they're fairly simple to implement, are supported by a lot of browsers, and are an effective way to heighten the feeling of interaction for Web site visitors.

## How rollovers work

To understand how a rollover works, you need to grasp a fundamental HTML concept. Web pages do not contain any images themselves — they only contain links to images. With an image, the link is referred to its source and is specified in the $<img>$ tag in HTML as the src attribute. As the user's mouse pointer hovers over the image — or in some cases, clicks the image — the src attribute is changed to another file. Because this happens very quickly, it appears as if the image itself is changing.

Before the rollover effect, a typical $<img>$ tag might read

```
<a href="home.html"><img src="button_regular.gif" height="100"
width="50" alt="home"></a>
```

After the rollover effect is applied, the code is

```
<a href="home.html"><img src="button_over.gif" height="100"
width="50" alt="home"></a>
```

As this code shows, the height, width, and alt text for the image doesn't change, nor does the link that the hyperlink is pointing to (in this example, "home.html"), as shown in the $<a>$ tag.

 **Caution**   Because only the src attribute changes with a rollover, the original image and any swapped images must have the same dimensions. You can't swap a smaller image with a larger one, or vice versa. If you do, the browser applies the height and width dimensions of the original image, leading to a distorted image.

Note that any $<img>$ can be modified, not just the $<img>$ that is rolled over. This is the foundation for disjointed rollovers, as discussed later in this chapter.

## Rollover states

Although a rollover actually switches one image for another, the illusion most often sought is one button that changes into different modes, or *states*. Before the user triggers the rollover effect, the image is in the Up state. When the rollover is triggered, the image changes to an Over state, because the user's mouse is over the image. In Fireworks, the easiest and most typical method of creating the different states for a rollover is with frames.

A basic rollover uses just two states (and thus two frames): Up and Over. A rollover may have up to four states. Table 20-1 details the rollover states and their typical associated frames.

| Table 20-1 | | |
| Rollover States | | |
| --- | --- | --- |
| *Frame* | *State* | *Description* |
| 1 | Up | The way the button looks when the user is not interacting with it. |
| 2 | Over | The button's appearance when the user's mouse is hovering over it. |
| 3 | Down | The button's appearance when it's "pressed." The Down state of a rollover button depicts the button's state on the destination Web page. For example, the Down state is commonly used to show which button was clicked to view the current Web page. |
| 4 | Over Down | The way a button that's in its Down state looks when the user's mouse hovers over it. |

## Creating rollover images

The first step in building a rollover is to create the separate rollover images that reside on the separate frames of a Fireworks document. I use either of two basic techniques to create images; which technique I choose depends on whether the rollovers are to be used by themselves or as part of a larger graphic. Both techniques involve creating an initial image, which is then duplicated and modified.

If your rollover buttons exists by themselves, use the following technique to create the images:

1. Create the initial button in Frame 1, as it should appear before being clicked by the user.

2. Click the button and choose Edit ➪ Clone to create a duplicate directly on top of it.

3. If your are going to create a Down state for this button, repeat Step 2. If you are also going to create an Over Down state, repeat Step 2 again, so that you have a total of four objects stacked on top of each other in Frame 1.

4. Select all of your button states by drawing a selection around them with the mouse. Click the Distribute to Frames button (which resembles the small movie strip) on the Layers panel.

   Your objects are distributed to separate frames, so that each button state is now in its own frame.

5. Frame 1 already contains a suitable Up state for your button. Go to Frame 2 and modify your button object slightly, to create an interesting Over state for the button. You might add a glow Live Effect to the Over state, or change the Fill or Stroke settings.

6. If you have Down and Over Down states, as well, modify them slightly on Frame 3 and Frame 4.

Tip    If the Over state of your button has a Live Effect bevel on it to give it a 3D appearance, a good way to modify subsequent states is to click the button object and modify the Look settings of the bevel Live Effect to create the impression of a 3D button moving up and down. For example, the Up state could have a Raised Look, the Over state a Highlighted Look, the Down state an Inset Look, and the Over Down state an Inverted Look.

If your rollovers are part of a larger graphic, use the following technique to create the images:

1. Create the basic image in Frame 1 of your document.

2. From the Options pop-up menu on the Frame panel, select Duplicate Frames.

   The Duplicate Frames dialog box appears.

3. In the Duplicate Frames dialog box, enter the number of frames that you want to add. In the Number text box, add one frame for each additional state used.

   For a simple rollover with just an Up and Over state, add one frame. For a rollover that also uses the Down and Over Down states, add three frames.

4. Make sure that the Insert New Frame After the Current Frame option is selected, and click OK when you're done.

   The duplicated frames are inserted.

Tip    If you're planning on using only two frames to create a simple rollover, you can also drag Frame 1 onto the New Frame button in the Frames panel.

5. In each new frame, modify the rollover section slightly to create a different image.

**Tip**    If you have multiple rollovers in the image (as with a navigation bar), you can modify them all simultaneously by selecting them and applying the changes through the Stroke, Fill, and/or Effects panel.

No matter which technique you use to create the separate rollover images, the best effect usually results from applying a degree of subtlety. If one image is too drastically different from another, the underlying image swap becomes overt and the effect of a button being clicked or highlighted is lost. Small shifts in position or an incremental change in an effect seem to work best, as shown by the examples in Figure 20-3.

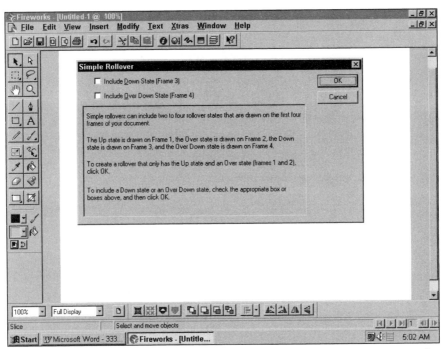

**Figure 20-3:** Fireworks offers many options for modifying one or more aspects of an image to create a successful rollover.

**Tip**    You can preview your rollover by clicking Play on the Frame controls. The frames of your image are then shown in rapid succession. Click the Stop button on the Frames control or press Esc to end the preview.

## Applying the Simple Rollover Behavior

The Fireworks engineers worked very hard to simplify the most commonly used rollover procedure, resulting in the Simple Rollover Behavior. Although Simple Rollover uses the same engine as the Swap Image Behavior, the interface has been streamlined. How simple is the Simple Rollover? For the most basic, two-state-type of rollover, you can assign a Simple Rollover to a selected slice with just two steps. Even the most complex variety of Simple Rollover takes only two additional steps. That's pretty simple.

To apply the Simple Rollover Behavior, follow these steps:

1. From the Web Layer of your image, select a slice.

2. From the Behavior inspector, choose Simple Rollover from the Add Action pop-up menu in the Behaviors panel.

   Fireworks displays the Simple Rollover dialog box (see Figure 20-4).

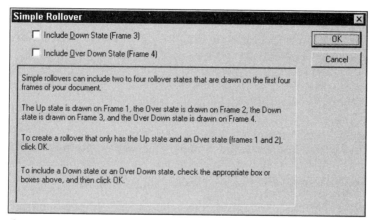

**Figure 20-4:** The Simple Rollover dialog box is the quickest way to add a rollover to your document.

3. If your rollover only uses the Up and Over states, click OK.

4. If the button has a Down state and/or an Over Down state, check Include Down State or Include Over Down State, as appropriate. Click OK when you're done.

5. To preview your rollover in your primary browser, press F12.

**Cross-Reference**    If you plan to use the rollover as a link, you need to assign a URL to it first. For detailed information on how to add a link to a Web object, see Chapter 19.

# Exporting Rollovers for the Web

Obviously, you can export images from Fireworks. When you create rollovers, the JavaScript code that controls the behavior of your images is exported within an

HTML file. The JavaScript itself is compatible with Netscape Navigator 3 and above, and Microsoft Internet Explorer 4 and above. The Macintosh version of Internet Explorer 3 will also display your rollover effects, but in Internet Explorer 3 on the Windows platform, your rollover effects will not be visible, although hyperlinks will still work.

**New Feature**

In the first version of Fireworks, only one type of rollover code was generated. Although quite effective, the style of the code was its own and did not conform with the code generated by any major Web-authoring tool. Fireworks 2 now offers a very flexible template system of outputting HTML, and allows you to pick the most suitable style of code. Fireworks comes with four different standard styles: Dreamweaver 2, Dreamweaver 2 Library, FrontPage, and Generic. The Generic code style closely resembles the code output by Fireworks 1, but even it has been enhanced.

To integrate your Fireworks-generated rollover in your Web page is a two-stage process:

✦ **Stage 1:** Export the code from Fireworks.

✦ **Stage 2:** Insert the code into your Web page.

The most difficult part of the first stage is determining which HTML style to use. For the most part, this choice is governed by the Web-authoring tool that you are using to lay out the Web page on which the rollover is being placed. The standard HTML styles included in Fireworks 2 are the following:

✦ **Generic:** The basic code, useful in hand-coded Web pages and the majority of Web authoring tools that work with standard HTML.

✦ **Dreamweaver 2:** Code stylized for Dreamweaver 2. Dreamweaver-style rollover code generated by Fireworks appears as Swap Image and Restore Swap Image in the Dreamweaver Behavior inspector.

✦ **Dreamweaver 2 Library:** HTML to be used in a Dreamweaver 2 Library has additional code that marks it as a Library item. This code must be saved in the site's Library folder. If you're using Dreamweaver 2, choosing this style of HTML makes inserting the code into a Web page extremely easy.

✦ **FrontPage:** FrontPage uses a series of *webbots* to format its code; Fireworks includes the code necessary for an image map webbot, as well as instructional code that displays when the document is opened in FrontPage.

**On the CD-ROM**

You'll find additional HTML templates on the CD-ROM accompanying this book.

# Exporting the code from Fireworks

To export a rollover — and its code — from Fireworks, follow these steps:

1. Choose File ➪ Export and optimize your image in the Export Preview dialog box. Click Next when you're ready to export.

   The Export dialog box, shown in Figure 20-5, appears.

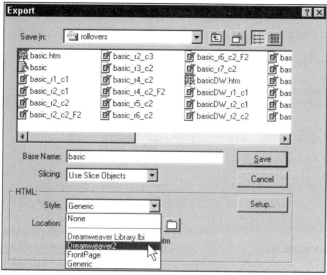

**Figure 20-5:** Choose the style of your HTML rollover code from the Export dialog box.

2. Set the filename and path of the Export in the upper part of the dialog box.

3. Choose either Use Slice Objects or Slice Along Guides from the Slicing option list.

**Note**    Most rollover situations require the Use Slice Objects option.

4. In the HTML area of the Export dialog box, select your preferred type of HTML output from the Style option list.

5. If you chose the Dreamweaver 2 Library HTML style, the Locate Site Library Directory opens, so that you can identify the Library folder of your site.

6. Choose the desired location for your HTML code:

- To output the code to the same folder as the images, select Same Directory from the Location option list.

- To output the code in the parent folder of the images, select One Level Up from the Location option list.

- To place the code in another folder, click the folder icon and select the path from the standard dialog box. Alternatively, you can open the dialog box by selecting Custom from the Location option list.

7. To alter any of the slice settings previously set, click Setup to reopen the Document Properties dialog box, and adjust your settings accordingly.

To review the possible slice settings, see Chapter 19.

8. After you make your selections, click Save to complete the Export.

## Inserting rollover code in your Web page

After you select your HTML style, Fireworks automatically outputs the requested type of code. However, Fireworks can't automatically insert the output code in an existing Web page — that chore is left to you. Luckily, it's not a tremendously complex task; in fact, in most cases, it's more on the order of cutting and pasting text than anything else.

The process for transferring rollover code to a Web page is essentially the same as that for transferring image maps or sliced images, with one very important exception; the code generated for rollovers — and all Behaviors — comes in two parts:

✦ The event portion of the code, which contains the `<img>` tags and their triggers, is stored in the `<body>` section of the Web page.

✦ The action portion of the code — with all the JavaScript functions — is kept in the `<head>` section.

You must transfer both parts of the code for the rollover to function properly.

With three out of the four HTML styles — Dreamweaver 2, FrontPage, and Generic — the process is very similar. Cut or copy the code from both the `<body>` and the `<head>` sections of the Fireworks-generated document and paste it into your existing Web page. (FrontPage does not separate the `<head>` and the `<body>` sections.) With Dreamweaver 2 Library-style code, however, the process is even simpler. Simply include the exported Library item.

For the Dreamweaver 2, FrontPage, and Generic styles of HTML rollover code, follow these steps to insert Fireworks code into your Web page:

1. Open the Fireworks-generated code in a text editor or in the text editor portion of your Web-authoring tool.

2. Select and copy to the Clipboard the section in the `<body>` tag that starts with

   `<!———— BEGIN COPYING THE TABLE HERE ————>`

   and ends with

   `<!———— STOP COPYING THE TABLE HERE ————>`

 **Note**    With Dreamweaver, you don't have to open the HTML inspector or other text editor. Just make sure that View ⇨ Invisible Elements is enabled and copy the icons representing the code.

3. Open your existing Web page in a text editor or in the text editor portion of your Web-authoring tool.

4. In the `<body>` section of your Web page, insert the code where you want the image to appear.

   If you're using the FrontPage template, your code transfer is complete and you can now preview your rollover.

5. For Generic-style and Dreamweaver 2-style HTML, return to the Fireworks-generated code and locate the `<head>` section of the HTML document.

6. Select and copy to the Clipboard the section in the `<body>` tag that starts with

   `<!———— BEGIN COPYING THE JAVASCRIPT SECTION HERE ————>`

   and ends with

   `<!———— STOP COPYING THE JAVASCRIPT HERE ————>`

7. Switch to your existing Web page.

8. Paste the copied code in the `<head>` section of the document.

   As long as the code is located in the `<head>`, placement is not critical. However, JavaScript code customarily is placed as the last element in the section.

 **Note**    Again, Dreamweaver 2 users don't need to access the HTML inspector to copy their code. Just choose View ⇨ Head Content and select the appropriate symbols. To paste the code, make sure that the Head section in the Document Window is highlighted.

After you insert both sections of the rollover code, you can preview your rollovers in any supported browser.

## Preloading Rollover Images

When the HTML document that contains your rollovers is first displayed, the Up state of your rollovers is visible, along with the other image files on the Web page. Ideally, as the user interacts with your document, the other states of the rollovers would be available from the browser cache — instead of from the Web — so that the actions happen instantaneously. Fireworks makes sure that this is the case by using JavaScript to "preload" the Over, Down, and Over Down images. If you inspect the JavaScript code output by Fireworks, you'll see functions for preloading the images and for displaying the different images `onMouseOver` and `onMouseOut`.

The addition of the Dreamweaver 2 Library-style HTML completely eliminates cutting and pasting code. As discussed in Chapter 19, the Dreamweaver Library feature allows a single repeating element to be inserted in multiple Web pages, which can then all be updated by modifying one item. Although Library items were available in the first version of Dreamweaver, Dreamweaver 2 adds the ability to associate JavaScript code with any item. This makes inserted Fireworks-generated Dreamweaver 2 Library code extremely straightforward. The only stipulation is that the rollover code must be stored in a special folder, called Library, for each local site during export. If you've never created a Library item for the current site, you need to make a new Library folder in the local site root.

After you export the HTML file as a Dreamweaver Library item, follow these steps to incorporate the rollover images and code:

1. In Dreamweaver, choose Window ➪ Library or click the Library button from the Launcher. Alternatively, you can use the keyboard shortcut, F6.

   The current site's Library palette is displayed.

2. Place your cursor in the document window where you want the rollover to appear.

3. In the Library palette, select your exported rollover from the list window.

   The preview pane of the Library palette displays the selected list items.

4. Click the Add to Page button or, alternatively, you can drag and drop the item from either the preview pane or the list window.

   The sliced image, and all the necessary code, is inserted into the Dreamweaver page.

# Advanced Rollover Techniques

The Simple Rollover is quick and easy, and I use it quite often. However, sometimes, a Web page needs more than just a Simple Rollover. Traditional rollovers can be extended with advanced techniques, to create interesting effects or even more navigation help for your users. The underlying engine for the Simple Rollover, the Swap Image Behavior, is key to these advanced techniques.

## Making disjointed rollovers

A *disjointed rollover* is one in which the user hovers their mouse over one part of an image (the event area) and another part of the image (the target area) is exchanged for the contents of another frame. A typical use for a disjointed rollover is to display details for each button in a navigation bar in a common area. Creating a disjointed rollover generally involves outlining the event and target areas with slice objects, although it is possible to trigger a disjointed rollover from a hotspot.

To create a disjointed rollover, follow these steps:

1. Create a slice object over the event area (the part of your image that the user should hover over to trigger the rollover).

2. Create a slice object over the target area (the part of your image that will seem to change).

3. Select the event area slice and choose Swap Image from the Add Action pop-up menu in the Behaviors panel.

   Fireworks displays the Swap Image dialog box (see Figure 20-6).

4. Choose the slice for the target area by choosing it from either the Target list of slice names or the Slice preview to the right of the Target list. Whichever you choose, the other is updated to reflect your choice.

5. Choose the Source for the swap by selecting a frame number from the Frame list. The area below the target slice on that frame will be used as the source for the image swap.

6. Check Restore Image onMouseOut to undo the swap again when the user moves their mouse away from the event area. Click OK when you're done.

To swap more than one slice simultaneously, repeat the preceding steps to apply multiple Swap Image Behaviors to the same Web Layer object. Through this technique, your navigation button can roll over itself and display a disjointed rollover at the same time.

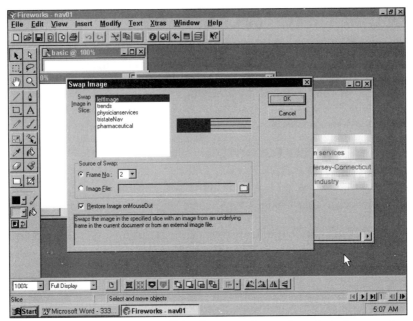

**Figure 20-6:** The Swap Image dialog box contains options that allow you to swap any slice in your document after any other slice is selected by the user.

## Creating external rollovers

Instead of using an object in another frame as the Over state for a rollover, Fireworks can also use external GIF images (regular or animated), JPEG images, or PNG images. When the rollover is viewed in a Web browser, the external file is used as the source file for a rollover, instead of using an area of a frame within your Fireworks document. External rollovers enable you to easily include animated GIF images into an existing image.

**Caution**　You can't swap one image file format for another, because of Web browser limitations. If you're going to export a slice as a GIF, make sure to use an external GIF or animated GIF only as the Over state. Similarly, if you're exporting a slice as JPEG or PNG, include only external JPEG images and PNG images, respectively, as the Over state.

Keep in mind that only the image source is changed (the `src` attribute of the `img` tag), so the browser will resize your external image to fit the size of the initial slice object it's being swapped for.

**Tip**

If you need to make a slice object the same size as an external image, so that you can swap that sliced area of your image for an external file, select the slice object, choose either Modify ➪ Transform ➪ Numeric Transform or the keyboard shortcut Ctrl+Shift+T, choose Resize from the list in the Numeric Transform dialog box, and then enter the desired width and height.

To create an external rollover, follow these steps:

1. Select the slice to trigger the external rollover.

2. Choose Swap Image from the Add Action pop-up menu in the Behaviors panel.

   Fireworks displays the Swap Image dialog box.

3. Choose the Source for the swap by clicking the Folder icon, to locate the external file through the standard Open dialog box.

4. Check Restore Image onMouseOut to undo the swap again when the user moves their mouse away from the event area.

5. Click OK when you're done.

**Caution**

When you create an external rollover, Fireworks does not preload the other button states to allow animated GIF images in the Over state of rollover buttons to play from the beginning when users trigger the rollover. If you want to preload the states of an external rollover, you have to customize Fireworks's HTML templates or the JavaScript output that you export along with your external rollover images. If you're using Dreamweaver, you can apply the Preload Images Behavior to the <body> tag and select the external file to preload.

## Working with hotspot rollovers

Hotspot rollovers enable you to create the effect of irregularly shaped rollovers. All images are rectangular boxes, so all image swaps involve swapping a rectangular area or slice. However, the image triggering the rollover does not have to be rectangular — any hotspot can be used. One limitation applies, though: the hotspots or slices can't overlap.

The key to the illusion of the hotspot rollover is Fireworks's ability to swap entire slices from different frames. Let's look at an example to see how this works. The illustration by Web designer Ruth Peyser in Figure 20-7 shows a brain with different areas outlined. Obviously, each area is far from rectangular, but the design requires that each area highlight independently when rolled over, and link to different pages on the Web site. To accomplish this goal, each area is outlined using the Polygon Hotspot tool and assigned a different URL. Then, a separate frame is made for each brain area; in the frame, just the one associated area is modified — here, it is made realistic with a highlighted type — all the other areas are left as they appear in the Up state. One large slice is created for each frame, encompassing the entire brain area. After all the frames have been created, a Swap Image Behavior is applied to each hotspot. In the Swap Image dialog box, the Source of the Swap is set to the corresponding frame number.

## Toggle groups

A *toggle group* is a way to turn a series of rollover buttons into a set of radio buttons. Each button is linked to the others, so that clicking one button and setting it to a Down state sets the other buttons to an Up state. Fireworks creates toggle groups by using JavaScript cookies. In JavaScript, a *cookie* is a small bit of information written to the user's computer. Cookies generally are used by Web sites to record visitors' selections as they travel from one Web page to another, as with a shopping cart on an e-commerce site. Fireworks uses this same technology to keep track of which button in a group has been selected.

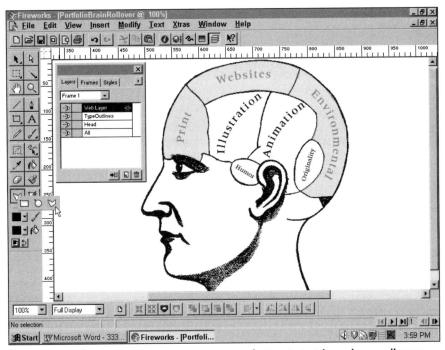

**Figure 20-7:** This brain navigation system uses hotspots to trigger large rollovers. (Courtesy of Ruth Peyser.)

Toggle groups and cookies might seem like advanced topics, but if you've implemented a three- or four-frame Simple Rollover Behavior, you've already used them. Fireworks automatically creates a toggle group (named "FwToggleGroup") for each Simple Rollover that uses a Down and/or Over Down state. You don't need to do anything else to get the toggle effect. However, if you use Swap Image to create your rollover, or want to toggle just the two Up and Over states of a Simple Rollover, you need to apply the Toggle Group Behavior explicitly.

To create a toggle group, follow these steps:

1. Create your rollover buttons, with appropriate states (Up, Over, Down, and Over Down) on the appropriate frames, one through four.

2. In Frame 1, draw a slice object over each rollover button.

3. Select each slice object, in turn, and turn it into a rollover by choosing Simple Rollover or Swap Image from the Add Action pop-up menu in the Behaviors panel.

4. Complete the Behavior as desired. Click OK when you're done.

   Your rollovers are now available to be turned into a toggle group.

5. Select all the slice objects to be included in the toggle group.

6. Choose Toggle Group from the Add Action pop-up menu in the Behaviors panel.

   Fireworks displays the Toggle Group dialog box (see Figure 20-8).

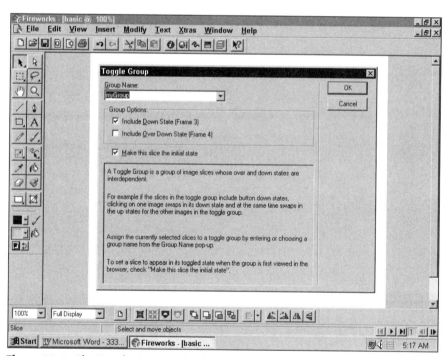

**Figure 20-8:** The Toggle Group Behavior makes any set of rollovers mutually exclusive, so that only one button can be selected at any time.

7. Enter a name for this Toggle Group Behavior in the Group Name drop-down list box. If you have included Down states in your rollovers, check Include Down State. If you have also included the Over Down state in your rollovers, check the Include Over Down State box. Click OK when you're done.

8. If you want one of the buttons to appear in its Down state by default, first deselect all the slices and then select the individual slice. Next, double-click the Toggle Group Behavior in the Behaviors panel, and check Make this Slice the Initial State. Click OK when you're done.

When you view your toggle group in a browser, the buttons change depending on which one is "clicked" (see Figure 20-9).

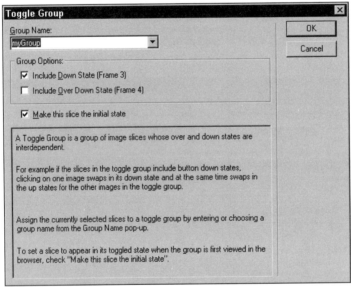

**Figure 20-9:** Clicking one button in a toggle group causes the other buttons to behave appropriately, to create the impression of a group of radio buttons, where only one button at a time can be in a Down state.

# Displaying a Status Message

You can provide the user with additional navigational assistance by supplying a message in the status bar. Status bar messages are often used with hotspots and image maps and are limited by the width of the viewer's browser. Because the browser window size can vary tremendously, lengthy messages are not recommended.

To add a status bar message to your document, follow these steps:

1. Select a slice object or hotspot and choose Display Status from the Add Action pop-up menu in the Behaviors panel.

   Fireworks displays the Display Status Message dialog box (see Figure 20-10).

2. Type in the Message box the message that you want to display when the user activates this slice.

3. Check Erase Message onMouseOut to have Fireworks remove your message when the user's mouse leaves the event area. Click OK when you're done.

4. Change the event from `onMouseOver` to `onMouseOut` or `onClick`, if necessary, by choosing that event from the event list.

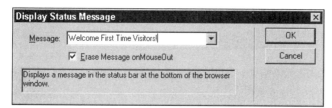

**Figure 20-10:** The Display Status Message dialog box enables you to add a status bar message to a slice or hotspot, to assist your users in navigating your site.

# Summary

Fireworks enables you to add dynamic JavaScript effects to your images, even if you don't know JavaScript, through the use of Fireworks Behaviors. When using Behaviors, keep these points in mind:

✦ The Behaviors panel is your control center for working with Behaviors.

✦ Behaviors are attached only to Web Layer objects (either hotspots or slices) and not to regular path or image objects on other layers.

✦ Rollovers can be rollover buttons, or they can be disjointed rollovers, wherein the image that changes is not the same as the one that triggered the event.

✦ Fireworks can also show text in the browser's status bar through the Display Status Message Behavior.

In the next chapter, we'll look at customizing Fireworks.

✦        ✦        ✦

# Customizing Fireworks

✦ ✦ ✦ ✦

**In This Chapter**

Fireworks automation essentials

Incorporating new export templates

Working with the Fireworks API

Building scriptlets

✦ ✦ ✦ ✦

**W**eb page designers have almost as many ways of working with code as with graphics. In addition to the increasing number of Web page authoring tools in use, different servers, IT departments, and even the coders themselves can all demand a particular flavor of HTML and/or JavaScript. It's not enough for a Web graphics tool to just output code — it's got to be flexible enough to output a wide variety of code. As flexible as Fireworks 2.

Fireworks 2 enables you to keep a full range of code styles on hand and select whichever is appropriate for a particular client, job, or even graphic. Moreover, there's an open source aspect to Fireworks 2's HTML and JavaScript output; you can customize your own export or batch processing files with Fireworks *scriptlets*. Under the hood, Fireworks 2 includes a full-featured JavaScript interpreter with custom extensions to address special Fireworks-only functions such as slices, hotspots, and behaviors. The very first part of this chapter describes how to incorporate new templates, and the balance of the chapter gives you all the details necessary to extend Fireworks to best fit the way you work.

## Understanding the HTML and JavaScript Engine

Part of the explosive growth of the Web is due to the relative accessibility of the underlying code. HTML is — as programming languages go — extremely easy to learn and abundantly available. Whereas JavaScript is more difficult, it is far more open than any compiled programming language, such as C or C++. The Fireworks engineers applied this accessibility to a novel approach: Fireworks uses JavaScript and HTML templates to output JavaScript and HTML code. The template approach makes it easy for a Web designer to choose a different style of code quickly. It also makes it feasible for the code to be easily updated or even completely customized.

**New Feature**

Fireworks 2 greatly expanded the openness of the program. In addition to a new system of interchangeable templates, any batch processing operation can be stored as a *scriptlet* and run as needed. Scriptlets — like the templates — are also written in JavaScript, and as such can be customized. In Fireworks 2, batch processing can entail find and replace, optimization, rescaling, or any other export procedure. You can even use a scriptlet to back up your files.

## Adding New Templates

Changing from one style of HTML to another is as easy as making a selection from a list of options. Adding new templates from which to choose is just as straightforward. An increasing number of Web designers, savvy in both design and code, are building HTML templates to fit a variety of circumstances. The open Fireworks HTML architecture enables multiple HTML styles to coexist, so you can switch from one to another whenever necessary.

Typically, a new HTML template consists of three files:

✦ **imagemap.htt:** This template creates the code necessary for making client-side image maps and for implementing the Display Status Message behavior, if no slices are used.

✦ **slices.htt:** Any exported image that uses slices accesses this template to create the necessary code.

✦ **Servermap.mtt:** Server-side image maps use this template to generate the required code.

**Note**

The file extensions are Fireworks originals: .htt stands for HyperText Template and .mtt is short for MapText Template.

Whereas all three are not necessary for every template — the Servermap.mtt file could be omitted if no server-side image map output was planned — a typical template includes them all.

**On the CD-ROM**

You'll find a variety of new templates to install on your system in the HTML Code folder on the CD-ROM accompanying this book.

To add a new HTML style template, follow these steps:

**1.** Using your system file manager, create a new folder within the Fireworks/Settings/HTML Code/ directory. The new folder should have a unique name to easily identify the template. This name appears in the HTML Style option list found on the Export dialog box.

2. Copy the new template files — imagemap.htt, slices.htt, and Servermap.mtt —
to your new folder.

3. Perform your export procedure as normal. When the Export dialog box
displays, choose your new template from the HTML Styles option list, as
shown in Figure 21-1.

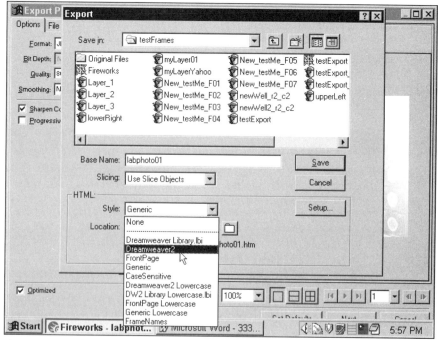

**Figure 21-1:** After adding the lowercase templates from Macromedia, the new
HTML Styles are instantly ready for use.

**Note**    It's not necessary to restart Fireworks to use the newly installed templates.

# Customizing HTML and JavaScript Output

Fireworks templates and scriptlets are all written in JavaScript. A firm
understanding of both JavaScript and HTML is necessary for customizing
Fireworks, as the templates create HTML documents.

When you begin working with Fireworks templates and scriptlets, keep these points in mind:

✦ Modifying existing code is the easiest way to get quick results and better understand Fireworks capabilities. Always work on a copy of the file you are customizing so that the original is still available.

✦ A custom export template must be saved with the identical name of the template being modified, but in a different folder. For example, if you were to create a custom slice template, the file would still be named slices.htt, but saved in a folder like myTemplates.

✦ All scriptlets must be named with the file extension .jsf.

**Note**

Macintosh users don't need to supply the .jsf file extension, except for those scriptlets in which the file type is changed to "TEXT."

✦ You can instantly test scriptlets in Fireworks by choosing File ➪ Run Script and selecting the script.

✦ You can run custom templates without relaunching Fireworks. Once the files have been copied to a folder within the Settings/HTML Code directory, the new files appear in the Export dialog box.

# Fireworks Extensions

How is a graphic engine like Fireworks able to process JavaScript code? Fireworks 2 has a JavaScript 1.2 interpreter built in. The Fireworks API (Application Interface) includes special objects with properties and methods for accessing and controlling a Fireworks document.

The Fireworks extensions are roughly divided by their two primary purposes: exporting and batch processing. Whereas some methods (also referred to as functions) or objects are only available during export operations, others are most useful for batch processing. An exporting template can include batch processing objects, but a scriptlet cannot generally use exporting methods such as WRITE_HTML(), because no output file is available.

**Tip**

Although automatic output is not available in a scriptlet as it is in the exporting templates, it is possible to use the File object to create, save, and close text files.

The exporting Fireworks extensions are further divided by which template uses them (slices.htt, imagemap.htt, or Servermap.mtt):

✦ **Global methods**: These functions are always available for debugging and user interaction; certain global methods are useful only when exporting.

✦ **Global objects**: These JavaScript objects generally handle application and file manipulation: App, Document, Find, Files, and Errors.

✦ **Hotspot objects**: These JavaScript objects are for the most part applicable to imagemap.htt and Servermap.mtt templates; the `behaviors` and `behaviorInfo` objects may also be used in the slices.htt template.

✦ **Slice objects**: These JavaScript objects are only applicable within the slices.htt template.

**Note**   The remainder of this chapter deals with advanced HTML and JavaScript concepts. If you're just getting started with JavaScript, you might want to keep a good resource nearby as you look over this chapter. I like and use *JavaScript Bible* by Danny Goodman, published by IDG Books Worldwide, Inc..

The Fireworks API employs both *static* method and properties, as well as *instance* methods and properties. A static method or property (also called a *class* method or property) is associated with the object itself, rather than an instance or copy of the object. As the name implies, an instance method or property is associated with an instance of the object. Instance methods and properties can therefore use the `this` keyword.

**Note**   In the following descriptions of each Fireworks API item, I've followed certain conventions. Arguments for methods are italicized; optional arguments are in square brackets.

# Global Methods

In the Fireworks API, global methods are used either to interact with the user or to write code. The user interaction functions are very helpful in debugging code and in helping to guide the user. The two file output functions — `WRITE_HTML()` and `write()` — are only available during an exporting operation.

## alert(*message*)

The `alert()` method displays a dialog box to the user with a Fireworks title and whatever the *message* variable or string evaluates to. The `alert()` dialog box must be dismissed before the user can continue; this type of dialog box is referred to as *modal*.

For example, the following code informs the user that the batch process job is completed:

```
alert("All done!")
```

## confirm(*message*)

The confirm() method displays a string in a modal dialog box and waits for the user to select either the OK or Cancel button, as shown in Figure 21-2. The function returns true if OK is selected and false if the user selects Cancel.

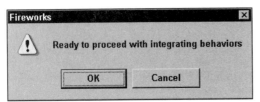

**Figure 21-2:** Use the confirm() method to get a confirmation from a user during an export or batch processing procedure.

The following code asks if the user is ready to proceed with a particular operation; if not, the operation is not carried through.

```
function doConfirm(curBeh){
  var message = "Ready to proceed with integrating " + curBeh
if (confirm(message)) {
  doFile(curBeh)
}
}
```

## prompt(*caption, text*)

The prompt() method enables the user to enter information in a modal dialog box that can be incorporated in the JavaScript code or HTML output. The prompt() dialog box includes both OK and Cancel buttons. If OK is selected, the contents of the text field are returned; otherwise null is returned.

In this example, the code lets the user select the exported slice's basename during the script's runtime.

```
function getName()
  var baseName = ""
prompt("Enter the basename for the slice now being exported",
baseName)
}
```

## WRITE_HTML(*arg1[, arg2, .... argN]*)

The WRITE_HTML() method converts each argument to a string and outputs the string to the currently open HTML file during export. This method is available only when exporting. The arguments are written one after the other, which enables you to easily concatenate text and variables. To create an end-of-line character, use \n, which is automatically converted to Carriage Return Line Feed (CR LF) for Windows and Carriage Return for Macintosh systems. Quotes within the string should be escaped with the backslash character, \.

For example, the following code writes out the <title> tag for an HTML page using a supplied filename and the first <meta> tag:

```
WRITE_HTML("<title>", exportDoc.filename, "</title>\n");
WRITE_HTML("<meta name=\"description\" content=\"Fireworks
Splice HTML\">\n");
WRITE_HTML("\n");
```

If the filename was MuseumPiece, this code would output:

```
<title>MuseumPiece</title>
<meta name="description" content="Fireworks Splice HTML">
```

## write(*arg1[, arg2, .... argN]*)

The write() method is exactly the same as the WRITE_HTML() method, and you'll find examples of it in the Servermap.mtt template. Macromedia recommends that WRITE_HTML() be used instead of write() to avoid confusion with the document.write() method of JavaScript.

# Global Objects

Fireworks API's global objects enable you to uncover most any detail about the current application settings or document, manage files, initiate a find-and-replace operation, and report errors in a localized language. These objects and their associated methods and properties are extremely valuable and used throughout templates and scriptlets alike. Any of the global objects can be used in any of the templates, without restriction.

# App

The App object accesses information about the Fireworks application as it is installed on the user's system. Through the App object, the programmer can determine the type of system (Windows or Macintosh) being used, where specific folders, such as the HTML Code folder, are located, and what files are currently open, among many other items.

Two of the most powerful methods of the App object are the getPref() and setPref() pair. With these two methods, you can control virtually every aspect of Fireworks's interface, setting and restoring options as needed.

## Properties

Most of the properties of the App object are read-only — in other words, you can get them, but you can't set them. The exceptions to the read-only rule are the three properties associated with the Batch Progress dialog box: batchStatusString, progressCountCurrent, and progressCountTotal.

### documentList

Attributes: Static property, read-only

The documentList property returns an array object with a Document object for every document currently open in Fireworks.

The following code makes the first Fireworks document active and brings it to the front for editing:

```
var editFirst = App.documentList[0].makeActive()
```

### platform

Attributes: Static property, read-only

The platform property returns win if Fireworks is running on a Windows system and mac, if on a Macintosh.

### appMacCreator

Attributes: Static property, read-only

On Macintosh systems, the appMacCreator property returns the string MKBY used in identifying the application that created the file.

### appMacJsfFileType

Attributes: Static property, read-only

On Macintosh systems, the `appMacCreator` property returns the string `JSFf` used in identifying the type of file, similar to a file extension on Windows systems.

**appDir**
Attributes: Static property, read-only

This property returns the pathname to the folder containing Fireworks.

**appBatchCodeDir**
Attributes: Static property, read-only

This property returns the pathname to the Batch Code folder.

**appExportSettingsDir**
Attributes: Static property, read-only

This property returns the pathname to the Export Settings folder.

**appFavoritesDir**
Attributes: Static property, read-only

This property returns the pathname to the URL Libraries folder.

**appHelpDir**
Attributes: Static property, read-only

This property returns the pathname to Fireworks's Help folder.

**appHtmlCodeDir**
Attributes: Static property, read-only

This property returns the pathname to the HTML Code folder.

**appPatternsDir**
Attributes: Static property, read-only

This property returns the pathname to the Patterns folder.

**appPresetsDir**
Attributes: Static property, read-only

This property returns the pathname to the Presets folder.

### appSettingsDir

Attributes: Static property, read-only

This property returns the pathname to the Settings folder.

### appTexturesDir

Attributes: Static property, read-only

This property returns the pathname to the Textures folder.

### appXtrasDir

Attributes: Static property, read-only

This property returns the pathname to the Xtras folder.

### batchStatusString

Attributes: Static property

The batchStatusString property is used to get the current string displayed in the Batch Progress dialog box. You can establish a new message in the dialog box by setting this property to the desired string. For example, the following code from the BatchTemplate.jst file displays the filename of each file as it is being processed:

```
App.batchStatusString = Files.getFilename(sourceDocumentPath);
```

### progressCountCurrent

Attributes: Static property

When a batch process is running, the dialog box keeps track of how many files have been completed, displaying something like "1 of 6 files processed." The progressCountCurrent represents the first number in this message and is used in a loop that increments the number each time a file is completed.

### progressCountTotal

Attributes: Static property

The progressCountTotal property represents the second number in the Batch Progress dialog box—the total number of files to be processed. This value can be set from the number of documents selected in the dialog box presented at the beginning of the operation; the chooseScriptTargetDialog() method returns such a list. Therefore, to get the total number of files to be processed, use code similar to this:

```
theDocList = App.chooseScriptTargetDialog(PNG);
App.progressCountTotal = theDocList.length;
```

### dismissBatchDialogWhenDone
Attributes: Static property

The default mode for Fireworks scriptlets is batch processing, so at the end of every scriptlet, Fireworks displays the Batch Progress dialog box. If a custom scriptlet does not require this dialog, set the `dismissBatchDialogWhenDone` property to true at some point in the code. Although it's customary to enter

```
App.dismissBatchDialogWhenDone = true
```

as the last line, that placement is not mandatory.

## Methods
The functions associated with the App object are all extremely useful. With them, you can do everything from open a specific file, to alter any Fireworks preferences, to close Fireworks itself.

**Note**     All of the App methods are static.

### findOpenDocument(*pathname*)
Attributes: Static method

The `findOpenDocument()` method checks to see if Fireworks already has the given pathname open in a document window. If so, that Document object is returned. If not, it returns null. Usually `findOpenDocument()` takes the pathname argument from an array of filenames, as in the following code:

```
theDocList = App.chooseScriptTargetDialog(App.getPref("PNG"))
for (var i = 0; i < theDocList.length; i++) {
theDoc = App.findOpenDocument(theDocList[i])
if theDoc == null {
  alert("No file found")
  }
}
```

### openDocument(*pathname[, openAsUntitled]*)
Attributes: Static method

The `openDocument()` method is used to open the specified file in the pathname argument. Because `openDocument()` opens another instance of an already opened file, the `openDocument()` method is often used in conjunction with `findOpenDocument()`. If the file cannot be opened, `openDocument()` returns null. If the optional `openAsUntitled` argument is set as true, the document is opened in a new Untitled window.

**Caution**

If you try to open a file by specifying the filename (rather than selecting it through a dialog box), be sure to escape each backslash character with another backslash, like this: **C:\\Fireworks\\borg.png**.

### quit()
Attributes: Static method

The quit() method, when invoked, closes Fireworks. No further confirmation is offered unless an open document has been modified, but not saved. You can use the confirm() global method to create a confirmation routine in this way:

```
if (confirm("Ready to Quit?")) App.quit()
```

### locateDocDialog(*maxnumdocs [, formatlist]*)
Attributes: Static method

The locateDocDialog() method presents the user with a dialog to choose one or more files. The maxnumdocs argument tells Fireworks whether to use the standard Open dialog box to open a single file or to use the Open Multiple Files dialog box for loading more than one. Use 1, 0, or -1 to open the standard Open dialog and any number higher than 1 to specify the Open Multiple Files dialog box. The number used as an argument does not limit the number of files that can be opened in any other way.

The formatlist argument is an optional list of acceptable file types to open. If formatlist is omitted, then all files will be listed. The formatlist argument is in the form of an array. For example, to specify just the PNG and TIFF file formats for a single file dialog box, use the following code:

```
var formats = [ "PNG", "kMoaCfFormat_TIFF" ];
var theFiles = App.locateDocDialog(1, formats);
for (f in theFiles) {
alert(theFiles[f]);
}
```

**Note**

The resulting dialog box also permits the user to select All Readable Files and All Files.

The locateDocDialog() method returns an array of filenames or null if the dialog box is canceled.

**Tip**

You can also access whatever file types the user's system has available by getting the MultiFileBatchTypes setting with code like this:

```
var thePrefs = App.getPrefs(MultiFileBatchTypes)
var theFile = App.locateDocDialog(1,thePrefs)
```

The `formatlist` arguments must take the following form:

| Argument | File Type |
|---|---|
| ADOBE AI3 | Adobe Illustrator |
| kMoaCfFormat_BMP | BMP file |
| kMoaCfFormat_FreeHand7and8 | Macromedia FreeHand 7.0 or 8.0 |
| kMoaCfFormat_GIF | GIF file |
| kMoaCfFormat_JPEG | JPEG file |
| kMoaCfFormat_LRG | Macromedia xRes LRG file |
| kMoaCfFormat_PICT | Macintosh PICT file |
| kMoaCfFormat_RTF | Rich Text file |
| kMoaCfFormat_Text | Plain text file |
| kMoaCfFormat_TIFF | TIFF file |
| PNG | PNG file |

### chooseScriptTargetDialog(*formatlist*)
Attributes: Static method

Similar to `locateDocDialog()`, the `chooseScriptTargetDialog()` method displays a dialog box (Figure 21-3) so that the user can select the files to be targetted for an operation. Unlike `locateDocDialog()`, here the formatlist is a required argument and no maximum number of documents can be specified. In this example, file formats are limited to BMP files:

```
var theFiles = App.chooseScriptTargetDialog("kMoaCfFormat_BMP")
```

**Tip**  To restrict the resulting dialog box from the `chooseScriptTargetDialog()` method to multiple file types, use the same array structure as `locateDocDialog()`.

**Figure 21-3:** Pop up a dialog box to enable users to select which files will be targeted for a custom operation with the `chooseScriptTargetDialog()` method.

**getPref(*prefname*) and setPref(*prefname, prefval*)**
Attributes: Static methods

The getPref() and setPref() methods enable you to read—and alter—the current program settings for almost every aspect of Fireworks. From the default fill color to the *x* and *y* coordinates for the Edit Gradient dialog box, these two methods provide a very powerful peek into the program. For an example of the powerful possibilities these methods bring, you don't need to look any further than the heart of the 2.02 upgrade, the scaling options. Each scaling option is invoked by running a scriptlet that alters the Image Resample and Transform modes, such as this one for Bicubic Interpolation:

```
App.setPref("ImageResampleMode", "2");
App.setPref("ImageTransformMode", "2");
```

The prefname and prefval arguments are set keywords contained in the Fireworks 2 Preferences file. As you can imagine, changing these values haphazardly can prove very disruptive to the program. Many of the preferences are not intended to be altered by the user, such as the DragTab positions. The primary settings are detailed in Table 21-1; all of the settings can be found in the Fireworks 2 Preferences file.

Caution

Macromedia strongly recommends that you do not alter any of these settings unless you are extremely confident of your abilities. Should you ever mistakenly damage your preferences, you can restore the defaults by deleting the Fireworks 2 Preferences text file found in the main Fireworks folder and restarting Fireworks.

| Table 21-1 Key Preferences and Their Settings | |
|---|---|
| **Preference** | **Value Type** |
| _kPref__BehaviorsPanel__ActionsWidth | Number |
| _kPref__BehaviorsPanel__EventsWidth | Number |
| _kPref__BehaviorsPanel__InfoWidth | Number |
| AllowPictRgba | True \| False |
| AlwaysAppendFileExtensions | True \| False |
| AnimGifDangerousOpt | True \| False |
| AntiAliasFillAmount | Number |
| ApplyNPreviewVisible | True \| False |
| AutoGenBehaviors | True \| False |

| Preference | Value Type |
|---|---|
| AutoGrowImages | True \| False |
| AutoImageEdit | True \| False |
| BatchDoBackup | Number |
| BatchDoExport | Number |
| BatchDoReplace | Number |
| BatchExpFileFitHeight | Number |
| BatchExpFileFitWidth | Number |
| BatchExpFileHeight | Number |
| BatchExpFileMod | Text |
| BatchExpFileModType | Number |
| BatchExpFilePct | Number |
| BatchExpFileScaleType | Number |
| BatchExpFileSettings | Export Setting |
| BatchExpFileWidth | Number |
| BatchGenName | Filename |
| BatchIncrementalBackup | True \| False |
| BatchTemplateName | Filename |
| BatchWhichFiles | Number |
| BezFitCornerAngle | Number |
| BezFitExtraTightTolerance | Number |
| BezFitExtraTightToleranceStep | Number |
| BezFitMaxPctLenDiff | Number |
| BezFitTolerance2 | Number |
| BezHandlePickDist | Number |
| BezInterpMaxErr | Number |
| BlackAndWhiteForDirector | True \| False |
| BrushCurrentColor | Red-Green-Blue-Alpha numbers |
| BrushDefaultColor | Red-Green-Blue-Alpha numbers |
| BucketFillsSelection | True \| False |

*Continued*

## Table 21-1 *(continued)*

| Preference | Value Type |
| --- | --- |
| BucketMouseOverPreview | True \| False |
| CheckAssociationOnStartup_jsf | True \| False |
| CheckAssociationOnStartup_png | True \| False |
| ColorMixerAutoApply | True \| False |
| ColorMixerColorModel | Number |
| CropTool_Constraint | Number |
| CropTool_Horiz | Number |
| CropTool_Vert | Number |
| CropToolStickiness | Number |
| CurrentFavoritesFile | URLs.htm |
| CustomCanvasColor | Red-Green-Blue-Alpha Numbers |
| DefaultDocColorState | Number |
| DefaultDocRes | Number |
| DefaultDocResUnit | Number |
| DefaultDocSize | X, Y coordinates |
| DisableUnicode | True \| False |
| DontShowWebHelpDialog | True \| False |
| DragOutThreshInPixels | Number |
| EditGradDialogPos | X, Y coordinates |
| EditURLChangesAll | True \| False |
| EraserToolDiameter | Number |
| EraserToolEraseMode | Number |
| EraserToolIsCircle | True \| False |
| EraserToolSoftEdge | Number |
| EraserToolStampSpacing | Number |
| ExpandAnimatedGifFrames | True \| False |
| ExpandCapType | Number |
| ExpandJoinType | Number |
| ExpandMiterLimit | Number |

| Preference | Value Type |
|---|---|
| ExpandWidth | Number |
| ExportPngWithAdam7Interlacing | True \| False |
| ExportPreviewPos | *X, Y* coordinates |
| ExportPreviewSize | *X, Y* coordinates |
| ExportSilently | True \| False |
| ExportSlicesImageFolder | Path |
| ExtraPatternsDir | Path and filename |
| ExtraPhotoshopPluginsDir | Path and filename |
| ExtraTexturesDir | Path and filename |
| EyeDropperExtraSamples | Number |
| FeedbackColor | Red-Green-Blue-Alpha Numbers |
| FFReplaceFont | Font name |
| FFSearchFont | Font name |
| FillCurrentColor | Red-Green-Blue-Alpha numbers |
| FillDefaultColor | Red-Green-Blue-Alpha numbers |
| FindReplaceOptions_BackupOpts | Number |
| FindReplaceOptions_LogChanges | Number |
| FindReplaceOptions_ReplaceThenFind | Number |
| FindReplaceOptions_SaveNClose | Number |
| FreeFormGravDiameter | Number |
| FreeFormGravDiameter_Sens | True \| False |
| FreeFormGravity_Preview | True \| False |
| FreeFormGravPower | Number |
| FreeFormGravPower_Sens | True \| False |
| FreeFormPushNPull_Preview | True \| False |
| FreeFormPushNPullLen | Number |
| FreeFormPushNPullLen_Sens | True \| False |
| GridGuideSnapDist | Number |
| GuidePickDist | Number |

*Continued*

## Table 21-1 *(continued)*

| Preference | Value Type |
| --- | --- |
| HideEdgesAutoResets | True \| False |
| HtmlCharSet | Label |
| ImageResampleMode | Number |
| ImageTransformMode | Number |
| InfoPanelColorModel | Number |
| InfoPanelPos | *X, Y* coordinates |
| InfoPanelRulerUnits | Number |
| InitialSettings_Alt | Text |
| InitialSettings_DoDemo | True \| False |
| InitialSettings_ExportUndefined | True \| False |
| InitialSettings_ImageMap | Number |
| InitialSettings_NameMode | Number |
| InitialSettings_ShimMode | Number |
| InitialSettings_URL | URL |
| InsetAmount | Number |
| InsetDirection | Number |
| InsetJoinType | Number |
| InsetMiterLimit | Number |
| InspectorsAutoApply | True \| False |
| InternalWinSetting06 | Number |
| InternalWinSetting07 | Number |
| JsInterpIdleThreshInMilliseconds | Number |
| LassoToolAntiAliased | True \| False |
| LassoToolFeatherAmount | Number |
| LastExportDirectory | Path |
| LegLookForPNG | Number |
| LockGuides | True \| False |
| LZWSmoothingAmount | Number |
| MainWindowDim | *X, Y* coordinates |

| Preference | Value Type |
|---|---|
| MainWindowMaximized | True \| False |
| MainWindowPos | *X, Y* coordinates |
| MakeDocsDirtyOnOpen | True \| False |
| MarqueeToolAntiAliased | True \| False |
| MarqueeToolFeatherAmount | Number |
| MarqueeToolMode | Number |
| MarqueeToolModeRatioX | Number |
| MarqueeToolModeRatioY | Number |
| MarqueeToolModeWidthX | Number |
| MarqueeToolModeWidthY | Number |
| MaxFolderDropDepth | Number |
| MaxUndos | Number |
| MoveBitsWithPtrToolUsesFillColor | True \| False |
| MultiFileBatchTypes | Format list |
| MultiFileSearchTypes | Format list |
| MultiFrameEditing | True \| False |
| NeverBugForRegistration | True \| False |
| NewDocHTMLTemplate | Filename |
| NewDocSlicing | True \| False |
| NewWindowsShowRulers | True \| False |
| NumericXformXformsBFE | True \| False |
| NumFloatingInspectors | Number |
| OnionSkin_AfterOpacity | Number |
| OnionSkin_BeforeOpacity | Number |
| OriginalFilesFolderName | Original Files |
| PasteExportOrder | Format list |
| PasteImportOrder | Format list |
| PencilAntiAlias | True \| False |
| PencilAutoErase | True \| False |

*Continued*

## Table 21-1 *(continued)*

| Preference | Value Type |
|---|---|
| PixelTrimThreshold | Number |
| PolygonToolIsAuto | Number |
| PolygonToolIsStar | True \| False |
| PolygonToolSides | Number |
| PolygonToolSpikiness | Number |
| PreviewDrag | True \| False |
| PreviewDragThreshInMilliseconds | Number |
| PrimaryBrowser | Path and filename |
| PrimaryScratchDisk | Path |
| RectToolCornerRadius | Number |
| ReplaceLogFileName | Filename |
| ResizeConstrain | True \| False |
| ResizeResample | True \| False |
| SaveAsMinimalFileWithBogusPngData | True \| False |
| SaveMkb1CompatFiles | True \| False |
| SavePngWithAdam7Interlacing | True \| False |
| ScriptFilesSaveAsText | True \| False |
| ScrubPressure | True \| False |
| ScrubRate | Number |
| ScrubVelocity | True \| False |
| SecondaryBrowser | Path and filename |
| SecondaryFeedbackColor | Red-Green-Blue-Alpha Numbers |
| SecondaryScratchDisk | Path |
| SelectionMouseOverPreview | True \| False |
| ShowAllFontsInMenu | True \| False |
| ShowGrid | True \| False |
| ShowGuides | True \| False |
| ShowSliceGuides | True \| False |
| SimplifyAmount | Number |

| Preference | Value Type |
|---|---|
| SingleLayerEditing | True \| False |
| SliceGuideColor | Red-Green-Blue-Alpha Numbers |
| SnapToGrids | True \| False |
| SnapToGuides | True \| False |
| StampToolEdge | Number |
| StampToolMode | Number |
| StampToolSize | Number |
| StampToolSource | Number |
| StampToolStampSpacing | Number |
| StopImageEditModeInPixels | Number |
| StylesOptions_LargePreview | Number |
| SwapFileChunkSize | Number |
| SwapFileReclaimThreshFraction | Number |
| SwapFileReclaimThreshInMegabytes | Number |
| Text_AntiAliasedFill | True \| False |
| Text_AutoKern | True \| False |
| Text_BaselineShift | Number |
| Text_Bold | True \| False |
| Text_Editor_DefaultFont | Font name |
| Text_Font | Font name |
| Text_HorizScale | Number |
| Text_Italic | True \| False |
| Text_Justification | Number |
| Text_Leading | Number |
| Text_LeadingMode | Number |
| Text_Orientation | Number |
| Text_RangeKerning | Number |
| Text_Size | Number |
| Text_Underline | True \| False |

*Continued*

| Table 21-1 *(continued)* | |
|---|---|
| **Preference** | **Value Type** |
| TextEditor_AutoApply | True \| False |
| TextEditor_AutoApplyTime | Number |
| TextEditor_RememberALLSettings | True \| False |
| TextEditor_ShowFont | True \| False |
| TextEditor_ShowSizeAndColor | True \| False |
| TextEditorPos | *X, Y* coordinates |
| TextEditorSize | *X, Y* coordinates |
| TextToolRevertsToPointer | True \| False |
| ToolInspPos | *X, Y* coordinates |
| ToolInspVis | True \| False |
| TransformConstrain | True \| False |
| TransformToolsAutoTrim | True \| False |
| Transmogrify | Number |
| TryInterleaveSwapFiles | True \| False |
| TryToRetainLayers | True \| False |
| TwainSource | Path |
| UseExtraPatternsDir | True \| False |
| UseExtraPhotoshopPluginsDir | True \| False |
| UseExtraTexturesDir | True \| False |
| UseLastExportDirectory | True \| False |
| UsePrecisionCursors | True \| False |
| UseSliceGuides | True \| False |
| UseSmallVectorImportPages | True \| False |
| WandToolAntiAliased | True \| False |
| WandToolFeatherAmount | Number |
| WandToolTolerance | Number |
| WarnOnFlattenPathForFilter | True \| False |
| WebsnapRange | Number |
| WriteThumbnailPreview | True \| False |
| XformToolXformsBFE | True \| False |
| XPDPaletteFeedback | True \| False |

# Document

The Document object in the Fireworks API is similar to the Document object in JavaScript. Both deal with the current, active document on a very precise exacting level. The Fireworks Document object is used to define the export parameters as well as the basis for a find-and-replace operation. Because most of this object is concerned with a specific document, it has no static properties and only two static methods, findExportFormatOptionsByName() and makeGoodNativeFilePath().

## Properties

The Document object has only five properties, but they all perform a very useful function. With them, you can determine whether a file is open, whether it's been modified, gather the current filename and — most importantly — describe how an document is to be exported.

Because all of the Document object properties work with specific documents, they must be associated with an instance of the Document object and not the Document object itself. To get an instance of the Document object, use an App method such as findOpenDocument() or openDocument(), as in this code:

```
var theDoc = App.openDocument(docPathname)
```

### isValid
Attributes: Read-only

The isValid property returns true if the current document is still open and false if it has been closed.

### isDirty
It's often necessary to determine whether a file has been modified before deciding how to act on it. The isDirty property returns true if the document has been modified since the last save or if it has never been saved; otherwise the property returns false.

### filePathForSave
The filePathForSave property is used to find and set the filename of the current document. This property is essential for creating backup files. If the file has never been saved, the result is null. The following code relies on the filePathForSave property to store a filename for later use during a backup operation.

```
function saveName(theDoc) {
  var sourcePath
  if (theDoc.filePathForSave != null) {
  sourcePath = theDoc.filePathForSave
  }
}
```

### filePathForRevert
Attribute: Read-only

The `filePathForRevert` property returns the pathname from which the Revert operation reads — in other words, the file opened to create the current document. Use `filePathForRevert` to get an original pathname for non-Fireworks native files or documents opened as "Untitled." This property returns null if the document was newly created and not read from a file.

### exportFormatOptions
Although all of the properties of any object are important, certainly the most complex — and arguably the most useful — property of the Fireworks Document object is `exportFormatOptions`. The `exportFormatOptions` property returns an object that contains the current export settings. Most of the export settings are expressed as a number rather than as a string. For example, the following code:

```
var theFormat = theDoc.exportFormatOptions.exportFormat
```

returns a 0 if the format is GIF and a 1 if JPEG. Several settings — `paletteInfo`, `paletteEntries` and `frameInfo` — are expressed as arrays.

Table 21-2 details the `exportFormatOptions` settings.

**Table 21-2**
**exportFormatOptions Settings**

| Setting | Possible Values |
|---------|-----------------|
| exportFormat | 0 (GIF), 1 (JPEG), 2 (PNG), 3 (Custom, including TIFF, xRes LRG, and BMP), or 4 (GIF-Animation) |
| macCreator | "XXXX," used to choose format if `exportFormat` = Custom |
| macFileType | "XXXX," used to choose format if `exportFormat` = Custom |
| colorMode | 0 (Indexed), 1 (24-bit color), or 2 (32-bit color) |
| paletteMode | 0 (Custom), 1 (Adaptive), 2 (Grid), 3 (Monochrome), 4 (Macintosh System), 5 (Windows System), 6 (Exact), or 7 (Web 216) |

| *Setting* | *Possible Values* |
|---|---|
| paletteInfo (array) colorModified colorLocked colorTransparent colorDeleted colorSelected | True \| False True \| False True \| False True \| False True \| False |
| paletteEntries (array) colorstring1 colorstring2 etc. | Red-Green-Blue-Alpha numbers where each number is in the range 0-255. Example: "255 0 0 255" If Alpha is 0, the color is transparent. |
| numCustomEntries | 0–256 |
| numEntriesRequested | 0–256 |
| numGridEntries | 0–256 |
| ditherMode | 0 (None), 1 (2-by-2), or 2 (Diffusion) |
| ditherPercent | 0–100 |
| paletteTransparency | 0 (None), 1 (Index), 2 (IndexAlpha), or 3 (RGBA) |
| transparencyIndex | 0–255, or -1 if none |
| webSnapTolerance | Always set to 14 |
| jpegQuality | 1–100 |
| jpegSmoothness | 1–8 |
| jpegSubsampling | 1–100 |
| percentScale | 1–100000 |
| xSize | -100000 to 100000 |
| ySize | -100000 to 100000 |
| cropTop | 0–Image Height minus 1 |
| cropLeft | 0–Image Width minus 1 |
| cropBottom | 0–Image Height minus 1 |
| cropRight | 0–Image Width minus 1 |
| applyScale | True \| False |
| useScale | True \| False |
| crop | True \| False |
| optimized | True \| False |

*Continued*

| Table 21-2 *(continued)* | |
|---|---|
| **Setting** | **Possible Values** |
| progressiveJPEG | True \| False |
| interlacedGIF | True \| False |
| animAutoCrop | True \| False |
| animAutoDifference | True \| False |
| localAdaptive | True \| False |
| webSnapAdaptive | True \| False |
| name | Text–Name of Setting |
| frameInfo (array) gifDisposalMethod delayTime | 0 (Unspecified), 1 (None), 2 (Background), or 3 (Previous) 0–1000000 |
| savedAnimationRepeat | 0–1000000 |

The useScale and applyScale settings of the Document object are dependent on each other to determine the type of scaling that is actually used. The following rules determine the scaling type:

✦ If useScale if false, and applyScale is false, no scaling is done on export.

✦ If useScale is true, then percentScale is used, regardless of the setting of applyScale.

✦ If useScale if false and applyScale is true, then xSize and ySize are used to determine the scaling as follows:

• If the value is positive, the value is used as specified for the *x* or *y* axis.

• If the value is zero, the *x* or *y* axis varies without limit.

• If the value is negative, the *x* or *y* axis varies, but may be no larger than the absolute value of the specified number.

Note that if one value is positive and one is negative, the positive value is always used.

### Methods
The Document object methods provide a great deal of functionality. These functions activate, save, and close files — and more. The findExportFormatOptions() and makeGoodNativeFilePath() methods are static, and the rest are instance methods.

### findExportFormatOptionsByName(*name*)
Attribute: Static method

This method is used to access any preset Export Settings. If an Export Setting is preset with the given name, a Document object is returned with the same settings as the `exportFormatOptions` property. If there is no preset by the given name, null is returned.

### makeGoodNativeFilePath(*pathname*)
Attribute: Static method

To make sure that a given pathname ends in a proper Fireworks .png extension, the `makeGoodNativeFilePath` method is applied. When used, it converts any file extension to a .png. For example, the following code snippets all return the same filename, C:\images\logo.png:

```
var theFile =
Document.makeGoodNativeFilePath("C:\\images\\logo.ping")

var theFile =
Document.makeGoodNativeFilePath("C:\\images\\logo.bmp")

var theFile =
Document.makeGoodNativeFilePath("C:\\images\\logo")
```

**Note**    As with other methods passing a filename, you must escape the backslash character if entering a literal filepath.

### makeActive()
Use the `makeActive()` method to make the referenced document the active one in Fireworks. The active document is then brought to the front of all other documents.

### save([*okToDoSaveAs*])
The `save()` method is used to store the document in its default location. If the optional `okToDoSaveAs` argument is true, then the user will be prompted for a file location if the document has never been saved. If `okToDoSaveAs` is false and the file has never been saved, the operation will fail and return `false`. Upon a successful save, the document's dirty flag is cleared. The `save()` method returns `true` if the save operation completes successfully, and `false` otherwise.

**Tip**   To force a Save As dialog box to appear, set the `App.filePathForSave` property to null before calling `Document.save()`.

### close([*promptUserIfDocIsDirty*])

Closing a document is accomplished with the `close()` method. By specifying the optional `promptUserIfDocIsDirty` argument as true, a confirmation dialog box appears to give the user an opportunity to save the document before it closes. If the argument is false, the file closes and any changes are lost.

**Caution**   Obviously, specifying the `promptUserIfDocIsDirty` argument as false is very risky and should only be used with extreme caution.

### saveCopyAs(*pathname*)

To store a duplicate of the current document, use the `saveCopyAs()` method. The full pathname, for example, "C:\\images\\logo.png," must be used. With this method, neither the `filePathForSave` nor `isDirty` property are affected.

### makeFind(*findParms*)

Within the Fireworks API, a separate Find object exists for running a find-and-replace operation. To link the Find object to a particular document, use the `MakeFind()` method to make the Find object and specify the criteria. As the Fireworks find-and-replace facility is capable of searching four different types of elements — text, font, color, and URLs — the `findParms` argument can take four different array forms.

For example, a text find-and-replace operation that searches for "FW" using the Whole Word option, and replaces it with "Fireworks," is defined with code like this:

```
var findParms = {
whatToFind: "text",
find: "FW",
replace: "Fireworks",
wholeWord: true,
matchCase: false,
regExp: false
};
var theFinder = Document.makeFind(findParms)
```

Note the use of quotation marks and parentheses to delineate the parameters. Once the Find object is defined, the actual operation is carried out with the Find object's `replaceAll()` method. Table 21-3 details the four types of Find parameters.

## Table 21-3
## Parameters for makeFind()

| Type of Find | Parameter | Possible Values |
|---|---|---|
| text | whatToFind | "text" |
| | find | "Any text string" |
| | replace | "Any text string" |
| | wholeWord | (True \| False) |
| | matchCase | (True \| False) |
| | regExp | (True \| False) |
| font | whatToFind | "font" |
| | find | "fontname-to-find" |
| | replace | "fontname-to-replace" |
| | findStyle | (-1 to 7) where -1 (StyleAnyStyle), 0 (StylePlain), 1 (StyleBold), 2 (StyleItalic), 3 (StyleBoldItalic), 4 (StyleUnderline), 5 (StyleBoldUnderline), 6 (StyleItalicUnderline), or 7 (StyleBoldItalicUnderline) |
| | replaceStyle | (-1 to 7) as described under findStyle |
| | findMinSize | (0–9999) |
| | findMaxSize | (0–9999) |
| | replaceSize | (0–9999, or -1 for "same size") |
| color | whatToFind | "color" |
| | find | "Red Green Blue Alpha values from 0–255" |
| | replace | "Red Green Blue Alpha values from 0–255" |
| | fills | (True \| False) |
| | strokes | (True \| False) |
| | effects | (True \| False) |
| URL | whatToFind | "url" |
| | find | "url-to-find" |
| | replace | "url-to-replace" |
| | wholeWord | (True \| False) |
| | matchCase | (True \| False) |
| | regExp | (True \| False) |

**Note**

When defining color strings for use in the color find-and-replace operation, it's often easier to define a few key variables to reuse again and again, such as these:

```
var kSolidWhite = "255 255 255 255";
var kSolidBlack = "0 0 0 255";
var kTransparent = "255 255 255 0";
var kRed = "255 0 0 255";
var kGreen = "0 255 0 255";
var kBlue = "0 0 255 255";
```

### exportTo(pathname [, exportOptions])

The actual export operation is handled by the `exportTo()` method. The full pathname argument is mandatory and if the optional `exportOptions` argument is omitted, the current export settings are used. Should `exportOptions` be specified, they are used without affecting the document's `exportFormatOptions` property. The `exportTo()` method returns `true` if it is successful.

## Find

There is only one property and one method for Fireworks's Find object, but — as you might expect — they're important.

### numItemsReplaced

Attributes: Read-only

The `numItemsReplaced` property enables you to get the number of items replaced during a find-and-replace operation. This value is then often reported to the user in the form of a dialog box, as with the code below:

```
var replaced = theFinder.numItemsReplaced
alert("All done. " + replaced + " items replaced.")
```

### replaceAll()

The engine of a find-and-replace operation is found in the `replaceAll()` method. Once applied to a Find object created by `Document.makeFind()`, `replaceAll()` returns `true` if any replacements were made and `false` if none were.

## Files

Manipulating files is a large part of any batch procedure, whether it involves exporting, scaling, or find-and-replace. The Files object of the Fireworks API is very robust and covers more than 20 functions that permit you to perform most any file operation. The vast majority (all but three) of these methods are static and must be called from the Files object itself. No properties are associated with the Files object.

## getLastErrorString()

Attribute: Static method

If the last call to a method in the Files object resulted in an error,
`getLastErrorString()` returns text describing the error. If the last call
succeeded, this method returns null. The following example code returns an error if
a copy operation was unsuccessful:

```
if (Files.copy(sourcePath, destPath) == false) return
Files.getLastErrorString();
```

The error returned is taken from the Fireworks API Errors object, described later in
this chapter. Note that `getLastErrorString()` is dedicated to errors committed
by methods of the Files object; the Errors object is used for displaying error
messages resulting from other situations.

## makePathFromDirAndFile(*dirname, filename*)

Attribute: Static method

Often, during a batch operation, Fireworks is called upon to take a directory from
one source and a filename from another and put them together to store a file. That
is exactly what `makePathFromDirAndFile()` does. The directory is specified in the
first argument, the filename in the second, as shown in this example:

```
var dirname = "c:\\Fireworks\\"
var filename = "borg.png"
theNewFile = Files.makePathFromDirAndFile(dirname, filename)
```

In this example, `c:\Fireworks\borg.png` is returned.

## getTempFilePath(*[dirname]*)

Attribute: Static method

The `getTempFilePath()` method returns a pathname in the system temporary
files directory. This function does not create a file; it simply returns a unique
pathname that does not conflict with any existing file. If the `dirname` argument is
given (and is not null), the pathname will indicate a file in the given directory rather
than in the temporary files directory. The `dirname` argument is taken literally and
no other path information is appended.

On a Windows system, `getTempFilePath()` returns `c:\windows\TEMP\00000001`
or `c:\TEMP\00000001` depending on your system; on a Macintosh it generally
returns `<BootDrive>:Temporary Items:00000001`, where *BootDrive* is the name
of your booting drive.

### createDirectory(pathname)

Attribute: Static method

It's not uncommon to need new directories when running batch procedures; the `createDirectory()` method handles this procedure for you. If the folder creation was successful, the function returns `true`; if not, it returns `false`.

### deleteFile(*pathname*)

Attribute: Static method

To remove a file or directory, use the `deleteFile()` method. If the deletion is successful, `true` is returned. `False` is returned if the pathname supplied in the argument does not exist or if the file or directory could not be deleted.

### deleteFileIfExisting(*pathname*)

Attribute: Static method

Rather than run a separate function to see if a file exists before removing it, you could use the `deleteFileIfExisting()` method. With this method, in addition to returning `true` if the file is successfully removed, `true` is also returned if the supplied pathname does not exist. The only circumstance in which `false` is returned is if the found file could not be removed.

### swap(*pathname, pathname*)

Attribute: Static method

Fireworks provides numerous methods for moving files around during an export operation; the `swap()` method switches the contents of one pathname for the contents of another. This function is helpful when you need to exchange a source file for a backup file.

**Note**

The `swap()` method has two limitations: first, you can only swap files, not folders, and second, both files to be swapped must be on the same drive. This routine sometimes failed inappropriately in Fireworks 2.0 when files were swapped on network drives under Windows, but the problem was fixed in version 2.02.

### copy(*sourcePathname, destinationPathname*)

Attribute: Static method

To copy a file to a new location quickly, use the `copy()` method. You can place the copy on a different drive, if necessary, but you can't copy folders with this function. This function also fails if the file named in the `destinationPathname` argument already exists; `copy()` won't overwrite a file.

### getExtension(*filename*)

Attribute: Static method

To retrieve just the filename extension, use the `getExtension()` method. For example, the code

```
var theExt = Files.getExtension("logo.png")
```

returns `.png`. If the filename has no extension, an empty string is returned.

### getFilename(*pathname*)

Attribute: Static method

To extract a filename from a fully qualified pathname, use the `getFileName()` method. The code,

```
var theFname =
Files.getFilename("C:\images\winter\seasonal.png")
```

returns `seasonal.png`.

### setFilename(*pathname, filename*)

Attribute: Static method

The `setFileName()` method replaces a filename in a pathname with another specified filename. For instance, the code

```
Files.setFilename("C:\images\winter\snowflake.png",
"snowstorm.png" )
```

returns `C:\images\winter\snowstorm.png`. Note that this function does not affect the file on disk in any way, but is just a convenient way to manipulate pathnames.

### getDirectory(*pathname*)

Attribute: Static method

The parallel function to `getFilename()` is `getDirectory()`, where just the directory portion of a pathname is extracted. In the example,

```
var theFname =
Files.getFilename("C:\images\winter\seasonal.png")
```

`C:\images\winter\` is returned.

### isDirectory(*pathname*)
Attribute: Static method

To verify that a supplied pathname is a directory and not a file, use the isDirectory() method. If the pathname is not a valid directory, true is returned.

### exists(*pathname*)
Attribute: Static method

You can check the existence of either a file or directory with the exists() method. True is returned unless the file or directory does not exist or the supplied pathname is invalid.

### rename(*pathname, filename*)
Attribute: Static method

Use the rename() method to change a full pathname to a new one. For example,

```
Files.setFilename("C:\images\logo.png", "newlogo.png")
```

Whereas setFileName() appears to perform the same operation in the same way, only rename() actually alters the name of the file on the drive.

### createFile(*pathname[, mactype [, maccreator]]*)
Attribute: Static method

To create a new file of any type, use the createFile() method. This method fails if the file already exists. The mactype and maccreator arguments are necessary for making a new permanent file on a Macintosh system.

### enumFiles(*pathname*)
Attribute: Static method

The enumFiles() method returns an array of pathnames for every file specified in the argument. The pathname argument should not, however, point to a file; if it does, enumFiles() returns just the single pathname for the file.

### open(*pathname, wantWriteAccess*)
Attribute: Static method

A very basic function of the Files object, the `open()` method opens a specified file for reading or writing. To write to a file, the `wantWriteAccess` argument must be true. If `open()` is successful, a Files object is returned, otherwise null is returned. The `open()` method is intended for use with text files.

### readline()

Attribute: Instance method

Text files are often read in one line at a time; in Fireworks, this function is handled by the `readline()` method. The lines are returned as strings without the end-of-line character. A null is returned when the end-of-file is reached (or if the line is longer than 2,048 characters).

### write(*string*)

Attribute: Instance method

To insert text in a file, use the `write()` method. No end-of-line characters are automatically appended after each string; it's necessary to attach a \n to generate a proper end-of-line character, as in the following code:

```
theString = "Log Report\n"
theFile.write(theString)
```

### close()

Attribute: Instance method

As you might suspect, the `close()` method closes the associated file. Although `close()` is not necessary because all files opened or created as a File object are closed when the script terminates, the `close()` method enables you to control access to a file programatically.

## Errors

To help keep the user informed when something goes wrong, the Fireworks API includes an Errors object. The Errors object includes 62 static properties, each of which returns a string localized for the language of the program. For example, the code

```
var theError = Errors.EFileIsReadOnly
```

returns "File is locked." in English. Table 21-4 lists all the Errors properties and their messages in English.

<table>
<tr><td colspan="2" align="center">Table 21-4<br>**Errors Properties**</td></tr>
<tr><td>**Property**</td><td>**English Message**</td></tr>
<tr><td>EArrayIndexOutOfBounds</td><td>An internal error occurred.</td></tr>
<tr><td>EBadParam</td><td>A parameter was incorrect.</td></tr>
<tr><td>EBufferTooSmall</td><td>An internal error occurred.</td></tr>
<tr><td>EDatabaseError</td><td>An internal error occurred.</td></tr>
<tr><td>EIllegalThreadAccess</td><td>An internal error occurred.</td></tr>
<tr><td>ENoSuchElement</td><td>An internal error occurred.</td></tr>
<tr><td>EInternalError</td><td>An internal error occurred.</td></tr>
<tr><td>EOutOfMem</td><td>Not enough memory.</td></tr>
<tr><td>EResourceNotFound</td><td>An internal error occurred.</td></tr>
<tr><td>EWrongType</td><td>An internal error occurred.</td></tr>
<tr><td>EUnknownReaderFormat</td><td>Unknown file type.</td></tr>
<tr><td>EUserCanceled</td><td>An internal error occurred.</td></tr>
<tr><td>EUserInterrupted</td><td>An internal error occurred.</td></tr>
<tr><td>ENotImplemented</td><td>An internal error occurred.</td></tr>
<tr><td>EFileNotFound</td><td>The file was not found.</td></tr>
<tr><td>EDiskFull</td><td>The disk is full.</td></tr>
<tr><td>EGenericErrorOccurred</td><td>An error occurred.</td></tr>
<tr><td>ENoSliceableElems</td><td>No paths were found.</td></tr>
<tr><td>ENotMyType</td><td>An internal error occurred.</td></tr>
<tr><td>EBadNesting</td><td>An internal error occurred.</td></tr>
<tr><td>EGroupDepth</td><td>An internal error occurred.</td></tr>
<tr><td>ESharingViolation</td><td>An internal error occurred.</td></tr>
<tr><td>ELowOnMem</td><td>Memory is nearly full.</td></tr>
<tr><td>EAppAlreadyRunning</td><td>An internal error occurred.</td></tr>
<tr><td>EDeletingLastMasterChild</td><td>A symbol must contain at least one object.</td></tr>
<tr><td>ENoNestedMastersOrAliases</td><td>Symbols may not contain Instances or other Symbols.</td></tr>
<tr><td>EBadFileContents</td><td>Unsupported file format.</td></tr>
</table>

| Property | English Message |
|---|---|
| EFileIsReadOnly | File is locked. |
| EAppNotSerialized | An internal error occurred. |
| ECharConversionFailed | An internal error occurred. |
| ENoFilesSelected | At least one file must be selected for scripts to operate. |

# Hotspot Objects

Hotspots — alternatively known as image maps — are one of two types of Web objects in Fireworks. Along with slices, hotspots enable a wide range of user interactivity to occur. The Fireworks API hotspot objects are, for the most part, read-only properties that enable you to gather any needed bit of information about image maps embedded in the Fireworks document.

**Note**     Because hotspots and slices employ many of the same mechanisms, several Fireworks API objects — exportDoc, behaviors, and behaviorInfo — listed under Hotspot Objects are also valid for use with slices.

## exportDoc

The exportDoc object is available for use in all the exporting templates — slices.htt, imagemap.htt, and Servermap.mtt. However, exportDoc cannot be outside of these files. All of its properties are read-only and relate to the current document and its Document Properties.

| Table 21-5 exportDoc Properties | | |
|---|---|---|
| **Property** | **Possible Value** | **Description** |
| height | Number | Height of the exported image in pixels. In slices.htt, it is the total height of the output images. |
| width | Number | Width of the export image in pixels. In slices.htt, it is the total width of the output images. |

*Continued*

## Table 21-5 *(continued)*

| Property | Possible Value | Description |
|---|---|---|
| filename | Relative URL | Simple URL for the exported image, relative to the HTML output—for example, images/Button.gif. In slices.htt, this property is the image basename plus the base extension—for example, Button_r2_c2.gif. |
| imagename | Text | The image basename, without a file extension—for example, Button. |
| pathBase | Pathname without extension | The filename with the extension removed—for example, images/Button. |
| pathSuffix | File Extension | The extension for the file name—for example, gif. |
| backgroundColor | Hexadecimal String | String that is the hex color for the document canvas. For example, "FF0000" is for a red background. Note that the hash (#) character is not included. |
| numFrames | Number | The number of frames in a file. |
| hasBackground Link | True \| False | True if a Background Link has been set through the Document Properties dialog box. |
| backgroundLink | URL | The relative or absolute URL for the Background Link. |
| hasAltText | True \| False | True if alternate text has been specified in the Document Properties dialog box. |
| altText | Text | The text string set as the Alt Text for the image. |
| clientMap | True \| False | True if the Client Side Image Map option is selected for the document. |
| serverMap | True \| False | True if the Server Side Image Map option is selected for the document. |
| backgroundIs Transparent | True \| False | True if the canvas is set to transparent, or if the export settings are a transparent GIF format. |

# imagemap

The imagemap object has one static property, eleven instance properties, and two methods — all read-only. Like several of the Fireworks API extensions, most of the work with the imagemap object is handled though an array. Each element in the imagemap array represents one hotspot in the current document. Get a particular imagemap object with code like this:

```
var theHotspot = imagemap[0]
```

## Properties

With the exception of the `numberOfURLs` property, described next, all imagemap properties are instance properties. Not only can the shape and number of coordinates of a hotspot be uncovered, but you can also determine what, if any, behaviors are linked to them.

### numberOfURLs

Attributes: Read-only, Static property

The `numberOfURLs` property is very important because it contains the number of hotspots in a particular imagemap. As such, `numberOfURLs` is often used to loop through an imagemap object array, as with this code:

```
var i = 0;
while (i < imagemap.numberOfURLs) {
  hasImagemap = true;
  }
  i++;
```

If there are no imagemaps in the document, the `numberOfURLs` returns zero.

The remaining imagemap properties are all read-only instance properties and are detailed in Table 21-6.

## Methods

The only imagemap methods are those concerned with gathering the *x* and *y* coordinates for the hotspot, `xCoord()` and `yCoord()`.

Both `xCoord()` and `yCoord()` work identically. Each gets one coordinate, in pixels, for the `index` point. These methods are used together in conjunction with the `numCoords` property to list the coordinates for the entire imagemap, as shown in this code:

```
for (var j=0; j<curImagemap.numCoords; j++) {
  if (j>0) WRITE_HTML(",");
  WRITE_HTML(curImagemap.xCoord(j), ",",
curImagemap.yCoord(j));
```

## Table 21-6
## imagemap Instance Properties

| Property | Possible Value | Description |
|---|---|---|
| shape | circle, rect, or poly | The type of hotspot |
| numCoords | 1 for circle, 2 for rect, and any number for poly | The number of coordinates used to describe the hotspot in HTML |
| radius | Number | The radius of the circle area hotspot |
| hasHref | True \| False | Returns true if the hotspot has a URL assigned |
| href | Relative or Absolute URL | The assigned URL |
| hasTargetText | True \| False | Returns true if the hotspot has a target specified |
| targetText | An HTML frame name. | The specified target |
| hasAltText | True \| False | Returns true if alternative text has been specified |
| altText | Text | The specified alternative text |
| behaviors | A behavior object (described later in this chapter) | Details regarding the behavior attached to the hotspot |

**Note**    The imagemap object has one other property associated with it: behaviors. Because the behaviors object can also work with slice objects, it is described in detail in the following section.

## Behaviors

Behaviors, in Fireworks, are effects that are exported as JavaScript code to include in an HTML page. A behavior is attached to a Web object (a hotspot or a slice) and triggered by a specific user event, such as a mouse click or rolling over an image. The behaviors object, in the Fireworks API, describes these effects by detailing their attributes and their triggering events.

Like the imagemap object, the behaviors object uses one static property and numerous instance properties. All of the properties are read-only and no methods are associated with the behaviors object.

Although the Behaviors panel lists four separate behaviors — Simple Rollover, Display Status Message, Swap Image, and Toggle Group — from the behaviors object perspective, there are only three different behaviors: Swap Image, Status Message, and Toggle or Radio Group. The Simple Rollover is actually a one or more Swap Image and possibly a Toggle Group behavior. Likewise, only three possible events are recognized: onMouseOver, onClick, and onMouseOut.

By default, if the user chooses Simple Rollover with just the first two frames (up and over) used, the Swap Image behavior is used. If either the third or fourth frames (down and overdown, respectively) are used, the Toggle Group behavior is called.

The one static property, numberOfBehaviors, is used with the behaviors object in the same fashion as numberOfURLs is used with the imagemap object, to determine how many behaviors are included in the current document. In the following code, the numberOfBehaviors property is used to loop through the array of behaviors:

```
for (var i=0; i<theCurBehaviors.numberOfBehaviors; i++) {
  var curBehavior = theCurBehaviors[i];
  if (curBehavior.action == kActionRadioGroup) {
    groupName = curBehavior.groupName;
  }
}
```

Table 21-7 lists the behaviors object properties and their possible values.

## Table 21-7
## Properties for the Behaviors Object

| Property | Possible Value | Description |
|---|---|---|
| action | 1 (Status Message), 2 (Swap Image), or 3 (Toggle Group) | The type of behavior. |
| event | 0 (onMouseOver), 1 (onClick), or 2 (onMouseOut) | The event that triggers the behavior. |
| restoreOnMouseout | True \| False | Used for the Swap Image and Status Message behaviors, returns true if the original image or blank status bar is to be restored onMouseOut. |
| statusText | Text string | The text used in the Status Message behavior. |

*Continued*

| | Table 21-7 *(continued)* | |
| --- | --- | --- |
| *Property* | *Possible Value* | *Description* |
| groupName | Unique name | For Toggle Group behaviors, the name of the group of buttons. |
| hasStatusText | True \| False | For Status Message behaviors, returns true if the status text is not empty. |
| hasHref | True \| False | For Swap Image behaviors, returns true if the swap image swaps in an external file as opposed to a Fireworks frame. |
| href | Relative or Absolute URL | For Swap Image behaviors, the URL for the swap image file for an external file swap image. |
| hasTargetFrame | True \| False | For Swap Image behaviors, returns true if the swap image swaps in another frame in the Fireworks file, as opposed to an external file. |
| targetFrameNum | Number (0 to number of frames minus 1) | For Swap Image behaviors, if hasTargetFrame is true, this is the frame number that will be swapped. The first frame is 0. |
| targetRowNum | Number | For Swap Image behaviors, the row in the slices table that will be swapped. |
| targetColumnNum | Number | For Swap Image behaviors, the column in the slices table that will be swapped. |

# Slices Object

Slices make it possible to divide one graphic into several — or many — different files, each of which can be saved separately with its own export settings or behaviors. The Fireworks API extension, the slices object, enables you to examine every aspect of those separate slices of an overall image. The slices object can access a wide range of both static and instance properties; all properties are read-only.

## Static properties

Several of the static properties of the slices object — doShimEdges, doShimInternal, and doSkipUndefined — refer to options. These options are all set in the Document Properties dialog box. To find out if the user has selected the No Shims option, use code like this:

```
if (slices.doShimInternal || slices.doShimEdges) {
//create shim code here
}
```

<table>
<tr><td colspan="3" align="center">Table 21-8<br>**Static Properties of the Slices Object**</td></tr>
<tr><td>*Property*</td><td>*Possible Values*</td><td>*Description*</td></tr>
<tr><td>numColumns</td><td>Number</td><td>The total number of columns, excluding the shim column, in the HTML table.</td></tr>
<tr><td>numRows</td><td>Number</td><td>The total number of rows, excluding the shim column, in the HTML table.</td></tr>
<tr><td>doDemoHTML</td><td>True | False</td><td>Returns true if the Generate Rollover Demos option is enabled.</td></tr>
<tr><td>shimPath</td><td>Relative URL</td><td>Path to the GIF file used for shims, for example, images/shim.gif.</td></tr>
<tr><td>imagesDirPath</td><td>Relative URL</td><td>Path to the folder used to store the images in the sliced table. If the images and the HTML file are in the same folder, returns an empty string.</td></tr>
<tr><td>doShimEdges</td><td>True | False</td><td>Returns true if the Table Shims option is set to Transparent Image.</td></tr>
<tr><td>doShimInternal</td><td>True | False</td><td>Returns true if the Table Shims option is set to Shims from Image.</td></tr>
<tr><td>doSkipUndefined</td><td>True | False</td><td>Returns true if the Export Undefined Slices is not enabled.</td></tr>
</table>

## Instance properties

Because slices exist in a table, each slice can be identified by its location in the row and column structure. A two-dimensional array holds these row and column values and marks each instance of a slice object. For example, the slice in the first row, first column position is slices[0][0]. To process all of the individual slices, use code similar to the following:

```
var curRow;
var curCol;
for (curRow = 0; curRow<slices.numRows; curRow++) {
for (curCol=0; curCol<slices.numColumns; curCol++) {
var curSlice = slices[curRow][curCol];
// do whatever processing with curSlice.
}
}
```

Notice how both the numRows and numColumns static properties must be used to properly loop through all of the slices. Once the individual slice has been identified by its two-dimensional array, the properties of the instance slice (described in Table 21-9) can be read.

### Table 21-9
### Instance Properties of the Slices Object

| Property | Possible Values | Description |
|---|---|---|
| skipCell | True \| False | Returns true if the table cell for the current slice is included in a previous row or column span. |
| hasImage | True \| False | Returns true if the current slice includes an image; text-only slices return false. |
| top | Number in pixels | The top of the cell in pixels, starting at 0. |
| left | Number in pixels | The left side of the cell in pixels, starting at 0. |
| width | Number in pixels | The width of the image in the slice, including column spans. |
| height | Number in pixels | The height of the image in the slice, including row spans. |
| cellWidth | Number in pixels | The width of the current HTML table column. |
| cellHeight | Number in pixels | The height of the current HTML table row. |
| imageSuffix | File extension | The file extension for the image in the current slice. |
| hasTargetText | True \| False | Returns true if a target is specified for the current slice. |
| targetText | HTML frame name | The specified target for the current frame. |
| hasHtmlText | True \| False | Returns true if the current cell is a text-only slice. |

| Property | Possible Values | Description |
|---|---|---|
| htmlText | Text | The text string for the current cell, marked as a text-only slice in the Object panel. |
| hasImagemap | True \| False | Returns true if hotspots are associated with the current slice. |
| hasHref | True \| False | Returns true if the slice has a URL. |
| href | URL | The URL for the current slice. |
| hasAltText | True \| False | Returns true if the slice has an alternative text description. |
| altText | Text | The alternative text for the current cell. |
| behaviors | A behaviors object | The behaviors object containing information describing any behaviors attached to the current slice. |
| imagemap | An imagemap object | The imagemap object containing information describing any hotspots attached to the current slice. |
| isUndefined | True \| False | Returns true if the current slice does not have a user-drawn slice associated with it. Fireworks automatically generates slices to cover such undefined cells. |

# Methods

The slices object has two methods associated with it: getFrameFileName() and setFrameFileName(). Both are instance methods.

### getFrameFileName(*frame*)

The getFrameFileName() method reads the filename for the slice and frame. The returned name does not include any path information, such as folder or file extension. For example, using the Fireworks defaults, the name of the first slice for a file named newLogo.gif would be newLogo_r1_c1. The first frame in an image file is 0; generally all slices in frame 0 are named. For frames 1 and over, only slices that are rollovers or are targeted by a swap image are named.

The following code shows how the getFrameFileName() method is used both with a constant and with a variable:

```
var curFile = slices[curRow][curCol].getFrameFileName(0);
for (var curFrame = 0; curFrame < exportDoc.numFrames;
curFrame++) {
var curFile =
slices[curRow][curCol].getFrameFileName(curFrame);
// processing code for each slice goes here
}
```

### setFrameFileName(*frame, filename*)

To change the filename of a slice, use the `setFrameFileName()` method. Specify the frame number and the new name of the slice in the two arguments, as in the following code:

```
slices[swapRow][swapCol].setFrameFileName(swapFrame, fileName);
```

**Note**    An interesting side effect of `setFrameFileName()` is that this method determines which images get written. By default, Fireworks sets it up so that all slices on frame 0 are named, and no other frames are named. If a swap image behavior uses a slice at row 2, column 3 on frame 2, the export templates set the frame filename so that that image gets written. You can also set slices on frame 0 to an empty string, and they won't get written. This is how the "Don't export undefined slices" option gets implemented.

## Developing Scriptlets

Scriptlets can be a very powerful automation tool when used properly. Perhaps the best way to develop scriptlets and learn more about their structure and possibilities is to modify one generated by Fireworks. You can save any batch processing procedure as a file by selecting the Script button on the Batch Process dialog. Open the saved .jsf file in any text editor and resave it under a new name before you make any changes. That way, you'll always have a clean version to refer to.

Here are some other points to keep in mind when you're developing scriptlets:

✦ Remember Fireworks has a JavaScript 1.2 interpreter built in, so you have a lot more commands than just those offered by the Fireworks API, as robust as that is. JavaScript 1.2 offers regular expressions, search and replace functions, and much more.

✦ When building scriptlets or modifying templates, be sure to end your script with a return on the final line of code. If you don't, Fireworks does not execute that line and errors could result.

✦ Fireworks always assumes that you're batch processing unless you explicitly tell it otherwise. For scriptlets where the progress of the batch processing is irrelevant, include this code:

```
App.dismissBatchDialogWhenDone = true
```

✦ Use the `prompt()` global object to interact with the user and permit a wider range of options with a single scriptlet. For example, you could use the following code to determine preset scaling options:

```
var theAnswer = prompt("Select Scale","Enter 1 for full-size,
2 for half-size or 4 for quarter-sized images"
switch(theAnswer) {
  case 1:
  // full-scale code goes here
    break;
  case 2:
  // half-scale code goes here
    break;
  case 4:
  // quarter-scale code goes here
    break;
}
```

## Summary

For me, the true power of any tool is demonstrated when it adapts to my own way of working. Fireworks 2 has been greatly extended to enable you to build custom scriptlets and automated batch processing files. When customizing Fireworks, keep these points in mind:

✦ It's very straightforward to include custom batch processing files. Just create a new directory in the HTML Settings folder and copy the files there. You don't even have to relaunch Fireworks to use them.

✦ Fireworks 2 includes a JavaScript 1.2 interpreter with a large number of API extensions to enable you to build custom slice, client-side imagemap, and server-side imagemap templates.

✦ Custom scriptlets can automate the power of Fireworks and enable you to repeat Web graphic production chores, such as creating thumbnails, just by running a script.

In the next chapter, you'll see how Fireworks integrates with Dreamweaver to create a unique Web page solution.

✦     ✦     ✦

# Integration with Dreamweaver

**N**ot all Web designers have the luxury — or the hardship — of just working on Web graphics. Many graphic artists create both the graphics and the layout for the Web pages they work on. And those designers who do just create imagery for the Internet must work closely with layout artists to incorporate their designs. No matter how you look at it, Fireworks is not — and was never intended to be — a standalone product. All graphics generated by Fireworks must be published to the Web by some other means.

Dreamweaver, the premier Web-authoring program from Macromedia, is the perfect partner for Fireworks. The earliest versions of the program complemented each other nicely, because both spoke a common language of PNG, hotspots, and HTML output. However, with the release of Fireworks 2 and Dreamweaver 2, new levels of integration have been achieved. Now, you can seamlessly optimize images with standard Fireworks controls from within Dreamweaver — without even opening Fireworks. This chapter delves into this and many other such features, including Fireworks commands that can be automatically issued from Dreamweaver.

## Integration Overview

As noted elsewhere in this book, Web graphics is as much about production and maintenance as it is about creation. The more efficiently you — or someone who works with you — can insert and update images into Web page layouts, the better the workflow. Because a Web page typically has numerous graphics, as well as text and other media, such as a Shockwave or QuickTime movie, the Web designer must be concerned with how all the elements work together. Not only must the overall design function aesthetically well, the Web page as a whole must be practical — that is, the download time must be kept to a minimum. All of these concerns require a constant back-and-forth between graphics and layout programs.

The integration between Fireworks 2 and Dreamweaver 2 goes a long way toward smoothing the transition between the two realms of content creation and layout. When Dreamweaver 2 was released in December, 1998, very few people realized that an entire feature set was patiently waiting to be revealed. With the release of Fireworks 2 a few months later, new menu items, such as Optimize Image in Fireworks, were suddenly available in Dreamweaver. New actions appeared in the Behaviors palette, as well. A new link between Web graphics creation and Web graphic layout was forged.

To take advantage of the additional benefits, the programs must be installed properly. In many cases, installation is a nonissue, because Dreamweaver 2 was installed prior to Fireworks 2. During the installation of Fireworks, the program looks for Dreamweaver and, if found, installs the needed files in the proper folders. However, if Fireworks was installed before Dreamweaver, you need to take special care to make the connection.

If you installed Fireworks 2 before you installed Dreamweaver 2, follow these steps to add the integration files to Dreamweaver:

1. Run the Fireworks installation program, either from the Fireworks CD-ROM or from the downloaded electronic distribution copy of Fireworks.

**On the CD-ROM** If you don't have a copy of Fireworks 2, use the trial version included on the CD-ROM accompanying this book.

2. After the Welcome and Legal disclaimer screen, the setup program asks you to confirm the file location for the installation. It is recommended that you accept the default path. Click Next to continue.

3. The next screen offers three choices for setup: Typical, Compact, and Custom. Click Custom and then Next to continue.

4. The following screen, shown in Figure 22-1, lists two sets of components to install: Fireworks Application and Files, and Dreamweaver 2 Compatibility Files. Deselect the Fireworks Application and Files option and leave the Dreamweaver 2 Compatibility Files option selected. Click Next to continue.

5. Continue the remainder of the installation, accepting the defaults. Click Finish to complete the installation.

The next time that you launch Dreamweaver, the integration commands and other files are made available. The installed files are detailed in Table 22-1.

**Figure 22-1:** During Fireworks installation, be sure the Dreamweaver 2 Compatibility Files option is selected, to gain the benefits of Fireworks/Dreamweaver integration.

## Table 22-1
## Integration Files Installed in Dreamweaver

| Location in Macintosh | Location in Windows | Files |
|---|---|---|
| Dreamweaver:Configuration: Behaviors:Actions | Dreamweaver\Configuration\ Behaviors\Actions | Group Down.htm Group Down.js Group Over.htm Group Over.js Group Restore.htm Group Restore.js |
| Dreamweaver:Configuration: Commands | Dreamweaver\Configuration\ Commands | Optimize in Fireworks.htm |
| Dreamweaver:Configuration: JSExtensions | Dreamweaver\Configuration\ JSExtensions | FWLaunch.dll (Windows) FWLaunch (Macintosh) |

The files inserted in the Actions folder add new Toggle Group Behaviors to Dreamweaver, which can be used with or without Fireworks. The Optimize in Fireworks command opens a special version of the Export Preview dialog box directly in Dreamweaver, without launching the full version of Fireworks; the FWLaunch file makes this possible.

# Optimizing Images with Fireworks

What's the most common modification needed for graphics being added to a layout? I don't know about everybody else, but I sure do an awful lot of resizing of images to get the right fit. To me, the term "resizing" encompasses rescaling an image, cropping it, *and* getting it to the smallest possible file size — all while maintaining the original image quality. The new Optimize Image in Fireworks command does just that, as well as allowing complete color and animation control. Best of all, you can do everything right from Dreamweaver in a standard Fireworks interface.

If you've never tried the Optimize Image command, that last statement might give you pause. How can you optimize an image "...from Dreamweaver in a standard Fireworks interface?" Aren't we talking about two different programs? Well, yes, and — most excitedly — no. You definitely need both programs for the command to work, but the full version of Fireworks does not have to be running. Instead, a special "light" version of Fireworks is launched, one that displays only the Export Preview dialog box, as shown in Figure 22-2.

The Optimize dialog box has all the features of Export Preview with one small change: an Update button sits in place of the Next button. In Fireworks, clicking Next from Export Preview opens the Export dialog box, in which you can select Slicing and HTML template options. The Optimize command relies on your last settings saved from within Fireworks for these options.

To optimize your image in Fireworks from within Dreamweaver, follow these steps:

**1.** In Dreamweaver, select the image you need to modify.

**Caution**    You must save the current page at least once before running the Optimize Image in Fireworks command. The current state of the page doesn't need to have been saved, but a valid file must exist for the command to work properly. If you haven't saved the file, Dreamweaver alerts you to this fact when you call the Optimize Image command.

**2.** Choose Commands ⇨ Optimize Image in Fireworks.

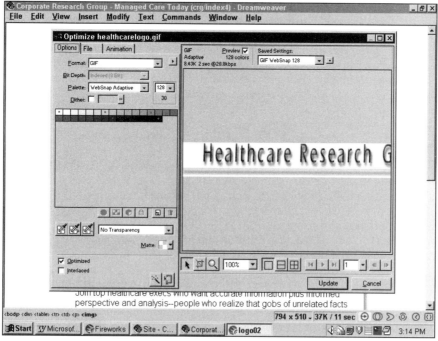

**Figure 22-2:** Choosing the Optimize Image in Fireworks command opens a dialog box equivalent to the Export Preview dialog box, but without running Fireworks.

3. If the selected image is not in PNG format, you're given the opportunity to select a Fireworks source file. Click Yes to select the PNG format source file from a standard Open dialog box.

   After the selected file is located, if appropriate, the Optimize Images dialog box appears.

4. Make whatever modifications you want from the Options, File, and Animation tabs of the Optimize Images dialog box.

5. When you're finished, click the Update button.

   If you're working with a Fireworks source file, the changes are saved to both your source file and exported file; otherwise, only the exported file is altered.

If you changed the scale, size, or cropping of the image during optimization, you need to adjust the height and width values in the Dreamweaver Property inspector. To do this, click the Refresh button.

**Caution**    If the image to be optimized is in PNG format — whether the enhanced PNG format that Fireworks uses to store all of its additional editing information or the
bitmapped PNG export — the Optimize Image in Fireworks command saves it as a
bitmapped file. In other words, Fireworks native files lose their editability. As
always, it's best to store your Fireworks source files in one directory and use your
exported Web page files — in GIF, JPEG, or PNG format — from another.

# Editing Images with Fireworks

For many purposes, optimizing an image is all you need to do — whether it's to crop
one side slightly or to reduce the file size. Often, though, you need to go further, such
as when the client has decided to change a department name on a navigation button.
Without Fireworks/Dreamweaver integration, in a situation like this, you'd need to
start up your graphics program, load in the image, make the change, save the image,
switch back to your Web-authoring tool, and reload the graphic. With Dreamweaver 2
and Fireworks 2, the process is greatly simplified:

1. Select image in Dreamweaver and choose Edit from the Property inspector.

   Image is automatically loaded into Fireworks, which is started if necessary.

2. Modify the image in Fireworks and click Update.

   The revised image is saved and automatically updated in Dreamweaver.

To take advantage of this enhanced connectivity, you first have to set Fireworks as
your graphics editor in Dreamweaver's Preferences. To do this, follow these steps:

1. In Dreamweaver, choose Edit ➪ Preferences

   The Preferences dialog box appears.

2. Select the External Editors category from the list on the left.

3. In the External Editors pane, shown in Figure 22-3, click the Image Editor
   Browse button to locate the main Fireworks program.

   The default location in Windows systems is C:\Program Files\Macromedia\
   Fireworks 2\Fireworks.exe; in Macintosh, it's applications:Fireworks 2:
   Fireworks 2. (The .exe extension may or may not be visible in your Windows
   system.)

Now, whenever you want to edit a graphic, select the image and click the Edit button
in the Property inspector. Fireworks will start up, if it's not already open. As with the
Optimize Image in Fireworks command, if the inserted image is a GIF or a JPEG, and
not a PNG format, Fireworks asks whether you want to work with a separate source
file. If you click Yes, you're given an opportunity to locate the file.

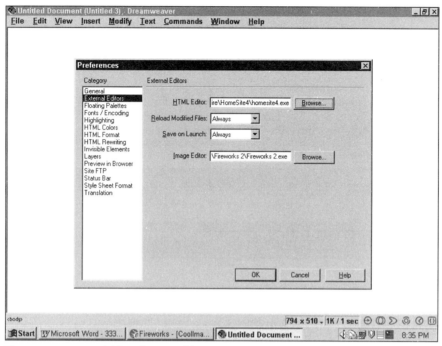

**Figure 22-3:** To quickly edit a graphic on a Dreamweaver page, set Fireworks as your graphic editor in Dreamweaver Preferences.

After you make your alterations to your file in Fireworks, choose either File⇨Update or the keyboard shortcut Ctrl+S (Command+S). If you're working with a Fireworks source file, both the source file and the exported file are updated and saved.

**Caution**   If you choose File⇨Update, make sure that your source file and exported file are the same dimensions. If your exported file is a cropped version of the source file, the complete source file is used as the basis for the export file, and any cropping information is discarded. To maintain the cropping, choose File⇨Export to re-export the file instead of saving it with File⇨Update.

# Exporting Dreamweaver Code

In its first release, Fireworks was only capable of outputting its own style of HTML. Although it was the very model of efficient code, it didn't mesh too well with Dreamweaver. It worked just fine, but you couldn't modify it within Dreamweaver — you had to return to Fireworks to make any changes. Not exactly an optimum situation.

**New Feature** Fireworks 2, on the other hand, speaks fluent Dreamweaver — and in two dialects, no less. For all export operations involving HTML output, including hotspots, slices, and Behaviors, Fireworks is capable of writing code either as Dreamweaver 2 or Dreamweaver 2 Library output.

The type of HTML output is set when exporting an image. In the Export dialog box, choose either Dreamweaver 2 or Dreamweaver 2 Library from the HTML Style option list, shown in Figure 22-4. The Fireworks and Dreamweaver engineers worked closely together to ensure that the code would match.

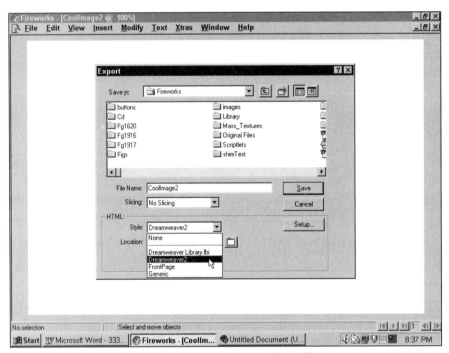

**Figure 22-4:** To output Dreamweaver-type code, select either Dreamweaver 2 or Dreamweaver 2 Library from the HTML Style list when exporting.

**Cross-Reference** For precise details on how to export Dreamweaver-style code from Fireworks and insert it into your Dreamweaver pages, see the chapters on Web objects — hotspots and slices — and Behaviors, Chapters 19 and 20, respectively.

## Working with Dreamweaver Libraries

The addition of Dreamweaver 2 Library code to Fireworks's output options is key. One of the most difficult tasks for graphic designers moving to the Web is handling code. With Generic or even Dreamweaver 2 output, all code must be cut and pasted from the Fireworks-generated page to the working Dreamweaver document. Although this is fairly straightforward in Dreamweaver (and Fireworks makes it as clear as possible, with concise HTML comments marking the code to move), it still involves working in an environment in which many designers aren't comfortable: code.

Dreamweaver Libraries eliminate the need for designers to handle code when inserting any Fireworks output, including even the most complex behaviors. What's a Dreamweaver Library? I like the explanation given to me by a Fireworks engineer, "Think of it as Encapsulated HTML." Designers routinely work with Encapsulated PostScript (EPS) files, and the metaphor fits. Like EPS files, a Dreamweaver Library item is capable of containing hundreds of lines of code, but the designer need only be concerned with one element — and a visual one, at that.

After an item has been exported as a Dreamweaver 2 Library item, it's extremely easy to insert in your page; here are the steps:

1. In Dreamweaver, open the document in which you want to insert the exported Fireworks code.

2. Choose Window ⇨ Library or click the Library icon from the Dreamweaver Launcher.

   The Library palette opens.

3. Select the exported item from the list pane.

**Tip**     I've found that I sometimes have to close the Library palette and reopen it before any newly added items from Fireworks will appear.

4. Insert the Library item on the page either by choosing Add to Page or by dragging and dropping the item from the list or preview pane.

   The Library item is added to your page and initially selected.

Feel free to move the Fireworks-generated Library item anywhere on the page; the code will move as well, if necessary.

A key feature of the Dreamweaver Library items is their updatability. Edit a single Library item, and Dreamweaver automatically updates all the Web pages using that item. This capability is a major time-saver. Unlike regular graphics, which can be modified at the click of the Edit button from Dreamweaver's Property inspector, Library item graphics first must be unlocked.

To edit a Library item, follow these steps:

1. In Dreamweaver, choose Window ⇨ Library to open the Library palette.

2. Select the Library item embedded in the page, either from the Web page or the Library palette.

3. From the Library palette (or from the Library Property inspector), click Open.

   The Library item opens in its own Dreamweaver window, shown in Figure 22-5. Note the <<Library Item> designation in the Dreamweaver title bar.

**Figure 22-5:** Before you can edit a Library item in Fireworks, you must unlock it in Dreamweaver.

4. Select the graphic and choose Edit from the Property inspector.

   If the file is not in PNG format, Fireworks asks whether you prefer to edit an original source file and gives you the chance to locate it. The selected PNG file is opened in Fireworks.

5. Modify the file, as needed.

6. When you're done, select File ➪ Update.

   The altered file is automatically updated in the Dreamweaver Library file.

7. In Dreamweaver, choose File ➪ Save.

   Dreamweaver notes that your Library item has been modified and asks whether you'd like to update all the Web pages in your site that contain the item. Click Yes to update all Library items (including the one just modified) or No to postpone the updates.

8. Close the editing window by selecting File ➪ Close.

If you opt to postpone the Library item update, you can do it at any time by selecting Modify ➪ Library ➪ Update Pages.

## Fireworks technique: adding CSS layers to Dreamweaver

Fireworks 2 features another type of export that—although not strictly a Dreamweaver feature only—fits so well in the Dreamweaver/Fireworks workflow that it's worth including in this chapter. Fireworks 2 is now capable of exporting images directly into Cascading Style Sheet (CSS) layers. A CSS layer is a free-floating structure that can be viewed in any version 4 or higher browser. CSS layers have several notable properties, including:

✦ **Position:** Layers—and thus, the content they hold—are precisely position-able. This makes layout far easier than with traditional HTML means.

✦ **Depth:** Layers can be stacked one upon another, and their depth can be changed, dynamically.

✦ **Visibility:** Layers can be hidden or revealed at will.

✦ **Movement:** Layers can be dynamically positioned and thus move across the screen.

I've exported CSS layers to use in Dreamweaver with two different methods: exporting Fireworks layers, and exporting Fireworks frames. The first method, using Fireworks layers, is very useful for determining a precise layout of images against a background. For one project, eight separate artworks needed to be placed in the proper position against a background. To ease the workflow, here's the technique that I followed:

1. In Fireworks, open the background graphic and lock it on the Layers panel.

2. Click the New Layer button on the Layers panel.

    A new layer is created.

Tip    If desired, give the layer a new, unique name; the layer names in Fireworks are used as the CSS layer names.

3. Choose Insert ➪ Image to open a foreground image.

    Alternatively, you can cut and paste an object or image from an open file.

4. Position the image against the background.

5. Repeat Steps 2-4, creating a new layer for each object.

    Although each object is placed in its own layer, they appear as if side by side, as shown in Figure 22-6.

6. When all the images are properly placed, hide the layer the background is on by deselecting the appropriate eye symbol in the Layers panel.

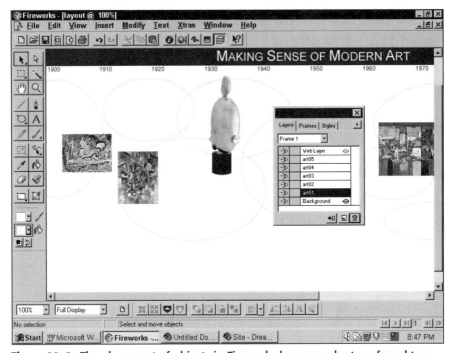

**Figure 22-6:** The placement of objects in Fireworks layers can be transferred to a Web page via CSS layers.

7. Choose File ⇨ Export ⇨ Special ⇨ Layers ⇨ Export as CSS Layers.

   The Export Special dialog box appears.

8. Select Layers from the Files From option list as the type of Fireworks component to export.

9. Make sure the Trim Images option is not selected.

10. Make sure that the HTML Style is set to CSS Layers.

11. Determine where the HTML file should be stored by selecting an option from the Location option list: Same Directory, One Level Up, or Custom.

12. Click Save when you're ready.

    Each Fireworks layer is saved as a separate image, and the CSS layer information is written out in HTML.

13. In Dreamweaver, open the Fireworks-generated HTML page.

14. Select all the CSS layers on the page by using one of the following methods:

    • From the Dreamweaver Layers palette, press Shift and select each layer.

    • In the Dreamweaver document window, press Shift and select each of the CSS layer symbols.

**15.** Choose Edit ⇨ Copy to copy the selected layers.

**16.** Open the target Web page for the layers.

**17.** Choose Edit ⇨ Paste to insert the layers.

The depth of the CSS layers is determined by the order of layers in Fireworks. In CSS layers, higher numbers are on top of lower numbers, just as an object in a higher-positioned layer in the Fireworks Layer panel places objects above those on lower layers.

The other method of using the CSS layer export feature of Fireworks, exporting Fireworks frames, comes in handy when you need to build complex Show-Hide Layer Behaviors in Dreamweaver. Often, the layers being alternately shown and hidden are in front of one another. You can take advantage of this positioning by setting up the separate objects as frames in Fireworks. Then, choose File ⇨ Export Special ⇨ Export as CSS Layers and select Frames as the Files From selection in the Export Special dialog box. Deselect the Trim Images option if you want each image to maintain its relative place in the frames; enable the option if you want the upper-left corner of each image to match.

**Tip**    If you are displaying separately saved images, you can use the Open Multiple command with the Open as Animation option enabled to place each image automatically in its own frame. Then, choose File ⇨ Export Special ⇨ Export as CSS Layers to output the frames as layers.

# Using Fireworks Behaviors in Dreamweaver

Fireworks 2 started writing Dreamweaver standard code so that the Behaviors would be recognized in Dreamweaver. What's the big deal about being recognized in Dreamweaver? If Dreamweaver can identify the Behavior as the same as its own, you can edit parameters in Dreamweaver that were defined in Fireworks. Now, if you apply a Display Status Message Behavior in Fireworks and want to change the message in Dreamweaver, you can.

Fireworks 2 exports code for three different Behaviors: Swap Image, Display Status Message, and Toggle Group. The Simple Rollover Behavior is actually the Swap Image Behavior with a different user interface.

**Note**    A fourth Behavior is automatically inserted for all Fireworks Behaviors: Preload Images. As the name implies, the Preload Images Behavior makes sure that the browser has all images ready for smooth rollovers.

To modify a Fireworks-applied Behavior in Dreamweaver, you must first open the Dreamweaver Behavior inspector, shown in Figure 22-7, which looks quite similar to the Behaviors panel in Fireworks. Select an object or tag in Dreamweaver, and any applied Behaviors are listed in the Behavior inspector.

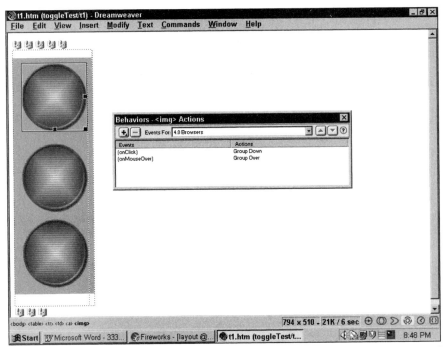

**Figure 22-7:** The Behavior inspector in Dreamweaver uses events and actions, just like the Behaviors panel in Fireworks.

Each of the Behaviors uses a different dialog box in Dreamweaver for modification; however, the overall procedure is the same. To modify any of the Fireworks-generated Behaviors in Dreamweaver, follow these steps:

1. In Dreamweaver, open the file incorporating your Fireworks-generated HTML code.

2. Choose Window ➪ Behaviors to open the Behavior inspector.

   Alternatively, you can click the Behavior button from the Launcher.

3. Select the image, object, or tag the Behavior is assigned to.

   The Behavior's event(s) and action(s) are displayed in the Behavior inspector.

4. To change to a different triggering event, click the desired Behavior option arrow and choose another option from the drop-down list.

**Tip** The list of available events changes depending on the associated tag.

5. To cause one action to be triggered before another action with the same event (for example, two `onClick` events), click the action and use the Up and Down buttons on the Behavior inspector to move the Behavior.

6. Double-click the Behavior that you want to modify.

The appropriate dialog box appears, such as the one for the Group Over Behavior, shown in Figure 22-8.

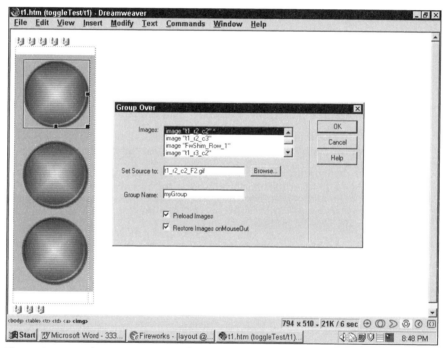

**Figure 22-8:** Make any necessary changes through the Dreamweaver-specific user interfaces for each Behavior.

7. Make any desired changes on the invoked dialog box.

8. Click OK when you're done.

The Toggle Group Behavior in Fireworks is translated into three separate Behaviors in Dreamweaver 2, each of which can be individually adjusted in Dreamweaver:

✦ **Group Over:** Controls rollovers for toggle groups

✦ **Group Down:** Controls the Down and highlighted Down state (typically, Frames 3 and 4 in a Fireworks rollover)

✦ **Group Restore:** Called whenever the Restore Image on MouseOut option is selected in the Fireworks Behaviors panel

## Summary

Fireworks and Dreamweaver integration is definitely a case of the whole being greater than the individual parts. Taken on their own merits, each program is a powerful Web tool, but together, they become a total Web graphics solution. As you begin to work with Fireworks and Dreamweaver together, consider these points:

✦ New features in Dreamweaver 2 become available when Fireworks 2 is installed.

✦ With the Optimize Image in Fireworks command, you don't even have to leave Dreamweaver to rescale, crop, or store your graphics in another format.

✦ After designating Fireworks as your graphics editor in Dreamweaver, selected images can be edited and updated automatically.

✦ Fireworks 2 outputs Dreamweaver-compliant code, making modifications within Dreamweaver seamless.

✦ Fireworks images exported as a Dreamweaver 2 Library item can be inserted in a Web page without additional cutting and pasting.

✦ You can retain positioning set in Fireworks by exporting Fireworks layers as CSS layers through the Export Special command.

In the next chapter, you'll learn about Fireworks's animation capabilities.

✦     ✦     ✦

# Animation

# Basic Animation Techniques

**A**nimation has become a prominent feature of the Web, and very few Web sites get by without at least a little of it. Animated GIF banner ads have long since proliferated from common to ubiquitous. Animated logos and buttons are an easy way to add spice to a site. Short, animated cartoons are increasingly popular as Web bandwidth increases.

This chapter looks briefly at some animation basics and then focuses on the Fireworks features that you use to create animations. We'll work with Fireworks frames and animated GIF export features, such as timing and looping. Next, we'll look at specific issues that you might confront when making animated banner ads, and then go through the process from start to finish.

 **Cross-Reference** You'll find information on importing animations and importing multiple files as animations in Chapter 15.

## Understanding Web Animation

Animation is a trick. Show me a rapid succession of similar images with slight changes in an element's location or properties, and I'll think that I see something moving. This movement can be very complex or very simple. The 24 frames per second of a motion picture aren't even required; in as little as 3 frames, an object can actually appear to be moving (with 2 frames, it just appears to be flashing).

Because Fireworks creates animated GIF images — the technical term for the format is *GIF89a* — this chapter focuses on that format. You'll find, though, that many of the ideas that go into creating good animated GIF images also apply when creating images in other Web animation formats.

# Bandwidth, bandwidth, bandwidth

Remember first and foremost that bandwidth is always an issue. Then, remember that bandwidth is always an issue.... I'll end up harping on that again and again, because bandwidth affects everything. Each and every bold, creative move must be analyzed for its eventual effect on the overall "weight" of the resulting animated GIF file (the total file size). Throughout the entire process of creating an animation for display on the Web, you need to balance carefully variables such as the number of colors you use, the number of frames, the timing of those frames, and how much area of your image is actually animated. If you want more colors, you may have to take out a few frames and settle for a less-fluid animation. If you're animating complex shapes that don't compress well, you may have to get by with fewer colors.

The 28 Kbps or 56 Kbps dial-up connection is the great equalizer. The Web is slow and generally static, and almost everybody knows it. If you can give your audience a quick, dynamic presentation, you'll score two times. Keep in mind the nature of GIF compression as you create your designs. Big blocks of cartoonish color and horizontal stripes compress much better than photographic images, vertical stripes, or gradients and dithers.

# Making a statement

So, maybe you're not going to win an Oscar with your animation; that doesn't mean you shouldn't give it a reason for existing. Every part of your animation needs to be focused and necessary, because each little movement that you add you also purchase with a corresponding amount of bandwidth. A short, tight, and concise animation will be much more popular with your audience. This applies whether you're creating a complex cartoon with an intricate story line, a flashy, abstract design, or even an animated logo. If you decide before you start what you want to accomplish creatively, you increase your chances of ending up with a tight, presentable result.

Animated GIF images are good at some things, but not so good at others. Consider those limitations carefully and focus on creating a good animated GIF — not just a good animation that happens to be forced into the framework on an animated GIF. Logos, buttons, and simple frame-by-frame animations work best. You might find that thinking of an animated GIF image as a slide-show rather than a movie is helpful. Typically, you work with fewer frames than a movie uses, and with slow, simple, animated elements. I find that thinking of animated GIFs as little PowerPoint-style presentations reminds me of the limitations of the format. You can make a little movement go a long way. You can show that something's moving either by smoothly animating it, frame by frame, across the entire width of the image, or you can place it once on the left side of the canvas, followed by a blurred version in the center, and then display it again at the right side.

Tip — Don't forget everything that you learned by watching Saturday morning cartoons or reading comic books. Techniques such as word balloons and lines that illustrate movement or action in still comics can help you to get your message across without adding significantly to the frame count (and the file size). Instead of moving an element off the canvas in ten smooth frames, replace it with a puff of smoke and some lines that point to which way the element went. Study animations for tricks like that and make lean, mean animations that really make an impression and get your message across.

As usual on the Web, you're at the mercy of the users' browsers — and you don't even know which browsers users will be using. However, generally, animated GIF images play back faster in Internet Explorer than in Navigator (and, naturally, play back faster on faster computers). Don't try to be too precise, attempting to measure the time between frames and worrying about it. Instead, embrace a little of the Web's anarchy and just try to find a middle ground. Trust the timing settings in Fireworks and hope for the best.

## Why animate a GIF?

Fireworks is the perfect place to create animated GIF images. Objects in Fireworks are always editable, so they are easy to move around the canvas, scale, or modify with effects. Finally, Fireworks unmatched image optimization enables you to create the lightest-weight animated GIF possible. (There's that bandwidth issue again.)

Tip — Although you usually create animated GIF animations directly in Fireworks, you also can export an animation as a series of files, by using File ⇨ Export Special ⇨ Export as Files. These files can then be modified in another application, or used in another animation format, such as an SMIL presentation in RealPlayer or an interactive Dynamic HTML (DHTML) slide-show.

The animated GIF has its share of limitations and gets its share of disrespect, especially when sized up feature for feature against some of the more "serious" animation formats used on the Web. Table 23-1 makes just such a comparison.

## Table 23-1
## Comparing Web Animation Formats

| Format | Sound | Interactivity | Streaming | Transparency | Palette |
|---|---|---|---|---|---|
| Animated GIF | No | No | No | Yes | 256 colors |
| Dynamic HTML | Yes | Yes | Yes | Yes | Unlimited |
| Java | Yes | Yes | Yes | No | Unlimited |
| Flash | Yes | Yes | Yes | Sometimes | Unlimited |

*Continued*

| Format | Sound | Interactivity | Streaming | Transparency | Palette |
|--------|-------|---------------|-----------|--------------|---------|
| Shockwave | Yes | Yes | Yes | No | Unlimited |
| QuickTime | Yes | Sometimes | Yes | No | Unlimited |
| RealPlayer | Yes | Sometimes | Yes | No | Unlimited |

Table 23-1 *(continued)*

Based on this table, the animated GIF seems like a pretty poor choice. Flash has much smaller file sizes. Other formats automatically stream or simulate streaming with multiple component files. Some have captured video, sound, and even interactivity.

So, why is the animated GIF used so often? Why haven't designers dropped it in favor of one or more of these other, seemingly superior methods? The answers to these questions, and more, can be found in Table 23-2, which details browser support for each format.

## Table 23-2
## Browser Support for Web Animation Formats

| Format | Navigator 2/3 and IE 3 | Navigator 4 and IE 4/5 | Navigator 5 | Most Other Browsers |
|--------|------------------------|------------------------|-------------|---------------------|
| Animated GIF | Yes | Yes | Yes | Yes |
| Dynamic HTML | No | Limited; user can disable | Yes; user can disable | No |
| Java | Yes; user can disable | Yes; user can disable | Yes; user can disable | No |
| Flash | Requires plug-in | Requires plug-in | Yes | No |
| Shockwave | Requires plug-in | Requires plug-in | Requires plug-in | No |
| QuickTime | Requires plug-in | Requires plug-in | Requires plug-in | No |
| RealPlayer | Requires plug-in | Requires plug-in | Requires plug-in | No |

When you compare the issues surrounding who can view some of these other animation formats, the animated GIF doesn't look so bad after all. Other formats may be sexier and flashier, but the animated GIF is "old reliable." No matter which platform or browser, the animated GIF is almost always available.

# The Fireworks Animation Toolkit

Animation in Fireworks focuses on these major tools:

✦ **Frames panel:** Where you manipulate Fireworks frames — like a director editing the frames of a film — and move and copy objects from frame to frame. This is the heart of the animation features of Fireworks.

✦ **Layers panel**: Where you manage each frame's layers. Organize your animation by keeping objects on the same layer from frame to frame, or share a layer across every frame, so that backgrounds or static objects can be created once for the entire animation.

✦ **Status bar VCR controls:** Where you flip through frames or play your entire animation right in the document window.

**New Feature**

Whereas Fireworks 1 enabled you to step through a series of frames with a Forward and Backward button on the Layers panel, Fireworks 2 improves upon your control of frames, offering First, Last, Next, and Previous frame buttons onscreen all the time, which you can use to play, stop, or move about an animation.

✦ **Export Preview dialog box's Animation tab:** Where you set options such as frame timing, visibility, looping, and optimization controls (frame-disposal methods, for example).

**Cross-Reference**

Another major animation tool in Fireworks is Symbols and Instances, which allows you to organize repeating objects and apply tweening effects. Chapter 24 examines these advanced animation techniques and effects.

## Managing frames

What separates an animation from a regular Fireworks document is that the animation has multiple frames. The relationship between layers and frames can be hard to understand when you first start animating in Fireworks. Understanding how they work — and work together — is essential, though.

Frames are like the frames of a traditional film strip (see Figure 23-1) that you might run through a movie projector. When you play your animation, only one frame is visible at a time. Frame 1 is shown first, and then Frame 2, Frame 3, and so on. When you add a frame to your document, you're extending the length of the film strip and making a longer movie. When you change the order of frames in the Frames panel, imagine that you're cutting a frame out of your film strip and splicing it back in at another point on the strip. If you move Frame 5 to the beginning of your movie, before Frame 1, all the frames are renumbered, so that what used to be Frame 5 is now Frame 1, what used to be Frame 1 becomes Frame 2, and so on.

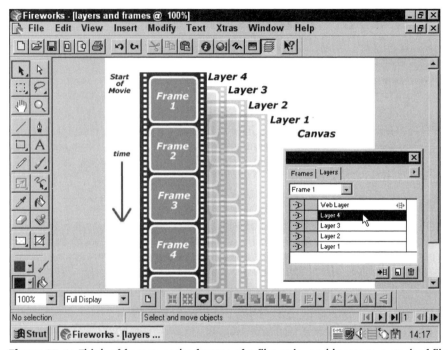

**Figure 23-1:** Think of frames as the frames of a film strip, and layers as a stack of film strips stuck together.

The layers in an animation are like separate film strips stacked together. When you play your animation, all the layers of Frame 1 are shown together, and then all the layers of Frame 2 are shown, and then Frame 3, and so on. Just like when you use layers in a static Fireworks document, layers provide a way to organize the order of objects and keep dissimilar objects separate from each other, for easier editing. When you add a layer to your document, you add a whole new film strip to the stack. Changing the order of layers in the Layers panel is like changing the order of that film strip in the stack of film strips.

**Note**    When you add a frame to your movie, it automatically has the same layers as all the other frames. To continue the film-strip metaphor, adding a frame to one film strip in the stack adds it to all the film strips. When you add a layer to your movie, it is added to every frame. Adding a layer adds a whole new film strip, the same length as the others.

One very useful interaction between layers and frames is the ability to share a layer. When a layer is shared, its content is the same on every frame, and no matter where you edit the objects in that layer, the changes appear on every frame. This is handy for static elements, such as backgrounds. We'll take a closer look at this later.

You do the bulk of your animation work in the Frames panel, so you need to have it open all the time while creating an animation. From there, you can add, delete, reorder, or duplicate frames. You can view and edit a single frame, a group of frames, or all of your frames simultaneously. You can copy or move objects from frame to frame. Take a closer look at each of these techniques in the following sections.

**Tip** You might want to dock your Layers panel with your Frames panel, if they aren't already (see Figure 23-2), so that you can easily move between them and manage their interactions as you animate. If you're not short on screen real estate, you could even keep them side by side. As long as they're both close at hand.

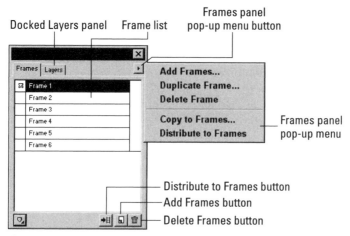

**Figure 23-2:** Manage Frames with the Frames panel and its handy pop-up menu.

## Adding frames

When you start creating an animation in Fireworks, your document has exactly one frame. Obviously, this has to change before you can simulate any kind of movement. At first, make a rough guess at how many frames your animation should contain, and then add that number of frames to your document. Later, you can add or remove frames as the need arises.

**Tip** I like to start with two frames: the first and the last. After you establish where your animation starts and finishes, filling in the intervening frames often is easier.

To add a frame to the end of the Frame list, click the Add Frames button (a blank sheet of paper icon) at the bottom of the Frames panel, or choose Insert ➭ Frame.

To add one or more frames at a specific point in the Frame list, follow these steps:

1. Choose Add Frames from the Frames panel pop-up menu.

   Fireworks displays the Add Frames dialog box (see Figure 23-3).

**Figure 23-3:** The Add Frames dialog box gives you careful control over how many frames you add and where you add them.

2. Enter the number of frames to add in the Number box, or use the slider to add up to ten frames.

3. Choose where to insert the new frames. The options are At the beginning, Before current frame, After current frame, and At the end. Click OK when you're done.

The new frames are created and added to the Frame list at the point you specified.

## Deleting a frame

The most important thing to remember when you delete a frame is that you also delete all the objects that it contains, except for those that are on a shared layer. Take care to identify and delete the correct frame.

**Tip**     If you delete a frame accidentally and want to restore it to the Frame list, choose either Edit ➪ Undo or the keyboard shortcut Ctrl+Z (Command+Z).

To delete a frame, select it on the Frame list and do one of the following:

✦ Click the Delete Frames button (a trashcan icon) at the bottom of the Frames panel.

✦ Drag the frame to the Delete Frames button at the bottom of the Frames panel.

✦ Choose Delete Frame from the Frames panel pop-up menu.

## Reordering frames

As you continue to work on your animation, you might want to change the order of your frames by moving them earlier or later in the animation.

To reorder a frame, click and drag it up or down the Frame list in the Frames panel.

**Note** From working with layers in the Layers panel, you may be accustomed to seeing the layer retain its name as you change its stacking order by dragging it up or down the layers list in a similar way. When you reorder a frame, though, all frames are renumbered to reflect their new positions. The first frame in your animation will always be Frame 1.

### Duplicating frames

One way to save a significant amount of time and effort is to copy a sequence of frames that you've already created and then modify the copies further. If you have created an animation sequence of a sunrise, you can copy those frames, flip the images horizontally and then reverse their order to get an automatic sunset. This not only saves you the time and effort of creating this animation from scratch, but also has the added advantage that the sun will set parallel to the place from which it arose in the canvas, and along the same path.

To duplicate a single frame, drag it from the Frame list onto the Add Frames button at the bottom of the Frames panel. The copy is inserted into the Frame list right after the original.

To duplicate one or more frames and place the copies in a specific place in the Frame list, follow these steps:

1. Choose Duplicate Frame from the Frames panel pop-up menu.

   Fireworks displays the Duplicate Frames dialog box.

**Note** The Duplicate Frames dialog box is very similar to the Add Frames dialog box, shown previously in Figure 23-3.

2. Enter the number of frames to duplicate in the Number box, or use the slider to duplicate up to ten frames.

3. Choose where to insert the copies. The options are At the beginning, Before current frame, After current frame, and At the end. Click OK when you're done.

The frames are duplicated and the copies are added to the Frame list at the point you specified.

## Animating objects

A significant part of creating animation is managing how objects in your document change over time. If you are creating a simple, animated sunrise, the sun starts out at a low point on the canvas and, over time (through later frames), moves to a higher point on the canvas. At the same time, a cloud might move from left to right, while the ground and sky stay the same.

You certainly don't want to draw each of these objects numerous times. Aside from being a lot of extra effort, you would probably end up with objects that are not exactly the same dimensions or properties from frame to frame. If the sun were to change size slightly in each frame, it would detract from the illusion that the animation has only one sun and that it's moving normally.

Instead, when you create animation, you draw objects once and then copy or distribute them from frame to frame, where they can be moved or modified to give the appearance of the same object moving or changing over time.

Keeping similar objects on their own layers makes working with just that object easier as you copy objects to frames. In the animated sunrise example, you might keep the sun on its own layer, and the clouds on another layer.

## Copying objects to frames

Most of the time, you'll be adding objects to other frames by copying them. To copy an object or objects to another frame, follow these steps:

1. Select the object(s).

2. Choose Copy to Frames from the Frames panel pop-up menu.

   Fireworks displays the Copy to Frames dialog box (see Figure 23-4).

3. Choose where the selection will be copied. The available options are All frames, Previous frame, Next frame, or Range, which is used to specify a specific range of frames. Click OK when you're done.

**Figure 23-4:** Use the Copy to Frames dialog box to copy objects to all of your frames or just a specific range of frames.

## Distributing objects to frames

When you choose to distribute a group of objects to frames, the objects are distributed after the current frame, according to their stacking order. The bottom object in the group stays on the current frame, the next one up goes to the next frame, the next one above that goes to the frame after that, and so forth. If you start with a blank canvas and create three objects, such as a square, circle, and star, the star will be on top, because it was created last. If you select those objects and distribute them to frames, the star — which was created last — will now be in the last frame of your animation. New frames are added to contain all the objects, if necessary. For example, if you distribute ten objects to five frames, five more frames will be added to contain all the objects.

You can quickly turn a static document into an animation in this way. Objects that were created first on the canvas end up first in the animation.

**Tip** If you're creating an animation that features an object that stays in the same place on the canvas, but its properties change over time, you can use Distribute to Frames to quicken the process. Create the object in the first frame and clone it by using Edit ➪ Clone, so that a copy is created on top of the original. Modify the copy and clone it again, and then modify that copy, and so on, until you end up with a stack of objects. Select them and choose Distribute to Frames from the Frames panel pop-up menu, and your stack of objects becomes an animation.

To distribute a selection of objects across multiple frames, select the objects and then do one of the following:

✦ Click the Distribute to Frames button (a filmstrip icon) at the bottom of the Frames panel.

✦ Choose Distribute to Frames from the Frames panel pop-up menu.

✦ Drag the blue selection knob on the object's bounding box to the Distribute to Frames button.

## Managing static objects

Fireworks simplifies management of the objects in your animation that aren't animated, because any layer can be shared across every frame of your animation. For example, if you create a background in Frame 1, you can share the layer the background is in, and that background will appear in every frame. After the layer is shared, you can modify the objects it contains in any frame, and the modifications will show up everywhere. Any static element in your animation needs to be created or edited only once.

To share a layer across all the frames of your animation, follow these steps:

1. In the Layer panel, double-click the layer that you want to share.

   Fireworks displays the Layer Options dialog box.

2. Check Share Across Frames and then click OK.

   Fireworks warns you that any objects on this layer in other frames will be deleted. Click OK to delete those objects and share the layer.

To stop sharing a layer across all frames of your animation, follow these steps:

1. In the Layer panel, double-click the layer that you want to stop sharing.

   Fireworks displays the Layer Options dialog box.

2. Uncheck Share Across Frames and then click OK.

Fireworks asks whether you want to leave the contents of the layer in all frames or just in the current frame. Choose Current to leave the contents of the layer just in the current frame. Choose All to leave the contents of the layer in all frames.

**Note**    Another way to modify whether or not a layer is shared is to select the layer in the Layers panel and check or uncheck Share Layer on the Layers panel pop-up menu.

## Using Onion Skinning

Most of the time, your document window displays the contents of a single frame. By flipping back and forth from frame to frame, you can get a feel for how the animation is flowing, but this is just a rough guide. To get a more precise view of the changes from one frame to the next, turn on Onion Skinning to view, and even edit, multiple frames simultaneously.

**New Feature**    "Onion skinning" is the traditional animation technique of drawing on translucent tracing paper to view a series of drawings simultaneously. Now, you can work with a range of frames simultaneously in Fireworks, as well, using the new Onion Skinning feature.

The Onion Skinning button in the lower-left corner of the Frames panel enables you to access the Onion Skinning pop-up menu (see Figure 23-5) and select which frames you want to view. You can choose to view any range of frames within your animation, or all of them.

Onion Skinning
range selector

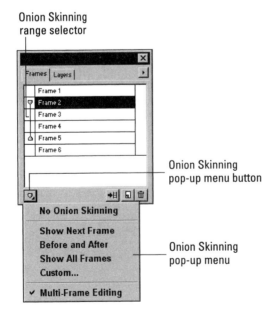

**Figure 23-5:** The Onion Skinning pop-up menu on the Frames panel provides various ways to select which frames you want to view, and even edit, simultaneously.

Onion Skinning
pop-up menu button

Onion Skinning
pop-up menu

When Onion Skinning is turned on, objects on the current frame are displayed normally, while objects on other frames are shown slightly dimmed. When playing an animation by using the Frame controls at the bottom of the document window, Onion Skinning is switched off temporarily.

## Setting the range of frames to onion skin

You can turn on Onion Skinning and choose a range of frames to display in any one of three ways:

✦ Specify a range of frames by using the Onion Skinning range selector, located in the Frame list's left margin in the Frames panel (refer to Figure 23-5). This is the quickest way to specify a range of frames, especially for shorter animations. To expand the range to include earlier frames, click inside an empty box above the selector. To expand the range to include later frames, click inside an empty box below the selector. To contract the range, click inside the selector itself. To turn off Onion Skinning, click the bottom end of the selector.

✦ Choose predefined ranges from the Onion Skinning pop-up menu on the Frames panel. To show the current frame and the next frame, choose Show Next Frame. To show the previous frame, the current frame, and the next frame, choose Before and After. To show all frames, choose Show All.

✦ Choose Custom from the Onion Skinning pop-up menu to display the Onion Skinning dialog box (see Figure 23-6), which gives you precise control over the frames that you view, all the way down to the opacity of other frames. Fill in the number of frames Before Current Frame and After Current Frame that you want to view, and specify an Opacity setting for those frames. A setting of 0 makes frame contents invisible, whereas a setting of 100 makes objects on other frames appear as though they're on the current frame.

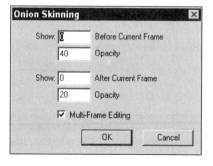

**Figure 23-6:** Select a specific range of frames to onion skin, and control the opacity of the onion-skinned frames with the Onion Skinning dialog box.

## Multi-Frame Editing

When Multi-Frame Editing is enabled, you can select and edit objects in the document window that are on different frames. Whether an object is on the current frame and displayed regularly or on another frame and dimmed makes no difference. You can easily select all versions of a particular object across multiple frames and move or scale them as one.

To enable multiframe editing, check Multi-Frame Editing on the Onion Skinning pop-up menu. To switch off multiframe editing, uncheck Multi-Frame Editing on the Onion Skinning pop-up menu.

## Using the VCR controls

While building your animations in Fireworks, you'll no doubt want to play them to get a feel for the motion between frames. Fireworks now has VCR-style controls available in the status bar on Windows, and on the document window on Macintosh, so that you can preview your animations (see Figure 23-7).

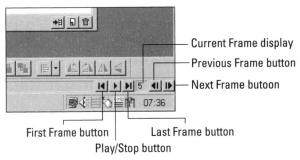

Current Frame display
Previous Frame button
Next Frame butoon

First Frame button
Play/Stop button
Last Frame button

**Figure 23-7:** The VCR controls in the Fireworks status bar enable you to control your multiframe Fireworks document like a movie.

When you click the Play button, your animation is played back, using the timing that is specified under the Animation tab of the Export Preview dialog box. While the animation is playing, the Play button turns into a Stop button. Fireworks also displays the current frame, and has buttons available to jump quickly to the previous or next frame, or to the first or last frame of your animation.

Tip    You can also stop a running animation by clicking your mouse inside the document window.

When you play your animation in the document window, it always loops, but you can change the timing of frames in the Export Preview dialog box, and the timing will be saved with the current file. If you don't set the timing, your animation plays at the default of $^{20}/_{100}$ of a second between frames. Setting this timing is discussed next.

## Export settings and options

Animation timing, looping, and some other format-specific options are built into the animated GIF image itself and are specified in the Export Preview dialog box when you create your animated GIF.

In addition to specifying playback options, exporting your animated GIF also involves reducing the file size. As usual, the last step before publishing Web media is to put that media on a "diet." For the most part, you can use Fireworks's default Export settings to produce very lightweight animated GIF images. Learning to tweak the Export settings will save you some kilobytes, depending on the type of animation you've created.

## Frame delay

The first thing to remember about controlling animation speed is that the settings you specify are approximate. Animated GIF images tend to play back faster in Internet Explorer than in Navigator, and faster computers play animations more quickly. Consider this when you choose a frame delay for each frame.

> **Tip** As if approximated GIF timing isn't enough, an animation that is currently downloading staggers along with no attention to timing, because each frame is displayed as it arrives. A couple of tricks for getting around the staggering playback of a downloading animated GIF are detailed later in this chapter, under "Web Design with Animated GIF Images."

The frame delay is specified in hundredths of a second, in the Frame Delay field. For example, a setting of 25 is a quarter second, 50 is a half second, and 200 is two seconds.

## Frame disposal

The frame disposal options described next are available from the Frame Disposal menu on the Animation tab of the Export Preview dialog box:

✦ **Unspecified:** Fireworks automatically selects the disposal method for each frame. This creates the lightest animated GIF images. Select this option unless you have a specific reason for selecting another.

✦ **None:** Overlays each frame on top of the previous frame. The first frame is shown, and then the next frame is added on top of it, and the following frame is added on top of that, and so forth. This is suitable for adding to a larger background a small object that won't move throughout the animation. For example, an animation that features parts of a logo that steadily appear until the animation is complete.

✦ **Restore to Background:** Shows the contents of each new frame over the background color. For example, to move an object in a transparent animated GIF.

✦ **Restore to Previous:** Shows the contents of each new frame over the contents of the previous frame. For example, to move an object across a background image.

In addition to the Frame Disposal menu, two related options greatly affect the export file size:

✦ **Auto Crop:** Causes Fireworks to compare each frame of the animation with the previous frame and then crop to the area that changes. This reduces file sizes by saving information in each animated GIF only once, and avoids a situation in which, for example, a patch of blue in a certain position is saved repeatedly in each frame.

**Tip**

If you are exporting your animated GIF for editing in another application, turning off Auto Crop is recommended. Some applications don't handle this type of optimization very well, and you may end up with artifacts. Macromedia's Director 7 is one such application.

✦ **Auto Difference:** Converts unchanged pixels within the Auto Crop area to transparent, which sometimes reduces file size further.

## Looping

When specifying looping, ask yourself whether you really need to make that animation run forever. If you're creating a banner ad, ten times may be enough looping before your ad settles down and lets the user read the page's content undistracted. Make sure the last frame of your animation has all the pertinent details, so that a user can return their attention to your ad later and still get the message. When your ad stops looping, the warm fuzzy feeling the viewer gets may translate to a click-through.

**Tip**

Each "click-through" refers to one specific time when a viewer is interested enough in a banner ad to click it and go to the advertiser's site. Although banner ads alone are an excellent way to get brand recognition, or "mindshare," advertisers love click-throughs, because they gauge how effective a particular banner ad or Web site is at attracting interest to the product. The Web average for click-throughs might be less than 1 percent.

If you're creating an animated rollover button, set looping to Forever for best results. Roll over to an animated GIF that plays once, and you may find that it doesn't play at all, or you may catch it in midplay. Different browsers treat preloaded animated GIF images in different ways.

## Step-by-step exporting

To export your animation as an animated GIF and specify settings for frame delay, frame disposal, and looping, follow these steps:

1. Choose File ➪ Export.

   Fireworks displays the Export Preview dialog box.

2. On the Options tab, choose Animated GIF from the format drop-down list.

3. On the Options and File tabs, specify settings such as Bit Depth and Transparency, just as you would for a regular, static GIF image.

4. On the Animation tab, choose each frame from the list, in turn, and enter a number (in hundredths of a second) in the Frame Delay field. Set the Frame Delay to 0 to make frames display as quickly as possible. Preview the results of your timing settings by using the VCR controls, located below the Preview window in the bottom-right area of the Export Preview dialog box.

**Cross-Reference**    For more about optimizing GIF Export settings, see Chapter 16.

5. If necessary, click the Frame View/Hide buttons (the eye icons) at the left of each frame on the list to show or hide a frame. If a frame is hidden, it isn't exported, and thus isn't shown when the animation is played in Fireworks.

**Note**    The Frame Delay setting is saved with your file after you export, or if you choose Set Defaults in the Export Preview dialog box. When you play your animation in the document window by using the VCR controls, Fireworks uses this Frame Delay setting.

6. Specify a method for frame disposal by clicking the Frame Disposal menu button (the trash-can icon next to the Frame Delay field) and choosing an option.

7. Choose whether or not your animation will loop, by clicking either the Play Once or the Loop button. If you click the Loop button, specify in the Number of Loops drop-down list the number of times to loop. You can either choose a number from the list, type another number, or choose Forever to loop continuously. Click the Next button when you're done.

   Fireworks displays the Export dialog box, shown in Figure 23-8.

8. Choose the target folder and filename for your animated GIF and then click Save.

Options tab    Animation tab    Frame Disposal menu button    Frame Delay field    Frame View/Hide buttons

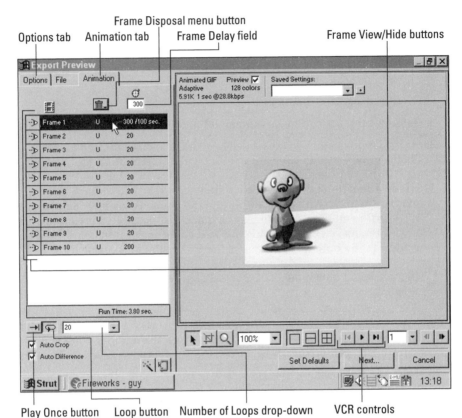

**Figure 23-8:** Specify in the Export Preview dialog box's Animation tab the speed and looping of the animated GIF images that you create.

Play Once button    Loop button    Number of Loops drop-down    VCR controls

# Web Design with Animated GIF Images

One of the nicest things about animated GIF images is that you can place them in a Web page just as easily as you can place regular GIF images. This section describes some ways you can incorporate animated GIF images into your Web pages to create a complete presentation.

## Animated background images

Version 4 and up browsers can display an animated GIF as a background image. A small, animated GIF will be tiled across the whole page, creating a very dynamic presentation with a very low weight.

## Reusing animations

A viewer has to download your animated GIF only once. If you use it again on the same page or on another page, it will play from their browser's cache. This is especially useful for an animated logo or for animated buttons.

## Scaling an animation

Use the height and width attributes of the img tag to present an animation at a larger size without increasing its weight. The slight reduction in quality that comes from scaling an image to double its size — in effect, you're halving its resolution — is a very small price to pay for the impact of a large animation. For example, if you create an animation that is 200 × 200 pixels, you can put it in a page at 400 × 400 pixels with the following img tag:

```
<img src="example.gif" width="400" height="400">
```

You can also use a percentage width or height to make an animation fit a page. This works better for some animations than others, but again, it can create quite an impact. Set the width and height to 100% and fill the entire browser window. The img tag would look like this:

```
<img src="example.gif" width="100%" height="100%">
```

## Using the browser's background image

One of the limitations of animated GIF images is the small number of colors that the GIF format can contain — and the high price you pay in weight for each extra color. However, you can give your animation a colorful background by making it transparent and then placing it in a Web page with a JPEG background. The weight of the whole presentation remains low, because you combine the strengths of the GIF format — animation and transparency — with the strengths of the JPEG format — lots of colors with a low weight.

## Preload an animation

Two ways exist that you can preload an animated GIF to avoid the staggering playback that you see when an animation plays while it's downloading:

✦ **Use the** lowsrc **attribute of the** img **tag.** The browser will show the lowsrc image until the regular image finishes downloading. The following line of code tells the browser "Show shim.gif until animated.gif has downloaded, and then replace shim.gif with animated.gif":

```
<img src="animated.gif" lowsrc="shim.gif" width="200"
height="200">
```

The file shim.gif is the transparent 1-x-1-inch image that Fireworks uses to space tables. You've seen it and have a few copies of it on your hard drive if you've ever exported a sliced image from Fireworks. If you haven't, you can make your own by creating a 1-x-1-inch image with a transparent canvas and exporting it. Because it's lightweight, it doesn't affect the weight of your page too much. Because it's transparent, the background color shows through until the animation starts.

**Note**  Internet Explorer does not support the img tag's lowsrc attribute.

✦ **Use JavaScript to preload the animated GIF and then swap it with another image, such as shim.gif, after the page loads.** This method is slightly more complex than the other method.

**Note**  You can preload and swap images with JavaScript by using a DHTML editor, such as Macromedia Dreamweaver, or by referring to one of the many JavaScript reference books or Web sites, such as www.javascripts.com.

## Animated rollovers

Replacing the Over state of a rollover button with an animation of the same size can create an exciting effect. When the viewer's mouse hovers over your button, the animation begins. When it stops hovering over your button, the animation stops.

**Caution**  Some browsers have problems with complex animated GIF images in rollovers. A small, simple animation that loops forever will likely work best.

To create a simple animated rollover, follow these steps:

1. Create a rollover button with at least three states (Up, Over, and Down) and export it as a GIF in the usual way. (A rollover with two states appears to flash rather than move.) Note the filename that Fireworks gives the Over state of your button; it will be something like button_r2_c2_f2, where f2 stands for frame 2, where you created the Over state.

**Cross-Reference**  For detailed instructions about creating rollover buttons, see Chapter 20.

After you export your file once as a rollover, you need to export it again as an animated GIF. The individual frames that served as each state of the rollover button will now serve as the frames of an animation.

2. To export your file again as an animated GIF, choose File ⇨ Export.

Fireworks displays the Export Preview dialog box.

3. On the Options tab, choose Animated GIF from the format drop-down list.

4. On the Animation tab, click the Loop button, choose Forever, and then click Next.

   Fireworks displays the Export dialog box.

5. Under Slicing, select No Slicing.

6. Under HTML Style, select None.

7. Choose the filename of the Over state of your rollover button and click Save to save your animated GIF with that name.

   Fireworks asks whether you want to replace the original file. Click Yes.

When you open the HTML file that Fireworks created when it created your rollover button, you'll find that hovering your mouse over the button makes the button start cycling through its Up, Over, and Down states.

**Tip**    You can also make an animated rollover button that stops animating when the user places their mouse over it. Instead of replacing the f2 image with an animation, as before, replace the f1 image. The animation plays as the page loads, but stops with a hover of the mouse over the button.

## Slice up animations

Don't be afraid to unleash Fireworks's formidable slicing tools on your animations.

**Caution**    In the Object panel, set static slices to GIF, JPEG, PNG, or whatever format you desire. Set animated slices to export as Export Defaults and then choose Animated GIF as the format when you export the whole document.

Some ideas for things you might do with slicing and animation:

✦ **Add extra colors:** Slice colorful, static areas and set the slice to export as a JPEG or PNG, and your animation will appear to have sections of 24-bit color.

✦ **Add interactivity:** Replace a blank slice of your animated GIF with an HTML form element, such as a drop-down list or a set of radio buttons.

**Cross-Reference**    For more information about slicing images in Fireworks, see Chapter 16.

# Fireworks Technique: Creating Banner Ads

Banner ads are where animated GIF images really shine. You want a Web advertisement to be eye-catching and viewable by all users, and animated GIF images are really the only choice. When does an animated GIF stop being an animated GIF and start being a banner ad? Three things are involved:

✦ It is a certain size in width and height.

✦ It is below a certain weight in kilobytes.

✦ It advertises a product or service or Web site.

We'll look at the issues involved as we go step by step through the process of creating a banner ad in Fireworks.

**Note** This step-by-step process assumes that you're creating a banner ad from start to finish, all by yourself. Although this is not always the case in the real world, where a chain gang of ad people, copywriters, producers, Web artists, and others might be involved in creating just one banner ad, this example enables you to work on a fictional banner ad, for practice.

**On the CD-ROM** You'll find the example banner ad created for this section in both the original Fireworks PNG format and the exported animated GIF.

## Step one: Set the stage

When banner ads started to proliferate on the Web, it became apparent that some sort of standard sizing scheme would benefit both the advertisers and the sites displaying the advertising. If you have a Web site on which you leave a $450 \times 50$ space in your design for a banner ad, and I then send you one that's $460 \times 60$, we have a problem. If ten other people send you ten other ads, all slightly different in size, then the problem becomes a big problem.

To solve this, the Standards and Practices committee of the Internet Advertising Bureau (IAB) and the Coalition for Advertising Supported Information and Entertainment (CASIE) got together, looked at the sizes everybody was using, and came up with a list of standard sizes. They offered this list as a recommendation to the ad buyers and sellers, who overwhelmingly accepted the list. Almost all ads on the Web now follow the IAB/CASIE standards.

**Note** For more about the IAB/CASIE standards, visit the IAB at www.iab.net or CASIE at www.casie.com.

Table 23-3 details the standard banner ad sizes and their names. Full Banner is by far the most common type of ad, with Micro Button probably in second place, but other sizes are gaining popularity as Web sites look to add advertising into newer and smaller spaces, such as margins and even inline with content. If you don't know which size to choose, choose Full Banner, $468 \times 60$.

**On the CD-ROM** You'll find on the companion CD-ROM a set of Fireworks PNG format files, one for each banner ad size, that you can use as templates when creating banner ads in Fireworks.

| Table 23-3 | |
| :-- | :-- |
| **IAB/CASIE Advertising Banner Sizes** | |
| *Dimensions* | *Name* |
| 468 × 60 | Full Banner |
| 392 × 72 | Full Banner with Vertical Navigation Bar |
| 234 × 60 | Half Banner |
| 125 × 125 | Square Button |
| 88 × 31 | Micro Button |
| 120 × 90 | Button 1 |
| 120 × 60 | Button 2 |
| 120 × 240 | Vertical Banner |

I'm going to follow these standards with my banner ad, and make a 468 × 60 Full Banner. Every Web site that has advertising accepts a Full Banner, so my banner can easily be displayed just about anywhere.

In addition to making sure your banner ads are the correct dimensions, you need to consider their weight. No "one true standard" exists for banner ad file sizes. Generally, Web sites set an upper limit on weight, beyond which they won't accept your ad. If you're designing an ad for a specific site, check with its owners first to see what their limit is, or at least check the weight of some of the ads that are already on that site. If you're not designing for a specific site, a general rule is to aim for less than 10K, and certainly keep it under 12K. If you can produce an exciting ad in 8K, so much the better. Your ad will be quick and your whole message will be seen by more viewers.

## Step two: Write the script

Now that you have a suitable "blank page" of the right size and shape, you are ready to sit and stare at it while you come up with an idea. All the same things that apply to regular animations apply to banner ads with regard to making a concise statement, planning ahead, and watching file size.

Let's face it: a 10K or 12K banner ad is not going to get into serious character development or include a lot of scene changes or scenery. If you can't express your idea in a few lines, it probably won't fit into the banner. Think "bumper sticker," and you'll probably be more successful.

My ad is for a fictional magazine called *Mundane Magazine*. It's a hip, youth-oriented magazine about the Web. I want to make something that attracts the attention of the target audience of young, hip Web surfers. Here's the pitch for my ad: "A UFO crash lands on a rocky alien landscape. The pilot thinks, 'Crap.'" Not much of a plot line, but I'm going to aim for 8K.

## Step three: Create the cast of characters

The movie now has a stage and a script—it now needs a cast.

Banner ads are deliberately sized as small as can be, and I find the dimensions a bit of a constraint when I'm drawing. Objects in banner ads are often cropped, scaled down, or halfway off the canvas anyway, so I like to draw and build objects in a second, larger document window (see Figure 23-9); sort of a scratchpad—or, to keep the showbiz analogy going, a backstage area where objects wait to be placed in their scenes. Because Fireworks objects always remain editable and can be dragged and dropped between documents, this backstage area also is a convenient way to work.

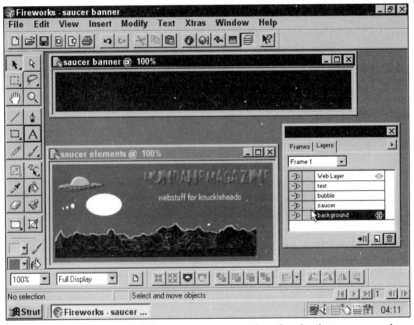

**Figure 23-9:** Use a second document as a scratchpad or backstage area when building objects for use in a banner ad, to avoid working entirely within the puny confines of the ad itself.

Recall that really complex objects with lots of effects, especially drop shadows and glows, increase the weight of the final animated GIF quite a bit. Concentrate on drawing good-looking objects, and leave the effects for later. If your final animation is underweight (yeah, right), then you can easily go back and add some effects to objects.

The following are the principal elements of my ad:

✦ Some rugged, otherworldly mountains to serve as a setting

✦ Some text of the magazine's name and catchphrase

✦ A flying saucer to do the crash-landing

✦ A thought bubble with the word "crap" in it

Each of these elements can be thought of as a cast member, an independent entity that we need to tell what to do as we make our ad.

## Step four: Direct the action

You are ready to start putting the objects where they go. Create a layer for each of your cast members. I have four cast members, and I have a pretty good idea of the order in which they should be stacked: the background should be on the bottom and the text should be on the top, so I made four layers:

✦ text          ✦ saucer

✦ bubble        ✦ background

Figure 23-10 shows these layers and shows that the mountains are placed into the layer called background, which is then shared so that it appears in every frame. I can lock the background layer now and forget about it.

Splitting up objects onto their own layers enables you to share a layer at any time, if you decide that a cast member should be static. I'm not sure yet whether the text with the name of the magazine and the catch phrase is going to be static. It probably will be, but I might get to change that after I see my animated GIF's weight. For now, I'll place the text in the banner and share its layer too.

At this point, the first frame is basically done. The mountains and logo are in place, and the UFO hasn't appeared yet. To finalize my design, I like to build the last frame next, which is where the animation rests before looping. I want to make sure that the UFO and the thought bubble are the right size, so that they hang together nicely in that frame, before I animate them through a bunch of middle frames (see Figure 23-11). After you create the first and last frames, filling in the middle frames may be a lot easier.

Finally, we're ready to start some serious animating. In the first frame, the UFO hasn't appeared yet; in the last frame, it has landed. I'm going to copy the UFO from the last frame, paste it into the first frame, and then move it to the top of the canvas, so that it's just peeking in.

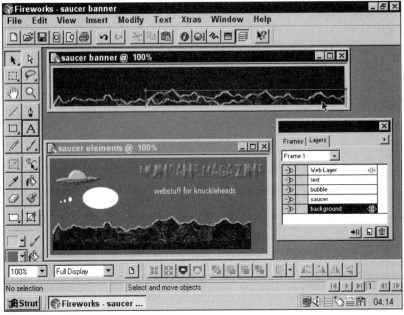

**Figure 23-10:** The background is going to stay the same throughout the animation, so the background layer is shared. This layer is now the same in every frame.

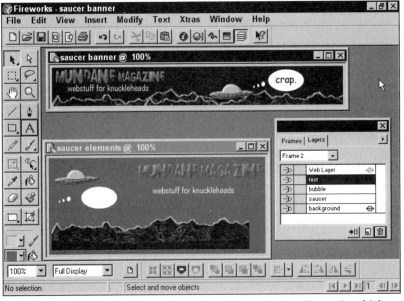

**Figure 23-11:** After you finish the first frame, create a new frame in which to build the last frame. Your two-frame animation now has a start and finish, which makes building the middle much easier.

So, in Frame 1, the saucer is just appearing. I want the next frame to be almost identical, except that the saucer should move a little bit closer to its landing site. The saucer doesn't have far to travel, and I'd like it to do so in seven or eight frames, so that the whole animation is nine or ten frames long. Keeping the animation in a small area and on a small number of frames limits its file size.

A quick way to make the next frame is to duplicate the current frame and then move the saucer a bit. Then, duplicate that one and move the saucer a bit more. The primary advantage to this procedure is that every time I move the saucer, I move it from the exact spot it's at in the previous frame. The other advantage is that I make a frame and copy the saucer with just one click and drag. The technique looks like this:

1. Duplicate Frame 1 by dragging it from the Frame list to the Add Frames button at the bottom of the Frames panel.

   A copy of Frame 1 is inserted as Frame 2.

2. Go to Frame 2, select the saucer, and move it a little closer to its landing site.

3. Repeat Steps 1 and 2, but this time start with Frame 2 and drag it to the Add Frames button, to make Frame 3. Go to Frame 3 and move the saucer a little closer again, and so on (see Figure 23-12), until the saucer appears to land about ten frames later.

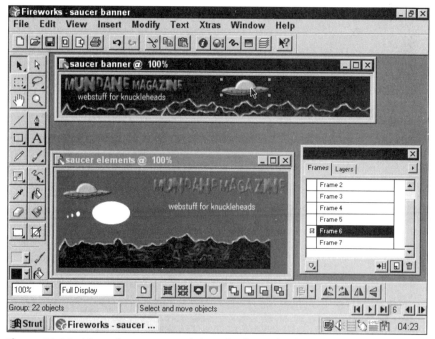

**Figure 23-12:** Move the saucer, and then duplicate the frame. Move the saucer in the duplicate, and duplicate again.

**Tip**    Another way to accomplish this would be to duplicate the saucer in Frame 1 by using Edit ⇨ Duplicate and then move the duplicate into the next position, but still within Frame 1. Duplicate the duplicate and move that one, still within Frame 1. Eventually, Frame 1 contains a bunch of saucers in the correct positions on the canvas, but in the wrong frames. Select all the saucers and choose Distribute to Frames from the Frames panel pop-up menu, and you instantly have an animation, because those saucers are distributed to new frames according to their stacking order.

Now, my saucer has landed; I can preview my animation by using the VCR controls, and tweak the saucer's descent by moving it a bit to the left or right in certain frames until I get the effect that I want, which is a bit of a rough landing. While previewing the animation, I decided that I didn't want the thought bubble to be the last frame. I want the last three frames to go like this: saucer lands, thought bubble appears, and then thought bubble disappears. The quickest way to get that extra frame on the end is simply to duplicate the last frame and then delete the thought bubble out of it.

The only thing that's left now is to set the frame timing so that the last three frames are a little slower. The frame timing, looping, and such are set on the Animation tab of the Export Preview dialog box. In Figure 23-13, you can see that I set the last three frames to one second, two seconds, and one second. I tested a few combinations of speeds by using the VCR controls in the Export Preview. I set looping to 10 times, which is long enough that it loops for about a minute, because my banner takes a little over five seconds to play. At that point, it becomes a static banner that still invites the viewer to visit Mundane Magazine, without annoying them by continuing to flash away.

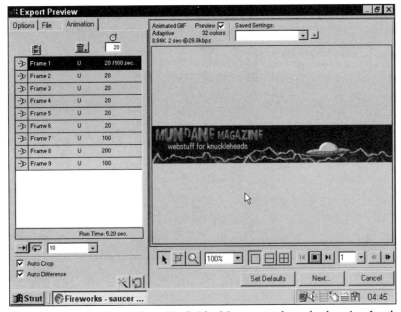

**Figure 23-13:** Set the timing of individual frames and set the looping for the whole animation. Note that the animation is playing in the Export Preview.

## Step five: Leave the excess on the cutting-room floor

Don't be afraid to be brutal when exporting your animation and creating the animated GIF image itself. Remember that your focus is to get a message across quickly—not to win awards for the most colors or the most profound use of animation. My banner is about 8K or so, but if it were 12K or more, I would definitely have to consider one of the following options:

✦ Cut some frames, which makes the animation less smooth.

✦ Move the saucers closer together from frame to frame, so that the area that's animated is smaller.

✦ Flatten some areas, such as the bumpy, textured mountains. Areas of solid, flat color compress better.

✦ Take out some colors by cutting the palette further.

✦ Remove effects, such as the inner bevel on the text and the saucer.

✦ Make some objects smaller, such as the text, so that more of the flat, blue background is showing, resulting in better compression.

Sometimes, swallowing your creative pride can lead to a better overall presentation and a fast-loading, attention-attracting banner ad that's ready to take a message to the Web (see Figure 23-14).

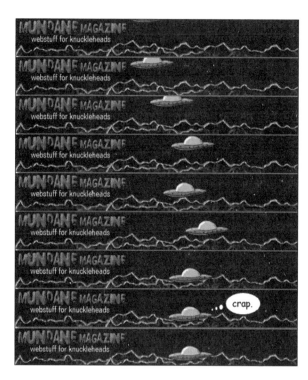

**Figure 23-14:** The finished banner ad keeps the animation in a small area and in a small number of frames. The background under the animated objects is a solid color that compresses well. The banner weighs 8.8K (about one second on a 56K connection).

# Summary

Fireworks enables you to create and edit animation by using a variety of techniques, most of which revolve around the Frames panel. When working with animation in Fireworks, keep these points in mind:

✦ The overall weight of your animated GIF is always a consideration. Every creative decision must be examined for its effect on file size.

✦ The Frames panel is the heart of Fireworks's animation tools, but the Layers panel is also important.

✦ Each frame in your Fireworks document is like a frame of a film strip. Copy objects to other frames by using the Frames panel, and then change the objects' locations on the canvas or their properties to create animation.

✦ Layers can be shared across multiple frames, to manage static objects better in an animation.

✦ Onion Skinning enables you to view and edit multiple frames simultaneously.

✦ The Web design opportunities for animated GIF images are numerous, such as animated rollover buttons, sliced animations, and animated browser backgrounds.

✦ Standard sizes exist for banner ads. Before you create a banner ad, make sure that you've selected the correct size, so that your banner ad can be used on the widest variety of Web sites.

In the next chapter, you'll look at how you can enhance your animation, especially large projects, with symbols and tweening.

✦    ✦    ✦

# Working with Symbols and Instances

**S**ymbols and Instances are time- and laborsaving devices for creating, editing, and managing multiple, similar objects. If you make an object into a Symbol, copies of it remain linked so that updating all the objects is easier. In addition, linked objects make advanced animation techniques possible.

**Note** Throughout this chapter, Symbols and Instances often are collectively referred to as "linked objects" when a distinction is unnecessary. For example, you can tween a Symbol and an Instance, or you can tween two Instances. To simplify the discussion, the text might call that "tweening two linked objects."

This chapter begins with a discussion of the basics of using Symbols and Instances in Fireworks. It covers how you can make, modify, and manage Symbols and Instances. Finally, it looks at how you can use tweening to change Instances over time and quickly create animations.

## Understanding Symbols and Instances

*Symbols* in Fireworks might just as well be called "object templates." The Symbol itself is a master copy, a rubber stamp, half a potato with a design carved in it and dipped in ink. You can use a Symbol to stamp out almost unlimited copies, called *Instances* (see Figure 24-1). Instances are simplified renderings of your original Symbol. Using linked objects instead of a bunch of independent objects improves performance, because Fireworks has to draw the more complex path object only once.

One symbol          Lots of Instances

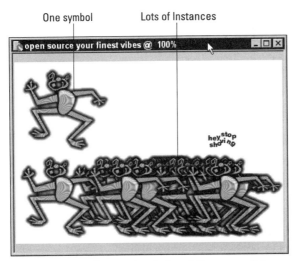

**Figure 24-1:** Make one Symbol and then copy it to create almost unlimited Instances. Because Instances are rendered like image objects, Fireworks doesn't have to draw this path object repeatedly, which speeds up performance.

Another advantage of Instances is that they remain linked to their parent Symbol and can inherit some of the edits that you make to the Symbol. After you create your Instances, you can change the fill or texture of the Symbol and its Instances will follow suit automatically. Rollover buttons are an example of a good place to take advantage of the easy editing of linked objects. The buttons in Figure 24-2 are all in the same frame, but they can be freely moved into other frames or stacked on top of each other without having to worry about selecting and editing them later. The fill, stroke, or texture can be changed quite easily just by changing the one on the top left, because it's a Symbol, and the rest are Instances.

Symbol

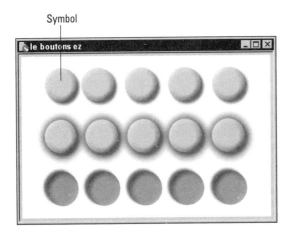

**Figure 24-2:** Change the fill, stroke, or texture of the Symbol, and the Instances update automatically. Managing rollover buttons is made simpler. Only one of these buttons is a Symbol and the rest are Instances of that Symbol.

The third major strength of linked objects is that Fireworks can tween two or more of them to create intermediate steps, which simplifies and speeds up the animation process. You make the first and last steps, and Fireworks fills in the middle steps. In Figure 24-3, I made the first head into a Symbol and copied it to make and modify the 5th, 9th, 13th, and 17th objects (the ones that are selected), and then Fireworks created the other objects for me. We'll look more closely at tweening later in this chapter.

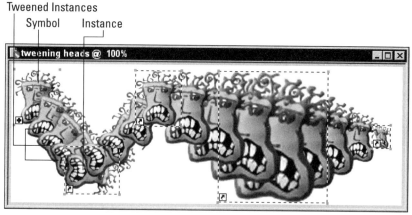

**Figure 24-3:** Linked objects become key frames, or resting points, and Fireworks does the dirty work of creating intermediate steps. The selected objects here were the key frames. The ones that aren't selected were made automatically by Fireworks.

# Creating Symbols and Instances

Making Symbols is very much like making groups. Both of these features work in Object mode only, and both allow you to bring together multiple objects and treat them as one object. In fact, you can subselect the component objects of a Symbol just like you can with a group.

**Cross-Reference** For more about groups, see Chapter 13.

Most of the time, you create and manage your linked objects by using the commands in the Insert menu, but the same commands are also available through the context menu that appears when you right-click (Ctrl-click) a Symbol or Instance.

**New Feature** In Fireworks 2, the commands for creating Symbols have moved from the Edit menu to the Insert menu.

## Creating Symbols

The first step in using Symbols and Instances is to create a Symbol. You can add and remove objects at any time, so you don't need to worry too much about making objects absolutely perfect before you give them the Symbol treatment.

Almost any object or group of objects can be made into a Symbol. The only thing that you can't make into a Symbol are objects that are already linked. In other words, they're already a Symbol or Instance.

To create a Symbol, follow these steps:

1. Select an object or objects.
2. Choose Insert ➪ Symbol to turn your selected objects into a Symbol.

You can identify a Symbol as a Symbol by the plus sign in the lower-left corner of its bounding box.

## Creating Instances

Creating Instances is as easy as copying the Symbol. That's all there is to it. Any of the methods that you're used to using to duplicate objects in Fireworks also work to duplicate a Symbol to make an Instance. You can also duplicate an Instance to make another Instance.

**Note**    The only time that you can duplicate a Symbol to produce another Symbol is when you copy a Symbol to another document. The copy in the target document is a Symbol, but it has no links to the original document.

To create an Instance, select a Symbol or an Instance and use one of the following methods:

◆ Choose either Edit ➪ Copy or the keyboard shortcut Ctrl+C (Command+C) to copy the Symbol to the Clipboard, and then paste an Instance into the document by choosing Edit ➪ Paste or the keyboard shortcut Ctrl+V (Command+V).

◆ Choose Edit ➪ Duplicate to create an Instance that's slightly offset from the original.

◆ Choose Edit ➪ Clone to create an Instance directly on top of the original.

◆ Select Copy to Frames from the Frames panel pop-up menu to create an Instance on another frame or range of frames.

◆ Click the Symbol and hold down the mouse button and, with the mouse button still held down, press and hold down the Alt (Option) key, and then drag an Instance off the Symbol. Let go of the mouse button, and then the Alt (Option) key, in that order.

The new Instance can be identified by the arrow icon in the lower-left corner of its bounding box (see Figure 24-4).

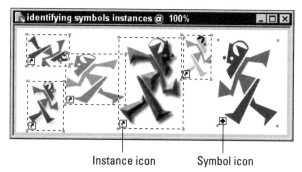

Instance icon          Symbol icon

**Figure 24-4:** You can identify linked objects by the icon in the lower-left corner of their bounding boxes. Symbols have plus signs and Instances have arrows.

# Modifying Linked Objects

When modifying linked objects, you need to consider which properties are passed on from Symbol to Instance, and which properties are not. Some changes to Symbols, such as the fill color, are automatically inherited by their Instances, but some changes, such as Live Effects, are not passed on. The semi-independence that Instances enjoy is what enables you to modify them enough that they can be tweened with their parent Symbols (see Figure 24-5). If an Instance mimicked its Symbol entirely — for example, when you scaled the Symbol, the Instance scaled, too — then linked objects would always look exactly alike.

**Figure 24-5:** Instances enjoy some independence from their parent Symbols, which enables you to tween from one to another. Here, an Opacity setting of 100 percent is tweened to an Opacity setting of 10 percent, because each Instance has its own setting.

**Tip**    If you want all of your linked objects to have a setting in common—such as the same drop shadow—modify that setting on the Symbol before you create the Instances.

Modifying any of the independent properties of a particular linked object has no effect on any other linked object. Modify the size of a Symbol, for example, and none of its Instances will change size. Similarly, modifying the size of an Instance affects only that particular Instance. You make these modifications in exactly the same way as you would for a regular object. Table 24-1 details the independent properties of linked objects.

| Table 24-1 | |
| **Independent Properties of Linked Objects** | |
| **Property** | **Description** |
| --- | --- |
| Transformations | The width, height, skew, distortion, and rotation, or flip it vertically or horizontally |
| Opacity | More or less transparency |
| Blending | A different blending setting |
| Live Effects | Effects such as drop shadow, inner bevel, or glow |

## Modifying a Symbol

When you want to modify a Symbol, you can treat it just like you treat a group. Apply Live Effects, scale or transform it, or change colors. All changes are applied to all component objects within the Symbol.

Changing the properties of just one of the objects within a Symbol also works just like it does with a group: hold down the Alt (Option) key and click component objects to subselect and then modify them.

When you add or remove objects from a Symbol, those changes are automatically applied to the Symbol's Instances. The same rules that apply to creating Symbols apply here, though: you can't include any object that is already a linked object.

To delete an object from a Symbol, hold down the Alt (Option) key, select the component object, and then delete it from the Symbol.

**Caution**    Make sure that you really want to delete objects from all of a Symbol's Instances before you delete an object from a Symbol.

To add objects to an existing Symbol, follow these steps:

1. Select the Symbol and the object or objects that you want to add to it.

2. Choose Insert ➪ Symbol Options ➪ Add to Symbol.

Your new objects are added to the Symbol, and all Instances of the Symbol are updated to include the new objects.

## Modifying an Instance

You can modify the independent properties of an Instance just as you would for a regular object. If Fireworks won't let you modify an Instance in a particular way, though, such as its color or stroke settings, then that's one of the linked properties that must be changed in the Symbol.

 **Caution** Applying an Xtra to an Instance turns it into an image object and causes it to stop being an Instance.

To modify an Instance, select it and change one of the following properties:

✦ **Transformations:** Alter settings such as width, height, and skew by choosing Modify ➪ Transform ➪ *option.*

✦ **Opacity:** Alter by adjusting the percentage slider in the Object panel.

✦ **Blending:** Alter in the Object panel.

 **Cross-Reference** For more about blending, see Chapter 11.

✦ **Live Effects:** Modify with the controls in the Effect panel.

 **Cross-Reference** For more about Live Effects, see Chapter 12.

You can't subselect the component objects within an Instance. Instances are renderings of a Symbol and are more like image objects than the original Symbol. To modify an object within an Instance, you must modify it within the Symbol.

## Trick Instance updates

Although you can't modify an independent property of a Symbol and have its Instances update automatically, you can trick them into doing so by adding a new object to the Symbol and deleting an old one. If the new object is similar to the old one, except that it has some independent property modified, then the end result will be that you've modified an independent property of your Symbol and all of its Instances.

For example, if you want to add a drop shadow to a Symbol and all of its Instances, follow these steps:

1. Select an Instance and break its link to the Symbol by choosing Insert ⇨ Symbol Options ⇨ Break Link.

   The Instance is now an independent object.

2. Add the drop shadow to the former Instance by selecting it and choosing Drop Shadow from the Effects panel.

3. Place the former Instance directly on top of the Symbol, select them both, and choose Insert ⇨ Symbol Options ⇨ Add to Symbol, to add the former Instance to the Symbol.

   The new object appears in all the Instances.

4. Pick up the Select Behind tool from the Toolbox or press the V key to select it automatically. Hold down the Alt (Option) key and double-click the Symbol to select the old object that's hiding underneath the new one. Press the Delete key to delete it.

   The old object disappears from all the Instances.

The Instances all seem to have inherited a drop shadow from the Symbol.

# Managing Symbols and Instances

In addition to creating and modifying Symbols and Instances, you have some options for changing Symbols back into regular objects, or finding the Symbol that belongs to a particular Instance.

## Finding linked objects

As a document becomes more and more complex, it gets easier to lose track of which linked object is the Symbol. You may not even know which frame it is on.

To find the parent Symbol of a particular Instance, select the Instance and choose Insert ⇨ Symbol Options ⇨ Find Symbol. Fireworks selects the Symbol for you. If it's in another Frame, Fireworks takes you to that frame.

## Unlinking linked objects

If you want to break the link between an Instance and its parent Symbol, select the Instance and choose Insert ⇨ Symbol Options ⇨ Break Link. The link is broken and your Instance is now a regular, independent object.

If you want break the link between a Symbol and its Instances, follow these steps:

1. Select the Symbol.

2. Choose Insert ➪ Symbol Options ➪ Break Link.

   Fireworks displays the Break Link dialog box (see Figure 24-6).

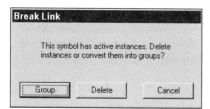

**Figure 24-6:** The Break Link dialog box enables you to choose how to dispose of Instances attached to the Symbol that you're attempting to unlink or delete.

3. Click the Group button to convert the Instances into regular groups. Click the Delete button to delete the Instances.

## Deleting linked objects

Deleting an Instance works just like deleting an unlinked object and has no effect on any other objects. Deleting a Symbol does have an effect on its Instances, though.

To delete just the Instances of a particular Symbol, select the Symbol and choose Insert ➪ Symbol Options ➪ Delete Instances. All Instances are deleted, while the Symbol itself is unaffected.

To delete a Symbol and all of its Instances, follow these steps:

1. Select the Symbol.

2. Press the Delete key or choose either Edit ➪ Cut or Ctrl+X (Command+X).

   Fireworks displays the Break Link dialog box (refer to Figure 24-6).

3. Click the Group button to convert the Instances into regular groups. Click the Delete button to delete the Instances.

# Tweening with Fireworks

After you learn how to create and modify linked objects, you can really unleash the advanced animation capabilities that Fireworks offers, by tweening those linked files to create exciting animation effects quickly and easily.

*Tweening* is an old-school animation term that refers to generating intermediate frames between two images to create the effect of the first image changing smoothly into the second image. The word itself evolved from "in-betweening." In Fireworks, all the Instance properties that you can modify can also be tweened. Each new Instance is slightly changed from the one before it, so that the first Instance seems to evolve into the last.

Any group of linked objects can be tweened. Fireworks tweens the group from bottom to top. In other words, it starts with the object that's closest to the canvas and then goes to the next one up, and then the next one up, and so on (see Figure 24-7). If you're tweening more than two objects, adjust their stacking order to make sure that they tween in the order that you want them to.

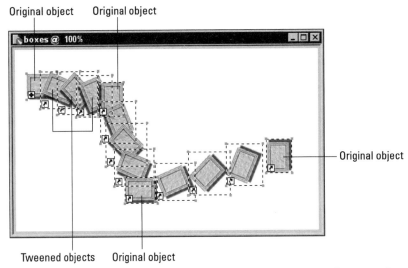

**Figure 24-7:** Four linked objects become an entire animation after tweening. Note that Fireworks tweened according to the object's stacking order. The start of the tween is the lowest point, and the end of it is at the highest point.

After you set the stacking order to determine the order that objects get tweened, you also have to decide how many steps Fireworks should fill in between each object. Refer again to Figure 24-7. The number of steps in that tween was three, so Fireworks filled in three objects between each of the objects that was already there.

Usually, you'll want to distribute your tweened objects to frames to create an animation. Fireworks offers to do this at the same time as it does the tweening, or you can select your tweened objects and click the Distribute to Frames button on the Frames panel to do it later. Fireworks distributes objects to frames from bottom to top, the same way that it tweens, so that your objects stay in the correct order.

To tween a Symbol and an Instance, follow these steps:

1. Create a Symbol and duplicate it to create an Instance.

2. The Instance is higher in the stacking order than the Symbol (further from the canvas), so it is the end of the tween. Move it to the spot on the canvas where you want the tween to stop. You can also modify one of its independent properties, such as its size or opacity, if you like.

**Tip**    If you try to tween a Live Effect between one object that doesn't have the effect applied and another that does, you'll notice that the effect doesn't graduate between the two, but instead seems to start after the object that doesn't have the effect. To get around this, apply the effect to both objects before you tween, and set the effect to 0 on one (it will still appear not to have the effect applied) and a higher setting on the other. In the beveling effects, this would be a depth of 0; in the glow or drop shadow, set the opacity to 0. When you tween, the effect's settings will tween as well.

3. Select the linked objects either by dragging a selection box around them with your mouse or by holding down the Shift key and clicking each one in turn.

4. Choose Insert ⇨ Tween Instances.

   Fireworks displays the Tween Instances dialog box (see Figure 24-8).

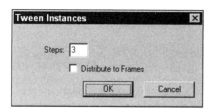

**Figure 24-8:** Set the number of steps to tween, and choose to distribute the objects to frames in the Tween Instances dialog box.

5. Enter the number of steps to tween. A setting of 3 makes Fireworks create three new objects between each original object.

6. Check Distribute to Frames to distribute the tweened objects to frames and make them into an animation. Click OK when you're done.

Fireworks creates the new objects, and you have instant animation (see Figure 24-9).

**Tip**    Fireworks can't tween shapes (morphing). If you want to tween shapes, you can do a blend in Macromedia Freehand 8 and then drag the shapes into Fireworks, ready to be distributed to frames. You can also do a shape tween in Macromedia Flash 3, although you have to save the result as an Adobe Illustrator document and then import that document into Fireworks in order to retain the vector information.

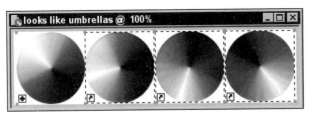

**Figure 24-9:** Two linked objects tweened with a Steps setting of 2. Fireworks creates two new objects between the original objects. The settings of the Inner Bevel Live Effect have also been tweened. The Symbol has the light source coming from the upper left. The final Instance has it coming from the lower right. The tweened objects fill in the gaps.

# Fireworks Technique: Fading In and Out

Fading an object in and out is a common effect that's easy to create in Fireworks. Tweening two linked objects, one with an Opacity setting of 0 percent and one with an opacity of 100 percent, produces a fade. Which way you go determines whether it's a fade in or a fade out. In this section, we create an animation in which the object fades in, and then fades back out, and then loops, so that it seems to fade in and out continuously.

To fade an object in and out, select the object and follow these steps:

1. Create the basic object or group to which you're going to apply the fade, and then make that object or group into a Symbol.

2. Select your Symbol and choose either Edit ⇨ Clone or Ctrl+Shift+C (Command+Shift+C) to create an Instance directly on top of the Symbol.

3. Open the Object panel and set the Opacity of the Instance to 0 percent. The slider only goes down to 1, so you have to type **0** into the field and hit Enter (Return).

**Note**
The Opacity setting might not seem to have any effect, because you will be able to see your Symbol directly through your Instance.

4. Choose Modify ⇨ Arrange ⇨ Send to Back to send the Instance directly behind the Symbol.

5. Select both the Symbol and the Instance by dragging a selection box around them. If they are the only objects in your document, you can alternatively select them by choosing either Edit ⇨ Select All or Ctrl+A.

6. Create Instances between your Symbol and Instance by choosing Insert ⇨ Tween Instances.

Fireworks displays the Tween Instances dialog box.

7. Set the number of steps to 5.

**Note**

You can choose a different number of steps, if you prefer, but during this example, I'll count steps and frames as if you've chosen 5.

8. Check the Distribute to Frames check box and then click OK.

Play your animation. Your object should appear to fade in. You should have seven frames. In the first frame, an Instance is completely transparent (opacity of 0), in the second frame, it fades in, and so on until the seventh frame, in which your Symbol is fully opaque. At this point, you can choose either to leave it as is or create some more animation after the object fades in. If you also want to fade out the object, continue on.

9. Open the Frames panel and select the final frame in your animation, to display it in the document window. This frame contains your Symbol; the fully faded-in version of your object.

10. Select your Symbol and choose either Edit ⇨ Clone or Ctrl+Shift+C (Command+Shift+C) to create an Instance directly on top of the Symbol.

11. Open the Object panel and set the Opacity of the Instance to 0 percent. Again, the slider only goes down to 1, so type a **0** into the field and press Enter (Return).

12. Select both the Symbol and the new Instance that's on top of it by dragging a selection box around them. If they are the only objects in this frame, you can alternatively select them by choosing either Edit ⇨ Select All or Ctrl+A.

13. Create Instances between your Symbol and Instance by choosing Insert ⇨ Tween Instances.

Fireworks displays the Tween Instances dialog box.

14. Set the number of steps to the same number you used when fading the object in (in this case, 5).

15. Check the Distribute to Frames check box and then click OK.

16. Select the final frame of your animation in the Frames panel and remove it by clicking the Delete Frame button (the trash-can icon). This final frame is redundant, because the first frame is also a fully transparent object. Your animation will loop more smoothly without it.

Click Play to preview your animation. The object appears to fade in and then fade out (see Figure 24-10). If you like, you can choose File ⇨ Export and adjust the timing of your animation on the Animation tab of the Export Preview dialog box, so that the pause between the fade in and fade out is longer.

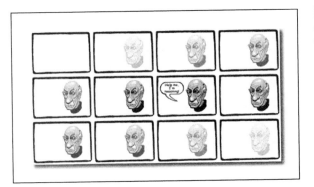

**Figure 24-10:** Fading an object in and out is easy with tweening.

**On the CD-ROM**  You'll find on the companion CD-ROM "Picasso heads," the animation from Figure 24-10, in both Fireworks PNG format and animated GIF.

# Fireworks Technique: Animating Xtras

Unlike Live Effects, you can't really tween Xtras, because they're applied directly to image objects only. Applying them to linked objects also breaks the link and leaves you with regular image objects. You can use tweening, though, to quickly create an animation in which the only changes are the settings of the Xtra as it's applied to each frame.

**Cross-Reference**  This example uses an Xtra called Fire, which is part of a third-party package called Eye Candy, from Alien Skin. If you don't have Eye Candy, try using any other standard filter in its place (but not the Blur, Invert, Other, or Sharpen Xtras—they won't work, because they treat all selections as groups). If you have only the Xtras that came with Fireworks available, try using CSI PhotoFilter to change a tint gradually from one color to another, or try CSI Noise to add noise gradually. Many Xtras are available for free on the Web that you might use, as well. For more information about Xtras and about Eye Candy, see Chapter 14.

To animate Xtras in Fireworks, follow these steps:

1. Create the basic object or group to which you're going to apply the Xtra, and then make the group or object into a Symbol.

2. Select your Symbol and create an Instance directly on top of it by choosing either Edit ➪ Clone or Ctrl+Shift+C (Command+Shift+C).

3. Select both the Symbol and the Instance by dragging a selection box around them. Alternatively, if they are the only objects in your document, you can select them by choosing either Edit ➪ Select All or Ctrl+A.

4. Create Instances between your Symbol and Instance by choosing Insert ⇨ Tween Instances.

   Fireworks displays the Tween Instances dialog box.

5. Set the number of steps to a small number, such as 5.

6. Uncheck the Distribute to Frames check box and then click OK.

   Now we have a stack of identical objects, to which we're going to apply an Xtra, changing the settings slightly each time so that each ends up looking slightly different.

7. Choose Insert ⇨ Symbol Options ⇨ Find Symbol.

   Fireworks selects the Symbol.

8. Drag the Symbol off the canvas, so that it no longer is part of your composition. You can use it later to create more Instances, because these Instances will end up as image objects.

9. Select all the Instances by dragging a selection around them with the mouse.

10. Choose Xtras ⇨ Eye Candy 3.0 ⇨ Fire.

    Fireworks displays the Fire dialog box for the first Instance.

11. Specify the settings that you want, and then click OK.

    Fireworks displays the Fire dialog box for the second Instance.

12. The controls are set the same way you left them after the first Instance. Modify the controls slightly to create a difference between this Instance and the previous one. Click OK when you're done.

    Fireworks displays the Fire dialog box for the third Instance.

13. Continue to change control settings slightly in each box as it appears, until you have modified all the Instances.

**Tip**    Clicking Cancel at any time in the Xtra's dialog box cancels the operation for all the Instances.

14. With your Instances still selected, click the Distribute to Frames button (the film-strip icon) on the Frames panel.

All Instances are distributed over frames to create an animation (see Figure 24-11). Preview your animation with the VCR controls in the status bar, or choose File ⇨ Export and preview your animation in the Export Preview dialog box, in which you can also specify the frame delay.

**On the CD-ROM**    You'll find on the companion CD-ROM the "hothead," the animation from Figure 24-11, in both Fireworks PNG format and animated GIF.

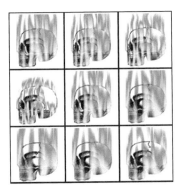

**Figure 24-11:** Tweening Xtras can be accomplished in relatively few steps. The difference in control settings for each Instance creates the animation. This animation depends entirely on the slight changes in the Fire effect applied to each Instance.

# Fireworks Technique: Tweening Depth

A quick and useful effect that you can create with linked objects is 3D depth, wherein your object appears to fly out from the canvas. You can do this by scaling down an Instance, altering its opacity to make it seem faded, moving it to the back, and then tweening the Symbol and Instance.

To create a depth effect with a Symbol and Instance, follow these steps:

1. Create a Symbol and place it near the top of the canvas.

2. Choose either Edit ➪ Clone or Ctrl+Shift+C (Command+Shift+C) to create an Instance directly on top of the Symbol.

3. Hold down the Shift key and, at the same time, use the arrow down key to move the Instance down the canvas without moving it left or right. A few hundred pixels is usually all you can get away with and still keep the depth effect looking like depth.

4. With the Instance still selected, choose Modify ➪ Transform ➪ Numeric Transform.

    Fireworks displays the Numeric Transform dialog box.

5. Scale the Instance to 30 percent of its size by selecting Scale from the drop-down list, checking Scale Attributes, checking Constrain Proportions, and entering **30** in one of the fields. Click OK when you're done.

6. Set the Instance's opacity to 10 percent by double-clicking it and entering 10 percent in the Opacity field of the Object panel.

7. With the Instance still selected, choose either Modify ➪ Arrange ➪ Send to Back or Ctrl+B (Command+B).

8. Hold down the Shift key and click the Symbol and the Instance to select them both. If they are the only objects in your document, you can choose Edit ➪ Select All or Ctrl+A.

9. Choose Insert ➪ Tween Instances.

Fireworks displays the Tween Instances dialog box.

10. Set the number of steps you want in between the Symbol and the Instance, uncheck Distribute to Frames, and the click OK.

Fireworks tweens the Symbol and the Instance.

**Tip** You can choose Edit ➪ Undo and then do Steps 12 and 13 again if you want to change the number of steps.

11. If you like, you can select the Symbol and make it stand out by adding a Live Effect such as glow or inner bevel to it.

Your object now appears to fly out from the canvas (see Figure 24-12).

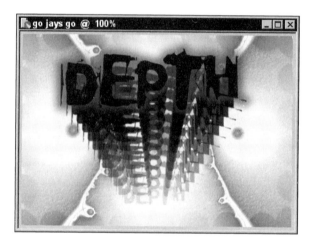

**Figure 24-12:** The front text object is a Symbol and the back text object is an Instance. Fireworks made the rest of them with tweening. A little of the Glow Live Effect was then added to the front object to make it stand out.

**Tip** To change this depth effect into an animation, select the Symbol and all the Instances by drawing a selection around them with the mouse (or, if they are the only objects in your document, choose either Edit ➪ Select All or Ctrl+A), and then click the Distribute to Frames button on the Frames panel. Your object animates its way toward you.

# Summary

Symbols and Instances are a way to manage multiple similar objects in your documents. When using Symbols and Instances, keep these things in mind:

✦ Symbols can contain any object or objects except for other Symbols or Instances.

✦ Every copy that you make of a Symbol is an Instance.

✦ Some properties of linked objects are independent, such as Live Effects, and transformations such as size. Changing these properties on a linked object has no effect on other objects. Some properties, such as fill and stroke, can be modified only on the Symbol, and are then inherited by its Instances.

✦ Tweening saves time and energy, because Fireworks fills in the middle elements of an animation automatically. Any selection of two or more linked objects can be tweened. Fireworks tweens from the bottom up.

✦ Distribute a tweened sequence to frames to create an instant animation.

✦ You can use tweening to create advanced effects, such as objects fading in and out or flying out from the canvas.

✦     ✦     ✦

# Keyboard Shortcuts

This appendix contains common Fireworks keyboard shortcuts.

## The File Menu

The File menu contains commands for file handling and import and export functions. Table A-1 details the commands and their keyboard shortcuts.

## Table A-1
## File Menu

| Command | Description | Windows | Macintosh |
|---------|-------------|---------|-----------|
| New | Displays the New Document dialog box before creating a new document. | Ctrl+N | Command+N |
| Open | Displays the Open dialog box before opening an existing document. | Ctrl+O | Command+O |
| Open Multiple | Displays the Open Multiple dialog box before opening multiple documents. | Ctrl+Shift+O | Command+Shift+O |
| Scan ⇨ Twain Acquire | Displays the interface dialog box for a Twain source, if one is available and has been, before acquiring an image from a Twain source. | n/a | n/a |
| Scan ⇨ Twain Select | Displays the Select Source dialog box before selecting a Twain source. | n/a | n/a |
| Scan ⇨ Photoshop Acquire Plug-In | Displays the options dialog box for a Photoshop Acquire plug-in, if one is available, before acquiring an image from the corresponding device (Macintosh only). | n/a | n/a |
| Close | Closes a document without closing Fireworks. | Ctrl+F4 | Command+F4 |
| Save | Saves a document, or displays the Save As dialog box for an unnamed document. | Ctrl+S | Command+S |
| Save As | Displays the Save As dialog box before saving a document. | Ctrl+Shift+S | Command+Shift+S |
| Save a Copy | Displays the Save Copy As dialog box . before saving a copy of a document | n/a | n/a |
| Revert | Replaces a document with the previously saved version of the same document. | n/a | n/a |
| Import | Displays the Import dialog box before importing a file for insertion into any open document. | Ctrl+R | Command+R |
| Export | Displays the Export Preview dialog before exporting a document. | Ctrl+Shift+R | Command+Shift+R |
| Export Special ⇨ Export as Files | Displays the Export Special – Files dialog box before exporting a document's layers, frames, or slices as files. | n/a | n/a |

| Command | Description | Windows | Macintosh |
|---|---|---|---|
| Export Special ⇨ Export as CSS Layers | Displays the Export Special – Files dialog box before exporting a document's layers, frames, or slices as files with HTML containing CSS layers. | n/a | n/a |
| Export Special ⇨ Export as Image Well | Displays the Export Special – Files dialog box before exporting a document's layers, frames, or slices as a Lotus Domino Designer Image Well. | n/a | n/a |
| Export Again | Exports a document using its previous Export settings. | Ctrl+Shift+X | Command+ Shift+X |
| Export Wizard | Displays the Export Wizard dialog boxes before exporting a document. | n/a | n/a |
| Batch Process | Displays the Batch Process dialog box before processing multiple documents. | n/a | n/a |
| Run Script | Displays the Open dialog box before running a batch processing script. | n/a | n/a |
| Preview in Browser ⇨ Preview in Primary | Previews a document in your primary browser. | F12 | F12 |
| Preview in Browser ⇨ Preview in Secondary | Previews a document in your secondary browser. | Shift+F12 | Shift+F12 |
| Preview in Browser ⇨ Set Primary (F12) Browser | Displays the Locate Browser dialog box before selecting a browser as your primary browser. | n/a | n/a |
| Preview in Browser ⇨ Set Secondary (Shift+F12) Browser | Displays the Locate Browser dialog box before selecting a browser as your secondary browser. | n/a | n/a |
| Print | Displays the Print dialog box before printing a document. | Ctrl+P | Command+P |
| Page Setup | Displays the Page Setup dialog box. | n/a | n/a |
| Document Properties | Displays the Document Properties dialog box. | n/a | n/a |
| Preferences | Displays the Preferences dialog box. | n/a | n/a |
| Recent Files | Displays the last four opened files; select any filename to reopen the file. | n/a | n/a |
| Exit | Closes Fireworks. | Alt+F4 | Option+F4 |

# The Edit Menu

The Edit menu enables you to move, copy, or duplicate objects. The Cut, Copy, and Paste commands are standard on all programs; others, such as Paste Attributes, are unique to Fireworks. Table A-2 details the commands and their keyboard shortcuts.

**Table A-2**
**Edit Menu**

| Command | Description | Windows | Macintosh |
|---|---|---|---|
| Undo | Reverses the last action; the number of Undo steps is set in Preferences. | Ctrl+Z | Command+Z |
| Redo | Reverses the last Undo. | Ctrl+Shift+Z | Command+Shift+Z |
| Cut | Places a copy of the current selection on the Clipboard and removes the selection from the document. | Ctrl+X | Command+X |
| Copy | Places a copy of the current selection on the Clipboard and leaves the selection in the document. | Ctrl+C | Command+C |
| Paste | Copies the contents of the Clipboard to the current cursor position. | Ctrl+V | Command+V |
| Clear | Removes the current selection from the document. | Delete | Delete |
| Paste Inside | Copies the contents of the Clipboard into a selected, closed path. | Ctrl+Shift+V | Command+Shift+V |
| Paste Attributes | Copies the attributes of the Clipboard to a selected object. | Ctrl+Alt+Shift+V | Command+Shift+Option+V |
| Select All | Selects all objects in a document, or all pixels in an image in Image Edit mode. | Ctrl+A | Command+A |
| Deselect | Deselects all objects or pixels. | Ctrl+D | Command+D |
| Superselect | Selects the entire group to which the current selection belongs. | Ctrl+Up arrow | Command+up arrow |
| Subselect | Selects all objects within the current selection. | Ctrl+down arrow | Command+down arrow |
| Select Inverse | Selects all deselected pixels, and vice versa, in Image Edit mode. | Ctrl+Shift+I | Command+Shift+I |

| Command | Description | Windows | Macintosh |
|---------|-------------|---------|-----------|
| Feather | Displays the Feather Selection dialog box before feathering the edges of a pixel selection in Image Edit mode. | n/a | n/a |
| Select Similar | Selects pixels that are similarly colored to the selection while in Image Edit mode. | n/a | n/a |
| Duplicate | Creates a copy of the selected object, offset slightly from the original. | Ctrl+Alt+D | Command+ Option+D |
| Clone | Creates a copy of the selected object, directly on top of the original. | Ctrl+Shift+C | Command+ Shift+C |
| Find & Replace | Displays the Find & Replace dialog box. | n/a | n/a |
| Crop Selected Image | Changes the size of a selected image object. | Ctrl+Alt+C | Command+ Option+C |

# The View Menu

With the commands on the View menu, you can zoom in or out on your work or view a grid or guides to assist with layout. Table A-3 details each command and its keyboard shortcut.

| Table A-3 View Menu | | | |
|---------------------|---|---|---|
| Command | Description | Windows | Macintosh |
| Zoom In | Increases the magnification level of a document by one setting. | Ctrl+Plus | Command+ Plus |
| Zoom Out | Decreases the magnification level of a document by one setting. | Ctrl+Minus | Command+ Minus |
| Magnification ⇨ 6% | Sets the magnification level of a document to 6 percent. | n/a | n/a |
| Magnification ⇨ 12% | Sets the magnification level of a document to 12 percent. | n/a | n/a |
| Magnification ⇨ 25% | Sets the magnification level of a document to 25 percent. | n/a | n/a |

*Continued*

## Table A-3 *(continued)*

| Command | Description | Windows | Macintosh |
|---|---|---|---|
| Magnification ⇨ 50% | Sets the magnification level of a document to 50 percent. | Ctrl+5 | Command+5 |
| Magnification ⇨ 100% | Sets the magnification level of a document to 100 percent. | Ctrl+1 | Command+1 |
| Magnification ⇨ 200% | Sets the magnification level of a document to 200 percent. | Ctrl+2 | Command+2 |
| Magnification ⇨ 400% | Sets the magnification level of a document to 400 percent. | Ctrl+4 | Command+4 |
| Magnification ⇨ 800% | Sets the magnification level of a document to 800 percent. | Ctrl+8 | Command+8 |
| Magnification ⇨ 1600% | Sets the magnification level of a document to 1,600 percent. | n/a | n/a |
| Magnification ⇨ 3200% | Sets the magnification level of a document to 3,200 percent. | Ctrl+3 | Command+3 |
| Magnification ⇨ 6400% | Sets the magnification level of a document to 6,400 percent. | Ctrl+6 | Command+6 |
| Fit Selection | Sets the magnification level of a document so that all selected objects are visible. | Ctrl+0 | Command+0 |
| Fit All | Sets the magnification level of a document so that all objects are visible. | Ctrl+Alt+0 | Command+ Option+0 |
| Full Display | Toggles Full Display. | Ctrl+K | Command+K |
| Hide Selection | Hides selected objects. | Ctrl+M | Command+M |
| Show All | Shows all hidden objects. | Ctrl+Shift +M | Command+ Shift+M |
| Hide Edges | Toggles display of marquee selection lines. | Ctrl+H | Command+H |
| Hide Panels | Toggles display of all open panels. | Ctrl+Shift+H | Command+ Shift+H |
| Rulers | Toggles display of rulers. | Ctrl+Alt+R | Command+ Option+R |
| Grid | Toggles display of the grid. | Ctrl+' | Command+' |
| Grid Options ⇨ Snap To Grid | Toggles whether or not objects snap to the Grid. | Ctrl+Shift+' | Command+ Shift+' |
| Grid Options ⇨ Edit Grid | Displays the Edit Grid dialog box. | Ctrl+Alt+G | Command+ Option+G |

| Command | Description | Windows | Macintosh |
|---|---|---|---|
| Guides | Toggles display of Guides. | Ctrl+; | Command+; |
| Slice Guides | Toggles display of Slice Guides. | Ctrl+Alt+ Shift+; | Command+ Option+ Shift+; |
| Guide Options ⇨ Lock Guides | Toggles whether or not Guides can be edited and moved. | Ctrl+Alt+; | Command+ Option+; |
| Guide Options ⇨ Snap to Guides | Toggles whether or not objects snap to Guides. | Ctrl+Shift+; | Command+ Shift+; |
| Guide Options ⇨ Edit Guides | Displays the Edit Guides dialog box. | Ctrl+Alt+ Shift+G | Command+ Option+ Shift+G |
| Status Bar | Toggles display of the status bar. | n/a | n/a |

# The Insert Menu

The Insert menu contains objects that you can insert into your documents. Table A-4 details the items available on the Insert menu and their keyboard shortcuts.

| Table A-4 | | | |
|---|---|---|---|
| **Insert Menu** | | | |
| Command | Description | Windows | Macintosh |
| Hotspot | Inserts a hotspot object. | Ctrl+Shift+U | Command+Shift+U |
| Slice | Inserts a slice object. | n/a | n/a |
| Behaviors | Displays the Behaviors inspec-. tor, focused on the currently selected slice or hotspot | n/a | n/a |
| Image | Displays the Import dialog box before importing an image into the document. | Ctrl+R | Command+R |
| Empty Image | Inserts an empty image object. | Ctrl+Alt+Y | Command+Option+Y |
| Symbol | Converts the selected object into a Symbol. | Ctrl+Alt+ Shift+M | Command+Option+ Shift+M |

*Continued*

## Table A-4 *(continued)*

| Command | Description | Windows | Macintosh |
|---|---|---|---|
| Tween Instances | Displays the Tween Instances dialog box before creating intermediate steps between two selected Symbol Instances. | Ctrl+Alt+ Shift+T | Command+Option+ Shift+T |
| Symbol Options ⇨ Break Link | Breaks the link between the selected Symbol and its Instances. | n/a | n/a |
| Symbol Options ⇨ Add to Symbol | Adds the selected object to the selected Symbol. | n/a | n/a |
| Symbol Options ⇨ Find Symbol | Finds the Symbol for the selected Instance. | n/a | n/a |
| Symbol Options ⇨ Delete Instances | Deletes all Instances of the selected Symbol (but not the Symbol itself). | n/a | n/a |
| Layer | Creates a new layer. | n/a | n/a |
| Frame | Creates a new frame. | n/a | n/a |

# The Modify Menu

The Modify menu lists all the commands for altering existing selections. Table A-5 details all the Modify options and their keyboard shortcuts.

## Table A-5
## Modify Menu

| Command | Description | Windows | Macintosh |
|---|---|---|---|
| Stroke | Displays the Stroke panel, focused on the currently selected object. | Ctrl+Alt+B | Command+ Option+B |
| Fill | Displays the Fill panel, focused on the currently selected object. | Ctrl+Alt+F | Command+ Option+F |
| Effect | Displays the Effect panel, focused on the currently selected object. | Ctrl+Alt+E | Command+ Option+E |
| Image Object | Switches to Image Edit mode. | Ctrl+E | Command+E |

| Command | Description | Windows | Macintosh |
|---|---|---|---|
| Exit Image Edit | Exits Image Edit mode. | Ctrl+Shift+D | Command+ Shift+D |
| Document ⇨ Image Size | Displays the Image Size dialog box. | n/a | n/a |
| Document ⇨ Canvas Size | Displays the Change Canvas Size dialog box. | n/a | n/a |
| Document ⇨ Canvas Color | Displays the Canvas Color dialog box. | n/a | n/a |
| Document ⇨ Trim Canvas | Removes empty rows or columns of pixels from the edges of a document. | n/a | n/a |
| Edge ⇨ Hard Edge | Removes antialiasing or feathering from the edges of a document. | n/a | n/a |
| Edge ⇨ Anti-Alias | Antialiases the edges of a document. | n/a | n/a |
| Edge ⇨ Feather | Feathers the edges of a document. | n/a | n/a |
| Free Transform | Toggles the display of an object's transformation handles | Ctrl+T | Command+T |
| Transform ⇨ Scale | Sets transformation handles to resize and rotate objects. | n/a | n/a |
| Transform ⇨ Skew | Sets transformation handles to slant and rotate objects, and change perspective. | n/a | n/a |
| Transform ⇨ Distort | Sets transformation handles to distort and rotate objects. | n/a | n/a |
| Transform ⇨ Numeric Transform | Displays the Numeric Transform dialog box. | Ctrl+Shift+T | Command+ Shift+T |
| Transform ⇨ Rotate 180° | Rotates an object 180 degrees. | n/a | n/a |
| Transform ⇨ Rotate 90° CW | Rotates an object 90 degrees clockwise. | Ctrl+9 | Command+9 |
| Transform ⇨ Rotate 90° CCW | Rotates an object 90 degrees counter-clockwise. | Ctrl+7 | Command+7 |
| Transform ⇨ Flip Horizontal | Flips an object horizontally. | n/a | n/a |
| Transform ⇨ Flip Vertical | Flips an object vertically. | n/a | n/a |

*Continued*

## Table A-5 (continued)

| Command | Description | Windows | Macintosh |
|---|---|---|---|
| Transform ➪ Remove Transformations | Removes all transformations from an object. | n/a | n/a |
| Arrange ➪ Bring to Front | Moves an object to the front of a layer. | Ctrl+F | Command+F |
| Arrange ➪ Bring Forward | Moves an object in front of the object just in front of it. | Ctrl+Shift+F | Command+Shift+F |
| Arrange ➪ Send Backward | Moves an object in back of the object just behind it. | Ctrl+Shift+B | Command+Shift+B |
| Arrange ➪ Send to Back | Moves an object to the back of a layer. | Ctrl+B | Ctrl+B |
| Align ➪ Left | Aligns selected objects to the left edge of the selection. | Ctrl+Alt+1 | Command+Option+1 |
| Align ➪ Center Vertical | Aligns selected objects to the vertical center of the selection. | Ctrl+Alt+2 | Command+Option+2 |
| Align ➪ Right | Aligns selected objects to the right edge of the selection. | Ctrl+Alt+3 | Command+Option+3 |
| Align ➪ Top | Aligns selected objects to the top edge of the selection. | Ctrl+Alt+4 | Command+Option+4 |
| Align ➪ Center Horizontal | Aligns selected objects to the horizontal center of the selection. | Ctrl+Alt+5 | Command+Option+5 |
| Align ➪ Bottom | Aligns selected objects to the bottom of the selection. | Ctrl+Alt+6 | Command+Option+6 |
| Align ➪ Distribute Widths | Distributes selected objects horizontally throughout the selection. | Ctrl+Alt+7 | Command+Option+7 |
| Align ➪ Distribute Heights | Distributes selected objects vertically throughout the selection. | Ctrl+Alt+9 | Command+Option+9 |
| Join | Joins two or more selected paths or endpoints. | Ctrl+J | Command+J |
| Split | Splits an object into component paths. | Ctrl+Shift+J | Command+Shift+J |
| Combine ➪ Union | Combines two or more selected closed paths into a single object. | n/a | n/a |
| Combine ➪ Intersect | Combines overlapping parts of two or more selected closed paths. | n/a | n/a |

| Command | Description | Windows | Macintosh |
|---|---|---|---|
| Combine ➪ Punch | Combines two or more selected closed paths by punching holes in the back object with the front object(s). | n/a | n/a |
| Combine ➪ Crop | Crops the back object of a selection with the front object of a selection of two or more closed paths. | n/a | n/a |
| Alter Path ➪ Simplify | Displays the Simplify dialog box before removing points from a path while keeping its overall shape. | n/a | n/a |
| Alter Path ➪ Expand Stroke | Displays the Expand dialog box. | n/a | n/a |
| Alter Path ➪ Inset Path | Displays the Inset dialog box before expanding or contracting one or more closed paths. | n/a | n/a |
| Merge Images | Merges one or more selected image objects into a single image object. | Ctrl+Shift+Alt+Z | Command+Shift+Option+Z |
| Merge Layers | Flattens visible layers, discarding hidden layers. | n/a | n/a |
| Group Command+G | Groups one or more selected objects. | Ctrl+G | |
| Mask Group | Groups one or more selected objects; the top object's grayscale values mask the underlying object(s). | Ctrl+Shift+G | Command+Shift+G |
| Ungroup | Ungroups a Group or Mask Group. | Ctrl+U | Command+U |

# The Text Menu

The Text menu enables you to change the formatting options for text objects, or convert them to paths. Table A-6 details the commands and their keyboard shortcuts.

## Table A-6
## Text Menu

| Command | Description | Windows | Macintosh |
|---|---|---|---|
| Font ⇨ Your Font List | Changes the selected text object's typeface, or the default typeface if no text object is selected. | n/a | n/a |
| Size ⇨ 8 to 120 | Changes the selected text object's type size, or the default type size if no text object is selected. | n/a | n/a |
| Style ⇨ Plain | Removes bold, italic, and underline formatting from the selected text. | Ctrl+Alt+Shift+P | Command+Option+Shift+P |
| Style ⇨ Bold | Makes the selected text bold. | Ctrl+Alt+Shift+B | Command+Option+Shift+B |
| Style ⇨ Italic | Makes the selected text italicized. | Ctrl+Alt+I | Command+Option+Shift+I |
| Style ⇨ Underline | Makes the selected text underlined. | Ctrl+Alt+Shift+U | Command+Option+Shift+U |
| Align ⇨ Left | Left-aligns the selected text. | Ctrl+Alt+Shift+L | Command+Option+Shift+L |
| Align ⇨ Center | Centers the selected text. | Ctrl+Alt+Shift+C | Command+Option+Shift+C |
| Align ⇨ Right | Right-aligns the selected text. | Ctrl+Alt+Shift+R | Command+Option+Shift+R |
| Align ⇨ Justified | Justifies the selected text. | Ctrl+Alt+Shift+J | Command+Option+Shift+J |
| Align ⇨ Stretched | Force-justifies the selected text. | Ctrl+Alt+Shift+S | Command+Option+Shift+S |
| Align ⇨ Top | Aligns vertically flowing text to the top of the text block. | n/a | n/a |

| Command | Description | Windows | Macintosh |
|---|---|---|---|
| Align ⇨ Center | Aligns vertically flowing text to the vertical center of the text block. | n/a | n/a |
| Align ⇨ Bottom | Aligns vertically flowing text to the bottom of the text block. | n/a | n/a |
| Align ⇨ Justified | Justifies vertically flowing text to the top and bottom of the text block. | n/a | n/a |
| Align ⇨ Stretched | Force-justifies vertically flowing text to the top and bottom of the text block. | n/a | n/a |
| Editor | Displays the Text Editor dialog box. | Ctrl+Shift+E | Command+Shift+E |
| Attach to Path | Attaches the selected text block to a selected path. | Ctrl+Shift+Y | Command+Shift+Y |
| Detach from Path | Detaches the selected text block from a path, if it's attached to one. | n/a | n/a |
| Orientation ⇨ Rotate Around Path | Orients attached text so that the bottom of each letter is closest to the path. | n/a | n/a |
| Orientation ⇨ Vertical | Orients attached text so that the side of each letter is closest to the path. | n/a | n/a |
| Orientation ⇨ Skew Vertical | Skews attached text vertically. | n/a | n/a |
| Orientation ⇨ Skew Horizontal | Skews attached text horizontally. | n/a | n/a |
| Reverse Direction | Reverses the direction of text attached to a path. | n/a | n/a |
| Convert to Paths | Converts text objects into vector objects. | Ctrl+Shift+P | Command+Shift+P |

# The Xtras Menu

Xtras are add-on features, such as Photoshop-compatible plug-ins, that expand the capabilities of Fireworks 2. Table A-7 details the standard Xtras that are included with Fireworks. Your Xtras menu may have additional options if you have installed third-party Xtras.

**Table A-7**
**Xtras Menu**

| Command | Description | Windows | Macintosh |
| --- | --- | --- | --- |
| Repeat Xtra | Repeats the most recently used Xtra. | Ctrl+Alt+Shift+X | Command+Option+Shift+X |
| Blur ⇨ Blur | Blurs the selected image object(s). | n/a | n/a |
| Blur ⇨ Blur More | Blurs the selected image object(s) across a larger radius than Blur. | n/a | n/a |
| Blur ⇨ Gaussian Blur | Displays the Gaussian Blur dialog box before blurring the selected image object(s). | n/a | n/a |
| Invert ⇨ Invert | Changes each color in the selected image object(s) to its mathematical inverse. | n/a | n/a |
| Other ⇨ Convert to Alpha | Converts the selected image object into an alpha mask. | n/a | n/a |
| Other ⇨ Find Edges | Identifies edges in the selected image object(s). | n/a | n/a |
| Sharpen ⇨ Sharpen | Sharpens the selected image object(s). | n/a | n/a |
| Sharpen ⇨ Sharpen More | Sharpens the selected image object(s) more than Sharpen. | n/a | n/a |
| Sharpen ⇨ Unsharp Mask | Displays the Unsharp Mask dialog box before sharpening the selected image object(s). | n/a | n/a |
| PhotoOptics ⇨ CSI GradTone | Displays the CSI GradTone dialog box before color-correcting an image object. | n/a | n/a |
| PhotoOptics ⇨ CSI HueSlider | Displays the CSI HueSlider dialog box before color-correcting an image object. | n/a | n/a |
| PhotoOptics ⇨ CSI Levels | Displays the CSI Levels dialog box before color-correcting an image object. | n/a | n/a |
| PhotoOptics ⇨ CSI MonoChrome | Displays the CSI MonoChrome dialog box before color-correcting an image object. | n/a | n/a |

| Command | Description | Windows | Macintosh |
|---|---|---|---|
| PhotoOptics ⇨ CSI Negative | Displays the CSI Negative dialog box before color-correcting an image object. | n/a | n/a |
| PhotoOptics ⇨ CSI Noise | Displays the CSI Noise dialog box before color-correcting an image object. | n/a | n/a |
| PhotoOptics ⇨ CSI PhotoFilter | Displays the CSI PhotoFilter dialog box before color-correcting an image object. | n/a | n/a |
| PhotoOptics ⇨ CSI PseudoColor | Displays the CSI PseudoColor dialog box before color-correcting an image object. | n/a | n/a |

# The Window Menu

The Window menu manages document windows as well as Fireworks panels and inspectors. Through this menu, detailed in Table A-8, you can open, close, arrange, bring to the front, or hide all of the additional Fireworks windows.

**Tip**  All the commands for the various panels and inspectors are toggles. Select them once to view the window; select again to close it.

| Table A-8 Window Menu | | | |
|---|---|---|---|
| Command | Description | Windows | Macintosh |
| New Window | Creates a duplicate of the current document window. | Ctrl+Alt+N | Command+Option+N |
| Toolbars ⇨ Main | Toggles display of the Main toolbar (Windows only). | n/a | n/a |
| Toolbars ⇨ Modify | Toggles display of the Modify toolbar (Windows only). | n/a | n/a |
| Toolbars ⇨ View Controls | Toggles display of the View Controls toolbar (Windows only). | n/a | n/a |

*Continued*

| Table A-8 *(continued)* | | | |
|---|---|---|---|
| *Command* | *Description* | *Windows* | *Macintosh* |
| Toolbox | Toggles display of the Toolbox. | Ctrl+Alt+T | Command+ Option+T |
| Object | Toggles display of the Object inspector. | Ctrl+I | Command+I |
| Stroke | Toggles display of the Stroke panel. | Ctrl+Alt+B | Command+ Option+B |
| Fill | Toggles display of the Fill panel. | Ctrl+Alt+F | Command+ Option+F |
| Effect | Toggles display of the Effect panel. | Ctrl+Alt+E | Command+ Option+E |
| Info | Toggles display of the Info panel. | Ctrl+Alt+I | Command+ Option+I |
| Tool Options | Toggles display of the Tool Options panel. | Ctrl+Alt+O | Command+ Option+O |
| Styles | Toggles display of the Styles panel. | Ctrl+Alt+J | Command+ Option+J |
| Color Mixer | Toggles display of the Color Mixer. | Ctrl+Alt+M | Command+ Option+M |
| Swatches | Toggles display of the Swatches panel. | Ctrl+Alt+S | Command+ Option+S |
| Layers | Toggles display of the Layers panel. | Ctrl+Alt+L | Command+ Option+L |
| Frames | Toggles display of the Frames panel. | Ctrl+Alt+K | Command+ Option+K |
| Behaviors | Toggles display of the Behaviors inspector. | Ctrl+Alt+H | Command+ Option+H |
| URL Manager | Toggles display of the URLs Manager. | Ctrl+Alt+U | Command+ Option+U |
| Find & Replace | Toggles display of the Find & Replace panel. | n/a | n/a |
| Project Log | Toggles display of the Project Log panel. | n/a | n/a |
| Cascade | Cascades the document windows (Windows only). | n/a | n/a |
| Tile Horizontal | Tiles the document windows horizontally (Windows only). | n/a | n/a |

| Command | Description | Windows | Macintosh |
|---|---|---|---|
| Tile Vertical | Tiles the document windows vertically (Windows only). | n/a | n/a |
| Your Open Documents | Displays a list of the currently open documents windows (Windows only). | n/a | n/a |

# The Help Menu

The final menu, Help, offers access to Fireworks HTML Help, comprehensive tutorials, and even the Fireworks Web site. Table A-9 explains each of the options.

| Table A-9 Help Menu | | | |
|---|---|---|---|
| Command | Description | Windows | Macintosh |
| Fireworks Help | Opens the Fireworks Help system in your primary browser. | F1 | n/a |
| Help Index | Opens the Fireworks Help system in your primary browser with the index visible. | n/a | n/a |
| Contacting Macromedia | Opens the Fireworks Help system in your primary browser with Macromedia contact information visible. | n/a | n/a |
| Using Hotspots and Slices | Displays the Web Objects Help dialog box. | n/a | n/a |
| Register Fireworks | Goes online to register your copy of Fireworks with Macromedia. | n/a | n/a |
| Fireworks Web Site | Goes online to view the Fireworks Web site. | n/a | n/a |
| About Fireworks | Displays the About Fireworks dialog box. | n/a | n/a |
| Tutorials | Opens a selection of tutorials in your primary browser, and sample documents in Fireworks. | n/a | n/a |

# The Toolbox

As well as providing key shortcuts for menu commands, Fireworks also enables you to use the keyboard to select and use the tools in the Toolbox quickly and easily. Table A-10 explains what each tool does and its keyboard shortcut.

| Table A-10 Toolbox | | | |
|---|---|---|---|
| *Tool* | *Description* | *Windows* | *Macintosh* |
| Pointer | Selects and drags objects. | V or 0 | V or 0 |
| Select Behind | Selects objects that are behind other objects. | V or 0 | V or 0 |
| Crop | Changes the size of the canvas. | C | C |
| Export Area | Exports a portion of a document. | J | J |
| Subselect | Selects an object within a group or points on a path. | A or 1 | A or 1 |
| Marquee | Selects a rectangular pixel area in Image Edit mode. | M | M |
| Ellipse Marquee | Selects an elliptical pixel area in Image Edit mode. | M | M |
| Lasso | Selects a freeform pixel area in Image Edit mode. | L | L |
| Polygon Lasso | Selects a polygonal pixel area in Image Edit mode. | L | L |
| Magic Wand | Selects pixel areas of similar color in Image Edit mode. | W | W |
| Hand | Pans the view of a document. | H or spacebar | H or spacebar |
| Magnify | Increases or decreases the magnification level of a document by one setting. | Z | Z |
| Line | Draws straight lines. | N | N |
| Pen | Draws paths by anchoring points. | P | P |
| Rectangle | Draws rectangles, rounded rectangles, and squares. | R | R |
| Ellipse | Draws ellipses and circles. | R | R |

| *Tool* | *Description* | *Windows* | *Macintosh* |
|---|---|---|---|
| Polygon | Draws polygons and stars. | G | G |
| Text | Creates text blocks. | T | T |
| Pencil | Draws 1-pixel pencil strokes. | Y | Y |
| Brush | Draws brush strokes using Stroke panel settings. | B | B |
| Redraw Path | Redraws portions of a selected path. | B | B |
| Scale | Resizes and rotates objects. | Q | Q |
| Skew | Slants and rotates objects, and changes perspective. | Q | Q |
| Distort | Distorts and rotates objects. | Q | Q |
| Freeform | Pulls or pushes a path segment using a resizable cursor. | F | F |
| Reshape Area | Reshapes a selected path within the area of the resizable cursor. | F | F |
| Path Scrubber (+) | Increases stroke characteristics controlled by pressure or speed. | U | U |
| Path Scrubber (−) | Decreases stroke characteristics controlled by pressure or speed. | U | U |
| Eyedropper | Samples a color and applies it to the active color well. | I | I |
| Paint Bucket | Fills objects with colors, gradients, or patterns and adjust fills with Paint Bucket handles. | K | K |
| Eraser | Removes or replaces portions of image objects and cut paths. | E | E |
| Rubber Stamp | Clones portions of an image object. | S | S |
| Rectangle Hotspot | Draws URL hotspots in the shape of rectangles or squares. | n/a | n/a |
| Circle Hotspot | Draws URL hotspots in the shape of circles. | n/a | n/a |
| Polygon Hotspot | Draws URL hotspots in the shape of irregular polygons. | n/a | n/a |
| Slice | Creates rectangular slice objects. | n/a | n/a |

✦     ✦     ✦

# What's on the CD-ROM

The CD-ROM that accompanies the *Fireworks 2 Bible* contains the following:

✦ Fully functioning trial versions of Fireworks 2, Dreamweaver 2, and Flash 4

✦ Fireworks-compatible filters from leading manufacturers, such as Alien Skin and MetaCreations

✦ A time-limited demo of Pantone's ColorWeb Pro

Also included is a wide range of strokes, gradients, textures, and custom HTML templates designed to make your work more productive. Finally, you'll also find several sample graphics from the book, for you to inspect, modify, and experiment with at your leisure.

## Using the CD-ROM

The CD-ROM is a "hybrid" CD-ROM, which means that it contains files that run on more than one computer platform — in this case, both Windows and Macintosh computers.

Several files, primarily the Macromedia trial programs and the additional commercial programs, are compressed. Double-click these files to begin the installation procedure. Most other files on the CD-ROM are not compressed and simply can be copied from the CD-ROM to your system by using your file manager. A few of the Fireworks extensions that include files that must be placed in different folders are also compressed.

Where possible, the file structure of the CD-ROM replicates the structure that Fireworks sets up when it is installed. For example, textures found in the Fireworks\Settings\Textures folder are located on both the CD-ROM and the installed program.

# Files and Programs on the CD-ROM

The *Fireworks 2 Bible* companion CD-ROM contains a host of programs and auxiliary files to assist your exploration of Fireworks, as well as your Web page design work in general. A description of the files and programs on the CD-ROM follows.

## Fireworks 2, Dreamweaver 2, and Flash 4 demos

If you haven't had a chance to work with Fireworks (or Dreamweaver or Flash), the CD-ROM offers fully functioning trial versions of three key Macromedia programs for both Macintosh and Windows systems. The demo can be used for 30 days; it cannot be reinstalled for additional use time.

To install the demo, simply double-click the program icon in the main folder of the CD-ROM and follow the installation instructions on your screen.

**Note** The trial versions of the Macromedia programs are very sensitive to system date changes. If you alter your computer's date, the programs will "time out" and no longer be functional.

The full Fireworks version comes with a wonderful assortment of clip art. To sample this work, visit the Fireworks Web site at `http://www.macromedia.com/products/fireworks`.

## Additional programs

Fireworks 2 is definitely one program that "plays well with others." Virtually any Photoshop-compatible plug-in can be used as a Fireworks Xtra—good news, unless you're not a Photoshop user. However, you don't need Photoshop to use the filters in Fireworks, and several of the leading filter developers have kindly loaned their programs for inclusion on this CD-ROM. In addition to the filters described in this section, the world-renown color specialist, Pantone, has contributed a program, ColorWeb Pro, to help ease the transition for designers from the world of print to the Web.

### Kai's Power Tools 5 from MetaCreations

Kai's Power Tools 5 includes 10 exciting, new plug-in tools, in addition to the original 18 KPT 3 filters. KPT 5's real-time 3D tools, particle growth effects, and professional blur suite will take your work to a new creative level, while enhancing productivity as you efficiently explore stunning creative options.

### Xenophone and Eye Candy 3 from Alien Skin

Alien Skin Software has contributed trials of two filter collections: Eye Candy 3 and Xenofex. Eye Candy 3 is a collection of 21 time-saving filters for use with Photoshop and other graphics programs. The set includes spectacular effects, such as Fire, Smoke, and Perspective Shadow, as well as frequently used production effects, such as Cutout, Carve, Drop Shadow, Inner Bevel, and Motion Trail.

Xenofex 1 is a collection of 16 inspirational special effects that will energize any graphics project. Realistic natural phenomena and sophisticated distortions have never been easier to create.

### Xaos Tools's Total Xaos Filters

Total Xaos is a bundle of three Fireworks-compatible plug-ins: Paint Alchemy, Terrazo, and TypeCaster. Paint Alchemy is great for painterly special effects, Terrazo makes superb seamless tiles, and TypeCaster turns any text into a 3D wonder — without any 3D experience required.

### ColorWeb Pro from Pantone

Many new Web designers are not new to design at all and bring a rich history — as well as a client list — from their print backgrounds. One constant in print color reproduction is the Pantone Color System. Many clients require that all of their graphics, whether intended for print or for the Internet, conform to a specific selection of Pantone colors. The ColorWeb Pro application translates Pantone colors into their RGB equivalents.

 You'll find a special technique for using ColorWeb Pro with Fireworks in Chapter 7.

## HTML templates and textures

Part of the power of Fireworks is the ability to extend both its image-creating capabilities and its HTML output. Making a set of textures available is as simple as copying a folder from one location to another. For the textures included with this CD-ROM, supplied by Massimo Foti and the Fantastic Corporation, you simply need to copy the images in the CD-ROM's Settings\Textures folder to the equivalent Fireworks folder and then relaunch Fireworks. The CD-ROM includes over 50 new textures.

Adding HTML templates is even easier. Just copy the entire template folder and all of its contents from the CD-ROM's Settings\HTML Settings folder to the similarly named Fireworks folder — you don't even have to relaunch Fireworks to use them. You'll find a full range of templates, including new ones from Macromedia, as well as one from myself and several from the prolific Massimo Foti.

## Gradients, strokes, and image libraries

Fireworks also gives you the ability to add many other components of an image, such as the stroke or gradient fill. For your graphic-creation pleasure, the CD-ROM includes a small, but useful compendium of various gradient fills, strokes, and image libraries, each in their own self-named folder. Although these are fairly simple to create in Fireworks, why reinvent the wheel when you have so much other work to do? Included in this collection is a wide variety of dotted and dashed strokes as well as an arrowhead library.

## *Fireworks 2 Bible* examples

Example images used in the *Fireworks 2 Bible* can be found in the Examples folder of the CD-ROM, organized by the chapter in which they appear in the book. You'll find examples of everything from PNG's Alpha Transparency mode to a pseudo banner ad, which conforms to industry-wide specifications.

## Web resource directory

The Web is a vital resource for any Web designer, whether you're a seasoned professional or a beginner. The CD-ROM contains an HTML page with a series of links to resources on the Web; the series contains general as well as Fireworks-specific references.

✦　　✦　　✦

# Index

*continued*

*continued*

# IDG BOOKS WORLDWIDE, INC.
# END-USER LICENSE AGREEMENT

<u>**READ THIS.**</u> You should carefully read these terms and conditions before opening the software packet(s) included with this book ("Book"). This is a license agreement ("Agreement") between you and IDG Books Worldwide, Inc. ("IDGB"). By opening the accompanying software packet(s), you acknowledge that you have read and accept the following terms and conditions. If you do not agree and do not want to be bound by such terms and conditions, promptly return the Book and the unopened software packet(s) to the place you obtained them for a full refund.

1. <u>**License Grant.**</u> IDGB grants to you (either an individual or entity) a nonexclusive license to use one copy of the enclosed software program(s) (collectively, the "Software") solely for your own personal or business purposes on a single computer (whether a standard computer or a workstation component of a multiuser network). The Software is in use on a computer when it is loaded into temporary memory (RAM) or installed into permanent memory (hard disk, CD-ROM, or other storage device). IDGB reserves all rights not expressly granted herein.

2. <u>**Ownership.**</u> IDGB is the owner of all right, title, and interest, including copyright, in and to the compilation of the Software recorded on the disk(s) or CD-ROM ("Software Media"). Copyright to the individual programs recorded on the Software Media is owned by the author or other authorized copyright owner of each program. Ownership of the Software and all proprietary rights relating thereto remain with IDGB and its licensers.

3. <u>**Restrictions On Use and Transfer.**</u>

    (a) You may only (i) make one copy of the Software for backup or archival purposes, or (ii) transfer the Software to a single hard disk, provided that you keep the original for backup or archival purposes. You may not (i) rent or lease the Software, (ii) copy or reproduce the Software through a LAN or other network system or through any computer subscriber system or bulletin-board system, or (iii) modify, adapt, or create derivative works based on the Software.

    (b) You may not reverse engineer, decompile, or disassemble the Software. You may transfer the Software and user documentation on a permanent basis, provided that the transferee agrees to accept the terms and conditions of this Agreement and you retain no copies. If the Software is an update or has been updated, any transfer must include the most recent update and all prior versions.

4. <u>**Restrictions On Use of Individual Programs.**</u> You must follow the individual requirements and restrictions detailed for each individual program in the "What's on the CD-ROM" appendix of this Book. These limitations are also

contained in the individual license agreements recorded on the Software Media. These limitations may include a requirement that after using the program for a specified period of time, the user must pay a registration fee or discontinue use. By opening the Software packet(s), you will be agreeing to abide by the licenses and restrictions for these individual programs that are detailed in the "What's on the CD-ROM" appendix and on the Software Media. None of the material on this Software Media or listed in this Book may ever be redistributed, in original or modified form, for commercial purposes.

5. **Limited Warranty**.

    **(a)** IDGB warrants that the Software and Software Media are free from defects in materials and workmanship under normal use for a period of sixty (60) days from the date of purchase of this Book. If IDGB receives notification within the warranty period of defects in materials or workmanship, IDGB will replace the defective Software Media.

    **(b)** **IDGB AND THE AUTHORS OF THE BOOK DISCLAIM ALL OTHER WARRANTIES, EXPRESS OR IMPLIED, INCLUDING WITHOUT LIMITATION IMPLIED WARRANTIES OF MERCHANTABILITY AND FITNESS FOR A PARTICULAR PURPOSE, WITH RESPECT TO THE SOFTWARE, THE PROGRAMS, THE SOURCE CODE CONTAINED THEREIN, AND/OR THE TECHNIQUES DESCRIBED IN THIS BOOK. IDGB DOES NOT WARRANT THAT THE FUNCTIONS CONTAINED IN THE SOFTWARE WILL MEET YOUR REQUIREMENTS OR THAT THE OPERATION OF THE SOFTWARE WILL BE ERROR FREE.**

    **(c)** This limited warranty gives you specific legal rights, and you may have other rights that vary from jurisdiction to jurisdiction.

6. **Remedies**.

    **(a)** IDGB's entire liability and your exclusive remedy for defects in materials and workmanship shall be limited to replacement of the Software Media, which may be returned to IDGB with a copy of your receipt at the following address: Software Media Fulfillment Department, Attn.: *Fireworks 2 Bible*, IDG Books Worldwide, Inc., 7260 Shadeland Station, Ste. 100, Indianapolis, IN 46256, or call 1-800-762-2974. Please allow three to four weeks for delivery. This Limited Warranty is void if failure of the Software Media has resulted from accident, abuse, or misapplication. Any replacement Software Media will be warranted for the remainder of the original warranty period or thirty (30) days, whichever is longer.

    **(b)** In no event shall IDGB or the authors be liable for any damages whatsoever (including without limitation damages for loss of business profits, business interruption, loss of business information, or any other pecuniary loss) arising from the use of or inability to use the Book or the Software, even if IDGB has been advised of the possibility of such damages.

(c) Because some jurisdictions do not allow the exclusion or limitation of liability for consequential or incidental damages, the above limitation or exclusion may not apply to you.

7. **U.S. Government Restricted Rights.** Use, duplication, or disclosure of the Software by the U.S. Government is subject to restrictions stated in paragraph (c)(1)(ii) of the Rights in Technical Data and Computer Software clause of DFARS 252.227-7013, and in subparagraphs (a) through (d) of the Commercial Computer — Restricted Rights clause at FAR 52.227-19, and in similar clauses in the NASA FAR supplement, when applicable.

8. **General.** This Agreement constitutes the entire understanding of the parties and revokes and supersedes all prior agreements, oral or written, between them and may not be modified or amended except in a writing signed by both parties hereto that specifically refers to this Agreement. This Agreement shall take precedence over any other documents that may be in conflict herewith. If any one or more provisions contained in this Agreement are held by any court or tribunal to be invalid, illegal, or otherwise unenforceable, each and every other provision shall remain in full force and effect.

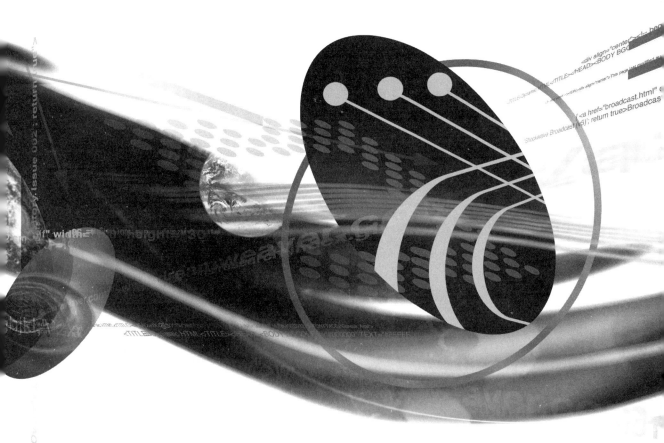

# Discover the Design Tool of Your Dreams!

Build great-looking Web sites in record time using drag-and-drop design, while Roundtrip HTML gives you total control over source HTML.

For Adobe Photoshop users, Dreamweaver is the fastest way to turn graphic comps into beautiful Web sites that run well across different browsers. Use Dreamweaver seamlessly with Macromedia Flash,

Fireworks, and Director to develop engaging Web content.

Develop sites collaboratively, separating content from design with XML and Dream Templates. Make complex site-wide changes quickly with a site map, global search and replace, and automatic link management.

Work smoothly with leading e-commerce and dynamic Web publishing solutions, including ASP, Apache, Cold Fusion, iCAT, and your own custom applications.

Drag and drop e-commerce objects to create great looking on-line stores in minutes. Get all this in one powerful and professional package with Macromedia Dreamweaver!

For more information, visit **www.macromedia.com/ dreamweaver.** To upgrade or order in the U.S. and Canada, call **800 457 1774**. For the name of a reseller near you, call **800 326 2128.**

**macromedia**®
add life to the web

# my2cents.idgbooks.com

## Register This Book — And Win!

## Discover IDG Books Online!

# CD-ROM Installation Instructions

The *Fireworks 2 Bible* CD-ROM contains a trial version of Fireworks as well as a full complement of auxiliary files and additional programs.

## Accessing the programs on the CD-ROM

Only the trial programs are compressed. Double-click these files to begin the installation procedure (Fireworks installation instructions are listed below). All other files on the CD-ROM are uncompressed and can simply be copied from the CD-ROM to your system by using your file manager.

The file structure of the CD-ROM replicates the structure that Fireworks sets up when it is installed. For example, HTML templates found in the Fireworks\Settings\ HTML Settings folder are located in both the CD-ROM and the installed program.

For a detailed synopsis of the CD-ROM contents, see Appendix B, "What's on the CD-ROM."

## Installing Fireworks

To install Fireworks on your Windows system, follow these steps:

1. Insert the Fireworks Bible CD-ROM into your CD-ROM drive.

2. Double-click the Fireworks.exe file to unpack it and begin the installation process.

3. Follow the onscreen instructions. Accept the default options for program location.

## Changing the Windows read-only attribute

You may not be able to access files on the CD-ROM after you copy the files to your computer. After you copy or move the entire contents of the CD-ROM to your hard disk or another storage medium (such as a Zip disk), you may get the following error message when you attempt to open a file with its associated application:

```
[Application] is unable to open the [file]. Please make sure
the drive and file are writable.
```

Windows sees all files on a CD-ROM drive as *read-only*. This normally makes sense because a CD-ROM is a read-only medium — that is, you can't write data back to the CD-ROM.

However, when you copy a file from a CD-ROM to your hard disk or to a Zip disk, Windows doesn't automatically change the file attribute from read-only to writable.

Installation software normally takes care of this chore for you, but in this case, because the files are intended to be manually copied to your disk, you have to change the file attribute yourself. Luckily, it's easy — just follow these steps:

1. Click the Start menu button.
2. Select Programs.
3. Choose Windows Explorer.
4. Highlight the filename(s) on the hard disk or Zip disk.
5. Right-click the highlighted filename(s) to display a pop-up menu.
6. Select Properties to display the Properties dialog.
7. Click the Read-only option so that it is no longer checked.
8. Click the OK button.

You should now be able to use the file(s) with the specific application without getting the annoying error message.